Thomas Osborne Davis, John Philpot Curran

The Speeches of the Right Honorable John Philpot Curran

Third Edition

Thomas Osborne Davis, John Philpot Curran

The Speeches of the Right Honorable John Philpot Curran
Third Edition

ISBN/EAN: 9783744713900

Printed in Europe, USA, Canada, Australia, Japan

Cover: Foto ©Thomas Meinert / pixelio.de

More available books at **www.hansebooks.com**

THE SPEECHES

OF

THE RIGHT HONORABLE

JOHN PHILPOT CURRAN.

EDITED,

WITH MEMOIR AND HISTORICAL NOTICES,

BY

THOMAS DAVIS, ESQ., M.R.I.A.,
BARRISTER-AT-LAW.

Third Edition.

DUBLIN:
JAMES DUFFY, WELLINGTON QUAY,
AND
22, PATERNOSTER ROW, LONDON.
1868.

PREFACE.

In 1807, a few of Curran's bar speeches were published. The edition, three thousand copies, was sold rapidly; and a second edition followed, in which some of his parliamentary speeches were added. In 1811, soon after his judgment in Merry v. Power, Stockdale published a third edition, containing that judgment; but otherwise unimproved from the second.

In 1843, a collection was published with ten speeches, not in any former edition, and a short memoir written by the present editor, but the writer of that memoir did not edit the speeches. They were printed, without correction, or notes, or arrangement, from Stockdale's volume, and the pamphlet reports, and they were struck off without having been ever seen by the writer of the memoir.

The present edition is arranged chronologically, with a single exception. It contains six of Curran's bar speeches, and thirty-three of his parliamentary speeches, not in any former edition, and no pains have been spared to get the best reports.

The illustrative matter may be thought too ample.

With most of the parliamentary speeches, some account is given of the state of politics connected with the question, and of the progress and result of the debate.

Prefixed to, or following, each of the legal speeches will be found, the facts and events of the case, and, in many instances, short biographies of Curran's clients

It was hoped by this to communicate to the reader some of the minute interest felt by a cotemporary, and to supply a better illustration of Curran's march through life, than could be given in a short memoir.

Great attention has been paid to fixing precise dates. Some documents, as the briefs in Sheares' case, dictated by John Sheares, being inaccessible to the public, have been largely quoted. To the historian of Curran's time, whenever he arises, some of these things may be useful.

There are, doubtless, many errors in the volume ; but as this really is the first attempt to illustrate and correct Curran's speeches, and as it has been made amid the anxieties and occupations of political life, perhaps they will be corrected and not cavilled at. Any correction however, no matter how offered, will be welcome.

T. D.

CONTENTS.

	PAGE
Memoir of John Philpot Curran	xi
Flood's Reform Bill, Nov. 29, 1783,	37
Privilege of Commons on Money Bills, Dec. 16, 1783,	38
Retrenchment, Feb. 14, 1785,	41
Militia v. Volunteers, Feb. 14, 1785,	ib.
On Attachments, Feb. 24, 1785,	42
Orde's Commercial Propositions, June 30, 1785,	46
The Same, July 23, 1785,	48
The Same, Aug. 11, 1785,	52
The Same, Aug. 12, 1785,	53
The Same, Aug. 15, 1785,	54
The Portugal Trade, March 11, 1786,	56
Pensions, March 13, 1786,	58
Outrages in the South, Jan. 19, 1787,	61
The Kingdom of Kerry, Jan. 23, 1787,	67
Right Boy Bill, Feb. 19, 1787,	68
The Same, Feb. 20, 1787,	70
Limitation of Pensions, March 12, 1787,	73
Tithes, March, 13, 1787,	76
Navigation Act, March 20, 1787	79
Contraband Trade, Feb. 19, 1788,	81
Madness of George III., Feb. 6, 1789,	82
Regency, Feb. 11, 1789,	88
The Same, Feb. 20, 1789,	90
Disfranchisement of Excise Officers, April 21, 1789	91

	PAGE
Dublin Police, April 25, 1789,	94
Stamp Officer's Salaries, Feb. 4, 1790	9?
Pensions, Feb. 11, 1790,	101
Election of Lord Mayor of Dublin—Before the Privy Council, on behalf of the Corporation—July 10, 1790,	103
Government Corruption, Feb. 12, 1791,	131
Catholic Emancipation, Feb. 18, 1792,	135
Egan v. Kindillan, (Seduction,) for Defendant,	143
War with France, Jan. 11, 1793,	147
Parliamentary Reform, Feb. 9, 1793,	152
For Archibald Hamilton Rowan, (Libel), Jan. 29, 1794,	153
The Same (to set aside Verdict,) Feb. 4, 1794,	182
For Drogheda Defenders (High Treason,) April 23, 1794,	190
For Northern Star (Libel), May 28, 1794,	205
For Doctor Drennan (Libel), June 25, 1794,	196
For Rev. William Jackson (High Treason), April 23, 1795,	211
Catholic Emancipation, May 4, 1795,	233
State of the Nation, May 15, 1795,	236
For Dublin Defenders (High Treason) Dec. 22, 1795,	221
Indemnity Bill, Feb. 3, 1796,	243
Channel Trade, Feb. 15, 1796,	244
Insurrection Bill, Feb. 25, 1796,	246
French War, Oct. 13, 1796,	248
Suspension of the Habeas Corpus, Oct. 14, 1796,	254
Catholic Emancipation, Oct. 17, 1796	256
Hoche's Expedition, Jan. 6, 1797,	261
Internal Defence, Feb. 24, 1787,	264
Disarming of Ulster, March 20, 1797,	266
Last Speech in the Irish Commons (on Parliamentary Reform), May 15, 1797,	270
For Peter Finnerty (Libel), Dec. 22, 1797,	276
For Patrick Finney (High Treason), Jan. 16, 1798,	299
For Henry Sheares (High Treason), July 4, 1798,	315
The Same, July 12, 1798,	327
For Oliver Bond (High Treason), July 24, 1798,	341

CONTENTS. ix

	PAGE
For Lady Pamela Fitzgerald and her Children—At the Bar of the Irish House of Commons—August 20, 1798,	355
For Napper Tandy (Outlawry), May 19, 1800,	362
Against Sir Henry Hayes (Abduction of Miss Pike), April 13, 1801,	370
Hevey v. Major Sirr (Assault and False Imprisonment), for Plaintiff, May 17, 1802,	384
For Owen Kirwan (High Treason), Sept. 1, 1803,	395
Against Ensign John Costley (Conspiracy to Murder), Feb. 23, 1804,	406
Massy v. Headfort (Criminal Conversation), for Plaintiff, July 27, 1804,	412
For Judge Johnson (Habeas Corpus), Feb. 4, 1805,	424
Merry v. Power (Decision when Master of the Rolls),	457
Newry Election, Oct. 17, 1812,	461

MEMOIR

OF

THE RIGHT HONORABLE
JOHN PHILPOT CURRAN.

In the north-west corner of the county of Cork stands the little town of Newmarket. It is in a land of moors and streams. Just north of it slope the Ure hills, part of the upland which sweeps forty miles across from Liscarroll to Tralee, and far south of it, over the valley of the Blackwater, frown the mountains of Muskerry, changing as they approach Killarney, into precipitous peaks. A brook tumbles on each side of it to the Avendala river and, a few miles off, the Avendala and Allo, and a dozen other tributaries swell the tide of the Blackwater.

In old times the town belonged to the M'Auliffes, a small but resolute clan. One of their castles was close by. They ranged their coatlined pikemen and hardy kerne under the banners of M'Carha or Desmond, and shared the fate of their suzerains in the days of Queen Elizabeth.

Then much was changed.

To the M'Auliffes succeeded the Aldworths, an Anglo-Saxon family. A grant and charter from James I., confirmed by Charles II., made them owners of a great estate and lords of a manor of 32,000 acres. Among their privileges was the right to hold a market on every Thursday, and, on this account, the town came to be called Newmarket. The castle of M'Auliffe fell to ruin—it is to this day empty and picturesque. The Aldworths built still nearer the town a great substantial "Newmarket House," and surrounded it with elm, and beech, and sycamore, and made a straight avenue of ash trees, which grew to be giants—for the family, though hospitable and good, were not so extravagant as their neighbours—a bridge succeeded the ford, and the parish church of Clonfert rose over the western brook. Some gentry of both races grew up around the town, and it went on improving, until several snug houses and a lot of cabins were clustered in it. Two roads—one from Mallow to Tralee, and the other from Charleville to Killarney—crossed in the town, and, therefore, not a few horsemen and footmen, fish-joulters and tinkers, lords and pedlars, going between Cork and Kerry, passed through Newmarket.

In this town Curran was born and bred.

John Philpot Curran was the son of a judge! It happened in this way. Early in the last century, "One Curran, from the North," settled in the town, and had a son James, who learned reading, writing, and cyphering, certainly, and it is said, some Greek and Latin. The son of a North-country Protestant, thus instructed, James Curran was patronized by the Aldworth family, and was finally appointed by them Seneschal of their Manor of Newmarket. As seneschal he had jurisdiction to the value of forty shillings, and thus the father of Curran was a judge.

This James Curran was an ugly man, for he bore a coarse likeness to his son, and 'tis certain he was an ordinary soul. Nevertheless, a judge and a scholar, he had honour in his native place, and won the hand of Sarah Philpot. She was of gentle blood, and, what is more to our purpose, she had a deep, fresh, womanly irregular mind; it was like the clear river of her town, that came gushing and flashing and discoursing from the lonely mountains—from the outlaw's and the fairy's home—down to the village. She had, under an exalted piety, a waste of passions and traditions lying grand and gloomy in her soul, and thence, a bright human love of her son came pouring out on him, and making him grow green at her feet. Well, then, did he place on her tomb in Newmarket this inscription:—

HERE LIES THE BODY OF

SARAH CURRAN;

She was marked by
Many Years, many Talents, many Virtues, few Failings, no Crime.
This frail Memorial was placed here by a Son whom she loved.*

On the 24th of July, 1750, when people in Newmarket were talking of Lucas's Popish plots, the Dublin Society, the war, and the Cork assizes, the house in which Seneschal Curran lived was agitated by the going in and out of midwife, nurse, and neighbours, and at a prosperous moment, his wife was delivered of her eldest born, who, some days after, was christened John Philpot.

He grew up a light-limbed, short, brown boy, with an eye like a live coal. He had a sensitive heart, loved his little brothers and sister; but he loved his mother best, and well he might. She doated on him, and petted him, and taught him much. She soothed him with soft lullabies that sent the passions of his country into his young heart; she flooded him with the stories and memories of the neighbourhood, she nursed up in him love, and truth, and earnestness, by her precept and her example, and she taught him his Bible.

His father's position threw him into contact with high and low, informed him of the ways of all the people in the country, and must have sharpened his sagacity.

There were in these days, too, more marked customs than there are now. Thrice in the autumn, and once in the summer in came cattle and pigs, horse dealers and frieze-dealers, cheese and hens, match-makers and pedlars, to the fair of Newmarket, and Curran got his toys and his share of the bustle and life with the rest. He was an early attendant at dances and wakes, and there he might gloat over traditions about the unfinished palace of Kanturk, and the hapless love of Catherine Ny Cormick; he might hear the old strollers and rapparees tell of William's wars, and the piper blow his merry jigs by the wild notes to which Alister M'Donnell marched to battle at Knocknanois, and the wilder ones with which the women mourned over his corpse.

Such was the atmosphere in which he lived—the hills and the streams, his father's court, the fairs and markets, and merry-makings, and his mother's lap. He learned much passion and sharpness, and some vices, too.

He went early to school, and it is said had a Kanturk boy, young Yelverton (afterwards Chief Baron Lord Avonmore) and Day his school-fellows; but he was a vehement boy, fonder of fun than books.

One morning he was playing marbles in the ball-alley, and playing tricks too (for he was wild with winning taws) when in strolled a large, white-haired, kind looking old man Seeing the young marble winner the centre of fun, and as hearty as his own laugh; the old man was attracted by him, began a gossip, and finally, by a few cakes induced him to go home to the Rectory This man was Mr. Boyse, who used to preach as earnestly as if he were pastor of the thousands of Roman Catholics who surrounded him, instead of ministering to the Aldworths, Allens, Currans, and a few more.

Mr. Boyse taught him reading, grammar, and the rudiments of the classics, "all he could."

---

* She died in a year or two after he had become Master of the Rolls.

Curran thrived under his care, and never forgot him. Once returning home to Ely Place, from a day of triumphant toil in court, he found a patriarch seated familiarly at his drawing-room fire. It was his benefactor. Curran grasped him; "You are right, sir," he said. "you are right; the chimney-piece is yours—the pictures are yours—the house is yours; you gave me all I have—my friend, my father!" That night Boyse went with the member for Kilbeggan to " the old house in College Green."

Curran was not "all work and no play" at Boyse's. He dashed out often—God bless him! One of his freaks was this:—A show was in the town, and the string-puller being ill, young Curran got leave to manage." He went on properly enough for a while with the courtship and quarrels of Punch and Judy, but gradually made that matron tell her husband all the cosherings of Newmarket, and ended by quizzing the priest! 'Twas a bold trick, for which he and the show-box were tumbled into the gutter. Whether he did this in Irish or English does not appear, for he spoke both languages before he could read either.

Still these were bursts; he was a willing pupil at Boyse's, and that kind, modest man, finding he could teach him no more, gave him a good man's advice, and sent him to Middleton school, partly at his own expense. One Carey kept this school. He was a passable man, who knew Greek and Latin well.

In that flat-land town he worked up classics for Trinity College. He was to enter the Church, for his mother hoped "John would be a bishop." There he learned to love the sweet-voiced romances of Virgil, the cold and exquisite lyrics of Horace, and the living deeds and men of Homer. He carried much of them in his head, and generally one of them in his pocket ever after. He used to read Homer once a year, and Phillips says he saw him reading the Æneid in a Holyhead packet, when every one else was deadly sick.

How far the gaieties of Horace and Ovid, or the example of Æneas, influenced his naturally fine qualities as a wit and a lover, it is easy to guess; but we see little other effect of these classics in his life. To be sure there are lots of his classical puns to be found in O'Regan and Phillips—some quotations in his speech for Judge Johnson—and a poem on a plate warmer, giving a history of "The Decline and Fall" of the Heathen Gods. But except the likeness between the exordium of his defence of Rowan and Cicero's of Milo, there is little of classic influence observable in his speeches. Surely, he owes more to the wakes, and his mother's stories about ghosts and heroes, and to the Bible and Sterne, than to all the classics; and he got still more from his loving and ambitious spirit—from the changeful climate of his country, and from the restless times which troubled him to action. Yet books of all kinds, English, French, and Latin, helped to give articulation to those laughs, and sighs, and curses. For 'tis of these his eloquence consists.

He was sufficiently ground at Middleton, to get a Sizarship in Trinity College. This was on the 16th June, 1767, when, therefore, he was not quite seventeen years old. His tutor was Doctor Dobbin, who did nothing for him. As a Sizar, he had free rooms and commons in College, and, thus rewarded, he read a little (unlike most young men about him)— got a Scholarship in 1770—and began reading for a Fellowship. He was then and ever an earnest, though not a monotonous student of men and books.

Being designed for the Church, he studied divinity, and got a little of the mannerism of his intended profession, as we see in a prosy letter of consolation, written to his dear friend "Dick Stack,"* in 1770. In his time he wrote two sermons. One was written for this Dick Stack, to preach before the Judges of Assize, at Cork. The other was preached in College Chapel, as a punishment, and in it he gloriously mimicked the Censor, Doctor Patrick Duigenan!—an eruption worthy of him who satirized Newmarket, when twelve years old. We cannot look at the College pulpit without fancying we see the giggling eye and hear the solemn voice of that wild boy.

Besides the classics and the Bible, he was fondest of Sterne, and of Rousseau's Eloisa. He liked metaphysical discussions, too, and they led him to a bargain with a friend, that

---

* This gentleman afterwards got a Fellowship, and wrote a Treatise on Optics, long a College Text-Book.

whoever died first should visit the other on the death night. His friend died first, and broke his word. Curran was also a lover, a punster, and a ready hand in the rows which "The Gownsmen" used to have every night with "The Townsmen." The students then were generally older than they are now, and society more dissipated and ferocious. The College gown was not only an uniform;—with a stone or a key slung in it, it became a weapon. Nor were the sticks and fists of "The Townsmen" idle. His son says that one night Curran was left senseless on the flags, and, doubtless, many a sore knock he gave and got. He was continually getting into scrapes with "The Board" by his humour and wildness, and getting out of them by his ready wit. In short, he was the wittiest and dreamiest, the most classical and ambitious, of the scamps of Trinity College.

He gave up all thoughts of the church on coming of age; and, having graduated, he went to London, and entered the Middle Temple, intending, like all law students, to be Lord Chancellor, and something more. His son's book contains a merry narrative—a little spoiled by imitations of Sterne—of his journey to London, in a letter, written from his lodgings, "31, Chandos-street." Part of this letter is important and characteristic:—

"I am determined to apply to reading this vacation with the utmost diligence, in order to attend the Courts next winter with more advantage. If I should happen to visit Ireland next summer, I shall spend a week before I go, in seeing the curiosities here (the King and Queen, and the lions); and if I continue in my present mood, you will see a strange alteration in your poor friend. That cursed fever brought me down so much, and my spirits are so reduced, that, faith, I don't remember to have laughed these six weeks. Indeed, I never thought solitude could lean so heavily on me as I find it does. I rise, most commonly, in the morning between five and six, and read as much as my eyes will permit me till dinner-time; I then go out and dine, and from that till bed-time I mope about between my lodgings and the Park. For heaven's sake send me some news or other (for, surely, Newmarket cannot be barren in such things) that will teach me once more to laugh. I never received a single line from any one since I came here. Tell me if you know anything about Keller; I wrote twice to that gentleman without being favoured with any answer. You will give my best respects to Mrs. Aldworth and her family; to Dr. Creagh; and don't forget my good friends, Peter and Will Connell.

"Yours sincerely,
"J. P. C.

"P.S.—I will cover this blank edge, with entreating you to write closer than you commonly do, when you sit down to answer this, and don't make me pay tenpence for a half-penny-worth of white paper."

What an odd fellow a cockney would think him; he had not seen the wonders of London (" the King, the Queen, and the lions"), and spoke of going to see them "next summer." This was one of those gloomy times, when the soul of Curran, thrown on itself, explored the mysteries of its own constitution—calculated its own magazines—and came out frowning, fresh, and keen for his work. There is a desperate humour in a letter written to Jerry Keller, by him, a little after:—

"If you cast your eyes on the thousand gilded chariots that are dancing the hayes in an eternal round of foppery, you would think the world assembled to play the fool in London, unless you believe the report of the passing bells and hearses, which would seem to intimate that they all made a point of dying here. It is amazing, that even custom should make death a matter of so much unconcern as you will here find it. Even in the house where I lodge, there has been a being dead these two days. I did not hear a word of it till this evening, though he is divided from me only by a partition. They visit him once a day, and so lock him up till the next (for they seldom bury till the seventh day), and there he lies without the smallest attention paid to him, except a dirge each night on the Jew's trump, which I shall not omit, while he continues to be my neighbour."

A grim joke this, and coming from a man with depths, and fuel in his soul. His "life in London" was a hard one. He spent his mornings in "reading even to exhaustion." He frequently attended the Courts, and though not a constant legal student, he made vigorous plunges into law," and mastered those elements of constitutional and equity jurisprudence, which were basis enough for his practical studies. The mistake (now a common) was then rare, of men supposing that they can leave their minds generally ignorant and without accomplishments or knowledge of life, provided they have read through piles of law books; mean hearts, who prefer gold to worthiness--blockheads, without sagacity to see that plenty of skill is of more value than plenty of tools.

It was not so with Curran. Besides his legal studies, he mastered the chief English and French writers, and saw what was going on about him in every court and theatre, club and cellar in London. Inclination, probably, more than design led him to this, and yet he was as much of a self-teacher as ever lived. His health had been bad, and his body weak. By cold baths, violent exercise, and attention to air and diet, he became robust; and thus, notwithstanding those excesses in drinking which were universal at the time. His oratorical training was as severe as any Greek ever underwent.

His voice was so bad that he was called at school "stuttering Jack Curran," and his manner was awkward and meaningless. By watching himself—by the daily habit of declaiming Junius, Bolingbroke, and Shakespeare, before a looking-glass—and by constant attendance at debating societies, he turned his shrill and stumbling brogue into a flexible, sustained, and divinely modulated voice; his action became free and forcible, and he acquired perfect readiness in thinking and speaking on his legs.

His first essay in a debating society was in The Devils, of Temple-bar. It amounted to saying, "Mr. Chairman," when he trembled, forgot, grew pale, grew red, grew hot, and sunk down in a fright. He attended the more regularly for a fortnight, and learned to say "aye" or "no," boldly and distinctly. One night he went there with Apjohn and Duhigg, after a dinner of mutton, with extra punch. A ragged, greasy blockhead, at whose anachronisms he smiled, attacked him as "Orator Mum." Curran, excited by wrath and whiskey, got up, and "dressed him better than he ever had been in his life." Loud applause, and a cold supper from the President, rewarded his vigour and confirmed it. Thenceforward he was a constant speaker at The Devils, The Robin Hood, and The Brown Bear. At this last he was known as "the little Jesuit of St. Omer," from wearing a brown coat outside a black, and making pro-Catholic speeches.

He used sometimes get into black melancholy about Ireland and Newmarket. Still oftener he suffered for want of money, and even thought of going to America. During his second year in London, he married Miss Creagh, daughter of Doctor Richard Creagh, of Newmarket, a cousin of his. With her he got a woman he loved, though she seems to have been lazy, and rather conceited. Her little fortune, and some money sent by his family, supported him till 1775, when he was called to the bar.

Curran's life has been made a long joke by the pleasant puerilities of his early biographers. Even his son's excellent book has over-much of this vice. What avails it us to know the capital puns he made in College, or the smart epigrams he said to Macklin; or, at least, they should take a small place in large biographies, instead of the chief place in sketches. These things are the empty shells of his deep-sea mind—idle things for triflers to classify. But for men who, though in the ranks of life, are anxious to order their minds by the stand of some commanding spirit—or for governing minds, who want to commune with his spirit in brotherly sympathy and instruction—to such men, the puns are rubbish, and the jokes chaff.

Pause then. oh! reader, while, on the first day of Michaelmas Term, 1775, this John Philpot Curran, the married man, aged twenty-five, is putting on his wig, or bowing to the Benchers, ere he sit down a candidate for briefs. Pause, reader, and recal what this young brown lawyer had in him.

The hills of Duhallow had laid lines of beauty and shades of wildness on his eye and soul he had been shapened by the position of his family—ennobled by the force of his mother's mind—instructed in Irish traditions and music. Knowing these, and such lore as Boyse could teach him, he left Newmarket. This wild, fanciful, earnest boy then picked up classics, experience, and ambition at Middleton, and was ennobled by generous companions, refined by study and society, and made fiery by love and pleasure in College.

In London, amid his melancholy and wildness, he had a strong resolve to be great and good. His melancholy grew glorious then, as sun-lit clouds; and poverty sustained his ambition against depression or dissipation. He was too proud to live, or shine, or love upon the toleration of mankind. He learned to labour, because he longed to enjoy. He continued to labour for labour's own great sake—for labour is practical power. His duties were great—his passions intense—his means nothing, save intellect. He knew that his soul was a treasury wherewith to give and to buy; a tongue, wherewith to win or persuade —a light to illumine—an army to conquer—a spirit to worship and be worshipped. Nobly he prepared it in life, and passion, and hard thought, even more than in books; and yet this man is called idle and careless. He worked hard during his Apprenticeship; but now he is a Master.

Thus trained, accomplished, strong, passionate, and surrounded by competitors, he came to the bar. Well may his son say, that "Instead of being surprised at his eminent success, the wonder would have been if such a man had failed."

Even when he was called, he was known and prized, not as a flashy and unblushing declaimer, but is an earnest and self-relying man, able to judge character and use knowledge.

His first brief was in a trivial Chancery motion, and the Devils' Club scene occurred over again. His imagination so mastered him, that when Lord Lifford bid him speak louder, he became silent, blushed, dropped his brief, and allowed a friend to finish the motion.

Phillips describes him as having attended the Cork assizes, and "walked the hall term after term, without either profit or professional reputation."

At this time Curran lodged in Redmond's-hill, a street between Cuffe-street and Digges-street. The neighbourhood was one frequented by his profession. The Solicitor-General lived in Cuffe-street, the Judge of the Prerogative in Bride-street, and Commissioners of Bankrupts were plenty as paving stones in Digges-street, as any one taking up that historical novel "an old almanack," can see. Mr. Phillips calls the place Hog-hill (there never was such a place in Dublin)? and makes a melo-dramatic picture of dirty lodgings, a starving wife, and a dunning landlady; and then brings Curran home to find his first brief, "with twenty gold guineas, and the name of old Bob Lyons on the back of it!"

Perhaps Mr. Lyons did, on Arthur Wolfe's recommendation, send twenty guineas and a brief, in "Ormsby v. Wynne, election petition." to Counsellor Curran's lodgings, and finding Curran a pleasant companion, asked him to Sligo,* for Lyons was in good business, a hospitable sharp fellow, and had his office in York-street, near Curran's lodgings. But Curran made eighty-two guineas his first year, between one and two hundred the second, and increased more rapidly every year after. With this, and what his wife had, he could not have been starving, though certainly he was not rich.

He rose rapidly and surely; and his reputation among his intimates was higher than with the public—a sign of a genuine man.

At last this matured genius found a great public opportunity, and used it. A cruel wrong had been done by one so high as to awe down all advocates, and corrupt the fountains of justice—there was need of an avenger, and he came.

The Cork summer assizes of 1780 are memorable, for there this Protestant lawyer appeared as voluntary counsel for a Roman Catholic priest against a Protestant nobleman. Was there ever such audacity?

To be sure, Lord Doneraile had acted like a ruffian.

He had seduced a country girl. Shortly after, her brother broke some rule of his church, and was censured by his bishop. The paramour sought Lord Doneraile's interference in her brother's favour. It was promptly given. Accompanied by a relative of his, a Mr. St. Leger, ex-captain of dragoons, his lordship rode to the cabin in which Father Neale, the parish priest, lived. Father Neale was an aged man, and a just and holy clergyman, but a very poor one. He was kneeling in prayer, when Doneraile's voice at the door ordered him out. Book in hand, with bare and hoary head and tottering step he obeyed, and heard at his lordship's stirrup a command to remove the censure from the convenient miscreant, whose sister Lord Doneraile favoured. The priest was half a slave; he muttered excuses,

---

* Lyons had a jolly house there on the fierce coast, amid a secluded Irish race, whom Curran mixed with and learned from

"he wished to and but for the bishop he would remove the censure,"—but he was only half a slave; he refused to break the rules to which he had sworn. A shower of blows from his lordship's horsewhip drove the old priest stumbling and bleeding into his hovel.

And yet every lawyer on the circuit had refused to act as counsel for this priest against that lord, when John Curran volunteered to plead his cause.

Reader! think over all this, and you will get at something of the man and the country then.

He did all that mortal could do, and more than any lawyer now or then would. He grappled with the baseness of Lord Doneraile, and dragged his character out on the table. He left his instructions, and described Captain St. Leger as "a renegade soldier," and "drummed-out dragoon." He heaped every scorn on Lord Doneraile's witnesses from their own story. He seemed to forget that he was speaking to tyrants—he treated the jury as men; he spoke as a man—virtuous, and believing others so. That jury, so adjured by genius, forgot penal laws, lordships, and ascendancy, remembered God and their oaths and gave a verdict for Father Neale.

Verily those thirty guineas damages were a conquest from the powers of darkness—the first spoils of emancipation.

On account of this trial, Curran fought a duel with Captain St. Leger, and endured the hostility of the Doneraile family; but, in exchange, he obtained the admiration and trust of his countrymen, and a glorified conscience. If he wanted more, he received it a few weeks after, in the dying and solemn blessing of Father Neale.

He had been five years at the bar, and now he was famous with the public. But he had been recognised long before. It is proof enough of this, that he was prior of the St. Patrick's Society in 1779. The reader looking at the note below, will see that the wisest, best, and most brilliant spirits of the island were there,* and that Curran was their honoured friend.

---

*LIST OF MEMBERS OF THE ST. PATRICK'S SOCIETY.

Founder.—†Barry Yelverton, M.P., afterwards Lord Viscount Avonmore, Lord Chief Baron.
Abbot.—†William Doyle, Master in Chancery.
Prior.—†John Philpot Curran, afterwards M.P., Privy Councillor, and Master of the Rolls.
Præcentor.—Rev. Wm. Day, S.F.T.C.D
Bursar.—Edward Hudson, M.D.
Sacristan.—†Robert Johnson, M.P., afterwards a Judge.

Arran, the Earl of.
*Barry, James, Painter, never joined.
†Brown, Arthur, M.P., and F.T.C.D.
†Burgh, Walter Hussey, Right Hon., and M.P.; afterwards Chief Baron.
*Burton, Beresford, K.C.
Carhampton, Earl of.
Caldbeck, William, K.C.
Chamberlayne, W. Tankerville, M.P.; afterwards a Judge.
Charlemont, Earl of.
Corry, Rt. Hon. Isaac, M.P.; afterwards Chancellor of the Exchequer.
Daly, Right-Hon. Denis, M.P.
*Day, Robert, M.P.; afterwards a Judge.
†Dobbs, Robert.
Doyle, John, M.P., afterwards a General in the Army, and a Baronet.
Dunkin, James.

†Duquery, Henry, M.P.
†Emmet, Temple.
†Finucane, Matthew, afterwards a Judge.
†Fitton, Richard.
†Forbes, John, M.P.
†Frankland, Richard, K.C.
†Grattan, Rt. Hon. H., M.P.
†Hacket, Thomas.
†Hardy, Francis, M.P. (Lord Charlemont's biographer.)
Harstonge, Sir Henry, Bart., and M.P.
†Herbert, Richard, M.P.
†Hunt, John.
†Hussey, Dudley, M.P. and Recorder of Dublin.
Jebb, Frederic, M.D.
Kingsborough, Lord Visct., M.P.
†Mocawen, ———
†Martin, Richard, M.P.
†Metge, Peter, M.P.; afterwards a Judge.
Mornington, Earl of.
†Muloch, Thomas.

Newenham, Sir Edward, M.P
Ogle, Rt. Hon. George, M.P.
*O'Leary, Rev. Arthur.
†O'Neill, Charles, K.C., M.P
Palliser, Rev. Dr. Chaplain.
†Pollock, Joseph.
†Ponsonby, Rt. Hon. George, M.P., afterwards Chancellor of Ireland.
†Preston, William.
Ross, Lieut.-Colonel, M.P
‡Sheridan, Charles Francis, M.P., Secretary at War.
†Smith, Sir Michael, Bart. M.P., afterwards Master of the Rolls.
‡Stawell, William.
Stack, Rev. Richard, F.T.C.D.
Townshend, Marquess of. (Elected, professed, and joined on his visit to Dublin, after his Vice-royalty.)
†Wolfe, Arthur, M.P., afterwards Lord Viscount Kilwarden, Chief Justice of the King's Bench.

[Thus marked (*) were Honorary Members; thus marked (†) were Barristers.]

From the title vulgarly given them, "Monks of the Screw,"* people suppose that this was a mere drinking club. Perhaps the names are answer enough. It was an union of strong souls, brought together, like electric clouds, by affinity, and flashing as they joined. They met, and shone, and warmed. They had great passions, and generous accomplishments, and they, like all that was good in Ireland, were heaving for want of freedom. They were men of wit and pleasure, living in a luxurious state of society, and probably did wild and excessive things. This was reconcileable *(in such a state of society)* with every virtue of head and heart.

This was the sunniest period, though not the grandest, of Curran's life. He was surrounded by wise and loving friends, and he saw his country striding to independence, and growing in wealth, in knowledge, and, better than all, in internal union. He was not an idle, though he was not a distinguished party during these events. He stood in the ranks of the Volunteers, armed as free men should ever be, to gain or guard their rights. His censure was dreaded by every corrupt judge and savage lawyer, and his counsel sought by Avonmore, Flood, and Grattan. At a special election in 1783, he entered the House of Commons. He sat for Kilbeggan, a borough belonging to Mr. Longfield, but he sat uncompromised; he sat as Henry Flood's colleague; he was returned under the guardian guns of the Volunteers, to enforce legislative independence. At the general election, in the spring of 1790, he came in for Rathcormac, and sat for it till the mad secession in 1797.

His parliamentary speeches reported are few and short. The first mentioned is on Flood's Reform Bill, in November, 1783. The next is introductory of a resolution, declaring the exclusive right of the Commons to originate Money Bills—an important resolution not likely to be trusted to a bad debater. The report of it seems like a newspaper sketch; still we see in it a sound historical argument. His appeal to the House to guard a right which was the palladium of liberty to a virtuous, and of corruption to a vicious Commons, was bold and original.

His speech in the House, on the 24th February, 1785, on the debate on the Abuse of Attachments by the King's Bench, led to a duel with Fitzgibbon, then Attorney-General.

Fitzgibbon had once been an intimate of Curran's, whose first brief-bag was a gift from John Fitzgibbon, "for good luck." But they were unlike: as the strong hard granite and the soft flashing wave. Fitzgibbon having, though a plebeian, taken the government side, gave it all the support that masculine talents, clear rhetoric, personal courage, and utter want of conscience enabled. Curran, the enthusiastic, the pure, the Irish, went with the people for liberty. They were not friends in 1785; and Fitzgibbon, it is said, had brought the Duchess of Rutland to hear him chastise the member for Kilbeggan. The fiery Cork man heard this, and would not wait for him. Fitzgibbon had fallen asleep, and Curran, on rising, attacked him as a "guilty spirit." Fitzgibbon answered with "puny babbler," and Curran retorted in an invective feebly resembling part of Grattan's against Flood. They

---

* The Monks of the Order of Saint Patrick, commonly called the Monks of the Screw, assembled at their Convent, in Saint Kevin-street, Dublin, on and after September the 3rd, 1779.

Curran wrote the Charter Song, of which Phillips gives a part:—

THE MONKS OF THE SCREW.

When Saint Patrick our order created,
And called us the Monks of the Screw
Good rules he revealed to our Abbot,
To guide us in what we should do

But first he replenished his fountain
With liquor the best in the sky;
And he swore, by the word of his Saintship,
That fountain should never run dry!

My children, be chaste—till you're tempted
While sober, be wise and discreet;
And humble your bodies with fasting
Whene'er you have nothing to eat.

Then be not a glass in the Convent,
Except on a festival found;
And this rule to enforce, I ordain it
A festival all the year round!

The Society dwindled away towards the end of the year 1785, according to Hardy. 1795, as printed in "Curran's Memoirs, by his Son," is an error, probably, of the printer.

exchanged shots, when Fitzgibbon did his best to bring Curran down, but failed, and they were deadly foes ever after, unless death has made them "Intimates" again.

The first of Curran's speeches displaying any remarkable ability, is a short one made on Orde's Commercial Propositions.

That on Catholic Emancipation, at p. 138, is perhaps the only one worthy of his reputation. In it, is the prophetic denunciation of an union with England as involving the "emigration of every man of consequence;" as "the participation of British taxes without British trade, and the extinction of the Irish name as a people." These sentiments he ever spoke and acted up to, and bore to his grave.

He used to account for the inferiority of these to his bar speeches, by saying they were made after the fatigue of court, and were badly reported, as he neglected them, and the reporters were government tools. But Curran was surely less qualified for Parliament than for the Bar. His education was forensic, not senatorial. The court did not require, as "the House" did, a minute investigation of the state and history of the country, a mastery of economic details, a power of foreseeing and organizing great political movements. His oratory, too, became too personal, both in reproof and exhortation, to be relished. He must have felt this, and neglected parliament.

The great bar speeches reported, begin with that for Alderman Howison, in 1790. Curran appeared before the Privy Council to sustain Howison's petition to be recognised as Lord Mayor, instead of Alderman James. This speech is less graceful, even in its humour, but far more lawyer-like in its arguments, than any other of his we possess. It is chiefly remarkable for the manner in which he bombarded Lord Clare from an old and irrelevant precedent. Before Clare's face, aye, at the Council board, he described him as a vain and petulant tyrant, and so ingeniously did he do so, that, though his object was palpable, Clare was obliged, after several struggles, to shut his teeth and endure the lash with as little writhing as possible.

But now we come to the state trial speeches. With some exceptions they constitute the whole of his reported bar speeches from thenceforth, and they constitute his *public* life. They were all made in cases arising out of the United Irish Conspiracy; and the history of that conspiracy is the history of the time. It is fully given in Dr. Madden, sufficiently stated in the general histories, and is, we trust, familiar to our readers. Yet we may briefly describe it.

When it was established in 1791, there were two agitations going on in Ireland; one was by the Protestants, the other by the Catholics. Gradually by the writings and acts of Molyneux, Swift, and Lucas, the Protestants of Ireland had come to distrust and quarrel with England. She looked on them as gaolers and bailiffs, and they were content, but sought freedom and riches too—impossible union! The Catholic serf became contemptible, and the Catholic merchant rich and convenient. Curry, Wise, and O'Connor had sustained their spirits. They sought for redress by the meanest supplications—they were refused and persecuted. They sought again in 1776. America had declared her independence, and they got the first emancipation act, allowing them to take leases of land. England grew more distressed when France joined her arms to America's. Ireland was left ungarrisoned, and the Volunteers—the armed Protestantism of Ireland—arose. Free trade followed the first click of their muskets; and Legislative Independence was yielded to their increased numbers, arms, discipline, and ferocity.

Thenceforward they got nothing more; for Charlemont was a weak and bigoted man. He was opposed to Catholic Emancipation, which Belfast demanded in 1782, and he broke up the Convention for Parliamentary Reform in 1783. Grattan, too, because of his insane trust in Charlemont, and his absurd quarrel with Flood, remained out of politics till 1785; and notwithstanding the splendid abilities he and Flood united on the Tithe Question, Orde's Propositions, Emancipation, Reform, and the Regency, there was a steady decline of the Volunteer organization, and of the strength of the liberal party to 1790. We have Tone's word that when the French Revolution broke out, both Catholic Committee and Whig Clubs—the Emancipation and Reform parties—were feeble and dispirited.

The Whig Club was founded in Dublin in the Summer of 1789, by Lord Charlemont.

A different race of men from Whig Club orators or Catholic Lords now began to act on the public.

In Dublin, John Keogh, the strong, rough-souled sagacious merchant, and men of his stamp, sent the Catholic nobles flying in slavish dread. And in Belfast, Neilson, Russel, M'Cracken, &c., headed a Protestant party, which advocated Reform, but began soon to think of Republicanism. The government rendered fearful by the Regency dispute, and desperate by the French Revolution, began to push corruption and the principles of disunion harder than ever.

Amongst the great men of the time, there was one greatest—Theobald Wolfe Tone. The son of a man half farmer, half coachmaker, a poor and briefless lawyer, with a wife and a pack of children, he resolved to redress the wrongs of the Catholic, restore representation in the Commons, and with these, or failing in them, to make his country an independent Republic. He did not publish his design. A few years before he had rashly hinted it in a pamphlet, which no one remembered. Now he wrote a pamphlet in favour of Catholic Emancipation, called "An Argument on behalf of the Catholics of Ireland, by a Northern Whig;" and received every mark of gratitude from his new clients.

In October, 1791, in Belfast, he founded the first United Irish Society. There is a passage in the 1st vol. of Tone's Memoirs, pp. 48-9, so remarkable, that it deserves insertion here:—

"The Dissenters of the North, and more especially of the town of Belfast, are, from the genius of their religion, and from the superior diffusion of political information among them, sincere and enlightened Republicans. They had ever been foremost in the pursuit of parliamentary reform; and I have already mentioned the early wisdom and virtue of the town of Belfast, in proposing the Emancipation of the Catholics, so far back as the year 1783. The French Revolution had awakened all parties in the nation from the stupor in which they lay plunged, from the time of the dispersion of the ever-memorable Volunteer Convention, and the Citizens of Belfast were the first to raise their heads from the abyss, and to look the situation of their country steadily in the face. They saw at a glance their true object, and the only means to obtain it; conscious that the force of the existing government was such as to require the united efforts of the whole Irish people to subvert it, and long convinced in their own minds that to be free it was necessary to be just, they cast their eyes once more on the long-neglected Catholics, and profiting by past errors, for which, however, they had not to accuse themselves, they determined to begin on a new system, and to raise the structure of the liberty and independence of their country on the broad basis of equal rights to the whole people.

"The Catholics, on their part, were rapidly advancing in political spirit and information. Every month, every day, as the Revolution in France went prosperously forward, added to their courage and their force; and the hour seemed at last arrived, when, after a dreary oppression of above one hundred years, they were once more to appear on the political theatre of their country."

The Belfast Society met publicly, as did all the United Irish Societies, until 1794, and its name told its object. They sought to unite Catholic and Protestant, and by this union of numbers and intelligence, to obtain perfect Emancipation for the Catholics, and Popular Representation for the men of both creeds. They exceeded the Catholics in the boldness of their Emancipation scheme; but their doctrines on representation, though inspired by the French Revolution, coincided with those of Fox and the English Whigs. These were the expressed and real opinions of the societies.

Tone, and others of the leading men, wished for an independent Republic, and doubtless framed its structure, and military organization was readily established. Had Government adopted just measures, these honest and sagacious Republicans would still have maintained a hard struggle, but would, for a time, at least, have been overruled by the Whigs, and outvoted in the societies.

The confederation extended to Dublin, received the support of the leading citizens, and of many of the Volunteer Corps. Its chief organ was the "*Northern Star.*" The first number of this paper was printed on the 4th of January, 1792. The manager was Samuel

---

(See Hardy's life of him, vol. ii. p. 195 to 219). The Northern Whig Club was founded by the same person in Belfast, in March, 1790, (History of Belfast. p. 334), to carry off and check the democratic feelings says Mr. Hardy. It were well if some one would cut the few useful facts out of Hardy, and throw the rest into the fire.

Neilson, and it occupied itself chiefly with French politics. The "*Evening Star*" appeared in Dublin soon after, but the "*Press*" did not commence till 28th September, 1797.

In March, 1792, the Catholic Committee, or rather Convention (for it was a body of delegates) met, and Tone was named its secretary. The agitation by means of these societies became most vigorous. The stirring progress of the French Revolution, and the organization of the political societies in England and Scotland aided them. The United Irishmen increased in numbers, the Catholics in confidence, and the Volunteer Corps began to restore their array, and improve their discipline. The ministry grew alarmed; or in Tone's words—

"The solid strength of the people was their union. In December the Catholics had thundered out their demands, the imperious, because unanimous, requisition of 3,000,000 of men; they were supported by all the spirit and intelligence of the Dissenters. Dumourier was in Brabant—Holland was prostrate before him; even London, with the impetuous ardour of the French, did not appear at an immeasurable distance; the stocks were trembling; war seemed inevitable; the minister was embarrassed; and under those circumstances it was idle to think that he would risk the domestic peace of Ireland to maintain a system of monopoly utterly useless to his views."

The Relief Bill was passed in April, 1793, admitting Catholics to the franchise, the bar, the university, and to all the rights of property; but excluding them from Parliament. from State Offices, and from all, indeed, that the Bill of 1829 conceded. It was a victory that encouraged, not a conquest that satisfied them. *They* continued their exertions for complete emancipation, and the United Irishmen grew more vehement and strong.

Meantime another conquest had repined. In December, 1792, a proclamation was issued against seditious associations. The United Irish Society rightly supposed it to be directed against the Volunteers, and they answered it in a publication which we must return to. A Volunteer Convention, said to represent 1,250,000 people, met at Dungannon on the 15th February, 1793, passed resolutions in favour of Emancipation and Reform, and named a permanent committee.

This, doubtless, assisted the carrying of the Relief Bill; but it made the ministry resolve to crush the Protestants, while it conciliated the Catholics. The reply of the United Irishmen to its proclamation was prosecuted; another proclamation, forbidding military societies, drilling, and the whole machinery of the Volunteers, without naming them, was issued on the 11th March, and the same Parliament which passed the Relief Bill, passed the Alien Act—the Militia, Foreign Correspondence, Gunpowder and Convention Acts—in fact, a full code of coercion.

Now the struggle became serious. Many, perhaps a majority of the United Irishmen turned their thoughts to force; and as Keogh and the leading Catholics were United, such a tendency was more formidable than even the anger of the Volunteers had been.

We have probably said enough to enable the reader, though otherwise ignorant of the history of the time, to understand the state of affairs when Curran's speeches for the United Irishmen commenced. The first of these speeches was delivered at the bar of the King's Bench, on the 29th January, 1794, for Archibald Hamilton Rowan.

We have stated that the United Irish Society had answered the government proclamation against seditious meetings. That answer was written by Dr. Drennan, and was a most brilliant and frantic document. Had the people been ready for it, nothing could have been better, otherwise it was most mischievous. It will be found at p. 154. Rowan, the chairman when the address was voted, was prosecuted for this as a libel, as also was Drennan. Drennan was acquitted on a point of form. We possess only one fragment of Curran's defence of him; but the speech for Rowan was amply and well reported. It bears every mark of labour; and yet if we were to trust the back of Curran's brief on the occasion, never was a speech more completely improvised. "Liberty of the Press," "Universal Emancipation," and half a dozen sentences besides, are written carelessly along it. They may, however, have been only marks to recal a prepared oration. The opening of the speech is too exactly like Cicero's exordium in Milo's case not to have been an imitation; and the ever-memorable passage on Universal Emancipation cannot claim originality of thought, though it is certainly unrivalled in rhetorical finish. But his vindication of

the Volunteers (beginning at p. 161), and the liberty of the press (from p. 174), are all his own, and unapproached by anything in Cicero or Erskine.
Rowan was convicted, and heavily sentenced, but he escaped to France.*
The agitation continued. The United Irish Society was changed into a secret and secretly organized body, and it made much progress. The Catholics still laboured; France had conquered: and her government aroused by the *Sans-Culottes* resolutions of Belfast, and by the suggestions of some Irish patriots, bethought herself of assisting the discontented Irish to effect a separation. Accordingly the Rev. William Jackson was sent there as an agent, and put himself in communication with Tone. But he was betrayed by one Cockayne, arrested and arraigned for treason. Curran was his leading counsel, but he ceeded none. He died in the dock of arsenic he had taken the night before.

Another glimmer of conciliation broke in. Lord Fitzwilliam came here early in 1795, with, 'twas said, a *carte-blanche* to carry Emancipation and Reform, and expel the undertakers and ascendancy party from office. Curran was to have been Solicitor-General. Had this policy been carried out, we would have been saved the horrors of 1798, and the conquest of 1800. Perchance the United Irish party would have continued their labours, and a war would have followed; but it would have been a national, not a civil war, and its result would have been separation, not provincialism. Lord Fitzwilliam was not rapid enough; he allowed the Beresfords to rally their friends, and when he came to dismiss one of them, whom he could not retain consistently with his policy, he was met by a court opposition, having the bigot and lunatic King at its head. Beresford was kept in—Fitzwilliam recalled—Emancipation and Reform spurned, and coercion resumed.

This was a triumph for the separation party. An Irish Republic now became the only object of the United Irish; and such being the case, the bulk of the Presbyterians of Down, Antrim, and Tyrone joined, as did multitudes of Protestants and Catholics in Leinster. At this time the Catholics of the North were Defenders or Ribbonmen. Both sides made ready for the worst. "The Union" was turned into a military confederation. An Insurrection Act passed, making it death for any one to take an oath of association; another allowing the Lord Lieutenant to proclaim counties, in which case no one could go out at night; and magistrates obtained the power of breaking into houses, and transporting to the navy all persons whom they suspected. Other acts, granting indemnity for magistrates guilty of any illegality—giving the Lord Lieutenant the power of arrest without bail—licensing the introduction of foreign troops, and establishing the Yeomanry Corps—followed in quick succession.

Government were in possession of information from 1786 out; but they thought it more politic to wait until they could ruin every one likely to join. But they were near overleaping. Tone had gone to America after Jackson's arrest, and thence he went to France. With only a few guineas, a few introductions, and but little French, so transcendent were his abilities and zeal, that he brought a noble French fleet, and sixteen thousand veterans, with Hoche at their head, out of Brest, in 1796. Had Hoche's frigate Christmassed, as Tone's ship did, in Bantry Bay, in 1796, the United Directory would have been the Irish Ministry in a month after. Again, in 1797, the Militia offered to seize Dublin, and were forbidden. Long delay and long coercion disarmed and disunited the people, and the insurrection of the 23rd of May, 1798, was partial and ineffective.

During all this time, Curran was engaged for the United Irish prisoners in every great case. The first regularly reported speech is that made in defence of Finnerty, on the 22nd of December, 1797.

To enable the reader to understand this consummate oration, we must premise some facts.

In September, 1796, William Orr, a Presbyterian farmer, was arrested, with many others, as a United Irishman, but was not tried till the 16th September, 1797. One of the witnesses against him was afterwards proved to have perjured himself; and some of the jurymen, wearied by long disagreement, had got drunk in their room, and in this state brought in the

---

* Drummond's Life of Rowan is not a useless nor disagreeable book; but that is all to be said of it.

verdict of "Guilty." Affidavits of the fact of drunkenness were made by three jurors next day, upon which Curran vainly moved an arrest of judgment. All the facts were laid before Government; yet, after two or three cruel respites, Orr was hanged at Carrickfergus, on the 14th October. He was a fine, handsome, gallant man—died true to his character and his country; and over his grave William Drennan uttered a lament of the most fiery beauty. No wonder he was looked on as a martyr. His name appeared on medals and flags, and in every patriot song; and, even in 1798, John Sheares could find no more forcible way of ending his stern proclamation than the words, "Remember Orr." A letter was published in the *Press*, the noble organ of the Union, addressed to Lord Camden, and narrating Orr's fate with much pathos and invective. The letter* was signed "MARCUS ' and was written by a Mr. Deane Swift.

Finnerty, the printer of the *Press*, was indicted for this as a libel. Curran defended him in a speech, which he himself preferred to any of his other speeches. He only got his brief a " few minutes before the cause commenced;" yet he never made an abler, nor did any other advocate ever make so able, a speech.

His account of the duties of the public writer deserves to be the very Bible of the press. 't so heroically directs and so wisely justifies them; and his narrative of Orr's fate goes on so tenderly, so gently, so grandly, that one hardly knows whether to admire its sagacity pause upon its lavish beauties, or weep over its sorrows. It is the lament of an angel.

"1798" came—that type of terror; and yet Curran's first effort in that year was crowned with success, and smiles, and pleasant greetings, and the thunders of the people followed the advocate home. Finney, and fifteen others, were indicted for High Treason. The chief witness was James O'Brien, a man who, by his own confession, had taken the United Oath, and had been guilty of many less equivocal crimes. Curran's cross-examination of him was equalled by his after address to the jury:—He tore O'Brien to pieces on the table; he put him together again, an image of the foulest treachery, of the fiercest love of blood, and of the most loathsome perjury. The jury refused to convict on the oath of this coiner and stabber, who came there to assassinate men with the word of God, and they acquitted the prisoners. O'Brien was still dear to the Castle, and continued in its pay; but about two years after, he committed a murder so indiscreetly, that he could not be any longer shielded. He was tried; and though Curran, who prosecuted, made a very temperate speech, he was found guilty, and hanged.

Alas! Curran prevailed no more. The Government would not go back, nor the people either. The Yeomanry consisted of the Tory gentry and their dependants. They were undisciplined and unprincipled; and not being checked by the people, who waited for command, they soon became a legal banditti, who brought local knowledge and old feelings to aid their crimes. No villany but was perpetrated by them. The house of whomsoever an of them disliked or suspected was surrounded at night:—If he were not at home it was burned: if found, he might consider himself lucky in being sent to serve in the navy, after being whipped or pitch-capped, instead of being half-hanged or whole-hanged, as the leisure or facilities of the officer allowed.

Still, still, still the Directory waited for foreign aid!—and waited in vain. One victory would have brought them more arms and officers from abroad or at home than any negociation.

The Directory consisted of Thomas Emmet, Arthur O'Connor, Oliver Bond, Doctor MacNevin, and Richard M'Cormick. Lord Edward was named Commander-in-Chief; and at length in March, in 1798, a rising was determined on, chiefly at the wish of Lord Edward, for Thomas Emmet wished to wait till the arrival of French troops, or, at least, of French officers.†

We must refer the reader to Dr. Madden's comprehensive work for the minutiæ of the events that followed. Suffice it here, that, on the 12th of March, fourteen United Delegates met at Oliver Bond's house, 13, Bridge-street, Dublin, and were arrested there on the aformation of Reynolds, the accursed. Many other arrests, chiefly of Northerns, had taken

---

* It appears in the indictment. page 277   † Madden's Memoir of Emmet.

place previously. Emmet, MacNevin, and other chiefs, were taken on the same day as those who attended the meeting at Bond's, and on the informat on of the same man, "whose name," says Doctor Madden, "sounds like a calamity." Other arrests followed:—On the 18th May, Lord Edward was arrested; on the 21st the Sheareses were taken; and on the 23rd was the rising.

We would not willingly follow the crash and waste of that explosion; we would rather follow the armed man striking in the open field for liberty, whether he won or lost. But this is not for us. Let us come to the dungeon, and survey the court; the public scaffold needs no painter.

An insurrection, which had not at its head one able tactician, and few men acquainted with the elements of war, or even the topography and statistics of the country, could hardly succeed. And yet it had almost conquered. Within twelve days from the first rising, the people of Wexford had cleared their county, with the exception of Ross and Duncannon, two places unfit to resist a skilful attack. Similar successes attended the Kildare insurrection. This was all that mere valour could do.

The leaders were brave, especially the few priests who fought. But all were ignorant to the last degree. No organization—no commissariat—no unity of action—no foreign aid—were attempted. To such men, victory brought drunkenness, waste, disputes, and want. Defeat could hardly bring worse.

Antrim and Down did not rise for a fortnight; and there, after similar blunders, and a shorter struggle, the Presbyterians were crushed.

The Wexford men protracted the war, partly from a vague hope of foreign assistance, but still more from despair, for they could not trust the faith of their persecutors; and not a few of these heroic men died on the plains of Meath, in an effort to force their way into Ulster.

It is said that fifty thousand insurgents and twenty thousand of the English party were slain. The amount seems exaggerated, as the details certainly were.

The soldier having done his own work, and that of the assassin and brigand, too—the civilian began to labour. The General's sword yielded to the bow-string of the Attorney General. Courts-martial hanged those taken in battle; and now courts civil slaughtered the prisoners. Most unaccountably, the insurgents did not retaliate; if they had a right to rise, they were entitled to the rights of war, and were weak, wicked, and impolitic in neglecting to enforce them. An insurgent chief should have shot the peasants who lifted their hands against property or person, without order; but he was equally bound to guard them against any but a soldier's hazards, by retaliating every execution, coolly, judicially, and uniformly.

But none of the older leaders of the United Irish were touched till after the insurrection was defeated. Then, in July, 1798, might you have seen the prison hovered round by anxious and mourning relatives, whom the guards of power repelled. Then might you have seen the crimson-clad judge—and the packed jury—and the ferocious prosecutor—and the military gangs from the Castle crush around the dock, wherein were the fearless and the true, and threaten, with voice and gesture, that little dark man who defended the prisoners. He scowled back upon their threats. "You may assassinate me," said he, when their bayonets were levelled at his breast, " but you shall not intimidate me!"* They could better have hoped to drive the stars from heaven by their violence, than force John Curran by threats to surrender one hair of his client's head.

They were not mere clients for whom he pleaded, to win fees and reputation. They were dear friends, for whose safety he would have coined his blood; they were brother patriots who had striven, by means which he thought desperate, or unsuited to him, to free their country. He was no hireling or adventurer. He came inspired by love, mercy, justice, and genius, and commissioned by heaven to walk on the waters with these patriots, and lend them his hand when they were sinking. He pleaded for some who, nevertheless,

---

* See page 343.

were slaughtered; but was his pleading vain, therefore? Did he not convert many a shaken conscience—sustain many a frightened soul? Did he not keep the life of genius, if not of hope in the country? Did he not help to terrify the Government into that compromise they so ill kept? Surely, he did all this at the time; and his speeches now and for ever will remain less as models of eloquence than as examples of patriotism and undying exhortations to justice and liberty.

The first trial after the insurrection was that of Henry and John Sheares. They wer two Cork gentlemen, barristers by profession, both men of liberal education, but of ver, unequal characters. Henry, the eldest, was mild, changeful, and weak; John was fiery and firm, and of much greater abilities. They had worked the United system in places having little connexion with the Executive Directory; but when some of the members o that Directory were seized on the 12th of March, the Sheareses stepped into the dangerous posts, and shared the same fate in ten days after.

On their arrest, a rough draft of a proclamation, written by John Sheares, was found in the writing-desk of Henry, who knew nothing of it. It was paraded in the front of the attack, and Captain Armstrong was the main force of the prosecution.

This frightful wretch had sought the acquaintance of the Sheareses—made it—encouraged their projects—assisted them with military hints—professed tender love for them mixed with their family—and used to dandle Henry Sheares's children. We hear the technical monster denies this little fact, though he admits all the rest.

He shared their hospitality—urged on their schemes—came to condole with them in prison—and then assassinated them with his oath.

They were first arraigned on the 4th of July, at the Green-street Commission; but legal difficulties occurred, and legal arguments, which will be found herein, and it was the 12th of July when they were tried. The case for the Crown closed at midnight. Curran applied for time; he had been racked by the contests and horrid excitement of a day in which he had to resist the royal bloodhounds, to cross-examine a demon, and gaze on the Sheareses —the one trembling for his brother, the other for himself. The delay was refused, and Curran opened his address with an earnest solemnity, which makes this part of this speech the most moving he ever uttered. But we cannot pause to criticise. He closed at daylight. That bright summer sun danced into the black court while Carleton sentenced these strong men to die, and long ere he set on the morrow they were swinging, without life, on the gallows.

On the 17th of July, M'Cann was tried, defended by Curran, condemned, and executed. Byrne shared the same fate in a few days after; but Curran's speeches in their defence were suppressed by Government.

On the 23rd of July, Oliver Bond was tried and convicted. Curran's speech for him is preserved. The chief topic in it was the character and testimony of Reynolds; a man with more crimes than Armstrong, but not of so deep a dye. He appears to have been a poisoner and robber, but he was a man of family, a gentleman, and the Government took care to make him a rich man. £6000 and a consulship rewarded his virtues, but could not increase his dignity.

Bond died of apoplexy or assassination; and shortly after, a compromise was made whereby the Government agreed to banish the rest of the prisoners upon getting *general* information as to the Union. They got the information, and then sent the prisoners to Fort George—prisoners still.

Curran, during this period, lived at The Priory, near Dundrum, and used to drive into town in a gig. He was in daily expectation of being shot. The trials ceased, and he went to England, but all was not over.

Humbert landed at Killala; the victory of Castlebar and the defeat at Collooney concluded the war, and caused a renewal of the military and civil massacres. Bartholomew Teeling, Humbert's aid-de-camp, surrendered with the French, and Tone was taken prisoner on board a French ship.

Tone passed as a Frenchman, till Sir George Hill, an old companion, ran him down. He was tried by a court martial in barracks; his defence is unrivalled for plain wise eloquence His last request, a soldier's death, was refused. He was sentenced to be hanged, but he w the Government anticipated the executioner. His threat was cut in prison. The wound, though mortal, did not produce immediate death, and in that state, they were going to hang him, when Curran came into court and obtained a habeas corpus. It was too late. Tone perished in a few days.

This was Curran's last struggle in 1798. But his griefs had not ended.

The Government, with arms victorious over the insurgents, advanced against the liberties of the people; a vanguard of villains, armed with gold and titles preceded them; terror was in their march, and falsehood pioneered the way. The Union was carried.

There were three other cases connected with the insurrection, in which Curran appeared to save or avenge. The first was his plea at the bar of the House of Commons for the widow and orphans of Lord Edward. The Government, malcontent that death should have secured the rebel's retreat, struck at those he left behind. They attainted him as a traitor, for Curran pleaded without effect, and they seized the fortunes of those dearest to him. Did they hope to disturb his shade by cruelty to those he loved? Curran spoke rather as a judge than a counsel. "Sir," said he to the Speaker, "I have no defensive evidence! I have no case! It is impossible I should: I have often of late gone to the dungeon of the captive, but never have I gone to the grave of the dead, to receive instructions for his defence, nor in truth have I ever before been at the trial of a dead man! I offer, therefore, no evidence upon this inquiry: against the perilous example of which I do protest on behalf of the public, and against the cruelty and injustice of which I do protest in the name of the dead father, whose memory is sought to be dishonoured; and of his infant orphans, whose bread is sought to be taken away." How gloriously he pleaded! With what potent scorn he flung aside the foulness of Reynolds. How profoundly, how nobly he disproved the policy of penal laws, and the prudence of cruelty! What imagery and wisdom united, as he described law and victim, each growing fiercer in the conflict, till the penalty could go no further, and the fugitive turned on his breathless pursuer. Does that man live who does not envy the Geraldines that beautifully true description of their blood, "nobler than the royalty which first ennobled it, that, like a rich stream, rose till it ran and hid its fountain?" Justice, humanity, and eloquence spoke idly to this red-handed government. They legislated Fitzgerald into a traitor, and then stooped to the mean barbarity of stripping his infant's cradle.

An act, called an act of most gracious pardon, passed in October, 1798, but it excepted every class of insurgents above the lowest, and by name attainted a crowd of leaders. Napper Tandy, the old commander of the Dublin Volunteer Artillery, was one of them. He was on the Continent, and after a fruitless effort to join Humbert, returned then and resided at Hamburgh. *Fifteen* days before he was bound to surrender, he was seized there, cast, ironed, into prison, and thence brought to Ireland. Curran chiefly relied on this technicality, that his time for surrendering had not expired when he was seized. Nominally on this ground, Tandy was acquitted; but he owed his escape to an advocate more eloquent than Curran. Tandy held a French commission, and had been seized on a neutral state, contrary to the law of nations, and Napoleon said, "if Tandy were hanged, he would hang two English officers for him, and so, "like case like rule," as the Chief Justice says. The reasoning was simple and conclusive, and Tandy was released. Would to God it had been used in time to save poor Tone!

The case of Hevey v. Major Sirr, which was tried in 1802, was one of those petty reactions against the insolence of petty tyrants wherewith vanquished men console themselves. Sirr had imprisoned and tortured hundreds—one too many. Hevey brought an action against him, and Curran stated Hevey's case with a galvanic energy, pouring out all the resources of persuasion, wit, and deepest pathos, till the jury were captivated into giving a verdict against the Castle minion. Doubtless, with all this, the Government could have defeated Hevey. They could have packed the jury to the right level. The desire to appear legal to England, or the fear of returning energy in Ireland, or some dim notion that Napoleon was beginning to see that there was waiting for him an ally more useful than Italy or Germany could give, or all combined, induced them to tolerate this one act of retribution. Their idemnity laws prevented the example from being inconvenient.

Still there was a storm mustering abroad, and a convulsion preparing at home. Thomas Addis Emmet was released in 1802, and went on the Continent. He and his younger brother, Robert, met at Amsterdam. Both adhered to their principles. Robert returned home, and communicated with several men of influence in Ireland. He obtained plenty of promises. All parties longed for redress, and perhaps for vengeance. The people were willing to sacrifice every thing for these objects, yet were depressed so much that it would have required the efforts of many leaders, or of many well-used years to restore their confidence. The upper ranks of the United were even more dispirited than the lower.

It was neither customary nor safe for any man then, nor though many a year after, to profess liberal or manly principles. The most vile and slavish doctrines echoed in Court, Church, 'Change and drawing-room. Agitation was as desperate as insurrection, and more dangerous.

Emmet had been absent. He thought the country ready; he only remembered the spirit of 1797. "If I get ten counties to rise," said he to Keogh, who still continued his safe counsel with the discontented, " ought I go on?" "You ought," said Keogh, "if you get five, and you will succeed."

Robert went on, but every bank broke under his feet. And though he was ardent and rapid as the mountain deer, he fell at last an easy prey. Napoleon was too busy, and money was scarce, and merchants cautious, Presbyterians irritated by the lies about Wexford massacres, and Catholics indignant at the supposed desertion of the North. Russell was seized after failing to raise the North,—he lies headless in Downpatrick. Emmet, too failed and suffered.

Curran defended Kirwan, one of the insurgents, and in his speech spoke of the French alliance in most eloquent anger, and of the insurrection in the bitterest scorn. We are not going to condemn Curran for what he did in 1803. He had gone to France in 1802, and was disgusted with its military government, and he meant doubtless to serve the people by warning them against trusting to strangers for redress. He was politically indignant at an explosion which wanted the dignity of even partial success, and yet had done vast injury to the country. Lord Kilwarden's death had irritated him, for he was his old friend; and last of all his own personal feelings had been severely tried by it.

Robert had won Sarah Curran's heart, and some of his letters were found in Curran's house. The rash chieftain had breathed out his whole soul to his love. Curran had to undergo the inquiries of the Privy Council, and accept the generosity of the Attorney-General.

What was still worse than any selfish suffering, he saw his daughter smitten, as with an edged sword, by the fate of her betrothed.

He refused to act for Robert, and he did well; but his refusal to see him was framed, we think, too harshly.

As Emmet himself said, "a man with the coldness of death on him need not be made to feel any other coldness."

That cold hand soon seized him—the tender, the young, the beautiful, the brave. Greater men died in the same struggle, but none so warmly loved, nor so passionately lamented.

It may be asked was Curran really no party to the United system? We have heard men rashly say that they *knew* that he and Grattan were united. But on being pressed, their proofs vanished. The only direct evidence we ever met was the fact, that in 1797, during some row or gathering in College green, Curran, muffled in his cloak, walked up to a gentleman, whose connexion with the Union was undoubted, and leaning up to his face, said, "when will it be?" Yet, surely this proves nothing but his anxiety on the subject. Doubtless, he, and many who like him took no part in the conspiracy, would not condemn its objects, though they might condemn or distrust the means used. Had it at all succeeded, we are sure the revolution would have received his enthusiastic support.*

---

* It is stated by the younger Tone, that so early as 1794, Curran expressed his anxiety for a *separation* from England, but that he was not United.—*Tone's Memoirs*.

And now the insurrections were over.

The prison had grown into a hopeless home, the exile had despaired, the widow and orphan were allowed to mourn without suspicion, the country rested in exhaustion and infamy—the dead rested better in their bloody graves. The gallant Fitzgerald, the romantic Emmet, and the matchless Tone were gone where there are no tears, nor tyrants, nor slaves. The ferocious Clare, too, had gone to his account. The visions of the one, and the crimes of the other had passed away. What wonder if Ireland lay down in despair, and said, "there is no hope for me." What wonder if Curran, the beloved and doating son of Ireland, should sink, and sorrow too. The mere might of intellect, the absolute trust placed in him, the old habit of exertion bore him along for some years, but his goal had sunk, there was nought before him, his mission was done. Yet his speeches afterwards were very great. His speech in Judge Johnson's case is a model of constitutional argument and persuasive advocacy. His decision in Merry v. Power, is full of impassioned justice; and that at the Newry Election has a mockery of hope in it. But what of these things? John Curran who came to the corrupt judge and hesitating jury, and awed them down before the spirits of liberty, heroism, and righteousness, which he invoked—John Curran, the avenger of the martyred, the divine man, who so often walked through the fiery furnace with those who trusted him—what had he to do in a country which ceased to hope, and ceased to strive, and was making its bed in the dungeon for a forty and odd years' sojourn?

We have no heart to scrutinize the trivial public events with which he was afterwards connected. These operas, after a solemn tragedy, do not suit honest men; better for them to go home and weep. But on the private life of Curran, we have something to say.

Let us now leave, therefore, the gowned monarch of the former, and go home with John Curran.

Of Curran's private life, during its morning and noon, little is before the public, yet some who could describe it must still be living.

About 1779, he took a glen near Newmarket, and built a cottage in it, which he called the Priory, from his rank as Prior of the Monks of St. Patrick. He used to spend his autumns here, after the Cork assizes, and his genius and pleasantry made his hospitality be well tried. Lord Avonmore, his friend, was a native of the town. His society, and that of the Creaghs and Kellers, would have been enough for a less enjoying and more fastidious man than Curran was. Of this place he had only a terminable lease, and in latter life he seldom visited Newmarket.

He was a great changer of his town residence. From Redmond's-hill he went to Fade-street, thence, in 1780 or 1781, to 12, Ely-place, afterwards called No. 4. In 1807, he took a house in Harcourt-street, and finally took the house No. 80, Stephen's-green, South, in which Judge Burton now resides.*

From 1790, however, his town house was a mere place of business. In that year he took a place called Holly Park, in the county of Dublin, and soon after changed its name to the Priory. The Priory contains about thirty-five acres, and lies on the road to White Church, about a mile beyond Rathfarnham, on the side of a moderately large hill, facing Dublin. From it, there is a beauteous view of the city, with the plains of Fingal on one side, and its bay and varied shores on the other. The house is a comfortable plain building, with a warm shrubbery, a garden, and a few fields about it. At the opposite side of the road is Marlay, the residence of the Latouches, and the country all round consists of wooded demesnes.

The place suited him perfectly habits there were very simple and uniform. He went to bed about one, and rose at seven o'clock, and spent a couple of hours dressing and lounging about. Immediately after breakfast he used generally to ride or drive in his gig

---

* Judge Burton was, we have heard, a clerk to an English Solicitor. Being in Ireland about some suit, he became professionally known to Curran, who induced him to stop here. Curran, it is said, gave Mr. Burton £500 a-year to note his briefs, during his, Mr. B.'s legal noviciate. It is needless to add, that Mr. Burton's profound knowledge and untouched honour justified Curran's predilection for him.

to Dublin. During term time, when he was a practising lawyer or a judge, this was of course necessary, as a matter of business; and, after he left the bench, he continued to go in to hear news, and see his old friends—hanging, as it would seem, on men's hearts, and hoping, like a lover, for some good tidings still.

Punctually at five o'clock he came up the avenue, often with his watch in hand; for though irregular in other things, he was childishly exact in his dinner-hour, and would not have waited for Washington.

When he did not go into town, he was fond of walking with a friend among the shaded roads about Rathfarnham and Dundrum: or oftener still he spent his hours in sauntering or strolling all alone through the garden and shrubbery of his little place. In one of these fields he had buried his little daughter Gertrude,* and upon her dear grave he used often lie down and weep, and wish to be with her. She had died in 1792, when his hopes were high, and his home untainted.

Of late years he grew close. He had been a man more irregular than lavish in money matters. Strange to say, he, the first lawyer at the bar, did not continue to keep a regular fee book, and excused himself by saying, the money came in so fast, he could not enter it. His irregularity continued, for, at the time when, it is said, he was miserly, he left his pecuniary concerns to be managed by a friend. He felt the weakness growing on him, and hated himself for it. His closeness must, however, have been over-rated by his friends and himself, or he would have died a richer man than he did.

He seldom dined without having some to share with him a meal that was occasionally too frugal. We have heard of his bringing Grattan and several others out to dine, when he had nothing useable but cold corned beef, and that one of the guests took to the kitchen and manufactured a dish of "bubble and squeak," which the party, assisted by plenty of good wine, declared to be capital.

Curran, when roused, used to run over jokes of every kind, good, bad, and indifferent. No epigram too delicate, no mimicry too broad, no pun too little, and no metaphor too bold for him. In fact he wanted to be happy, and to make others so, and he rattled away, not for a Boswell to note, but for mere enjoyment. These after-dinner sittings were seldom prolonged very late, but they made up in vehemence what they wanted in duration. Curran played the violin and violoncello, and when the fit took him, played with great feeling and nature; but if asked to show off, he was timid and stiff in his performance. The same difference was observable in talking over any of his own speeches or writings.

Often, after his company had left him, he used to walk about the room, soliloquizing aloud, until he got into very high or very low spirits.

This habit of soliloquy he had fallen into when a young speaker. He *never wrote* his speeches, and hardly ever wrote even passages of them. There is no orator, living or dead, of whom this can be said to the same extent.†

Curran's avoidance of written speeches was deliberate. He thought that no foresight could enable you to calculate beforehand how to shape your discourse exactly, and he felt in himself the rare power of doing, on the spur of the occasion, whatever his genius, if allowed repose, could have planned. But though he wrote none of his speeches, he generally *prepared them with the most intense and passionate care.* Walking about his grounds, in his driving into and out from Dublin, and in those stray hours which intervened between the departure of his guests and the coming of the welcomer guest, sleep, he most frequently bethought himself how to shape his coming speech most persuasively; and then, and in walking in the hall, or when rambling over his violoncello, his happiest and most glorious

---

* On a diamond-shaped flag is the inscription—"Here lies the body of Gertrude Curran, fourth daughter of John Philpot Curran, who departed this life October the 6th, 1792, age twelve years." She lies under a little group of limes, ash, and laburnums, in a very safe untroubled looking spot.

† When we say orators, we do not mean public talkers, but men whose speeches are great combinations of reasoning or plausibility, fancy or passion, and owe their success to the literary excellence and oratorical address, and not to other circumstances. This makes the orator occasionally rank below the speechless man of business and character.

thoughts used to come. He had a fine and well-practised memory, and it carried for him to court the frame and topics, and leading illustrations of his speech, but no more. The speech was an original effort upon these previous materials, and what the events in court added to them. His notes were mere catch words, as we mentioned in Rowan's case; nor were they needed, as the speeches for Finnerty and the Sheareses prove.

His library was small, but very good, especially in classics. He says in one of his letters that he was fond of metaphysical and theological studies, but he appears not to have had settled opinions on these subjects. From his letters one would say, that Sterne was a greater favourite than Berkley or Virgil, and the Bible supplies his speeches with more illustrations than any book, save nature's.

Alas, for poor Curran! his country's dishonour was not his only cause of woe. Just as the time sorrow for Ireland most pressed him down, his wife, the companion of twenty-five years, deserted him for a man whom he had long welcomed as a friend—the Rev. Mr Sandys.

It has been said that Curran was dissipated, that he was apt "to hang up his merriment with his hat when he came home," and that he ought not to have so trusted a man of Mr. Sandys' character. We have neither leisure nor inclination to inquire whether he was too confiding, too careless, or too self-indulgent; suffice it, the separation took place under circumstances of peculiar pain, not only to him, but to his children. Curran recovered but trifling damages in an action against Mr. Sandys, and this certainly shows that he was to some extent faulty. The occurrences of this trial estranged him from many of his old friends.

This event is said to have given a most cruel interest to his speech in the case of Massy and Headfort. His speech against Lord Headfort is beyond comparison the most persuasive pleading ever uttered in a case not involving national interests or public passions. By his ability and his personal sympathy for the case, he made it a great contest between virtue and vice. The safety of the juror's family, the character of the country, the fate of society itself, seem to depend on their making an example of this "hoary criminal." How he leads them over the whole chronicle of dishonour, yet never compromises their dignity or his own for one instant. His reply to the palliations offered by Lord Headfort's counsel sends them back in coals of fire. He represents the judge as interposing to prevent the victim's flight with her seducer, and puts in his mouth every argument that reason, passion, mercy, and Scripture could give to prevent this crime. He warns him that he cannot marry this fugitive; for, between him and the marriage altar, there are two sepulchres to pass. He tears away the miserable pretext of love from an indulgence which would as surely cause the ruin, as it proved the dishonour, of its object; and under his burning eloquence he makes the lordly sinner blacken into a selfish, cowardly violator of hospitality, and a traitor to public morals.

This was Curran's last great achievement at the bar.

In 1806, on Pitt's death, Fox and the Whigs came in. It had been settled for seventeen years before, that when they should come in, Ponsonby was to have the first, and Curran the second, legal appointment. Ponsonby was made Chancellor; Curran was entitled to the Chief Justiceship if it could be vacated, and if not, to the Attorney-Generalship. He got neither, but was put off with the Mastership of the Rolls, encumbered by the officers of Sir Michael Smith; for Mr. Ponsonby had agreed to leave these officers in, or pension them before Sir Michael would retire. Curran was not consulted on this, and very naturally refused to be bound by it, and dismissed the officers. This led to a quarrel between him and Ponsonby which was never healed. Both parties seem to have acted with just intentions. Curran explained the facts in a letter to Grattan, and to that published letter no reply was given, nor could any. Ponsonby very honourably provided for these people out of his own estate.

Curran was unsuited to the technicalities and minute business of the Rolls. He had neither knowledge nor taste for it. He felt this, and the moment when he could rise was one he anxiously looked for. It may be guessed that his orders on details were not very sound nor convenient The only memorable decision he made was that in Merry v Power

The expulsion of his party from office in 1807, forced him into communication with men whose policy he condemned as much as their principles.

In the vacations, he often went to England. Some of his letters during these trips are precious tokens of the swell and depth of his ebbing mind One dated from Godwin's house. 41, Skinner-street, London, in 1810, tells us something of his habits and feelings.

"I am glad to hear you are letting yourself out at Old Orchard; you are certainly unwise in giving up such an inducement to exercise, and the absolute good of being so often in good air. I have been talking about your habit without naming yourself. I am more persuaded that you and Egan are not sufficiently afraid of weak liquors. I can say, from trial, how little pain it costs to correct a bad habit. On the contrary, poor nature, like an illused mistress, is delighted with the return of our kindness, and is anxious to show her gratitude for that return, by letting us see how well she becomes it.

"I am the more solicitous upon this point from having made this change, which I see will make me waited for in heaven longer than perhaps they looked for. If you do not make some pretext for lingering, you can have no chance of conveying me to the wherry; and the truth is, I do not like surviving old friends. I am somewhat inclined to wish for posthumous reputation; and if you go before me, I shall lose one of the most irreclaimable of my trumpeters; therefore, dear Mac, no more water, and keep the other element, your wind, for the benefit of your friends. I will show my gratitude as well as I can, by saying handsome things of you to the saints and angels before you come. Best regards to all with you. "Yours, &c., "J. P. C."

He visited Scotland this autumn, and praises the knowledge, independence, and hospitality of all classes there. In one of these letters he thus speaks of having visited Burns' cabin:—

"Poor Burns!—his cabin could not be passed unvisited or unwept; to its two little thatched rooms—kitchen and sleeping-place—a slated sort of parlour is added, and it is now an ale-house. We found the keeper of it tipsy; he pointed to the corner on one side of the fire, and with a most *mal-a-propos* laugh, observed, 'there is the very spot where Robert Burns was born.' The genius and the fate of the man were already heavy on my heart; but the drunken laugh of the landlord gave me such a view of the rock on which he foundered, I could not stand it, but burst into tears."

A more affecting sight could not well be.— No man could sympathize better with the genius and failings of Robert Burns, than John Curran. In the whole range of literature, there are no two men more like. They had the same deep, picturesque genius; the same absolute control over language; the same love of country and kind; the same impassionate, womanishly sensitive hearts; now plunging into difficulties from their loving, generous, and social hearts, and springing out of them by strength of intellect, and then, alas! both sinking under the tyranny of imagination, and seeking relief from intense melancholy in undue social excitement. There are several minuter points of resemblance, and any one familiar with the two men, must feel the likeness in their lives and works.

Some other bits of the letters show how playful he could be in all this depression. From Cheltenham he writes in September 1811—

"During my stay here, I have fallen into some pleasant female society; but such society can be enjoyed only by those who are something at a tea-table or a ball. Tea always makes me sleepless; and as to dancing, I tried three or four steps that were quite the cream of the thing in France at one time, and which cost me something. I thought I might be the gaiters that gave them a piperly air; but even after putting on my black silk stockings, and perusing them again before the glass, which I put on the ground for the purpose of an exact review, I found the edition was too stale for re-publication."

Talking of Irish parties, in the same letter he says—

"The smoke is thickest at the corners furthest from the chimney, and, therefore, near the fire we see a little more distinctly; but as things appear to me, I see not a single ticket in the wheel that may not be drawn a blank, poor Paddy's not excepted. To go back to the fire—each party has the bellows hard at work; but I strongly suspect that each of them does more to blind their rivals, and themselves too, by blowing the ashes about, than they do in coaxing or cherishing the blaze for the comfort or benefit of their own shins."

From London, 1811, he says—

"I have little doubt that Perceval is as warlike a hero as Grenville, and just as capable of simplifying our government to the hangman and the tax-gatherer."

In a P.S. from Holland House he writes—

"Some more lies from the Continent. Another victory—three legs of Bonaparte shot away, the fourth very precarious. I really suspect that you have been here *incog.*, and bit every body; for they will believe nothing, even though authenticated by the most respectable letters from Gottingen."

The next letter is strong on an important point-

"As to our miserable questions, they are not half so interesting as the brolls in the Caraccas. What a test of the Union! and what a proof of the apathy of this blind and insolent country! They affect to think it glorious to struggle to the last shilling of their money, and the last drop of their blood, rather than submit their property and persons to the capricious will of France; and yet that is precisely the power they are exercising over us—the modest authority of sending over to us laws, like boots and shoes ready made for exportation, without once condescending to take our measure, or ask whether or where they pinch us."

In October, 1812, he was asked to stand for Newry, but was beaten, after a six days contest, by General Needham. The Catholic agitation was then at its height, and yet, by the votes and labours of some Roman Catholics, he was beaten. His picture of these miserable men is such as to justify the cruel charity with which he bids the people "forgive them, for they will not forgive themselves."

Every part of this speech deserves close attention. It is the perfect oratory of a matured patriot. But we more especially ask the reader to study the principle announced in pages 406-7,—a most emphatic announcement of the power of agitation to achieve its ends.

His son's memoir contains a long treatise of his, on the then state of Irish politics, in a letter to the Duke of Sussex—we have not space to publish it, nor is it equal to his less formal letters, in thought or style.

Curran resigned the Mastership of the Rolls in 1814, in consequence of his wretched health, which grew worse and worse every day.

But sickly as his body had grown, it was healthier than his mind.

Grief of every kind weighed upon that wild sensitive heart of his. The purest by whose side he had striven for Ireland, were dead or banished; the bitterest with whom he contended, were no longer there to excite anger and exertion. There was no more a corrupt Irish party to be exposed, or an audacious ministry to be confronted and beaten back. His dearest child had withered under the last blow that struck his country, and all that remained of home had been poisoned by a villain. He had ever been easily affected, and mirth and melancholy divided his restless being. Now these tendencies became diseased and excessive.

Memory, to him, wore "a robe of mourning" and came in "a faded light."

Dublin, at that time, had been emptied of its genius; it had not acquired the education which, in our day *begins* to make its society tolerable—and politically it was a blank.

He rallied every young man of promise about him; and many are living who have no greener recollection than the nights they spent at The Priory, when his mind, roused by friendship and sympathy, broke loose from its sorrows. Nor can we wonder, though we must grieve, at the influence which men who had no merit but coarse gaiety and a knowledge of his character, sometimes exercised over his seared and trusting spirit.

Even from amid the excitements of London and Paris, where he was cherished and honoured, he looked back to Ireland and wept bitterly.

In a letter to Mr. Lubé, he says—

"Everything I see disgusts and depresses me; I look back at the streaming of blood for so many years; and every thing every where relapsed into its former degradation. France rechained—Spain again saddled for the priests—and Ireland, like a bastinadoed elephant, kneeling to receive the paltry rider; and what makes the idea the more cutting, her fate the work of her own ignorance, no' fury. She has completely lost all sympathy here, and

I see no prospect for her, except a vindictive oppression and an endlessly increasing taxation. God give us, not happiness, but patience!"

The same letter has most plaintive and beautiful thoughts on the value of hearty loving intercourse among friends, and the dull hollowness of "general" society—that wretched cheat. His account of English society is bitter enough too

"Since my arrival here, my spirits have been wretchedly low: though treated with great kindness, I find nothing to my mind. I find heads without thinking, and hearts without strings, and a phraseology sailing in ballast—every one piping, but few dancing. England is not a place for society; it is too cold, too vain, without pride enough to be humble, drowned in dull fantastical formality, vulgarised by rank without talent, and talent foolishly recommending itself by weight rather than by fashion—a perpetual war between the disappointed pretensions of talent and the stupid overweening of affected patronage; means without enjoyment, pursuits without an object, society without conversation or intercourse: perhaps they manage this better in France—a few days, I think, will enable me to decide.'

This feeling about England confirmed him in refusing to enter the Imperial Parliament, which he had been repeatedly urged to do. Thank God he refused to be handed in by a corrupt patron, to exhibit a genius impotent to convince and able only to excite and gratify that hard-hearted senate.

His letters from Paris continue to express the same view of Irish affairs, and display the same mixture of jest and woe.—

"Patriotic affectation is almost as bad as personal, but I declare I think these things do a good deal in sinking my health, which is far from good; my spirits quite on the ground; and yet as to Ireland, I never saw but one alternative—a bridewell or a guard-house; with England the first, with France the other. We might have had a mollification and the bolts lightened, and a chance of progression; but that I now give up."

That his grief was not the striving of a worldly spirit against the orders of nature, might be judged from a most fearfully humorous description of a visit to the Catacombs of Paris, to see "a dead population equal to four times the living." It has contrasts as terrible as Goethe's. There was a vain woman of the party—

"I asked her whether it gave her a sentiment of grief, or fear, or hope? She asked me what room I could see for hope in a parcel of empty skulls? 'For that reason, madam', and because you know they cannot be filled with grief or fear, for all subjects of either is past.' She replied, 'oui, et cependant c'est jolie.' It did not raise her in my mind, though she was not ill-looking; and when I met her above ground, after our resurrection, she appeared fit enough for the drawing-rooms of the world, though not for the undercellar. I do not remember even to have had my mind compressed into so narrow a space: so many human beings, so many actors, so many sufferers, so various in human rank, so equalized in the grave! When I stared at the congregation, I could not distinguish what head had raved, or reasoned, or hoped, or burned. I looked for thought, I looked for dimples,—I asked, whither is all gone—did wisdom never flow from your lips, nor affection hung upon them—and if both or either, which was the most exalting—which the most fascinating? All silent. They left me to answer for them, 'So shall the fairest face appear.'"

On the 22nd of August, 1814, he mentions his anxiety to live amongst the French, whom he preferred to the English, but he seems to have doubted his power of living much longer any where. Yet he feared not death.—

"I do not like the state of my health; if it was merely *maladie* under sailing orders for the undiscovered country, I should not quarrel with the passport. There is nothing gloomy in my religious impressions, though I trust they are not shallow: I ought to have been better—I know also that others have been as blameable: and I have rather a cheerful reliance upon mercy than an abject fear of justice. Or were it otherwise, I have a much greater fear of suffering than of death."

Then he bore up, and for two years more he shared his time between a Dublin circle, including Mr. Sheil, and all that was worth knowing here, and a London one, too large for an intimacy out of whom the dearest to him were Moore and Godwin.

During the same interval, he fiddled a little with memoirs of his time,* and a note which he had commenced. He occasionally appeared too at public dinners.

His time was at last come. The body could no longer endure that deep corroding sorrow. He was attacked by paralysis, in the summer of 1817, at Moore's table, and was immediately ordered to the South of Europe. He, however, thought it necessary to go to Ireland to settle his affairs.

Leaving Dublin, he felt it was for the last time. "I wish it was all over," said he to one friend; and as he grasped another's hand on the packet's deck, he said, "you will never see me more."

He returned to London—but Ireland, enslaved Ireland was like a vision before him. He burst into tears at a large dinner party on some slight allusion to Irish politics.

On the 8th of October he was attacked by apoplexy, and became speechless. On the 14th of October, 1817, at nine at night, his spirit went to another home. Several of his children, and his dearest friend, Mr. Godwin, watched his painless death.

Round the grave he sanctifies, before the effigy of that inspired face which was but the outside of his soul, and oftenest of all, in communion with his undying thoughts, let the young men of Ireland bend.

His life was full of labour, daring patriotism and love. He shrunk from no toil, and feared no peril for country, and fame, and passion. He was no pedant—good by rule, or vicious from calculation. He strove, because he felt it noble and holy and joyous to be strong, and he knew that strength comes from striving. He attained enormous power, power of impassionate eloquence, and he used that power to comfort the afflicted, to guard the orphan, to rescue his friend, and avenge his country.

A companion unrivalled in sympathy and wit; an orator, whose thoughts went forth like ministers of nature, with robes of light and swords in their hands; a patriot who battled best when the flag was trampled down, and a genuine earnest man, breathing of his climate, his country, and his time; let his countrymen study what he was and did, and let his country guard his fame.

His burial possesses more interest than commonly clings round the coffin of the greatest. He had written in one of his letters, expressing anxiety, that the exiles of 1798 should be allowed to return. "But," he says—

"They are destined to give their last recollection of the green fields they are never to behold, on a foreign death bed, and to lose the sad delight of fancied visits to them in a distant grave." * * * *

He little thought it would be his own fate.

"The last duties (he pathetically observed in one of his latest letters) will be paid by that country on which they are devolved; nor will it be for charity that a little earth shall be given to my bones. Tenderly will those duties be paid, as the debt of well-earned affection, and of gratitude not ashamed of her tears."

From some cause or other, his executors would not or could not do so, and he was buried in one of the vaults of Paddington church. There his dust lay for twenty years, when his remains were resumed by his mother earth.† Ever honoured be they, for they are all this is mortal of one of the purest, loveliest, and most potent spirits this land of ours eve nursed.

---

* His feeling of duty as to such memoirs was strong, and is well said in the fragment we have of them. "You that propose to be the historian of yourself, go first and trace out the boundary of your grave—stretch forth your hand and touch the stone that is to mark your head, and swear by the Majesty of Death, that your testimony shall be true, unwarped by prejudice, unbiassed by favour, and unstained by malice; so mayest thou be a witness not unworthy to be examined before the awful tribunal of that after time, which cannot begin, until you shall have been numbered with the dead."

† Curran now lies buried in Glasnevin cemetery. His funeral to it was public, and so is his tomb. There is a monument to him in St. Patrick's church—a bust by Moore, on a sarcophagus. It is copied from Lawrence's picture, and is the finest monument, so simply made, I ever saw. Let the reader look at it when the setting sun comes upon it, and he will recognise lineaments of power. It is most like him in his glorified mood, full of thought and action. In an Irish Pantheon our greatest orator should be represented at full length, and the bass reliefs of his sarcophagus should be his receiving Father Neale's blessing, his rising to defend the Shearses, his delivery of the judgment in Merry and Power and his weeping for Ireland near his child's grave at the Priory

SPEECHES

OF THE

RIGHT HONOURABLE

JOHN PHILPOT CURRAN.

FLOOD'S REFORM BILL.

November 29th, 1783.

CURRAN, as we have stated in the Memoir, entered Parliament for Kilbeggan, in 1783, as Flood's colleague.

The first time his name appears in the Parliamentary Debates,* is on the 12th of November, 1783, objecting to the issue of a new writ for Enniscorthy; but his remarks are limited to two sentences, and were unavailing.—*Debates,* vol. ii., p. 116.

His next appearance is, on the 18th of November, casually recommending immediate attention to the claims of some distressed manufacturers.—*Debates,* voL ii., p. 176.

His speech in favour of Flood's motion for leave to bring in a bill for Parliamentary Reform, is reported at but little more length, yet it seems to have been vigorous, though, perchance, extravagant. Flood's mode of bringing the subject on was clumsy, as he neither gave it the actual weight, nor freed it from the political odium of being a message from the Volunteer Convention, then seated in the Rotunda. Flood's own speech—a fearless and profound one—was made in the middle of the debate, after the Attorney-General. (Yelverton) had damaged the bill very cleverly. Langrishe, George Ponsonby, Fitzgibbon, Bushe, and Hutchinson followed, and opposed Flood, one with epigrams, another with dogmas, another with crafty doubts, and Fitzgibbon with powerful scorn. The weakest and most stupidly insolent speech was made by Hardy, (afterwards Lord Charlemont's biographer,) and to him Curran replied:—

I am surprised to see a man rising up, with the violence of a maniac, to tell us that this bill ought not to be received while the convention is sitting ; but that convention, and The Volunteers in general, you will not find your enemies ; they have no other enemies but the enemies of their country. That a reform has long been necessary the history of this country evinces. Why were you so long slaves, but because the parliament wanted a reform ? Why, just after your hearts throbbed at your newly-acquired constitution, at the glory of Ireland, did you sink

* Previously to 1782 our only Parliamentary Reports are two volumes, for 1763-4, by a "Military Officer" (Sir James Caldwell). From 1781 to 1799 we have eighteen volumes of Commons' Debates, of various degrees of excellence, and two volumes of Lords' Debates. The eighteenth volume of the Commons' Debates is very scarce ; Byrne, the printer, it is said, shipped the stock to America, and it was lost at sea. The Union debates are only in pamphlets ; a good volume of them reprinted would be a great convenience.

C

that glory in the slavery of an adulatory address, but that you wanted a reform? The man who so violently opposes this day a reform, was once the patron of such a measure; but, perhaps, we shall soon behold him seated where no storms shall fret him.

What have we been doing since we met? We have been talking of retrenchment, and running a course of the most profligate profusion, while our miserable fellow-creatures are roaming the streets for bread. [Here he gave a most pathetic picture of the distress of the poor.*] But some of our new statesmen would guide the government, if it were as easy to be managed as a carriage with four horses by an expert charioteer. Your argument that if the measure come from the Volunteers you will reject it, is a denunciation that you consider them as enemies; I caution the house not to make a public declaration of war against them!—*Debates*, vol. ii., pp. 255, 6.

After a slight speech from Grattan for the motion, leave to bring in the bill was refused by a majority of 158 to 49. The Attorney-General then moved—"That it is now become necessary to declare that this House will maintain its just rights and privileges against all encroachments whatsoever." This latter was carried by 150 to 68, and Mr. Thomas Conolly moved, and carried with unanimity, a "life and fortune" address to the King, in support of "our present happy constitution." The Convention was then wheedled and lied into a dissolution. (See MacNevin's History of The Volunteers, Grattan's Memoirs, &c.)

PRIVILEGE OF COMMONS ON MONEY BILLS.

December 16*th*, 1783.

On this day Curran moved—"That it is the sole and undoubted privilege of the Commons of Ireland to originate all bills of supply and grants of public money, in such manner, and with such clauses as they shall think proper." This motion was called out by two resolutions of the House of Lords, stated in the speech itself:—

While I reflect that the motion I am now going to make is of the utmost importance to the honour, and even existence of this house, and that I have given full notice of my intention, I am much surprised at the little regard that seems intended to be paid to it, as is manifest from the emptiness of those benches. This, sir, is not a question of party; I am no party man—I despise the principle; I never did, nor ever will attach myself to party, and, though I mean to move the resolution from this side of the house, yet it concerns both sides equally; it goes to assert the privileges of the people of Ireland, represented in this house of commons? and I say, every party, and every description of men in this house is equally concerned in supporting it. I say it is the sole and exclusive right of the commons of Ireland to originate and frame money bills in such manner as they shall think proper; and the resolution I intend to propose is only to vindicate this privilege from the encroachments of a neighbouring assembly, which has lately by cer-

* In our transition from the artificial prosperity given by the Irish Manufacture pledge of 1788-9, to the genuine prosperity consequent on independence there was some distress, and much complaint in Dublin.

tain resolutions, invaded this right, this palladium of the constitution, which I trust every man in the house will think himself bound to defend.

I am sorry to say that the constitution of Ireland is so young, that I need not go back to a very remote period to prove that the exclusive right of originating and framing money bills, has always resided in this house; but, for thirty years back, it certainly has, and in England, from whence we derive our constitution, it always has been the practice. The peers and the crown possess an undoubted right of rejecting such bills *in toto*, but in the commons alone resides the power of originating or framing them; the very mode of giving the royal assent to such bills, demonstrates that the commons alone are the source from which they flow. His Majesty thanks his faithful commons, accepts their benevolence, and wills it to be so, and this mode obtains both in Britain and here. To whom should the people of Ireland look for the redress of grievances, for the encouragement of arts, for the promotion of commerce, but to their representatives in this house? What powerful engine has this house, by which it can obtain the redress of grievances, the encouragement of arts, or the promotion of commerce, but by including those objects in the bill of supply? If the right be once given up, or wrested from the commons, they cease to be the patrons and representatives of the people; another assembly will assume that power; the people will learn to look for that encouragement and support from the aristocratic, which they now receive from the democratic branch of the state; this house will become a very cypher, and its members, instead of possessing the power of encouraging arts, rewarding merit, or, in a word, of serving the country, will become the humble solicitors of another assembly.

From the reign of Henry the Third, the power of annexing the redress of grievances to money bills, has been the constitutional privilege of the commons of England; the practice of inserting such clauses as the commons have deemed proper, has obtained in Ireland for more than thirty years, and, to any person acquainted with our constitution, must, at the slightest view, appear to be their inherent right. I cannot, therefore, suppose this house will be silent when this privilege is invaded by another assembly. No man entertains a higher opinion of that assembly than I do; and I am persuaded that so great is their lordships' wisdom, that when this matter is duly considered by them, they will see the impropriety of two resolutions which appear upon their journals of the fourth of the present month, to this effect: " That all grants for the encouragement of particular manufactures, arts, and inventions, or for the construction or carrying on of any public or other works, ought to be made in separate acts; and that the practice of annexing such grants to bills of aid or supply, for the support of his Majesty's government, is unparliamentary, and tends to the destruction of the constitution." " That this house will reject any bill of aid or supply to which such clauses shall be annexed." That the illustrious assembly to which I allude has passed such resolutions, is notorious, and cannot be denied; they are inserted in its journals, and have been seen by many members of this house. The formality, therefore, of appointing a committee to respect their lordships' journals is unnecessary, and all that remains for the commons is to vindicate their own privileges by a mild and temperate resolution, which I shall propose to the house ; for, even admitting that sometimes a house of commons has erred in making improper grants, we should rather reform ourselves, and determine not to err again, than submit to have a monitor over us.

If I were addressing a house of commons, the most virtuous or the most corrupt, I should expect to be supported in this measure ; for I would say to a virtuous house of commons—the privilege of originating and framing money bills is the palladium of your liberty, the great engine to restrain oppression, to redress grievances, or to encourage merit : I would say to a corrupt house of commons—it is the palladium of your corruption, the security of the wages of your venality, the means by which you may obtain the reward of your prostitution ; or if I were addressing a house containing both descriptions, both kinds of argument would be applicable ; but to the house before which I stand, surely the arguments which I have first used, the arguments of virtue and of honour, will be sufficient ; to them, therefore, I shall trust.

I lament that a learned and right honourable member,* with whom I once had the happiness of living on terms of friendship, is now absent; because I think I might rely upon his supporting the resolution I intend to propose ; that support would, perhaps, renew the intercourse or our friendship, which has lately been interrupted. And I must beg the indulgence of the house to say, that that friendship was upon the footing of perfect equality, not imposed by obligation on the one side, or bound by gratitude on the other ; for I thank God, when that friendship commenced, I was above receiving obligation from any man, and, therefore, our friendship, as it was more pure and disinterested, as it depended on a sympathy of minds and congeniality of sentiments, I trusted would have endured the longer. I think myself bound to make this public declaration, as it has gone forth from this house, that I am a man of ingratitude, and to declare, that for any difference of opinion with my learned and right honourable friend, I cannot be taxed with ingratitude; for that I never received any obligation from him, but lived on a footing of perfect equality, save only so far as his great talents and erudition outwent mine.

I confess my obligation to the house for this indulgence of speaking a few words foreign to the debate, but which every man must think I owed to my own character ; and that I may detain gentlemen no longer, I shall briefly move :—

" That it is the sole and undoubted privilege of the commons of Ireland to originate all bills of supply and grants of public money, in such manner and with such clauses as they shall think proper."—*Debates*, vol. ii., pp. 333, 4, 5.

Mr. Parsons seconded the motion, and, after a short debate, it was negatived, by 68 to 11. Curran then moved that a Committee to examine the Lords' Journals be appointed, which motion was also rejected.

---

* Barry Yelverton. The reference is thus interpreted by Leonard MacNally, in a note on the passage, in a copy of the 1811 edition of Curran's Speeches, now in my possession. This copy was a present to MacNally from Curran and contains several notes by the former, which I shall use.

RETRENCHMENT.

February 14th, 1785.

On the 14th of February, on the motion for a Committee of Supply, Flood, in an admirable debating speech, moved, as an amendment—"That an immediate and effectual retrenchment of our expenses is necessary." Curran supported the amendment, which was lost. The following fragment of his speech remains:—

I am surprised gentlemen will press the order of the day before they agree to a resolution which is to be directory to the committee of supply. The question is, in fact, is economy to take place or not? for I laugh at men who say it is for the order of the day. I hope ministers will not be found formidable only in numbers, and tremble at argument; the people cannot be easily satisfied that they have got great advantages by giving up the protection of their trade in hopes of an extension of it, unless the parliament, who are bound in honour to do so, declare that no new tax or heavy burthens are to be laid upon them. One gentleman says it is now too late to look for economy; the same gentleman says it is too early, and thus we are bandied about between too late and too early, and nothing effectual is to be done. I therefore hope ministers will not have their strength in numbers, but will advance some argument why economy should not take effect.—*Debates,* vol. iv. p. 217.

The amendment was lost.

MILITIA *v.* VOLUNTEERS.

On the same day Mr. Gardiner moved a grant of £20,000 for clothing the militia. This motion was levelled at The Volunteers, and was therefore violently debated. Curran opposed it, and we give his reported speech:—

I would not, at first, have known that the question was undoubtedly ministerial, had I not perceived, on the first stir of it, the little advocate* drawing out his brief from his pocket, prepared to support it. I am the more warranted in this expression of calling it a brief, as it is evident the instructions are false. The high character and honour of The Volunteers, is a reason why the right honourable gentleman should not persist in a motion which will not add to his honour; I wish him to consider, that what he may gain in splendour he may lose in respect and I adjure him not to lose the favourable wish of the people. The honourable gentleman has been unsuccessful in a motion, in which he had my support; and I confess that I wish him to be unsuccessful on the present question, as it is one which is injurious to the nation, dishonourable to The Volunteers, these great saviours of their country, and increases the influence of the crown, which has been already much, too much, increased. It is probable that the right honourable gentle-

* The Right Honourable Luke Gardiner—Lord Mountjoy by the Union.

man undertook this ministerial business in hope of being rewarded, by being raised to a higher rank.—*Debates*, vol. iv., pp. 232, 3.

This last allusion caused a wrangle with Gardiner, and then Fitzgibbon, the Attorney General, spoke a few words, which we print, as characteristic of his insolence:—

"Sir, having heard such an unintelligible rhapsody of words, in which the honourable member has stated the danger of embodying a militia of gentlemen, in which he has applauded the zeal of the lowest order of the people, and called upon them to continue their noble exertions—in which he has poured forth a studied panegyric on the volunteers—and in which he has uttered a general miscellany of all sorts of things, I will pass by all that he has said, making the greatest allowance for his intemperance, because he is labouring in the cause of his constituents; and so constitutional a representative of the people ought to have the privilege of saying whatever he thinks fit. But as I feel myself in a very different situation from that honourable member, I shall even intrust the defence of the country to gentlemen, with the King's commission in their pockets, rather than to his friends, the beggars in the streets."—*Debates*, vol. iv., pp. 233, 4.

Unfortunately, Grattan went with the government, and the motion was carried by 149 to 63.

ON ATTACHMENTS

February 24th, 1785.

RENEWED efforts were made in 1784 for Reform. In consequence of a requisition, Henry Reilly, Esq., Sheriff of the county of Dublin, summoned his bailiwick to the court-house of Kilmainham, for the 25th of October, 1784, to elect members to a national congress. For this Mr. Reilly was attached by the King's Bench, on a crown motion, and, on the 24th of February, 1785, the Right Hon. William Brownlow moved a vote of censure on the judges of that court, for the attachment.

I hope I may say a few words on this great subject, without disturbing the sleep of any right honourable member [the Attorney-General* had fallen asleep on his seat]: and yet, perhaps, I ought rather to envy than blame the tranquillity of the right honourable gentleman. I do not feel myself so happily tempered, as to be lulled to repose by the storms that shake the land. If they invite rest to any, that rest ought not to be lavished on the guilty spirit. I never more strongly felt the necessity of a perfect union with Britain, of standing or falling with her in fortune and constitution, than on this occasion. She is the parent, the archetype of Irish liberty, which she has preserved inviolate in its grand points, while among us it has been violated and debased. I now call upon the house to consider the trust reposed in them as the Great Inquest of the people.

I respect judges highly; they ought to be respected, and feel their dignity and freedom from reprehension, while they do what judges ought to do; but their stations should not screen them, when they pass the limit of their duty. Whether they did or not, is the question. This house is the judge of those judges; and it would betray the people to

---

* John Fitzgibbon. He was made Solicitor-General on the 9th of November, 1783, and on the 20th of December, 1783, succeeded Yelverton as Attorney-General. This latter office he retained till he was raised to the Chancellorship, on the 12th of August, 1789, thus making way for Arthur Wolfe, afterwards Lord Kilwarden.

tyranny, and abdicate their representation, if it do not act with probity and firmness.

In their proceedings against Reilly, I think they have transgressed the law, and made a precedent, which, while it remains, is subversive of the trial by jury, and, of course, of liberty. I regard the constitution, I regard the judges, three of that court at least: and, for their sakes, I shall endeavour to undo what they have done.

The question is, whether that court has really punished its own officer for a real contempt; or whether it has abused that power, for the illegal end of punishing a supposed offence against the state, by a summary proceeding, without a trial by jury?

The question is plain, whether as a point of constitution, or as of law; but I shall first consider it in the former view. When I feel the constitution rocking over my head, my first anxiety is to explore the foundation, to see if the great arches that support the fabric have fallen in; but I find them firm, on the solid and massy principle of Common Law. The principle of legal liberty is, that offence, and trial, and punishment, should be fixed; it is sense, it is Magna Charta—a trial by jury, as to fact, an appeal to judges as to law.

I admit Attachment an exception to the general rule, as founded in necessity, for the support of courts, in administering justice, by a summary control over their officers acting under them; but the necessity that gave rise to it is also the limit. If it were extended farther, it would reach to all criminal cases not capital; and, in the room of a jury, crimes would be created by a judge, the party accused by him, found guilty by him, punished by the utter loss of his liberty and property for life, by indefinite fine and imprisonment, without remedy or appeal. If he did not answer he was guilty; even if he did, the court might think, or say it thought, the answer evasive, and so convict him for imputed prevarication.

The power of Attachment is wisely confined by the British laws, and practised within that limit. The crown lawyers have not produced a single case where the King's Bench in England have gone beyond it. They have ranged through the annals of history; through every reign of folly and of blood: through the proud domination of the Tudors, and the blockhead despotism of the Stuarts, without finding a single case to support their doctrine.

I consider the office of sheriff as judicial and ministerial. Reilly's offence did not fall within any summary control, in either capacity. It was not a judicial act, it was not *colore officii*. An act *colore officii* must either be an act done by the actual exercise of an abused or an usurped authority—neither of which can it be called; for where the sheriff summons his county, he does it by command, by authority, under pain of fine and imprisonment to those who disobey.

Was the appointment of a meeting any such active exertion of authority? Does any man suppose he was obliged to attend? that he would be fined if he refused to attend? No. Did the sheriff hold out any such colourable authority? Clearly not. The contrary: he explained the purpose of the intended meeting; he stated at whose instance he appointed such meeting; and thereby showed to every man in his senses that he was not affecting to convene them by colour of any compulsive authority.

If, then, there was any guilt in the sheriff's conduct, it was not punishable by Attachment. They who argue from its enormity, are guilty of a shabby attempt to mislead men from the question, which is not whether he ought to be punished at all, but whether he had been punished according to law.

You have heard no man adduce a single case to support their assertion; but we have the uniform practice of the King's Bench in England in our favour, the uniform practice, both there and here, during these last years. Had they not meetings there and here? Did not the crown receive petitions and addresses from such assemblies? Why, during that time, was there no motion for an Attachment in either kingdom?

If an English Attorney-General had attempted such a daring outrage on public liberty and law, he must have found some friend to warn him not to debase the court, and make it appear to all mankind as the odious engine of arbitrary power; not to put it into so unnatural a situation, as that of standing between the people and the crown, or between the people and their representatives.

I warn him not to bring public hatred on the government, by the adoption of an illegal prosecution. If he show himself afraid of proceeding against offenders by the ordinary mode, then offenders will be exalted by arbitrary persecution of them; they will become suffering patriots, from being mere petty offenders; their cries will become popular. Let him be warned how he leads the court into an illegality, which the commons can never endure. No honest representative can sacrifice his fame and his duty, by voting in support of a proceeding subversive of liberty. I should shrink from the reproach of the most insignificant of my constituents, if that constituent could say to me— "When thou sawest the thief of the constitution, thou consentedst unto him."

Such would be the caution suggested to an English Attorney-General; and, accordingly, we find no instance of his ever venturing on such a measure.

Without case, then, or precedent, or principle, what is the support of such a conduct here?—the distinction of a judge? And what is that distinction? It is different in different men; it is different in the same man at different times: it is the folly of a fool and the fear of a coward; it is the infamy of the young, and the dotage of age: in the best man it is very weakness that human nature is subject to; and in the worst, it is very vice. Will you then tell the people that you have chosen this glorious distinction in the place of fixed laws, fixed offences, and fixed punishments, and in the place of that great barrier between the prerogative and the people—Trial by Jury?

But it is objected that the resolution is a censure on the judges, and a charge of corruption:—I deny it, and I appeal to your own acts.

Mr. Curran then called to the clerk, who read from the journals a vote of censure passed upon Mr. Justice Robinson, for imposing a fine illegally in a county. when on circuit, without view or evidence.

Was your resolution founded on any corruption of that judge? No you would, if so, have addressed to remove him. I called for the resolution, therefore, not to charge him with guilt—I am persuaded he acted merely through error ; but to vindicate him, to vindicate you, and to exhort you to be consistent. You thought a much smaller violation of the law was deserving your reprobation. Do not abandon yourselves and your country to slavery, by suffering so much a grosser and more dangerous transgression of the constitution, to become a precedent for ever. In tenderness even to the judges, interpose. Their regret, which I am sure they now feel on reflection, cannot undo what they have done: their hands cannot wash away what is written in their records ; but you may repair whatever has been injured :—if your friend had unwillingly plunged a dagger into the breast of a stranger, would you prove his innocence by letting the victim bleed to death? The constitution has been wounded deeply, but, I am persuaded, innocently ; it is you only, who, by neglecting to interpose, can make the consequences fatal, and the wound ripen into murder.

I would wish, I own, that the liberty of Ireland should be supported by her own children ; but if she is scorned and rejected by them, when her all is at stake, I will implore the assistance even of two strangers ; I will call on the right honourable Secretary to support the principles of the British constitution. Let him not render his administration odious to the people of Ireland, by applying his influence in this house, to the ruin of their personal freedom. Let him not give a pretence to the enemies of his friend in a sister country, to say that the son of the illustrious Chatham is disgracing the memory of his great father ; that the trophies of his Irish administration are the introduction of an inquisition among us, and the extinction of a trial by jury ; let them not say that the pulse of the constitution beats only in the heart of the empire, but that it is dead in the extremities.

Mr. Curran concluded with declaring his hearty concurrence in the resolution proposed.

The Attorney-General (Fitzgibbon), in a speech of much personality, opposed Curran's motion.

Mr. Curran, in reply —I thank the right honourable gentleman for restoring me to my good humour, and for having, with great liberality and parliamentary decency, answered my arguments with personality. Some expressions cannot heat me, when coming from persons of a certain distinction. I shall not interrupt the right honourable gentleman in the fifth repetition of his speech. I shall prevent his arguments by telling him that he has not in one instance alluded to Mr. Reilly. The right honourable gentleman said I had declared the judges guilty; but I said no such thing. I said, if any judge was to act in the manner I mentioned, it would be an aggravation of his guilt. The right hon. gentleman has said, that the house of commons had no right to investigate the conduct of judges ; if so, I ask the learned Sergeant why he sits in that chair ? I ask why the resolution has been just read from the journals ? The gentleman has called me a babbler ; I cannot think that was meant as a disgrace, because, in another Parliament, fore I had the honour of a seat in this house, but when I was in the gallery, I heard a young lawyer named Babbler. I do not recollect that there were sponsors at the baptismal font; nor was there any occasion, as the infant had promised and vowed so many things in his own name. Indeed I find it difficult to reply, for I am not accustomed to pronounce panegyrics on myself; I do not know well how to do it; but since I cannot tell you what I am, I shall tell you what I am not :— I am not a man whose respect in person and character depends upon the importance of his office ; I am not a young man who thrusts himself into the foreground of a picture, which ought to be occupied by a better figure ; I am not a man who replies with invective, when sinking under the weight of argument; I am not a man who denied the necessity of a parliamentary reform, at the time he proved the expediency of it, by reviling his own constituents, the parish clerk, the sexton, and the grave-digger ; and if there be any man who can apply what I am not to himself, I leave him to think of it in the committee, and to contemplate it when he goes home.—*Debates,* vol. iv., pp. 402—10.

The resolution was negatived by 143 to 71.

ORDE'S COMMERCIAL PROPOSITIONS.

June 30th, 1785.

WAS the interest of Ireland to be subordinate to England, when her parliament had ceased to be so? This Mr. Pitt tried to adjudicate against, by deceit, in 1785, and failing, he resolved to reach the same end by abolishing our parliament, and this he unhappily accomplished in 1800.

There is no political event from 1782 to the Union, of greater importance than the discussion of Orde's Propositions. In Grattan's Memoirs, vol. iii., and in Seward's *Collectanea Politica,* valuable elements of a judgment on this matter will be found. I tried to sum up the history of the transaction in the *Citizen* Magazine for September, 1841, in reviewing Grattan's Memoirs. On looking over that paper, I find I cannot condense the description of the propositions and their fate, given there, so I shall simply copy it:—

"Partly from a belief that protection alone would secure a beginning to trade, and partly out of retribution on England, an attempt was made, in April, 1784, to impose severe import duties on manufactures Mr Gardiner's motion for that purpose was negatived in parliament by nearly four to one ; of that the Commons were the enemies of protection, but the creatures of England

"In May in the same year, 1784, a proposal of Mr. Griffith's, for *inquiry* on the commercial intercourse between Britain and Ireland, was taken out of his hands by government. He desired to show that Irish trade should be protected from English competition : the opposite was the direction given to the inquiry by the adopting parents; *he* sought to inquire how Ireland might be served even at the expense of England ; *they,* how England might be pampered on the spoil of Ireland Accordingly, they solved it in their own way, and on the 7th of February, 1785, Mr Orde, the Chief Secretary, announced, and on the 11th moved the eleven propositions on trade, commonly called the *Irish* propositions, to distinguish them from the twenty proposed as amendments thereon by Pitt, a few months after, called the *English* propositions, though, in fact, both were English in contrivance and purport. There were four principles established in the Irish propositions:—1st, that the taxes upon all goods, foreign and domestic, passing between the two countries, should be equal. Secondly, that taxes on foreign goods should always be higher than on the same articles produced in either island. Thirdly, that these regulations should be unalterable. Fourthly, that the surplus of the hereditary revenue (hearth tax, and certain customs and excises, over £656,000 a year) should be paid over to the English treasury, for the support of the Imperial (English ?) navy. The first principle went to place a country with immense capital, great skill, and old trade, on the same footing with one without any of these, and therefore went to ruin the latter, unless private came forward, as it had don oefore, and supplying the defects of the law, rescued the country from the alien, the aristocrat, and the placeman. The second article sacrificed the realities of French, Spanish, and American trade, then increasing, to (the profits?) of English competition. The third and fourth were assumptions of a power beyond law-making; they abdicated legislation. The last, especially, paid for English strength—that is, Irish misery; and purchased protection, that is slavery, at a price which, as Grattan afterwards said, might amount to any share of the national revenue, to which a tricking financier wished to raise it. To pay black mail was to lay Ireland at the mercy of England, yet not secure her against other foreign states by any lasting or effectual means. An old treaty, or the convenience of a conqueror, are no substitutes for the safety, of which national pride and home passions and interests are the true guardians. Your own sword is a better protection than another's shield; for if he be endangered, you are left unarmed and undefended. Besides, between nations, guardianship means plunder; and the ward is an impoverished drudge. Yet this plan was proffered as a boon, and, what is stranger still, it was paid for as such—£140,000 of new taxes were asked for, and voted in return for the prospective favours of the minister. Flood almost alone opposed it; he asked for time to let himself—to let the nation reflect on the propositions: he exposed some of the propositions; he expressed confidence in only a few." * *

"On the 22nd of February, Pitt, in a speech full of hopes for this country, moved the resolution which declared that Ireland should be allowed the advantages (i.e. competition) of British commerce as soon as she had 'irrevocably' granted to England an 'aid' (i.e. tribute) for general defence. Thus we were promised an equivocal boon at the cost of independence. Such was the generosity of Pitt, and it was too much for the opposition, too much for North and the Tories, too much for Fox and the Whigs. They were in opposition, and they saw in English jealousy to Ireland a sure resource against the 'heaven-born minister.' He, to be sure, had not done good to Ireland, but he gravely promised to serve her, and this was suspicious, at the least, especially when coming from one who still had a character. None of the leaders cared for Ireland, nor were they bigotted against her; but they flung her in each other's faces." * ▼ * *

"Fox obtained adjournments; and all England 'spoke out,' from Lancashire to London, from Gloucester to York. During the twenty years of Pitt's supremacy, the liberal opposition had his apostacy from principle, his suppression of opinion in England, his hostility to freedom all over the globe, his bloody and constant wars,—all these had they, and what came nearer still to the soul (stomach?) of England, they had his exhausting taxation to bring against him; yet he repelled them without difficulty, even led by Fox, when armed with these grievances. In 1785 the opposition united under a more exciting banner-cry; 'jealousy of Ireland,' and England rallied beneath their flag. Pitt was borne back, but he was skilful and unscrupulous; he saw his danger, and sounded a parley; he submitted to some of their terms; he succeeded in retaining all that was adverse to the Irish constitution, suffered the loss of all that could be by any ingenuity supposed serviceable to Irish trade, and returned the act *approved of by him* in this form. The opposition kept up a little clamour about the invasion of Irish rights; it served for declamation, but England was now content: there being no fear of benefit to Ireland, the intended wrongs were soon forgotten in England.

"We have before us the Report of the Committee of Trade, and Plantations, on the equalization of duties. That report includes the examinations of the chief manufacturers of England, and a more valuable evidence could not be got of English dread and jealousy, and assumption: fearing that free trade may make Ireland able to compete with them, they deprecate her prosperity, and assume a right to control her improvement. They all assert the success of the Irish non-importation agreement."

"The eleven propositions had been increased in England to twenty, each addition a fresh injury. Half the globe, namely, all between Magellan and Good Hope, was (by articles 3 and 9) interdicted to Ireland's ships: interdicts were also laid on certain goods. The whole customs legislation of Ireland was taken away by clauses which forced her (by article 4) to enact (register) all navigation laws passed or to be passed by England; (by articles 5 and 8) to impose all colonial duties that England did; (by 6 and 7) to adopt the same system in custom houses that England did; and finally, (by 17 and 18) to recognise all patents and copyrights granted to England."

The propositions were returned thus changed, and on Thursday, the 30th of June, 1785, the Right Honourable Thomas Orde moved the adjournment of the house till Tuesday fortnight. Against this Curran spoke as follows:—

I can easily excuse some inconsistencies in the conduct of the right honourable Secretary [Orde]; for some accidents have befallen him. When we met last, he desired us to adjourn for three weeks; we did so; and now he wants above a fortnight more; but will that help forward the business before the house? Will it expedite the progress of the bill, to say, "Let us wait till the packet comes in from England, and perhaps we shall have some news about the propositions?" Did the British minister act in this manner? No: when he postponed, from time to time, the consideration of the propositions, he did not postpone the other business of the house: he did not say, let it wait till the packet comes from Dublin. This the Irish minister is forced to do: I say forced, for I am sure it is not his inclination; it must distress him greatly, and I sincerely feel for, and pity his distress.

When we had the eleven propositions before us, we were charmed with them. Why?—because we did not understand them! Yes, the endearing word reciprocity rang at every corner of the streets. We then thought that the right honourable gentleman laid the propositions before us by authority: but the English minister reprobates them as soon as they get to England, and the whole nation reprobates them. Thus, on one hand we must conclude, that the English minister tells the Irish minister to propose an adjustment, and, when it goes back, alters every part; or, that the Irish minister proposed it without any authority at all. I am inclined to believe the latter; for it would add to the gentleman's distress to suppose the former.

Now let us mark another inconsistency into which the right honourable gentleman is driven, no doubt against his will. Time to deliberate was refused us, when we had something to deliberate upon; and now, when we are told we have nothing before us to consider, we are to have a fortnight's recess, to enable us to think about nothing. And time, indeed, it will take, before we can think to any purpose. It will take time for the propositions to go through, and, perhaps, to be again altered in the house of lords. It will take time for them to be re-considered in the British commons. It will take time for them to come over here. It will take time for us to consider them, though that time is likely to be very short. It will take time to send them back to England. It will take time for them to be returned to us again; and then time will be required to carry them into execution.

But a rumour hath gone abroad, of a studied design to delay the discussion of this business until there shall be no members in town. Away with such a suspicion; I think too honourably of the right honourable gentleman; though I should be glad to hear him say there is not even an idea of the base design of forcing them down our throats.

July 23rd, 1785.

Mr. Secretary Orde havi.g this day moved that the house do adjourn to Tuesday se'nnight, with a proviso that the further delay of a week or more might be needed, Mr. Curran rose and spoke to the following effect:—

Sir, the adjournment proposed is disgraceful to parliament, and disgraceful to the nation I must explain myself by stating a few facts, though they relate to a subject that I own I cannot approach but with reluctance. The right honourable gentleman, early in the session, produced a set of propositions, which he said he was authorised to present to us, as a system of final and permanent commercial adjustment between the two kingdoms. As a compensation for the expected advantages of this system, we were called upon to impose £140,000 a-year on this exhausted country. Unequal to our strength, and enormous as the burden was, we submitted; we were willing to strain every nerve in the common cause, and to stand or fall with the fate of the British empire. But what is the event? I feel how much beneath us it would be to attend to the unauthenticated rumours of what may be said or done in another kingdom; but it would be a ridiculous affectation in us not to know that the right honourable gentleman's system has been reprobated by those under whose authority he was supposed to act, and that he himself has been deserted and disavowed

I cannot, for my own part, but pity the calamity of a man who is exposed to the contempt of the two countries as an egregious dupe, or to their indignation as a gross impostor; for even he himself now abandons every hope of those propositions returning to this house in the form they left it. On the contrary, he now only hopes that he may be able to bring something forward that may deserve our approbation on some future day. He requests an adjournment for ten days, and he promises that he will give a week's notice when the yet undiscovered something is to be proposed, which something he promises shall be agreeable to this nation, and authorised by the English minister.

On what his confidence of this is founded I know not; unless he argues, that because he has been disavowed and exposed in his past conduct by his employers, he may rely on their supporting him in future. But however the right honourable gentleman may fail in drawing instruction from experience or calamity, we ought to be more wise; we should learn caution from disappointment.

We relied on the right honourable gentleman's assurances—we found them fallacious: we have oppressed the people with a load of taxes, as a compensation for a commercial adjustment;—we have not got that adjustment: we confided in our skill in negotiation, and we are rendered ridiculous by that confidence. We looked abroad for the resources of Irish commerce, and we find that they are to be sought for only at home, in the industry of the people, in the honesty of parliament, and in our learning that negotiation must inevitably bring derision on ourselves, and ruin on our constituents. But you are asked to depend on the right honourable gentleman's regard for his own reputation. When the interest of the people is at stake, can we be honest in reposing on so despicable a security? Suppose this great pledge of the right honourable gentleman's character should chance to become forfeited, where will you look for it? When he sails for England, is it too large to carry with him? Or, if you would discover in what parish of Great Britain it may be found, will the sacrifice be an atonement to a people who have already been betrayed by trusting to so contemptible a pledge?

See, then, what we do by consenting to this short adjournment: we have been abused already and we neglect every other duty, in order to solicit a repetition of that abuse. If this something should arrive at all, it will be proposed when the business of the country will engage every county member at the assizes; for, as to his week's notice, it either cannot reach him in time, or, if it should, he cannot possibly obey it. Is it, then, our wish to have a new subject, of such moment as a contract that is to bind us for ever, concluded in half a house, and without even a single representative for a county in the number? Is it wise to trust to half the house, in a negotiation in which the wisdom of the whole has been already defeated?

But what is the necessity that induces us to acquiesce in a measure of so much danger and disgrace? Is this nation brought to so abject a condition by her representatives, as to have no refuge from ruin but in the immediate assistance of Great Britain?

Sir, I do not so far despair of the public weal; oppressed as we were, we found a resource for our constitution in the spirit of the people: abused as we now find ourselves, our commerce cannot fail of a resource in our virtue and industry, if we do not suffer ourselves to be diverted from those great and infallible resources, by a silly hope from negotiation, for which we are not adapted, and in which we can never succeed. And if this great hope still is left, why fill the public mind with alarm and dismay? Shall we teach the people to think, that something instantly must be done, to save them from destruction? Suppose that something should not, cannot be done, may not the attempt, instead of uniting the two countries, involve them as its consequence, in discord and dissension?

If your compliance with the right honourable gentleman's requisition do not sink the people into despair of their own situation, does it not expose the honour and integrity of this house to suspicion and distrust? For, what can they suppose we intend by this delay? The right honourable gentleman may find it worth his while to secure his continuance in office by an expedient. however temporary and ineffectual: but, sir, if we are supposed to concur in such a design, our character is gone with the people; for, if we are honest, it can be of no moment to us whether this secretary or that minister shall continue in office or not.

I know it has been rumoured that the right honourable gentleman may take advantage of a thin house, to impose upon this country the new set of resolutions that have passed the commons of Great Britain. I do not suspect any such thing, nor would I encourage such a groundless apprehension. I do not think it would be easy to find a man who would stand within the low-water mark of our shore, and read some of those resolutions above his breath, without feeling some uneasiness for his personal safety; neither can I think if a foreign usurpation should come crested to our bar, and demand from the treachery of this house a surrender of that constitution which has been established by the virtue of the nation, that we would answer such a requisition by words.

But, sir, though the people should not apprehend such extreme perfidy from us, they will be justly alarmed, if they see us act with needless precipitation; after what is past, we cannot be surprised at not meeting with the most favourable interpretations of our conduct.

On great objects, the magnitude of the ideas to be compared may cause some confusion in the minds of ordinary men; they will therefore examine our conduct by analogy to the more frequent occurrences of common life; such cases happen every day. Will you permit me to suppose a very familiar one, by which our present situation may be illustrated to a common mind.

I will suppose then, sir, that an old friend that you loved, just recovering from a disease, in which he had been wasted almost to death, should prevail upon you to take the trouble of buying him a horse for the establishment of his health; and I the more freely presume to represent you for a moment in an office so little corresponding with the dignity of your station, from a consciousness that my fancy cannot put you in any place, to which you will not be followed by my utmost respect. I will, therefore, suppose that you send for a horse-jockey, who does not come himself but sends his foreman. Says the foreman, Sir, I know what you want; my master has a horse that will exactly match your friend; he is descended from Rabelias' famous Johannes Caballus, that got a doctor of physic's degree from the College of Rheims; but your friend must pay his price. My master knows he has no money at present, and will therefore accept his note for the amount of what he shall be able to earn while he lives; allowing him, however, such moderate subsistence as may prevent him from perishing. If you are satisfied, I will step for the horse and bring him instantly, with the bridle and saddle, which you shall have into the bargain. But friend, say you, are you sure that you are authorised to make this bargain? What, sir, cries the foreman, would you doubt my honour? Sir, I can find three hundred gentlemen who never saw me before, and yet have gone bail for me at the first view of my face. Besides, sir, you have a greater pledge; my honour, sir, my renown is at stake. Well, sir, you agree—the note is passed; the foreman leaves you, and returns without the horse. What, sir, where is the horse? Why, in truth, sir, answers he, I am sorry for this little disappointment, but my mistress has taken a fancy to the horse, so your friend cannot have him. But we have a nice little mare that will match him better; as to the saddle, he must do without that, for little master insists on keeping it: however, your friend has been so poor a fellow, that he must have too thick a skin to be much fretted by riding barebacked; besides the mare is so low that his feet will reach the ground when he rides her; and still further to accommodate him, my master insists on having a chain locked to her feet, of which lock my master is to have a key, to lock or unlock, as he pleases; and your friend shall also have a key, so formed that he cannot unlock the chain, but with which he may double-lock it, if he thinks fit. What, sirrah! do you think I'll betray my old friend to such a fraud? Why really, sir, you are impertinent, and your friend is too peevish; it was only the other day that he charged my master with having stolen his cloak, and grew angry, and got a ferrule and spike to his staff. Why, sir, you see how good-humouredly my master gave back the cloak. Sir, my master scorns to break his word, and so do I ; sir, my character is your security. Now, as to the mare, you are too hasty in objecting to her, for I am not sure that you can get her : all I ask of you now is, to wait a few hours in the street, that I may try if something may not be done ; but let me say one word to you in confidence—I am to get two guineas, if I can bring your friend to be satisfied with what we can do for him ; now, if you assist me in this, you shall have half the money ; for to tell you the truth, if I fail in my undertaking, I shall ither be discharged entirely, or degraded to my former place of helper n the stable.

Now, Mr. Speaker, as I do not presume to judge of your feelings by my own, I cannot be sure that you would beat the foreman, or abuse him as an impudent, lying impostor ; I rather think you would for a moment be lost in reflecting, and not without a pang, how the rectitude of your heart, and the tenderness of your head, had exposed you to be the dupe of improbity and folly. But, sir, I know you would leave the wretch who had deceived you, or the fool who was deceived by his master, and you would return to your friend. And methinks you would say to him, we have been deceived in the course we have adopted ; for, my good friend, you must look to the exertions of your own strength, for the establishment of your health. You have great stamina still remaining—rely upon them, and they will support you. Let no man persuade you to take the ferrule or spike from your staff. It will guard your cloak. Neither quarrel with the jockey, for he cannot recover the contents of the note, as you have not the horse ; and he may yet see the policy of using you honestly, and deserving to be your friend. If so embrace him, and let your staff be lifted in defence of your common safety, and in the meantime, let it be always in readiness to defend yourself.

Such, sir, is the advice you would offer to your friend, and which I would now offer to this house. There is no ground for despairing ; let us not, therefore, alarm the people. If a closer connexion with Great Britain is not now practicable, it may be practicable hereafter ; but we shall ruin every hope of that kind by precipitation. I do therefore conjure gentlemen not to run the risk of forcing us, at a week's notice, to enter on a subject on which every man in the nation ought to be allowed the most unlimited time for deliberation. I do conjure them not to assent to a measure that can serve nobody but the proposer of it ; that must expose the members of this house to the distrust of their constituents, and which may, in its consequences, endanger the harmony of two kingdoms, whose interests and fortunes ought never to be separated.
—*Debates*, vol. v., pp. 299—304.

The adjournment was, however, carried.

August 11th, 1785.

Ir. Curran entered the house late, and spoke to the following effect :—

He demanded of the secretary what was become of the eleven propositions of the Irish parliament, as of them only that parliament could trent. He had no fear, he said, that the house would be so base, or the nation so supine, as to suffer any others to be the grounds of a treaty; and as to the fourth resolution of the British parliament, he understood too well what the conduct of the house would be, was anything to be founded on it, to fear from that quarter. But he again desired to know what was become of the eleven propositions, as it was impossible to negotiate, until the fate of them was known. He said, though it seemed to be the present fashion to urge the house forward, without giving the least time for reflection or consideration, yet he would not suppose the house would, in this instance, precipitate itself into the absurdities of an address, without knowing upon what ground; much less could he fear that it would fall into the greatest of all absurdities, the negotiating by a bill—binding themselves, and leaving the other parties at liberty. However, as to-morrow was so near, he would listen to what the right honourable Secretary had to offer, convinced that no man would dare to bring forward anything founded on the British resolutions.—*Debates*, vol. v., p. 328.

August 12*th*, 1785.

On this day Orde moved his bill, and was opposed by Grattan and Flood, in speeches of eminent force and brilliancy. Curran's speech is short, and his exhaustion seems to have been excessive:—

I am too much exhausted to say much at this hour [six o'clock] on the subject. My zeal has survived my strength. I wish my present state of mind and body may not be ominous of the condition to which Ireland would be reduced, if this bill should become a law. I cannot therefore, yield even to my weakness—it is a subject which might animate the dead. [He then took a view of the progress of the arrangement, and arraigned the insidious conduct of the administration.*] In Ireland it was proposed by the minister; in England it was reprobated by the same minister. I have known children learn to play at cards, by playing the right hand against the left; I never before heard of a negotiation being carried on in that way. A bill is not a mode of negotiating; our law speaks only to ourselves—binds only ourselves; it is absurd, therefore, to let the bill proceed. The commercial part is out of the question; for this bill portends a surrender of the constitution and liberty of Ireland. If we should attempt so base an act, it would be void, as to the people. We may abdicate our representation, but the right remains with the people, and can be surrendered only by them. We may ratify our own infamy; we cannot ratify their slavery. I fear the British minister is mistaken in the temper of Ireland, and judges of it by former times. Formerly the business here was carried on by purchase of majorities. There was a time when the most infamous measure was sure of being supported by as infamous a majority but things have changed. The people are enlightened and strong they will not bear a surrender of their rights, which would be the con-

* So in the original report.

sequence, if they submitted to this bill. It contains a covenant to enact such laws as England should think proper; that would annihilate the parliament of Ireland. The people here must go to the bar of the English house of commons for relief; and for a circuitous trade to England we are accepting a circuitous constitution.

It is different totally from the cases to which it has been compared, the settlement of 1779, or the Methuen treaty; there all was specific and defined, here all is future and uncertain. A power to bind externally, would involve a power also of binding internally. This law gives the power to Great Britain, of judging what would be a breach of the compact, of construing it; in fact, of taxing us as she pleased; while it gives her new strength to enforce our obedience. In such an event, we must either sink into utter slavery, or the people must wade to a re-assumption of their rights through blood, *or be obliged to take refuge in a union, which would be the annihilation of Ireland, and what, I suspect, the minister is driving at.* Even the Irish minister no longer pretends to use his former language on this subject; formerly we were lost in a foolish admiration on the long impedimented march of oratoric pomp, with which the Secretary displayed the magnanimity of Great Britain. That kind of eloquence, I suppose, was formed upon some model, but I suspect that the light of political wisdom is more easily reflected than the heat of eloquence; yet we were in raptures even with the oratory of the honourable gentleman. However, he now has descended to an humble style; he talks no more of reciprocity, no more of emporium.

[He then went into general observations, to show that this treaty would give no solid advantages to Ireland, but was a revocation of the grant of 1779.] He said—I love the liberty of Ireland, and shall therefore vote against the bill, as subversive of that liberty. I shall also vote against it as leading to a schism between the two nations, that must terminate in a civil war, or in a union at best. I am sorry that I have troubled you so long, but I feared it might be the last time I should ever have an opportunity of addressing a free parliament; and, if the period is approaching, when the boasted constitution of Ireland will be no more, I own I feel a melancholy ambition to deserve that my name be enrolled with those who endeavoured to save it in its last moment. Posterity will be grateful for the last effort, though it should have failed of success.—*Debates* vol. v., pp. 421, 2, 3.

The introduction of the bill was carried by 127 to 108.

August 15th, 1785.

Mr. Orde, on presenting the bill, abandoned it for the session, and for ever Thereon Flood moved the following resolution:—

" Resolved—That we hold ourselves bound not to enter into any engagement to give up the sole and exclusive right of the parliament of Ireland to legislate for Ireland in all cases whatsoever, as well externally as commercially and internally "

Curran supported him :—

I shall support the resolution proposed by the honourable member, because I think it necessary to declare to the people, that their rights have not been solely supported by one hundred and ten independent gentlemen, but that, if eight or ten of them had been absent, those who had countenanced the measure, would have abandoned every idea of prosecuting it further.

It has ever been the custom of our ancestors, when the constitution has been attacked, to take some spirited step for its support. Why was Magna Charta passed? It was passed not to give freedom to the people, but because the people were already free. Why was the repeal of the 6th of George I.? Not to give independence to the men of Ireland, but because Ireland was in itself an independent nation. This resolution does not go to give rights, but to declare that we will preserve our rights. We are told to be cautious how we commit ourselves with the parliament of Great Britain; whether this threat carry with it more of prudence or timidity, I leave gentlemen to determine. I rejoice that the cloud which had loured over us has passed away. I have no intention to wound the feelings of the minister, by triumphing in his defeat; on the contrary, I may be said to rise with some degree of self-denial, when I give to others an opportunity of exulting in the victory.

The opposition in England has thrown many impediments in the way, but I shall remember, with gratitude, that the opposition there has supported the liberties of Ireland. When I see them reprobating the attacks made upon the trial by jury, when I see them supporting the legislative rights of Ireland, I cannot refrain from giving them my applause. They well know that an invasion of the liberty of Ireland would tend to an attack upon their own.

The principle of liberty, thank heaven! still continues in those countries: that principle which stained the fields of Marathon, stood in the pass of Thermopylæ, and gave to America independence. Happy it is for Ireland, that she has recovered her rights by a victory unstained by blood—not a victory bathed in the tears of a mother, a sister, or a wife—not a victory hanging over the grave of a Warren or a Montgomery, and uncertain whether to triumph in what she had gained, or to mourn over what she had lost!

As to the majority, who have voted for bringing in the bill, the only way they can justify themselves to their constituents, is by voting for the resolution. As to the minority, who have saved the country, they need no vindication: but those who voted for the introduction of the bill must have waited for the committee, to show the nation that they would never assent to the fourth proposition. That opportunity can never arrive—the bill is at an end. The cloud that had been collecting so long, and threatening to break in tempest and ruin on our heads, has passed harmlessly away. The siege that was drawn round the constitution has been raised and the enemy is gone—"*Juvat ire, et Dorica castra, desertosque videre locos;*" and they might now go abroad without fear, and trace the dangers they had escaped: here was drawn the line of circumvallation, that cut them off for ever from the eastern world; and there the corresponding one, that inclosed them from the west.

Nor let us forget, in our exultation, to whom we are indebted for the deliverance. Here stood the trusty mariner [Mr. Conolly] on his old station, the mast-head, and gave the signal. Here [Mr. Flood] all the wisdom of the state was collected, exploring your weakness and your strength, detecting every ambuscade. and pointing to the hidden battery that was brought to bear on the shrine of freedom. And there [Mr Grattan] was exerting an eloquence more than human, inspiring, forming, directing, animating, to the great purposes of your salvation.

But I feel that I am leaving the question, and the bounds of moderation ; but there is an ebullition in great excesses of joy, that almost borders on insanity. I own I feel something like it in the profuseness with which I share in the general triumph.

It is not, however, a triumph which I wish to enjoy at the expense of the honourable gentleman who brought in the bill, I am willing to believe with the best intention. Whatever I may have thought before, I now feel no trace of resentment to the honourable gentleman. On the contrary, I wish that this day's intercourse, which will probably be our last, may be marked, on our part, with kindness and respect. I am for letting the right honourable gentleman easily down ; I am not for depressing him with the triumph, but I am for calling him to share in the exultation.

Upon what principle can the gentlemen who supported the previous question defend their conduct, unless it was in contradiction to the general rule of adhering to measures, not to the man? Here it is plain they were adhering to the man, not to the measure ; the measure had sunk, but the man was still afloat. Perhaps they think it decent to pay a funeral compliment to his departure ; yet I warn them how they press too eagerly forward ; for, as there cannot be many bearers, some of them might be disappointed of the scarf or the cypress. I beseech them now to let all end in good humour, and, like sailors who have pursued different objects, when they get into port, shake hands with harmony.—*Debates*, vol. v., pp. 453, 4, 5.

Flood withdrew his motion, the House adjourned, and Orde's Propositions merged in a secret design for a Union.

PORTUGAL TRADE.

March 11th, 1786.

In 1782 the Irish Commons had addressed the Crown to negociate a relaxation of the duties then recently imposed on certain Irish manufactures, but nothing was done. On the 11th of March, 1786, Mr. Longfield moved another address to the same effect, and sought exact information from the government, which was refused. Mr. Toler (afterwards Lord Norbury) defended the Methuen treaty, and to him Curran alludes in the middle of the following speech :—

I am convinced that not one good end can be derived from withholding the information required. What! is Ireland ever to be obliged to console herself with explaining the enigmas of an English secretary, solving his political problems, and expressing her astonishment at his sagacious paradoxes? If it be decided that the right of Ireland refused by the court of Portugal to trade to her dominions, then, I apprehend, it would be a question for Great Britain herself, if she were sincere in her declarations towards this country. It is the highest nonsense to say that a treaty, which we are told is soon to be made public, is a matter of secrecy; the honourable gentleman may also say that the exportation of beef and butter is a secret. It is, indeed, a matter of amazement that his extreme caution does not also prompt him to warn the house not to make that circumstance public. Thus we find the nation to be amused, because a secretary rising, with much solemnity, in his place, declares he has now reason to believe, from what he has not reason to comprehend, that matters would be brought to a conclusion favourable to this country; an assertion which, it is evident, he cannot, with any degree of authenticity, support, from his manifest ignorance of the negotiation which he evasively pronounces on foot. This, indeed, is highly ridiculous; but not more so than my learned friend's getting up to construe the Methuen treaty, or, in fact, than what the honourable gentleman within a few feet of him has advanced; the task he confessed a difficult one; his merit was therefore the greater, for stepping forward, to rescue from oblivion, or develop the previous arguments of his friend; but, however I may admire him as a commentator, yet I am sorry to find myself still in the dark, notwithstanding my learned friend's laudable exertions. I do not wish to give way to levity, but the absurdities of some persons have the unfortunate knack of turning matters of the most serious nature into ridicule. The present opposition given to the motion before the house falls under that description, and it would be extremely ludicrous to treat that opposition seriously. If the trade of Portugal is to be abandoned, let the humanity of the honourable gentleman declare it, that we may find out another market for the exportation of our butter and woollens, and not continue, in the course of six years, to be deceived from day to day, and be the ridicule of Europe, by suffering ourselves to be thus easily duped by designing and illiberal ministers. I now ask the secretary if there be positively a negotiation on foot?

Mr. Orde said he had repeatedly told gentlemen that the treaty was drawing to a conclusion, and, let the event be what it would, they would very soon know it.

Mr. Curran—However great the honour I may have received from the honourable gentleman's condescension in giving me an answer, yet I must beg leave to proceed. He has told us there is a treaty on foot; now, if there be, what injury can be done the cause by disclosing that a proposal has been made to the court of Portugal? If circumstances favourable to us are included in that proposal, the information will quiet the minds of the people, and not disserve the honourable gentleman or his cause.

I have indeed, heard of a game of chess going from one generation to another, but, in a commercial negotiation, I humbly apprehend a similar procrastination is unnecessary. I would be happy to be informed of a simple question, whether the interruption is to be on the exportation of cloth to Portugal? If we sleep over this business any longer, will not Portugal laugh at our pusillanimity? Your prohibition of por-wine is a tax of revenue upon yourselves; you make us pay double for a glass of wine, to revenge yourselves on the Portuguese. For this tax I am no advocate; not from a motive of luxury so much as to prove that we are not so inconsistent as to take revenge on the Portuguese, for the misconduct of the English ministers. If the question of adjournment be put, it will tell the Portuguese that the House of Commons has given up the circumstance; therefore I will, in consequence of this opinion, vote against the adjournment, and for the motion of my ɒonourable friend.—*Debates*, vol. vi., pp 269, 70, 71.

The address was withdrawn.

PENSIONS.

March 13th, 1786.

THE endeavour to regain by corruption what was surrendered to force, began in 1782, and increased greatly after the defeat of Orde's Propositions. To restrain this, Mr. Forbes, on the 13th of March, 1786, moved for leave to bring in a bill to limit the amount of pensions. It was read a first time, and he then moved that it "be read a second time to-morrow." Sir Hercules Langrishe moved the adjournment of the question to August (*i.e.* altogether), in a speech full of Hanoverian doctrines, and was supported by (amongst others) Sir Boyle Roche, in an absurd speech, which, as a specimen of his *celebrated* style, we insert:—

"Sir Boyle Roche—I opposed this bill at its first rising in this house, in the shape of a motion. [The house called to Sir Boyle to speak up.] Indeed I think it necessary that I should overcome my bashfulness, and I lament that I was not brought up to the learned profession of the law, for that is the best remedy for bashfulness of all sorts.

"The just prerogative of the crown and the rights of parliament are the main pillars that support the ponderous pile of our constitution. I never will consent to meddle with either, lest I should bring the whole building about my ears.

"I would not stop the fountain of royal favour, but let it flow freely, spontaneously and abundantly as Holywell in Wales, that turns so many mills. Indeed some of the best men have drank of this fountain, which gives honour as well as vigour. This is my way of thinking; at the same time I feel as much integrity and principle as any man that hears me. Principle is the fair ground to act upon, and that any man should doubt the principle of another, because he happens to differ with him in opinion, is so bad an act that I do not choose to give it a name."—*Debates*, vol. vi., pp. 280, 81.

Mr. Curran said—I object to adjourning this bill to the first of August, because I perceive in the present disposition of the house, that proper decision will be made upon it this night. We have set out upon our inquiry in a manner so honourable, and so consistent, that we have reason to expect the happiest success, which I would not wish to see baffled by delay.

We began with giving the full affirmative of this house, that no grievance exists at all; we considered a simple matter of fact, and adjourned our opinion; or rather, we gave sentence on the conclusion, after having adjourned the premises. But I do begin to see a great deal of argument in what the learned Baronet has said; and I beg gentlemen will acquit me of apostacy, if I offer some reasons why the bill should not be admitted to a second reading.

I am surprised that gentlemen have taken up such a foolish opinion, as that our constitution is maintained by its different component parts, mutually checking and controlling each other; they seem to think, with

Hobbes, that a state of nature is a state of warfare: and that, like Manomet's coffin, the constitution is suspended between the attraction of different powers. My friends seem to think that the crown should be restrained from doing wrong by a physical necessity; forgetting, that if you take away from man all power to do wrong, you, at the same time, take away from him all merit of doing right; and, by making it impossible for men to run into slavery, you enslave them most effectually. But if, instead of the three different parts of our constitution drawing forcibly in right lines, in different directions, they were to unite their power, and draw all one way, in one right line, how great would be the effect of their force, how happy the direction of this union! The present system is not only contrary to mathematical rectitude, but to public harmony; but if, instead of privilege setting up his back to oppose prerogative, he were to saddle his back, and invite prerogative to ride, how comfortably they might both jog along! and therefore it delights me to hear the advocates for the royal bounty flowing freely, and spontaneously, and abundantly, as Holywell in Wales. If the crown grant double the amount of the revenue in pensions, they approve of their royal master, for he is the breath of their nostrils.

But we shall find that this complaisance, this gentleness between the crown and its true servants, is not confined at home; it extends its influence to foreign powers. Our merchants have been insulted in Portugal, our commerce interdicted: what did the British lion do? Did he whet his tusks? did he bristle up, and shake his mane? did he roar? No; no such thing: the gentle creature wagged his tail for six years at the court of Lisbon; and now we hear from the Delphic oracle on the treasury bench, that he is wagging his tail in London to Chevalier Pinto, who, he hopes soon to be able to tell us, will allow his lady to entertain him as a lap-dog; and when she does, no doubt the British factory will furnish some of their softest woollens, to make a cushion for him to lie upon. But though the gentle beast has continued so long fawning and couching, I believe his vengeance will be great as it is slow; and that posterity, whose ancestors are yet unborn, will be surprised at the vengeance he will take!

This polyglot of wealth, this museum of curiosities, the pension list, embraces every link in the human chain, every description of men, women, and children, from the exalted excellence of a Hawke or a Rodney, to the debased situation of the lady who humbleth herself that she may be exalted. But the lessons it inculcates form its greatest perfection: it teacheth, that sloth and vice may eat that bread which virtue and honesty may starve for after they have earned it. It teaches the idle and dissolute to look up for that support which they are too proud to stoop and earn. It directs the minds of men to an entire reliance on the ruling power of the state, who feed the ravens of the royal aviary, that cry continually for food. It teaches them to imitate those saints on the pension list that are like the lilies of the field, they toil not, neither do they spin, and yet are arrayed like Solomon in his glory. In fine, it teaches a lesson, which, indeed, they might have learned from Epictetus, that it is sometimes good not to be over tuous: it shows, that in proportion as our distresses increase, the munificence of the crown increases also; in proportion as our clothes are rent, the royal mantle is extended over us.

Notwithstanding that the pension list, like charity, covers a multitude of sins, give me leave to consider it as coming home to the members of this house—give me leave to say, that the crown, in extending its charity, its liberality, its profusion, is laying a foundation for the independence of parliament; for hereafter, instead of orators or patriots accounting for their conduct to such mean and unworthy persons as freeholders, they will learn to despise them, and look to the first man in the state; and they will, by so doing, have this security for their independence, that while any man in the kingdom has a shilling, they will not want one.

Suppose at any future period of time the boroughs of Ireland should decline from their present flourishing and prosperous state—suppose they should fall into the hands of men who would wish to drive a profitable commerce, by having members of parliament to hire or let; in such a case a secretary would find great difficulty, if the proprietors of members should enter into a combination to form a monopoly: to prevent which, in time, the wisest way is to purchase up the raw material. young members of parliament, just rough from the grass; and when they are a little bitted, and he has got a pretty stud, perhaps of seventy, he may laugh at the slave merchant; some of them he may teach to sound through the nose, like a barrel organ; some, in the course of a few months, might be taught to cry, "Hear! hear!" some, "Chair! chair!" upon occasion—though those latter might create a little confusion, if they were to forget whether they were calling inside or outside of those doors. Again he might have some so trained that he need only pull a string, and up gets a repeating member: and if they were so dull that they could neither speak nor make orations (for they are different things), he might have them taught to dance, *pedibus iræ in sententia*. This improvement might be extended: he might have them dressed in coats and shirts all of one colour; and, of a Sunday, he might march them to church two by two, to the great edification of the people, and the honour of the Christian religion; afterwards, like ancient Spartans, or the fraternity of Kilmainham, they might dine all together in a large hall. Good heaven! what a sight to see them feeding in public, upon public viands, and talking of public subjects, for the benefit of the public! It is a pity they are not immortal; but I hope they will flourish as a corporation, and that pensioners will beget pensioners, to the end of the chapter.—*Debates*, vol. vi., pp. 281—4.

The adjournment was, however, carried. We shall presently find that the bill was renewed, and supported by Curran, in the next year.

OUTRAGES IN THE SOUTH

January 19th, 1787.

Persons of all politics are now agreed that the disturbances which have broken out so often in the south, for the last hundred years, were caused by the misery of the people. How far, at any period of this time, the misery was caused peculiarly by excessive rents, bad tenures, harsh treatment, oppressive tithing, or absenteeism, we need not distinguish; but it is certain that all contributed. As little need we examine how far French interests (connected, as they were with this country, by "The Brigade," the clerical schools, and the legal and contraband trades,) availed themselves of these disturbances, in the middle of the last century, or how far political parties united with them towards the close of that period. 'Tis sufficient and necessary to allude to these topics.

In the Lord Lieutenant's opening speech, in 1786, he referred to the "frequent outrages," and Mr. Seward (*Collectanea Politica*, p. 82,) applies this to the "Right Boys" of Kilkenny and quotes a pastoral of Dr. Troy's, to his Clergy in Ossory, stating that any person refusing to abjure the Right Boy oath, should be refused the rights of his church, living or dead. Yet the only bill on disturbances brought in by government was a Dublin Police Bill, against which the city petitioned.

In 1787, however, the speech from the Viceroy referred more positively to the Southern outrages, and, on the address in reply to it, a most vehement debate occurred. Curran's speech is one of his best in parliament, but has been omitted in all former editions of his works. During this debate the government party treated the disturbances as against the clergy, accused the landlords of grinding the people and abetting the disturbances, and asked fresh powers. In an after discussion, Fitzgibbon, the Attorney-General, made the following interesting statements with reference to these disturbances:—

"Their commencement was in one or two parishes in the county of Kerry, and they proceeded thus:—The people assembled in a mass house, and there took an oath to obey the laws of Captain Right, and to starve the clergy. They then proceeded to the next parishes, on the following Sunday, and there swore the people in the same manner, with this addition, that they (the people last sworn) should, on the ensuing Sunday, proceed to the chapels of their next neighbouring parishes, and swear the inhabitants of those parishes in like manner.

"Proceeding in this manner they very soon went through the province of Munster. The first object of their reformation was tithes: they swore not to give more than a certain price per acre—not to take from the minister at a great price—not to assist or allow him to be assisted in drawing the tithe, and to permit no proctor. They next took upon them to prevent the collection of parish cesses—then to nominate parish clerks, and, in some cases, curates—to say what church should or should not be repaired; and in one case, to threaten that they would burn a new church if the old one was not given for a mass house.

"At last they proceeded to regulate the price of lands, to raise the price of labour, and to oppose the collection of the hearth money and other taxes.

"Bodies of five thousand of them have been seen to march through the country unarmed, and if met by any magistrate, who had spirit to question them, they have not offered the smallest rudeness or offence; on the contrary, they have allowed persons charged with crimes to be taken from amongst them, by the magistrates alone, unaided with any force.

"I am very well acquainted with the province of Munster, and I know that it is impossible for human wretchedness to *exceed that of the miserable peasantry in that province*. I *know that the unhappy tenantry are ground to powder by relentless landlords*—I know that, far from being able to give the clergy their just dues, they have not food or raiment for themselves, the landlord grasps the whole: and sorry I am to add, that, not satisfied with the present extortion, some landlords have been so base as to instigate the insurgents to rob the clergy of their tithes, not in order to alleviate the distresses of the tenantry, but that they might add the clergy's share to the cruel rack-rents already paid. I fear it will require the utmost ability of parliament to come to the root of those evils. The poor people of Munster live in a more abject state of poverty than human nature can be supposed able to bear—their miseries are intolerable, but they do not originate with the clergy; nor can the legislature stand by and see them take the redress into their own hands. Nothing can be done for their benefit while the country remains in a state of anarchy."—*Debates,* vol. vii., p. 57.

But Mr. Longfield, a county Cork gentleman, stated that the disturbances were exaggerated, though the distress was not. He accused the government of looking for a year at the disturbances, for a political purpose, and used these strong words—"none but the lowest wretches, who groan under *the most intolerable oppressions*, were engaged in any disturbance."

Curran moved an amendment to the address thus:—

Had this address been, (as were all addresses that I have ever read or heard of,) composed of unmeaning stuff, I should not rise to speak to it. But, Sir, it is an address that tends to inspire the mind of the chief governor with indignation for the wretched people of this country—an address tending to impress the father of his people with the idea of their being in open revolt, to divert the royal mind from listening to the complaints of afflicted subjects, or alleviating their miseries. I cannot give my consent to such gross invective. To say it is necessary, is only adding irony to invective.

But you wish to compliment his grace—and do you? No; you praise him for the exertion of force that was never exerted; and, if you suppose it exerted, you must confess yourself disappointed in your expectations of it; and surely this can be no compliment.

Sir, this country has been represented as in a state little short of oper rebellion. As subjects of the country, it is the business of all gentlemen to consider the real state of the case, and if ever there was a time when party bias should be thrown aside, it is the present. We should not brand the nation in our address with words of course.

Sir, when you speak of popular disturbances, you should search for the source of them; the people are oppressed, and before you pour the last drop into the vessel, and cause the waters of bitterness to overflow on them, consider well what you are about. If the representatives of the nation have been remiss, if the magistrates throughout the kingdom have been criminally supine, lay the blame at the right door; cease to utter idle complaints of inevitable effects, when you yourselves have been the causes. Sir, the man who would say, that the constitution in church and state was in danger, from the simple insurrection of a parcel of peasants, without order, without a head, without a leader, undisciplined, unarmed, or only partially so, I would not take to be a very wise man; and the man who would say so from anything, save an error in judgment, I would not take to be either a wise or an honest man. What, Sir, is the tendency of this paragraph? Why, Sir, it is to create civil discord between subject and subject—to arm the hand of one man against another!

It is unusual with me, Sir, to offer any captious opposition. My opposition to this part of the address is not of this nature. I have in my breast a feeling which will not suffer me to hear the cry of public calamity interpreted as the shout of rebellion, and this is now attempted to be done. You have no rebellion cresting her head in the nation. But a deliberate scheme is said to be on foot, for the extirpation of the Protestant religion and of the constitution. Were it the case, I should expend the last drop of my blood in defence of both; but it is not the fact. I will tell gentlemen the causes from whence the present disturbances originated. An idea has been disseminated, but I hope in God it will never take root, that, though a man labours, he is not entitled to enjoy the emoluments of his labour and industry. This is said to be the case, but I hope, without justice. Sir, the patience of the people has been totally exhausted; their grievances have long been the empty song of this house, but no productive effect has ever yet followed. But it may be asked, what are the grievances of the people? Why, one is non-residence of the landholders. By their absence the unfortunate tenant becomes subject to the tyranny of an intermediate landlord— and when this matter came before you, what did you do? Why, you denied the existence of the grievance, and refused redress. You are deprived, by the non-resident landholder, of your specie—your gold and silver—but this is not the worst of the mischief. Every incentive to order or industry is withdrawn, and hence one great reason for the present disturbances.

Is it any wonder that the wretches whom woful and long experience has taught to doubt, and with justice to doubt, the attention and relief of the legislature—wretches, that have the utmost difficulty to keep life and soul together, and who must inevitably perish, if the hand of assistance is not stretched out to them—should appear in tumult? No, Sir, it is not. Unbound to the sovereign by any proof of his affection— unbound to government by any instance of its protection, unbound to the country, or to the soil, by being destitute of any property in it, 'tis no wonder that the peasantry should be ripe for rebellion and revolt; so far from being matter of surprise, it must naturally have been expected.

Will any man dare to say, that there is a single man of property, a single man of consequence, connected with the insurgents? Or that any such men afford them support? No; and with what justice, then, can the paragraph stand in the address?

When a body of men stood forward, in the moment of general consternation and dismay—in that perilous moment, when it was a question whether you should long sit as a House of Commons, for government was unable to defend you—they, The Volunteers, defended you; and, to be sure, you held out a good encouragement to loyalty! What did you do? You thanked them first, and dismissed them afterwards! This was attended with the blessed effects we are now witnesses of. Fired with honest indignation, they withdrew themselves from the service of their country, and left it exposed to all the consequences of intestine commotion. It is true you talked of substituting a militia bill—but, Sir, this was a mere farce, to amuse for the present moment: and you should not have deprived the country of one support, until you had actually supplied her with another.

You were called on, Sir, solemnly called on for a proper reformation in the representation of the people; did you grant it? No; and how does it at present stand? Why, Sir, seats in this house are bought and sold. They are set up to public sale; they are become an absolute article of commerce—a traffic of the constitution. I have a doubt, whether, if a member of this house should become a bankrupt, his seat in this assembly would not be claimed by his assignees, as a part of his property, and whether they might not put it up to public cant.

The legal and constitutional idea is, that a member should represent his constituents, by virtue of the property he has. Now, members for these saleable rotten boroughs represent their constituents, or the peo ple, by virtue of the property which they have not, for they represent them in virtue of the two thousand pounds which they give the proprietor for his seat. Nothing, then, can be more clear than that they do not represent the people in virtue of the property they have.

Certainly as they have bought the people for a sum of money, it is natural they should sell them—and so they do! and make the most they can of the bargain. The mandate of a borough-monger can return any man,—however contemptible—however obnoxious, to this house, and I ask you should this be tolerated?

There is a race in this country, between public prodigality and connivance. Prodigality is everywhere to be seen, and connivance affords it the means of existence, and hence the race between public prodigality and public connivance, and the fact of their both keeping pace together. I do not blame a certain right honourable gentleman [Mr. Orde]; I see him look grave at what I say; I am sure he feels it with regret. Sir, that right honourable gentleman knows, that the people have no power of control over their representatives; and what is the consequence? Why, it is in the power of a few borough-mongers to impede the necessary motions of government—to obstruct the necessary business of the nation! And hence, Sir, expectants and demandants must be gratified with places and pensions, or we should have, in fact, no government! And hence are the people victims. I know what I say may be offensive to many gentlemen; individually and personally, I have as much respect for them, perhaps, as any man can have, but private respect must give way to public necessity.

Unless something is done, what will be the end of all this? Why, government will be necessitated, at length, to imitate the policy of Henry the Seventh, who broke the neck of an abominable aristocracy, and caused the property they had accumulated to circulate amongst the people. In this case, it would only be restoring to the people their own property—the right of election.

Nor are the evils I speak of seen in theory only, but in practice. You have now near one hundred thousand pounds on your pension list; and this should surprise and alarm every man who is not dead to all real subjects of surprise and alarm.

The peasantry have formed hopes of relief; and will you dash the cup of comfort, or snatch the bread of hope from the mouth of affliction? People, when oppressed—though oppressed by law—will make reprisals; and these are the real causes of disturbance.

I have been a resident of this county, spoken of as in open insurrection; and, since gentlemen are in the habit of speaking of themselves, I shall do myself the same honour. I could not perceive any of the outrages spoken of; and I am certain that they were nothing more than the offspring of the most abject misery. They were all forlorn wretches, who, were they inclined to become danglers, and to pin themselves to the petticoat of administration, so poor, so naked are they, that administration would not find on them a rag whereby to pin them to their petticoat.

I have a thought the accounts of disturbances faith-'

ful and unexaggerated, can it be fairly supposed I would wish to withhold protection from them? But, in such a light do I hold insurrection, whatever provocatives might have been to it, that as a counsel I refused to be concerned for two men charged with the crime;* and this, I think, should entitle me to a little credit.

Still, I can see no necessity for creating a dictatorship, in the person of our chief governor. Do we not possess the means of punishing any crime that may be committed against society? Will any man hold out such an incentive to rebellion, as to say we do not? The insurrection is not so great. The man who says it is, despairs of the commonwealth and I insist that there is nothing in the present times that will justify a departure from the ordinary proceedings and established forms of government.

The supineness of the magistrates, and the low state of the commissions of the peace throughout the kingdom, but particularly in the county of Cork, are the things that should be rectified. At the last assizes there, I prevailed on two unworthy magistrates, Butler and Wogan, to resign their commissions, (which they had abused), by freeing them from a prosecution.

A system of vile jobbing is one of the misfortunes of this country. It extends even to commissions of the peace; how else can the report of the four and twenty commissions of the peace sent down to the county of Clare in one post (I don't mention it as a fact) be accounted for. Even the appointment of sheriffs, is notoriously in the hands of government. Through jobbing the sheriffs themselves cannot be trusted; two sheriffs ran away last year with executions in their pockets, and the late high sheriff of the county of Dublin has absconded.

Disorders should be remedied; but, in that remedy, do not pronounce a sentence of excommunication against the people. Suppose all the people of Ireland should come to your house, and tell you they were aggrieved, and wanted redress, let me ask you what would you say? Many independent men are waiting with patience for your decision—waiting quietly, with their hands before them—men, whose influence may make insurrection dreadful indeed. We have a most elegant custom-house, and for what? To afford palaces for the servants of the crown. One palace has been built in it, and I understand it was a matter of contention, that there were not two. All this is jobbing—and now I am given to understand that palaces must be built for all the officers of police, under the description of resident-houses.

I have read the history of other nations, and I have read the history of yours; I have seen how happily you emerged from insignificance, and obtained your constitution. But when you washed this constitution with the waters which were to render it invulnerable, like the mother of Achilles, you forgot that the part by which you held it was untouched in the immersion; it was benumbed, and not rendered invulnerable, and therefore it should attract your nicest care.

You may talk of commerce extending—of a freedom of trade; but

* His refusing to act as counsel seems strange and indefensible.

what, in God's name, have they to do with the wretched peasantry?—and when the peasantry complain, and when I hear such language, I consider it as a solemn and an insulting mockery.

Let me examine what government has done to suppress those disturbances. They sent down the crown solicitor to Cork! Was the crown solicitor a person to quell rebellion? They sent down four hundred soldiers! was it to fugle for the body of rebels? If it was not, where are the conquests they made? But what did both solicitor and army do? They empannelled twelve of the wretches to try a thirteenth—they found him guilty, and they whipped him through the town at a cart's tail! For shame! for shame! Cease thus to expose the King's government to the ridicule of the whole world, by this trumpeting of alarm, when such is the only foundation for it.

I have, on a former day, opposed Attachments; but I think the magistrates who have neglected their duty, should and ought to be attached; and that it would be a better measure than to augment the offences of our criminal code, already too numerous.

He concluded by moving the following amendments :—

To the second paragraph of the address, by inserting between the word *kingdom* and the word *and* the following words :—" Though it is a great consolation to us to think that these outrages have not originated in any disaffection in your Majesty's subjects of this kingdom to your Majesty's government, or in any concerted design of disturbing our present happy constitution either in Church or State, but they had been wholly .onfined to some individuals of the lowest class of the people, whose extreme indigence and distress may be the occasion, though they cannot be a justification, of such illegal proceedings ; and it is a further consolation to us to know, that the ordinary powers of the law now in being are fully adequate, if duly exerted, to punish and restrain such excesses.

To the third paragraph, by adding after the word *government* the following words :—" At the same time we humbly beg leave to represent to your Majesty, that the public expenses of this country have increased to a degree so far beyond the ability of the people to bear, that we feel ourselves called upon by our duty to our constituents to reduce those expenses, by every mode of retrenchment, consistent with such honourable and necessary support to your Majesty's government, within such limits as may be compatible with the very exhausted resources of a distressed people. And we do not doubt of having your Majesty's gracious approbation of a measure so essential to the commercial hopes of your kingdom of Ireland, as well as conducive to the permanent peace and prosperity of this kingdom."—*Debates*, vol. vii., pp. 25—31.

The amendments were lost without a division.

THE KINGDOM OF KERRY.

January 23rd, 1787.

The following fragment of a speech on the 23rd of January, seems to have originated this phrase:—

I admit that there may be local circumstances which would justify the withholding of a writ of election, but they should be of notoriety, and well ascertained. I know of no whiteboys, at present, impeding the freedom of election. Since disturbances have been spoken of, I declare that I sincerely wish the offenders may be punished, but I most sincerely wish that the cause of these disturbances may be removed. For my part I have done everything as a magistrate, and as a man to restore order. The low and contemptible state of your magistracy is the cause of much evil, particularly in the Kingdom of Kerry. I say Kingdom, for it seems absolutely not a part of the same country.

Sir, I will relate to you a circumstance that will give you an idea of the vigilance of the magistrates in that quarter. One Seely, a notorious offender, for whom a reward had been offered by government, appeared openly in the county. A poor cottager was met by a person one morning, when going to pay his rent. The person asked him was he not distressed to make up the money. The poor cottager innocently replied—why should I want money, when I can, at any time, get fifty pounds for informing against Seely? For having dropped this expression, the wretch's cabin was that night broken open by six armed men, and as himself, his wife, and children, sat round a little table, at their tasteless and scanty meal of dry potatoes, a blunderbuss was discharged on them. Scarcely one of the children escaped being wounded; the father died on the spot. In Tralee another fellow broke gaol, and they are both walking about the country, not skulking or hiding, but in the face of day. To my own knowledge, informations were laid before a magistrate—a very respectable person—but no step has been taken to apprehend them, and the murderer and the outlaw stalk about the land, laughing at the sleeping laws.—And I say, Sir, to suffer those men again to return into the mass of the people, is the severest reproach upon your magistracy

In saying this I do not mean to throw the smallest imputation on the venerable character from whom the magistrates receive their commissions. A man of higher integrity never existed; but it is impossible for him personally to know every man recommended—he must take them upon the credit of the recommender, and he only is to blame, who, for any base purposes, clothes in authority a wretch, unworthy, perhaps, to be a footman or a groom.—*Debates,* vol. vii., pp. 41, 2.

RIGHT BOY BILL.

February 19th, 1787

On the motion for the Committtal of the Bill, a hot debate occurred. Mr. Burgh, of Old-town, interrupted the reading of the bill at the clause for pulling down Roman Catholic Chapels. This clause was afterwards abandoned, but Fitzgibbon's defence of it is worth notice:—

"I am now come to the clause which, upon the first reading, drew forth such a string of feverish epithets from some honourable gentlemen—the clause directing magistrates to demolish mass-houses at which combinations shall be formed, or unlawful oaths administered. I am as unwilling as any man to abolish Christianity; for I know if religion is abolished, there is no longer any tie over the minds of men. I am unwilling as the right honourable gentleman to stab them through the sides of their God; but if they will make their places of worship places of combination, they should be prostrated; if they will pervert them to the vilest purposes, they ought to be demolished. However, though I should not press this clause, I am glad it has appeared in print; it will show the bulk of the people what they are likely to draw upon themselves, by perverting their places of worship and it will rouse those who are most interested in their preservation to exert themselves for the prevention of combinations, and administering unlawful oaths in them. Nor can I give up the principle on which the clause is founded; for we are told, from the highest authority, that when the temple had become a den of thieves. the doors therefore were shut. Besides, I have known this very punishment inflicted in Catholic countries, and have actually seen churches shut up by an order of the king of France, for offences of political nature. However, I shall not press the clause, being convinced, that by appearing in print, it has answered the purpose intended."—*Debates*, vol. vii., p. 185.

Grattan opposed the excesses of the bill; Curran resisted it altogether:—

Mr. Curran said—I came to the house impressed with the insignificant figure to which the house has been reduced, in the course of this business. A committee has been appointed to consider this great subject—they meet, not to inquire into the real state of the country, but blindly to accede to a resolution proposed. Without hearing one single evidence of any fact, we are now called upon to treat this kingdom as if it were in actual rebellion, and to add a new list to the catalogue of capital punishments. If we are reduced to the necessity of adding oppression to misery, and that we must condemn the wretched peasantry of this country unheard, the more blindly we are driven forward the better—our degradation ought to be matter of consolation to us, as it must be of excuse. I will, however, beseech the house to consider the danger contained in the principle of the bill, before they suffer it to go into a committee. [He then went into a view of the state of Ireland previous to and subsequent to 1782.*] In the former period we were treated as a conquered country by Great Britain; cramped in our industry by her jealousy: bound by laws to which we never assented; kept in a state of weakness; unable to resent, by the divisions artfully fomented among us; our peasantry reduced to the most abject misery; our employments, of every description, bestowed upon strangers; our nobles paid without being trusted; the kingdom, of consequence, weak, idle, ignorant, and licentious, and all this because of the civil and religious disunion among the people. A happy change occurred. We have witnessed the increase of knowledge and of industry, emancipation from unconstitutional power, a happy escape from religious intolerance,

* This and all similar abridgements are so in the original reports.

the admission of our Catholic brethren to the national rights of fellow-subjects and fellow-Christians. [He then contrasted the former weakness of a divided people with the state of strength and respect to which Ireland had advanced by her unanimity, in the last war.] When England left you to guard yourselves, the spirit of a people, then happily united, sent into the field an army of citizens, without distinction of sects or tenets, and united in the common and glorious cause of defending their country. Your enemies were dismayed; and Europe saw us start from a sleep of centuries, and reclaim that station which we so long had relinquished in the scale of nations.

[He then proceeded to state more particularly the present state of the nation, and observed on the general effect of severe laws.] The people are too much raised by a consciousness of their strength and consequence to be proper objects of so sanguinary a code as that now proposed. The overstrained severity of a law amounts universally to the impunity of the offender, for every good and social principle in the heart of man obstructs its execution. The witness, the jury, the judge concur, by every practicable artifice, to save the wretch from a punishment inadequate to his crime. On general principles, therefore, I will oppose the principle of a bill that is written in blood. But the general principle receives double strength from the circumstances of the time. The disturbances of the south are not only exaggerated beyond the truth, by every misrepresentation of artful malignity, but are held up to the public mind in so silly or so wicked point of view, as to make it impossible for parliament to proceed, without the most imminent danger of sacrificing every advantage we have acquired. And here let me advert for a moment to the state of our ecclesiastical policy for centuries past.

The church of Ireland has been in the hands of strangers, advanced to the mitre, not for their virtues or their knowledge, but quartered upon this country, through their own servility or the caprice of their benefactors, inclined naturally to oppress us, to hate us, and to defame us, while the real duties of our religion have been performed by our own native clergy, who, with all the finer feelings of gentlemen and scholars, have been obliged to do the drudgery of their profession for forty, or at most fifty pounds a year; without the means of being liberal, from their poverty, and without the hope of advancing themselves by their learning or their virtues, in a country where preferment is notoriously not to be attained by either. On this ground I vindicate the great body of the native acting clergy of Ireland, from any imputation because of the small progress which Protestantism has made among us. The pride of Episcopacy, and the low state to which our ministers of the Gospel are reduced, abundantly accounts for it. Their distresse and oppression are the real objects of parliamentary consideration; and we cannot interfere in the manner now proposed, without exposing them to the most imminent danger

[He then adverted to the nature of the disturbances in the south.] I cannot justify these outrages; they ought to be punished, but we ought not to forget that we have ourselves expressly admitted that they had proceeded from the supineness of magistrates, and the oppression of landlords. Now an act like this would be a proclamation of a religious war in this kingdom. A publication has been industriously circulated through a number of editions, stating that a scheme has been formed between the Catholics and the Presbyterians, for the subversion of the established religion and constitution; and the former are gravely informed that their religion absolves them from all tie of allegiance to the state, or observance of their oaths. And this is not an opinion pronounced upon light authority; it is the deliberate assertion of a reverend prelate, whose judgment on one of the abstrusest points of our common law has been opposed, with success, to that of our venerable chancellor, who is, perhaps, the ablest common lawyer in either kingdom, except only those gentlemen who are not of the profession. [He then examined the justice of the learned author's publication, which he condemned, as founded on illiberality and misrepresentation, and tending to obstruct the advancement of our religion, and to annihilate the provision of the established clergy; and tending also manifestly to revive the dissensions from which we had so recently emerged, and to plunge us into the barbarism from which we were emerging, or, perhaps, to imbrue us in the bloodshed of a religious war.]*

However the public may excuse the effects of mistaken zeal in the reverend writer, the house will be degraded below itself, if it adopt so silly an intolerance, or so abject a panic. This law would render the established church odious to the country, and, of course, prevent the progress of the established religion; it would expose the great body of the clergy to be stripped of the scanty pittance to which the cruelly unequal distribution of church revenues has confined them; it would involve us in all the horrors of a religious war; it would throw us back into the miseries of a weak, a licentious, and a divided people; and it would be a repeal of the acts which our wisdom has made in favour of our Catholic brethren, in admitting them to the natural rights of fellow-subjects and fellow-Christians. I therefore think myself bound, as a man anxious for the rights of the country, for its peace, its religion, and its morals, to vote against the committal of this bill.—*Debates,* vol. vii., pp. 192, 3, 4.

The Bill was committed by 192 to 31.

February, 20th, 1787.

On this day, a Committee, Mr. John O'Neill moved that the application of the Bill should be limited to Cork, Kerry, Limerick, and Tipperary. In order to explain Curran's opening, we must refer to a passage in his speech of the 19th of January (see page 65, par. 4th), and quote Major Hobart's speech in this debate:—

" I rise to observe upon what fell from an honourable gentleman on the other side, as every thing that falls from him deserves notice. He says he is not prepared to pass a riot act;

---

* This refers to a bulky, able, and insolent pamphlet, by Dr. Woodward, Bishop of Cloyne, in defence of Tithes. It is easily procured, and is worth reading.

that the outrages are confined to the lowest of the people; but that there are people of higher class watching the event, and ready to take advantage of it. I know that th_ honourable gentleman has communicated these circumstances for the most laudable purposes, and I hope the house will not be intimidated, but take proper advantage of this communication, and act with greater vigour and energy."—*Debates*, vol. vii., p. 212.

I consider myself called on. What I intended in the sentences alluded to by Mr. Hobart was that many gentlemen would have done more to suppress the insurgents, if they did not consider them as labouring under grievances. That was my meaning on that day, and my belief at the present.

An honourable member has indulged himself in an episodical plenitude; but I shall not imitate him, nor talk of the commander of the church, or the commander of the army, as he has done. I am sorry that when disposed to diffuse the rays of his panegyric, they were not vertical; like the beams of the morning, that courted the tops of the mountain, and left the valleys unilluminated, they applied only to the great, while the distressed poor were left in the shade. I consider the clergy of the south an oppressed and unfortunate body of men—confined to poverty by the cruel policy of their own laws; I should be sorry to be thought as seeking for causes of complaint; I have purposely avoided speaking on many. I could have proved that much of the disturbances arise from clerical neglect, and the motives of the insurgents might excuse, though not justify their conduct. I will mention a circumstance of disturbance—in the very diocese from whence the publication, so much reprobated, issued—in a parish worth eight or nine hundred pounds a year—which should make the house blush. It was a rising to banish a seraglio of prostitutes, kept by a rector who received near a thousand pounds a year from the church, and to reinstate the unoffending mother and innocent children in the polluted mansion. Perhaps I am not keeping the secrets of the church as closely as I ought. Two questions arise upon this. Did the learned proclaimer of dissension know this? and if he did not, why did he write upon the state of the country, when he was ignorant of that of his own diocese?

I object to the universality of the bill, as the severity of it should only fall where it is merited; and so far from any danger to the constitution, in church or state, existing, it is my decided and rooted opinion, that there is no Roman Catholic in the kingdom, possessed of five pounds property, that does not wish for the due observance of the laws; but such is the abject misery and distress of the very lower orders, that they may consider, and I do not doubt that they may be right, even the being employed to act against the laws, as a favourable change in their condition.

As to the arguments of a riot act existing in England, I reply that it was adopted in the time of rebellion, in the days of Edward the Sixth, when the sacred religion of the country was attacked. It was continued by his bloody successor, for the establishment of a different religion. From the time of Elizabeth to the reign of George the First, it remained in that oblivion which it ever should, but it was then revived, to guard the crown, and to prevent the Protestant religion from sinking under the ruins of the throne. Such causes cannot be alleged in this kingdom. [Having answered this argument, he entered upon the locality of the law, and demonstrated that its limitation would be highly salutary.] If the north were excluded it would hold out the highest encouragement to peaceability and decorous demeanour, to the inhabitants of the south. They would then see that this had merited the punishment, by having been singled out for its operation. The people of the north might say to those of the south—come from under that bondage which has been imposed on you, and be like us; in order to do so, you need only be peaceable. This would be alarming their pride, and if a man's pride be once raised, it has more effect than can be well conceived. It has been mentioned that in 1772 there were riots in the north, but none since. Surely, then, the honour of the amendment should do away the remembrance of the transgression, and consign it to oblivion. You should not visit the crimes of the fathers upon the children; and I think that, after a trial of fourteen years, the north should be entitled to the confidence of a wise legislature. But it is said that the insurgents would emigrate to the north. If they did, when they would behold the moderation and industry of the people of that quarter, it is more than probable they would be struck with a sense of their folly, and they would return from it the missionaries of virtue, as they had come into it the incendiaries of rebellion.

There is another great vice in this bill—the disproportion between the crime and the punishment. If murder be punished no higher than a petty transgression, it will impress the lower orders with a dangerous idea, and banish all distinction of crimes. It will look as if the legislature thought no more of the preservation of the life of a man, than they did of the preservation of his hedge; and it would be strange if the legislature would decree, that the tendering of an oath to a man was as henious a crime as holding a knife to his throat. The laws should have force, but that force should never be seen; there should be a kind of superstition in the people, which would prevent their discovering it. Omnipotence was an attribute of parliament; but to pass such a law as this would be the impotence of parliament; for if the jury commiserate the criminal—if the judge melt into tears, and his humanity suffer that the man escape, the law enacted by this bill will be like the thunder, which makes a great noise, but rolls over the head innoxious.

[He made other observations of this nature, and returned to the subject of including the whole kingdom in the act.] It is only by the body being diseased that the administration of medicine is harmless, and so, coercive laws are only harmless where there is a resistance from tumult—as in the body a resistance from disease. If medicine were administered, therefore, where there is no disease to resist it, the consequences would be destructive; and so, if coercive laws are enacted, when there is no tumult to resist them, the consequences must be equally fatal. I fear that, as the coercion is so great, and as no means are taken for the relief of the poor, rebellion will go in the dark, and, as in arbitrary countries, stalk abroad at midnight, and add its solitary faggot to the heap, until the blaze shall be at length kindled, and the whole kingdom set in a flame.*—*Debates*, vol. vii., pp. 214, 15, 16.

The limiting motion was rejected by 176 to 42.

LIMITATION OF PENSIONS.

March 12th, 1787.

Mr. Forbes renewed his bill for limiting Pensions, this session, and Curran supported him thus:—

I feel too much respect for the excellent mover of the bill, and too strong a sense of the necessity of the measure, to give it only a silent support. I rejoice in the virtuous perseverance of my honourable friend in labouring for the establishment of our constitution, by securing the independence of parliament. I shall offer some reasons in defence of the bill, though I feel the full force of the policy adopted by administration to make any attempt of that kind either ridiculous or impossible. I observed gentlemen consulting whether to bury the question under a mute majority, or whether to make a sham opposition to it, by setting up the old gladiator of administration, new polished and painted for the field. They expected, I suppose, that men should shrink in silence and disgust from such a competition. I shall defend the principle of the bill on the ground of economy, but, still more, of constitution. The frame of our civil state depends on an exact balance of its parts ; but, from our peculiar situation, that equipoise on which our liberty depends, must be continually losing ground, and the power of the crown continually increasing. A single individual can be vigilant and active, improving every occasion of extending his power: the people are not so ; they are divided in sentiment and in interest ; without union, and therefore without co-operation. From hence the necessity of bringing the constitution frequently back to its first principles ; but this is doubly necessary to do by law, in a country where a long system of dividing the people has almost extinguished that public mind that public vigilance and jealousy, with which the conduct of the crown watched over in Great Britain.

Further, it is rendered necessary by the residence of our king in another country. His authority must be delegated first to a Viceroy, and next it falls to a Secretary, who can have no interest in the good of the people, no interest in future fame, no object to attract him, but the advancement of his dependants. Then the responsibility that binds an English king to moderation and frugality is lost here in the confusion of persons, or in their insignificance.

This may be deemed an unusual language in this house ; but I assure the right honourable Secretary I do not speak with any view of disturb-

* The reader will recognise a metaphor afterwards employed by Curran in his speech for Hamilton Rowan.

ing his personal feelings. I do not admire, nor shall I imitate the cruelty of the Sicilian tyrant, who amused himself with putting insects to the torture. I am merely stating facts. What responsibility can be found or hoped for in an English Secretary? Estimate them fairly not according to the adulation that lifts them into a ridiculous importance while they are among you, or the alike unmerited contumely that s heaped upon them by disappointment and shame when they leave you. But what have they been, in fact?—why, a succession of men, sometimes with heads, sometimes with hearts, oftener with neither.

But as to the present right honourable Secretary, it is peculiarly ridiculous to talk of his responsibility, or his economy to the people. His economy is only to be found in reducing the scanty pittance which profusion has left for the encouragement of our manufactures; or in withholding from the undertakers of a great national object that encouragement that had been offered them on the express faith of parliament; unless, perhaps, it were to be looked for in the pious plan of selling the materials of houses of religious worship, on a principle of economy. But where will you look for his responsibility as a minister? You will remember his Commercial Propositions. They were proposed to this country on his responsibility. You cannot forget the exhibition he made; you cannot have yet lost his madrigal on reciprocity; but what was the event? He went to Great Britain with ten propositions, and he returned with double the number; disclaimed and abandoned by those to whom he belonged, and shorn of every pretension to responsibility.

Then look for it in the next leading feature of his administration. We gave an addition of £140,000 in taxes, on the express compact and condition of confining expense within the limits of revenue. Already has that compact been shamefully evaded; but what says the responsible gentleman? Why, he stood up in his place, and had the honest confidence boldly to deny the fact! Now I should be glad to ask, who that right honourable member is? Is he the whole House of Commons?—if he be, he proposed the compact. Is he the king?—he accepted it by his viceroy. Is he the viceroy?—he accepted it by himself. In every character that could give such a compact either credit, or dignity, or stability, he has either proposed or ratified it. In what character, then, does the right honourable gentleman deny it?—why, in his own; in that of a *right honourable gentleman.*

Is any man, then, so silly as to think that a barefaced spirit of profusion can be stopped by anything less than a law? Or can any man point out any ground on which we can confide in the right honourable gentleman's affection to the interest or even the peace of this country? At a time when we are told that the people are in a state of tumult little short of rebellion, when you ought to wish to send an angel to recall the people to their duty, and restore the credit of the laws, what does he do?—he keeps three judicial places, absolutely vacant, sinecure places,—as if in this country not officers, but offices, are to become superannuated; and he sends the commission, with a job tacked to it, to be displayed in the very scene of this supposed confusion. Would this contemptuous trifling with the public be borne in Great Britain? No, Sir; but what the substance of an English minister, with all his talents, would not dare to attempt in that country, his fetch is able to achieve, and with impunity, in this.

A right honourable member opposes the principle of the bill, as being in restraint of the royal bounty. I agree with him in this sentiment, but I differ from his argument. It becomes the dignity and humanity of a generous people, to leave it in the power of the sovereign to employ some part of the public wealth for honourable purposes, for rewarding merit, for encouraging science. Nor would it become us to inquire too narrowly into every casual or minute misapplication; but a gross and general application of the people's money to the encouragement of every human vice, is a crying grievance, that calls on every man to check it —not by restraining the bounty of the crown, but by curbing the profusion of Irish administrations. The pension list, at the best of times, was a scandal to this country; but the present abuses of it have gone beyond all bounds. If a great officer of state, for instance, finds that the severity of business requires the consolation of the tender passion, he courts through the pension list; and the lady, very wisely, takes hold of the occasion, which, perhaps, could not be taken of the lover, and seizes time by the forelock. Why, Sir, we may pass over a little treaty of that sort; it may naturally enough fall under the articles of concordatum or contingencies; but that unhappy list has been degraded by a new species of prostitution that was unknown before: the granting of honours and titles, to lay the foundation for the grant of a pension the suffering any man to steal a dignity, for the purpose that a barren beggar steals a child. It was reducing the honours of the state from badges of dignity to badges of mendicancy.

[He then adverted to the modern practice of doubling the pensions of members of that house, who were, unhappily, pensioners already.] Is the Secretary afraid of their becoming converts? Is it necessary to double bolt them with pensions? Is there really so much danger that little Tricksey will repent, and go into a nunnery, that the kind keeper must come down with another hundred to save her from becoming honest?

But a right honourable gentleman made another objection, rather inconsistent with his former one; he feared it would take away the control of parliament over pensions within the limits of the act proposed. The objection is not, however, founded in fact; at the same time this argument admits that the unlimited power of pensioning is a grievance that ought to be remedied by some effectual control.

Such is the principle and the effect of this bill, if carried into a law. It would not restrain the crown; it would not restrain a Lord Lieutenant; it would only restrain a Secretary from that shameful profusion of the public treasure, unimputable and unknown to his majesty or his viceroy, which was equally disgraceful to the giver and receiver. It is a bill to preserve the independence of parliament; it is a bill to give us the constitution of Great Britain, where we had it not before. It is similarly necessary, when we have adopted a penal law of Great

Britain, giving a new force to the executive magistrate, that we should also adopt that law of Great Britain, which might secure the rights of the people. It is a law necessary, as a counterpoise to the riot act. It is a law of invention, and, if necessary, prevention ; for, if you wait till the evil, which my right honourable friend is anxious to guard against, shall have actually fallen upon this country, the corruption will be uni versal, and the remedy impossible.—*Debates*, vol. vii., pp. 332—6.

TITHES.

March 13*th*, 1787.

Mr. Grattan having moved a resolution that if tranquillity were restored, at the opening of the next session, the house would consider the Tithe question, Curran said :—

I support the resolution as indispensably necessary at the present juncture—the circumstances of the time make it necessary. The disturbance of the public tranquillity, and the light in which some gentlemen thought proper to represent that disturbance, have brought upon this country a law of pains and penalties severe beyond all example of any former period. We should have remembered that the offence was local and partial, but that the causes of such offence were universal. The very offence, therefore, should have turned our attention to those causes—the abject and miserable state of the peasantry of Ireland. But the right honourable Secretary declares he is a stranger to their distresses ; that they have not petitioned this house ; that if they did offer petitions he would reject them ; that he will not consent to any change in the constitution, and that, therefore, he will not hold out any hope that the distresses of the poor of this kingdom shall ever be considered by parliament. I am happy to find that the right honourable gentleman has so good an excuse for language so little consistent with either wisdom or humanity, in that ignorance of the state of this country which he so ostentatiously got up to declare. I am happy, too, to find that the only man in the house who is a stranger to the misery of the people, is also a stranger to their interest and their country. I own I am surprised to find the right honourable gentleman so ready to believe their offences, and yet such a stranger to their sufferings, when I recollect that both have been stated to the house at the same moment, and by the same person.

But the right honourable gentleman will not parley with their mutiny Were the kingdom really in that state of insurrection, which can be the only fact on which such an argument could be founded, I doubt much if the right honourable gentleman has nerves to hold such a language ; but if the fact be notoriously false, what does the assertion come to ? Because a few have offended, we are afraid to tell the whole body of the people that when tranquillity shall be restored, we will consider their grievances. This may be reconciled with that utter ignorance which the right honourable gentleman has been so anxious to display; but for this house to give weight to such reasoning, would be to say, that we are deterred from speaking the language of truth and justice, by a paltry panic, which the magnanimity of parliament could not entertain, or its wisdom confess. Mean as the idea is, the honourable gentleman has brought it forward, and has reduced you to the necessity of sinking under the imputation, or of disclaiming it by concurring in this resolution. The honourable gentleman ought to know that the people have a constitutional right to have their grievances considered and redressed by their representatives; but the honourable gentleman has, by an unfortunate alacrity in declaring his sentiments, filled the mind of the nation with dismay on that subject. They would naturally have hoped, that when the application of an unusal legislative security had restored the peace of the public, we would listen to the call of duty and compassion, and take their calamity into consideration, at a proper time; but the honourable gentleman could not let the riot act pass without accompanying it with an express disavowal of all intention to alleviate, or even at any period, however distant, to deign to listen to their complaints.

When a right honourable gentleman of so much consequence comes forward wantonly to toll out the knell of separation to the people, it becomes the duty of every man to disclaim all participation in so abominable a sentiment. The resolution is necessary even to the execution of the law that we passed; for who are the objects of it? The whole peasantry of the south? And who are to execute it? That very body of men in the class above them, who have been represented as adverse to the rights of the clergy, and are said to have connived at these offences. If, then, you make both those classes of the people desperate on the subject, do you hope that the law can ever be executed? I am, therefore, as a friend to the clergy, in this point of view, a friend to the resolution.

The gentleman will not consent to an innovation in the constitution but he ought to reflect that if that argument has not prevailed against the introduction of enormous penalties into our law, it can scarcely be an objection to any rational plan for removing the distress of the people. The gentleman has, probably taken his ideas of innovation from a school in which the principles of Irish administration were founded on an uniform system of plunder and oppression. But whatever may be the idea of an English Secretary, this house must be too wise to say that inveterate evils can receive any sanction from length of time. A change for the better is not innovation, it is reformation, it is renovation.

As to the idea of commutation, I cannot think it would be found impracticable; as, for my part, I have no idea of stripping the clergy of their legal rights, or of making any change that would not serve them as well as ease the people. To such an alteration I am sure they are too wise to make any objection; but if they be so mistaken as to make an ill-advised opposition, suggested only by mistake, and persevere in this obstinacy, the wisdom of the legislature ought not to suffer an opposition of that kind to stand in the way of their own solid interests and those of the community

The resolution is objected to, as containing no specific plan of any kind; that I think an argument strongly in its favour. To pledge myself to anything specific, without a thorough examination, might be pledging myself to temerity—to impossibility; but I have no objection to pledge myself to give the complaints of the people a patient hearing, and to give them effectual relief in such a way as on a perfect investigation may be found just and practicable ; that is only pledging myself to the right of the people, and the duty of their representatives.

I think there remain other reasons to show the expediency of the resolution. Though the misery of the people has produced only a local outrage, the inconsiderate zeal of individuals has raised a general ferment. It is difficult and delicate to speak any thing on this subject, peculiarly so to me, who, I know, have been grossly misrepresented, as an enemy to the rights of the church. I disclaim the charge—I respect the clergy. I will never hear of any attempt to injure their legal rights. I love their religion ; there is only one religion under heaven which I love more than the Protestant, but I confess there is one—the Christian religion. As the subject has been forced into this debate, I cannot help saying that I think it incumbent on the members of this house to show themselves untainted by the intolerant principles of certain publications. In doing so I am persuaded they will perfectly concur with the respected author[*] of one of them. I am satisfied that good and pious man has long since regretted the precipitate publication of those hasty sentiments, and rejoiced that their natural tendency had been happily frustrated by the good sense of the public. But I see no reason for introducing the name of his adversary,[†] as a subject of censure in this house. Mr. O'Leary is, to my knowledge, a man of the most innocent and amiable simplicity of manners in private life. The reflection of twenty years in a cloister has severely regulated his passions, and deeply informed his understanding. As to his talents, they are public; and I believe his right reverend antagonist has found himself overmatched in him, as a controversialist. In this instance it is just that he should feel his superiority. It is the superiority not of genius only, but of truth, of the merits of the respective causes. It is the superiority of defence over aggression. It is the victory of a man, seeing the miseries of his country, like a philosopher and a tolerant Christian, and lamenting them like a fellow-subject, obtained over an adversary who was unfortunately led away from his natural gentleness and candour, either not to see these miseries, or to represent them through a fallacious medium. It is a victory in which, I am persuaded, the vanquished rejoices, and of which the victor rather bewailed the occasion, than exulted in the achievement. I am sorry that those subjects should be introduced into a debate of this kind, but as they are, I think it is right to show the public that we are not inflamed against our fellow-subjects by that persecuting and suspicious spirit, which has been relinquished even by those who first caught, and incautiously endeavoured to propagate the infection. I am

[*] Dr. Richard Woodward, Bishop of Cloyne, author of the Pamphlet entitled "The present state of the Church of Ireland," before alluded to.
[†] The Rev. Arthur O'Leary.

against withdrawing the resolution; if it were withdrawn the people might suspect the sincerity of those who supported it, or be ignorant how many gentlemen of this house feel compassion for their distress, and are anxious to relieve them; I will therefore heartily give my support to the resolution. It will, I hope, remove the ill impression of what the right honourable Secretary has, rather incautiously, spoken, and what others have as incautiously written. It will prevent the people from being worried into despair: it will adopt the wise policy of every free government, of deterring outrage by punishment, and encouraging obedience by reward; it will show the people that they have representatives by whom neither their misconduct can be overlooked, nor their grievances forgotten.—*Debates*, vol. vii., pp. 354—58.

Grattan's motion was lost, without a division.

NAVIGATION ACT.

March 20th, 1787.

THE English Navigation Law, originated by Cromwell, in 1650 (*vide* Scobell's Collection of Acts, p. 132), and carried out by 12th Charles II., c. 18, was now sought to be introduced into Ireland in lump. The Dublin merchants petitioned against this, but Fitzgibbon insulted their petition. Grattan this day moved an amended clause, that the Act should only bind Ireland, while the benefits and restraints of it were equal in the two countries. Curran said:—

The Navigation Act was founded on principles of imperial monopoly—to depress the rivals of Great Britain, and to advance the power of her navy. It sought to obtain more objects; first, by confining the whole export and import of her colonies to English ships; secondly, by prohibiting all importation of colonial produce into the central ports of the empire, save in English ships; and thirdly, it prevented her European rivals from establishing staples for that produce, by prohibiting importation, save directly from the place of the growth: but this was never intended at first to be a system of prohibition or restraint, as between the several parts of the European British empire. It left the freedom of commercial intercourse between England and Wales, or between Wales and Berwick; in which latter cases it cannot be contended that any restraint ever existed under that act; it was therefore, in its origin, an act equally affecting England and Ireland in its construction; but the system soon changed its principle. By the 12th of Charles II., Ireland was cast off from all export to the Western plantations, except the export of her inhabitants; and by the 23rd of that reign, by leaving the word Ireland out of the bond, she was completely cut off from import of every kind.

[He then stated the other laws that establish the exclusion of Ireland from the circuitous import into England, which he considered as equally unwise and unjust. He proceeded to state the trade granted to this country by the English Act of 1780, which, he said, was granted in the time of war, and for a great compensation by a monopoly of our market in exclusion of cheaper ones, and of a considerable revenue.] It is a trade, of which we have reaped very little benefit—it is at best, perhaps, only a capability; but even that is reduced to nothing, if England persist in the injustice of refusing to admit the import of colonial produce from us. While our own consumption is the limit of our import from the West, speculation is at an end, and the trade will be equally unproductive as it has been.

Under these circumstances I consider the clause and the amendment. A petition has been presented by the merchants against the re-enactment of the Navigation Act, whilst a construction so injurious to their trade is founded upon it, and carried into effect against them. I condemn the disrespectful manner in which that petition was received. It has been treated in a way not very becoming the dignity of parliament, or the character of the petitioners, who are the first merchants in Ireland. Their interest is a pledge for their integrity in what they have advanced, and their acquisitions are a proof of their knowledge of commercial subjects. This clause enacts by reference a foreign act. Where is that act to be found, if pleaded in our courts? This mode of adoption may have answered the reign of Henry the Seventh, when the power of England to bind us was admitted; it was necessary, from the urgency of the occasion, in 1782, but it is not now necessary, and therefore ought not to be done. If you enact it by reference, you also enact it subject to that construction against you, of which you have notice, that is, you enact a prohibition of your own trade.

This is an objection to form, but it is a form in which the dignity of parliament is interested. I object to the general adoption of the act, on grounds more substantial, as it comprehends the trade of the whole British empire, which it is ridiculous in us to affect any power over. We ought not to meddle in any community of legislation with England. Her power secures her, but our weakness exposes us to the danger of every thing like a precedent. I cannot accede to the argument that we are bound to do so by the condition of the grant of 1780. [He read the words of that act.] It requires us to lay equal duties with those of England; but it says not a word of the Navigation Act. But, further, that condition could only extend to what we got in 1780, which was only a part of the colonial trade, the rest we had since the reign of George the First. I ask, on what ground we are now called upon, after seven years' possession of that trade, to adopt the Navigation law?

Does England demand it? Does the minister demand it? Is it not, therefore, madness in us, voluntarily to adopt this law, whilst our commerce is unjustly confined by the construction of it? It is objected, that the exclusion is reciprocal between England, and is under the words of that law; and that England is enabled, by our act of customs, to import colonial produce. This I deny. The act of customs reduces the duty, but does not expressly authorise the admission, by a repeal of the prohibition, if, in fact, by any construction of the Navigation law, they were prohibited. It has been argued that this law is already in force. The arguments in support of that assertion are far from conclusive; but if so, why enact it again?

The reason of enacting it now has been fairly avowed by a right honourable gentleman, who, it seems, heard some extra-judicial opinion that it is in force. Is there, then, a doubt, which Great Britain wishes to remove? Do you not, in order to do that, give up your own act, the claim of your merchants to an equal construction of the law? It was said, there must be soon an arrangement between the two countries. I do not approve of Ireland making any advances on the subject; her dignity requires that she should not. It would be folly in the extreme to advance, not by a demand of her right, but by an undemanded surrender of it. The adoption of the Navigation Act, without the amendment, would amount to a decent surrender of the claim—to a surrender of a great point of commercial right.

The petition of the merchants was founded in the utmost prudence, and was conceived in a manner that deserved a better reception. A virtuous parliament would always be happy in seeing and encouraging the subjects to consider topics of great public moment, and to communicate with them; but I fear some persons are disposed to discountenance the inquiries, and to stifle the voice of the people. It has been done on constitutional subjects; I fear the same will be the fate of commercial investigation. If such a system should succeed, the people would give up all attention to their rights, and the constitution itself would moulder away. Our late acquisitions in that way would sink, one after another; the temple we had erected to liberty would be demolished, in order to build sheds for our commerce from the materials; and the unfortunate architect might live to see the ruin of that structure which he fondly hoped would have survived his labour, and have been the monument of his fame.—*Debates*, vol. vii., pp. 388—90.

Grattan's motion was lost, by 127 to 52.

CONTRABAND TRADE.

February 19th, 1783.

THE following morsel is too good to be lost sight of:—

I have always considered a high duty on any commodity as a premium, to the contraband trader. This house has been repeatedly moved to lower the duty on tobacco from ten to six-pence per pound. The conduct of the gentlemen who conduct the revenue department reminds me of a circumstance which happened in our university some time ago. The lads had got a custom of breaking the lamps; for a long time there could be found no remedy for this grievance, but mending them when broken, till at length a very sagacious member of the board of Fellows hit upon a very extraordinary expedient. "The lamps," said he, "cannot be well broken in the day without immediate detection, wherefore if they were taken down at nightfall every evening, and put up every morning, the mischief might be prevented." The learned doctor's argument has been adopted by the gentlemen of the revenue; they find that smuggling has risen to a great height, they then shut up the ports, thereby making them of no use.

I am sorry to find that the practice of changing the revenue officers from time to time, which was successfully followed in England, was not adopted here; nay, so long are they allowed to remain in one situation, that they are incorporated with the people, and become of the same common interest, and such root do they take in some places, that they are even returned as members of parliament to this house.

Mr. Beresford assured Mr. Curran that three-fourths of the officers of the port of Derry had been changed from time to time.

Mr. Curran—But, not to trouble the house any longer, I will add but one argument more: in the memorable year 1688, the citizens of Derry shut their gates against a tyrant, in defence of your religion and constitution; and shall it be said that in 1788 the doors of this house were shut against their prayers?—*Debates*, vol. viii., pp. 273, 4.

MADNESS OF GEORGE THE THIRD.

February 6th, 1789.

GEORGE III. had for some time been mad; but this calamity (to him, not to the country) had been concealed. In the end of 1788 it could be no longer hid—a regency became necessary. In the ministers' draft of the address in answer to the Lord Lieutenant, they praised themselves, and Grattan moved an amendment, substituting a general expression of loyalty. On this Curran said:—

I oppose the address, as an address of delay. The public calamity of the king's indisposition is not so welcome a tale to us as to call for any thanks to the messenger that brought. If it be the fact, instead of thanks for communicating it now, it should be resented as an outrage upon us not to have communicated it before. As to thanks for his wishes for Ireland, it is a strange time for the noble marquis to call for it. I do not wish that an untimely vote of panegyric should mix with the voice of a people's lamentation; it is a picture of general mourning, in which no man's vanity ought to be thrust in as a figure; but, if it be pressed, what are his pretensions? One gentleman [Mr. Boyd] had lost hundreds a year by his arts, and defended him on that ground. Another [Mr. Corry] praised his economy for increased salaries in the ordnance. The economy of the noble lord is then to be proved only by public or by private losses. Another right honourable member [the Attorney-General] has painted him as a man of uncouth manners, much addicted to vulgar arithmetic, therefore entitled to praise. But what have his calculations done? They have discovered that a dismounted trooper might be stripped of his boots as a public saving; or that a mutilated veteran might be plundered of half the pittance of his coals, or a stoppage for that wooden leg, which, perhaps, the humane marquis might consider as the most proper fuel to keep others warm.

But a learned gentleman (Mr. Wolfe) has defended the paragraph as in fact meaning nothing at all. I confess I find the appeal to the compassion of the public stronger than to their justice. I feel the reverses of human fate. I remember this very supplicant for a compliment, to which he pretended only because it was no compliment, drawn into this city by the people harnessed to his chariot, through streets blazing with illuminations; and, after more than a year's labour at computation, he has hazarded on a paragraph stating no one act of private or of public good—supported by no man that says he loves him—attested by no act that says he ought to be loved—defended not by an assertion of his merit, but an extenuation of his delinquency.— The house would degrade itself, if such a proposal can be a subject of serious consideration.

For my part, I am but little averse to accede to the sentiment of an honourable friend, who observed that he was soon to leave us, and that it was harsh to refuse him even a smaller civility than every predecessor for a century had got. I do not oppose his being borne away in the common hearse of his predecessors; I do not wish to pluck a single faded plume from the canopy, nor a single rag of velvet that might flutter on the pall. Let us excuse his manners, if he could not help them. Let us pass by a little peculation, since, as an honourable member says, it was for his brother; and let us rejoice that his kindred were not more numerous. But I cannot agree with my learned friend who defends the conduct of the noble lord on the present occasion. The Viceroy here, under a party that had taken a peculiar line in Great Britain, should not have availed himself of his trust to forward any of their measures. He should have considered himself bound by duty and by delicacy to give the people the earliest notice of their situation, and to have religiously abstained from any act that could add to the power of his party, or embarrass any administration that might succeed him; instead of that, he abused his trust by proroguing the two houses, and has disposed of every office that became vacant in the interval, besides reviving others, that had been dormant for years. Yet the honourable member says he acted the part of a faithful steward. I confess I do not know what the honourable gentleman's idea of a good steward is; —I will tell him mine. A good steward, if his master were visited by infirmity or by death, would secure every article of his effects for his heir; he would enter into no conspiracy with his tenants; he would remember his benefactor, and not forget his interest. I will also tell him my idea of a faithless, unprincipled steward: he would avail himself of the moment of family distraction; while the filial piety of the son was attending the sick bed of the father, or mourning over his grave, the faithless steward would turn the melancholy interval to his private profit; he would remember his interest, and forget his benefactor; he would endeavour to obliterate or conceal the title deeds; to prevent cabals among the tenants on the estate, he would load it with fictitious incumbrances; he would reduce it to a wreck, in order to leave the plundered heir no resource from beggary, except continuing him in a trust which he had been vile enough to betray. I will not appropriate either of their portraits to any man; I wish earnestly to God, that no man may be found in the community whose conscience would acknowledge the resemblance of the latter.

I now revert to the question which alone calls on your deliberations. The third estate is said to be incapable of its functions. Our first care is to inquire instantly into the fact. Oddly as the document appear, I will not object to them. An honourable member objected to them, as not authenticated by the English houses; with me it would be an objection if they had been offered under any such authority. The Commons act not by the ordinary rules of courts of law. The grand inquest of the nation knows facts of its own knowledge; it contains its own evidence, and therefore it can administer no oath. Here the fact is simple; all England has attested it; the Viceroy here has announced it; we have evidence of it on our table. We ought not to lose a moment. A right honourable member [the Attorney-General] says we ought to pay great attention to England, and do nothing hastily or rashly. A party, then, has taken its line. Is it meant that we are to be bound by any act of their two houses of convention? Is it supposed that this country will adopt that line? I hope the contrary. Is it for our honour or the good of the public, to hold us up as the partisans of a faction in Great Britain? It might be party there, but here it would have all the meanness and absurdity of faction. If the third estate have become incapable, what is our duty? When the natural protector of that estate is disabled, it becomes our duty to guard its powers with the most scrupulous care; to put them into a way of being exercised in their full former vigour, unimpaired and undiminished; and for that purpose, it is our task to inquire whether the trustee of them is appointed by any express law, or whether, by any necessary inference from our constitution, and from our inseparable union with Great Britain, that trustee was pointed out by any designation so clear and so cogent as not to be overlooked or resisted. This is our duty to our constituents and the public. While the powers of the third estate are suspended, we are no parliament, can make no law; we are not the national depository of those powers; a fatality has thrown them on our mercy, and we are bound by every tie of political and constitutional faith not to associate ourselves with any cabal whatsoever, to destroy or impair them, but to restore them, with all practical expedition, in their former state, into the hands of their natural protector. If we do not that, we may assume on ourselves to make a new constitution, but we should destroy the old.

We are called upon by an additional motive for despatch. Every man sees the change of public administration that is approaching. It has been delayed and opposed by a party in another kingdom. Upon what principle of wisdom or justice can Ireland enlist herself in that opposition? On the contrary, when it is obvious to every man what ought to be done, it is his duty to do it promptly, unreluctantly, cordially, and with confidence, that the governor and people may not be divided by suspicion and distrust, but be cemented by mutual confidence and mutual affection; and those, who recommend a different system to our imitation, ought not to overlook the distractions it has occasioned nor to hazard, for any interest of theirs, the arising of such distractions as may ruin this country. A right honourable baronet [the Chancellor of the Exchequer]* argued for delay on the precedent of the revolution, and because the case is of importance. As to the latter argument, if your friend that you love were in danger of being drowned, the case is important; will you, therefore, postpone your assistance? Here the constitution that you ought to love is struggling for its life: does such an emergency as that call upon you for a despatch by which all may be saved, or a cold unfeeling delay, by which all may be lost? At the revolution was there delay? Not a moment. Yet how did that case differ from ours in favour of delay? There the powers to be considered were unascertained, and the trustee of them to be chosen. Can any man suppose either of these points unsettled in the present instance? Gentlemen have advised us to go on with the ordinary business. We cannot decently postpone the settlement of the constitution to any thing which, however important, must be of such inferior moment. But the thing is impossible; we cannot legislate. We can only deliberate till the executive power is put into action.— However, the state of the public business is another and pressing call on our diligence. On the 25th of next month our army will be disbanded, and our public credit at an end, if the mutiny-bills and money-bills shall not be revived before that day. I do not think the pitiful compliment in the address worthy of a debate, or a division; if any gentleman has a mind to stigmatise the object of it by a poor, hereditary, unmeaning, unmerited panegyric, let it pass; but I cannot consent to a delay that I think at once dangerous and disgraceful.—*Debates*, vol. ix., pp. 18—22.

Grattan's amendment was carried without a division. (although he called the Lord Lieutenant, Buckingham,† "a jobber in a mask.") so prostrated was The Castle at the prospect of the Prince's Regency, with Fox as premier. Mr. Fitzherbert‡ presented the report of the King's physicians. On Grattan's moving for a Committee of the House thereon, for the 11th of February, he voted with 128 to 74, Curran and himself being Tellers.

REGENCY.

February 11th, 1789.

On this day ministers tried to postpone the discussion on the Regency. Their motive (real and avowed) was to hare from England the Resolutions of the British houses, appointing the Prince Regent of Great Britain, but with limited powers—(he was not to make peers; not to grant offices or pensions, save during *royal* pleasure; not to make leases; not to have the care of the King's person; not to administer but in the King's name). These

* Sir J. Parnell.
† George Temple, Marquis of Buckingham, had become Viceroy in December, 1/87. The country had been governed by Lords Justices from the previous October, when the Duke of Rutland had died.
‡ He had succeeded Thomas Orde as Chief Secretary to the Lord Lieutenant, in 1787 The Right Honourable John Hely Hutchinson was Secretary of State for Ireland. The two offices here referred to are often confounded; at the Union the latter office was abolished.

resolutions had passed on the 23r of January, and been accepted by the Prince on the 31st of January, but had not reached the Irish government. The postponement was refused by the house, and then Mr. Thomas Conolly, of Castletown, moved—" That it is the opinion of this Committee that an humble address be presented to his Royal Highness the Prince of Wales, humbly to request his Royal Highness to take upon himself the government of this realm, during the continuation of his Majesty's present indisposition, and no longer; and, under the style and title of Prince Regent of Ireland, in the name of his Majesty to exercise and administer, according to the laws and constitution of this kingdom, all regal powers, jurisdiction and prerogatives to the Crown and government thereof belonging." This resolution was supported by C. F. Sheridan, Lord Henry Fitzgerald, Sir Henry Cavendish, Curran, Bushe, and Grattan: and opposed by Hobart, Corry, and, in repeated speeches, by the Attorney-General, Fitzgibbon. In an after part of the night he had a serious wrangle with Grattan, but it was in reply to his first speech that Curran spoke. He had prefaced the speech by calling for the reading of the 4th William and Mary, c. 1, sec. 1, expressive (by recital) of Irish dependence, and he went into much abuse of the Irish leaders, saying that if separation were the alternative, he would be for an Union. Curran's speech seems meagrely reported:—

I rise to support the address. Much irrelevant matter has forced itself into the debate on a subject the most simple and obvious that ever came before the house. The fact of incapacity is ascertained; the two houses must provide for the deficiency. The principle of the British constitution in either kingdom simply is, that the third estate should be certain, and not elective. The right of election is the right of ambition, of faction, of intrigue, of shedding civil blood. But this is a question to be considered on another principle also, the compact that unites the crowns of England and Ireland; the compact is, that the executive power of the two kingdoms shall be ever the same. If either country has a wild, arbitrary right of election, both have the same; and if so, the absurdity follows, that they are bound to have the same third estate, and yet have a right of choosing different third estates; that is gross and unconstitutional nonsense. To avoid that absurdity, we should seek for some striking circumstances that point out to both nations the common Regent: they are, evidently, the full age and the capacity of the heir apparent; there could, here, be no other. England agrees in the unanswerable necessity of choosing the prince—Ireland is unanimous in the same choice. They both confess it is clearly right to do so; it follows of course it would be clearly wrong to do otherwise. It follows, at least, that the two countries think it their indispensable duty to make that choice; and I know no other quality of a right than a claim that cannot be overruled by the tribunal competent to decide upon it. All disputations on that point so confessed, can be only the refinement of verbal sophistry, or the pretext of faction. The person, then, is evidently designated. The next question is, what trust is to be delegated to him? I think the entire power of the third estate. I disavow the idea of doing this on any principle but a constitutional one. I think of his royal highness, as the house seem to think, with all confidence in his virtue; but I act not from any motive of confidence in his virtue; but I respect the personage; he is the representative of the people; and caution, not confidence, should be the principle of his conduct. But here I do not think I have a legal right of yielding to diffidence, even if I found any reason to diffide. The constitution debars me from any exercise of any fancied prudence. The law of the constitution says, that no estate of parliament can be abridged, without its own consent.

Here it cannot consent; it cannot be abridged but by act of parliament. We can make no act of parliament; for to that the three estates are necessary. We are but two; to abridge the third estate now, would be to steal the sceptre, when the hand from which it had fallen could not protect it; it would be to become judges in our own cause, when our opponent could not speak for himself.

I see clearly that this kingdom has much to reform, but this is no time. I would arm the third estate with its constitutional shield, and then attack it with constitutional weapons; to do anything else would be to obtain a victory by robbery, not by virtue; to redress the people by theft and plunder, not by law. I will support your rights; I think you have great claims for redress of many crying grievances, but I will not redress them by betraying the constitution, by thieving from the third estate, and by provoking it to reprisals perhaps beyond the measure of what it had lost. This might be called rash, and was called criminal by a right honourable member [the Attorney-General]; but I confide more in that learned member as a prophet, than a lawyer; for that honourable member premised that he despaired of finding the house concur in his opinion. The only point that remains is, how these full powers should be delegated, by address or by act. The latter is impossible. We are but two estates, they cannot legislate; they may deliberate; they may declare the incapacity of the king—the right of the prince; but they can do it only by address. I have heard strange doctrines from a right honourable member [the Attorney-General]. Does that gentleman think two estates can legislate? He said the affixing the great seal of England makes an Irish law; that an act coming to our lords so authenticated, was, *ipso facto*, law. Does the honourable member think a third estate supplied by a creature of the two houses, by a forgery on the constitution, by a phantom that has no interest to guard, no will to consult, no power to rescue? It is taking seals for crowns, and baubles for sceptres: it is worshipping wafers and wax in the place of a king; it is substituting the mechanical quibble of a practising lawyer for the sound deduction of a philosopher, standing on the vantage ground of science: it is more like the language of an Attorney particular than that of an Attorney-General; it is that kind of silly fatuity that, on any other subject I would leave to be answered by silence and contempt; but when blasphemy is uttered against the constitution, it cannot pass under its insignificance, because the offence should be reprehended, though the doctrine could not make a proselyte. The right honourable member has said that we are competent to make an act; if so, a Regent is unnecessary. With respect to us, our third estate does not make alliances, or peace, or war; it only legislates; if we can, without it, legislate, we want no Regent. The learned member said the Regent of England might put the seal, and so give the Royal assent. If so, he might refuse it—if so, he might refuse us a Regent. But who is the Regent of England? One elected. If so, England's two houses has a right to elect a third estate for Ireland. But the right honourable member has said that England gives up all pretensions to legislate for us. What follows, then, from both his arguments? that neither England nor Ireland could resuscitate our constitution.

[Here he went at large into the acts of Henry the Eighth, of William and Mary, and the modern act brought in by Mr. Yelverton, and argued from them that the crown of Ireland was annexed to, not merged in the crown of England: that no law could be law here by virtue of the seal of England, but by virtue only of the royal assent, by a real third state, given in full parliament; and that the king of England, as such, affixed the seal of England, but that he gave the royal assent as king of Ireland. He proceeded to state further objections to attempting an act of legislation.]

First, it is impossible; any fiction of a third estate is a conditional forgery, and I will never consent to it. The frame of the state is composed of two great segments of arches, and the crown is the key-stone if that key-stone, by any fatality, fall out, what is to be done? Shall the separated parts be brought to meet, so as to supply its place? If you do that, every joint must be severed, every point of support must be changed, in so desperate an experiment; and if in that convulsion it falls not into ruin, the key-stone can never be restored. In other words, I like not the affectation of legislating by two estates; it is holding out an idea to the people, that you can do altogether without the third; it is making a silly experiment by which the third estate, the only security of our liberty, is brought into disrepute, possibly into disuse, and by which our glorious constitution may be lost for ever. But the learned member has protested against giving up the question of restrictions on the Regent. I admit that the two houses being incompetent to legislate, cannot restrict by address; if they have a mind to adopt the contitutional improbity of mutilating the regal power, it must be by the semblance of an act; and, therefore, such a sacrilege upon the constitution can be achieved only by a profanation of its forms. In this house I do not think it necessary to go into such detail of restriction; no man here espouses his doctrine. He is a solitary and unprevailing preacher; but absurdities may go abroad, and may be thought unanswerable, merely because they have not been thought worthy a reprehension; and particularly when other persons, that ought to have weight with the public, have not zeal enough for the cause, against which those calumnies are levelled, to disavow them, but think they act more wisely by giving them the authority of a silent implied approbation.

[Here he went into a variety of observations, and ridiculed the arguments of the Attorney-General's threatening us with the consequences of separation; where, even if there was a right of election, that election had so happened as to secure our union.] I disdain even the advantage of an union that can be preserved only by our servility. Our union is of common, of equal interest, and is to be supported by mutual justice and good faith. The argument of the right honourable member, that a Regent of England could supersede the Regent of Ireland, is an outrage upon our independence, and must excite the contempt of every Irishman. So far am I from thinking the two houses competent to make any act, previous to the regency, I think they ought to make no act on the subject, even when the Regent is in possession of his functions. A right honourable member for whom I have the highest respect [Mr. Grattan] seems to compare the present case to the revolution; but the cases are different; there the throne was vacant—here not; there a restricted power was to be given to the prince—here an unlimited one; there the person to receive the regal powers was purely elected—here he is received from the authority of an irresistible constitutional designation; there it was a compact made by negotiation with the people—here it is a trust pointed out by the constitution. But the right honourable member thinks the law necessary to ascertain the period of the power to the continuance of the incapacity. First, he must be completely Regent, before he can assent to such a bill: and if so, he may refuse that assent. Are we, then, without any security, in case of his Majesty's recovery? Clearly not unless we trust it to an act. The constitutional necessity that creates the Regent limits his continuance. If the King is restored, his right to the regal power revives with his capacity; and the exercise of it by any other individual would be usurpation and treason. The case is then provided for by a higher authority, the law of Edward the Third. We would not be wise in seeking to give authority to the first principle of the constitution, and to the statutes that secure the crown, by a compact with the Regent, which ultimately he might refuse to ratify and justly refuse, when he is in possession of a power to which it is incident to assent or dissent at discretion. For my part, I think it is that kind of apprehension which it is scarcely decorous to anticipate. No man can suppose even the possibility of such a danger, considering the part that illustrious personage has already acted; but if it is at all to be looked at, the laws already in force have abundantly provided for it. No new law can add to that provision. I therefore hope the house will not adopt a measure that can have no possible operation. As to a subsequent law, I throw out these remarks merely for the consideration of gentlemen; as to the present, I am decided The house, too, seems decided, with a very few exceptions, that an act is impossible and absurd, and that the address proposed is the only expedient that can be adopted.—*Debates*, vol. ix., pp. 58—62.

The motion passed without a division. On the 12th of February Mr. Conolly moved and carried, without division, the adoption of this address:—

"To his Royal Highness George, Prince of Wales.
'The humble address of the Knights, Citizens, and Burgesses, in Parliament assembled.

"MAY IT PLEASE YOUR ROYAL HIGHNESS,

"We his Majesty's most dutiful and loyal subjects, the Commons of Ireland in Parliament assembled, beg leave humbly to request that your Royal Highness will be pleased to take upon you the government of this realm during the continuation of his Majesty's present indisposition, and no longer, and under the style and title of Prince Regent of Ireland, in the name and on the behalf of his Majesty, to exercise and administer, according to the laws and constitution of this kingdom, all regal powers, jurisdictions, and prerogatives to the crown and government thereof belonging."

On the 17th, the concurrence of the Lords to this address (with some additional words of condolence) was brought up and agreed to. On the 19th of February this joint address presented by the Lords and Commons in state, was refused to be transmitted by the Lord Lieutenant, and on returning to College-green the Commons adjourned.

February 20th, 1789.

In consequence of the Lord Lieutenant's refusal to transmit the address, the Commons agreed, this day, on transmitting it by deputation. The Duke of Leinster and the Earl of Charlemont were named by the Peers, and the Right Honourable Thomas Conolly, John O'Neill, and W. B. Ponsonby, with James Stewart (M.P. for Tyrone), Esq., were named by the Commons on this deputation. On the same day Grattan moved—" That in addressing his Royal Highness the Prince of Wales to take upon himself the government of this country, on the behalf, and in the name of his Majesty, during his Majesty's present indisposition, and no longer, the Lords and Commons of Ireland have exercised an undoubted right, and discharged an indispensable duty, to which, in the present emergency, they alone are competent." Curran supported the resolution thus:—

I congratulate the other side of the house on having recovered their voices; they have shown the most sympathetic feeling for the infirmity of their beloved sovereign. When the people despaired of his recovery they were dumb; drowned in sorrow they could find no utterance; but now that some hopes are held out to them, their oratory is restored; it does not yet venture on its legs—it is confined to "Hear him"—it is oratory sitting in parliament. The question has been deserted: we are not inquiring whether an address is expedient or legal: all that has been decided before, and it is indecent to argue it over again. A right honourable member has gone over the same arguments that have already been urged in vain. You are now called upon to vindicate your own honour. The Marquis of Buckingham has insulted you—you are bound to answer the insult. He has not been satisfied with simply refusing to transmit your address, but he has insulted you by a lecture equally unreasonable and ill-founded. If the King deny his assent, he does it in the modest language of doubt—" he will advise ;" but the pride of mock majesty, of burlesque royalty, must show its plumes, its glory, its learning. For my part, I would not have regretted the noble lord's refusal, had I been the bearer to the prince of the greeting of the two houses; the latter might possibly have said to him—would they had sent it by a better messenger! But he has added outrage to his refusal. From such a character it would not be worth your while to resent this misconduct; but the insult is upon record, and would remain a stigma upon you, when the memory of the noble lord will not live to be your justification. I give my hearty assent to the motion.—*Debates,* vol. ix., p. 151.

The Resolution was carried, by 130 to 74.

In order to close this subject, we subjoin the following extract from the Journals of the 2nd of March:—

The Speaker informed the house that the following letter had been delivered to him in the chair this day, which he read to the house:—

"To the Right Honourable the Speaker of the House of Commons, Ireland.

"SIR—We have the honour to acquaint you, for the information of the House of Commons, that in pursuance to their order we have presented the address of both houses to his Royal Highness the Prince of Wales, who was graciously pleased to give us the enclosed answer, from which it will appear to the house that it is our duty to wait his Royal Highness's further commands.

"We have the honour to be, Sir,
"Your most obedient humble servants,
"THOMAS CONOLLY, W. B. PONSONBY
JOHN O'NEILL, JAMES STEWART.

"London, February 27th, 1789."

"MY LORDS AND GENTLEMEN,
"'The address from the Lords spiritual and temporal, and Commons of Ireland, which you have presented to me, demands my warmest and earliest thanks.
" If anything could add to the esteem and affection I have for the people of Ireland, it would be the loyal and affectionate attachment to the person and government of the King, my father, manifested in the address of the two houses.
" What they have done, and their manner of doing it, is a new proof of their undiminished duty to his Majesty, of their uniform attachment to the house of Brunswick, and of their constant care and attention to maintain inviolate the concord and connexion between the kingdoms of Great Britain and Ireland, so indispensably necessary to the prosperity, the happiness and liberties of both.
" If, in conveying my grateful sentiments on their conduct in relation to the King, my father, and to the inseparable interests of the two kingdoms, I find it impossible adequately to express my feelings on what relates to myself, I trust you will not be the less disposed to believe that I have an understanding to comprehend the value of what they have done, a heart that must remember, and principles that will not suffer me to abuse their confidence.
" But the fortunate change which has taken place in the circumstances which gave occasion to the address agreed to by the Lords and Commons of Ireland, induces me for a few days to delay giving a final answer, trusting that the joyful event of his Majesty's resuming the personal exercise of his royal authority, may then render it only necessary for me to repeat those sentiments of gratitude and affection for the loyal and generous people of Ireland which I feel indelibly imprinted on my heart."

It was ordered that the letter, and his Royal Highness's answer, be entered in the journals of the house.

On the 20th of March a still more fervid letter, announcing his father's recovery, was read.

Thus, for the time, ended the Regency dispute, wherein the Irish maintained the common constitution against the English parliament, which yet was used to deprive Ireland of that constitution; but it may be as well to remind the reader that in 1799, when the Union was contemplated, a bill making the *de facto* Regent of England, Regent *de jure* of Ireland, was pressed by the patriots, and rejected by Castlereagh.

DISFRANCHISEMENT OF EXCISE OFFICERS.

April 21st, 1789.

CURRAN supported the bill for this purpose:—

I think such a bill at all times necessary, but now more so than ever. The arguments against it would have convinced me, if my mind had not been decided before. One member objects that the principle goes too far—another that it does not go far enough—thus inconsistent with itself is the opposition to this measure—consistent only in this, that it comes from the avowed servants of the crown, and of every administration. One of those, deservedly of much respect [the Chancellor of the Exchequer], has hazarded the assertion that there is not too much influence in Ireland; that gentleman has distinguished very rightly. I do not complain of the influence of the crown—I complain of that insulated sort of influence not flowing from the body of the people, or of the nobility—not belonging to the crown, but the personal property of every administration. The excess of this is manifest in the history of past times, and in the picture of the present. Observing on the state of Ireland for a century past, we find the succession of its viceroys, as almost to a man uniformly ignorant and rapacious; followed by a train of dependants and servants, insolent surly and worthless—the government of course oppressive—the parliament weak as venal, and the people undone. If, in that interval of darkness and misery, the wretched people felt that a law existed, they felt it not in protection, but in penalty; the religion of the country spoke to them only by the mouth of the tithe-proctor or bailiff. Gentlemen may suppose that Ireland has been weighed down by the great talents or virtues of its successive rulers. No; no such thing. On the contrary, the men sent to grind us are, in general, the refuse of Great Britain: but it is the fashion of Ireland to despise and hate our fellow-subjects, because they are hated and despised in England; it is the fashion to venerate the maxims of which we are the victims, and to admire and respect the contemptible instruments by which we are plundered and disgraced. This silly infatuation was felt as it ought, many years ago, by Dean Swift; I will read it to you, in his own words:—" I knew another person, who was in England the common standard of stupidity, where he was never heard a minute in any assembly, or by any party, with common Christian treatment; yet, upon his arrival here, could put on a face of importance and authority, talk more than six, without either gracefulness, propriety, or meaning, and, at the same time, be admired as a pattern of eloquence and wisdom"

What a pity that the picture of such a master should find no resemblance, except in the age in which he lived! Excess of influence was never more legible than in the present administration. The present viceroy came over here, making a parade of economy. Has he reduced a single establishment? Has he abolished a single useless place? You had the faith of government, when you gave them £140,000 a year additional in taxes, in 1784, that your expenses should not exceed your revenue; they have now exceeded it by more than £30,000. Has he adopted any plan for alleviating any of these grievances? No! Where you have been active, has he co-operated? No! When the voice of a nation's morality and a nation's want called upon you to correct the shameful abuse of the pension-list—when the odious monster was condemned, and led forth to execution, it found a reprieve from the Marquis of Buckingham. But why should we wonder at it, for what crime has not had the mercy of a pious and religious king wasted upon it in this adminstration of economy and mercy? Has not rape? Has not murder? Has not forgery? Let it not be supposed that I mention those things, merely to bear hard upon the name of a Lord Lieutenant; if they are reproaches, I cannot change their nature; I mention them as incontrovertible arguments, that no governor, without a most dangerous degree of unconstitutional influence, could pursue such a system. I defend the power of parliament to correct abuses in elections. Every election law is an exercise of that power. England has passed exactly such a law. But, it is said, England has done so upon evidence of an offence committed. This is not the principle. To punish a body of men for the delinquency of a few, would be absurd. England did not so; it was not an *ex post facto* law of punishment—it was a law of prevention! But do gentlemen look for offence? What do they say of a cavalcade of upwards of one hundred voters collecting from every corner of the nation, and taking possession of boroughs on the eve of an election. A right honourable member has stated that fact as a necessary retaliation. But the very justification admits the fact; and what a picture may gentlemen anticipate of the marches of those revenue troops, when they shall be put in motion on the next general election! A simpleton will be apt to ask, if these cart-loads of vagrants are on their way to the sea-side, to be transported for their offences? No; they are cart-loads of the raw material of members of parliament! I am sorry to find that such a picture can excite a laugh. I cannot laugh when I consider that it is not at Swords, or Irishtown, or Dungarvan, only, that these strolling companies of constituents will be called on to act; no, there is not a borough nor a county in Ireland where you will not see a temporary stage erected, in which the comedians' *fisc* shall hold the mirror up to the constitution of the land

At this time the law is peculiarly necessary. You have a governor now, whose conduct towards you has been treated as it merited—the stigma you have imprinted is indelible; so is his resentment—he never will forgive what he has drawn upon himself. He feels his government deserted by the body of the nobles—by the body of the people. Corrupt influence is his only resource; and you see his confidence in it, in his contempt of the reprobation of both houses; in an open distrust of the proudest of your nobles and gentry, and in their dismissal from office: and who succeed them?—his countrymen, his creatures. His clerks and runners are preferred to the rank, the virtue, the talents, and the responsibility of this country. Yes; the fairest and the tallest trees in the forest are overshadowed by the luxuriance of exotics—exotics of the worst kind, that would not grow in their native mould; hungry and barren, they drain the soil—they bear no blossom, yield no fruit—while you are stunted and shorn, to make room for the fantastic wreathings of their sterile exuberance. I do not make these remarks from any wish to mortify the gentlemen to whom I am supposed to allude. To some of them the nation is bound by the tenderest ties of necessities on one side, and liberality on the other. I cannot regard with partiality any gentleman whom I have been accustomed to see a gleaner in the field, sharing the scanty straw, that falls from the binder, with the birds of heaven, though he should be put at the head of the reapers. On the contrary, I pity the awkwardness of his situation; for why are the sages of the law brought in in the arms of their nurses? Why do the Burleighs of the day escape from the austerer labours of the toilet, to unbend in the government of a great nation? It is a plan of vengeance; it is not merely the viceroy's wanton desire of advancing his dependants, or making them ridiculous by promotion—it is to stigmatise you in his turn; and effectually he will succeed, if he can hold you up to the eyes of England and Europe, by your submitting to such a rule. You may read your resolutions, and talk of the authority of your houses; he will exhibit his runners and clerks as an answer; and it will be more than a refutation. In truth, if he shall succeed in this curious project, he will probably, by next session, think it a pity to have such rare talents wasted upon you; and will send to Tavistock-street for a cabinet of milliners to manage the affairs of Ireland.—*Debates*, vol. ix., pp. 385—88.

The bill was rejected by 148 to 93. Curran's prophecy was fulfilled. The English executive inflicted incompetent men and corrupt measures on Ireland, then took advantage of her own crime and our misfortunes to provincialise us, and now uses these very events as arguments against our independence.

DUBLIN POLICE

April 25th, 1789.

Sir Henry Cavendish, as Chariman of the Committee on Police Accounts, moved two resolutions, to the effect that the Dublin Police system was attended with waste, and useless patronage. Ministers opposed the resolutions.

[Mr. Curran supported the resolutions, and stated the history of the police at large.] Advantage had been taken of some disturbances in 1784, to enslave the capital by a police. A watch of old men, at fourpence per night, was naturally ineffectual. They had not youth, nor strength, nor pay; their imperfection should have been removed by choosing proper persons, and paying them reasonably. The present system does more—it pays them too much. It appears by the report, that for actual protection we pay £9,500 per annum; but added to that you pay £10,500 for patronage, that is, for corruption. Instead of £10,000 which the old watch would have cost in two years and a half, the present plan has stood the city in £51,000. Let any man lay his hand to his heart, and when he considers how this sum is produced—that it is extracted from the little means of comfortable support that are left to the labourer and tradesman, let him say if such an extraction is not a grievous exaction upon this city. But it is not merely the expense that the city complains of; you had your floor covered last session with petitions from the citizens of the most reputable description; you heard their case; you heard it moved at your bar: often heard uncontroverted evidence, that instead of protection, they had derived only insolence and exaction from this system and then, what did you do? When the enormity and the shamefulness of this petty system of tyranny and oppression stared you in the face, what did you do? You turned your face another way, and you did nothing; still, however, the rankness of the measure has forced itself again upon you. You ordered a committee—and when was that committee ordered? When the viceroy was in his humiliation—at the time that he was canonized on the records of both houses. As he declined, economy began to appear; as he recovers, economy declines. What kind of measure is it, that he is now forcing us to support? It is an act for enslaving the population; it is not like the carnal profusion that arises from a general wastefulness of administration; it is not the dole that is thrown to those who are paid for calling "question;" nor to those whose talents are shown in observing in what corner of the house a gasping orator may want the critical aid of a "hear him!"—those ventriloquists of the treasury bench. It is not the pay that allures a mechanic from his shop, and stations him in our gallery to make speeches for one side, and suppress them for another*—to extol his feeders, and vilify the characters who feel for, and speak for the rights of their country. No, Sir, this bill enacts a permanent system. on a principle that makes it immortal; it enacts a grievance into a battery—and gives the command of it to some unhappy wretch who must defend the post, or starve. Let me ask, is there a man in this house that does not know, that by the police board, with a very little aid from another of the same description, a certain majority of the aldermen are gagged? Let me ask would the city of London bear to have a system imposed upon them, by which every pulsation of public virtue was to be extinguished in the heart of the nation? No, Sir, there is not a mechanic, there is not a porter, in whom the minister would not fear and find a libel, if he hazarded such an attempt. He would not care to exhibit the representation of London as a miserable senatorial mummy, preserved in the poison of public corruption. As to me, I feel for the unhappy situation of a worthy man, who must be desperate, to be honest; who, instead of uttering the sentiments of a great and enlightened body of constituents, must sit mute and frozen to his seat, till the secretary, or the prompter of the secretary (if his ignorance should require a prompter), shall give him the signal to move. I should feel still more for him, if I did not feel so much for those constituents whose dignity, whose rights, whose wrongs, whose complaints are all sunk and lost in his personal calamity. It is these wrongs that are now forced upon your attention and stare you in the face once again.

Read the report of your committee. Is there an item that would not rouse the indignation of any man that hears it? £150 for lookingglasses for those midnight Adonises, to admire themselves; Wilton carpets for those delicate gentlemen to walk upon; hundreds of pounds for gilt paper and sealing-wax; a library, not of spelling-books, but of geography, of morality, of tactics. They would not have ventured on such barefaced, insolent dissipation of the money of the city, if they did not expect as barefaced a protection in another place. Whether they were right or wrong in the honourable opinion they conceived of us, must be this night decided; we cannot evade it—you cannot blink it. As to the objections, I am sorry they have been made by gentlemen at the other side: they would act a part of more spirit by saying boldly, —this is a job of government; we do not wish to have the city of Dublin unbound or ungagged,—than by offering unfounded objections, that require only to be stated, to appear ridiculous. One gentleman says the report is garbled. On what evidence does he say so? None; the only answer such an observation deserves is, that it is unjust as it is illiberal. But, says another right honourable member [the AttorneyGeneral] we have not the evidence on which the report was founded. And how does he prove this charge? Why, by producing the minutes in his hand! Give me leave, Sir, to say, that we are not treating that

* Curran complained that the reporting was in government hands, and that his speeches were mangled; but one may ask why did not he and his friends get up a corps of reporters?

committee in a decent or parliamentary way; they are not to be talked to as a gang of invaders, making an attack on a fortress of corruption that we are resolved to defend; they acted under our order—they are yet subject to our authority. If you want a special report, send them back—they will make it; if you want their minutes, call for them; but do not hope, if you are determined to screen an odious set of delinquents—if you are determined to stifle the complaints of the city—do not expect that such arguments can impose upon its understanding: the charge has been proved upon them. If you acquit them, you must do it in defiance of proof, in the face of the fact, and of your own conviction; your resolution in their favour will be a ridiculous outrage upon demonstration, not unlike the verdict of a Welsh jury that said to the judge—"My lord, we find the man, that stole the mare, not guilty."

I must now notice a new ground that has been, I fear rather indiscreetly, taken by a learned gentleman [Mr. Sergeant Toler] that it is not safe to come to any harsh resolution against the police. I desire to know if the honourable gentleman spoke the sentiments of administration, when he sought to intimidate the house from doing their duty to the public? The learned gentleman would have us silent, not because they are innocent, but because they are formidable. Does the learned member perceive, that he is unluckily putting the conduct of administration on the most odious ground he could possibly find? I will agree with the honourable member that his argument is as tenable as those of others, but scarcely as discreet. I ask, do gentlemen sincerely wish to let their conduct stand on so despicable a defence? If they do, they hope to have it believed by the people that they acted under the influence of a panic, equally mean and incredible, rather than of an unpardonable connivance at unconstitutional patronage and unbounded rapacity, of which the nation has had so many examples. But why do I fatigue you or myself with this subject? Is it to tire the public eye with a miserable and disgusting picture? Is it with the hope of making proselytes to my opinion? No, Sir; but the desertion of public duty, or the trampling on public rights, I recoil from with that indignation and abhorrence which you ought to feel—and, as to converting, I am not so vain. With nothing to rely upon but truth and justice, I feel the imbecility of my allies. I may refute gentlemen's arguments; I may expose their positions; but I cannot hope to weaken their motives. The motives to giving countenance to rapacity and extortion; the motives that can induce us to deliver up the metropolis to be enslaved by an unfeeling administration, or plundered by a legalized banditti, are impregnable to exposure or refutation. They may be counterpoised; but I am too poor to balance the weight of arguments that depend, not on reason, but arithmetic. I speak at least to redeem myself from the imputation of concurring in principles that I detest; and that, however they may triumph for a season, cannot fail, at length, of meeting the reprobation they deserve.—*Debates*, vol. ix., pp. 413—16.

The resolutions were rejected by 132 to 78.

Had Curran lived to see all the refinements of continental despotism introduced - a standing army permanently enacted, without a mutiny law, and indefinitely increaseable at the will of a deputy minister—a metropolitan "gens d'armerie"- a "Detective" or "Spy Force"--how he had thundered! but our orators were silent.

STAMP OFFICERS' SALARIES.
February 4th, 1790.*

On this day Curran spoke and proposed as follows:—

I rise with that deep concern and melancholy hesitation, which a man must feel who does not know whether he is addressing an independent parliament, the representatives of the people of Ireland, or whether he is addressing the representatives of corruption: I rise to make the experiment; and I approach the question with all the awful feelings of a man who finds a dear friend prostrate and wounded on the ground, and who dreads lest the means he should use to recover him may only serve to show that he is dead and gone for ever. I rise to make an experiment upon the representatives of the people—whether they have abdicated their trust, and have become the paltry representatives of castle influence: it is to make an experiment on the feelings and probity of gentlemen, as was done on a great personage, when it was said "Thou art the man." It is not a question respecting a paltry viceroy; no, it is a question between the body of the country and the administration; it is a charge against the government, for opening the batteries of corruption against the liberties of the people. The grand inquest of the nation are called on to decide this charge; they are called on to declare whether they would appear as the prosecutors or the accomplices of corruption: for though the question relative to the division of the Boards of Stamps and Accounts is in itself of little importance, yet will it develop a system of corruption tending to the utter destruction of Irish liberty, and to the separation of the connexion with England.

I bring forward an act of the meanest administration that ever disgraced this country. I bring it forward as one of the threads by which, united with others of similar texture, vermin of the meanest kind have been able to tie down a body of strength and importance. Let me not be supposed to rest here; when the murderer left the mark of his bloody hand upon the wall, it was not the trace of one finger, but the whole impression which convicted him.†

The Board of Accounts was instituted in Lord Townshend's administration;‡ it came forward in a manner rather inauspicious; it was questioned in parliament, and decided for by the majority of the five members who had received places under it. Born in corruption, it could only succeed by venality. It continued a useless board until the granting of the stamp duties, in Lord Harcourt's time :§ the management of the stamps was then committed to it, and a solemn compact was made that the taxes should not be jobbed, but that both departments

---

* It is right to mention here, that on the 5th of January, 1790, John Fane, Earl of Westmoreland, succeeded the Marquis of Buckingham as Viceroy, and Mr. R. Hobart (afterwards Earl of Buckinghamshire), became Secretary to the Lord Lieutenant.
† Alluding to a notable conviction by circumstantial evidence.
‡ From 1767 to 1772.
§ Lord Harcourt succeeded Lord Townshend.

should be executed by one board. So it continued till it was thought
necessary to increase the salaries of the commissioners, in the Marquis
of Buckingham's famous administration.*

Then nothing was held secret: the increase of the Revenue Board,
the increase of the Ordnance, thirteen thousand pounds a year added to
the infamous Pension List—these were not sufficient, but a compact
which should have been held sacred, was violated, in order to make
places for members of parliament. How indecent! two county members
prying into stamps! What could have provoked this insult? I will
tell you: you remember when the sceptre was trembling in the hand of
an almost expiring monarch; when a factious and desperate English
minister attempted to grasp it, you stood up against the profanation of
the English, and the insult offered to the Irish crown; and had you not
done it, the union of the empire would have been dissolved. You
remember this; remember then, yourselves; remember your triumph: it
was that triumph which exposed you to submit to the resentment of the
Viceroy; it was that triumph which exposed you to disgrace and flagella-
tion. In proportion as you rose by union, your tyrant became appalled:
but when he divided, he sunk you, and you became debased. How this
has happened no man could imagine; no man could have suspected
that a minister without talents could have worked your ruin. There is
a pride in a great nation that fears not its destruction from a reptile;
yet is there more than fable in what we are told of the Romans, that
they guarded the Palladium, rather against the subtlety of a thief, than
the force of an invader.

I bring forward this motion, not as a question of finance, not as a
question of regulation, but as a penal inquiry; and the people will now
see whether they are to hope for help within these walls, or turning
their eyes towards heaven, they are to depend on God and their own
virtue. I rise in an assembly of three hundred persons, one hundred of
whom have places or pensions; I rise in an assembly, one-third of
whom have their ears sealed against the complaints of the people, and
their eyes intently turned to their own interest; I rise before the
whisperers of the treasury, the bargainers and runners of the castle: I
address an audience before whom was held forth the doctrine, that the
crown ought to use its influence on this house. It has been known
that a master has been condemned by the confession of his slave, drawn
from him by torment; but here the case is plain: this confession was
not made from constraint; it came from a country gentleman, deservedly
high in the confidence of administration, for he gave up other confidence
to obtain theirs.

I rise, Sir, to try, when the sluices of corruption have been let loose
upon us, whether there are any means left to stem the torrent. Were
our constituents now to behold us, defending the influence which has
been avowed, they would suppose we were met to vote the robbery of
the people, and to put the money into our pockets; that under the blas-

* The Marquis of Buckingham was Lord Lieutenant from the 15th of September, 1782,
to the 3rd of June, 1783, as Earl Temple, and from the 16th of December, 1787, to the 5th
 1 January, 1790, as Marquis of Buckingham.

phemous pretence of guarding the liberty of the country, we were working for our own emolument.

I know I am speaking too plain; but which is the more honest physician, he who lulls his patient into a fatal security, or he who points out the danger and the remedy of the disease? I, Sir, am showing the danger that arises to our honour and our liberty, if we submit to have corruption let loose among us.

I should not be surprised if bad men of great talents should endeavour to enslave a people; but, when I see folly uniting with vice, corruption with imbecility, men without talents attempting to overthrow our liberty, my indignation rises at the presumption and audacity of the attempt. That such men should creep into power, is a fatal symptom to the constitution; the political, like the material body, when near its dissolution, often bursts out in swarms of vermin.

In this administration a place may be found for every bad man, whether it be to distribute the wealth of the treasury, to vote in the house, to whisper, and to bargain, to stand at the door and note the exits and the entrances of your members, to mark whether they earn their wages, whether it be for the hireling who comes for his hire, or for the drunken aide-de-camp who swaggers in a brothel; nay, some of them find their way to the treasury-bench, the political musicians, or hurdy-gurdy men, to grind the praises of the viceroy.

Notwithstanding the profusion of government, I ask, what defence have they made for the country, in case it should be invaded by a foreign foe? They have not a single ship on the coast. Is it, then, the smug aide-de-camp, or the banditti of the pension-list, or the infantine statesmen, who play in the sunshine of the castle, that are to defend the country? No, it is the stigmatised citizens. We are now sitting in a country of four millions of people, and our boast is, that they are governed by laws to which themselves consent; but are not more than three millions of the people excluded from any participation in making those laws? In a neighbouring country,* twenty-four millions of people were governed by laws to which their consent was never asked; but we have seen them struggle for freedom; in this struggle they have burst their chains, and, on the altar erected by despotism to public slavery, they have enthroned the image of public liberty.

But are our people merely excluded? No; they are denied redress. Next to the adoration which is due to God, I bend in reverence to the institutions of that religion, which teaches me to know his divine goodness; but what advantage does the peasant of the South receive from the institutions of religion? Does he experience the blessing? No; he never hears the voice of the shepherd, nor feels the pastoral crook, but when it is entering his flesh, and goading his very soul.

In this country, Sir, our King is not a resident; the beam of royalty is often reflected through a medium, which sheds but a kind of disastrous twilight, serving only to assist robbers and plunderers We have no security in the talents or responsibility of an Irish ministry; injuries which the English constitution would easily repel, may here be fatal. Ttherefore call upon you to exert yourselves, to heave off the vile incumbrances that have been laid upon you. I call on you not to a measure of finance or of regulation, but of criminal accusation, which you may follow with punishment. I therefore, Sir, most humbly move :—

" That an humble address be presented to his Majesty, praying that he will order to be laid before this house the particulars of the causes, considerations, and representations, in consequence of which the Boards of Stamps and Accounts have been divided, with an increase of salary to the officers; also, that he will be graciously pleased to communicate to this house the names of the persons who recommended that measure."

After a long debate, Curran replied; the conclusion of the following observations refers to some vulgarly intemperate and threatening language, held towards him in the house, by Sir Boyle Roche and others:—

One member has boldly advanced and justified corruption as the engine of government; it is the first time that open bribery has been avowed, in even the worst of times, in this country; but the people now are fairly told that it is lawful to rob them of their property, and divide the plunder among the honest gentlemen who sell them to administration. As to the honourable member not finding much force in my arguments, I am not much surprised at it; they labour under much disadvantage when compared with the honourable member's. My arguments are not all on the same side—they are not stamped with that current impression which has so visible an effect on the honourable member's opinion—they are not arguments equally despised by those to whom he deserted, and those from whom he apostatized. They are not arguments compensated and disavowed, hired and abhorred. The honourable member [the Solicitor-General] has talked of intimidation. I see no intimidation in talking of the conduct of France. A great country asserting her freedom against the vices and corruption of a court, is a glorious object of generous emulation in every free assembly; it is only to corruption and prostitution that the example can be terrible. But from what quarter of the house has intimidation dared to come?

We have been told this night in express words, that the man who dares to do his duty to his country in this house, may expect to be attacked without these walls by the military gentlemen of the castle. If the army had been directly or indirectly mentioned in the course of the debate, this extraordinary declaration might be attributable to the confusion of a mistaken charge, or an absurd vindication; but without connection with the subject, or pretence of connection with the subject, a new principle of government is advanced, and that is the bayonet; and this is stated in the fullest house, and the most crowded audience I ever saw. We are to be silenced by corruption within, or quelled by force of arms without. If the strength of numbers or corruption should fail against the cause of the public, it is to be backed by assassination. Nor is it necessary that those avowed principles of bribery and arms should come from any high personal authority; they have been delivered by the known retainers of administration, in the face of that bench, and heard even without a murmur of dissent or disapprobation.

For my part, I do not know how it may be my destiny to fall; it may be by chance, or malady, or violence; but should it be my fate to perish the victim of a bold and honest discharge of my duty, I will not shun it. I will do that duty; and if it should expose me to sink under the blow of the assassin, and become a victim to the public cause, the most sensible of my regrets would be, that on such an altar there should not be immolated a more illustrious sacrifice. As to myself, while I live, I shall despise the peril. I feel in my own spirit the safety of my honour, and in my own and the spirit of the people do I feel strength enough to hold that administration, which can give a sanction to menaces like these, responsible for their consequences to the nation and the individual.—*Debates* vol. x., pp. 108—11, and 132, 3.

The resolution was rejected by 141 to 81.
One of the consequences of this speech was the duel between Curran and the Right Honourable Major Hobart (afterwards Earl of Buckinghamshire) of which I have spoken in the preliminary Memoir.

PENSIONS.

February 11th, 1790.

GOVERNMENT corruption and patriot opposition proceeded, the public daily being more convinced that nothing but a reform of the Commons could save the constitution of 1782 from the foul policy of ministers. Mr. Forbes moved an address describing and censuring several recent pensions. Curran supported it:—

An honourable friend behind me wishes to direct the indignation of the house against the Irish cabinet, but I do not exactly know who or what the Irish cabinet is, considering the fugitive and fugacious race of ministers who occasionally compose it. I think, however, it comes in some measure under Lord Hood's description of a corporation. "A corporation," says Lord Hood, "cannot go to a brothel—cannot be carried before a justice for a bastard child—cannot get drunk (though the mayor and aldermen may be now and then a little fuddled); cannot be whipped through the town, or put in the stocks, &c." For these reasons I think the punishment of the Irish cabinet not practicable, according to the idea of my honourable friend. Sometimes, however, when the political vessel is in danger of sinking, and those at the helm desert their duty and betray their trust, they are, by a kind of common consent, thrown overboard: at present, indeed, the ship seems to be abandoned by its constitutional pilot, and left to the mercy of a few solitary salvagers.

An honourable military friend of mine [Mr. Johnson, the barrack-master] has adduced a very brilliant simile about an Italian painter, with a knife in one hand, and a brush in the other, which, he said, put him strongly in mind of that instrument with a knife at one end and a brush at the other; but I recollect it had also a screw at the centre, which teaches me to imagine that the honourable gentleman was about to draw a cork instead of a picture.

I shall now proceed to trace the ground on which the resolution is opposed. There are certain chains in which gentlemen on the other side of the house seem to be restricted; but finding themselves obliged to speak on the question, endeavoured to compromise the matter, and made only half a defence. One gentleman [the Chancellor of the Exchequer] has objected to the address as unnecessary, because it is to be followed by a bill, to which he means to object also; this kind of reasoning I ridicule.

The public exports which have been spoken of as symptoms of our prosperity, may be thought in many instances to be traits of our misery; those of corn, for instance, where the miseries of the peasantry oblige them to sell the bread they ought to eat: it has been a trade forced in the hot-bed of public bounty, supported by public taxation.

[He next adverted to Mr. Orde's administration, and proceeded to refute the arguments which had been urged in support of it.] In reply to the objection of Mr. Bushe against the address, as stating matters not of fact, I state the fact that a salary of £300 has been annexed to a useless place, for the purpose of accommodating a member of parliament. I do not rise to answer the pitiful kind of arguments which are offered on the other side. Of many instances of parliamentary infidelity and ministerial profusion, the facts are not denied, nor arguments offered in refutation; but I am aware the arguments on my side of the house will be repelled, not by reason, but by vote.

The hardihood of ministers is like that obduracy which I have observed in felons in the courts, in the course of my profession, who, on the first charge of criminality, were struck dumb with remorse and terror, but, in a little time, ventured to argue in defence of their crimes. The first day of this session was a day of public procession of the grievances of the country before the house. Ministers were then a little abashed; they now stand boldly forward, and avow, and defend their corruption; but there is a tribunal, and it is that of the people, before which our conduct is to be judged. If we obey their instructions, as faithful representatives, they will approve; but if not, they have a right from God, the law, and the constitution, to resist and correct our conduct.

I turn to the speech of Mr. Duquery. I lament the misapplication of his splendid talents, in a cause so unworthy. He has acted the part of a humane advocate for his client; for when his brief afforded no argument in favour of the criminal, it was charitable to become his preacher. In that part of Mr. Duquery's speech, where he spoke in a rhapsody of the blessings of a free trade, I remarked he was supported by the "hear him, hear him!" of the very men who fought against this free trade. But has the honourable member looked into the public accounts? there he can see the vouchers of that corruption, which may be read in the living mummies of this house—in the public profusion of ministers—in the sale of peerages, where animal is trucked against animal; but the people shall know it, and the refusal of inquiry shall be the record of the fact. I deny the danger of insurrection. The people are a great tribunal, who have a right to scrutinize and check the conduct of their representatives; and I pledge myself to bring forward the grievances of the people day after day. I wish to give them a chance of redress, and administration a chance of acquittal.—*Debates* vol. x., pp. 212—14.

The motion was rejected by 136 to 92.

ELECTION OF LORD MAYOR OF DUBLIN.

July 10th, 1790.

The first speech of Curran's *out* of Parliament, of which we have a readable report, is the following, made before the Privy Council. The occasion was a disputed election for the Mayoralty of Dublin; but it was connected closely with the subject so discussed in previous speeches—the attempt of the English government to govern or provincialize Ireland by corruption. In consequence of this notorious design, the burgesses of Dublin in their guilds pledged themselves not to return any one as Lord Mayor or member of Parliament for the city, who held place or pension from government. Alderman James was a Police Commissioner, obnoxious as a place-holder to this pledge, and doubly so from the character of his office, which we have previously seen described. Under the old Corporation Laws the Lord Mayor and Aldermen sat and voted in one chamber, the Sheriffs and Common Councilmen in a second. On the 16th of April, 1790, the former sent down Alderman James's name, as that of the Lord Mayor elect, for the ensuing year; but the Common Council rejected him on a ballot, by 65 votes to 61. Seven *other* names afterwards sent down were similarly rejected. On the following day the Common Council elected Alderman Howison, by 81 votes to 8. Napper Tandy led the popular party; Gifford, the "dog in office," led the opposition, in the Common Council. The Aldermen repeated their election of Alderman James. This dispute came before the Privy Council on the 24th of April, on Alderman James's petition, which set out the facts, and relied on the 33rd of George II. c. 16, to show that the Common Council could not reject without *assigning* a cause. The attendance was full, including the Right Hon. Henry Grattan, Lord Charlemont, Lord Pery, Lord Carhampton, the Chancellor (Lord Fitzgibbon, afterwards Earl of Clare), the Lord Lieutenant, &c. Michael Smith and Downes argued for James, the petitioner, and called witnesses to prove the occurrences in the Boards, and the pledge against officials. Curran and Ponsonby replied for Howison, or, rather, for the Sheriffs and Common Council, for Howison disclaimed his council at the Privy Chamber. The only Report of that speech of Curran's which I could get was quite mangled, and was limited to the arguments included in the speech here given. The Privy Council, after some deliberation, decided for a new election. The result was the re-election of James by the Aldermen, and of Howison by the Common Council, and two petitions. These petitions gave rise to a hearing, on Monday, the 7th of June, wherein Duigenan and Smith were counsel for James, and Curran and George Ponsonby for Howison. The former decision was repeated. The agitation became violent. On the 24th of June the Aldermen re-elected James, and on the 26th the Commons re-elected Howison. On the 10th of July the question came again before the Privy Council, and then the following noble speech was made

While Fitzgibbon was in the Commons, we have seen that he and Curran were bitterly hostile. Fitzgibbon carried his passions to the Woolsack,* and insulted and injured Curran in the Court of Chancery. An opportunity for vengeance now came, without danger to his client (for the Privy Counsel would certainly approve of Alderman James), and Curran used it sternly. The counsel for James were—Patrick Duigenan, Esq., LL.D., and Michael Smith, Esq., LL.D.; for Howison, John P. Curran, Esq., K.C., and George Ponsonby, Esq., K.C. Dr. Duigenan opened, in a clumsy, weak, and arrogant speech, urging that the Common Council could not reject, without assigning a reason. James Napper Tandy and Mr. Purcell, Clerk of the Common Council, were examined, to prove the *facts* of the ballot (stated above) and then Curran rose, and spoke as follows:—

My Lords,—I have the honour to appear before you as counsel for the Commons of the Corporation of the metropolis of Ireland, and also for Mr. Alderman Howison, who hath petitioned for your approbation

---

* He had become Chancellor in June, 1789, succeeding Lord Lifford, who died in April that year. By this Arthur Wolfe became Attorney, and the infamous Toler, Solicitor General. His first title was Baron Fitzgibbon.

of him as a fit person to serve as Lord Mayor, in virtue of his election by the Commons to that high office; and in that capacity I rise to address you, on the most important subject that you have ever been called upon to discuss. Highly interesting and momentous, indeed, my lords, must every question be, that, even remotely and eventually, may affect the well-being of societies, or the freedom or the repose of nations; but that question, the result of which, by an immediate and direct necessity must decide, either fatally or fortunately, the life or death of that well-being, of that freedom and that repose, is surely the most important subject on which human wisdom can be employed, if any subject on this side the grave can be entitled to that appellation.

You cannot, therefore, my lords, be surprised to see this place crowded by such numbers of our fellow-citizens; heretofore they were attracted hither by a strong sense of the value of their rights, and of the injustice of the attack upon them; they felt all the magnitude of the contest; but they were not disturbed by any fear for the event; they relied securely on the justice of their cause, and the integrity of those who were to decide upon it; but the public mind is now filled with a fear of danger, the more painful and alarming, because hitherto unforeseen; they are now taught to fear, that their cause may be of doubtful merits, and disastrous issue; that rights which they considered as defined by the wisdom, and confirmed by the authority of written law, may now turn out to be no more than ideal claims, without either precision or security; that acts of parliament themselves are no more than embryos of legislation, or, at best, but infants, whose first labours must be, not to teach, but to learn; and which, even after thirty years of pupilage, may have thirty more to pass under that guardianship, which the wisdom of our policy has provided for the protection of minors. Sorry am I, my lords, that I can offer no consolation to my clients on this head: and that I can only join them in bewailing, that the question, whose result must decide upon their freedom or servitude, is perplexed with difficulties of which we never dreamed before, and which we are now unable to comprehend: yet surely, my lords, that question must be difficult, upon which the wisdom of the representative of our dread sovereign, aided by the learning of his chancellor and his judges, aided also by the talents of the most conspicuous of the nobles and the gentry of the nation, has been twice already employed, and employed in vain. We know, my lords, that guilt and oppression may stand irresolute for a moment ere they strike, appalled by the prospect of danger, or struck with the sentiment of remorse.; but to you, my lords, it were presumption to impute injustice: we must therefore suppose that you have delayed your determination; not because it was dangerous, but because it was difficult to decide.

And indeed, my lords, a firm belief of this difficulty, however undiscoverable by ordinary talents, is so necessary to the character which this august assembly ought to possess, and to merit from the country, that I feel myself bound to achieve it by an effort of my faith, if I should not be able to do so by any exertion of my understanding.

In a question, therefore, so confessedly obscure as to baffle so much regnicity, I am not at liberty to suppose that certainty could be attained by a concise examination. Bending, then, as I do, my lords, to your high authority, I feel this difficulty as a call upon me to examine it at large; and I feel it as an assurance that I shall be heard with patience

The Lord Mayor of this city hath, from time immemorial, been a magistrate, not appointed by the crown, but elected by his fellow citizens; from the history of the early periods of this corporation, and a view of its charters and bye-laws, it appears that the Commons had, from the earliest periods, participated in the important right of election to that high trust; and it was natural and just that the whole body of citizens, by themselves or their representatives, should have a share in electing those magistrates who were to govern them, as it was their birthright to be ruled only by laws which they had a share in enacting. The Aldermen, however, soon became jealous of this participation, encroached by degrees upon the Commons, and at length succeeded in engrossing to themselves the double privilege of eligibility and of election of being the only body out of which, and by which the Lord Mayor could be chosen.

Nor is it strange that, in those times, a board consisting of so small a number as twenty-four members, with the advantages of a more united interest, and a longer continuance in office, should have prevailed, even contrary to so evident principles of natural justice and constitutional right, against the unsteady resistance of competitors so much less vigilant, so much more numerous, and, therefore, so much less united. It is the common fate of the indolent to see their rights become a prey to the active. The condition upon which God hath given liberty to man is eternal vigilance, which condition if he break, servitude is at once the consequence of his crime, and the punishment of his guilt.

In this state of abasement the Commons remained for a number of years; sometimes supinely acquiescing under their degradation; sometimes, what was worse, exasperating the fury, and alarming the caution of their oppressors, by ineffectual resistance. The slave that struggles, without breaking his chain, provokes the tyrant to double it; and gives him the plea of self-defence for extinguishing what, at first, he only intended to subdue.

In the year 1672, it was directed by one of the New Rules, made by the Lord Lieutenant and Privy Council, under the authority of the Act of Explanation, that "No person should be capable of serving in the office of Lord Mayor, until approved of by the Lord Lieutenant and Council;" and this was a power given after the unhappy civil commotions in this country, to prevent any person, who was not a loyal subject, from holding so important a trust; and upon this single ground, namely, *disloyalty*, have you, my lords, any authority to withhold your approbation.

From that time till the year 1759, no further alteration appears to have taken place in the mode of electing the chief magistrate; at this latter period the act of the 33rd of George the Second was passed; the occasion and the object of that law are universally known. A city so increased in population, in opulence, and in consequence, could not tamely submit to have its corporate rights monopolized by a few, who were at once the tyrants of the metropolis, and the slaves of the government. Magistrates elected by the Board of Aldermen were, in fact, nominated by the court, and were held in derision and abhorrence by the people. The public peace was torn by unseemly dissensions; and the authority of the law itself was lost in the contempt of the magistrate. The legislature felt itself called upon to restore the constitution of the city, to restore and ascertain the rights of the Commons, and thereby to redeem the metropolis from the fatal effects of oppression, of servitude, and anarchy. In saying this, my lords, I am founded on the preamble of the act itself:—" Whereas dissensions and disputes have from a dissatisfaction as to some parts of the present constitution of the Corporation of the city of Dublin, arisen, and for some years past subsisted among several citizens of the said city, to the weakening the authority of the magistrates thereof, who are hereby rendered the less able to preserve the public peace within the said city: therefore, for remedying the aforesaid mischiefs and inconveniences, and for restoring harmony and mutual good will among the citizens of the said city, and for the preserving peace and good order therein : at the humble petition of the Lord Mayor, Sheriffs, Commons, and Citizens of the city of Dublin, be it enacted," &c. Here are stated the mischief acknowledged, and the remedy proposed ; with this view, the statute has ascertained the constituent parts of the Corporation, their respective members, their rights, and the mode of their election, with so minute and detailed an exactness, as even to enact many of those regulations which stood upon the authority of the new rules, or the ancient charters and bye-laws, and in which no alteration whatsoever was intended to be made ; and this it did, that the city might not be left to explore her rights by uncertain deductions from obscure or distant sources, but that she might see the whole plan in a single view, comprised within the limits of a single statute ; and that so intelligibly to every common understanding, as to preclude all possibility of doubt, and thereby all future danger of cavil or dissension.

For this purpose it enacts—" That the Common Council of the city of Dublin, consisting of the Lord Mayor and twenty-four Aldermen, sitting apart by themselves as heretofore, and also of the Sheriffs of the said city for the time being, and Sheriffs' Peers not exceeding forty-eight, and of ninety-six freemen who are to be elected into said Common Council out of the several Guilds or Corporations of the said city, in manner hereafter mentioned, be and for ever hereafter shall be deemed and taken to be, the Common Council of the said city and the representative body of the Corporation thereof."

It then prescribes the mode of electing representatives of the several Guilds, and the time of their service, in which the right of the Commons is exclusive, and without control.

It then regulates the election of Sheriffs: the Commons nominate eight freemen, the Mayor and Aldermen elect two from that number.

Then of Aldermen: the Mayor and Aldermen nominate four Sheriffs' Peers ; the Commons elect one of them.

And here, my lords, give me leave to observe, that this exclusive right of electing their own representatives, and this participation in the election of their magistrates, is given to the popular part of the Corporation to be exercised, as all right of suffrage is exercised by the constitution of this country, that is, according to the dictates of judgment or of affection, and without any authority vested in any human tribunal, of catechising as to the motives that may operate on the mind of a free elector in the preference of one candidate, or the rejection of another.

I will now state to your lordships that part of the statute which relates to the subject of this day :—

" And be it enacted, by the authority aforesaid, that the name of every person, who shall hereafter be elected by the Lord Mayor and Aldermen of the said city, or the usual quorum of them, to serve in the office or place of Lord Mayor of the said city, shall be returned by them to the Commons of the Common Council of the city for their approbation ; without which approbation such person shall not be capable of serving in the office or place of Lord Mayor ; and if it shall happen that the said Commons shall reject or disapprove of the person so returned to them, the Lord Mayor and Aldermen of the said city, or the usual quorum of them, shall, from time to time, elect another person to serve in the office or place of Lord Mayor, and shall, from time to time, return the name of the person so by them elected, to the Commons of the Common Council of the said city, for their approbation, and so, from time to time, until the said Commons shall approve of the person returned by the Lord Mayor and Aldermen of the said city, or the usual quorum of them ; provided always, that such election into the said office of Lord Mayor shall be of some person from among the Aldermen, and that the Commons shall approve of some one person, so elected and returned to them for their approbation.

" And for the preventing the mischiefs and inconveniences which may arise from a failure of the Corporation of the said city, in the appointment of necessary officers, be it enacted, by the authority aforesaid, that if either the Lord Mayor and Aldermen, or the Commons, shall omit or refuse to assemble at or within the usual times for the electing the Lord Mayor, Aldermen, and Sheriffs respectively ; or being assembled shall omit or refuse to do what is hereby required to be done by them respectively, for the election and appointment of the said officers ; then and as often as the case shall happen, it shall and may be lawful for the Commons, in case such default shall be in the Lord Mayor and Aldermen, or for the Aldermen, in case such default shall be in the Commons, or for the usual quorum of them respectively, without any summons for that purpose, to assemble themselves at the Tholsel of the said city on next following day, not being Sunday, or, in case the same shall happen to be a Sunday, then on the Monday next following, and then and there to elect the said officers respectively, as the case shall require and every such election, so made, shall and is hereby declared to be valid and effectual to all intents and purposes.

" Provided always, and be it further enacted, by the authority aforesaid, that every election by the said several Guilds, for the constituting of their representatives in the Common Council of the said city, and every election made or approbation given by the Commons of the said Common Council, by virtue of this act, shall be by ballot, and not otherwise.

"Provided always, that notwithstanding any thing in this act contained, no person or persons shall be enabled or made capable to serve in or execute the office or place of Lord Mayor or Sheriff, Recorder or Town Clerk of the said Corporation, until he or they shall respectively be approved of by the Lord Lieutenant or other Chief Governor or Governors and Privy Council of this kingdom, in such manner as hath heretofore been usual."

Under this act, at the Easter Quarter Assembly, held on the 16th of April, 1790, the Lord Mayor and Aldermen sent down the name of Mr. Alderman James to the Commons, who rejected him; the Lord Mayor and Aldermen elected seven other persons, who were sent down to the Commons, and successively rejected; the Lord Mayor and Aldermen then broke up their meeting, without sending down the name of any other person, or conceiving that they had any right whatsoever to question the Commons touching their reasons for rejecting those who had been so rejected.

The Sheriffs and Commons, thinking that the Lord Mayor and Aldermen had omitted to do what was required of them by the statute to do, namely, to proceed by sending down the name of another person, and so, from time to time, &c., assembled and elected Mr. Alderman Howison, whom they returned, for the approbation of this Board. The Lord Mayor and Aldermen returned Mr. James also as duly elected; the claims of both parties were heard by their counsel, and this Board did not think proper to approve of either candidate; the city proceeded to a new election; the name of Mr. James was again sent down, and rejected as before; a message was then sent to demand of the Commons the reason of their disapprobation; they declined giving any answer but that it was their legal right to do so; Mr. James was accordingly returned as duly elected by the Lord Mayor and Aldermen; the Sheriffs and Commons, as before, elected and returned Mr. Howison; the claims of the candidates were again debated before this honourable Board, but nothing was decided.

A third assembly has since been held, in which the Lord Mayor and Aldermen have acted as before, and returned Mr. James; the Sheriffs and Commons have elected Mr. Howison, who has petitioned for your approbation in virtue of that election.

I trust, my lords, you will think it now time to decide the question: my client calls for that decision; his opponents cannot wish for longer procrastination; in the progress of their pretensions hitherto they have found the fears, and odium, and reprobation of the public increasing upon them.

It is full time to compose the disquietude of that public—the people do not always perceive the merits or the magnitude of a question at a single glance, but they now completely comprehend its merits and importance; they are now satisfied that every thing that can be of value to men may be lost or secured by the event of the present contest.

The claim of my clients has been impeached upon an alleged meaning of this act, and also upon certain facts stated by the learned counsel on the other side, and admitted as proved; of which facts, and the arguments upon them, I will take notice in their proper place.

As to the invective so liberally bestowed upon my fellow-citizens, it best becomes the unhired voluntary advocate* of their rights to pass them without remark. I feel them of too high respect to be protected by panegyric, or avenged by invective; I shall therefore treat those sallies of the learned gentlemen's imaginations as I would the flights of doves; they come abroad only *animo revertendi*, and ought to be suffered to return unmolested to their owners.

The right of Mr. Howison is confessed by the counsel for his opponents, to be warranted by the letter of the law. The Mayor and Aldermen sent down Mr. James; he was rejected by the Commons, who sent to request that another might be sent down; the Board did not send down another, but demanded a reason for the rejection of Mr. James, which, by the letter of the Act, they were certainly not warranted in doing; but it is said that, by the sound construction of that law, the Commons have a right to reject only for good cause, and that having refused to assign such cause, they have been guilty of a default which has transferred the sole right of election to the Lord Mayor and Aldermen, who have accordingly elected Mr. James.

Lord Chancellor—The question here is, "can a mere right of rejection or approbation supersede a right of election?"

Mr. Curran—If I can satisfy this Board that that is not the question, I trust I shall be heard with patience, as to what I conceive to be the question.

I say, my lords, that is not the question, because—

1st. The mode and the rights of election in this case turn not upon any general doctrine of the common law, but upon an express statute, which statute would never have been made, had it not been intended by the legislature to prescribe rules of direction different from those of the common law.

2ndly. The rule alluded to relates to officers in Corporations, (as in the case cited), who have a naked authority to admit, but can reject only for a plain defect of right in the candidate, and who, if a mandamus is directed to them requiring them to admit, must return a legal cause of their disapprobation, that the truth of the fact, or the validity of the cause, may be duly tried.

But there is clearly no analogy between such an officer and the great body of the Commons of this city:—

1st. That officer has no elective authority whatsoever; it is admitted that the act gives to the Commons at least a concurrent elective control and, if the Mayor and Aldermen "make default," an exclusive right to elect, which shall be "valid to all intents and purposes!"

* Curran and Ponsonby were unfeed.

2ndly. That officer has a sort of judicial power which is well placed in a single permanent individual, who is capable of and responsible for the exercise of a judicial power—but it would be monstrous to give a judicial power to a fluctuating multitude; for they cannot be presumed capable of exercising it; nor could they be responsible for such exercise by any course of law; for, suppose a mandamus directed to them, requiring them to approve; how is it possible to make any true return to such writ? How can any man assign a cause for that rejection which the law requires to be by ballot, and, consequently, secret? Or suppose a party of the Commons are practised upon to return a cause, and that designedly an invalid one, how shall the residue of the Commons be able to justify themselves by alleging the true and valid cause of their disapprobation?

To try it, therefore, by such a rule, is to try it by a rule clearly having no general analogy to the subject, nor even a possible application, except so far only as it begs the question.

My lords, it is absurd to ask how a simple power of approbation or rejection for cause shall be controlled, unless it is first determined whether the Commons have that simple power only, or whether they have, what I think they clearly have under the statute, a peremptory right of approving or rejecting, without any control whatsoever.

If they have, but a simple right to reject for cause, and ought to have assigned such cause under the law, they have been guilty of a default, and the sole right to elect devolves to the Board of Aldermen, who, of course, have duly elected. If they are not bound to assign such a reason, manifestly the Aldermen have acted against law, and by their default have lost this power, and the Commons have duly elected Mr. Howison.

Now, my lords, in examining this question, you must proceed by the ordinary rule of construction, applicable alike to every statute; that of expounding it by the usual acceptation and natural context of the words in which it is conceived. Do the words, then, my lords, or the natural context of this act, describe a limited power of rejecting only for cause to be assigned, or a peremptory power of rejecting, without any such cause? Says the act, "If it shall happen that the Commons shall reject or disapprove." The law describes this accidental rejection in language most clearly applicable to the acts of men assembled, not as judges, but as electors; not to judge by laws which they have never learned, but to indulge their affections, or their caprice; and therefore justly speaks of a rejection, not the result of judgment, but of chance.

"If it shall happen that they shall *reject* or *disapprove*." My lords, you cannot say these words are synonymous; in acts every word must have its meaning, if possible. To "*reject*" contradistinguished to "*disapprove*," is to reject by an act of the will: to disapprove supposes some act of the judgment also.

The act, then, clearly gives a right of rejecting, distinct from disapprobation, which, by no possibility, can be other than a peremptory right, without limit or control.

But here, if a reason must be had, the law would naturally prescribe some mode of having it demanded; this, however, unluckily cannot be done without a direct violation of the act, which enjoins that the two bodies shall "sit apart," and "by themselves, as heretofore;" but at least it might have left the Board of Aldermen the means of making a silent struggle for the approbation of their favourite candidate, by sending him down again for re-consideration. But, on the contrary, the law is express, that "if the Commons shall happen to reject or disapprove the first," they must then proceed to send down the name, not of *him*, but of *another*, and so on. How long, my lords? Until a good reason shall be assigned for the rejection of the first? No, my lords, it is "until the Commons shall approve of *some one person*, so sent down;" and to this right of rejection, which the law has supposed might happen so often, the law has opposed the limit of a single proviso only, applicable enough to a peremptory right of rejection, but singular indeed, if applied to rejection for cause:—"Provided always, that such election into the said office of Lord Mayor, shall be of some person from among the Aldermen, and that the Commons shall approve of some one person, so elected and returned to them for their approbation." A rejection without cause to be assigned, being a mere popular privilege, may be limited in its extent by reasons of expediency; but a judicial power of rejecting for legal cause cannot be so controlled, without the grossest absurdity. It is like a peremptory challenge, which is given to a prisoner by the indulgence of the law, and may be therefore restricted within reasonable bounds. But a challenge for cause is given of common right, and must be allowed as often as it shall be found to exist, even though the criminal should remain for ever untried, and the crime for ever unpunished.

Permit me now, my lords, to try this construction contended for, by another test. Let us put it into the form of a proviso, and see how it accords with the proviso which you find actually expressed:—"Provided always that the Commons shall be obliged to approve of the first person whose name shall be sent down to them, unless they shall assign good legal cause for their rejection." The proviso expressed is—"Provided that they shall approve, not of the first person, but of some one person so elected." Can anything be more obvious than the inconsistency of two such provisos?

Give me leave, my lords, to compare this supposed proviso with the enacting part of the statute. It says, that if the first person sent down be rejected, the Lord Mayor and Aldermen shall "then proceed to elect another, and send down his name;" but if this supposed proviso were to make a part of the act, they would not be obliged to send down "another name," but would be authorised to insist upon the claim of the first candidate, by demanding a reason for his rejection. This supposed proviso, therefore, and, of course, this superinduced construction, is directly incompatible both with the body and the proviso of the statute itself.

But see further, my lords, what you do by such a construction; you declare that the benefit of this statute, which is given expressly to the

Commons, is given upon a tacit condition, by the breach of which that benefit is utterly forfeited. Do you think, my lords, you shall act consistently with the spirit of the constitution, or of the law of Ireland, if you declare and enforce a cause of forfeiture, written in no law whatsoever, and devised only by your own interpretation; or do you not feel, my lords, to what a wretched state of servitude the subject is reduced, if criminality and forfeiture are to depend, not on the plain and permanent meaning of the law, but upon the dreams and visions of capricious interpreters? If a constructive cause of forfeiture can be warranted, by which any part, or any individual, of a corporation, shall be adjudged to have lost their franchise; by the same principle may a constructive offence and forfeiture be devised, by which a whole corporation shall be stripped of its charter. Says the law, "if they shall omit or refuse to do what they are required to do by this act," they lose the benefit thereof: but this curious construction would declare, that the Commons have forfeited the benefit of the statute, by refusing to do that which they are not required by this, or any other act, to do.

If, then, my lords, you call this power of rejection or disapprobation a power to be regulated by technical maxims of the common law, and to be exerted only for legal cause to be assigned; what is it but to give the law a meaning which the legislature never spoke? what is it but to nullify a statute made for the benefit of the people, by an arbitrary construction, supported only by the most pitiful of all argumentative fallacies—an assumption of what cannot be proved; or to describe it in terms more suited to its demerit, that mixture of logical poverty and ethical meanness, which stoops to beg what it has not industry to acquire, nor craftiness to steal, nor force to extort.

But see, my lords, whether this infallible rule of the common law, upon which the whole merits of this case have been rested, will not, if admitted, be subversive of the authority which it would seem to support. By one of the new rules, and by a clause in this act of parliament, no person can serve as Mayor without the approbation of this Board. This power of approving was notoriously given for the security of the government; and hath now, for upwards of a century, been exercised upon no other ground whatever. By a clause in this act, no person can serve as Mayor without the approbation of the Commons, and this right of approbation, as notoriously, was given to increase the power of the people; and the Commons have accordingly so exercised it uniformly for thirty years; it is observable that this right of approbation is given to them in language more emphatic than it is to your lordships; but for argument sake, I will suppose the words the same; now, if, by the common law, all right of approving or rejecting can be founded only on legal cause to be assigned, what becomes of your lordships' decision? You have already refused your approbation to the two present petitioners, having both had exactly the same pretensions to your approbation which they have at present; you have refused your approbation, and you have assigned no cause; but let me ask a much more material question—what, in that case, becomes of your lordships' power? The same words, in the same act of parliament, cannot have two different constructions; if the Commons are bound to assign a legal cause for rejection, you, my lords, must be similarly bound, and the law will then coerce the Commons, and coerce your lordships, in a manner directly contrary to the intention of the act; it will then cease to be a law for the protection of liberty, on the one hand, or the security of the government on the other; for, being equally confined to a rejection for legal cause, the Commons may be obliged to approve a candidate, not legally disqualified, though an enemy to their liberty, and your lordships be restrained from rejecting a candidate, not legally disqualified, though an enemy to the state. See, then, my lords, to what you will be reduced: you must either admit, that the statute has confined you both equally to decide upon the mere question of legal capacity or incapacity only, of which they are clearly incapable of judging, and on which it is here admitted you are incompetent to decide, and has thus elevated them, and degraded your lordships from good citizens and wise statesmen, into bad judges; or if, in opposition to this construction, you do your duty to your sovereign, and refuse to admit to the magistracy, a man whom you have good reason to believe disaffected to the state, though subject to no legal incapacity, what do you do, my lords? You give two different expositions to the same words, in the same act of parliament; that is, an enlarged exposition in favour of yourselves, and a confined one against the people; that is, in fact, you are driven to incur the odium of repealing the law, as against the crown, and enforcing it against the subject. See, on the other hand, my lords, how, by the plain and hitherto adopted construction, all these mischiefs are avoided. You judge of the candidate with respect to his loyalty—the Commons with regard to his integrity and independence; neither of you with any relation to his legal capacity or incapacity; thus will every object of the law, of the people, and of the government, be completely obtained; the Commons will enjoy their power, in deciding upon the popularity of the candidate for magistracy, you will do your duty, in deciding upon his loyalty, and the courts of justice will retain their natural exclusive jurisdiction in every question that can touch his legal qualification; thus will it be impossible for any man to have the power of the city in his hands, who is not free from all legal objections, and who is not also deserving the confidence of his Sovereign, as well as of his fellow-subjects.

Thus far, my lords, have I examined this law, with respect to the present question, by the general rule of construction, applicable generally to all statutes, that is, of seeking for the meaning of the legislature in the ordinary and natural context of the words which they have thought proper to adopt; and this, I thought, I might do with still more confidence, in a law professedly made for the direction of men unacquainted with legal difficulty, unversed in the subtlety of legal distinction, and acting in a situation which precludes them from the advantage of all legal assistance; but I feel that what hath been satisfactory to my mind hath not been so to some of your lordships. I feel myself, therefore, obliged to enter upon a more minute examination of this statute, upon principles and circumstances peculiar to itself.

I am sorry, my lords, to trespass upon your patience; but I am speaking upon a subject in which, if I do not succeed, the people of this country will have lost what is of infinitely more value than any time, however precious, that may be wasted in their defence.

This act, my lords, professes to be a remedial act, and, as such, must be construed according to the rules peculiar to remedial laws; that is, in three points of view; first, the former state of the law; secondly, the mischief of such former state; and thirdly, the remedy proposed for the cure of that mischief.

As to the first point; at the time of this statute, the Lord Mayor and Aldermen exercised the exclusive power of election to the Chief Magistracy, without any interference of the Commons. The immediate mischief of such a constitution, with respect to the metropolis itself, I have touched on before; the people were borne down, the magistracy was depraved, the law was relaxed, and the public tranquillity was at an end. These mischiefs were more than enough to induce the citizens of Dublin to call loudly, as they did, upon the justice of the legislature for parliamentary redress. But the wisdom of that legislature formed an estimate of the mischief from consideration that, probably, did not enter into the minds of the contending parties; namely, from the then state of Ireland as an individual, and as a connected country; as an individual depressed in every thing essential to the support of political or civil independency; depressed in commerce, in opulence, and in knowledge; distracted by that civil and religious discord, suggested by ignorance and bigotry, and inflamed by the artifice of a cruel policy, which divided, in order to destroy, conscious that liberty could be banished only by disunion, and that a generous nation could not be completely stripped of her rights, until one part of the people was deluded into the foolish and wicked idea that its freedom and consequence could be preserved or supported only by the slavery or depression of the other. In such a country it was peculiarly necessary to establish at least some few incorporated bodies, which might serve as great repositories of popular strength: our ancestors learned from Great Britain to understand their use and their importance; in that country they had been hoarded up with the wisest forecast, and preserved with a religious reverence, as an unfailing resource against those times of storm, in which it is the will of Providence that all human affairs should sometimes fluctuate; and, as such, they had been found at once a protection to the people, and a security to the crown. My lords, it is by the salutary repulsion of popular privilege that the power of the monarchy is supported in its sphere; withdraw that support, and it falls in ruin upon the people, but it falls in a ruin no less fatal to itself, by which it is shivered to pieces.

Our ancestors must, therefore, have been sensible that the enslaved state of the corporation of the metropolis was a mischief that extended its effects to the remotest borders of the island. In the confederated strength, and the united councils of great cities, the freedom of a country may find a safeguard which extends itself even to the remote inhabitant who never put his foot within their gates.

But, my lords, how must these considerations have been enforced by a view of Ireland, as a connected country, deprived, as it was, of almost all the advantages of an hereditary monarchy; the father of his people residing at a distance, and the paternal beam reflected upon his children through such a variety of mediums; sometimes too languidly to warm them; sometimes so intensely as to consume; a succession of governors, differing from one another in their tempers, their talents, and their virtues; and, of course, in their systems of administration; unprepared, in general, for rule, by any previous institution, and utterly unacquainted with the people they were to govern, and with the men through whose agency they were to act. Sometimes, my lords, 'tis true a rare individual has appeared among us, as if sent by the bounty of Providence, in compassion to human miseries, marked by that dignified simplicity of manly character which is the mingled result of an enlightened understanding and an elevated integrity; commanding a respect that he laboured not to inspire, and attracting a confidence which it was impossible he could betray. It is but eight years, my lords, since we have seen such a man* amongst us, raising a degraded country from the condition of a province to the rank and consequence of a people, worthy to be the ally of a mighty empire; forming the league that bound her to Great Britain, on the firm and honourable basis of equal liberty and a common fate, "standing and falling with the British nation," and thus stipulating for that freedom which alone contains the principle of her political life, in the covenant of her federal connexion. But how short is the continuance of those auspicious gleams of public sunshine, how soon they are passed, and perhaps for ever! In what rapid and fatal revolution has Ireland seen the talents and the virtues of such men give place to a succession of sordid parade and empty pretension, of bloated promise and lank performance, of austere hypocrisy, and peculating economy! Hence it is, my lords, that the administration of Ireland so often presents to the reader of her history, not the view of a legitimate government, but rather of an encampment in the country of a barbarous enemy, where the object of the invader is not government, but conquest; where he is, of course, obliged to resort to the corrupting of clans, or of single individuals, pointed out to his notice by public abhorrence, and recommended to his confidence only by a treachery so rank and consummate as precludes all possibility of their return to private virtue or to public reliance, and therefore only put into authority over a wretched country, condemned to the torture of all that petulant unfeeling asperity with which a narrow and malignant mind will bristle in unmerited elevation; condemned to be betrayed, and disgraced, and exhausted, by the little traitors that have been suffered to nestle and to grow within it, making it at once the source of their grandeur, and the victim of their vices, reducing it to the melancholy necessity of supporting their consequence, and of sinking under their crimes, like the lion perishing by the poison of a reptile that finds shelter in the mane of the noble animal, while it is stinging him to death.

* William Henry Bentinck, Duke of Portland, was Lord Lieutenant from the 13th of December, 1780, to the 14th of April, 1782, and was erroneously believed to have acted with good faith to Ireland, in that momentous period. His correspondence, recently published, proves the reverse.

By such considerations as these, my lords, might the makers of this statute have estimated the danger to which the liberty of Ireland was exposed ; and, of course, the mischief of having that metropolis enslaved, by whose independence alone those dangers might be averted ; but in this estimate they had much more than theory, or the observation of foreign events, to show them that the rights of the sovereign and of the subject were equally embarked in a common fate with that independency When, in the latter part of the reign of Queen Anne, an infernal conspiracy was formed, by the then Chancellor [Sir Constantine Phipps] and the Privy Council, to defeat that happy succession which, for three generations hath shed its auspicious influence upon these realms, they commenced their diabolical project by an attack upon the corporate rights of the citizens of Dublin, by an attempt to impose a disaffected Lord Mayor upon them, contrary to the law. Fortunately, my lords, this wicked conspiracy was defeated by the virtue of the people : I will read to your lordships the resolutions of a committee of the House of Commons on the subject.

" First, Resolved, that it is the opinion of this committee, that soon after the arrival of Sir Constantine Phipps, late Lord Chancellor, and one of the Lords Justices in this kingdom, in the year 1710, a design was formed and carried on to subvert the constitution and freedom of elections of magistrates of Corporations within the new rules, in order to procure persons to be returned for members of parliament, disaffected to the settlement of the crown or his Majesty and his royal issue.

" 2nd. Resolved, that it is the opinion of this committee, that in pursuance of that design, indirect and illegal methods were taken to subvert the ancient and legal course of electing magistrates in the city of Dublin.

" 3rd. Resolved, that it is the opinion of this committee, that the said Sir Constantine Phipps, and those engaged in that evil design, in less than five months, in the year 1711, procured six Aldermen, duly elected Lord Mayors, and fourteen substantial citizens, duly elected Sheriffs, all well known to be zealously affected to the Protestant succession, and members of the Established Church, to be disapproved, on pretence that Alderman Robert Constantine, as senior Alderman, who had not been Mayor, had a right to be elected Lord Mayor.

" 4th. Resolved, that it is the opinion of this committee, that the senior Alderman who had not served as Mayor, had not any right by charter, usage, or by law, in force in the city of Dublin, as such, to be elected Lord Mayor.

" 5th. Resolved, that it is the opinion of this committee, that tl said Sir Constantine Phipps, and his accomplices, being unable to support the pretended right of seniority, did, in the year 1713, set up a pretended custom or usage for the Mayor in being, to nominate three persons to be in election for Lord Mayor, one of whom the Aldermen were obliged to choose Lord Mayor."

Lord Chancellor—Can you think, Mr. Curran, that these resolutions of a committee of the House of Commons, can have any relation whatsoever to the present subject?

Mr. Curran—I hope, my lords, you will think they have much relation, indeed, to the subject before you: the weakness of the city was the mischief which occasioned the law in question; to give it strength was the remedy. You must construe the law, so as to suppress the former and advance the latter. What topics, then, my lords, can bear so directly upon the point of your inquiry as the perils to be apprehended from that weakness, and the advantages to be derived from that strength? What argument, then, can be so apposite, as that which is founded on undeniable facts? Or what authority so cogent as the opinion of the representative wisdom of the nation, pronounced upon those facts, and transmitted to posterity upon record? On grounds like these—for I can conceive no other—do I suppose the rights of the city were defended in the time to which I have alluded; for it appears by the records which I have read, that the city was then heard by her counsel; she was not denied the form of defence, though she was denied the benefit of the law. In this very chamber did the Chancellor and Judges sit, with all the gravity of affected attention to arguments in favour of that liberty and those rights which they had conspired to destroy. But to what end, my lords, offer arguments to such men? A little and a peevish mind may be exasperated; but how shall it be corrected by refutation? How fruitless would it have been to represent to that wretched Chancellor, that he was betraying those rights which he was sworn to maintain—that he was involving a government in disgrace, and a kingdom in panic and consternation—that he was violating every sacred duty, and every solemn engagement that bound him to himself, his country, his sovereign, and his God! Alas, my lords, by what argument could any man hope to reclaim or to dissuade a mean, illiberal, and unprincipled minion of authority, induced by his profligacy to undertake, and bound by his avarice and vanity to persevere? He would probably have replied to the most unanswerable arguments by some curt, contumelious, and unmeaning apophthegm, delivered with the fretful smile of irritated self-sufficiency and disconcerted arrogance; or even if he could be dragged by his fears to a consideration of the question, by what miracle could the pigmy capacity of a stunted pedant be enlarged to a reception of the subject? The endeavour to approach it would have only removed him to a greater distance from it than he was before; as a little hand that strives to grasp a mighty globe is thrown back by the reaction of its own effort to comprehend. It may be given to a Hale, or a Hardwicke, to discover and retract a mistake. The errors of such men are only specks that arise for a moment upon the surface of a splendid luminary; consumed by its heat, or irradiated by its light, they soon purge and disappear. But the perversenesses of a mean and narrow intellect are like the excrescences that grow upon a body naturally cold and dark; no fire to waste them, and no ray to enlighten, they assimilate and coalesce with those qualities so congenial to their nature, and acquire an incorrigible permanency in th union with kindred frost and kindred opacity. Nor, indeed, my lords, except where the interest of millions can be effected by the folly or the vice of an individual, need it be much regretted that to things not worthy of being made better, it hath not pleased Providence to afford the privilege of improvement.

Lord Chancellor—Surely, Mr. Curran, a gentleman of your eminence in your profession must see that the conduct of former privy councils has nothing to do with the question before us. The question lies in the narrowest compass; it is merely whether the Commons have a right of arbitrary and capricious rejection, or are obliged to assign a reasonable cause for their disapprobation. To that point you have a right to be heard, but I hope you do not mean to lecture the council.

Mr. Curran—I mean, my lords, to speak to the case of my clients and to avail myself of every topic of defence which I conceive applicable to that case. I am not speaking to a dry point of law, to a single judge, and on a mere forensic subject; I am addressing a very large auditory, consisting of co-ordinate members, of whom the far greater number is not versed in law. Were I to address such an audience on the interests and rights of a great city, and address them in the hackneyed style of a pleader, I should make a very idle display of profession, with very little information to those that I address, or benefit to those on whose behalf I have the honour to be heard. I am aware, my lords, that truth is to be sought only by slow and painful progress; I know, also, that error is in its nature flippant and compendious—it hops with airy and fastidious levity over proofs and arguments, and perches upon assertion which it calls conclusion.

[Here the Lord Chancellor moved to have the chamber cleared. After some time the doors were opened, and Mr. Curran proceeded.*]

My lords, I was regretting the necessity which I am under of trespassing so much on that indulgent patience, with which I feel I am so honoured. Let me not, however, my lords, be thought so vainly presumptuous as to suppose that condescension bestowed merely upon me; I feel, my lords, how much more you owe it to your own dignity and justice, and to a full conviction that you could not be sure of deciding with justice, if you did not hear with temper.

As to my part, my lords, I am aware that no man can convince by arguments which he does not clearly comprehend, and make clearly intelligible to others; I consider it, therefore, not only an honour but an advantage to be stopped whenever I am not understood. So much confidence have I in the justice of the cause, that I wish any noble lord in this assembly would be pleased to go with me step by step through the argument. One good effect would inevitably result; I should either have the honour of convincing the noble lord, or the public would, by my refutation, be satisfied that they are in the wrong. With this wish, and, if I may presume to say so, with this hope, I will proceed to a further examination of the subject.

It is a rule of law, that all remedial acts shall be so construed, as to suppress the mischief and advance the remedy. Now, a good cause of rejection can mean only a legal cause; that is, a cause working an incapacity in the person executing a corporate franchise—that is, of course, such a cause as would justify a judgment of ouster against him by a court of law, if actually in possession of such franchise, or warrant

Lord Clare. It is said, moved the Council that Mr. Curran should be restrained from this course of observation, and that they decided against the motion.

his amoval by an act of the corporation itself. There are three sorts of offences for which a corporator may be amoved:—first, such as have no immediate relation to his office, but are in themselves of so infamous a nature as to render the offender unfit to exercise any public franchise: secondly, such as are *only* against his oath and the duty of his office as a corporator, and amount to a breach of the tacit condition annexed to his franchise or office; the third sort of offence, for which an officer or corporator may be displaced, is of a mixed nature, as being an offence not only against the duty of his office, but also a matter indictable at common law.

For the first species of offences, a corporation can in no case amove without a previous indictment and conviction in a court of common law For the other offences, it has a power of trial, as well as amotion.

To this let me add, that the office of Alderman is as much a corporate office as that of Lord Mayor, and the legal cause that disqualifies the one must equally disqualify the other; but the person chosen to be Mayor must be an Alderman at the time of his election, and the law of course, cannot suppose a man actually in possession of a corporate franchise, to labour under any corporate or legal incapacity. Does it not then, my lords, follow irresistibly, that the law cannot intend to confine the power of rejection, which it expressly gives, to a legal incapacity, which without the grossest absurdity it cannot suppose to exist?

But let us assume, for argument sake, however in defiance of common sense, that the legislature did suppose it possible that such an incapacity might exist, what does a power of rejection for such cause give to the Commons? And it is admitted by the learned counsel, "that this statute made a great enlargement, indeed, in their powers."

Before the act was made, any corporator subject to a personal disqualification was removeable by the ordinary course of law. To give the Commons, therefore, only a power of preventing a man legally disqualified from serving a corporate office, was giving them nothing which they had not before. What sort of construction, then, my lords, must that be which makes the legislature fall into the ridiculous absurdity of giving a most superfluous remedy, for a most improbable mischief? And yet it is not in a nursery of children, nor a bedlam of madmen but it is in an assembly, the most august that this country knows of, that I am obliged to combat this perversion of sense and of law. In truth, my lords, I feel the degradation of gravely opposing a wild chimera, that could not find a moment's admission into any instructed or instituted mind; but I feel, also, that they who stoop to entertain it only from the necessity of exposing and subduing it, cannot, at least, be the first object of that degradation.

Let me, then, my lords, try this construction contended for by another test. If the act must be construed so as to say that the Commons can reject only for a legal cause to be assigned, it must be so construed, as to provide for all that is inseparably incident, and indispensably necessary to carrying that construction into effect: that is, it must provide a mode, in which four things may be done:

First, a mode in which such cause shall be assigned.

Secondly, a mode in which the truth of the fact of such cause shall be admitted or controverted.

Thirdly, a mode by which the truth of such fact, if controverted, shall be tried; and

Fourthly, a mode by which the validity of such cause, when ascertained in fact, shall be judged of in law. To suppose a construction, requiring a reason to be assigned, without providing for these inevitable events, would be not the error of a lawyer, but would sink beneath the imbecility of an infant.

Then, my lords, as to the first point, how is the cause to be assigned. The law expressly precludes the parties from any means of conference, by enacting, that they shall "sit apart and by themselves." The same law says, that "the rejection or disapprobation shall be by ballot only, and not otherwise." Now, when the law gives the Commons a power of rejecting by ballot, it gives each individual a protection against the enmity which he would incur from the rejected candidate. But if you say that the rejection shall be null and void, unless fortified by the assignment of legal cause, see, my lords, what you labour to effect: under this supposed construction, you call upon the voters who reject by a secret vote to relinquish that protection of secrecy which the law expressly gives them, unless, my lords, the sagacity that has broached this construction can find out some way by which the voter can justify why he voted against a particular candidate, without disclosing, also, that he did, in fact, vote against that candidate.

Let me, however, suppose that inconsistency reconciled, and follow the idea.

The name of Alderman James is sent down, and the Commons certify his rejection. An ambassador is then sent to demand of the Commons the cause of this rejection. They answer, "Sir, we have rejected by ballot, and they who have voted against him are protected by the law from discovering how they voted." To which the ambassador replies, "Very true, gentlemen, but you mistake their worships' question; they do not desire you to say who rejected Mr. James, for in that they well know they could not be warranted by law; they only desire to know why a majority has voted against Mr. Alderman James." This, my lords, I must suppose to be a mode of argument not unbefitting the sagacity of aldermen, since I find it gives occasion to a serious question before so exalted an assembly as I have now the honour to address. I will, therefore, suppose it conclusive with the Commons. A legal reason must be assigned for their rejection. Pray, my lords, who is to assign that legal reason? Is it the minority who voted for the rejected candidate? I should suppose not; it must be then the majority who voted for the rejection. Pray, my lords, who are they? By what means shall they be discovered?

But I will suppose that every member of the Commons is willing to adopt the rejection, and to assign a cause for it. One man—suppose a friend of the rejected candidate—alleges a cause of a rejection, in which he did not in reality concur, and which cause he takes care shall be invalid and absurd—as for instance, the plumpness of the person of Mr James. If he did not vote for the rejection he can have no right to assign a cause for it. The question then is, did he vote for the rejection? I beg leave, my lords, to know how that is to be tried?

But suppose, to get rid of a difficulty, otherwise insurmountable, it shall be agreed, in direct contradiction to common sense and justice. that every member of the Commons shall be authorized to assign a legal cause of rejection; ....., in truth, if he may assign one he may assign more than one, if he is disposed to do so. Suppose then, my lords, that one hundred and forty-six causes are assigned, for such may be the number, though no one member assigns more than a single cause. If they may be all assigned, they must be all disposed of according to law. But which shall be first put into a course of trial?—how shall the right of precedence be decided? But I will suppose that also settled, and a single cause is assigned; that cause must be a legal disability of some of the kinds which I have already mentioned, for there cannot be any other. The cause, then, assigned, in order to prevail, must be true in fact, and valid in law, and amount to a legal incapacity. And here let me observe, that a legal cause of incapacity, as it can be founded only on the commission of an infamous crime, or of some fact contrary to the duty and oath of a corporator, must, if allowed, imprint an indelible stigma on the reputation of the man so rejected. I ask, then, is the accusation of malignity, or credulity, or folly, to be taken for true? Or shall the person have an opportunity of defending himself against the charge? The cause for which he can be rejected is the same with the cause for which he can be disfranchised; they are equally causes working an incapacity to hold a corporate franchise; their consequences are the same to the person accused—loss of franchise, and loss of reputation. The person accused, therefore, if by the construction of a statute he is exposed to accusation, must by the same construction be entitled to every advantage in point of defence, to which a person so accused is entitled by the general law of the land. What, then, are those advantages to which a corporator is entitled, when charged with any fact as a foundation of incapacity or disfranchisement? He must have due and timely notice of the charge, that he may prepare for his defence; every corporator must have timely and express notice of the specific charge against him, that nothing may be done by surprise on either side. Now, my lords, you will condescend to observe, that the time supposed by this statute for the whole business of election is a single day. Is it, then, possible to give every member of the Board of Aldermen—for each of them may be a candidate—due notice of every charge of legal disability that may possibly be made against them? Or if it be not, as it manifestly is not, will you, my lords, create a construction which exposes any subject of the land to trial without notice, and to conviction and forfeiture without that opportunity of defence to which he is entitled of natural justice and common right? But I will suppose that your lordships may adopt this construction, however it may supersede the right of the subject and the law of the land; I will suppose that the candidate may be accused at a moment's warning—is bare accusal tion to hold the place of conviction? Shall the alderman whose name is sent down, and who is rejected for an alleged personal disability, have an opportunity of defending himself against the charge of the Commons? He cannot have the privilege of the meanest felon, of standing before his accusers, for, as an alderman, he must remain with his brethren, " separate and apart by themselves." He cannot then plead for himself in person, nor by the law can he depu— an attorney to defend in his name, for the Commons are not authorized to admit any strangers among them. It is, therefore, utterly out of his power to deny the charge against him, however false in fact it may happen to be. But I will suppose, if you please, that the charge is denied, and issue joined upon the fact; I beg leave to ask, if this supposed construction provides any mode of calling the jury, or summoning the witnesses, on whose testimony, and on whose verdict a citizen is to be tried upon a charge of corporate or legal culpability? But let me, my lords, with the profoundest respect, press this wicked and silly nonsense a little farther. Suppose the charge admitted in fact, but the validity of it denied, who, my lords, is to judge of it by virtue of this construction? A point of law is to be decided between the Lord Mayor and Aldermen who have chosen, and the Commons who have rejected. What is the consequence? If the Lord Mayor and Aldermen decide, they judge in their own cause; if the Commons decide, they judge in their own cause, contrary to the maxim, that "*Nemo Judex in propriâ causâ.*" Can you then, my lords, think yourselves warranted in adopting a construction which supposes a legal charge to be made, in which the accused has not the advantage of notice, or the means of defence, or of legal trial; and on which, if any judgment be pronounced, it must be pronounced, in direct opposition to the law of the land, by the parties in the cause.

But, my lords, it seems all these defects in point of accusation, of defence, of trial, and of judgment, as the ingenious gentlemen have argued, are cured by the magical virtue of those beans, by whose agency the whole business must be conducted.

If the law had permitted a single word to be exchanged between the parties, the learned counsel confess that much difficulty might arise in the events which I have stated; but they have found out that all these difficulties are prevented or removed by the beans and the ballot According to these gentlemen, we are to suppose one of the unshaven demagogues, whom the learned counsel have so humourously described, rising in the Commons when the name of Alderman James is sent down; he begins by throwing out a torrent of seditious invective against the servile profligacy and liquorish venality of the Board of Aldermen—this he doth by beans. Having thus previously inflamed the passions of his fellows, and somewhat exhausted his own, his judgment collects the reins that floated on the neck of his imagination, and he becomes grave, compressed, sententious and didactic; he lays down the law of personal disability, and corporate criminality, and corporate forfeiture, with great precision, with sound emphasis, and good discretion, to the great lelight and edification of the assembly—and this he does by beans. He then proceeds, my lords, to state the specific charge against the unfortunat candidate for approbation, with all the artifice and malignity of accusation—scalding the culprit in tears of affected pity—bringing forward the blackness of imputed guilt through the varnish of simulated commiseration—bewailing the horror of his crime, that he may leave it without excuse—and invoking the sympathy of his judges, that he may steel them against compassion—and this, my lords, the unshaved demagogue doth by beans. The accused doth not appear in person, for he cannot leave his companions, nor by attorney, for his attorney could not be admitted—but he appears and defends by beans. At first humble and deprecatory, he conciliates the attention of his judges to his defence, by giving them to hope that it may be without effect; he does not alarm them by any indiscreet assertion, that the charge is false, but he slides upon them arguments, to show it improbable. By degrees, however, he gains upon the assembly, and denies and refutes, and recriminates and retorts—all by beans—until at last he challenges his accuser to a trial, which is accordingly had, in the course of which the depositions are taken, the facts tried, the legal doubts proposed and explained by beans; and in the same manner the law is settled with an exactness and authority that remains a record of jurisprudence, for the information of future ages; while at the same time the "harmony" of the metropolis is attuned by the marvellous temperament of jarring discord, and the "good will" of the citizens is secured by the indissoluble bond of mutual crimination and reciprocal abhorrence.

By this happy mode of decision, one hundred and forty-six causes of rejection (for of so many do the Commons consist, each of whom must be entitled to allege a distinct cause) are tried in the course of a single day, with satisfaction to all parties.

With what surprise and delight must the heart of the fortunate inventor have glowed, when he discovered those wonderful instruments of wisdom and of eloquence, which, without being obliged to commit the precious extracts of science or persuasion to the faithless and fragile vehicle of words or phrases, can serve every process of composition or abstraction of ideas, and every exigency of discourse or argumentation, by the resistless strength and infinite variety of beans, white or black, or boiled or raw; displaying all the magic of their powers in the mysterious exertions of dumb investigation and mute discussion—of speechless objection and tongue-tied refutation!

Nor should it be forgotten, my lords, that this notable discovery does no little honour to the sagacity of the present age, by explaining a doubt that has for so many centuries perplexed the labour of philosophic inquiry, and furnishing the true reason why the pupils of Pythagoras were prohibited the use of beans. It cannot, I think, my lords, be doubted that the great author of the Metempsychosis found out that those mystic powers of persuasion, which vulgar naturalists supposed to remain lodged in minerals or fossils, had really transmigrated into beans; and he could not, therefore, but see that it would have been fruitless to preclude his disciples from mere oral babbling, unless he had also debarred them from the indulgence of vegetable loquacity.

My lords, I have hitherto endeavoured to show, and, I hope, not without success, that this act of parliament gives to the Commons a peremptory right of rejection: that the other construction gives no remedy whatsoever for the mischief which occasioned its being passed, and cannot, by any possible course of proceeding, be carried into effect. I will take the liberty now of giving an answer to some objections relied upon by the counsel for Mr. James, and I will do it with a conciseness, not, I trust, disproportioned to their importance.

They say, that a peremptory rejection in the Commons takes away all power whatsoever from the Board of Aldermen. To that I answer, that the fact and the principle is equally against them:—the fact, because that board is the only body from which a Lord Mayor can be chosen, and has, therefore, the very great power that results from exclusive eligibility; the principle, because, if the argument be that the Lord Mayor and Aldermen ought to have some power in such election, by a parity of reason, so ought the Commons, who, if they can reject only for a legal incapacity, will be clearly ousted of all authority whatsoever in such election, and be reduced to a state of disfranchisement by such a construction.

The gentlemen say, that your lordships can only inquire into the *prima facie* title, and that the claim of Mr. James is, *prima facie*, the better claim.

I admit, my lords, you are not competent to pronounce any judgment that can bind the right. But give me leave to observe, first, that the question upon which you yourselves have put this inquiry, is a question applicable only to the very right, and by no possibility applicable to a *prima facie* title.

One of your lordships has declared the question to be, "Whether, by the common law, a mere power of approbation or rejection can supersede a power of election?" If that question is warranted in assuming the fact, give me leave to say, that the answer to it goes directly to the right, and to nothing else: for if the Commons are bound by law to assign a cause of rejection, and have not done so, Mr. James has clearly the legal right of election, and Mr. Howison has no right or title whatsoever.

But I say further, the mode of your inquiry makes it ridiculous to argue that you have not entered into any disquisition of the right Why, my lords, examine witnesses on both sides? Why examine the books of the corporation? Why examine into every fact relating to the election?

I cannot suppose, my lords, that you inquired into facts, upon which you thought yourselves incompetent to form any decision; I cannot suppose you to admit an extra judicial inquiry, by which the members of a corporation may be drawn into admissions, that may expose them to the future danger of prosecution or disfranchisement.

I hope, my lords, I shall not be deemed so presumptuous as to take upon me to say why you have gone into these examinations; it is not my province to justify your lordships' proceeding. It stands upon your own authority; I am only answering an argument, and I answer it by showing it inconsistent with that proceeding.

Let me, my lords, pursue the idea a little further. Are you only inquiring into a *prima facie* title? What is a *prima facie* title? I conceive it to be a title, not which may possibly be found a good one upon future examination, but which is good and valid, and must prevail, unless it be opposed and defeated by another, which may possibly be adduced, but which does not then appear. So in ejectment, for instance, a plaintiff must make a title, or he is non-suited. If he makes out a legal title *in omnibus*, the court declares it a *prima facie* title—that is a title conclusive as to the right, unless a better shall be shown; and accordingly, calls on the defendant to show such better title, if he can. The moment the defendant produces his title, the question of *prima facie* title is completely at an end, and the court has no longer any question to decide upon but the very merits; and this for a plain reason: the question, whether *prima facie* a good title or not, is decided upon the single ground that no other title then appears with which the title shown can be compared. In short, my lords, " whether *prima facie* good," is a question confined only to the case of a single title, and cannot be applied, without the grossest absurdity, to a case where you have both the titles actually before you. It may be the question in case of a single return; in case of a double return, as here, it cannot by any possibility be the question.

But, my lords, let me carry this a little farther yet. You have both the titles before you. You have yourselves declared that the question turns upon the construction of this act of parliament, which enacts also, " that it shall be deemed a public act in all courts, and in all places."

Now it is contended, the construction of the act is *prima facie*, in favour of Mr. James.

May I presume to ask, what does the *prima facie* construction of statute import? It must import, if it import any thing, that meaning which, for aught then appearing, is true; but may possibly, because of something not then appearing, turn out not to be so. Now, nothing can possibly be opposed to that *prima facie* construction, save the act itself. A *prima facie* construction of a statute, therefore, can be nothing but the opinion that rises in the mind of a man, upon a single reading of it, who does not choose to be at the trouble of reading it again. In truth, my lords, I should not have thought it necessary to descend to this kind of argumentation, if it had not become necessary for me to do so, by an observation coming from your lordships—" That the letter of the act would bear out the Commons in their claim, but that the sound construction might be a very different thing." I will, therefore, add but another word upon this subject: if a *prima facie* construction be sufficient to decide, and if the Commons have the letter of the law in their favour, I would ask, with the profoundest humility, whether your lordships will give the sanction of your high authority to a notion, that in statutes made to secure the liberties of the people, the express words in which they are written, shall not be at least a *prima facie* evidence of their signification?

My lords, the learned counsel have been pleased to make a charge against the citizens of Dublin " for their tests and their cavalcadings" on a late occasion; and they have examined witnesses in support of their accusation. It is true, my lords, the citizens did engage to the public and to one another, that they would not vote for any candidate for corporate office, or popular representation, who had any place in the Police establishment. But I would be glad to know by what law it is criminal in freemen to pledge themselves to that conduct which they think indispensably necessary to the freedom of their country? The city of Dublin is bound to submit to whatever mode of defence shall be levised for her by law, while such law shall continue unrepealed.; but would be glad to learn, by what law they are bound not to abhor the Police institution, if it appears to them to be an institution, expensive and ineffectual, inadequate to their protection, and dangerous to their liberty; and that they do think it so, cannot be doubted. Session after session has the floor of the senate been covered with their petitions praying to be relieved against it, as an oppressive, a corrupt, and therefore an execrable establishment.

True it is, also, my lords, they have been guilty of those triumphant processions, which the learned counsel have so heavily condemned. The virtue of the people stood forward to oppose an attempt to seize upon their representation, by the exercise of a dangerous and unconstitutional influence, and it succeeded in the conflict; it routed and put to flight that corruption which sat, like an incubus, on the heart of the metropolis, chaining the current of its blood, and locking up every healthful function and energy of life. The learned counsel might have seen the city pouring out her inhabitants, as if to share the general joy of escaping from some great calamity, in mutual gratulation and public triumph. But why does the learned counsel insist upon this subject before your lordships? Does he think such meetings illegal? He knows his profession too well not to know the reverse. But does he think it competent to the Lord Lieutenant and Council of Ireland, to take cognizance of such facts, or to pronounce any opinion whatever, concerning the privileges of the people? He must know it is not. Does he then mean that such things may be subjects of your resentment, though not of your jurisdiction? It would have been worth while, before that point had been pressed, to consider between what parties it must suppose the present contest to subsist. To call upon the government of the country to let their vengeance fall upon the people for their resistance of unconstitutional influence, is surely an appeal not very consistent with the virtuous impartiality of this august assembly. It is only for those who feel defeat to feel resentment, or to think of vengeance.

But suppose for a moment, (and there never ought to be reason to suppose it) that the opposition of the city had been directly to the views or the wishes of the government. Why are you, therefore, called upon to seize its corporate rights into your hands, or to force an illegal magistrate upon it? Is it insinuated that it can be just to punish a want of complaisance, by an act of lawless outrage and arbitrary power? Does the British constitution, my lords, know of such offences, or does it warrant this species of tyrannical reprisal? But, my lords, if the injus tice of such a measure is without defence, what argument can be offered in support of its prudence or policy? It was once the calamity of England to have such an experiment made by the last of the Stuarts, and the last of that unhappy race, because of such experiments. The several corporations of that country were stript of their charters; and what was the consequence? I need not state them; they are notorious yet, my lords, there was a time when he was willing to relinquish what he had so weakly and wickedly undertaken; but there is a time when concession comes too late to restore either public quiet or public confidence; and when it amounts to nothing more than an acknowledgment of injustice; when the people must see, that it is only the screen behind which oppression changes her attack, from force to fraud—from the battery to the mine. See, then, my lords, how such a measure comes recommended; its principle, injustice; its motive, vengeance; its adoption sanctioned by the authority of a tyrant, or the example of a revolution.

My lords, the learned counsel has made another observation which I cannot pass without remark; it is the last with which I shall trouble you. He says the Commons may apply to the law, and bring an information in *quo warranto*, against Mr. James, though you should give him your approbation; that is, my lords, your judgment does not bind the right, it only decides the possession of the office. To this I answer, that, in this case, to decide on the possession is, in fact, to decide the contest; and I found that answer on the high authority of the noble lord,* who was pleased to say, that "when the city had spent three years in the King's Bench, she would probably grow sick of the contest." I was not surprised, my lords, to hear an expression of that regret which must arise in every worthy mind, and I am sure the noble lord sincerely felt, at the distress of a people reduced to defend those rights which ought never to have been attacked, and to defend them in a way by which they could not possibly succeed. The truth is, as the noble lord has stated, the time of Mr. James's mayoralty would expire in year, and the question of law could not be terminated in three; the present contest, therefore, cannot be decided by law. How, then, my lords, is it to be decided? Are the people to submit tamely to oppression, or are they to struggle for their liberties? I trust, my lords, you will think they have not done any thing so culpable as can justify the driving them to so calamitous a necessity; for fatal must that struggle be, in whatsoever country it shall happen, in which the liberties of a people can find no safety but in the efforts of vindictive virtue, fatal to all parties, whatever may be the event. But, my lords, I feel this to be a topic on which it is neither my province nor my wish to expatiate; and I leave it the more willingly, because I know that I have already trespassed very long upon your patience, and also, because I cannot relinquish a hope, that the decision of your lordships, this day, will be such as shall restore the tranquillity of the public mind, the mutual confidence between the government and the people, and make it unnecessary for any man to pursue so painful a subject

* The Lord Chancellor

Ponsonby followed on the same side, and Smith replied The Privy Council in a few days, decided for Alderman James, but he resigned, and on the 5th of August Howison's name was sent down from the Aldermen, approved by the Common Council (the numbers being 97 to 6), approved by the Privy Council, too, and thus this strange struggle ended in the utter defeat of the government.

It is right to add some other facts. On the 16th of July, in the Common Council, Mayor Tandy carried (after violent opposition from Gifford) seventeen resolutions censuring the Privy Council, Aldermen, and, among other things, summoning a meeting of freemen and freeholders at the Exchange. This meeting was held on the 20th of July. Hamilton Rowan in the chair, was addressed by many persons of influence, and, after appointing a committee to prepare a state of facts, adjourned to the 3rd of August. On the latter day the State of Facts was read (an admirable document, which I subjoin, as an epitome of the prevalent opinions) and Alderman James's resignation was announced. The meeting was addressed at great length by Sir Edward Newenham, in reply to an audacious speech delivered by Lord Chancellor Fitzgibbon, in the House of Peers, on the 24th of July, and published in Faulkner's Journal. Of course Newenham treated it as a pamphlet of the printer's, and lashed it well. On the previous day (the 2nd of August), the Whig Club had met, and, in a report, drawn up apparently by Grattan, had attacked Fitzgibbon, with still greater severity. This was natural; for, in his speech, Fitzgibbon, having read a resolution of the Whig Club, approving the conduct of the Common Council, had proceeded to insult the club, until Lords Charlemont and Moira avowed the resolution, and drove him to the appearance of argument. The following, from the *Whig Club* Report is interesting.—

"That we have been charged by the author of the speech with the crime of looking to power, we make no assertion. Instead of assertion we set forth the following measures to which we are all pledged.

"A Place bill,—a Pension bill,—a bill to repeal or modify the City Police bill,—a bill to restrain the minister from arbitrarily extending the County Police,—a Responsibility bill, —a bill to disqualify the dependant Officers of the Revenue from voting for members of Parliament. We are pledged to disallow the corrupt charges of the Marquis of Buckingham and his successor. We are pledged against the sale of peerages, and for the liberty of the press, and the personal liberty of the subject against arbitrary and illegal bail. We are pledged to the principles whereon the late parliament addressed his Royal Highness the Prince of Wales to take on himself the Regency, and against the assertions and principles that advanced and maintained, in the appointment of a Regent, the authority of the parliament of another country, and would have denied to the Irish crown its legislative power, and, of course, its imperial dignity. We are pledged against a Union: we are pledged against the memorable Propositions; and we are now pledged to oppose the misconstruction or the alteration of the act of the 33rd of Geo. II., whereby the Commons of this city have peremptory right of rejection, which peremptory right we will support. If any thing is here omitted, it will be found in our original declaration; and we have already appointed a committee to procure copies of the bills already mentioned, that the country may, if she leases, adopt them, or at least may know how far, and how specifically we are embarked in her interest. We have no personal animosity; but should any of the ministers of the crown attempt to trample on the people, WE ARE READY TO DEFEND THEM."

Fitzgibbon had made himself so unpopular, that the guild of merchants, who had, in the previous winter, voted him an address in a gold box, for services to their trading interests, expunged the resolutions on the 13th of July, as "disgraceful."

Here is the state of facts above referred to :—

* *Aggregate Meeting of the Citizens of Dublin, held at the Royal Exchange, on Tuesday, the 3rd of August*, 1793, *pursuant to the adjournment of the 20th of July last*

ARCHIBALD HAMILTON ROWAN, Esq., in the chair.

"The report of the Committee appointed to draw up a State of the Case of the Citizens of Dublin, was delivered in by Sir Edward Newenham, one of the representatives of the county, and was read by the Chairman.

"That it appears that the citizens of Dublin at large had originally the election of its magistrates, until ousted by a bye-law.

"That in the reign of Charles II., when the revenues were surrendered to the crown for ever, the power of making regulations for the different Corporations was given to the Lord Lieutenant and Council, and certain new rules were made accordingly.

"That by one of those rules the right of electing a Chief Magistrate, for the City of Dublin, was given to the Board of Aldermen, subject to the approbation of the Lord Lieutenant and Council.

"That in the latter part of the reign of Queen Anne, the use which the Lord Lieutenant and Council made of this power, was an attempt to introduce disaffected men into the magistracy, and to exclude men of Whig principles, and well affected to the constitution and the present Royal Family, 'and, in their place, to introduce men devoted to the their administration.

ELECTION OF LORD MAYOR OF DUBLIN.

"That this constitution, which had not proved sufficient to secure to the magistracy proper and safe men, was the cause of great discontent among the citizens, to remedy which a bill in the 33rd year of the late King passed into a law.

"That by this bill no man can be Mayor who is rejected by the Commons of the Common Council. That on certificate of that rejection, the Board of Aldermen must send down another person, and so on, from time to time, until the Commons shall approve. That there is no restriction in the act on the rejection by the Commons, save only that they must approve of some one Alderman.

"That if the Board of Aldermen or the Commons offend against the requisites set forth in the act, the body offending loses, for that turn,—the right of election, if the Board of Aldermen; and of rejection, if the Commons: and the other body, that has conformed to the law, acquires the absolute right of choosing the Lord Mayor.

"That notwithstanding these clauses, an opinion has been advanced by the Board of Aldermen and their Counsel, which supposes that the Commons cannot reject any Alderman without assigning, as grounds for their rejection, some corporate or legal disability.

'That we have examined the act, and can find no such clause.

'That we have examined precedents, and we find that there is no precedent for any such thing; on the contrary, the precedents are against it.

"That in 1763, soon after making the act, the Commons rejected Alderman Barré, and assigned no reason.

"That they rejected him a second time in the said year, and assigned no reason; and that the Board of Aldermen submitted, and sent down Alderman Forbes, who was approved of and was Lord Mayor.

"That in this year the Commons in April rejected Alderman William James, and the Board sent down another and another Alderman, without demanding reasons.

"That the Council act under words the same as those under which the Commons proceed, save only that there are some further clauses and stronger expressions in favour of the right of the Commons, and yet the Council did, in the year 1711, repeatedly reject the Lord Mayor of Dublin, without assigning reasons: that they rejected in 1763 the Lord Mayor, sent up by the Board on one part, and by the Commons on the other, and assigned no reasons. That in the present year, they in May rejected both Alderman James and Alderman Howison, and assigned no reasons. That in June they rejected the same, and assigned no reasons: that they have now rejected Alderman Howison, and assigned no reason.

"That if the Commons must assign, as ground for their rejection, corporate or legal incapacities in the person so rejected, the Commons receive from the clause in the act, no power or authority whatsoever.

"That we cannot find the cause or this construction in the act, and must look for it somewhere else; that we apprehend the citizens have given offence to his Majesty's Ministers, and particularly those who at present direct the government of this country.

"That we have examined our conduct and our hearts, and we declare to God and to our country, that however conscious we are of coming under the displeasure of those men, we are not conscious of having deserved it.

"That we do acknowledge, that for the last ten or eleven years the citizens of Dublin did take an active part for the liberty of their country; that in 1780 they supported, to the utmost of their power, a Declaration of Right, which those who now principally direct the government of this kingdom resisted, but that we do not repent the part we then acted; on the contrary, we rejoice in it, and aver, with all humility, but with truth, that if the people of Ireland in general, and the citizens of Dublin in particular, had not taken an active part on that occasion, we do conceive that the exertions and abilities of those who now principally direct our government, and enjoy a superior degree of power and profit under that free constitution which they opposed, would have prevailed against the liberties of their country.

"That we do acknowledge, in 1785, when those very persons proposed to give back that liberty, in a scheme, consisting of twenty Propositions, the citizens of Dublin did take a very decided part against said system, and bore their share in the honour of defeating and confounding that wicked attempt; and though they might have given cause by that conduct to the resentment of the abettors of that project, and also to certain low and insolent expressions at that time pronounced, yet we do not repent of our conduct. We had rather suffer in common with the rest of our countrymen, under any description of abuse, however opprobrious and petulant, than under the stings of our conscience, reproaching us for supporting that most disgraceful surrender of our rights, which was proposed in said twenty propositions.

"That on the late question of the Regency, the citizens of Dublin took an humble and dutiful, but a firm and constitutional part, and made their protest against those dangerous and slavish doctrines, which affected to say, that the British Parliament could make a Regent for Ireland, and that his Majesty legislated in Ireland, not as King of Ireland, but as King of Great Britain; and that the great seal of England had powers in this country superior to the imperial crown thereof.

"That in protesting against such doctrines, we conceive we only did our duty, and we

Low repeat our entire approbation of these principles, on which his Royal Highness the Prince of Wales was called upon by the two Houses of the Irish Parliament, to take on himself the Regency of this country without unconstitutional and capricious restrictions; and in opposition to the above-mentioned unconstitutional and arbitrary notions—notions tending to prejudice the dignity of the Royal Family, and, at the same time, to deprive this country of a proud opportunity of exercising the powers of her free constitution, and also of manifesting her affection and loyalty.

"That we do also acknowledge to have expressed our approbation of the conduct of the minority of the two Houses of the late Parliament in the last session, and so far to have taken a part in condemning the attempts on the liberty of the Press, and on the personal liberty of the subject, by holding him to arbitrary and illegal bail; attempts made by the ministers of justice, and screened from inquiry by those of the crown. We also acknowledge by that approbation to have taken a part in condemning the late corruption and profusion practised by our Ministers, in the creation of useless offices, salaries, and pensions, and likewise in the sale of peerages, in order to buy seats in the House of Commons, by selling those in the House of Lords.

"That the citizens appear justified in entertaining such a conviction, viz. :—That those measures had no other view, meaning, or object, save corruption only: first, because said measures bespoke nothing else; secondly, because the nation was told so by the highest authority, in a threat, signifying that members of parliament should be made victims of their vote, which accordingly was the case; and afterwards again told by another very high authority, in a declaration which averred, that in order to defeat an opposition in parliament, this nation had been, in the administration of his late Excellency the Marquis of Townshend, bought in by the government, and sold by the members of parliament for half a million, and that if opposition continued to the present administration, this nation must be bought and sold again.

"That under such authority we could not but think ourselves warranted in expressing our approbation of those who resisted such a wicked practice; for we cannot conceive a stronger challenge or summons to the people than such a declaration.

"That we do acknowledge the Freedom of the city of Dublin refused to his Excellency the Earl of Westmoreland, was refused because it was perceived that the measures, the men, and the principles which had disgraced his predecessors, were countenanced and continued under his government; and in those disgraceful circumstances of his government it was imagined that any testimony of approbation would not have given credit or dignity to Lord Westmoreland, but would have lessened the character of the city.

"That we do not deny that many among us did, on a former occasion, favour the scheme of Protecting Duties, but we utterly deny and disclaim having any share in approving of the outrages which followed that proposal; nor can we imagine how our approbation of laying Protecting Duties, can, without great inconsistency, render us obnoxious to his Majesty's ministers, seeing that the person who was the author of the attempt, and the cause of what followed it, has since received the encouraging marks of Royal favour and bounty.

"But that the chief cause of the displeasure of his Majesty's ministers seems to be our opposition to the corruption intended by an act, entitled an act for the better regulating the police of the city of Dublin—That we do solemnly declare it to be our sincere opinion, that the great object and design of the contrivers of the police bill was to extend over the city of Dublin corruption both in the corporation and among the citizens thereof; and we are authorized in entertaining such an opinion, because we know such corrupt influence to have been exercised over both, and such a criminal and corrupt use to have been made of that bill by its contrivers and abettors; and if on the last election such attempts did not succeed, it was because the virtue of the citizens of Dublin was superior to that of those persons who had pretended to frame bills for their regulation.

"That we beg leave to mention, that this bill has cost, since the establishment of the police, about £20,000 a year, and we leave it to our fellow-subjects whether the protection received from said police has been adequate to the expense thereof. We beg leave also to mention that notwithstanding the various extravagant and criminal charges proved to have been made under colour of said bill, no one commissioner nor divisional justice has been discharged by government, but has continued—they to give their votes for government, and government to give them every countenance and approbation, notwithstanding said scandalous expenditure of the public money.

"That however inadequate the Police bill has been to destroy the free representation of the city, it has proved fully equal to the purpose of securing a part of the corporation to all the purposes of the minister, and if that minister shall succeed in destroying the right of the Commons to reject an Alderman elected Mayor by the board, in that case, the minister (having a majority at the board) does in truth and in effect appoint the Lord Mayor for the city of Dublin.

"That we do acknowledge that tests were taken and circulated, relative to said police—that, in consequence thereof, different corporations have been threatened with the loss of their franchises, their books sent for; and their freemen examined, in order to find out criminal matter to subject the corporation to the loss of franchise; so that we have reason to apprehend this attack on one particular privilege to be but a beginning, and that there is an intention, if not speedily checked, of a more general seizure of the franchises of the city.

"That we apprehend, if tests and associations against the corrupt purposes of power are punishable, that every association, and particularly those some years since entered into—the Non-Consumption, and the Non-import Association, and, likewise, the Volunteer Association—may be held a ground for criminal prosecution; and we fear, also, that every test proposed to candidates for a seat in parliament, and every resolution touching their election or conduct, may be held illegal and criminal; nor do we know of any description of men who have taken a part in the business of the public, that may not be included in said crime.

"That it is now above one hundred years since the charters of the subjects of Great Britain and Ireland were attacked; that we are not conscious of giving any pretence for reviving such desperate practices; that so little are we conscious of giving such a pretence, so convinced are we of our innocence, and the innocence of those tests which have been taken, that we do, with much humility, adopt and repeat them, and we, accordingly, declare, that we approve of the conduct of the Commons of the Common Council, in withholding their approbation in favour of any police magistrate; and, further, that in every capacity in which we shall be, we will endeavour to procure the repeal of that mischievous act of parliament. And, further, as we conceive the corruption and violence of ministers have not been confined to the city, but have extended to the kingdom at large · to defend the same, we solemnly declare—

"That we will not vote for any person who will not support a place bill; a pension bill: a bill to make his Majesty's ministers responsible; a bill to disqualify revenue officers from voting for members to serve in parliament; a repeal of the police acts. Nor shall we vote for any person who does not support the redress of grievances, viz.:—tho war charges imposed by the late Lord Lieutenant, and continued by the present; the sale of honours arbitrary and illegal imprisonment; arbitrary and illegal demands of bail; infringement of the privileges of the Commons of the city of Dublin. Finally, we declare, we will not vote for any person who does not promise that he never will assent to the misconstructions of the statute of the 33rd of George II., whereby no person can be the Lord Mayor of Dublin, who is rejected by the Commons.

"Resolved unanimously—That this meeting do most heartily concur with the report of the committee, and do submit the same to the consideration of our fellow-subjects at large.

"Resolved unanimously—That the warmest thanks of this meeting be presented to those respectable personages, his Grace the Duke of Leinster, the Earls of Charlemont and Moira, and other members of the Whig Club, for their manly, spirited, and constitutional support of the laws of the land, and the privileges of the citizens of Dublin; and we cannot avoid expressing our concern that any thing disrespectful should have been offered to them in the discharge of their duty to their country.

"Resolved unanimously—That the thanks of this meeting be voted to the independent jury who refused to find TRUTH A LIBEL, on the late prosecution of a printer.

"Sir Edward Newenham, at the request of the meeting, having taken the chair,

"Resolved—That the thanks of this meeting be given to our worthy chairman, Archibald Hamilton Rowan, Esq., for his spirited and proper conduct in the chair.

"Mr. Rowan having resumed the chair,

"Resolved unanimously—That the report of the committee, and the proceedings of this day, be published; and that this meeting do now adjourn.

Signed by order,
"MATT. DOWLING. Sec."

GOVERNMENT CORRUPTION.

February 12th, 1791.

On this day Curran made another attempt to probe the impurities of government.

[Mr. Curran observing the house thin, and the gallery crowded, began by lamenting that curiosity seemed to act more powerfully on the public than a sense of duty on the members of the house. After saying a few words on his motives in making the intended motion, he stated its importance as going to induce inquiry into a crime which must, if not punished and prevented, ultimately effect the destruction of the society in which it was suffered; it was raising men to the peerage for money, which was disposed of to purchase the liberties of the people.]

A man who stands forth an accuser in a case like this ought to be received by the house as its best friend, or, if his accusation should prove unfounded and malicious, then the heaviest indignation of the house should fall on him. When a motion of similar import was proposed on a former day, I could not suppose that it would have met with opposition; but finding it has been opposed, I think the house must have objected to its form, and that they were unwilling to enter into an inquiry wherein the honour and privileges of the Lords, as well as those of this house, are concerned, without their lordships' concurrence.

I am not inclined, after what has passed so recently on this subject, to expatiate on the enormity of the act, nor on the wretched situation of those miserable men who are, by it, introduced into this house, like beasts of burden, to drudge for their employers—the humble instruments and pliant tools of power. Still less am I inclined to depict the situation of those who are introduced into the other, clothed in the robes of justice, to frame laws, and dispose of the property of the kingdom, under the direction of that corruption by which they have been raised. It would be more useful to consider what should be done at such a crisis, and what is the duty of the house: and this duty is not difficult to be ascertained—it is not to be cited from volumes of law; we are the grand inquest of the nation—it is, therefore, our duty to inquire into the alleged offence. Every man capable of sitting on a Grand Jury is adequate to the inquiry; the oath of the Grand Juror suggests their duty—*not to suppress from malice, nor find from favour.*

I have heard it affirmed that common fame is not sufficient ground to nstitute this inquiry; but, on the principle of the constitution, I do assert that common fame is a full and sufficient ground of inquiry; and I appeal to the house—to the kingdom—whether any report can be more prevalent, or more credited, than that such corrupt contract as I have mentioned, was entered into by administration.

But I rest not on common fame—I have PROOF, and I stake my character on producing such evidence to a committee as shall fully and incontrovertibly establish the fact, that a contract has been entered into by the present ministers to raise to the peerage certain persons, on condition of their purchasing a certain number of seats in this house. This evidence, however, I will not produce, till a committee shall be appointed; for no man can suppose that a man who is rich enough to purchase a peerage is not rich enough to corrupt the witnesses, if I should produce them at the bar, before an inquiry is instituted.

I call on any lawyer to say, whether a man professing himself ready to prosecute, and staking himself to convict, would not, in any court, be admitted to go into trial? I call on lawyers to answer this question, for on this it depends, not whether the culprits shall be tried, but whether the Commons of Ireland shall be acquitted. I call on you to be cautious in your decision of this question, for you are in the hearing of a great number of the people of Ireland.

The Speaker called to order, and informed him it was unparliamentary to allude to strangers—that there was a standing order, which excluded strangers, and if any allusions are made by a member, he must enforce the order. Sir H. Cavendish also spoke to order, and censured Mr. Curran's language as highly disorderly.

Mr. Grattan did not think this doctrine was consistent with the nature of a popular assembly, such as the House of Commons. He quoted an expression of Lord Chatham's, in support of this opinion, who, in the House of Peers, where such language was certainly less proper than in a House of Commons, addressed the Peers:—" My Lords, I speak not to your Lordships—I speak to the public and to the constitution." The expression, he said, was, at first, received with some murmurs, but the good sense of the house and the genius of the constitution justified him.

Mr. Curran—I do not wish to use disorderly language, but I am concerned for the honour of the house, which is degraded by becoming accomplices in a crime so flagrant ; this induces me to remind you that you are in the presence of the public.

Chair again called to order, and must clear the house if any allusion to strangers

I do not allude to any strangers in the gallery, but to the *constructed presence* of the people of Ireland. I call on the house to fix their eyes on four millions of people, whom a sergeant-at-arms cannot keep unacquainted with your proceedings. I call on you to consider yourselves as in the presence of the majesty of the people—in the immortal presence—and not to give impunity to guilt, either from consciousness of participation, or from favour to the criminal.

I direct your attention to the people without doors, because that people must now have contracted a habit of suspicion at what passes within these walls. In the course of two sessions the constitution of Britain has been demanded in the name of the people and refused. It is the wisdom of Great Britain to restrain the profusion of public money for corrupt purposes, by limiting her pension-list. It is the wisdom of Great Britain to preclude from her senate men whose situations afford ground to suspect that they would be under undue influence. It is the wisdom of Britain that certain individuals should be responsible to the people for public measures. These were demanded by the people of Ireland, but the wisdom, certainly not the corruption, of this house has denied them.

To have claims of alleged right continually overborne by a majority may induce credulous minds to suppose the house corrupt. Another circumstance may contribute to give strength to the suspicion. We have enjoyed our constitution, such as it is, but eight years, and in the course of that time, there has been twice that number of attacks made on it ; and now those very gentlemen spend their nights in patriotic vigils to defend that constitution, whose patriotic nights were formerly spent in opposing its acquisition. These circumstances naturally lead the public mind to suspicion—they are corroborated by another no less remarkable. An honourable baronet*—a man *fleshed* in opposition—one who had been emphatically called the *arithmetic* of the house—to see such a man march to join the corps of the minister, without any

S.r Henry Cavendish, the notorious slave of Government, as Tone calls him.

assignable motive for the transition—as if tired of explaining the orders of the house—of talking of the majesty of the people, of constitution, and of liberty—to-day glorying in his strength, rejoicing like a giant to run his course, and to-morrow cut down; and nothing left of him but the blighted root from which his honours once had flourished. These are circumstances which, when they happen, naturally put the people on their guard. I exhort the house to consider their dignity, to feel their independence, to consider the charge I lay before you, and to proceed on it with caution and with spirit. If I charge a member of your house, with a crime which I am ready to prove, if you give me an opportunity, and am ready to submit to the infamy of a false accuser if I fail—then to screen such a man, and not permit me to prove his guilt—is yourselves to convict him, and convict him of all the guilt and baseness of a crime, allowing him no chance of extenuation from the circumstances of the case.

Now I say again, we have full proof to convict; I have evidence unexceptionable, but if you call on me to declare this evidence, I will not do it until you enter on the inquiry. I have some property in this country; little as it may be, it is my all: I have children, whom I would not wish to disgrace—I have hope—perhaps more than I have merit; all these I stake on establishing my charge. I call on you to enter on the trial. [After a very long and able speech, Mr. Curran moved—" That a committee be appointed, consisting of members of both houses of parliament, who do not hold any employment, or enjoy any pension under the crown, to inquire, in the most solemn manner, whether the late or present administration have, directly or indirectly, entered into any corrupt agreement with any person or persons, to recommend such person or persons to his Majesty, for the purpose of being created Peers of this kingdom, on consideration of their paying certain sums of money, to be laid out in the purchase of seats for members to serve in parliament, contrary to the rights of the people, inconsistent with the independence of parliament, and in direct violation of the fundamental laws of the land."]

[He afterwards made an observation or two on the declaration of the Lord Chancellor, when he sat in that house, that it cost government half a million to beat down the aristocracy, and would cost them another to beat down the present, and concluded by saying, that should the motion be agreed to, it would be necessary, in the next place, to send a deputation to the Lords, to desire their concurrence.]—*Debates*, vol xi., pp. 154—7

A debate of great length and ability followed, wherein Barrington made a furious speech against the motion; after which Mr. Curran again rose, and replied:—

The subject of the present motion, however diffused or perplexed in the course of this debate, whether through ignorance or design, has yet reduced itself within a very narrow extent; and I am fortified in my opinion of the necessity of the resolution by the idle arguments and the indiscreet assertions which have been urged against it. Administration has resisted it with every tongue that could utter a word; every legal gentleman has spoken, but all agree on the criminality of selling the independency of this house for the honours of the other,—of trafficking an abject and servile commoner for a plebeian peerage,—of selling the representatives of the people like beasts of labour,—and of exalting to the high dignity of the other assembly a set of scandalous purchasers, a disgrace to the nobility, and a dishonour to the crown. The guilt, then, being confessed, the question must be, whether we have sufficient foundation for inquiry into the fact. We have stated that we are in possession of evidence to convict the actual offenders, by proving the fact upon them. I stand here in my place, a member of your house, subject to your power, subject to the vengeance which your justice shall let fall upon my head, the accuser of that which you confess to be a crime of the basest and blackest enormity. I stand forth, and I repeat to you, that there have been very lately direct contracts entered into for selling the honours of the peerage for money, in order that the money so obtained should be employed in buying seats for persons to vote for the sellers of these honours. I assert the fact, and I offer, at the expense of every thing that can be dear to man, to prove the charge. Will the accused dare to stand the trial, or will they admit the charge by their silence, or will this house abandon every pretence to justice, to honour, or to shame, by becoming their abettors? But perhaps gentlemen give weight and credit to the objections of those who have opposed my motion. Late as I see it is, perhaps they may wish to have their objections examined. A right honourable gentleman [the Attorney-General] has objections, he says, to the substance, and also to the form. We have not grounds, he says, for such an inquiry: on a former night he thought common fame was no ground for parliamentary inquiry; he thought at that time, the parliament of the first and second of Charles the First a riotous assembly: he now only thinks the authority of that parliament which differs directly from his opinion, is lessened by the disturbance of the times. Does the learned gentleman think that the commotion occasioned by the desperate violence of state offenders can diminish the authority of those proceedings by which they are brought to justice? If he does not think so, his objection has no weight, even in his own opinion, and ought to have as little in yours. But let me take the liberty of telling him that the answering my proposition upon only part of its merits, is but a pitiful fallacy. Yet into such has that very respectable member, I must suppose unintentionally fallen. I have not moved upon common fame only; I move on the offer of proving the fact by evidence in my possession. But if I had moved merely on common fame—I say that if no parliamentary precedent had existed, you ought to make the precedent now. Unless you abdicate the power, or abandon your duty as the grand inquest of the nation, you must inquire on weaker grounds than those on which I have now proposed to you. If you will not inquire until, as the learned member says, there has been proof of the charge, he should have told you that an offender should be convicted before his trial: if this principle were carried further, in capital cases the offender should be hanged, before you bring him to trial. Or does he think you have at least as much power, and as strong a duty as an ordinary grand jury? Yes, Sir, the great principle is very little different; like them, you ought not to present from malice, or suppress from favour; like them, a probability of guilt is sufficient to put the accused on his trial; like them, you may present on your own knowledge, without any evidence upon oath; like them, you ought to collect that probability from the ordinary grounds of probability that will impress themselves on any reasonable mind. Now, I ask, can any good ground be stronger than the universal belief of the nation? Is there a man in this house that has not heard the minutest circumstances of those scandalous transactions? Has any honourable member in this house laid his hand on his heart and declared his disbelief of the fact? Will any member now say, upon his honour, he does not believe it? But he says it is a libel on the King, the Lords, and Commons: I answer, it is, if false; I answer, it is a scandal, whether false or not.

I add, if it be, you have a false accuser before you, or a guilty criminal, whom in common justice you ought to punish. You can convict the former only by trying the latter. I challenge that trial. But are there no circumstances to corroborate the common fame that is dinning this libel into the ears of the people? or to justify them in suspecting that unfair practices have been used in obtaining the present influence of administration. During the whole of last session we have, in the name of the people of Ireland, demanded for them the constitution of Great Britain, and it has been uniformly denied. We would have passed a law to restrain the shameful profusion of a pension-list— it was refused by a majority. We would have passed a law to exclude persons who must ever be the chattels of the government, from sitting in this house—it was refused by a majority. A bill to make some person, resident among you, and therefore amenable to public justice, responsible for the acts of your governors, has been refused to Ireland by a majority of gentlemen calling themselves her representatives. Can we be so vain as to think that the bare credit of those majorities can weigh down the opinion of the public on the important subject of constitutional right. Or must not every man in his senses know that the uniform denial of what they look upon to be their indefeasible rights, must become a proof to them that the imputation of corrupt practices is founded in fact. Now, Sir, if the honourable gentleman's objections in point of substance are not to be supported—if, in short, the fact charged is highly criminal—if you are competent to inquire into it— if you have all the ground that can be expected—does he treat himself or the house as he ought, when he makes objections of form? But see what those are. We cannot, he says, appoint a committee of both houses—we have power only over our own members. I answer the fact of the objection does not exist. We affect no authority over the Lords by the resolution I propose. The parliamentary course in Great Britain is first to move for a joint committee, and then to send a message to the Lords to apprise them thereof, and to request their concurrence. But he says it is interfering with their privileges. I answer, the offence I state is an outrage upon them as well as upon us, and therefore it is peculiarly proper to invite their lordships to join us in an inquiry that affects both houses equally. The man must be wretchedly ignorant indeed, who does not know that such joint committees have been appointed in England, on various occasions, both before and since the revolution. Such a committee you find on their journals so early as the reign of Henry the Fourth—such you find previous to the prosecution of Lord Strafford—such you find on the subject of the India charter, previous to the impeachment of the Duke of Leeds, in 1695. What, then, becomes of those objections in form or in substance? But another right honourable gentleman [the Prime Sergeant*] put his objection on a single point, which, if answered, he will vote for my motion. I accept the condition, and I claim the promise. I ask him, where he found the distinction? Lawyers here seem fond of authorities. But he has cited none. Having, then, none of his own, let him submit to profit by mine. In those I have already cited there was no previous ascertainment of the fact any more than of the offenders, save what arose from public common notoriety. [Here Mr. Curran adverted to the particular circumstances of those transactions, to show that there was not and could not have been any evidence, either as to the crimes or the delinquents, until the inquiry actually began.] But the learned member seems to think the crime should first be proved by witnesses. I ask him if he was prosecuting for the crown would he be so incautious as to disclose his evidence before the actual trial? The honourable gentleman, then, has opposed me upon a distinction unsupported by precedent, and unsupportable by argument or principle. [Mr. Curran then examined the arguments of the Solicitor, which went nearly on the same ground that had already been taken.] One new observation which the learned member has produced from a legal man, I am sorry is not to the question in debate. The learned member, it seems, was surprised to find a motion for reforming the senate, come from the representative of a borough. If the mover of such a resolution was a man who had, in any instance, since he was a member of this house, deserted the principles he professed, or betrayed his trust, the observation would have weight, however the honourable member is mistaken in thinking the fault of the representative a demerit in the constitution; but if I have done none of those things, I cannot but regret the strange simplicity of argument of the honourable gentleman, who comes forward with a weapon which can wound nobody but himself. [Mr. Curran then went through a number of less important objections, which had been advanced by gentlemen on the other side.] I am sorry to find the honourable gentlemen of my own profession have not given more ground to vindicate the constitutional independency of that profession. The science of the law inspires a love of liberty, of religion, of order, and of virtue. It is like every seed, which fails or flourishes, according to the nature of the soil. In a rich, and fertile, and ardent genius, it is ever found to refine, to condense, and to exalt. In milder temperaments it cannot be fairly judged of at a particular side in a popular assembly. Far from thinking the silence or the unsuccessful speeches of some of my learned

* Hon James Fitzgerald.

brethren as a stain upon their profession, I think the reverse. I think it proves how strongly they are impressed with the demerits of their cause, when they support it so badly; and I feel pleasure in seeing what honourable testimony is borne by the disconcertion of the head, to the integrity of the heart. If, indeed, those professional seeds had been sown in a poor, gross, vulgar soil, I would expect nothing from it but a stupid, graceless, unprincipled babble—the goodness of the seed would be destroyed by the malignity of the soil, and the reception of such a profession into such a mind could form only a being unworthy of notice, and unworthy of description, unless, perhaps, the indignation of an indiscreet moment, observing such an object wallowing in its favourite dirt, should fling it against the canvass, and produce a figure of it depicted in its own filth. As for my part, if such a description of unhappy persons could be found to exist, and should even make me the subject of their essays, I would pass them with the silence they deserve, happy to find myself the subject, and not the author of such performances. I cannot sit down without reminding gentlemen of one curious topic in which I have been opposed. It has been stated that, in a former administration, the Peerage and the Bench were actually exposed to sale. If so, the motion cannot be resisted, without an indelible stain upon the character of the house. I am willing to extend the limits of the inquiry, to take in those persons who may have been guilty of such a crime: let them be the subjects of the same inquiry, and, if they be guilty, of the same punishment.—*Debates*, vol. xi., pp. 183—8.

Curran's motion was lost, by 147 to 85.

CATHOLIC EMANCIPATION

February 18th, 1792.

Curran was the unchanging friend of religious liberty. The Catholics had vainly prayed for a relaxation of the Penal Code, till the destruction of the British armies in America—then they succeeded. Again they prayed for further relaxation; their prayer was supported by Grattan and Curran, and failed, till, in 1792-3, when Wolfe Tone had worked up Catholic organization, and the French armies began to conquer, when they gained fresh privileges.

The proceedings on the 18th of February, on the Roman Catholic Relief Bill, are most remarkable. They began by the presentation of a petition from the Protestants of the County Antrim for the bill. A conversation on their admission to Trinity College then occurred, which is so important as to deserve quotation:—

Mr. Grattan gave notice, that in addition to the privileges now about to be granted to the Roman Catholics, the power of becoming Professors of Botany, Anatomy, and Chemistry, should be given.

Hon. Mr. Knox said, he also intended to propose that they should be permitted to tak the academic degrees in the University of Dublin.

Hon. Denis Browne rose to say, he would second both these intentions.

The Attorney-General said, under the present laws of the University, Roman Catholics could not be admitted to take degrees without taking the oaths usually taken by Protestants. As the University is a corporation deriving by charter under the crown, and governed by laws prescribed by its founder, it would not be very decorous for parliament to break through those laws; but the king might, if such was his pleasure, direct the College to dispense with these oaths; and, in his opinion, it would be wise to do so.

Mr. Knox said, it was not his intention to infringe upon any prerogative of the crown, but he could not see how this proposal was an infringement, as the bill must, in its ultimate stage, pass under the inspection of the crown, and receive the royal assent. Nevertheless, if any gentlemen of the University would rise and say, that the wish of the University was to have these impediments removed, he would then not think it necessary to make the motion.

Sir Hercules Langrishe—The bill is intended to remove certain disabilities which the Catholics (by law) labour under. Now, there is no law as to this point: When it became necessary for me, in framing the bill, to search through the laws relative to education, I found there was no law to prohibit Roman Catholics from taking degrees, but the rules o the University itself; these rules can be changed, whenever the crown shall think proper, but it would be very unbecoming for the parliament to interfere. As to the principle there can be no difference of opinion; we differ only as to the mode of carrying it into effect.

Doctor Browne (of the College)—I am unable to say what the sentiments of the heads of the College are upon this subject, as they have not informed me; but the reason the right honourable gentleman has stated is certainly the true reason why Roman Catholics are not admitted to degrees. If it shall be deemed expedient to admit them, the College must be much enlarged, and a greater number of governors must be appointed. My own sentiment is, that such a measure would tend much to remove prejudices, and to make them coalesce with Protestants. This is my own sentiment, and the sentiment of several persons of the University; but I cannot say whether it be the sentiment of the majority. If the house shall think the measure expedient, they may address his Majesty to remove the oath which bars them from taking degrees.

After the presentation of a petition, by Mr. Egan, for the restoration of the elective franchise, the discussion on the bill proceeded. The speeches of Michael Smith, Hutchinson Grattan, and Curran, gave the bill most powerful support. One of the boldest and finest speeches was that of the Hon. George Knox—a man too little remembered.

Mr. Curran—I would have yielded to the lateness of the hour, my own indisposition, and the fatigue of the house, and have let the motion pass without a word from me on the subject, if I had not heard some principles advanced which could not pass without animadversion. I know that a trivial subject of the day would naturally engage you more deeply than any more distant object of however greater importance but I beg you will recollect, that the petty interest of party must expire with yourselves, and that your heirs must be not statesmen, nor placemen, nor pensioners, but the future people of the country at large. I know of no so awful call upon the justice and wisdom of an assembly, as the reflection that they are deliberating on the interests of posterity. On this subject, I cannot but lament, that the conduct of the administration is so unhappily calculated to disturb and divide the public mind, to prevent the nation from receiving so great a question with the coolness it requires.

At Cork, the present viceroy was pleased to reject a most moderate and modest petition from the Catholics of that city. The next step was to create a division among the Catholics themselves; the next was to hold them up as a body formidable to the English government, and to their Protestant fellow-subjects; for how else could any man account for the scandalous publication which was hawked about this city, in which his Majesty was made to give his royal thanks to an individual of this kingdom, for his protection of the state. But I conjure the house to be upon their guard against those despicable attempts to traduce the people, to alarm their fears, or to inflame their resentment. Gentlemen have talked, as if the question was, whether we may, with safety to ourselves, relax or repeal the laws which have so long coerced our Catholic fellow-subjects? The real question is, whether you can, with safety to the Irish constitution, refuse such a measure? It is not a question merely of their sufferings or their relief—it is a question of your own preservation. There are some maxims which an honest Irishman will never abandon, and by which every public measure may be fairly tried. These are, the preservation of the constitution upon the principles established at the revolution, in church and state; and next, the independency of Ireland, connected with Britain as a confederated people, and united indissolubly under a common and inseparable crown. If you wish to know how these great objects may be affected by a repeal of those laws, see how they were affected by their enactment. Here you have the infallible test of fact and experience; and wretched, indeed, must you be, if false shame, false pride, false fear, or false spirit, can prevent you from reading that lesson of wisdom which is written in the blood and the calamities of your country. [Here Mr. Curran went into a detail of the Popery laws, as they affected the Catholics of Ireland.] These laws were destructive of arts, of industry, of private morals and public order. They were fitted to extirpate even the Christian religion from amongst the people, and reduce them to the condition of savages and rebels, disgraceful to humanity, and formidable to the state.

[He then traced the progress and effects of those laws from the revolution in 1779.] Let me now ask you, how have those laws affected the Protestant subject and the Protestant constitution? In that interval were they free? Did they possess that liberty which they denied to their brethren? No, Sir; where there are inhabitants, but no people, there can be no freedom; unless there be a spirit, and what may be called a pull, in the people, a free government cannot be kept steady, or fixed in its seat. You had indeed a government, but it was planted in civil dissension, and watered in civil blood, and whilst the virtuous luxuriance of its branches aspired to heaven, its infernal roots shot downward to their congenial regions, and were intertwined in hell. Your ancestors thought themselves the oppressors of their fellow-subjects, but they were only their gaolers, and the justice of Providence would have been frustrated, if their own slavery had not been the punishment of their vice and their folly. But are these facts for which we must appeal to history? You all remember the year one thousand seven hundred and seventy-nine. What were you then? Your constitution, without resistance, in the hands of the British parliament: your trade in many parts extinguished, in every part coerced. So low were you reduced to beggary and servitude as to declare, that unless the mercy of England was extended to your trade, you could not subsist. Here you have an infallible test of the ruinous influence of those laws in the experience of a century: of a constitution surrendered, and commerce utterly extinct. But can you learn nothing on this subject from the events that followed? In 1778 you somewhat relaxed the severity of those laws, and improved, in some degree, the condition of the Catholics. What was the consequence even of a partial union with your countrymen? The united efforts of the two bodies restored that constitution which had been lost by their separation. In 1782 you became free. Your Catholic brethren shared the danger of the conflict, but you had not justice or gratitude to let them share the fruits of the victory. You suffered them to relapse into their former insignificance and depression. And, let me ask you, has it not fared with you according to your deserts? Let me ask you if the parliament of Ireland can boast of being now less at the feet of the British minister, than at that period it was of the British parliament? [Here he observed on the conduct of the administration for some years past, in the accumulation of public burdens, and parliamentary influence.] But it is not the mere increase of debt; it is not the creation of one hundred and ten placemen and pensioners that forms the real cause of the public malady. The real cause is the exclusion of your people from all influence upon the representative. The question, therefore, is, whether you will seek your own safety in the restoration of your fellow-subjects, or whether you will choose rather to perish than to be just? I now proceed to examine the objections to a general incorporation of the Catholics. On general principles no man can justify the deprivation of civil rights on any ground but that of forfeiture for some offence. The Papist of the last century might forfeit his property for ever, for that was his own, but he could not forfeit the rights and capacities of his unborn posterity. And let me observe, that even those laws against the offender himself, were enacted while injuries were recent, and while men were, not unnaturally, alarmed by the consideration of a French monarchy, a Pretender, and a Pope; things that we now read of, but can see no more. But are they disaffected to liberty? On what ground can such an imputation be supported? Do you see any instance of any man's religious theory governing his civil or political conduct? Is Popery an enemy to freedom? Look to France, and be answered. Is Protestantism necessarily its friend? You are Protestants; look to yourselves, and be refuted. But look further: do you find even the religious sentiments of sectaries marked by the supposed characteristics of their sects. Do you not find that a Protestant Briton can be a bigot, with only two sacraments, and a Catholic Frenchman a Deist, admitting seven? But you affect to think your property in danger, by admitting them into the state. That has been already refuted; but you have yourselves refuted your own objection. Thirteen years ago you expressed the same fear, yet you made the experiment; you opened the door to landed property, and the fact has shown the fear to be without foundation.

But another curious topic has been stated again; the Protestant ascendancy is in danger. What do you mean by that word? Do you mean the rights, and property, and dignities of the church? If you do, you must feel they are safe. They are secured by the law, by the coronation oath, by a Protestant Parliament, a Protestant king, a Protestant confederated nation. Do you mean the free and protected exercise of the Protestant religion? You know it has the same security to support it. Or do you mean the just and honourable support of the numerous and meritorious clergy of your own country, who really discharge the labours and duties of the ministry? As to that, let me say, that if we felt on that subject as we ought, we should not have so many men of talent and virtue struggling under the difficulties of their scanty pittance, and feeling the melancholy conviction that no virtues or talents can give them any hope of advancement. If you really mean the preservation of every right and every honour that can dignify a Christian priest, and give authority to his function, I will protect them as zealously as you. I will ever respect and revere the man who employs himself in diffusing light, hope, and consolation. But if you mean by ascendancy the power of persecution, I detest and abhor it. If you mean the ascendancy of an English school over an Irish university, I cannot look upon it without aversion. An ascendancy of that form raises to my mind a little greasy emblem of stall-fed theology, imported from some foreign land, with the graces of a lady's maid, the dignity of a side-table, the temperance of a larder, its sobriety the dregs of a patron's bottle, and its wisdom the dregs of a patron's understanding, brought hither to devour, to degrade, and to defame. Is it to such a thing you would have it thought that you affixed the idea of the Protestant ascendancy? But it is said, admit them by degrees, and do not run the risk of too precipitate an incorporation. I conceive both the argument and the fact unfounded. In a mixed government, like ours, an increase of the democratic power can scarcely ever be dangerous. None of the three powers of our constitution act singly in the line of its natural direction; each is necessarily tempered and diverted by the action of the other two; and hence it is, that though the power of the crown has, perhaps, far transcended the degree to which theory might confine it, the liberty of the British constitution may not be in much danger. An increase of power, to any of the three, acts finally upon the state with a very diminished influence, and, therefore, great indeed must be that increase in any one of them which can endanger the practical balance of the constitution. Still, however, I contend not against the caution of a general admission. Let me ask you can you admit them any otherwise than gradually? The striking and melancholy symptom of the public disease is, that if it recovers at all, it can be only through a feeble and lingering convalescence. Yet even this gradual admission your Catholic brethren do not ask, save under every pledge and every restriction which your justice and wisdom can recommend to your adoption.

I call on the house to consider the necessity of acting with a social and conciliatory mind. Contrary conduct may perhaps protract the unhappy depression of our country, but a partial liberty cannot long subsist. A disunited people cannot long subsist. With infinite regret must any man look forward to the alienation of three millions of our people, and to a degree of subserviency and corruption in a fourth. I am sorry to think it is so very easy to conceive, that in case of such an event, the inevitable consequence would be an union with Great Britain. And if any one desires to know what that would be, I will tell him. It would be the emigration of every man of consequence from Ireland; it would be the participation of British taxes, without British trade; it would be the extinction of the Irish name as a people. We should become a wretched colony, perhaps leased out to a company of Jews, as was formerly in contemplation, and governed by a few tax-gatherers and excisemen, unless, possibly, you may add fifteen or twenty couple of Irish members, who may be found every session sleeping in their collars under the manger of the British minister.—*Debates*, vol. vii., pp. 174—178.

EGAN v. KINDILLAN

Mr. Charles Phillips, from whose brilliant "Recollections of Curran" I print this speech, gives the following account of the case in which it was made. I could not find the date.

" 'The case of 'Egan against Kindillan' for seduction, was tried before Lord Avonmore. It was a case of a very singular nature. Miss Egan was a young lady of some accomplishments, and great personal beauty. Mr. Kindillan was then a dashing young officer in a dragoon regiment, nearly related to the late Lord Belvidere. The reader will find the principal circumstances of the trial detailed indignantly in Mr. Curran's speech; but it is necessary to apprise him that Kindillan was first vindictively prosecuted for the offence in a criminal court, and escaped through the great exertions and genius of his immortal advocate, who, however, in the civil action, was only able to mitigate the damages down to £500. After the plaintiff had gone through his case, Mr. Curran proceeded:—"

My lords, and gentlemen of the jury—I am in this case counsel for the defendant. Every action to be tried by a jury, must be founded in principles of law; of that, however, the court only can determine, and upon the judgment of the court, you, gentlemen, may repose with great confidence. The foundation of this action is built upon this principle of law, and this only, that the plaintiff suffered special damage by losing the service of his daughter, who has been taken away from him; for you, gentlemen, will err egregiously, and the court will tell you so, if you imagine that the law has given any retribution by way of damages for all the agony which the father may suffer from the seduction of his child. However, I do not mean to make light of the feelings of a parent; he would be a strange character, and little deserving the attention of a court, who could act in that manner; to see his gray hairs brought with calamity to the grave, and yet hold him out as a subject of levity or contempt. I do no such thing; but I tell you soberly and quietly, that, whatever his feelings may be, it is a kind of misery for which the law does not provide any remedy. No action lies for debauching or seducing a daughter, but only for the loss of her service it the same time, over and over again, that the only ground is the special circumstance of the loss of her service—at the same time, gentlemen, I agree implicitly in the idea of letting the case go at large to you. In every injury, which one man sustains from another, it is right to let all circumstances, which either aggravate or diminish the weight of it, go to the jury. This case has been stated in evidence by two persons. Miss Egan has told, I think, the most extraordinary story—

Lord Chief Baron—The most artless story I ever heard.

Mr. Curran—I do not allude to her credit; I only say I never heard so extraordinary a story, because I never heard of an instance of a young woman, decently bred, arrived at eighteen, going away with a man, after a single conversation; having no previous acquaintance—

no express promise; abandoning her father's house, protection, and care, after two conversations, in which there was not one word of marriage; without a previous opportunity of engagement: without a possibility of engaging her affections or seducing her from her father, she embraces the first opportunity which was given to her; therefore, indeed, I am astonished. I said, gentlemen, the case ought rightly to go before you—I tell you why—circumstances which compose the enormity of an offence of this kind can be judged by you. If you receive a man into your house, give him access to any female in your family, and he converts that privilege to abuse her virtue, I know nothing of greater enormity. If you admit a man to your house and your table, and he avails himself of that confidence to abuse the virtue of your daughter or your wife, I know of no length to which the just indignation of a jury might not be carried. But if there be no such criminality on the part of the defendant? if he was rather the follower than the mover of the transaction? His conduct may be palliated, it cannot be condemned. Look at this case, even as stated by the witness herself. Who was the seducer? Mr. Kindillan! Where was the single act to inspire her with a single hope, that he intended to marry her? Why steal away from her father's house—why go to a public inn, at a common sea-port, even at that age, and with that degree of understanding you see her possess? She confesses she suspected there was no design of marriage; that at Aungier-street he spent a night with her, and no design of marriage; they cohabited week after week, and no conversation of marriage till they leave their mother country, and arrive at the Isle of Man—and then from whom does it move? not from her who might have talked even with a degree of pride, if she thought he took her away from her father:—"You have robbed me of a father, under the promise of becoming my husband—give me that protector!" No: you find it moving from him, from his apprehension of her dissatisfaction. If you can believe that, what kind of education must she have received? She throws herself into the arms of the first officer she ever saw; flies into a hackney-coach, and goes to another country, and never talks of marriage till she arrives there. To talk of the loss of a father is a very invidious subject; every father must feel an argument of that kind. But it is not because that one man suffers, another must pay. It is in proportion to his own guilt that he must be punished, and therefore it is that the law denies the right of the father to receive compensation. It is an injury which can rarely arise, when the father has discharged the precedent part of his duty. It is wise, therefore, that the law should refuse its sanction to an action of that sort, because it calls upon the father to guard against that event, for which he knows he can have no reparation. I guards more against the injury by discountenancing the neglect which may give it birth; it refuses a compensation to reward his own breach of duty. Only see what would be the consequence if the law gave its sanction to an action of this sort. This man is in the army. I am not here to preach about morals; I am talking to men who may regret that human nature is not more perfect than it is but who must take men as they are. This man goes to a watering-place; he sees this young woman, full of giddiness and levity—no vice possibly, but certainly not excusable in any female; see how she conducts herself.— "Have you considered the proposal?" "No," says she, "our acquaintance is too short;"—but the second conversation, and she is gone. How would any of you, gentlemen, think of your child, if she picked up a young buck whom she never saw before? what would your wife say, if she was told her daughter had picked up a man she did not know? But you know mankind—you know the world. What would you think of a woman, unmarried, who held a conversation on these terms? If at Philipsborough you addressed a young woman, with whom not a word of marriage passed, and yet she accompanied you without hesitation—would you suppose her a girl of family and education, or would you not rather suppose her to be one of those unfortunate, uneducated creatures, with whom a conversation very different from that of marriage takes place? This, then, is the situation of the defendant; he yields, more seduced than seducing. It is upon this the father calls to you for damages! For an injury committed—by whom? from what cause? From the indiscreet behaviour, the defective education, and neglected mind of his daughter. He can have no feeling, or he would not have exposed both her and himself; or, if he have any feelings, they are such as can be gratified by you, gentlemen of the jury—they are such as can be calmed by money! He can find more enjoyment in pecuniary compensation, than in other species of retribution! I speak harshly—I am obliged to do so; I feel it. It is to be decided by you with liberality and justice between such a father and the defendant. I am stating these things, supposing you believe her. Her story is well delivered—it would be extraordinary if it were not, when it has been so often repeated. The defendant was tried for his life, and twelve men upon their oaths acquitted him of the charge, though the fact was sworn to by her. Her sufferings and her beauty may make an impression upon your minds; but, gentlemen, you are not come here to pity, but to give a verdict; not from passion, but which may be the calm result of deliberation between party and party. There is a kind of false determination of mind, which makes dupes of judicial men upon cases which involve more sentiment than speculation. If you can feel any such sensation in your minds, glowing and heating to a degree of violence in which reason may be consumed, let me entreat you to guard against its falling upon the head which ought not to suffer. We are not to determine by zeal, but judge by discretion. It is not her tears, her heavings, her sighs, that must influence your sentence. She has been brought up a second time by her father, and exhibited before you, the unhappy object of vice and of wantonness. She has thus been exhibited by that father, whose feelings are represented as so tender—an exhibition which ought to have been avoided by a sincere parent. But let me expose the silly trap, that you may not be the dupes of such artifice. It was a simple case it could have been proved without her testimony; the leaving her father's house could have been proved by many; and of the finding her in the defendant's possession there was sufficient evidence, and the service could be proved as well by any person as herself. But the circumstances are proper for consideration: give me leave to say, there are no circumstances more proper for consideration than the motives of the man who brings the action. What his conduct was, appears by her own evidence; she goes away with a man—he is seized and called upon to marry her, under the terror of a prosecution for his life, a species of inducement such as never was heard of. Let it not be told, that a case of this kind,—that the unsolicited elopement of a young, unfortunate woman yielding to criminal desires, going off with an officer upon a first acquaintance, is an example to be held up by a court and jury, or to be sanctioned by a verdict; that a loose girl, coming back from the cloyed appetite of her paramour, should make welcome her return to her father's house by the golden showers of compensation. If you wish to hold up examples to justify elopements of your children, establish it by your verdict! and be answerable for the consequence; you will resolve yourselves into a fund for unportioned wantons, whose fathers will draw upon you for fortunes; you will establish an example. I am not ashamed to be warm—I do not sell my warmth, though I may my talents; but give me leave to tell you that an example of this kind, where no abuse of confidence can be pleaded, no treachery alleged, would go thus far, that every miserable female who parades about your streets in order to make a miserable livelihood by the prostitution of her person, will come forward under the imposing character of a witness, because there is scarce any of them who has not a father that may bring an action. Let me warn you against another case: you will establish an example by which the needy father is encouraged, first, to force the man into marriage under the apprehension of a prosecution, or afterwards to compel him from the dread of a verdict, unless you think that the man could be reconciled to marry a girl he is tired of, and who has added perjury to the rest of her conduct. It is hard to talk of perjury; but how will they answer for the verdict of twelve honest men upon their oaths? Impeach her credit, because she is swearing this day to the fact, in opposition to the verdict of twelve men; she swore to it upon the prosecution, because of terror from her father, expecting to receive death from his hands, unless she warded it off by perjury. Have you not heard her swear that he forced her into the King's Bench with a knife in his hand? After he has failed to affect the life of the defendant, he makes a desperate attempt at his property, through the means of a jury—is this a case for a jury? She goes off unsolicited, she seeks the opportunity, and yet Mr. Kindillan is to be the victim! A young man who meets a woman, goes to a tavern, and indulges his appetites at the expense of the peace, quietness, and happiness of a family, you may wish to see reformed; but be he whose son he may, he cannot be punished in this way for such conduct. Will you lay your hands on your hearts and say, whether the defendant has been more to blame than Miss Egan herself? She has suffered much—her evidence shows it; at first from her terror of her father, now in preserving her consistency, to see her exposed as she was on the table. But has the defendant suffered nothing? Is it suffering nothing to be put in fear of his life? to have the horrors of a prison to encounter? Is it nothing, what he must have suffered in point of property? He comes now, to resist this last attempt, after all the others, to drive him, by robbing him of his property, to marry the daughter. Would you, gentlemen, advise your sons to marry under such circumstances? I put it boldly to you—answer it. and your answer will be your verdict. After ten weeks voluntary cohabitation, would you advise him to marry? or would you ensure a reasonable prospect of conjugal fidelity afterwards? Let me not take up your time; we will call witnesses to discredit what she has sworn; let me say in excuse for her, for what she said upon her oath, that she came forward under the terror of her father's power. Certain it is, that a sense of female honour should not have had more influence upon her when in the other court, where she was vindicating herself, than here where she comes to put money into her father' pocket. The consequence of large damages is this: you will encourage every man to neglect the education of his child; making a fortune by dropping a seed of immorality in the mind of the female, which may ripen into that tree of enormity, that will be cut down, not to be cast into the fire, but for the father's benefit. A girl of eighteen, whose father forced her upon this table, whose sufferings have been brought upon her by the leprosy of her morals, is not to be countenanced. If you wish to point out the path to matrimony through dishonour, and you think it better that your daughter should be led to the altar from the brothel, than from the parent's arms, you may establish that by your verdict. If you think it better to let the unfortunate author of her own misery benefit by the example she may hold up, you will do it by such a verdict as your understanding, not your passion, dictates

WAR WITH FRANCE.

January 11th, 1793.

On the 10th of January, Lord Westmoreland opened Parliament with a speech full of momentous statements, and notable omissions. It complained of the discontent of Ireland, but said nothing of the corruption, extravagance, and alien policy of Ministers, which had provoked the fierce cry for Reform. It complained of the invasion of Holland by France, but was silent of the European conspiracy against the young Republic—a conspiracy which, having been defeated in a war which it had opened with a view to level Paris, prepared larger forces to avenge itself and the Bourbons. And it recommended a relaxation of Catholic fetters, but did not connect therewith the motives of the advice:— Custine had conquered the Rhine,* Dumourier had won the battle of Jemappes,† and annexed Belgium. The speech also stated that government had increased the military establishment, and it recommended the formation of a Militia. This last was a stroke at the Volunteers. The Address, moved by Lord Tyrone, and seconded by John O'Neill, was, of course, an echo to the speech. Grattan moved a trivial amendment. His speech was eminently bold and able, and I give one passage, illustrative of the time:—

"I have heard of seditions writings of Mr. Paine, and other writers. These writings may be criminal, but it is the declarations of the ministers of the crown that have made

---

* October 21st, 1792. † November 6th, 1792.

them dangerous. Mr. Paine has said monarchy is a useless incumbrance, a minister of the crown comes forth, and says he is right—monarchy cost this country, to buy the Parliament, half a million at one period, half a million at another. Mr. Paine has said an hereditary legislative nobility is an absurdity—our minister observes he has understated the evil; it is a body of legislators whose seats are sold by the ministers to purchase another body of legislators to vote against the people; but here is the difference between Mr. Paine and our authors—the latter are ministers, and their declaration evidence against their royal master. They say we love monarchy—we love the king's government, which, however, we must acknowledge, governs by selling one house, and buying the other. So much more powerful agents of republicanism are the Irish ministers than such authors as Mr. Paine, that if the former wished to go into rebellion in '93 as in '82—some of them went into sedition—they could not excite the people to high treason, by stronger provocation than their own public declarations; and the strongest arguments against monarchial government, are those delivered by themselves, in favour of their own administration."—*Debates*, vol. xiii. pp. 7, 8.

Before giving the meagre report which exists of Curran's speech, it is needful to remind the reader of the form which the political elements of Ireland had taken. The majority of the people—the Catholics—whose petition of 1790 had been kicked out of the Commons, had acquired spirit and organization. The latter they peculiarly owed to Wolfe Tone, and both in a great degree to him, to John Keogh, Byrne, Todd Jones, and M'Cormick. The Catholic Committee negotiated with the government, and as the successes of France compensated to them for the baseness of their aristocracy, they seemed about to obtain all they sought —complete Emancipation. Powerfully assisting them, though formed primarily to gain Parliamentary Reform, were the United Irishmen. The bolder Dissenters of Belfast, sympathising with France, and inspired by the possession of a Volunteer army, looked to forming an Irish Republic; so did Tone, the founder of the Club: but the purpose of the mass of members was limited to Reform, till Ministers showed they preferred rebellion.

In opposition to the Catholic Committee, and the United Irishmen, the government stimulated Protestant bigotry and Catholic division. Out of doors they got the exclusive Corporation of Dublin to address the other Irish Corporations against Emancipation, and they intrigued with the aristocracy (lay and clerical) of the Catholics. In parliament they found the relics of the old exclusion party. Flood was no longer there* to repent of his error in resisting the increase of his nation by three millions; but those who had not his genius, or his virtue, or his capacity for improvement, were there to misquote his example; and there were crowds besides who were ready to mimic the contortions of fanaticism for money, place, or title. The Minister got an Emancipation bill passed which left division and weakness behind—left the Protestants some wrongs, to guard—the Catholics many favours to cringe for. He got 20,000 regulars and 16,000 militia, a Gunpowder bill, and a Secret Committee. Thus armed he commenced his crusade of prosecuting and persecuting, obtained fresh laws from time to time, and, after the truce of 1795, drove the quarrel to an insurrection and an Union.

Mr. Curran—I wish to call the attention of the house to our public situation abroad and at home. We are on the eve of a war with France, and are the part of the empire most likely to be the scene of it, and to feel its dreadful effects. It is a war of that kind which resembles nothing in the memory of man. It is not a war of any definite object; nor does it look to peace on any definite terms. The mode of carrying it on is as novel as its object: a war, in which a strange political fanaticism was the precursor of arms; a war to be resisted only by the union of the British empire, and probably encouraged on the part of France by a sense of its disunion. For, at the moment when the British minister should have held out to French ambition the united resistance of the British empire, at that moment the voice of three millions of the Irish nation was heard declaring to the throne, that they laboured under a slavery which was too terrible to be long endured, and that, of course, our enemies had not any such united resistance to apprehend. Our object, then, is, in the first instance, to take away such a hope from our enemies, and such a danger from ourselves, by making that union com-

* Flood died December 2nd, 1791.

ple. By no other means can the empire act with the necessary energy; by no other means can the executive power of the empire provide for its preservation. To this great end every jealousy should be laid aside. The smallest attack from without must bring you to the earth, if you are already unpoised and reeling with intestine discord. You must make your government strong; and to do that, you must unite your people—and to do that, you must destroy those foolish distinctions that have separated them from each other—and you must change that conduct that has destroyed their confidence in this house and in this administration.

An honourable baronet [Sir John Parnel] has very fairly admitted that even the parliament has become unpopular in the country. I have a very high opinion of that gentleman's talents and integrity, but I differ with him in thinking that the speeches of opposition have occasioned that unpopularity; on the contrary, the government has become unpopular and odious by its corruption and weakness, and the credit of parliament has become a victim to the same cause. How could the credit of parliament survive its independency? And where is the latter to be found? What portion of the property or sense of the people can be found in the present deplorable state of this house? Deplorable I will call it; for I differ much from those who reproach gentlemen for not acting with more principle than they showed. A great number—much more than half of us—have no manner of connexion with the people. We represent their money. But what money? That of which the possession makes them rich and independent? No; but that which they have parted with, and thereby become poor and dependent. What, then, can we represent but that poverty, and the cries of those wants which we have lost the honest means of relieving—the cries of nature for that bread which we have sold in order to become senators? Let no man blame us for acting as we do. As little let any other trader think this political traffic more beneficial than his own. If he should, let him observe the progress and the profit of this traffic:—Sir Francis sells his estate and buys a seat; brings madam and miss to town, where, I dare say, they are likely to make many edifying discoveries; is introduced to a minister, who, as the right honourable secretary says of himself—and, I am sure, justly—knows not how to be uncivil to any man. Well, Sir, Sir Francis takes a squeeze for a promise, and, full of future place, comes down and speaks for the good of the nation. He soon finds he has unluckily neglected one necessary preparation—the learning to read: his eloquence cannot live long upon "hear him." He finds he is better anywhere than on his legs; he, therefore, betakes himself to his seat—pops his chin upon his stick—listens and nods with much sapience—repays his "hear him," and walks forth among the "ayes," with good emphasis and sound discretion. Thus he works on for seven sessions, and, at last, gets not one place, but three places ——in the stage-coach, for himself, and madam, and miss, to go back to a ruined farm, with ruined healths, and ruined morals; unworthy and unfit for the only society they can have; a prey to famished wants and mortified pretensions; with minds exactly like their faded Castle silks

—the minds too feeble to be reformed, and the gowns too rotten to be scoured. Sir, I join in the laugh, that, I find, I have unintendingly drawn upon this melancholy picture. I intended it as an appeal to compassion and forgiveness. I intended it as an answer to the obloquy which has been, unthinkingly, cast upon us. How can the people, Sir, blame a man for acting unwisely or unworthily for the nation, who does not act wisely or worthily for himself? Or what right have the people to question the conduct of any man who does not represent them? Sir, it comes shortly to this: the disunion of the people from this house arises from this—the people are not represented. And to restore the union, you must have the people restored to a fair representation; in other words, by a radical reform of the Commons.

Sir, a most important question next arises; namely, what is the people? Is it the soil of Ireland, or the men who live upon it? I do not know of any moral or political quality that an acre of land can possess. And, therefore, for my part, I have no other idea of any country, with respect to its rights, than the aggregate of its inhabitants. In Ireland we have tried an experiment on another principle—namely, whether she could be free upon the exclusion of three fourths of her population; and we have found that she is not free, and that, therefore, she is disunited and infirm. Sir, upon this question, respecting our Catholic brethren, my opinion is most materially changed since the last session. I was then actuated by a compassion for their depressed and unhappy state. I knew and loved their virtues, their order, and their loyalty; and I was among the very small number who endeavoured to open the gates of the constitution, and receive them as my fellow-subjects and fellow-Christians. But I thought I was acting merely from regard to them; I now think that without them the country cannot be saved. The nation has felt this necessity, and I am a convert to it now. Bind them to equal exertion in the public cause, by giving them equal interest in it. Give them no qualified emancipation. I would not rely upon that man's defence of liberty, who can himself be content with equivocal freedom. Do this—emancipate your fellow-subjects, and reform their representation, and you unite Ireland with herself and with Great Britain, and you restore the energy of the empire when it needs it most.

Nor is this the first time that we have laboured in this house for this necessary reform. This reform consists of two parts: the one, external, by restoring the franchise of the elector; the other, as essential, by securing the independency of the representative. This we have laboured for in years past, but in vain; for this have we, in vain, pressed a place, a pension, a responsibility bill. In vain shall the people vote without for a member, if there is no law to guard his independency within. No, Sir, the vital principle of parliamentary reform was contained in those measures which we have pressed, and, therefore, has the whole force of administration been exerted to defeat them. [He then adverted to what had been said respecting the strength of administration.] I agree perfectly. It is the crisis of internal and external danger. A hated government, an unpopular parliament, a discontented people. I do not believe Great Britain is fairly apprised of our state.

If she were, I am confident she could not be so infatuated as to suffer these abuses, which have kindled the present flame in Ireland, and endanger the union between the two countries. [He then took a view of the persons and measures of the present administration, which, he said, was a system of incapacity and profligacy. He inveighed against the sale of the peerages, the attack on the charter of Dublin, and the corruption which, he said, was openly avowed in that house.] What avails your strengthening the people, by restoring their rights and their union, if you strengthen not the executive hand at this moment of danger, by restoring confidence in the administration? And how can you give them confidence in a set of simpletons, or clerks, or avowed enemies of the people, who are at once hated and despised? Talk not of union with England while such obstacles remain; think not of joining two nations with less skill than a carpenter must have in joining two boards together. He cannot glue them till he has cleaned the joint; nor can we unite two nations without removing the depravity that must eternally prevent their cohesion. Let us, therefore, have a government that can be honest and respected, and a senate that represents the people, and our union with England will be saved, in spite of all the efforts of fanaticism and sedition. Those who abuse their trust are they who render government odious, and give too specious a pretence to those incendiaries who wish to subvert all order, and introduce the despotism of anarchy and robbery under the name of reformation. Without such preachers, as the clerks who form this government become by their practices, the true principles of British constitution could never be defamed with effect; without the flagrant abuses that we see, sedition could have no pretext.

The Catholic petition has been rejected by the influence of the Irish administration. The principle of that rejection has been disavowed by the throne. Administration has now an interest distinct from the united wishes of the people and their sovereign. The present question, I feel is between a sovereign who has saved the people, and an administration who would have destroyed it. I will vote for that sovereign and that people. Their petition was rejected by those who called themselves their representatives; the next year that same petition passed over that parliament, and approached the throne. Had it been rejected there, there remained only one other throne for misery to invoke, and from that last and dreadful appeal, let it never be forgotten by Irish gratitude, that we have been saved by the piety and compassion of the father of his people. The opposition to the amendment I, therefore, consider conveys the sentiment which we feel of the profligacy which exposed us, and of the gracious interposition by which we have so providentially been preserved.—*Debates*, vol. xiii., pp. 43—6.

The amendment was carried unanimously.

PARLIAMENTARY REFORM.

9th February, 1793

ON the 29th January, we find Curran unsuccessfully resisting the Attorney-General (Arthur Wolfe's) motion, for the committal of M'Donnell, the printer of the *Hibernian Journal*, for publishing that the house was not free and independent; but his speech is not given. On the 14th of January, (so persuasive were French victories), Grattan obtained a Committee of the whole House on Parliamentary Representation; and on th day moved these moderate resolutions:—

"Resolved—That the representation of the people is attended with great and heavy charges and payments, in consequence of elections and returns of members to serve in parliament, and that said abuses ought to be abolished.

"Resolved—That of the three hundred members elected to serve in parliament, the counties, and counties of cities, and towns, together with the university, return eighty-four members, and that the remaining two hundred and sixteen are returned by boroughs and manors.

"Resolved—That the state of the representation of the people in parliament requires amendment."

But the opposition had yielded to Ministers indemnity for their violent proclamations against the Republican Volunteers; they had consented to Militia and Gunpowder Bills; and, therefore, the resolutions were resisted. There are two solemn lessons in this, as in the history of every one of our great epochs before or since: 1st—*That England's offers should be the signal for increased precaution and jealousy.* 2ndly—*That hypocritical loyalty in Ireland pioneers the way for genuine servility.*

Curran's speech is slightly reported:—

I was sorry to hear the sentiments delivered by Mr. Bushe, because I think them wrong; and, next, because I consider them as speaking the opinion of administration. The result of that gentleman's speech was to reprobate the idea of parliamentary reform altogether. This is not a time for sophistry or quibble. A member of parliament ought to leave his ingenuity at the door, and bring into the house nothing but his ingenuousness and integrity. We must be bespotted, indeed, if we think sophisms, which could not impose upon ourselves, can make dupes of the public. The question before us is the simplest imaginable. The house has come to a resolution of inquiring " into the state of the representation." The committee has now met accordingly. What did they meet to inquire into? Is it the merits of the House of Commons? No; every man knows the contrary: it is the defects of the representation complained of by the people, and admitted by the house itself. What, then, can the Chancellor of the Exchequer mean, by proposing a fulsome panegyric on the merits of a body, into whose defects they were ordered to inquire? If we do this we shall deceive nobody; not ourselves; not the people—they will despise and detest us, for the hypocrisy and effrontery of such a procedure. Parliament is at the very moment of crisis. The hope we held out of constitutional redress has held the disquiet of the public mind in suspense. Our present conduct must be decisive; it must fix the public hope of reform to parliament, or show the people they must look only to themselves. We have brought forward the first necessary step—the avowed abuse of parliament—the sale of boroughs. Is this a fact? If you deny it, we will show you that the great body of this house are sitting here for money, and not by election. If you admit the fact, will you say that it is not an abuse? If you stifle this by artifice, I say again, we shall become odious and contemptible to the nation, and they will look to themselves, and Ireland must take her chance of such constitution as may be made for her. If you do your duty, you may now form it yourselves.

A fair representation of the landed and commercial property of the nation, ought to be accomplished forthwith, as cautiously as may be, but certainly within this session; otherwise, it must be lost. The state of Ireland, at war, divided and dissatisfied, makes this peculiarly necessary at this juncture. But gentlemen desire a plan. I feel much indignation at this demand; to deny the disease, and demand the remedy, is ridiculously absurd. I should be sorry to see a plan introduced until the necessity was confessed; it would be silly while that necessity was denied. But I have another objection to the introduction of a plan; I think it ought to be subject to all the consideration within and without this house which the session will allow, and I think the house ought to ensure the continuance of the session for that great object. I have also another; the Catholic question must precede a reform. Their place in the state must be decided first.

The question is short, and will be decisive. Ireland feels, that without an immediate reform her liberty is gone   I think so, too. While a single guard of British freedom, either internal or external, is wanting, Ireland is in bondage. She looks to us for that great emancipation; she expects not impossibilities from us, but she expects honesty and plain dealing; and if she finds them not, remember what I predict —she will abominate her parliament and look for a reform to herself — *Debates*, vol. xiii., pp. 185—6

The motion was lost by 71 to 153.
A few days after (15th February) a Volunteer Convention met at Dungannon, and passed resolutions for Reform and Emancipation;—for arms and gunpowder would have been wiser.

HAMILTON ROWAN.

29th January, 1794

The Government proclamation, in the Autumn of '92, against the Volunteers, who had assumed French forms, was answered by the United Irishmen, in an address, written by Dr. Drennan, and signed by Rowan, as Secretary. For this, Rowan and Drennan were prosecuted. Rowan wanted Thomas Addis Emmet, and the Hon. Simon Butler, members of the society, to defend him; but they preferred Curran. The back of Curran's brief (I saw it a few years ago in a copy of this trial sold at an auction) contained these catchwords:—" To Arms—2nd. Reform—3rd. Catholic Emancipation—4th. Convention—now unlawful—Consequence of Conviction—Trial before Revolution—Drowned—Lambert - Muir—Character of R.—Furnace, &c.—Rebellion smothered stalks—Redeeming Spirit."
Here is the accusation:—

FOR ARCHIBALD HAMILTON ROWAN, ESQ.
COURT OF KING'S BENCH. JANUARY 29, 1794.

LIBEL.
ABSTRACT OF THE INFORMATION.
Be it remembered, that the Right Honourable Arthur Wolfe, Attorney-General of our present Sovereign Lord the King, gives the court here to understand and be informed, that Archibald Hamilton Rowan, of the city of Dublin, Esq., being a person of a wicked and tur

bulent disposition, did, on the 16th day of December, in the thirty-third year of the reign of our present Sovereign Lord George the Third, publish a certain false, wicked, malicious, scandalous, and seditious libel, that is to say:—

"'The Society of United Irishmen at Dublin, to the Volunteers of Ireland. William Drennan, chairman; Archibald Hamilton Rowan, secretary.

"'CITIZEN SOLDIERS—You first took up arms to protect your country from foreign enemies and from domestic disturbance; for the same purposes it now becomes necessary that you should resume them. A proclamation has been issued in England, for embodying the militia; and a proclamation has been issued by the Lord Lieutenant and Council in Ireland, for repressing all seditious associations. In consequence of both these proclamations, it is reasonable to apprehend danger from abroad and danger at home. From whence but from apprehended danger are these menacing preparations for war drawn through the streets of this capital? From whence, if not to create that internal commotion which was not found—to shake that credit which was not affected—to blast that volunteer honour which was hitherto inviolate—are those terrible suggestions, and rumours, and whispers, that meet us at every corner, and agitate, at least, our old men, our women, and our children? Whatever be the motive, or from whatever quarter it arises, alarm has arisen; and you, Volunteers of Ireland, are, therefore, summoned to arms at the instance of government, as well as by the responsibility attached to your character, and the permanent obligations of your institution. We will not at this day condescend to quote authorities for the right of having and of using arms; but we will cry aloud, even amidst the storm raised by the witchcraft of a proclamation, that to your formation was owing the peace and protection of this island; to your relaxation has been owing its relapse into impotence and insignificance; to your renovation must be owing its future freedom, and its present tranquillity. You are, therefore, summoned to arms, in order to preserve your country in that guarded quiet, which may secure it from external hostility, and to maintain that internal regimen throughout the land, which, superseding a notorious police or a suspected militia, may preserve the blessings of peace by a vigilant preparation for war. Citizen Soldiers, to arms! Take up the shield of freedom and the pledges of peace—peace, the motive and end of your virtuous institution. War, an occasional duty, ought never to be made an occupation; every man should become a soldier in the defence of his rights—no man ought to continue a soldier for offending the rights of others. The sacrifice of life in the service of our country is a duty much too honourable to be entrusted to mercenaries; and at this time, when our country has, by public authority, been declared in danger, we conjure you by your interest, your duty, and your glory, to stand to your arms, and, in spite of a police—in spite of a fencible militia—in virtue of two proclamations, to maintain good order in your vicinage, and tranquillity in Ireland. It is only by the military array of men in whom they confide—whom they have been accustomed to revere as the guardians of domestic peace—the protectors of their liberties and lives—that the present agitation of the people can be stilled, that tumult and licentiousness can be repressed, obedience secured to existing law, and a calm confidence diffused through the public mind, in the speedy resurrrection of a free constitution, of liberty, and of equality—words which we use for an opportunity of repelling calumny, and of saying, that by liberty we never understood unlimited freedom, nor by equality the levelling of property, or the destruction of subordination. This is a calumny invented by that faction, or that gang, which misrepresents the King to the people, and the people to the King; traduces one half of the nation, to cajole the other; and, by keeping up mistrust and division, wishes to continue the proud arbitrators of the fortune and fate of Ireland. Liberty is the exercise of all our rights, natural and political, secured to us and our posterity by a real representation of the people; and equality is the extension of the constituent to the fullest dimensions of the constitution—of the elective franchise to the whole body of the people—to the end that government, which is collective power, may be guided by collective will, and that legislation may originate from public reason, keep pace with public improvement, and terminate in public happiness. If our constitution be imperfect, nothing but a reform in representation will rectify its abuses; if it be perfect, nothing but the same reform will perpetuate its blessings. We now address you as citizens, for to be citizens you became soldiers; nor can we help wishing that all soldiers, partaking the passions and interests of the people, would remember that they were once citizens - that seduction made them soldiers, but nature made them men. We address you without any authority, save that of reason, and if we obtain the coincidence of public opinion, it is neither by force nor stratagem; for we have no power to terrify, no artifice to cajole, no fund to seduce. Here we sit, without mace or beadle—neither a mystery, nor a craft, nor a corporation. In four words lies all our power—universal emancipation, and representative legislature; yet we are confident, that on the pivot of this principle, a convention, still less, a society, still less, a single man, will be able first to move and then to raise the world. We, therefore, wish for Catholic emancipation without any modification, but still we consider this necessary enfranchisement as merely the portal to the temple of national freedom; wide as this entrance is—wide enough to admit three millions - it is narrow when compared to the capacity and comprehension of our beloved principle, which takes in every individual of the Irish nation, casts an equal eye over the whole island, embraces all that think, and feels for all that suffer. The Catholic cause is subordinate to our cause, and included in it; for, as United Irishmen, we adhere to no sect, but to society—to no cause, but Christianity—to no party, but the whole people. In the sincerity of our souls do we desire Catholic emancipation; but were it obtained to-morrow, to-morrow would we go on as we do to-day, in the pursuit of that reform, which would still be wanting to ratify their liberties as well as our own. For both these purposes it appears necessary that provincial conventions should assemble preparatory to the convention of the Protestant people. The delegates of the Catholic body are not justified in communicating with individuals, or even bodies of inferior authority; and, therefore, an assembly of a similar nature and organization is necessary to establish an intercourse of sentiments, an uniformity of conduct, an united cause, and an united nation. If a convention on the one part does not soon follow, and is not soon connected with that on the other, the common cause will split into the partial interest—the people will relapse into inattention and inertness—the union of affection and exertion will dissolve—and, too probably, some local insurrections, instigated by the malignity of our common enemy, may commit the character, and risk the tranquillity of the island, which can be obviated only by the influence of an assembly arising from, assimilated with the people, and whose spirit may be, as it were, knit with the soul of the nation. Unless the sense of the Protestant people be on their part as fairly collected, and as judicially directed—unless individual exertion consolidates into collective strength—unless the particles unite into one mass—we may, perhaps, serve some person or some party for a little, but the public not at all. The nation is neither insolent, nor rebellious, nor seditious: while it knows its rights, it is unwilling to manifest its powers; it would rather supplicate administration to anticipate revolution by well-timed reform, and to save their country in mercy to themselves. The Fifteenth of February approaches—a day ever memorable in the annals of the country as the birth day of new Ireland. Let parochial meetings be held as soon as possible; let each parish return delegates; let the sense of Ulster be again declared from Dungannon, on a day auspicious to union, peace, and freedom; and the spirit of the north will again become the spirit of the nation. The civil assembly ought to claim the attendance of the military associations; and we have addressed you, Citizen Soldiers, on this subject, from the belief that your body, uniting conviction with zeal, and zeal with activity, may have much influence over your countrymen, your relations, and friends. We offer only a general outline to the public, and, meaning to address Ireland, presume not at present to fill up the plan, or pre-occupy the mode of its execution. We have thought it our duty to speak; answer us by actions. You have taken time for consideration; fourteen long years have elapsed since the rise of your associations; and in 1782 did you imagine that in 1792 this nation would still remain unrepresented? How many nations in this interval have gotten the start of Ireland? How many of your countrymen have sunk into the grave?'

"In contempt of our said Lord the King, in open violation of the laws of this kingdom, to the evil and pernicious example of all others in the like case offending, and against the peace of our said Lord the King, his crown and dignity. Whereupon the said Attorney-General of our said Lord the King, who for our said Lord the King in this behalf prosecutes, prays the consideration of the court here in the premises, and due process of law may be awarded against him, the said Archibald Hamilton Rowan, in this behalf, to make him answer to our said Lord the King touching and concerning the premises aforesaid.
"ARTHUR WOLFE.

"THOMAS KEMMIS, Attorney.
'Received the 8th of June 1793."

To this information Mr. Rowan appeared, by Matthew Dowling, gent., his attorney, and pleaded the general issue—Not Guilty; and the court having appointed Wednesday, the 29th day of January, 1794, for the trial of the said issue, the undernamed persons were sworn upon the jury:—

Sir F. Hutchinson, Bart.,	Richard Manders,	Richard Fox,
Frederick Trench, Esq.,	George Palmer,	Christopher Harrison,
William Duke Moore,	John Read,	George Perrin,
Humphry Minchin,	Robert Lea,	Thomas Sherrard.

Counsel for the Prosecution—Mr. Attorney-General, Prime Sergeant, Solicitor-General Mr. Frankland, Mr. Ruxton. Agent—Mr. Kemmis.

Counsel for the Defendant—Mr. Curran, Mr. Recorder, Mr. Fletcher. Agent—Mr. Dowling.

Mr. Ruxton opened the pleadings.

The Attorney-General (Arthur Wolfe) stated the case. The following passage from statement describes the proclamation and meeting:—

"The troops are summoned to meet, the guards are summoned to assemble, and the first battalion of National Guards were to have paraded, clothed like Frenchmen. The day before, the Lord Lieutenant had summoned the council of the kingdom; upon that night a proclamation issued, stating that there were intentions to assemble men in arms with seditious signs, and apprehending danger from their so assembling. It prohibited their meeting. The proclamation issued on a Saturday night, and it produced that satisfaction which all good men desirous of order seek to enjoy; and they felt once more the pleasurable assurance that they had a government. Appalled by this proclamation, the corps did not meet on the 8th of December, as it was intended, though some few were seen dressed in the National Guard uniform, parading the streets, with a mob crowding at their heels; but, however, nothing followed.

"A few days after—I am not aware of the particular day—but a few days after the issuing the proclamation, the society assembled. The proclamation was upon the 7th, the address I speak of was published the 16th of December; the meeting, therefore, must have been between the 7th and the 16th of December. The society, I say, assembled, and they agreed upon a certain address to the Volunteers of Ireland, and Dr. Drennan is there stated to have been in the chair, and the traverser secretary. At that meeting the address to the Volunteers was agreed upon, which is the libel charged against Mr. Rowan, as being guilty of publishing it. Under that address, this was to be done. The Volunteers of Dublin were to be called into action, and those papers were to be dispersed among them. For that purpose, the several Volunteer corps at that time existing in Dublin were summoned to assemble in a house in Cope-street, belonging to Purdon, a fencing-master; upon the 16th of December. Accordingly, upon that day the several corps of Volunteers did go with side-arms to this fencing-school in Cope-street. The traverser was, I believe, at the head of one of these corps; another very celebrated name was at the head of another of them, James Napper Tandy. Who was at the head of the others I am not able to inform you. But in the afternoon of the 16th of December, several Volunteers, with uniforms and side arms, assembled in the fencing-school. In this fencing-school, gentlemen, there was a gallery, and into that gallery there was such public access, that what passed below may be said to have passed in the face of the world."

Witnesses were examined, who fully connected Rowan with the document, and then Curran thus spoke for the defence:—

Gentlemen of the jury, when I consider the period at which this prosecution is brought forward; when I behold the extraordinary safeguard of armed soldiers resorted to, no doubt for the preservation of peace and order;* when I catch, as I cannot but do, the throb of public anxiety which beats from one end to the other of this hall; when I reflect on what may be the fate of a man of the most beloved personal character, of one of the most respectable families of our country—himself the only individual of that family—I may almost say of that country—who can look to that possible fate with unconcern? Feeling, as I do, all these impressions, it is in the honest simplicity of my heart I speak, when I say, that I never rose in a court of justice with so much embarrassment as upon this occasion.

If, gentlemen, I could entertain a hope of finding refuge for the disconcertion of my mind in the perfect composure of yours—if I could suppose that those awful vicissitudes of human events, which have been stated or alluded to, could leave your judgment undisturbed, and your hearts at ease, I know I should form a most erroneous opinion of your character. I entertain no such chimerical hope—I form no such unworthy opinion. I expect not that your hearts can be more at ease than my own—I have no right to expect it; but I have a right to call upon you, in the name of your country, in the name of the living God, of whose eternal justice you are now administering that portion which dwells with us on this side of the grave, to discharge your breasts, as far as you are able, of every bias of prejudice or passion, that if my client be guilty of the offence charged upon him, you may give tranquility to the public, by a firm verdict of conviction; or, if he be innocent, by as firm a verdict of acquittal; and that you will do this in defiance

* A few moments before Mr. Curran entered into his client's defence, a guard was brought into the Court-house by the Sheriff (Gifford).

of the paltry artifices and senseless clamours that have been resorted to, in order to bring him to his trial with anticipated conviction. And, gentlemen, I feel an additional necessity in thus conjuring you to be upon your guard, from the able and imposing statement which you have just heard on the part of the prosecution. I know well the virtues and talents of the excellent person who conducts that prosecution ;* I know how much he would disdain to impose on you by the trappings of office ; but I also know how easily we mistake the lodgment which character and eloquence can make upon our feelings, for those impressions that reason, and fact, and proof, only ought to work upon our understandings.

Perhaps, gentlemen, I shall act not unwisely in waiving any further observation of this sort, and giving your minds an opportunity of growing cool and resuming themselves, by coming to a calm and uncoloured statement of mere facts, premising only to you, that I have it in strictest injunction from my client, to defend him upon facts and evidence only, and to avail myself of no technical artifice or subtlety that could withdraw his cause from the test of that inquiry which it is your province to exercise, and to which only he wishes to be indebted for an acquittal.

In the month of December, 1792, Mr. Rowan was arrested on an information, charging him with the offence for which he is now on his trial. He was taken before an honourable personage now on that bench, and admitted to bail.†

He remained a considerable time in this city, soliciting the present prosecution, and offering himself to a fair trial by a jury of his country. But it was not then thought fit to yield to that solicitation ; nor has it now been thought proper to prosecute him in the ordinary way, by sending up a bill of indictment to a grand jury.

I do not mean by this to say that informations *ex-officio* are always oppressive or unjust ;‡ but I cannot but observe to you, that when a petty jury is called upon to try a charge not previously found by the grand inquest, and supported by the naked assertion only of the King' prosecutor, that the accusation labours under a weakness of probability which it is difficult to assist. If the charge had no cause of dreading the light—if it was likely to find the sanction of a grand jury—it is not easy to account why it deserted the more usual, the more popular, and the more constitutional mode, and preferred to come forward in the ungracious form of an *ex-officio* information.

If such a bill had been sent up and found, Mr. Rowan would have been tried at the next commission ; but a speedy trial was not the wish of his prosecutors. An information was filed, and when he expected to be tried upon it, an error, it seems, was discovered in the record. Mr. Rowan offered to waive it, or consent to any amendment desired. No, that proposal could not be accepted : a trial must have followed. That information, therefore, was withdrawn, and a new one filed ; that is, in

---

* The late Lord Kilwarden, then Attorney-General Wolfe.
† The Honourable Justice Downes, afterwards Lord Downes, and Chief Justice of the King's Bench.
‡ M'Nally notes that in Curran's private opinion they were

fact, a third prosecution was instituted upon the same charge. This last was filed on the 8th day of last July.

Gentlemen, these facts cannot fail of a due impression upon you. You will find a material part of your inquiry must be, whether Mr. Rowan is pursued as a criminal, or hunted down as a victim. It is not, therefore, by insinuation or circuity, but it is boldly and directly that I assert, that oppression has been intended and practised upon him, and by those facts which I have stated. I am warranted in the assertion.

His demand, his entreaty to be tried, was refused, and why? A hue and cry was to be raised against him; the sword was to be suspended over his head; some time was necessary for the public mind to become heated by the circulation of artful clamours of anarchy and rebellion these same clamours which, with more probability, but not more success, had been circulated before through England and Scotland. In this country the causes and the swiftness of their progress were as obvious as their folly has since become to every man of the smallest observation. I have been stopped myself with—" Good God, Sir, have you heard the news?" "No, Sir, what?" "Why one French emissary was seen travelling through Connaught in a post-chaise, and scattering from the window, as he passed, little doses of political poison, made up in square bits of paper; another was actually surprised in the fact of reducing our good people from their allegiance, by discourses upon the indivisibility of French robbery and massacre, which he preached in the French language, to a congregation of Irish peasants."

Such are the bugbears and spectres to be raised to warrant the sacrifice of whatever little public spirit may remain amongst us. But time has also detected the imposture of these "Cock-lane apparitions;" and you cannot now, with your eyes open, give a verdict, without asking your consciences this question:—Is this a fair and honest prosecution? is it brought forward with the single view of vindicating public justice, and promoting public good? And here let me remind you, that you are not convened to try the guilt of a libel, affecting the personal character of any private man. I know no case in which a jury ought to be more severe, than where personal calumny is conveyed through a vehicle which ought to be consecrated to public information. Neither, on the other hand, can I conceive any case in which the firmness and the caution of a jury should be more exerted, than when a subject is prosecuted for a libel on the state. The peculiarity of the British constitution (to which, in its fullest extent, we have an undoubted right, however distant we may be from the actual enjoyment), and in which it surpasses every known government in Europe, is this, that its only professed object is the general good, and its only foundation the general will; hence the people have a right, acknowledged from time immemorial, fortified by a pile of statutes, and authenticated by a revolution that speaks louder than them all, to see whether abuses have been committed, and whether their properties and their liberties have been attended to as they ought to be.

This is a kind of subject by which I feel myself overawed when I approach it; there are certain fundamental principles which nothing but necessity should expose to public examination; they are pillars, the depth of whose foundation you cannot explore, without endangering their strength; but let it be recollected, that the discussion of such subjects should not be condemned in me, nor visited upon my client: the blame, if any there be, should rest only with those who have forced them into discussion. I say, therefore, it is the right of the people to keep an eternal watch upon the conduct of their rulers; and in order to that, the freedom of the press has been cherished by the law of England. In private defamation, let it never be tolerated; in wicked and wanton aspersion upon a good and honest administration, let it never be supported. Not that a good government can be exposed to danger by groundless accusation, but because a bad government is sure to find, in the detected falsehood of a licentious press, a security and a credit, which it could never otherwise obtain.

I said a good government cannot be endangered; I say so again; for whether it be good or bad, it can never depend upon assertion: the question is decided by simple inspection; to try the tree, look at its fruit: to judge of the government, look at the people. What is the fruit of a good government? the virtue and happiness of the people. Do four millions of people in this country gather those fruits from that government, to whose injured purity, to whose spotless virtue and violated honour this seditious and atrocious libeller is to be immolated upon the altar of the constitution? To you, gentlemen of the jury, who are bound by the most sacred obligation to your country and your God, to speak nothing but the truth, I put the question—do the people of this country gather those fruits?—are they orderly, industrious, religious, and contented?—do you find them free from bigotry and ignorance, those inseparable concomitants of systematic oppression? Or, to try them by a test as unerring as any of the former, are they united? The period has now elapsed in which considerations of this extent would have been deemed improper to a jury: happily for these countries, the legislature of each has lately changed, or, perhaps, to speak more properly, revived and restored the law respecting trials of this kind.* For the space of thirty or forty years, a usage had prevailed in Westminster hall, by which the judges assumed to themselves the decision of the question, whether libel or not; but the learned counsel for the prosecution is now obliged to admit that this is a question for the jury only to decide. You will naturally listen with respect to the opinion of the court, but you will receive it as a matter of advice, not as a matter of law; and you will give it credit, not from any adventitious circumstances of authority, but merely so far as it meets the concurrence of your own understandings.

Give me leave now to state the charge, as it stands upon the record: it is, "that Mr. Rowan, being a person of a wicked and turbulent disposition, and maliciously designing and intending to excite and diffuse among the subjects of this realm of Ireland, discontents, jealousies, and

---

* Erskine and Fox procured this amendment, or restoration of the law of libel.

suspicions of our Lord the King and his government, and disaffection and disloyalty to the person and government of our said Lord the King, and to raise very dangerous seditions and tumults within this kingdom of Ireland, and to draw the government of this kingdom into great scandal, infamy, and disgrace, and to incite the subjects of our said Lord the King, to attempt, by force and violence, and with arms, to make alterations in the government, state, and constitution of this kingdom, and to incite his Majesty's said subjects to tumult and anarchy, and to overturn the established constitution of this kingdom, and to overawe and intimidate the legislature of this kingdom by an armed force;" did "maliciously and seditiously" publish the paper in question.

Gentlemen, without any observation of mine, you must see, that this information contains a direct charge upon Mr. Rowan; namely, that he did, with the intents set forth in the information, publish this paper; so that here you have, in fact, two or three questions for your decision. First, the matter of fact of the publication; namely, did Mr. Rowan publish the paper? If Mr. Rowan did not in fact publish that paper, you have no longer any question on which to employ your minds; if you think that he was in fact the publisher, then, and not till then, arises the great and important subject to which your judgments must be directed. And that comes shortly and simply to this. Is the paper a libel? and did he publish it with the intent charged in the information? For whatever you may think of the abstract question, whether the paper be libellous or not, and of which paper it has not even been insinuated that he is the author, there can be no ground for a verdict against him, unless you also are persuaded that what he did was done with a criminal design.

I wish, gentlemen, to simplify, and not to perplex; I therefore say again, if these three circumstances conspire, that he published it, that it was a libel, and that it was published with the purposes alleged in the information, you ought unquestionably to find him guilty: if, on the other hand, you do not find that all these circumstances concurred; if you cannot upon your oaths say that he published it; if it be not in your opinion a libel; and if he did not publish it with the intention alleged: I say upon the failure of any one of these points, my client is entitled, in justice, and upon your oaths, to a verdict of acquittal.

Gentlemen, Mr. Attorney-General has thought proper to direct your attention to the state and circumstances of public affairs at the time of this transaction; let me also make a few retrospective observations on a period at which he has but slightly glanced; I speak of the events which took place before the close of the American war.

You know, gentlemen, that France had espoused the cause of America, and we became thereby engaged in a war with that nation.

"Heu nescia mens hominum futuri!"

Little did that ill-fated monarch know that he was forming the first causes of those disastrous events, that were to end in the subversion of his throne, in the slaughter of his family, and the deluging of his country with the blood of his people. You cannot but remember that, at time when we had scarcely a regular soldier for our defence, when the old and young were alarmed and terrified with apprehensions of descent upon our coasts, that Providence seemed to have worked a sort of miracle in our favour. You saw a band of armed men come forth at the great call of nature, of honour, and their country. You saw men of the greatest wealth and rank; you saw every class of the community give up its members, and send them armed into the field, to protect the public and private tranquillity of Ireland. It is impossible for any man to turn back to that period, without reviving those sentiments of tenderness and gratitude, which then beat in the public bosom to recollect amidst what applause, what tears, what prayers, what benedictions, they walked forth amongst spectators, agitated by the mingled sensations of terror and of reliance, of danger and of protection, imploring the blessings of heaven upon their heads, and its conquest upon their swords. That illustrious, and adored, and *abused* body of men, stood forward and assumed the title, which I trust the ingratitude of their country will never blot from its history,—" THE VOLUNTEERS OF IRELAND."

Give me leave now, with great respect, to put this question to you :— Do you think the assembling of that glorious band of patriots was an insurrection? Do you think the invitation to that assembling would have been sedition? They came under no commission but the call of their country; unauthorized and unsanctioned, except by public emergency and public danger. I ask, was that meeting insurrection or not? I put another question :—If any man then had published a call on that body, and stated that war was declared against the state; that the regular troops were withdrawn; that our coasts were hovered round by the ships of the enemy; that the moment was approaching, when the unprotected feebleness of age and sex, when the sanctity of habitation, would be disregarded and profaned by the brutal ferocity of a rude invader; if any man had then said to them—" Leave your industry for a while, that you may return to it again, and come forth in arms for the public defence :" I put the question boldly to you (it is not the case of the Volunteers of that day; it is the case of my client at this hour, which I put to you), would that call have been then pronounced in a court of justice, or by a jury on their oaths, a criminal and seditious invitation to insurrection? If it would not have been so then, upon what principle can it be so now? What is the force and perfection of the law? It is, the permanency of the law; it is, that whenever the fact is the same, the law is also the same; it is, that the letter remains written, monumented and recorded, to pronounce the same decision, upon the same facts, whenever they shall arise. I will not affect to conceal it: you know there has been artful, ungrateful, and blasphemous clamour raised against these illustrious characters, the saviours of the king of Ireland. Having mentioned this, let me read a few words of the paper alleged to be criminal : " You first took up arms to protect your country from foreign enemies, and from domestic disturbance.— For the same purposes, it now becomes necessary that you should resume them."

I should be the last man in the world to impute any want of candour to the right honourable gentleman, who has stated the case on behalf of the prosecution; but he has certainly fallen into a mistake, which, if not explained, might be highly injurious to my client. He supposed that this publication was not addressed to those ancient Volunteers, but to new combinations of them, formed upon new principles, and actuated by different motives. You have the words to which this construction is imputed upon the record; the meaning of his mind can be collected only from those words which he has made use of to convey it. The guilt imputable to him can only be inferred from the meaning ascribable to those words. Let his meaning then be fairly collected by resorting to them. Is there a foundation to suppose that this address was directed to any such body of men as has been called a banditti (with what justice it is unnecessary to inquire), and not to the old Volunteers?

As to the sneer at the words *citizen soldiers*, I should feel that I was treating a very respected friend with an insidious and unmerited kindness, if I affected to expose it by any gravity of refutation. I may, however, be permitted to observe, that those who are supposed to have disgraced this expression by adopting it, have taken it from the idea of the British constitution, " that no man in becoming a soldier ceases to be a citizen." Would to God, all enemies as they are, that that unfortunate people had borrowed more from that sacred source of liberty and virtue; and would to God, for the sake of humanity, that they had preserved even the little they did borrow! If ever there could be an objection to that appellation, it must have been strongest when it was first assumed.* To that period the writer manifestly alludes; he addresses " those who first took up arms." " You first took up arms to protect your country from foreign enemies and from domestic disturbance. For the same purposes, it now becomes necessary that you should resume them." Is this applicable to those who had never taken up arms before? " A proclamation" says this paper, " has been issued in England for embodying the militia, and a proclamation has been issued by the Lord Lieutenant and Council of Ireland, for repressing all seditious associations. In consequence of both these proclamations, it is reasonable to apprehend danger from abroad, and danger at home." God help us from the situation of Europe at that time; we were threatened with too probable danger from abroad, and I am afraid it was not without foundation we were told of our having something to dread at home.

I find much abuse has been lavished on the disrespect with which the proclamation is treated, in that part of the paper alleged to be a libel To that my answer for my client is short: I do conceive it competen to a British subject, if he thinks that a proclamation has issued for the purpose of raising false terrors; I hold it to be not only the privilege, but the duty of a citizen, to set his countrymen right, with respect to such misrepresented danger; and until a proclamation in this country

* In the resolutions and addresses of the old Volunteers, at and prior to 1783, the *citizen soldiers* and *citizen soldiery*, were no uncommon appellations.

shall have the force of law, the reason and grounds of it are surely at least questionable by the people. Nay, I will go farther; if an actual law had passed, receiving the sanction of the three estates, if it be exceptionable in any matter, it is warrantable to any man in the community to state, in a becoming manner, his ideas upon it. And I should be at a loss to know, if the positive laws of Great Britain are thus questionable, upon what grounds the proclamation of an Irish government should not be open to the animadversion of Irish subjects.

"Whatever be the motive, or from whatever quarter it arises," says this paper, "alarm has arisen." Gentlemen, do you not know that to be a fact? It has been stated by the Attorney-General, and most truly, that the most gloomy apprehensions were entertained by the whole country. "You, Volunteers of Ireland, are therefore summoned to arms, at the instance of government, as well as by the responsibility attached to your character, and the permanent obligations of your institution." I am free to confess, if any man, assuming the liberties of a British subject to question public topics, should, under the mask of that privilege, publish a proclamation, inviting the profligate and seditious, those in want, and those in despair, to rise up in arms to overawe the legislature—to rob us of whatever portion of the blessing of a free government we possess; I know of no offence involving greater enormity. But that, gentlemen, is the question you are to try. If my client acted with an honest mind and fair intention, and having, as he believed, the authority of government to support him in the idea that danger was to be apprehended, did apply to that body of so known and so revered a character, calling upon them by their former honour, the principles of their glorious institution, and the great stake they possessed in their country: if he interposed, not upon a fictitious pretext, but a real belief of actual and imminent danger, and that their arming at that critical moment was necessary to the safety of their country, his intention was not only innocent, but highly meritorious. It is a question, gentlemen, upon which you only can decide; it is for you to say, whether it was criminal in the defendant to be misled, and whether he is to fall a sacrifice to the prosecution of that government by which he was so deceived. I say again, gentlemen, you can look only to his own words as the interpreters of his meaning; and to the state and circumstances of his country, as he was made to believe them, as the clue to his intention. The case, then, gentlemen, is shortly and simply this; a man of the first family, and fortune, and character, and property among you reads a proclamation, stating the country to be in danger from abroad, and at home; and, thus alarmed, thus, upon the authority of the prosecutor, alarmed, applies to that august body, before whose awful presence sedition must vanish, and insurrection disappear. You must surrender, I hesitate not to say, your oaths to unfounded assertion, if you can submit to say, that such an act, of such a man, so warranted, is a wicked and seditious libel. If he was a dupe, let me ask you, who was the impostor? I blush and shrink with shame and detestation from that meanness of dupery and servile complaisance, which could make that dupe a victim to the accusation of an impostor.

You perceive, gentlemen, that I am going into the merits of this publication before I apply myself to the question which is first in order of time, namely, whether the publication, in point of fact, is to be ascribed to Mr. Rowan or not. I have been unintentionally led into this violation of order. I should effect no purpose of either brevity or clearness, by returning to the more methodical course of observation. I have been naturally drawn from it by the superior importance of the topic I am upon, namely, the merit of the publication in question.

This publication, if ascribed at all to Mr. Rowan, contains four distinct subjects: the first, the invitation to the Volunteers to arm: upon that I have already observed; but those that remain are surely of much importance, and, no doubt, are prosecuted, as equally criminal. The paper next states the necessity of a reform in parliament: it states, thirdly, the necessity of an emancipation of the Catholic inhabitants of Ireland; and, as necessary to the achievement of all these objects, does, fourthly, state the necessity of a general delegated convention of the people.

It has been alleged, that Mr. Rowan intended by this publication, to excite the subjects of this country to effect an alteration in the form of your constitution. And here, gentlemen, perhaps you may not be unwilling to follow a little farther than Mr. Attorney-General has done, the idea of a late prosecution in Great Britain, upon the subject of a public libel. It is with peculiar fondness I look to that country for solid principles of constitutional liberty and judicial example. You have been impressed in no small degree with the manner in which this publication marks the different orders of our constitution, and comments upon them. Let me show you what boldness of animadversion of such topics is thought justifiable in the British nation, and by a British jury. I have in my hand the report of the trial of the printers of the *Morning Chronicle*, for a supposed libel against the state, and of their acquittal; let me read to you some passages from that publication, which a jury of Englishmen were in vain called upon to brand with the name of libel:—

"Claiming it as our indefeasible right to associate together in a peaceable and friendly manner, for the communication of thoughts, the formation of opinions, and to promote the general happiness, we think it unnecessary to offer any apology for inviting you to join us in this manly and benevolent pursuit; the necessity of the inhabitants of every community endeavouring to procure a true knowledge of their rights, their duties, and their interests, will not be denied, except by those who are the slaves of prejudice, or interested in the continuation of abuses. As men who wish to aspire to the title of freemen, we totally deny the wisdom and the humanity of the advice, to approach the defects of government with 'pious awe and trembling solicitude.' What better doctrine could the pope or the tyrants of Europe desire? We think, therefore, that the cause of truth and justice can never be hurt by temperate and honest discussions; and that cause which will not bear such a scrutiny, must be systematically or practically bad. We are sensible that those who are not friends to the general good, have attempted to inflame the public mind with the cry of 'Danger, whenever men have associated for discussing the principles of government; and we have little doubt but such conduct will be pursued in this place; we would therefore caution every honest man, who has really the welfare of the nation at heart, to avoid being led away by the prostituted clamours of those who live on the sources of corruption. We pity the fears of the timorous, and we are totally unconcerned respecting the false alarms of the venal.

"We view with concern the frequency of wars. We are persuaded that the interests of the poor can never be promoted by accession of territory, when bought at the expense of their labour and blood; and we must say, in the language of a celebrated author, 'We, who are only the people, but who pay for wars with our substance and our blood, will not cease to tell kings,' or governments, 'that to them alone wars are profitable; that the true and just conquests are those which each makes at home, by comforting the peasantry, by promoting agriculture and manufactures, by multiplying men and the other productions of nature; that then it is that kings may call themselves the image of God, whose will is perpetually directed to the creation of new beings. If they continue to make us fight, and kill one another in uniform, we will continue to write and speak, until nations shall be cured of this folly.'

"We are certain our present heavy burdens are owing, in a great measure, to cruel and impolitic wars, and therefore we will do all on our part, as peaceable citizens, who have the good of the community at heart to enlighten each other, and protest against them.

"The present state of the representation of the people calls for the particular attention of every man who has humanity sufficient to feel for the honour and happiness of his country, to the defects and corruptions of which we are inclined to attribute unnecessary wars, &c. We think it a deplorable case when the poor must support a corruption which is calculated to oppress them; when the labourer must give his money to afford the means of preventing him having a voice in its disposal; when the lower classes may say—'We give you our money, for which we have toiled and sweat, and which would save our families from cold and hunger; but we think it more hard that there is nobody whom we have delegated, to see that it is not improperly and wickedly spent; we have none to watch over our interests; the rich only are represented.' An equal and uncorrupt representation would, we are persuaded, save us from heavy expenses, and deliver us from many oppressions; we will therefore do our duty to procure this reform, which appears to us of the utmost importance.

"In short, we see, with the most lively concern, an army of placemen, pensioners, &c., fighting in the cause of corruption and prejudice, and spreading the contagion far and wide.

"We see, with equal sensibility, the present outcry against reforms, and a proclamation (tending to cramp the liberty of the press, and discredit the true friends of the people), receiving the support of numbers of our countrymen.

"We see burdens multiplied, the lower classes sinking into poverty,

L

disgrace and excesses, and the means of those shocking abuses increased for the purpose of revenue.

"We ask ourselves, 'Are we in England?' Have our forefathers fought, bled, and conquered for liberty? And did they not think that the fruits of their patriotism would be more abundant in peace, plenty, and happiness?

"Is the condition of the poor never to be improved?

Great Britain must have arrived at the highest degree of national happiness and prosperity, and our situation must be too good to be mended, or the present outcry against reforms and improvements is inhuman and criminal. But we hope our condition will be speedily improved, and to obtain so desirable a good, is the object of our present association: an union founded on principles of benevolence and humanity; disclaiming all connexion with riots and disorder, but firm in our purpose, and warm in our affections for liberty.

"Lastly, we invite the friends of freedom throughout Great Britain to form similar societies, and to act with unanimity and firmness, till the people be too wise to be imposed upon; and their influence in the government be commensurate with their dignity and importance. *Then shall we be free and happy.*"

Such, gentlemen, is the language which a subject of Great Britain thinks himself warranted to hold, and upon such language has the corroborating sanction of a British jury been stamped by a verdict of acquittal. Such was the honest and manly freedom of publication; in a country, too, where the complaint of abuses has not half the foundation it has here. I said I loved to look to England for principles of judicial example; I cannot but say to you that it depends on your spirit, whether I shall look to it hereafter with sympathy or with shame. Be pleased, now, gentlemen, to consider whether the statement of the imperfection in your representation has been made with a desire of inflaming an attack upon the public tranquillity, or with an honest purpose of procuring a remedy for an actually existing grievance.

It is impossible not to revert to the situation of the times; and let me remind you, that whatever observations of this kind I am compelled thus to make in a court of justice, the uttering of them in this place is not imputable to my client, but to the necessity of defence imposed upon him by this extraordinary prosecution.

Gentlemen, the representation of our people is the vital principle of their political existence; without it they are dead, or they live only to servitude; without it there are two estates acting upon and against the third, instead of acting in co-operation with it; without it, if the people are oppressed by their judges, where is the tribunal to which their judges can be amenable? without it, if they are trampled upon and plundered by a minister, where is the tribunal to which the offender shall be amenable? without it, where is the ear to hear, or the heart to feel, or the hand to redress their sufferings? Shall they be found, let me ask you, in the accursed bands of imps and minions that bask in their disgrace, and fatten upon their spoils, and flourish upon their ruin? But let me not put this to you as a merely speculative question. It is a plain question of fact: rely upon it, physical man is everywhere t'e same; it is only the various operations of moral causes that gives variety to the social or individual character and condition. How otherwise happens it that modern slavery looks quietly at the despot, on the very spot where Leonidas expired? The answer is, Sparta has not changed her climate, but she has lost that government which her liberty could not survive.

I call you, therefore, to the plain question of fact. This paper recommends a reform in parliament: I put that question to your consciences; do you think it needs that reform? I put it boldly and fairly to you, do you think the people of Ireland are represented as they ought to be? Do you hesitate for an answer? If you do, let me remind you, that until the last year, three millions of your countrymen have, by the express letter of the law, been excluded from the reality of actual, and even from the phantom of virtual representation. Shall we then be told that this is only the affirmation of a wicked and seditious incendiary? If you do not feel the mockery of such a charge, look at your country; in what state do you find it? Is it in a state of tranquillity and general satisfaction? These are traces by which good are ever to be distinguished from bad governments, without any very minute inquiry or speculative refinement. Do you feel that a veneration for the law, a pious and humble attachment to the constitution, form the political morality of the people? Do you find that comfort and competency among your people, which are always to be found where a government is mild and moderate, where taxes are imposed by a body who have an interest in treating the poorer orders with compassion, and preventing the weight of taxation from pressing sore upon them?

Gentlemen, I mean not to impeach the state of your representation; I am not saying that it is defective, or that it ought to be altered or amended; nor is this a place for me to say, whether I think that three millions of the inhabitants of a country whose whole number is but four, ought to be admitted to any efficient situation in the state. It may be said, and truly, that these are not questions for either of us directly to decide; but you cannot refuse them some passing consideration at least; when you remember that on this subject the real question for your decision is, whether the allegation of a defect in your constitution is so utterly unfounded and false, that you can ascribe it only to the malice and perverseness of a wicked mind, and not to the innocent mistake of an ordinary understanding; whether it may not be mistake; whether it can be only sedition.

And here, gentlemen, I own I cannot but regret, that one of our countrymen should be criminally pursued, for asserting the necessity of reform, at the very moment when that necessity seems admitted by the parliament itself; that this unhappy reform shall, at the same moment, be a subject of legislative discussion and criminal prosecution. Far am I from imputing any sinister design to the virtue or wisdom of our government; but who can avoid feeling the deplorable impression that must be made on the public mind, when the demand for that orm is answered by a criminal information'

I am the more forcibly impressed by this consideration, when I consider, that when this information was first put on the file, the subject was transiently mentioned in the House of Commons. Some circumstances retarded the progress of the inquiry there, and the progress of the information was equally retarded here. On the first day of this session, you all know, that subject was again brought forward in the House of Commons, and, as if they had slept together, this prosecution was also revived in the court of King's Bench, and that before a jury taken from a panel partly composed of those very members of parliament, who, in the House of Commons, must debate upon this subject as a measure of public advantage, which they are here called upon to conider as a public crime.*

This paper, gentlemen, insists upon the necessity of emancipating the Catholics of Ireland, and that is charged as part of the libel. If they had waited another year, if they had kept this prosecution impending for another year, how much would remain for a jury to decide upon, I should be at a loss to discover. It seems as if the progress of public nformation was eating away the ground of the prosecution. Since the commencement of the prosecution, this part of the libel has unluckily received the sanction of the legislature. In that interval our Catholic brethren have obtained that admission, which, it seems, it was a libel to propose; in what way to account for this, I am really at a loss. Have any alarms been occasioned by the emancipation of our Catholic brethren? has the bigoted malignity of any individuals been crushed? or has the stability of the government, or that of the country been weakened; or is one million of subjects stronger than four millions? Do you think that the benefit they received should be poisoned by the sting of vengeance? If you think so, you must say to them—" You have demanded emancipation, and you have got it; but we abhor your persons, we are outraged at your success, and we will stigmatise by a criminal prosecution the adviser of that relief which you have obtained from the voice of your country." I ask you, do you think, as honest men, anxious for the public tranquillity, conscious that there are wounds not yet completely cicatrized, that you ought to speak this language at this time, to men who are too much disposed to think that in this very emancipation they have been saved from their own parliament by the humanity of their sovereign? Or do you wish to prepare them for the revocation of these improvident concessions? Do you think it wise or humane at this moment to insult them, by sticking up in a pillory the man who dared to stand forth as their advocate? I put it to your oaths; do you think that a blessing of that kind, that a victory obtained by justice over bigotry and oppression, should have a stigma cast upon it by an ignominious sentence upon men bold and honest enough to propose that measure? to propose the redeeming of religion from the abuses of the church, the reclaiming of three millions of men from bondage, and giving liberty to all who had a right to demand it; giving, I say, in the so much censured words of this paper, giving " UNIVERSAL

---

* The names of several members of parliament were included in the panel.

EMANCIPATION!" I speak in the spirit of the British law, which makes liberty commensurate with and inseparable from British soil; which proclaims even to the stranger and sojourner, the moment he sets his foot upon British earth, that the ground on which he treads is holy, and consecrated by the genius of UNIVERSAL EMANCIPATION. No matter in what language his doom may have been pronounced; no matter what complexion incompatible with freedom, an Indian or an African sun may have burnt upon him; no matter in what disastrous battle his liberty may have been cloven down; no matter with what solemnities he may have been devoted upon the altar of slavery; the first moment he touches the sacred soil of Britain, the altar and the god sink together in the dust; his soul walks abroad in her own majesty; his body swells beyond the measure of his chains, that burst from around him; and he stands redeemed, regenerated, and disenthralled, by the irresistible genius of UNIVERSAL EMANCIPATION.

A sudden burst of applause from the court and hall, which was repeated for a considerable length of time, interrupted Mr. Curran. Silence being at length restored, he proceeded:—

Gentlemen, I am not such a fool as to ascribe any effusion of this sort to any merit of mine. It is the mighty theme, and not the inconsiderable advocate, that can excite interest in the hearer. What you hear is but the testimony which nature bears to her own character; it is the effusion of her gratitude to that Power which stamped that character upon her.

And permit me to say, that if my client had occasion to defend his cause by any mad or drunken appeals to extravagance or licentiousness, I trust in God I stand in that situation that, humble as I am, he would not have resorted to me to be his advocate. I was not recommended to his choice by any connexion of principle or party, or even private friendship; and saying this, I cannot but add, that I consider not to be acquainted with such a man as Mr. Rowan, a want of personal good fortune. But upon this great subject of reform and emancipation, there is a latitude and boldness of remark, justifiable in the people, and necessary to the defence of Mr. Rowan, for which the habits of professional studies, and technical adherence to established forms, have rendered me unfit. It is, however, my duty, standing here as his advocate, to make some few observations to you which I conceive to be material.

Gentlemen, you are sitting in a country which has a right to the British constitution, and which is bound by an indissoluble union with the British nation. If you were now even at liberty to debate upon that subject; if you even were not, by the most solemn compacts, founded upon the authority of your ancestors and of yourselves, bound to that alliance, and had an election now to make; in the present unhappy state of Europe, if you had been heretofore a stranger to Great Britain, you would now say—We will enter into society and union with you:—

"Una salus ambobus erit, commune periculum."

But to accomplish that union, let me tell you, you must learn to become like the English people. It is vain to say you will protect their freedom, if you abandon your own. The pillar whose base has no foundation, can give no support to the dome under which its head is placed; and if you profess to give England that assistance which you refuse to yourselves, she will laugh at your folly, and despise your meanness and insincerity. Let us follow this a little further—I know you will interpret what I say with the candour in which it is spoken. England is marked by a natural avarice of freedom, which she is studious to engross and accumulate, but most unwilling to impart; whether from any necessity of her policy, or from her weakness, or from her pride, I will not presume to say, but so is the fact; you need not look to the east nor to the west; you need only look to yourselves.

In order to confirm this observation, I would appeal to what fell from the learned counsel for the crown,—" that notwithstanding the alliance subsisting for two centuries past between the two countries, the date of liberty in one goes no further back than the year 1782."

If it required additional confirmation, I should state the case of the invaded American, and the subjugated Indian, to prove that the policy of England has ever been, to govern her connexions more as colonies than as allies; and it must be owing to the great spirit indeed of Ireland, if she shall continue free. Rely upon it, she shall ever have to hold her course against an adverse current; rely upon it, if the popular spring does not continue strong and elastic, a short interval of debilitated nerve and broken force will send you down the stream again, and reconsign you to the condition of a province.

If such should become the fate of your constitution, ask yourselves what must be the motive of your government? It is easier to govern a province by a faction, than to govern a co-ordinate country by co-ordinate means. I do not say it is now, but it will always be thought easiest by the managers of the day, to govern the Irish nation by the agency of such a faction, as long as this country shall be found willing to let her connexion with Great Britain be preserved only by her own degradation. In such a precarious and wretched state of things, if it shall ever be found to exist, the true friend of Irish liberty and British connexion will see, that the only means of saving both must be, as Lord Chatham expressed it, " the infusion of new health and blood into the constitution." He will see how deep a stake each country has in the liberty of the other; he will see what a bulwark he adds to the common cause, by giving England a co-ordinate and co-interested ally, instead of an oppressed, enfeebled, and suspected dependant; he will see how grossly the credulity of Britain is abused by those who make her believe that her interest is promoted by our depression; he will see the desperate precipice to which she approaches by such conduct; and with an animated and generous piety, he will labour to avert her danger.

But, gentlemen of the jury, what is likely to be his fate? The interest of the sovereign must be for ever the interest of his people, because his interest lives beyond his life: it must live in his fame; it must live in the tenderness of his solicitude for an unborn posterity; it must live in that heart-attaching bond, by which millions of men have united the destinies of themselves and their children with his, and call him by the endearing appellation of king and father of his people.

But what can be the interest of such a government as I have described? Not the interest of the king—not the interest of the people; but the sordid interest of the hour; the interest in deceiving the one, and in oppressing and defaming the other; the interest of unpunished rapine and unmerited favour: that odious and abject interest, that prompts them to extinguish public spirit in punishment or in bribe, and to pursue every man, even to death, who has sense to see, and integrity and firmness enough to abhor and to oppose them. What, therefore, I say, will be the fate of the man who embarks in an enterprise of so much difficulty and danger? I will not answer it. Upon that hazard has my client put every thing that can be dear to man, his fame, his fortune, his person, his liberty, and his children; but with what event your verdict only can answer, and to that I refer your country.

There is a fourth point remaining. Says this paper,—" For both these purposes, it appears necessary that provincial conventions should assemble, preparatory to the convention of the Protestant people. The delegates of the Catholic body are not justified in communicating with individuals, or even bodies, of inferior authority; and therefore an assembly of a similar nature and organization is necessary to establish an intercourse of sentiment, an uniformity of conduct, an united cause, and an united nation. If a convention on the one part does not soon follow, and is not soon connected with that on the other, the common cause will split into the partial interests; the people will relax into inattention and inertness; the union of affection and exertion will dissolve; and, too probably, some local insurrection, instigated by the malignity of our common enemy, may commit the character, and risk the tranquillity of the island, which can be obviated only by the influence of an assembly arising from, and assimilated with the people, and whose spirit may be, as it were, knit with the soul of the nation. Unless the sense of the Protestant people be, on their part, as fairly collected and as judiciously directed; unless individual exertion consolidates into collective strength; unless the particles unite into one mass, we may, perhaps, serve some person or some party for a little, but the public not at all. The nation is neither insolent, nor rebellious, nor seditious; while it knows its rights, it is unwilling to manifest its powers; it would rather supplicate administration to anticipate revolution by well-timed reform, and to save their country in mercy to themselves."

Gentlemen, it is with something more than common reverence, it is with a species of terror that I am obliged to tread this ground. But what is the idea, put in the strongest point of view? We are willing not to manifest our powers, but to supplicate administration to anticipate revolution, that the legislature may save the country, in mercy to itself.

Let me suggest to you, gentlemen, that there are some circumstances, which have happened in the history of this country, that may better serve as a comment upon this part of the case, than any I can make. I am not bound to defend Mr Rowan, as to the truth or wisdom of the opinions he may have formed. But if he did really conceive the situation of the country such, as that the not redressing her grievances might tend to a convulsion; and of such an opinion not even Mr. Rowan is answerable here for the wisdom, much less shall I insinuate any idea of my own upon so awful a subject; but if he did so conceive the fact to be, and acted from the fair and honest suggestion of a mind anxious for the public good, I must confess, gentlemen, I do not know in what part of the British constitution to find the principle of his criminality.

But, be pleased further to consider, that he cannot be understood to put the fact on which he argues on the authority of his assertion. The condition of Ireland was as open to the observation of every other man, as to that of Mr. Rowan. What, then, does this part of the publication amount to? In my mind, simply to this:—

"The nature of oppression in all countries is such, that, although it may be borne to a certain degree, it cannot be borne beyond that degree. You find that exemplified in Great Britain; you find the people of England patient to a certain point, but patient no longer. That infatuated monarch, James II., experienced this. The time did come, when the measure of popular sufferings and popular patience was full— when a single drop was sufficient to make the waters of bitterness to overflow. I think this measure in Ireland is brimful at present; I think the state of the representation of the people in parliament is a grievance; I think the utter exclusion of three millions of people is a grievance of that kind, that the people are not likely long to endure, and the continuation of which may plunge the country into that state of despair, which wrongs, exasperated by perseverance, never fail to produce." But to whom is even this language addressed? Not to the body of the people on whose temper and moderation, if once excited, perhaps not much confidence could be placed; but to that authoritative body, whose influence and power would have restrained the excesses of the irritable and tumultuous, and for that purpose expressly does this publication address the Volunteers.

"We are told that we are in danger. I call upon you, the great constitutional saviours of Ireland, to defend the country to which you have given political existence, and to use whatever sanction your great name, your sacred character, and the weight you have in the community, must give you, to repress wicked designs, if any there are. We feel ourselves strong—the people are always strong; the public chains can only be rivetted by the public hands. Look to those devoted regions of southern despotism: behold the expiring victim on his knees, presenting the javelin, reeking with his blood, to the ferocious monster who returns it into his heart. Call not that monster the tyrant; he is no more than the executioner of that inhuman tyranny, which the people practise upon themselves, and of which he is only reserved to be a later victim than the wretch he has sent before. Look to a nearer country, where the sanguinary characters are more legible—whence you almost hear the groans of death and torture. Do you ascribe the rapine and murder in France to the few names that we are execrating here? or do you not see that it is the frenzy of an infuriated multitude, abusing its own strength, and practising those hideous abominations upon itself? Against the violence of this strength, let your virtue and influence be our safeguard."

What criminality, gentlemen of the jury, can you find in this? What, at any time: but I ask you, peculiarly at this momentous period, what guilt you can find in it? My client saw the scene of horror and blood which covers almost the face of Europe: he feared that causes, which he thought similar, might produce similar effects; and he seeks to avert those dangers, by calling the united virtue and tried moderation of the country into a state of strength and vigilance. Yet this is the conduct which the prosecution of this day seeks to punish and stigmatize; and this is the language for which this paper is reprobated to-day, as tending to turn the hearts of the people against their sovereign, and inviting them to overturn the constitution.

Let us now, gentlemen, consider the concluding part of this publication. It recommends a meeting of the people, to deliberate on constitutional methods of redressing grievances. Upon this subject I am inclined to suspect that I have in my youth taken up crude ideas, not founded, perhaps, in law; but I did imagine that, when the bill of rights restored the right of petitioning for the redress of grievances, it was understood that the people might boldly state among themselves that grievances did exist; I did imagine it was understood that people might lawfully assemble themselves in such manner as they might deem most orderly and decorous. I thought I had collected it from the greatest luminaries of the law. The power of petitioning seemed to me to imply the right of assembling for the purpose of deliberation. The law requiring a petition to be presented by a limited number, seemed to me to admit that the petition might be prepared by any number whatever, provided, in doing so, they did not commit any breach or violation of the public peace. I know that there has been a law passed in the Irish parliament of last year, which may bring my former opinion into a merited want of authority. The law declares that no body of men may delegate a power to any smaller number, to act, think, or petition for them. If that law had not passed, I should have thought that the assembling by a delegate convention was recommended, in order to avoid the tumult and disorder of a promiscuous assembly of the whole mass of the people. I should have conceived, before that act, that any law to abridge the orderly appointment of the few, to consult for the interest of the many, and thus force the many to consult by themselves, or not at all, would, in fact, be a law not to restrain but to promote insurrection. But that law has spoken, and my error must stand corrected.

Of this, however, let me remind you: you are to try this part of the publication by what the law was then, not by what it is now. How was it understood until last session of Parliament. You had, both in England and Ireland, for the last ten years, these delegated meetings. The Volunteers of Ireland, in 1783, met by delegation: they framed a plan of parliamentary reform; they presented it to the representative wisdom of the nation. It was not received; but no man ever dreamed that it was not the undoubted right of the subject to assemble in that manner. They assembled by delegation at Dungannon; and to show the idea then entertained of the legality of their public conduct, that same body of Volunteers was thanked by both Houses of Parliament, and their delegates most graciously received at the throne. The other day you had delegated representatives of the Catholics of Ireland, publicly elected by the members of that persuasion, and sitting in convention in the heart of your capital, carrying on an actual treaty with the existing government, and under the eye of your own Parliament, which was then assembled; you have seen the delegates from that convention carry the complaints of their grievances to the foot of the throne, from whence they brought back to that convention the auspicious tidings of that redress which they had been refused at home.

Such, gentlemen, have been the means of popular communication and discussion, which, until the last session, have been deemed legal in this country, as, happily for the sister kingdom, they are yet considered there.

I do not complain of this act as any infraction of popular liberty; I should not think it becoming in me to express any complaint against a law, when once become such. I observe only, that one mode of popular deliberation is thereby taken utterly away, and you are reduced to a situation in which you never stood before. You are living in a country, where the constitution is rightly stated to be only ten years old—where the people have not the ordinary rudiments of education. It is a melancholy story, that the lower orders of the people here have less means of being enlightened than the same class of people in any other country. If there be no means left by which public measures can be canvassed, what will be the consequence? Where the press is free, and discussion unrestrained, the mind, by the collision of intercourse, gets rid of its own asperities; a sort of insensible perspiration takes place in the body politic, by which those acrimonies, which would otherwise fester and inflame, are quietly dissolved and dissipated. But now, if any aggregate assembly shall meet, they are censured; if a printer publishes their resolutions, he is punished: rightly, to be sure, in both cases, for it has been lately done. If the people say, let us not create tumult, but meet in delegation, they cannot do it; if they are anxious to promote parliamentary reform in that way, they cannot do it; the law of the last session has for the first time declared such meetings to be a crime.

What then remains? The liberty of the press *only*—that sacred palladium, which no influence, no power, no minister, no government, which nothing, but the depravity, or folly, or corruption of a jury, can ever destroy. And what calamities are the people saved from, by having public communication left open to them? I will tell you, gentlemen, what they are saved from, and what the government is saved from; I will tell you also to what both are exposed by shutting up that communication. In one case, sedition speaks aloud and walks abroad: the demagogue goes forth—the public eye is upon him—he frets his busy hour upon the stage; but soon either weariness, or bribe, or proishment, or disappointment, bears him down. or drives him off, and he appears no more. In the other case, how does the work of sedition go forward? Night after night the muffled rebel steals forth in the dark, and casts another and another brand upon the pile, to which, when the hour of fatal maturity shall arrive, he will apply the torch. If you doubt of the horrid consequence of suppressing the effusion even of individual discontent, look to those enslaved countries where the protection of despotism is supposed to be secured by such restraints. Even the person of the despot there is never in safety. Neither the fears of the despot, nor the machinations of the slave, have any slumber—the one anticipating the moment of peril, the other watching the opportunity of aggression. The fatal crisis is equally a surprise upon both the decisive instant is precipitated without warning—by folly on the one side, or by frenzy on the other: and there is no notice of the treason, till the traitor acts. In those unfortunate countries—one cannot read it without horror—there are officers, whose province it is, to have the water which is to be drunk by their rulers, sealed up in bottles, lest some wretched miscreant should throw poison into the draught.

But, gentlemen, if you wish for a nearer and more interesting example, you have it in the history of your own revolution. You have it at that memorable period, when the monarch found a servile acquiescence in the ministers of his folly—when the liberty of the press was trodden under foot—when venal sheriffs returned packed juries, to carry into effect those fatal conspiracies of the few against the many—when the devoted benches of public justice were filled by some of those foundlings of fortune, who, overwhelmed in the torrent of corruption at an early period, lay at the bottom, like drowned bodies, while soundness or sanity remained in them; but, at length, becoming buoyant by putrefaction, they rose as they rotted, and floated to the surface of the polluted stream, where they were drifted along, the objects of terror, and contagion, and abomination.*

In that awful moment of a nation's travail, of the last gasp of tyranny, and the first breath of freedom, how pregnant is the example! The press extinguished, the people enslaved, and the prince undone. As the advocate of society, therefore—of peace—of domestic liberty—and the lasting union of the two countries—I conjure you to guard the liberty of the press, that great sentinel of the state, that grand detector of public imposture; guard it, because, when it sinks, there sinks with it, in one common grave, the liberty of the subject, and the security of the crown.

Gentlemen, I am glad that this question has not been brought forward earlier; I rejoice, for the sake of the court, of the jury, and of the public repose, that this question has not been brought forward till

---

* "It may not be ungratifying to hear the manner in which this passage was suggested to the speaker's mind. A day or two before Mr. Rowan's trial, one of Mr. Curran's friends showed him a letter that he had received from Bengal, in which the writer, after mentioning the Hindoo custom of throwing the dead into the Ganges, added, that he was then upon the banks of that river, and that, as he wrote, he could see several bodies floating down its stream. The orator shortly after, while describing a corrupted bench, recollected this fact and applied it as above."—*Life of Curran, by his Son*, vol. i., p. 316.

now. In Great Britain, analogous circumstances have taken place. At the commencement of that unfortunate war which has deluged Europe with blood, the spirit of the English people was tremblingly alive to the terror of French principles; at that moment of general paroxysm, to accuse was to convict The danger looked larger to the public eye, from the misty region through which it was surveyed. We measure inaccessible heights by the shadows which they project, where the lowness and the distance of the light form the length of the shade.

There is a sort of aspiring and adventurous credulity, which disdains assenting to obvious truths, and delights in catching at the improbability of circumstances, as its best ground of faith. To what other cause, gentlemen, can you ascribe, that in the wise, the reflecting, and the philosophic nation of Great Britain, a printer has been gravely found guilty of a libel, for publishing those resolutions to which the present minister of that kingdom had actually subscribed his name?— To what other cause can you ascribe, what in my mind is still more astonishing, in such a country as Scotland—a nation cast in the happy medium between the spiritless acquiescence of submissive poverty, and the sturdy credulity of pampered wealth—cool and ardent—adventurous and persevering—winging her eagle flight against the blaze of every science, with an eye that never winks, and a wing that never tires—crowned, as she is, with the spoils of every art, and decked with the wreath of every muse, from the deep and scrutinizing researches of her Hume, to the sweet and simple, but not less sublime and pathetic, morality of her Burns—how, from the bosom of a country like that, genius, and character, and talents, should be banished to a distant barbarous soil, condemned to pine under the horrid communion of vulgar vice and base-born profligacy, for twice the period that ordinary calculation gives to the continuance of human life?*

But I will not further press an idea that is so painful to me, and I am sure must be painful to you. I will only say, you have now an example, of which neither England nor Scotland had the advantage: you have the example of the panic, the infatuation, and the contrition of both. It is now for you to decide, whether you will profit by their experience of idle panic and idle regret; or whether you meanly prefer to palliate a servile imitation of their frailty, by a paltry affectation of their repentance. It is now for you to show, that you are not carried away by the same hectic delusions, to acts, of which no tears can wash away the fatal consequences, or the indelible reproach.

Gentlemen, I have been warning you by instances of public intellect suspended or obscured; let me rather excite you by the example of that intellect recovered and restored. In that case which Mr. Attorney-General has cited himself—I mean that of the trial of Lambert, in England—is there a topic of invective against constituted authorities, is there a topic of abuse against every department of British government, that you do not find in the most glowing and unqualified terms

---

* Alluding to Scotland, where sentence of transportation for fourteen years, had been passed upon Mr. Muir, Mr. Palmer, and others. Recently public monuments have been erected to these patriots in Edinburgh and London.

in that publication, for which the printer of it was prosecuted, and acquitted by an English jury? See, too, what a difference there is between the case of a man publishing his own opinion of facts, thinking that he is bound by duty to hazard the promulgation of them, and without the remotest hope of any personal advantage, and that of a man who makes publication his trade. And saying this, let me not be misunderstood. It is not my province to enter into any abstract defence of the opinions of any man upon public subjects. I do not affirmatively state to you that these grievances, which this paper supposes, do, in fact, exist; yet I cannot but say, that the movers of this prosecution have forced this question upon you. Their motives and their merits, like those of all accusers, are put in issue before you; and I need not tel. you how strongly the motive and merits of any informer ought to influence the fate of his accusation.

I agree most implicitly with Mr. Attorney-General, that nothing can be more criminal than an attempt to work a change in the government by armed force; and I entreat that the court will not suffer any expression of mine to be considered as giving encouragement or defence to any design to excite disaffection, to overawe or to overturn the government. But I put my client's case upon another ground: if he was led into an opinion of grievances, where there were none, if he thought there ought to be a reform, where none was necessary, he is answerable only for his intention. He can be answerable to you in the same way only that he is answerable to that God, before whom the accuser, the accused, and the judge, must appear together; that is, not for the clearness of his understanding, but for the purity of his heart.

Gentlemen, Mr. Attorney-General has said, that Mr. Rowan did by this publication (supposing it to be his) recommend, under the name of equality, a general indiscriminate assumption of public rule, by every the meanest person in the state. Low as we are in point of public information, there is not, I believe, any man, who thinks for a moment, that does not know that all which the great body of the people of any country can have from any government, is a fair encouragement to their industry, and protection for the fruits of their labour. And there is scarcely any man, I believe, who does not know, that if a people could become so silly as to abandon their stations in society, under pretence of governing themselves, they would become the dupes and the victims of their own folly. But does this publication recommend any such infatuated abandonment, or any such desperate assumption? I will read the words which relate to that subject—"By liberty, we never understood unlimited freedom; nor by equality, the levelling of property, or the destruction of subordination." I ask you, with what justice, upon what principle of common sense, you can charge a man with the publication of sentiments the very reverse of what his words avow, and that, when there is no collateral evidence, where there is no foundation whatever, save those very words, by which his meaning can be ascertained? Or, if you do adopt an arbitrary principle of imputing to him *your* meaning, instead of his own, what publication can be guiltless or safe? It is a sort of accusation that I am ashamed and sorry to see introduced in a court acting on the principles of the British constitution.

In the bitterness of reproach it was said, "Out of thine own mouth will I condemn thee." From the severity of justice I demand no more. See if, in the words that have been spoken, you can find matter to acquit or to condemn—"By liberty, we never understood unlimited freedom; nor by equality, the levelling of property, or the destruction of subordination. This is a calumny invented by that faction, or that gang, which misrepresents the King to the people, and the people to the King—traduces one half of the nation, to cajole the other—and, by keeping up distrust and division, wishes to continue the proud arbitrator of the fortune and fate of Ireland." Here you find that meaning, disclaimed as a calumny, which is artfully imputed as a crime.

I say, therefore, gentlemen of the jury, as to the four parts into which the publication must be divided, I answer thus. It calls upon the Volunteers. Consider the time, the danger—the authority of the prosecutors themselves for believing that danger to exist—the high character, the known moderation, the approved loyalty of that venerable institution—the similarity of the circumstances between the period at which they were summoned to take arms, and that in which they have been called upon to re-assume them. Upon this simple ground, gentlemen, you will decide, whether this part of the publication was libellous and criminal, or not.

As to reform, I could wish to have said nothing upon it; I believe I have said enough. If Mr. Rowan, in disclosing that opinion, thought the state required it, he acted like an honest man. For the rectitude of the opinion he was not answerable; he discharged his duty in telling the country that he thought so.

As to the emancipation of the Catholics, I cannot but say that Mr. Attorney-General did very wisely in keeping clear of that subject. Yet, gentlemen, I need not tell you how important a figure it was intended to make upon the scene; though, from unlucky accidents, it has become necessary to expunge it during the rehearsal.*

Of the concluding part of this publication, the convention which it recommends, I have spoken already. I wish not to trouble you with saying more upon it. I feel that I have already trespassed much upon your patience. In truth, upon a subject embracing such a variety of topics, a rigid observance either of conciseness or arrangement could, perhaps, scarcely be expected. It is, however, with pleasure I feel I am drawing to a close, and that only one question remains, to which I would beg your attention.

Whatever, gentlemen, may be your opinion of the meaning of this publication, there yet remains a great point for you to decide upon:— namely, whether, in point of fact, this publication be imputable to Mr Rowan, or not?—whether he did publish it or not? Two witnesses are called to that fact—one of the name of Lyster, and the other of the name of Morton. You must have observed that Morton gave no evi-

---

* Referring to the Emancipation Act of 1793.

dence upon which that paper could have even been read; he produced no paper—he identified no paper—he said that he got some paper, but that he had given it away. So that, in point of law, there was no evidence given by him, on which it could have gone to a jury; and, therefore, it turns entirely upon the evidence of the other witness. He has stated that he went to a public meeting, in a place where there was a gallery crowded with spectators, and that he there got a printed paper the same which has been read to you. I know you are well acquainted with the fact, that the credit of every witness must be considered by, and rest with the jury. They are the sovereign judges of that; and I will not insult your feelings by insisting on the caution with which you should watch the testimony of a witness that seeks to affect the liberty, or property, or character of your fellow-citizens. Under what circumstances does this evidence come before you? The witness says he has got a commission in the army, by the interest of a lady, from a person then high in administration. He told you that he made a memorandum upon the back of that paper, it being his general custom, when he got such papers, to make an indorsement upon them—that he did this from mere fancy—that he had no intention of giving any evidence on the subject—" he took it with no such view." There is something whimsical enough in this curious story. Put his credit upon the positive evidence adduced to his character. Who he is I know not—I know not the man; but his credit is impeached. Mr. Blake was called; he said he knew him. I asked him, " Do you think, sir, that Mr. Lyster is or is not a man deserving credit upon his oath?" If you find a verdict of conviction, it can be only upon the credit of Mr. Lyster. What said Mr. Blake? Did he tell you that he considered him a man to be believed upon his oath? He did not attempt to say that he did. The best he could say was, that he " would hesitate." Do you believe Blake? Have you the same opinion of Lyster's testimony that Mr. Blake has? Do you know Lyster? If you do know him, and know that he is credible, your knowledge should not be shaken by the doubts of any man. But if you do not know him, you must take his credit from an unimpeached witness, swearing that he would hesitate to believe him. In my mind, there is a circumstance of the strongest nature that came out from Lyster on the table. I am aware that a most respectable man, if impeached by surprise, may not be prepared to repel a wanton calumny by contrary testimony. But was Lyster unapprised of this attack upon him? What said he? " I knew that you had Blake to examine against me—you have brought him here for that purpose." He knew the very witness that was to be produced against him—he knew that his credit was impeached—and yet he produced no person to support that credit. What said Mr. Smyth? " From my knowledge of him, I would not believe him upon his oath."

Mr. Attorney-General—I beg pardon, but I must set Mr. Curran right. Mr. Lyster said he had heard Blake would be here, but not in time to prepare himself.

Mr. Curran—But what said Mrs. Hatchell? Was the production o. that witness a surprise upon Mr. Lyster? Her cross-examination shows the fact to be the contrary. The learned counsel, you see, was perfectly apprised of a chain of private circumstances, to which he pointed his questions. This lady's daughter was married to the elder brother of the witness Lyster. Did he know these circumstances by inspiration? No; they could come only from Lyster himself. I insist, therefore, that the gentleman knew his character was to be impeached; his counsel knew it, and not a single witness has been produced to support it. Then consider, gentlemen, upon what ground can you find a verdict of conviction against my client, when the only witness produced to the fact of publication is impeached, without even an attempt to defend his character? Many hundreds, he said, were at that meeting. Why not produce one of them, to swear to the fact of such a meeting? One he has ventured to name; but he was certainly very safe in naming a person, who, he has told you, is not in the kingdom, and could not, therefore, be called to confront him.

Gentlemen, let me suggest another observation or two, if still you have any doubt as to the guilt or innocence of the defendant. Give me leave to suggest to you what circumstances you ought to consider, in order to found your verdict. You should consider the character of the person accused; and in this your task is easy. I will venture to say, there is not a man in this nation more known than the gentleman who is the subject of this prosecution; not only by the part he has taken in public concerns, and which he has taken in common with many, but still more so, by that extraordinary sympathy for human affliction, which, I am sorry to think, he shares with so small a number. There is not a day that you hear the cries of your starving manufacturers in your streets, that you do not also see the advocate of their sufferings—that you do not see his honest and manly figure, with uncovered head, soliciting for their relief—searching the frozen heart of charity for every string that can be touched by compassion, and urging the force of every argument and every motive, save that which his modesty suppresses, the authority of his own generous example. Or if you see him not there, you may trace his steps to the private abode of disease, and famine, and despair—the messenger of heaven, bringing with him food, and medicine, and consolation. Are these the materials of which you suppose anarchy and public rapine to be formed? Is this the man on whom to fasten the abominable charge of goading on a frantic populace to mutiny and bloodshed? Is this the man likely to apostatize from every principle that can bind him to the state—his birth, his property, his education, his character, and his children? Let me tell you, gentlemen of the jury, if you agree with his prosecutors, in thinking that there ought to be a sacrifice of such a man on such an occasion—and upon the credit of such evidence you are to convict him—never did you, never can you give a sentence, consigning any man to public punishment, with less danger to his person or to his fame: for where could the hireling be found to fling contumely or ingratitude at his head, whose private distresses he had not endeavoured to alleviate, or whose public condition he had not laboured to improve?

I cannot, however, avoid reverting to a circumstance that distinguishes the case of Mr. Rowan from that of the late sacrifice in a neighbouring kingdom.*

The severer law of that country, it seems—and happy for them that it should—enables them to remove from their sight the victim of their infatuation. The more merciful spirit of our law deprives you of that consolation; his sufferings must remain for ever before our eyes, a continual call upon your shame and your remorse. But those sufferings will do more ; they will not rest satisfied with your unavailing contrition —they will challenge the great and paramount inquest of society—the man will be weighed against the charge, the witness, and the sentence —and impartial justice will demand, why has an Irish jury done this deed? The moment he ceases to be regarded as a criminal, he becomes of necessity an accuser ; and let me ask you, what can your most zealous defenders be prepared to answer to such a charge? When your sentence shall have sent him forth to that stage, which guilt alone can render infamous, let me tell you, he will not be like a little statue upon a mighty pedestal, diminishing by elevation ; but he will stand a striking and imposing object upon a monument, which, if it does not (and it cannot) record the atrocity of his crime, must record the atrocity of his conviction.

Upon this subject, therefore, credit me when I say, that I am still more anxious for you than I can possibly be for him. I cannot but feel the peculiarity of your situation. Not the jury of his own choice, which the law of England allows, but which ours refuses ; collected in that box by a person certainly no friend to Mr. Rowan†—certainly not very deeply interested in giving him a very impartial jury. Feeling this, as I am persuaded you do, you cannot be surprised, however you may be distressed, at the mournful presage with which an anxious public is led to fear the worst from your possible determination. But I will not, for the justice and honour of our common country, suffer my mind to be borne away by such melancholy anticipation. I will not relinquish the confidence that this day will be the period of his sufferings ; and, however mercilessly he has been hitherto pursued, that your verdict will send him home to the arms of his family, and the wishes of his country. But if, which heaven forbid! it hath still been unfortunately determined, that because he has not bent to power and authority, because he would not bow down before the golden calf, and worship it, he is to be bound and cast into the furnace ; I do trust in God, that there is a redeeming spirit in the constitution, which will be seen to walk with the sufferer through the flames, and to preserve him unhurt by the conflagration.

Upon leaving the court, Mr. Curran was drawn home by the populace, who took the horses from his carriage.

At the close of Curran's speech there was another shout of admiration and sympathy, which Lord Clonmel with difficulty stopped. The Attorney-General (most irregularly) spoke in defence of his own character, against the charge of oppressive delay, and then Prime-Sergeant the Hon. James Fitzgerald replied to Curran. Lord Clonmel (Chief Ju-

* Scotland, from whence Messrs. Muir, Palmer, and others, were transported for sedition
† Gifford, the Sheriff.

nie, charged the jury violently against Mr Rowan. In this charge he used the following words, omitted in the editions of the trials, but given in Curran's Memoirs, by his Son, vol. i., p. 347 :—
"One hundred and fifty Volunteers, or United Irishmen, and not one comes forward! Many of them would have been proud to assist him (the traverser.) *Their silence speaks a thousand times more strongly than any cavilling upon this man's credit—the silence of such a number is a volume of evidence in support of the prosecution.*"

Justice (afterwards Lord) Downes also charged, and the Jury, in t minutes, found a verdict of Guilty. The following scene then occurred:—

"Lord Clonmel—Do the Counsel for the defendant desire four days' time to move in arrest of judgment?

"Mr. Curran—The only instructions I have from my client are to disclaim any application of that kind: he does not wish to take advantage of errors in the record, if any there be; but is now ready to attend to receive what sentence the court may be pleased to pronounce.

"Lord Clonmel—(After conferring with the other judges)—We will not pronounce judgment till four days. Mr. Sheriff, take care of your prisoner.

"The Counsel for Mr. Rowan here objected, that he was not a prisoner—he had not been in custody; he had not given bail upon this information; he was bound in no recognizance; was served with no process; he had appeared to the information by attorney; he pleaded by attorney; the issue was tried after the manner of a civil action, a word merely of the record being read, and the defendant was not given in charge to the jury, as the practice is, where he appears in custody. Mr. Rowan attended the trial, it is true, but the court had no judicial cognizance of him; the information could have been tried in his absence; he attended as a common auditor, and the witness being called upon to point him out at the desire of the bench, might have been a satisfaction to them to see that the witnesses were speaking of the same person, but it was altogether unprecedented in such cases as the present. Mr. Rowan was ready for sentence; he claims no indulgence, does not insist upon the four-day rule; but if the court, for their own accommodation, choose to defer the sentence for four days, they have no legal authority for sending Mr. Rowan to prison, until sentence is pronounced, or the usual and accustomed process issued against him.

"Lord Clonmel—If the Attorney-General consents. I have no objection.

"The Attorney-General had left the court, and the Solicitor for the Crown remained silent.

"Lord Clonmel—The defendant is a convict, as such he is a prisoner; the law must have its course. Adjourn the court.

"Accordingly the court was adjourned.

"Mr. Rowan was conveyed to the New Prison, attended by both the Sheriffs and a formidable array of horse and foot guards."—*Mac Nevin's State Trials*, p. 122.

February 3rd, 1794.

Affidavits were read in court, to prove that one of the jury was avowedly hostil

February 4th, 1794.

The Recorder applied to set aside the verdict given in the case of Archibald Hamilton Rowan, Esq. The application was grounded upon different affidavits sworn in court, charging, 1st—One of the jurors with a declaration against Mr. Rowan, previous to trial. 2ndly—Partiality in one of the high sheriffs. 3rdly—That John Lyster, the principal evidence, was not to be believed upon his oath he, as the affidavits stated, having been guilty of perjury. And 4thly—upon which the learned gentleman rested his case—the misdirection of the court. After much discussion, Mr. Curran followed on the same side, and said:—

It was an early idea, that a verdict in a criminal case could not be set aside *inconsulto rege;* but the law had stood otherwise, without a doubt to impeach its principle, for the last two reigns. Common sense would say, that the discretion of the court should go at least as far in criminal as in civil cases, and very often to go no further would be to stop far short of what was right, as in those great questions where the prosecution may be considered either as an attempt to extinguish liberty, or as a necessary measure for the purpose of repressing the virulence of public licentiousness and dangerous faction ; where there can be no alternative between guilt or martyrdom ; where the party prosecuted must either be considered as a culprit sinking beneath the punishment of his own crimes, or a victim sacrificed to the vices of others. But when it clearly appears that the party has fallen a prey to persecuting combination, there remains but one melancholy question—how far did that combination reach?

There have been two cases lately decided in this very court ; the King and Pentland, where the motion was made and refused ; and the King and Bowen, where it was granted ; both of which show, that captious sophistry and technical pedantry have here, as well as in England, given way to liberal and rational inquiry ; and that the court will not now, in their discretion, refuse a motion of this kind, unless they can, at the same time, lay their hands upon their hearts, and say, they believe in their consciences, that justice has been done : such was the manly language of one of your lordships [Mr. Justice Downes], and such the opinion of the court on a former occasion.

He then cited 7 Modern 57, as referred to in Bacon *tit*. Trial, to show, that where there was good ground of challenge to a juror, not known at the trial, it was sufficient cause for setting aside the verdict.

In England they have a particular act of parliament, entitling the party to strike a special jury to try the fact, and then he has time between the striking and the trial to question the propriety of that jury; here my client had no information, till the instant of trial, who his jurors were to be.

There are certain indulgences granted at times, perhaps by the connivance of humanity, which men who are not entitled to demand them in an open court, obtain, nevertheless, by sidelong means ; and perhaps the little breach which affords that light to the mind of the man accused, is a circumstance concerning which the court would feel pain, even if called upon to say, that it should in all cases be prevented ; but to overturn principles and authorities, for the purpose of oppressing the subject, is what this court will never do.

The first of the affidavits I shall consider, is that of the traverser.— I do not recollect whether it states the sheriff, in avowed terms, to be an emissary or a hireling agent of the castle, therefore I do not state it from the affidavit ; but he swears that he does believe that he did labour to bring into the box a jury full of prejudices, and of the blackest impressions ; instead of having, as they ought, fair and impartial minds, and souls like white paper.

This sheriff now stands in court ; he might have denied it, if he would ; he had an opportunity of answering it ; but he has left it an undenied assertion—he was not certainly obliged to answer it ; for no man is bound to convict himself. But there is a part of that charge which amounts at least to this :—" Your heart was poisoned against me, and you collected those to be my judges, who, if they could not be under the dominion of bad dispositions, might be, at least, the dupes of good." The most favourable thing that can be said is this, you sought to bring against me honest prejudices, but you brought against me wicked ones

The very general charge that he sought for persons who, he knew, were most likely to bring prejudices with them into the jury box, is a part of the affidavit that it was incumbent on him to answer if he could.

I do not contend, that what is charged in the affidavit would have been a ground of principal challenge to the array; but I hold it to be the better opinion, that a challenge to the array for favour does well lie in the mouth of the defendant. The ancient notion was, you shall not challenge the array for favour, where the King is a party; the King only can challenge for favour; for the principle was, that every man ought to be favourable to the crown: but, thank God, the advancement of legal knowledge, and the growing understanding of the age, have dissipated such illiberal and mischievous conceptions.

But I am putting too much stress upon such technical, discarded, and antiquated scruples. The true question has been already stated from the authority of Mr. Justice Downes, and that question is—" Has justice been done?"

It is a matter upon which scarce any understanding would condescend to hesitate, whether a man had been fairly tried, whose triors had been collected together by an avowed enemy, whose conduct had been such as to leave no doubt that he had purposely brought prejudiced men into the box.

In every country where freedom obtains, there must subsist parties. In this country, and Great Britain, I trust there never will be a time when there shall not be men found zealous for the actual government of the day. So, on the other hand, I trust there will never be a time, when there will not be found men zealous and enthusiastic in the cause of popular freedom, and of the public rights. If, therefore, a person in public office suffers his own prejudices, however honestly anxious he may be for a prosecution carried on by those to whom he is attached, to influence him so far as to choose men, to his knowledge devoted to the principles he espouses, it is an error which a High Court of Judicature, seeking to do right justice, will not fail to correct.

A sheriff, in such a case, might not have perceived the partiality of his conduct, because he was surveying through the medium of prejudice and habitual corruption; but it is impossible to think that this sheriff meant to be impartial; it is an interpretation more favourable than his conduct will allow of; if he deserves any credit at all, it is for not answering the charge made against him; at the same time, that, by not answering it, he has left unimpeached the credit of the charge itself.

The sheriff here tendered some form of an affidavit, which the court would not allow to be sworn or read, for the same reason, that those sworn and tendered by the defendant's counsel, had been before refused. Mr. Curran, however, consented to its being sworn and read, which the Attorney-General declined, being unacquainted with the contents, and uninstructed as to its tendency; it, therefore, was not sworn.

Mr. Curran proceeded—Is this, then, the way to meet a fair application to the court, to see whether justice has been done between the subject and the crown? I offer it again, let the affidavit be read.— And let me remind the court, that the great reason for sending a cause back to a jury is, that new light must be shed upon it; and how must your lordships feel, when you see that indulgence granted to the conscience of the jury denied to the court?

Mr. Attorney-General—I am concerned that any lawyer should make a proposition in the manner Mr. Curran has done; he proposes to have an affidavit read, provided we consent that others, which the court have already refused, should be now read.* I did not hear it offered; but is it to be presumed that I will consent to have an affidavit read, about which I know nothing? Yesterday, without any communication with a human being, I did say, that I conceived it unnecessary to answer any of the affidavits, thinking that they were not sufficient to ground the application made to the court. And it is presumed I am so mad as to consent to the reading of affidavits which I have not seen.

Some altercation here took place, when Lord Clonmel, Chief Justice, interposed, and said, that the counsel had certainly a right to argue it on the ground that the sheriff was biassed, and did return a jury prejudiced against the traverser.

Mr. Curran was about to observe upon the expression of one of the jury, sworn to in another affidavit, "that there would be no safety in the country, until the defendant was either hanged or banished," when it was asked by the court, whether the time of its coming to the knowledge of the traverser, that the sheriff was biassed, was stated in his affidavit?

Mr. Curran—He was in prison, and could not have the attendance of those counsel whose assistance he had in court; and, besides, from the nature of the circumstances, it was impossible he could have been sufficiently apprised of its consequences, for he saw not that panel till the day of the trial, when he could not have had time to make any inquiry into the characters, dispositions, or connexions of the jury.

If triors had been appointed to determine the issue, favourable or not, what would have been their finding? Could they say upon their oaths, that he was not unfavourable to that party against whom he could make such a declaration?

Favour is not cause of principal challenge, which, if put upon a pleading, would conclude the party. Favour is that which makes the man, in vulgar parlance, unfit to try the question. And as to the time these facts came to his knowledge, he has sworn that he was utterly ignorant of them at the time of his coming into court to take his trial.

I will not glance at the character of any absent noble person, high in office; but let it be remembered, that it is a government prosecution, and that the witness has, from a low and handicap situation, scraped himself into preferment, perhaps—for I will put the best construction upon it—by offering himself as a man honestly anxious for the welfare of his country; in short, it is too obvious to require any comment, what the nature of the whole transaction has been, that he got his commission as a compensation *pro labore impendendo*, and came afterwards into court, to pay down the stipulated purchase.

Had this, then, been an unbiassed jury, was there not something in all these circumstances, that might have afforded more deliberation than that of one minute per man, for only so long was the jury out? and, had this been a fair witness, would he have lain down under a charge which, if true, ought not only to damn this verdict, but his character for ever? What would a corps of brother-officers think of a person, charged upon oath with the commission of two wilful perjuries, and that charge remaining undenied? Here is an undenied charge, in point of fact; and although I do not call upon the court to say, that this is a

* Mr. Attorney-General, it may be proper to observe, mistook Mr. Curran's proceed. which was an unqualified offer to have Mr. Gifford's affidavit read.

guilty and abominable person, yet surely the suspicion is strongly so, and must be considered. This was at least a verdict where the evidence went to the jury, under slighter blemishes than it will if my client has the advantage of another trial; for then he will put it out of the power of man to doubt that this witness has been perjured—this witness, who has had notice both here and at the trial, of the aspersions on his character, and yet has not called a human being to say that he entertained a contrary opinion of him.

Was he known any where? Did he crawl unobserved to the castle? Was it without the aid or knowledge of any body that that gaudy plumage grew on him, in which he appeared in court? If he was known for any thing else than what he is stated to be, it was, upon that day, almost a physical impossibility, in a court-house, which almost contained the country, not to have found some person, to give some sort of testimony respecting his general character. For though no man is bound to be ready at all times to answer particular charges, yet every man is supposed to come with his public attestation of common and general probity. But he has left that character, upon the merits of which my client is convicted, unsupported, even by his own poor corporal swearing. You are called upon, then, to say, whether, upon the evidence of a being of this kind, such a man as that is to be convicted, and sentenced to punishment, in a country where humanity is the leading feature even of the criminal law.

I have now to deal with the evidence of the second witness. A man coming to support the credit of another collaterally, is himself particularly pledged; then, what was his testimony? He did not know whether Mr. Gifford was concerned in the newspaper! And now, you have the silence of Gifford himself, in not answering Mr. Rowan's affidavit, to contradict that. And next, he did not know whether his own cousin-german was the relation of their common uncle! I call upon you, my lords, in the name of sacred justice and your country to declare whether the melancholy scenes and murderous plots of the Meal tub and the Rye-house are to be acted over again; and whether every Titus Oates that can be found is to be called into your courts, as the common vouchee of base and perjured accusation.

I also conceive, my lords, that the direction of the court was not agreeable to the law of Ireland. The defence of my client was rested upon this: that there was no evidence of the fact of publication; upon the incredibility of the fact; and the circumstances of discredit in the character of the witness: yet the court made this observation: "Gentlemen, it scarcely lies in the mouth of Mr. Rowan to build a defence upon objections of this kind to the characters of witnesses, because the fact was public; there were many there; the room was crowded below, the gallery was crowded above; and the publicity of the fact enabled him to produce a number of witnesses to falsify the assertion of the prosecutor, if, in fact, it could be falsified!" Is that the principle of criminal law? Is it a part of the British law, that the fate of the accused shall abide, not the positive establishment of guilt by the prosecutor, but the negative proof of innocence by himself? Why has it been said in foolish old books, that the law supposes the innocence of every man, till the contrary is proved? How has it happened that that language has been admired for its humanity, and not laughed at for its absurdity, in which the prayers of the court are addressed to heaven for the safe deliverance of the man accused? How comes it that so much public time is wasted in going into evidence of guilt, if the bare accusation of a man did call upon him to go into evidence of his innocence? The force of the observation is this. Mr. Rowan impeaches the credit of a witness, who has sworn that he saw him present, and doing certain acts, at a certain meeting; but it is asked, has he substantiated that discredit, by calling all the persons who were present to prove his absence from that meeting, which is only stated to have existed by a witness whom he alleges to have perjured himself? I call upon the example of judicial character; upon the faith of that high office, which is never so dignified as when it sees its errors and corrects them, to say, that the court was for a moment led away, so as to argue from the most seductive of all sophisms, that of the *petitio principii*.

See what meaning is to be gathered from such words: we say the whole, that this man has sworn, is a consummate lie; show it to be so, says the court, by admitting a part of it to be true. It is a false swearing; it is a conspiracy of two witnesses against this defendant; well, then, it lies upon him to rebut their testimony, by proving a great deal of it to be true! Is conjecture, then, in criminal cases, to stand in the place of truth and demonstration? Why were not some of those (I will strip the case of the honour of names which I respect), but why were not some of those, who knew that these two persons were to be brought forward, and that there were to be objections to their credit, if, as it is stated, it happened in the presence of a public crowd, rushing in from motives of curiosity, why were not numbers called on to establish that fact? On the contrary, the court have said to this effect: Mr. Rowan, you say you were not there; produce any of those persons with whom you were there, to swear you were not there! You say it was a perjury; if so, produce the people, that he has perjured himself in swearing to have been there! But as to your own being there, you can easily show the contrary of that, by producing some man that you saw there! You say you were not there! Yes. There were one hundred and fifty persons there: now produce any one of those to swear they saw you there!

It is impossible for the human mind to suppose a case, in which infatuation must have prevailed in a more progressive degree, than when a jury are thus, in fact, directed to receive no refutation nor proof of the perjury of the witness, but only of his truth. We will permit you to deny the charge, by establishing the fact: we will permit you to prove that they swore falsely to your being there, by producing another witness to prove to a certainty that you were there.

Mr. Curran was here interrupted by Lord Chief Justice Clonmel.

Lord Clonmel—The reasoning of the court was strong upon that point: this is a transaction stated by the witness to have happened in open day, in a crowded assembly, in the capital, amidst a number of persons dressed in the uniform of Hamilton Rowan. There has been nothing suddenly brought forward to surprise the traverser; yet what has he done? Did no offer, as in the common course to prove an alibi? It is stated to be at such a day, the witness swears at such an hour; the place is sworn to have been full of people, of Mr. Rowan's friends; but if there was even a partial assembly, it would be easy still to produce some one of those persons who were present, to say, that the fact did not happen which has been sworn to; or if you say Mr. Rowan was not there, it is easier still to prove it, by showing where he was; as thus: I breakfasted with him, I dined with him, I supped with him; he was with me, he was not at Purdon's ;disprove that assertion, by proving an affirmation inconsistent with it.

Mr. Curran—I beg leave to remind the court of what fell from it. "He may call," said the court, "any of those persons; he has not produced one of them;" upon this, I think, a most material point does hang. "He might have called them, for they were all of his own party."

Lord Clonmel—That is, if there were such persons there, or if there was no meeting at all, he might have proved that.

Mr. Curran—There was no such idea put to the jury, as whether there was a meeting or not: it was said they were all of his party, he might have produced them; and the non-production of them was a "volume of evidence" upon that point. No refinement can avoid this conclusion, that, even as your lordship now states the charge, the fate of the man must depend upon proving the negative.

Until the credit of the witness was established, he could not be called upon to bring any contrary evidence. What does the duty of every counsel dictate to him, if the case is not made out by his adversary or prosecutor? Let it rest; the court is bound to tell the jury so, and the jury are bound to find him not guilty. It is a most unshaken maxim, that *nemo tenetur prodere seipsum*. And it would indeed be a very inquisitorial exercise of power, to call upon a man to run the risk of confirming the charge, under the penalty of being convicted by *nil dicit*. Surely, at the criminal side of this court, as yet, there has been no such judgment pronounced. It is only when the party stands mute from malice, that such extremes can be resorted to. I never before heard an intimation from any judge to a jury, that bad evidence, liable to any and every exception, ought to receive a sanction from the silence of the party. The substance of the charge was neither more nor less than this: that the falsehood of the evidence shall receive support and credit from the silence of the man accused. With anxiety for the honour and religion of the law, I demand it of you, must not the jury have understood that this silence was evidence to go to them? is the meaning contained in the expression, "a volume of evidence," only insinuation? I do not know where any man could be safe; I do not know what any man could do to screen himself from prosecution; I know not how he could be sure, even when he was at his prayers before the throne of heaven, that he was not passing that moment of his life, on which he was to be charged with the commission of some crime, to be expiated to society by the forfeiture of his liberty or of his life; I do not know what shall become of the subject, if a jury are to be told that the silence of the man charged is a "volume of evidence" that he is guilty of the crime: where is it written? I know there is a place where vulgar frenzy cries out, that the public instrument must be drenched in blood; where defence is gagged, and the devoted wretch must perish. But even there, the victim of such tyranny is not made to fill, by voluntary silence, the defects of his accusation; for his tongue is tied, and therefore, no advantage is taken of him by construction; it cannot be there said that his not speaking is a volume of evidence to prove his guilt.

But to avoid all misunderstanding, see what is the force of my objection: is it, that the charge of the court cannot receive a practicable interpretation, that may not terrify men's minds with ideas such as I have presented? No; I am saying no such thing: I have lived too long, and observed too much, not to know, that every word in a phrase is one of the feet upon which it runs, and how the shortening or lengthening of one of those feet will alter the progress or direction of its motion. I am not arguing that the charge of the court cannot by any possibility be reconciled to the principles of law; I am agitating a more important question; I am putting it to the conscience of the court whether a jury may not have probably collected the same meaning from it which I have affixed to it; and whether there ought not to have been a volume of explanation, to do away the fatal consequences of such mistake.

On what sort of a case am I now speaking? on one of that kind with which it is known the public heart has been beating for many months; which, from a single being in society, has scarcely received a cool or tranquil examination. I am making that sort of application which the expansion of liberal reason and the decay of technical bigotry have made a favoured application.

In earlier times, it might have been thought sacrilege to have meddled with a verdict once pronounced; since then, the true principles of justice have been better understood; so that now, the whole wisdom of the whole court will have an opportunity of looking over that verdict, and setting right the mistake which has occasioned it.

Mr. Curran made other observations, as well in corroboration of his own remarks, as in answer to the opposite counsel, of which it is impossible to give an exact detail, and concluded:—

You are standing on the scanty isthmus that divides the great ocean of duration, on one side of the past, on the other of the future; a ground that, while you yet hear me, is washed from beneath our feet. Let me remind you, my lords, while your determination is yet in your power, "*Dum versatur adhuc intra penetralia Vestæ*," that on that ocean of future you must set your judgment afloat. And future ages will assume the same authority which you have assumed; posterity feel the same emotions which you have felt, when your little hearts have beaten, and your infant eyes have overflowed, at reading the sad history of the sufferings of a Russell or a Sidney.

Similar applause followed this speech. On the 5th the crown counsel argued at much length against the application, and on the 7th Clonmel and Boyd gave judgment against it; and then Boyd sentenced Rowan to a fine of £500, and two years' imprisonment, from the 29th of January, 1794, and to find security, himself in £2,000, and two sureties in £1,000 each. Rowan escaped, and went to France.*

---

* See Mac Nevin's State Trials, Madden's United Irishmen, and Rowan's Autobiography, edited by Dr. Drummond.

DROGHEDA DEFENDERS.

Spring Assizes, Drogheda, April 23rd, 1794.

THE Lords' Committee of 1793, thus describes the Defenders:—
" The people at this time called Defenders are very different from those who originally assumed that appellation, and are all, as far as the Committee could discover, of the Roman Catholic persuasion; in general poor ignorant men labouring men, sworn to secrecy, and impressed with an opinion that they are assisting the Catholic cause; in other respects they do not appear to have any distinct particular object in view, but they talk of being relieved from hearth-money, tithes, county cesses, and of lowering their rents. They first appeared in the county of Louth in considerable bodies in April last; several of them were armed; they assembled mostly in the night, and forced into the houses of Protestants, and took from them their arms. The disorders soon spread through the counties of Meath, Cavan, Monaghan, and other parts adjacent; at first they took nothing but arms, but afterwards they plundered the houses of every thing they could find."

Premising that the "Protestants" were the rich class in these districts, we feel no difficulty in recognizing the same grievances and consequent outrages which have existed in Munster from the beginning of the last century to this day; but the Secret Committee tried to connect them with Catholic gentlemen, and the crown prosecutors tried to trace them to United Irish organization,* and French gold.

On Monday, the 21st of April, 1794, Roger Hamill, James Bird, Casimir Delahoyde, Patrick Kenny, Matthew Read, Bartholomew Walsh, and Patrick Tiernan were put to the bar and arraigned, before the Honourable Mr. Justice Downes, one of the Judges of his Majesty's Court of King's Bench, upon the following

INDICTMENT.

County of the town of } The Jurors for our Lord the King, upon their oath say and present that Patrick Kenny, of Drogheda, yeoman, Matthew Read
Drogheda to wit. of the same, yeoman, Bartholomew Walsh of the same, yeoman, Patrick Tiernan, of Turfeckan, in the county of Louth, yeoman, Roger Hamill, James Bird and Casimir Delahoyde, all of Drogheda, in the county of the town of Drogheda, merchants, being wicked, seditious, and evil-minded persons, and of wicked and turbulent dispositions, and contriving, designing, and intending unlawfully, unjustly, maliciously, turbulently and seditiously, the peace of our said Lord the King and the common tranquillity of this his realm of Ireland to disquiet, molest, and disturb, and, as far as in them lay, to stir up cause, incite and procure sedition, insurrection, and rebellion within this realm, and to bring the government of our said Lord the King within this realm into manifest danger, on the 14th day of December, in the thirty-third year of the reign of our sovereign Lord George the Third, King of Great Britain and soforth, at Drogheda, in the county of the town of Drogheda, and on divers other days and times, as well before as after, with force and arms their aforesaid wicked, malignant, and seditious purposes and designs to fulfil and effect, did then and there together with divers other wicked, seditious, and ill-minded persons to the jurors of our Lord the King at present unknown, meet, assemble, agree, conspire, confederate and treat of and about the accomplishing and effecting of their aforesaid malignant and seditious purposes and designs, and of, for, and about causing, procuring, inciting and effecting an insurrection and rebellion within the realm of Ireland; and for, about, and concerning the raising, providing, and procuring of arms and armed men to be ready and prepared in different places within this realm, their aforesaid wicked, malignant, seditious, and rebellious designs and purposes to effect, accomplish and fulfil, in contempt of the laws of this realm, to the evil example of all others in the like case offending, and contrary to the peace of our said Lord the King, his crown and dignity.

And the jurors of our Lord the King, do further present and say, that the said Patrick Kenny, Matthew Read, Bartholomew Walsh, and Patrick Tiernan, James Bird, Roger Hamill, and Casimir Delahoyde, being such wicked, ill-minded, and seditious persons as aforesaid, and wickedly, factiously, and seditiously, contriving and intending the peace of our said Lord the King, and the common tranquillity of this his realm of Ireland to molest, disquiet, and disturb, and to cause and incite a wicked rebellion within this realm, and the laws and government of our said Lord the King to bring into danger, on the said 14th day of December, in the said thirty-third year of the reign of our said Lord the King, and at divers other days and times, as well before as after, at Drogheda aforesaid, in the county of the

---

* See Mac Nevin's State Trials, Madden's United Irishmen, and Rowan's Autobiography, edited by Dr. Drummond.

said town of Drogheda aforesaid, with force and arms, did then and tl ere wickedly, factiously, seditiously and contemptuously meet, associate, consult, conspire, confederate and agree together, and to and with divers other wicked and ill-disposed persons to the jurors aforesaid at present unknown, of, for, concerning, and about the raising, causing, and levying of insurrection, rebellion, and war against our said Lord the King, within this his realm of Ireland; and of, for, concerning, and about the procuring and providing of arms and armed men, to be prepared within this realm, their aforesaid wicked, malignant, and diabolical designs and purposes aforesaid to accomplish and effect; in contempt of the laws of this realm, and to the evil example of all others in the like case offending, and contrary to the peace of our said Lord the King, his crown and dignity.

To this indictment the accused traversed, and the court ordered their trial for the following day.

On Wednesday, the 23rd of April, 1794, the several traversers before mentioned were again put at the bar in order of trial.

After several witnesses were examined, Cur. un said:—

Being counsel for the traversers, Mr. Bird, Mr. Hamill, and Mr Delahoyde, now on trial, I find it necessary, without proceeding further, to offer to your lordships and this very respectable jury, some general observations in the extraordinary case of my clients, and the singular preposterousness of the charges in this accusation, as laid before you in evidence.

It is an accusation, that, of its nature, must involve a black degree of enormity in any country. It implies a criminal intention, that if carried into effect must loosen every bond of society, and plunge that country which should unhappily be the theatre of such atrocity, into the most inconceivable state of calamity and wretchedness, no matter how rich and prosperous might be its previous condition. The existence of a state is like the existence of life in man; and to take existence from the political body is similar to taking the life of an individual; with this difference, that the consequence of the one is so vastly superior to that of the other, that to determine the proportionate criminality, would be as visionary as impossible.

The charge against my clients is, that they are enemies to their country and its government; that they are adverse to its settlement, its peace, and its prosperity: that they have formed plans to spread general discontent, confusion and divisions, for the purpose of destroying the advantages derived to the nation from a state of well-ordered tranquillity; and that, for carrying such an abominable project into execution, they have employed for their agents, the greatest miscreants in society!

It is that sort of guilt that, at countenancing which, every man of character and sensibility must recoil. But it is for you, gentlemen, to consider, that an offence of such great enormity is not lightly to be believed, and requires to be proved by the strongest evidence.

It is n t my intention at present to enter into any very minute observations on the evidence which has been this day laid before you; if that shall be necessary, one of the learned gentlemen here will do so.

There are few general circumstances upon which to observe, from the facts related in evidence. The state of the country, for some time past, and particularly the state of that body of your fellow-subjects against whom suspicion and calumny seem to have been directed, are circumstances that must here be observed upon, and cannot fail of exciting it your minds some of the tenderest feelings.

In last year's parliament, one of the most glorious triumphs that ever this country witnessed, was obtained by that body, over the blackest prejudice and injustice, exasperated by imaginary wrongs. That fatal disunion, from which for centuries great individual calamity and public disquietude had arisen, had the axe laid to its root by the senate of the nation. And there was no good man in the community, that did not look to the consequences of it to be the security of the peace, industry, and happiness of the country, and an exemption from the calamities of the nations around us. Upon such a great occasion, there must necessarily be diversity of opinons; but I am sorry to say, that prejudices are not yet removed from persons of a lower description.

There was, at that time, an obloquy thrown out against the committee of our Catholic brethren sitting at Dublin; but I speak in the presence of a Protestant jury and a Protestant judge, and I say that in history there is no example of any such proceeding being carried on with more decorous tranquillity and strictly legal propriety. Their orderly, decent, and respectful perseverance was crowned with that success, which, it was imagined, would confer happiness on themselves, and on those that were to come after them. It was expected the disturbances which had been occasioned by a ruinous system of law would be done away; and that there would be a coalition of all parties, formed into one united phalanx, and feeling that their country could never be prosperous and happy, without a general participation of freedom to all its people.

A privileged order in a state may, in some sort, be compared to a solitary individual separated from the society, and unaided by the reciprocal converse, affections or support of his fellow-men. It is like a tree standing singly on a high hill, and exposed to the rude concussions of every varying blast, devoid of fruit or foliage. If you plant trees around it to shade it from the inclemency of the blighting tempest, and secure to it its adequate supply of sun and moisture, it quickly assumes all the luxuriance of vegetation, and proudly rears its head aloft, fortified against the noxious gales which agitate and wither the unprotected brambles lying without the verge of the plantation.

Upon this principle acted the dying man whose family had been disturbed by domestic contentions. Upon his death-bed he calls his children around him; he orders a bundle of twigs to be brought; he has them untied: he gives to each of them a single twig; he orders them to be broken—and it is done with facility. He next orders the twigs to be united in a bundle, and orders each of them to try their strength upon it. They shrink from the task as impossible. Thus, my children continued the old man, it is UNION alone that can render you secure against the attempts of your enemies, and preserve you in that state of happiness which I wish you to enjoy.

Such should be the effects of the liberty conferred by the act of the last session of parliament; and such I believe they would be, if not for the misconceptions of a lower description of people, who may have imagined that a more respectable order of persons had the same passions and dispositions as themselves. I cannot attribute the accusation altogether to the irregular proceedings going forward for some time in this part of the country, but rather to vague charges, which I have read with concern, brought against a description of persons, the calamities of whose ancestors must have peculiarly influenced to a demeanour directly the contrary.

However ruinous the charges against the individuals may be, that alone does not terminate the mischief. These reports will go abroad—they will be carried to the seat of government; and it is impossible to say what impressions may be made there to the disadvantage of a great portion of our countrymen. But would to God the powers in England were present this day, to hear the charges made against a respectable body of persons, and the manner in which they have been *attempted* to be proved.

It belongs to me to speak only of three persons—Mr. Bird, Mr. Hamill, and Mr. Delahoyde. It is not the unhoused villain and profligate vagabond upon whom you sit in judgment. It is the opulent and respectable merchant—the man who owes every thing to his public character. This is the description of men to be tried.

It cannot possibly be imagined, that the plan had been forced to excite previous prejudices in their favour. If it was, the manner of their arrest and subsequent treatment shows them to have been much disappointed. Mr. Bird was taken out of his bed at eleven o'clock at night, and brought to the capital under a military guard, after a very uncomfortable imprisonment of one night in the Town-house. He was not indulged in the common decencies of imprisonment—nor suffered to enjoy the visits of his friends!—an indulgence permitted to the most flagitious criminals however low the description. Pen and ink were denied him; and he was brought to the capital, and there lodged among the vilest malefactors. He applied to the court of King's Bench to be admitted to bail, fancying from his character he would be admitted. That was denied him. From this, it might be imagined that there was some respectable witness or prosecutor of character to criminate him. You have all seen and heard them.

I certainly consider, that when crimes of this kind are committed, it must be necessary that some of the parties concerned should turn approver. I am well aware, that to shut out such from examination, would be to stop public justice; but yet, I did imagine, that in the present case some respectable witness would come forward to disclose the turpitude of the offence. To support the enormous charges in the indictment, one Murphy has been produced. But, as gentlemen who are chosen to decide on a matter, upon the issue of which the safety of a great part of the population of Ireland depends, I ask you, is there safety for the life of any man, if the testimony of such a witness has weight in a court of justice? Upon his examination he declared to the learned judge, that he had been examined before at Dundalk, and acknowledged that there the jury showed no respect to his evidence, and, therefore, he did not wish to be examined. On the evidence of a man having such apprehensions of himself, a jury should decide with extreme caution. The man to be believed by a respectable jury, against respectable persons, is Murphy, confessedly a robber by character, tried twice in another county upon charges of a flagitious nature, and discharged out of court by proclamation. If you believe him, you must credit the testimony of a man who acknowledges himself to have fired shots into the house of Mr. M'Clintock, with an intent to commit murder. When the prosecutor lodged these examinations, it appears, he was in gaol, in actual custody. It is now for you to consider, whether, in your unbiassed judgment, the story hangs well together. Mr. Bird and Mr. Hamill, it is well known, exerted themselves much in forwarding the cause of the Roman Catholics. You are told these gentlemen formed committees in ale-houses—that they there associated with the vilest miscreants, to assassinate the Protestants of the land, at a time when the object they had in view was going on prosperously in the legislature of the nation! Is it likely that, at such a period, they would form a plot for the extermination of their Protestant fellow-subjects? Such a supposition is contrary to common sense. Is it likely, that a country reduced to such an unhappy state, that manufacturers are in a state of requisi*' *n *'*" the fabrication of arms, should be considered an eligible marke for their purchase? It is to me peculiarly nauseous to take up much of your time in describing the character of a wretch like Murphy; I sh*'*d, therefore, proceed to the matter most worthy of your consideratio*'*. Some of the jury who sit here to-day sat in this court yesterday. They must have heard the observations made by the learned judge wh preside*'* "If (said the learned judge) a witness forswears himself in any material circumstance, making a substantive part of the accusation upon which the prosecution is grounded, the rest of his evidence, although it may be true, should be discredited." I speak this in the recollection of several gentlemen present. If I have stated it wrong, I am sure they will set me right. Gentlemen, I now call upon you to put this principle in practice. Murphy swore in his examinations that he saw money distributed at the committee upon several times and occasions, and that all the persons charged gave the examinant money at several times. Does not all this appear from his own evidence to be false?

Gentlemen, upon such an occasion as this, there is no man but may be drawn beyond the line of calm discussion. For that reason, I have studiously endeavoured to argue the subject coolly, and, therefore, to come to a cool examination of facts. Did Murphy, in his examination, swear he got money from all the traversers at the bar, and did he, on the table, swear he got money but from one? And is there any jury that will be so base as to found a conviction upon such evidence? I am well aware, gentlemen, that nothing is more strongly corroborative of the truth of an evidence, than little accidental deviations in immaterial circumstances. The present must appear to you, however, quite a contrary case.

What has he said of arms? In his examination it is stated that he saw a box of arms landed at Amagassin, and distributed. What has he said himself on the table? That he did not see them distributed, but laid against a wall. Is this no material circumstance in the prosecution? If you ask is it material, I tell you it is. It is a part of the charge, for procuring and distributing arms for the abolition of the

Protestant government. I speak in the presence of the court, and in the presence of a right honourable gentleman, my personal respect for whom prevents me from saying what he knows I think of his conduct. The procuring of arms for the purpose specified is a circumstance highly material to the prosecution; it amounts to an act of High Treason.— I mention this, to show, upon that fact, you have certain evidence of perjury. You have better evidence of the fact, than if he had been indicted for perjury—you have the man confronted by his own oath.— When a man swears two ways upon the same fact, it is physically impossible that he should not be perjured.

There is another person brought forward as a witness in this prosecution, whose state in society it is difficult to ascertain. He was indicted—tried—convicted—pardoned—enlisted—deserted—retaken—brought to gaol—and becomes an approver! If, gentlemen, you apply the same rule to this man, you are to consider has he also perjured himself in a material fact. Gentlemen, it is for you to exercise your judgment in this affair. I had not the informations. It was impossible for me to know any thing about Tiernan—impossible for me to be acquainted with the fact of his having lodged an information against him, as he denied it on the table. In the information read by his lordship, the examinant says, he knew the place of Tiernan's abode—that he has been acquainted with him intimately for six years—and saw him frequently at the Defenders' committees, in company with the traversers. What is his evidence now? Directly the reverse. You have heard him swear that he never saw Tiernan at any of the meetings. You have heard more—you have heard him swear that he never swore so. His lordship asked him, could he have sworn to that effect and forgotten it? He swears positively not. Here is a direct and irreconcileable contradiction between his examination, sworn before a magistrate, and his testimony on this table. And here, gentlemen, you must be convinced that it is impossible he could be forsworn in so material a fact, if not intentionally. You must see clearly that he is deliberately forsworn.

Indeed, if it was not known by unfortunate experience, and particularly in many recent instances, it could scarcely be conceived that such abominable turpitude could find place in any human being. It could scarcely be conceived, that any being, endued with a rational and immortal soul, would deliberately come forward to forswear himself in a court of justice, and, in the face of heaven, to "bear false witness against his neighbour," under such circumstances, as if credited, must cause the life of the accused to be forfeited. Such acts can only proceed from minds the most obdurate. If you see this done in the present case, you must consider it a crime against a great body of your fellow-subjects, and tending directly to disunite the people. It must be of high consideration to you, that when you acquit, you will be able to say, you do not merely acquit because you cannot condemn; but you acquit from a secondary motive, of discountenancing the persecution of any particular description of people.

The gentlemen here to-day at your bar are merchants—men, whose most valuable property is the integrity of their characters. They have correspondents in foreign countries—in Great Britain, for instance.— What effect, then, must it have, when read in foreign newspapers, that such and such men were taken up, to be tried for rebellion against the laws of the country where they live? How will any merchant in England be able to discover, whether they may not really be guilty of the crime against society with which they are charged?

I know, from recent experience, that an acquittal, however honourable, does not wipe off the aspersion which such charges cast on men's characters. I have particularly experienced it in a neighbouring county. I have there been asked, did I not think Fay had a lucky escape! I am aware, gentlemen, you must have a conviction that what has been brought forward in evidence is false; but where allegations of this sort are made, it is proper to try them in the most public manner. I know your characters, and I think you will not content yourselves with a mere acquittal. It should not be alone; it should be accompanied by something calculated to do away the unjust imputations upon the characters of the accused. If, however, you consider further evidence necessary, or feel any dissatisfaction upon your minds, we can produce two or three witnesses.

Curran examined several witnesses, the Attorney-General replied, the judge charged, and the jury, in a few minutes, returned a verdict of *Not Guilty*.
The following slip from the back of this report may be interesting:—
"On Wednesday, the 23rd of April, 1794, came on also the trial of James Skelton, Esq., M.D., of the town of Drogheda, on an Indictment for having, on the 30th day of January, in the 33rd year of his Majesty's reign, taken an unlawful oath, to be a true Defender, not being compelled thereto by any necessity.
"To this indictment Mr. Skelton pleaded the general issue—Not Guilty.
"No evidence being produced on behalf of the crown,
"Mr. Curran said—As I understand the learned counsel on behalf of the crown do not mean to bring forward any evidence on the present trial. I must consider that circumstance to be an unanswerable justification of the gentleman accused.
"Mr. M'Cartney—My lord, we have reasons for not bringing them forward.
"Mr. Skelton was then acquitted, and discharged."

DOCTOR DRENNAN.

June 25th, 1794.

WILLIAM DRENNAN, Esq., M.D., was one of the ablest writers and truest patriots during the long struggle for Irish independence. One of his earliest works was Orellana, or the Letters of an Irish Helot, published in 1779, advocating a free constitution, and written with a passionate vigour, which greatly aided the cause, and made the writer famous. He was an intimate of Tone's, who speaks highly of his powers and resolve,—was an early member of the United Irish Society,—and, as we have seen in the introduction to Curran's defence of Rowan, was the writer of the famous counter-proclamation, beginning "Citizen Soldiers!" He was chairman of the meeting (to which Rowan was secretary), at which that document was passed, and was indicted for a seditious libel for having published it. The indictment was found by the City of Dublin Grand Jury in Easter Term, 1794, and contained nine counts, but only two were rolled on, viz., the 2nd count, charging him with publishing the libel in "The Hibernian Journal, or Chronicle of Liberty," on the 17th of December, 1792, and the 8th count, charging publication generally.

To this indictment, Dr. Drennan was in the same term called upon to plead.
The Hon. Mr. Butler, and Mr. Emmet, applied to the court for four days' time to plead, and a copy of the indictment.

the Attorney-General, on behalf of the crown, opposed the motion for time to plead, which he insisted was never allowed in case of an indictment. As to the copy of the indictment, if Dr. Drennan had, as his counsel contended, a right to it, he would obtain i of course, without any such application as this now made.
The court was of opinion with the Attorney-General; and Dr. Drennan, having been arraigned, traversed the indictment.
The 25th of June (in Trinity term) was appointed for the trial.

Wednesday, June 25, 1794.

The court sat at half past ten. Mr. Justice Boyd, having been taken ill, did not preside.
Dr. Drennan appeared in court with his bail.
Counsel for the Crown—Right Hon. Prime-Sergeant, Right Hon. Attorney-General Solicitor-General, Mr. Frankland, and Mr. Ruxton. Solicitor—Mr. Kemmis.
Counsel for the Traverser—Mr. Curran, Mr. Fletcher, Mr. Emmett. Solicitor—Mr. Dowling.
The High Sheriffs returned the *venire facias*, with a panel thereto annexed. The panel having been called over, and twenty-six gentlemen having answered to their names, the Clerk of the Crown proceeded to swear the jury.
Sir John Trail, Knight, was called.
Mr. Curran—My lord, I understand that this gentleman has declared an opinion on the subject of this prosecution.
Right Hon. Attorney-General—I wonder to see these things practised again. I thought they would be ashamed of such artifices. I am sure the learned gentleman has been instructed to do this. These things are intended to go abroad, and have an effect on the public mind. If this is a cause of challenge—if it is law, that this is cause of challenge—let it be made ; let us have the opinion of the court upon it.
Mr. Curran—My lord, I stand upon nothing but the rule of law. If what I said be fact, surely he is not a proper juror to try the cause. If he has a pre-conceived opinion on the subject, I would put the question in the mode which the law warrants, by swearing the juror. It is true, he is not bound to answer anything to his prejudice; but it cannot be to his prejudice to say that he has formed an opinion. Forming an opinion is not a culpable matter in our law ; I, therefore, desire to have him sworn.
The Attorney-General—The gentleman has a right to challenge if he has good ground.
Mr. Curran—I move, my lord, that Sir John Trail may be sworn to answer.
Lord Clonmel—It cannot be done ; it is not a legal practice.
Mr. Justice Downes—I looked into the books on this point on a former occasion. It is laid down expressly, in Hawkins, that this ought not to be done.
Mr. Curran—I cannot support the objection by any other evidence than the gentleman's own.
Attorney-General—Surely you might by your informer's testimony.*

Sir John Trail was sworn.	Peter Roe, merchant, sworn.
Robert Alexander, merchant, sworn.	William Beeby, merchant, sworn.
Mark White, merchant, sworn.	Jeffrey Foot, merchant, sworn.
William Lindsay, merchant, sworn.	James Hamilton, merchant, sworn.
Benjamin Woodward, merchant, sworn.	William Little, merchant, sworn.
Mark Bloxham, merchant, sworn.	William Galway, merchant, sworn.

The indictment was then read by the Clerk of the Crown, and Dr. Drennan given in charge to the jury.
The several counts were deliberately read, and the different copies of the libel scrupulously and accurately compared with the record by the traverser's counsel. No variance however appeared.
Mr. Ruxton opened the indictment.
The Attorney-General stated the case for the prosecution, and called five witnesses to prove that Drennan was chairman of the meeting at which the address was passed, and that it was published by his (Drennan's) direction. The chief witness was William Paulet Carey, printer and publisher of the "National Evening Star." The Prime-Sergeant examined him in a series of loading questions, to which Curran objected, and got favourable decisions, *after* the questions were answered. Curran cross-examined him at great length, making him contradict himself, and fail in his evidence of the identity of the document read by Drennan and that in the indictment. It appeared that the address was printed in a hand-bill by one M'Allister, but this could not be got. However, Carey acknowledged that he was a United Irishman: that after the address, he had in the society proposed taking up arms, but had been resisted by Dr. Drennan, and that being under prosecution, the society had failed to support him, for which reason he was hostile to its members, and especially to Dr. Drennan.

---

* Trail proved the propriety of the challenge by his audacious speech at the close of the trial.

Mr. Thomas M'Donnell was also examined, to prove the printing in the "Hibernian Journal," but broke down under the direct examination.
The first witness for the defence was Thomas Traynor, who answered Mr. Fletcher as follows :—

Do you know Mr. William Paulet Carey? I do.
What are you, Sir? I am a merchant, and live in Poolbeg-street.
Had you ever any conversation with Carey respecting the traverser? I had: I was mentioning to some person that I thought Carey was much aggrieved; and that I would set or foot a subscription for his relief——
How long since is this? This was about the 1st of April last: I did not know Carey before; he waited on me next day; he told me he was much obliged to me for my intention — that he had been much aggrieved by the United Society of Irishmen—but that if they would pay his bail, he would quit the kingdom; he added, that he did not like either to turn informer against Drennan or lose his liberty, and that a few guineas would be of infinite service to him.
Did he threaten the traverser at all? He said that if he did leave the kingdom, he would give Drennan a *flailing* before he went: said I, "Drennan is a delicate little man, and a stroke from a strong man would kill him; he answered that, "By Jesus, he would think it no crime to assassinate such a villain, who had ruined his peace for ever, and made a motion to expel him from the United Society of Irishmen, just at the time they should have supported him;" some time after this I heard Dr. Drennan was taken up.
Did you see Carey at any time after? He never came near me since.
Attorney-General—You may go down, Mr. Traynor; I shall not cross-examine you.

After some other evidence for the defence, Curran spoke as follows :—

My Lord, and Gentlemen of the Jury—I am of counsel for Doctor Drennan, the traverser; and, gentlemen, I do not, for the sake of my client, regret that my state of health prevents me trespassing long on your time, or that of the court; for my heart tells me, that if he is reduced to stand in need of any effort from talent, that it is impossible, under the circumstances of the case, that he can hope for any assistance from an advocate, where, if there is any danger of conviction, it must arise from what passes in the minds of the jury, and not from any thing which has passed in this court.

It may be a loss to the traverser that he is not aided by the personal exertions of those who are connected with him by habits of life and uniformity of pursuits. Such a person I am not; to him I am a perfect stranger. I never, to my knowledge, exchanged a word with him, save once in the public street. I never was under the same roof with him that I know of; and the reason why I yielded to an ordinary application to become his counsel, was, because I had been personally defamed for acting as counsel in the defence of another, who was charged with the same libel. I felt that my character in the world, little as it may be, was owing all to my professional talents; and I feel that, if a barrister can act so mean and despicable a part as to decline, from personal apprehension, the defence of any man accused, he does not deserve to be heard in any court of justice.

I will state shortly what I conceive the question to be, and the evidence brought in support of the charge.

The indictment is, that Dr. Drennan, the traverser, did publish the libel, and that he did print and publish the paper, with the base and seditious intentions there stated. To this he has pleaded not guilty and one question to be tried is, did he, in point of fact, publish the paper? The next, upon which I shall trouble you but very little, is as to the nature of the paper—whether it is a seditious libel or not?

The law of libels in this country and in Great Britain has lately, (by the perseverance and exertions of two men—Mr. Fox and Mr. Erskine—being at last crowned with success), undergone a most fortunate change.

There is said, gentlemen, to be an instinct in animals, which directs them to those medicines which relieve their disorders ; and it seems as if, in the public malady of the three kingdoms, this only medicine had been discovered, and carried into effect by this law.

For part of the court which I address, I have infinite regard and esteem. To extend that profession would, perhaps, be as presumptuous, as it would flatter my vanity ; but let me not by this be understood to profess any contrary feeling. I merely disavow the arrogance of affecting to feel, where I have no claim to any interest.

But, gentlemen, the law has taken the power of decision in those cases from the court, and vested it in you. And you are not only to inquire into the fact of publication, but into the question of "libel or not." Upon the latter question I have said I would make a few observations ; but I will be frank with you, and will say, that if you have any disposition to believe the fact of publication, I would advise the traverser to prepare with a fatal facility to receive your opinion, that the paper is whatever the prosecutors please to call it. For, if you believe it, it must be from some perversion of mind—some gangrene of principle, with which I disdain to hold parlance or communication ; and this I say, from a proud conviction, that there will be no law in this country, when such monstrous facts are swallowed by juries, and the country disgraced by such convictions.

As to the liberty of the press, I have heard and I have read of something relative to it lately, at which I am truly astonished. I have heard, that an English Attorney-General could say, " that the guilt or innocence of a man depends on the candour with which he writes."— I feel that this must have been an imposition ; I cannot believe that it could have been said. The liberty of the press does not consist in reasoning right—in candour—or in weighing the preponderancy of arguments, as a grocer weighs his wares : it is founded in the principle, that government is established for the happiness of the people—that the people have a kind of superintendant, or inquisitorial power, to watch over government, that they may be satisfied that the object is truly sought. The liberty of the press is not for expressing merely argument, but to convey the feelings of personal discontent against the government, that the passions of the governors may be checked ; and if any one is bold enough to tell them they over-bound their duty, they may be tortured into rectitude, by being held up as objects of odium, abomination, horror, or ridicule.

If you confine the liberty of the press to fair argument—if you condemn, as libellous, every publication, where invective may be a little too warm—where it may go beyond the enormity, or, the complaint beyond the grievance—you destroy it.

Every man knows what is a public crime : the maliciously pointing out grievances so as to disturb the quiet of the country : such a crime will never find protection from a court or a jury. If the traverser did intend "to diffuse among the subjects of this realm, discontents, jealousies, and suspicions of our sovereign lord the king, and his government; disaffections and disloyalties to his person and government; and to raise very dangerous seditions and tumults within this kingdom," &c. he ought to be found guilty—if he did not, he is entitled to acquittal. Having said this, I dismiss the subject; because, I trust in God, so fatal an example to the liberties of this country, as a condemnation upon such evidence, will never be given.

What has Carey sworn?—that he was at a meeting on the 14th of December; that Dr. Drennan was there; that the question was put on an address; that he himself was desired to publish that address; that the manuscript could not be given him, but that he should take it from the *Dublin Journal** of the next Monday; that he sent for that paper a great deal of his evidence went to proving the *Star*, but that was not read, and is out of the question. The question is therefore narrowed to the publication in the *Dublin Journal;* is there any evidence that this was the paper read in the society? No. What is it?—Carey has told you—indeed he told you the impossibility of his swearing it; I read the address in the paper—he could not swear even to the substance, he could not tell that it was the same. Coiling and twining about me, as you saw that wretched man, he could not prove this; therefore, all the evidence on this part, comes to this, that Dr. Drennan did produce some address in that meeting, but of what it contained you have no evidence before you. And, as to the publication in the *Hibernian*, the evidence is so vague, that it can give no aid whatever to the former proof; so that the evidence stops at the meeting in Back-lane.

I asked Carey what address he was desired to publish—he answered that agreed to by the society; what proof have you that he did so?—it will be ingeniously endeavoured to impress upon your minds, that a general power to publish was given by the traverser to Carey, and that he thereby made himself personally liable for Carey's acts.

The consequence of such a doctrine as that a man could commit himself for any future publication, made without his privity, would be so wild and desperate, that it is unnecessary to do more than offer it to you in its true light.

But Carey has pinned the authority to a particular publication of the particular paper read in the society. What question are you trying? are you trying the traverser for every possible publication which might have been sent to M'Donnell's paper? do you live in a country where such unlimited power is given to informers? Suppose Carey to have taken from M'Donnell's paper a libel which Dr. Drennan never saw— he is, by this doctrine, responsible—is it not too ridiculous? and does it not come to this, that Carey was tied down to publish that particular paper read in the society, and no other; has he said, then, that it was the same paper which appeared in the *Dublin Journal?* where is the

---

* "It is evident that Mr. Curran meant the *Hibernian Journal*, but these were certainly his words." The foregoing note appears in the pamphlet report, which is plainly hostile to Drennan and his counsel throughout.—T. D.

evidence that it was the same paper, and where is the guilt of Dr. Drennan?

But, it will be said, by his declaration of an intent to publish it, he made himself answerable. Did he give it to M'Donnell to be published by him? or, to take a previous question, did M'Donnell publish it himself? Has he said so? No such thing. But, what did he tell you?—that any other printer might have published the paper produced, if he had had the materials; but it is highly probable that he printed it. What! is a man to be sent for two years to gaol, because you believe it *highly probable* that M'Donnell published this paper? Are you prepared by any impression whatsoever, so far to humble your minds, as to swear that M'Donnell did publish this very paper, though the man himself cannot say so? Where is your honesty, or where is your common sense, if they can be *flattened* down into a verdict founded on nothing but your own credulity?

If Dr. Drennan had given the paper to M'Donnell, the acts of the printer might derive credit from the original author; as it is, see how far this would be carrying constructive authority. What, my lord, is the act of the third person?—Is it the law, that the act of a printer, with the witness Lestrange, should affect the traverser, who knew nothing of the transaction? The argument is, that the delivery by M'Donnell to Lestrange was, no doubt, a publication by the traverser; but I say that nothing he does or says can affect Dr. Drennan.

Suppose I were charged with committing murder, and that I had employed the crier of the court for the purpose; if he did the fact by my directions, he is guilty; but no confession of his can be evidence against me. So the publication of M'Donnell, with the authority of Dr. Drennan, might be evidence; but no declaration of M'Donnell's can be evidence. The argument is, that M'Donnell admitted the fact, by giving the paper to the stamp officer; but was this admission on oath? Is what he said to a petty officer of stamps to be evidence against my client? But M'Donnell does not recollect this transaction—he does not, on his oath, confirm the statement by Lestrange—and yet you are desired to take Lestrange's evidence of what M'Donnell did. If you do, purposes may, indeed, be answered; and we have heard that there are many prosecutions in *petto*—many persons over whom the arm of the law is only suspended.

This may be policy, to keep the abandoned informer haunting the slumbers of the innocent man; but it is for you to consider, is such a time as this proper for it. In the present melancholy of the public mind, how far will it heal the grief which afflicts society? Or, will it not rather answer the immediate and selfish objects of those whom a small gale may waft to that point, where the recollection of the country and its situation will never assail their ears?

But of the *probability* of this evidence how shall I speak? What does it depend on? The integrity of the man who swears it. Do you think, gentlemen, that in every case an oath is a sufficient measure to weigh down life and liberty?—where a miscreant swears guilt against man, must you convict him?

The declaration that the paper would appear in the *Hibernian Journal* stands on the single evidence of Carey. Was he consistent with himself? If he did not appear to you upon that table a perjured man, believe every word he said. This man was under two prosecutions for this and another libel; this charge is to rest as well on his memory as his credit. He received a summons, signed by the Lord Chief Justice of Ireland! ! Do you believe, gentlemen, that Lord Clonmel's name was to it? Examine Mr. Kemmis.

What is the answer? That he thought it was—he could not answer—he was sure it was. And this man, who comes to tell of words *spoken* two years ago, makes this silly mistake about the Chief Justice's name. Again, "Who are you?" "I was under prosecution"—" I was a member of the society"—" I do not know whether I would have prosecuted or not, if they had kept their word." Three different things he swore as to my lord's name:—he did recollect; next, he did not; and, last of all, he could not tell. Does he not appear that kind of man, on whose evidence no man ought to be convicted. Scarce ever have I known a conviction on the mere evidence of an informer. But see what motives this man has: under prosecution for the same crime, he has not only his own safety to consult, but the most avowed and rancorous malice to Doctor Drennan. He swore he had none. Did you not hear of his declaration of vengeance? A gentleman comes and swears that he said he thought it no crime to assassinate Drennan, for a refusal to support him under a criminal prosecution—to support the man who proposed to the society to arm against the government.

I asked him why he proposed this? Merely, to try character. Was he himself sincere? He was!—he was perfectly sincere; and yet it was a mere fetch to try character.

As to the influence of his situation on his evidence, what did he say?—he was not sure of a pardon, but he hoped for one. If you give credit to this man, you make a fine harvest for informers; a fine opportunity you give to every ruffian in society; and you may go home in the comfortable conviction, that it is far from impossible that the next attack shall be on yourselves; and if your wives are superstitious, or your children undutiful, you may have them going to fortune-tellers to inquire "when Mr. Carey shall be unmuzzled against you."

So far as Bell's testimony was appealed to, he contradicted Carey He did not believe that the words of the address stood any part of the paper read, and no human being has given evidence of the general substance. Bell contradicted him again; for he said there were no orders made to print it in any paper. And what did Wright say. That it was after the publication in the *Hibernian Journal* that Carey complained to him of having been neglected, and asked should he publish the paper. "How shall I publish it?" says he; "the *Evening Post* is nonsense." Says Wright, "take it from the *Hibernian Journal*." Here is the positive oath of this unimpeached witness contradicting Carey's evidence. Unfortunate, perjured man, he makes a complaint that he received no instructions; he complains of the whole society. Gentlemen, do you believe Wright?

But there is a way in which you may get out of this   It will be said. "God forbid that a man should not perjure himself in one or two little points, and tell truth in the whole ;" an old woman may say, that oaths are but wind—he might tell truth at other times.   Did you ever, gentlemen, hear of a point in which a perjured witness might be believed.   Yes, there is one—when he says he is perjured.   The principle is as strong in our hearts, as if it had been written by the finger of that God who said, "*thou shalt not bear false witness.*"   The law of the country has said that the man once convicted of false swearing shall not a second time contaminate the walls of a court of justice ; and it is the very essence of a jury, that if a man appears (though not yet marked out by the law as a perjurer) to have soiled his nature by the deliberate commission of this crime, that moment his credit shall cease with the jury—his evidence shall be blotted from their minds, and leave no trace but horror and indignation.

I feel the hardship of their situation, when grave and learned men are brought forward to support such a prosecution.   I have great respect for them—for some of them I have had it from my boyish days—but his respect does not prevent my saying, that, as officers of state, their private worth is not to weigh with you.   It is for their credit to deceive you.   They have no power to control a prosecution—if one is commanded, they must carry it on ; and when they talk of their character, what do they say ?—" If the evidence is insufficient, take a little of our dignity to eke it out."   What their feelings are is nothing to you, gentlemen ; they may have feelings of another kind to compensate for them.

But while I lament this, I will show that your sympathy is not called forth for nothing.   Why do we hear such expressions as these—" I speak under the authority of a former jury?"   Has that verdict been given in evidence ?   No.   Could it govern you if it had ?   No.   Here you see the necessity of an appeal to official dignity.   We heard of clubs formed in this city ; we had no evidence of them that their object was to separate the countries.   Does this appear ?   To pull the king from his throne ; what can I say, but " how does this appear."   Not a word of it has been proved ; and here let me mention the impolicy of such expressions, and say that the frequent recital of such circumstances will rather reconcile profligate minds to them than deter them.

As to the Society of United Irishmen, I have had the misfortune, from my strong reprobation of their conduct, to incur much contumelious animadversion.   But where is their desperate purpose to be found ?   Is it in the rejection of Carey's proposal to arm ?   Does this show their design to pull the king from the throne, or to separate the countries ?   But it comes down to the *horrible blasphemy* of reviling the police.   To make their case more hideous and more aggravated, you are told of their blaspheming the *sanctified* police—the *holy, prudent,* and *economical* police.

Did they suppose that they were addressing the liquorish loyalty of a guzzling corporation ?   Or do you suppose, gentlemen, that there is a collation of custards prepared for you when you leave the jury box, when they wished to excite your compassion for the abused police? But it is said, that they not only attack existing establishments, but sully the character of the *unborn* militia ; that they hurl their shafts against what was to be raised the next year. " So, *Gossip,*" says the flatterer to *Timon.* " What," says he, " I did not know you had children.' "Nay, but I will marry, shortly, and my first child shall be called Timon, and then we shall be gossips." So this wizard, Drennan, found out that a militia was to be raised the next year, and he not only abused the corporation but the police and the militia.

Do they think you are such buzzards—such blind creatures—do they think you are only fit to go to school—or rather to go where one part would be punished, for no other reason, than its exact similarity to the other ?

I protest I have been eighteen years at this bar, and never, until this last year have I seen such witnesses supporting charges of this kind with such abandoned profligacy. In one case, where men were on trial for their lives, I felt myself involuntarily shrinking under your lordships' protection, from the miscreant who leaped upon the table, and announced himself a witness. I had hoped the practice would have remained in those distant parts of the country where it began ; but I was disappointed. I have seen it parading through the capital, and I feel that the night of unenlightened wretchedness is fast approaching, when a man shall be judged before he is tried—when the advocate shall be libelled for discharging his duty to his client; that night of human nature, when a man shall be hunted down, not because he is a criminal, but because he is obnoxious.

Punish a man in the situation of Dr. Drennan, and what do you do? what will become of the liberty of the press? you will have the newspapers filled with the drowsy adulations of some persons who want benefices, or commissions in the revenue, or commissions in the army; here and there, indeed, you may chance to see a paragraph of this kind :—

" *Yesterday came on to be tried, for the publication of a seditious libel, Dr. William Drennan. The great law-officer of the crown stated the case in the most candid and temperate manner. During his speech every man in court was in an agony of horror ; the gentlemen of the jury—many of them from the rotation office, were all staunch whigs, and friends to government. Mr. Carey came on the table, and declared that he had no malice against the traverser, and most honourably denied the assertion in his next breath. It was proved, much to his honour, that he had declared his intention to assassinate the traverser. The jury listened with great attention. Mr. Curran, with his usual ability, defended the traverser ;*"—for he must have been ably defended. " *Dr. Wright was produced, a bloody-minded United Irishman—he declared, he could not say but that Dr. Drennan was the author of the libel; and that the types were very like each other in the face. An able speech was made in reply by his Majesty's Prime-Serjeant. He said, with the utmost propriety, that the jury knew little of him, if they supposed him to prosecute without a perfect conviction of the traverser's guilt ; that Mr. Curran's great abilities had* been spent in jests on the subject; that the perjuries were more little inconsistencies, the gentleman having much on his mind. He made many pertinent observations on the aspersions thrown out on the corporation of Dublin.

"Here Mr. Curran interposed, and assured him he intended no such aspersions. The Prime-Sergeant declared he thought he had heard them. That, as to the Police, they were a most honourable body of men; that a number of looking-glasses, and other articles of furniture, were highly necessary for them; and as to the militia, the attack on that was abominable, for that it was shameful to asperse a body intended to be raised by government next year.

"The Jury—a most worshipful worthy jury, retired for a few minutes, and returned with a verdict of GUILTY, much to the satisfaction of the public."

To this sort of language will you reduce the freedom of public discussion, by a conviction of the traverser: and if the liberty of the press is destroyed for a supposed abuse, this is the kind of discussion you will have.

The Prime-Sergeant replied angrily. Lord Clonmel charged strongly, that the document was a libel, but with some fairness as to Carey's contradictions, and the doubt thereby thrown on the fact of Drennan's having ordered the publication. Justices Downes and Chamberlain concurred with Earl Clonmel, and at 10 o'clock at night the jury retired. At a quarter past 11 they came into court, and (the judges being absent) in reply to the officer, the foreman, Sir John Trail, said the verdict was *Not Guilty*. A burst of applause followed, whereon the foreman retired, and returned again and gave in to one of the judges the verdict, with the following indecent comment:—

"My lords, as I consider this a trial of the first importance to the peace of the country and the happiness of society, I must conceive such indecent conduct as we have experienced, to bespeak a spreading pernicious spirit, which by an exertion of power, ought to be suppressed. For my own part, timidity has no influence on my mind—I act without fear—I despise the resentment, and disregard the approbation of an unruly and seditious rabble : and I can assure them, they have no cause for exultation in meeting favour from the jury; for they regret at seeing a criminal they cannot reach, and guilt which they cannot punish."

The other counts were then severally put to the jury, and a verdict of *Not Guilty*, received upon all.

The report adds:—

"In the course of the tumult in the outer hall, one of the High Sheriffs (Mr. Giffard) selected an opulent citizen, (Mr. S. Gardiner of Church-street) who appeared an active disturber. Complaint was made to the Court next day by the Sheriff, and a rule put upon Gardiner to show cause why an attachment should not issue against him for the contempt; whereupon he filed an affidavit, in which he relied much upon the court's having been, at the time of his apprehension, adjourned. Counsel was heard for him; but the court was pleased to make the rule absolute for attaching him."

Drennan afterwards wrote in "The Press" both prose and verse. His "Wake of William Orr" is one of the finest laments, and his "When Erin first rose," one of the best lyrics we have. His Letters to Pitt against the Union rank with the pamphlets of Goold, Grattan, Taaffe, and Bushe. A life of him, and a collection of his writings, are much wanted.

NORTHERN STAR

28th May, 1794.*

THE best introduction I can give to Curran's very short speech is that prefixed to the pamphlet report of the trial:—

"The measures which government have taken against the proprietors of the *Northern*

* This should have gone before Drennan's case, but was received by the editor too late for insertion in the proper place

Star having excited a considerable share of public curiosity, and it being of importance that the nature and extent of proceedings by information, on the part of the crown, should be generally known, a brief narrative of the prosecution, previous to the following trial cannot but be interesting.

"The alarming circumstances with which this business commenced are worthy of particular notice. The following account of the ARREST is, therefore, copied from the *Northern Star* of January 2, 1793:—

"'For several days past, rumours prevailed that government meditated an attack on the proprietors of this paper. The reports gained considerable ground on Sunday last; and on the evening of that day a troop of light dragoons, which had been stationed at Banbridge, arrived here, in consequence of an express from this town. At the same time, all the other companies belonging to the regiment quartered here were ordered in with all possible dispatch.

"'These menacing appearances, in a time of perfect peace, and without any previous tumult or disturbance whatever to give the faintest colour of propriety to, or necessity for, such a measure, induced in the proprietors a doubt, whether some very extraordinary act of arbitrary power was not intended against them, the more especially as a general officer had been sent here to take the command of the troops in this part of the kingdom.

"'Under these impressions, one of the proprietors wrote a letter to the sovereign of this town early on Monday morning, of which the following is a copy:—

"'Belfast, December 31, 1792.

"'MR. SOVEREIGN—It is affirmed that a troop of light horse came to this town last night, and that more are on their way, in consequence of an application from you, as chief magistrate, demanding aid in the execution of certain warrants or orders against individual inhabitants of the town; and it is farther said, that you have represented the town to be in such a state, that said orders could not be executed without the protection of a strong military force.

"'Now, Sir, as an inhabitant of Belfast, anxious to maintain the high character of the town—as a Volunteer, who has, in conjunction with my companions, manifested an ardent desire to support the civil magistrate in the due execution of the law—but above all, as a proprietor of a newspaper, which is said to be one object of attack on the present occasion -I call upon you to do away so foul a calumny on the town, over the peace of which you preside; I call upon you to avow the fact, *that the civil power of Belfast is capable of supporting the magistrate in the legal execution of his office;* and, in my latter capacity, I will add, that the printer of the paper I allude to, will instantly and cheerfully submit to and obey any *legal* summons, order, or arrest. But any proceeding against him contrary to the law of the land will be resisted, and he will throw himself in such a case for protection on his fellow-citizens, who have declared that they will maintain law, peace, and order, equally against 'a *mob* or a *monarch*, a riot or a proclamation.'

"'Candour—a regard to your character—but more particularly to the peace and character of the town of Belfast, demand of me this communication.

"'I am, Sir, yours truly, &c.

"'To the Rev. W. Bristow, Sovereign of Belfast.

"'Just as this letter was dispatching to the chief magistrate, he called on the gentleman who wrote it—told him there was an order or warrant in town, for the purpose of holding the proprietors to bail, for a certain publication in the *Northern Star*, of the 5th of December last; and that he would earnestly recommend a peaceable obedience to the law, in order that the matter might come fairly to issue. It was replied that if the order was in the nature of a judge's warrant or any other *legal* proceeding, it would meet a prompt obedience. The sovereign said that the order was strictly legal, and by no means a proceeding of an extraordinary nature.

"'On reading the letter, the sovereign *most solemnly* declared, that the calling in the troops was not a measure of his, and even done without his knowledge—that the officer from the King's Bench was instructed not to use force—and, farther, that he (the sovereign) was determined not to use military aid on any such occasion.

"'It was then stated, that, as the proprietors were numerous, and all, less or more, engaged in mercantile pursuits, it would be at once a cruel and unnecessary exercise of power to hurry them away eighty-two miles, from their homes and their business, to enter into a recognizance in Dublin; that they were now ready to do so before the chief magistrate, or would surrender at due time before the justices of the King's Bench, previous to the time of trial.

"'The sovereign, struck with the force of these remarks, took some time to consider, and, finally, agreed to write to government, requesting power might be sent to him, and such other magistrates as might be thought proper, to take bail of the proprietors in Belfast, they, at the same time, pledging themselves to appear in Dublin, for the purpose of giving security, in case this application should prove fruitless.

" 'After the business was thus arranged, the officer who had the warrant was admitted, and received the *voluntary submission* of the proprietors, in the presence of the sovereign.'

"The application from the chief magistrate having been refused by government, the proprietors repaired to Dublin, and entered into recognizances on the 7th of January, before Lord Chief Justice Clonmel, themselves in £100, and two sureties in £50 each. When before his lordship, it was entreated that the proprietors might be informed what the publication was for which they had been arrested? His lordship said it was for a publication inserted in the *Northern Star* of the 5th of December, but did not recollect precisely of what nature it was. Counsel then asked his lordship for a copy of the warrant, which was refused.

"Next term the King's Attorney-General filed *six* informations against the proprietors, for having inserted so many seditious publications, including one inserted on the 5th of December. The assizes shortly after succeeded: but Mr. Attorney-General did not think proper to come to trial on any of the informations. During the next term (Easter) no step whatever was taken; but early in Trinity Term, a *seventh* information was filed for publishing the resolutions of the town of Belfast in the preceding December.

"During this term, the Court of King's Bench was moved, on the part of the defendants, that their recognizances should be vacated, inasmuch as the Attorney-General had proceeded by information, instead of indictment; that he had not come to a trial, although an assizes had intervened; and that the recognizances only related to the execution and warrant on which they had been bound over This application was refused

"On the 19th of July, the proprietors' agent was served with notice of trial on *two* out of the *seven* informations, at the ensuing assizes for the county of Antrim, the publication of the 5th of December *not* being one. In consequence of this notice, the proprietors prepared for their trial, engaged a respectable bar, gave out their briefs, and had Mr. Curran retained, to come down specially on the occasion from Dublin: but on the 3rd of August (only five days before the assizes . they were informed that the crown lawyers *did not think fit to proceed.*

"In Michaelmas Term, 1793, the Attorney-General came into court and moved, *as a matter of right*, for a trial at bar, on the 4th of February, 1794. To this motion the court acceded. The Attorney-General did not give any reason why the sheriff, jury, and defendants should be taken to Dublin, to try a cause which originated in the county of Antrim.

"A motion, on behalf of the proprietors, during this term, had the effect of obtaining an order to the crown solicitor, that he would give notice what information he meant to proceed upon.

"On the 1st of February last, the Court of King's Bench (on an application on behalf of the defendants) ordered the trial to stand for the 19th of May, at bar the Attorney-General refusing to permit it to be tried at Carrickfergus, the last assizes.

"On the 19th of May, the jury were called; but the cause was ordered to stand over for Friday, owing to a civil action, which was then pending in the court; and on Friday, after some slight opposition on the part of the defendants, it was for the same reason further postponed until Wednesday, the 28th, when it proceeded, as is hereafter related.

"And thus has terminated a prosecution upon *one* out of the *seven* informations filed, which has been attended (from the peculiar manner in which it has been carried on) with an expense, perhaps exceeding that of any criminal prosecution upon record; the fees alone for obtaining copies of the informations, stamps and fees of office, and license for Mr. Curran to plead against the crown, have been little short of ONE HUNDRED POUNDS!!!"

On Wednesday, the 28th of May, 1794, this cause came on to be tried at the bar of the court of King's Bench, before Lord Chief Justice Clonmel and Mr. Justice Downes. The following is a copy of the Information:—

"County of Antrim, to wit.—Be it remembered that the Right Honourable Arthur Wolfe, Attorney-General of our present Sovereign Lord the King, who for our said present sovereign Lord the King, prosecutes in this behalf, in his proper person, comes into the court of our said present Lord the King, before the King himself, at the city of Dublin, in the county of the said city, the 28th day of January in this same term, and for our said Lord the King giveth the court to understand and be informed that William M'Cleery, of Belfast, tanner, William Tennent, of the same, merchant, John Haslett, of the same, wholesale woollen-draper, Henry Haslett, of the same, broker and merchant, William Magee, of the same, printer and stationer, Samuel Neilson, of the same, wholesale woollen-draper, John Boyle, of the same, merchant. William Simms, of the same, tanner, Robert Simms, of the same, tanner, Gilbert M'Ilveen, jun. of the same, linen-draper, John Tisdall, of the same, printer, and John Rabb, of Belfast, printer, and Robert Callwell, of the same, printer, all in the county of Antrim, being *wicked, seditious*, and *ill-disposed persons*, and being *greatly disaffected* to our *said Sovereign Lord the King*, and his administration of the government of this kingdom, and *wickedly, maliciously*, and *seditiously intending, devising*, and seditiously intending, devising, and contriving to stir up and excite discontent and *sedition* among the subjects of our Lord the King, and to cause it to be believed, that there a not any *government* lawfully constituted in this kingdom of Ireland, on the 15th day of December, in the 33rd year of the reign of our present Lord George the Third, by the grace of God, of Great Britain, France and Ireland, King, Defender of the Faith, and soforth, with force and arms, at Belfast, in the county of Antrim, they, the said William M'Cleery, William Tennent, John Haslett, Henry Haslett, William Magee, Samuel Neilson, John Boyle, Robert Simms, William Simms, Gilbert M'Ilveen, John Tisdall, John Rabb, and Robert Callwell, wickedly and seditiously printed and published a certain false, wicked, malicious, scandalous, and seditious libel, of and concerning the government, state and constitution of this kingdom of Ireland, according to the tenor and effect following:—

"'IRISH JACOBINS OF BELFAST.

"'At a meeting of the Irish Jacobins of Belfast, the 15th instant, (December, 1792), Mr. Rowley Osborne, jun., in the chair, the following declaration and address to the public, was unanimously agreed to, and ordered to be published:—

"'DECLARATION.

"'1st. Resolved—That this kingdom [meaning the kingdom of Ireland] has no national government, inasmuch as the great mass of the people are not represented in parliament. 2nd. Resolved—That the people of Ireland, of every religious description, have an inherent and indefeasible right from God and nature, to constitute laws for their internal and external welfare. 3rd. Resolved—That the people of Ireland can never effectually constitute their own laws, without an extension of the elective franchise to all its citizens. 4th. Resolved—That the elective franchise can never be obtained without a cordial, steady, and persevering union of all the Irish people of every denomination. 5th. Resolved—That the penal code of statutes which have for upwards of a century doomed our fellow-citizens, the Roman Catholics of this kingdom [meaning Ireland] to a state little inferior to the unlettered African, is a disgrace to the land we live in. 6th. Resolved—That as irreligious prejudices have given and are giving way in every quarter of the globe, the justice of God and the natural rights of man demand of Ireland not to be the last in the annals of freedom. 7th. Resolved—That to obtain this most desirable end, we entreat our fellow-citizens of every denomination in Ireland, England, and Scotland, to turn their thoughts to a National Convention, in order to collect the sense of the people as to the most effective means of obtaining a radical and complete Parliamentary reform, an object without which these kingdoms must for ever remain wretched, and the attainment of which will raise them to a state of freedom, happiness, and glory. 8th. Resolved—That impressed with these sentiments, we have determined to form an association, for the purpose of uniting ourselves with our countrymen, and of disseminating these principles among them, and we pledge ourselves to each other and to our country, that we will individually and collectively exert every means in our power to carry the same into effect.

"'ADDRESS.
"'*The Irish Jacobins of Belfast to the Public.*

"'At this decisive crisis, when it becomes the duty of every individual to step forward and avow his principles, we deem it incumbent on us to explain to our fellow-citizens, our country, and the world at large, the motive and intention of our association. The first thing that struck us, was the manifold grievances the majority of this land, [meaning Ireland] which has falsely been denominated free, labour under from the irreligious distinctions our present constitution [meaning thereby the constitution of Ireland] has imposed on the major part of its inhabitants. According to our ideas, a constitution is nothing else than a fixed and established order in the manner of governing; this order cannot exist if it be not upheld by fundamental rules, enacted by the free and formal consent of the whole nation, or of those it has chosen for its representatives: thus a constitution is a precise and constant form of government; or it is the expression of the rights and obligations of the different powers which compose it. Where the mode of government is not derived from all the people clearly expressed, that nation has no constitution: need we say this is the case with Ireland: it possesses only an acting government which varies according to circumstances, and which gives way to all events; in such a government the supreme authority has more power to oppress the subject than to defend his rights. It ever has been an acknowledged constitutional principle that Irishmen cannot be taxed but with their own consent,—how absurd and false the assertion, for out of five millions of people [meaning the people of Ireland] ninety individuals actually return a majority of the House of Commons [meaning thereby the House of Commons of Ireland], who instead of representing the voice of the nation, are influenced by English interests, and that aristocracy whose baneful exertions have ever tended to sap the vital principles, the rising greatness and native genius of this unhappy and wretched country [meaning Ireland]. Shall we then profane the sacred name of liberty by calling this [meaning Ireland] a land of freedom? The question answers itself. It may be asked by some, do we not at present enjoy civil liberty, or where is the period in our history in which we enjoyed more. We answer that we [meaning his Majesty's subjects of this kingdom] do not at present enjoy real, substantial liberty, neither is there a period in our history from which we would wish to date its era. The present momentous period is the time we could wish to date it from, when the great bulk of the people begin to know their rights, and to feel their wrongs. By unanimity and perseverance this divided land [meaning Ireland] will be liberated from the shackles of tyranny. Yet we do not desire a tempestuous liberty, we desire not a liberty without rule, which places an arbitrary authority in the hands of the multitude, disposes it to error, to precipitation, to anarchy, and has despotism always in its train, ready to seize its prey. Even those who maintain that we have a constitution, acknowledge that it is necessary to restore it to its pristine state. The thing desired is a happy and free constitution, the object of our association, and when we renounce this object, may the Disposer of events and our country renounce us. There is no evil so great which the possession of liberty, we trust, will not make us support; nor is there any advantages that will compensate for its loss: let us seize, then, this auspicious moment; let us hasten to procure by our individual and collective exertions this benefit for our country [meaning Ireland]. Where liberty is once fixed, good laws will present themselves of course. It is by procuring a renovated representation that liberty will be established in this country [meaning Ireland]; this can only be accomplished by a National Convention. The Roman Catholics are already convened: let the Protestants follow their peaceable example. Then, and not till then, the voice of an indignant nation will and must be heard—'For a people to be free it is sufficient that they will it.' Our undisguised sentiments are now before the Tribunal of our country; we submit them with cheerfulness, and if all good citizens be satisfied with them, there can be no doubt but similar associations will be formed in every corner of the nation. Finally, may all Irishmen contract between themselves and their country an alliance equal, firm and eternal. — 'S. KENNEDY, 3c.

"Whereupon the said Attorney-General of our Lord the King, who, for our said Sovereign Lord the King, prosecutes in this behalf, prays the consideration of the court here in the premises, and that due process of law may be awarded against the said persons in this behalf, to make them answer our said present Sovereign Lord the King, touching and concerning the premises aforesaid.

"ARTHUR WOLFE.

"THOMAS KEMMIS, Attorney.
"Received 28th January, 1793."

At eleven o'clock the jury were called over, when Hugh Lyle and John Haltridge having been objected to by the crown, without cause, and no challenge having been taken by the defendants, the following gentlemen were sworn in:—

Thomas Morris Jones, of Moneyglass, Esq.
Sampson Moore, of Springmount, Esq.
James Stewart Moore, of Ballydivity, Esq.
Langford Heyland, of Cromlin, Esq.
Francis Shaw, of Carrickfergus, Esq.
Stafford Gorman, of Brewmount, Esq.
Robert Gage, of Rathlin. Esq.
Jackson Clark, of Antrim, Esq.
Henry C. Ellis, of Prospect, Esq;
Alexander M'Auley, of Glenville, Esq.
George Stewart, of Glenarm, Esq.
Edmund M'Ildowney, of Ballycastle, Esq.

Mr. Ruxton opened the pleadings. The Attorney-General stated the case, and called evidence to prove proprietorship and publication. An argument arose out of the evidence as to the proof of proprietorship, on which, in reply to the crown, Curran said:—

I regret that we are come to such an era in criminal justice, that four gentlemen of high distinction should be gravely listened to, in arguing whether there was a shadow of evidence to go to a jury against twelve of the King's subjects, to charge them with a very heinous crime. I insist that, according to the ordinary practice, where a number of parties are included in a criminal charge, those against whom there is no evidence should be sent to the jury with directions to acquit them, that those who are to be tried may have the benefit of their evidence, if it should be necessary. The counsel for the crown have set out upon erroneous principles; they seem to take the question to be, whether these people are proprietors or not. There is no law of this country, by which every man entitled to share the profits of a certain trade shall be criminally responsible for the exercise of that trade by his agent. If several people employ a ship, and the navigator of it shall commit piracy or treason upon the high seas, shall those who are entitled to share the profits be criminally responsible? Is that the principle of

Irish law. If not, it is absurd to say that this question depends upon the proprietorship of the parties, or has anything to do with it. There is no rule of law better established than that distinction between being criminally and civilly responsible for the acts of an agent. If a servant of his own head commit a criminal act, his master certainly will not be involved in the crime, however he might be if it was fully proved to be by his express command, for then the employer would be involved in the guilt. But the bare act is not *prima facie* evidence to charge the master; nothing short of evidence of commandment can do that. Otherwise there would be no safety in society, and every man here might, for what he never knew, be answerable for as many crimes as he had servants. By intendment of law, the master is only supposed to give authority for that which is lawful; unless there is some privity or commandment shown, there is no evidence of guilt in the master. I should be ashamed to insist further from the very elementary principles of a study in which I have been employed for seventeen years. Evidence that these men whose names have crowded the information, are proprietors of a newspaper, is not evidence that they are guilty of a deed not done by themselves. The act of parliament itself makes a clear distinction between the printer and proprietor, and the proprietors come under a clause or designation different from the publisher or printer.— This irresistibly shows the fallacy attempted to be imposed upon the court. The stating a man's name and residence and other collateral circumstances, is not for the purpose of making him be considered as printer or publisher, but to let in certain lights which may be advantageous to the public, or any individual who shall be aggrieved.

This affidavit, made pursuant to the act of parliament, states Rabb to be the sole printer; and yet it is offered in evidence, to show that others were the printers or publishers: it is true these gentlemen have not made an affidavit to the contrary, although it might have been a wise thing for them to have made a purgative and preventative affidavit every day as to the case cited: I meant to have quoted it in our favour, as directly establishing the principle, that their barely being entitled to receive a portion of the profits, or being proprietors, is not evidence of their being printers or publishers, but that there must be evidence of the act charged to be criminal being done by the party himself or by his immediate commandment. In Topham's case there was evidence of buying a paper at the office when he was sole proprietor, there was besides an affidavit, of payment for the stamps used, in printing this very paper; there it was clearly done with his privity, under his control; here it is clear that there has been no evidence given of personal interference so as to amount to such authority or command, as would render any of the parties criminally liable.

After other counsel were heard, the jury, under direction of the court, found a verdict of acquittal for all the *proprietors* except John Rabb, the actual printer. The case was then proceeded with against him. Mr. Dobbs defended him on the ground that the publication was not a libel. Clonmel and Downes charged against the prisoner, and the jury, "after five minutes' consideration, brought in their verdict—GUILTY."

REV. WILLIAM JACKSON.

April 23rd, 1795.

Mr. W. H. Curran, in the Memoirs of his Father, thus describes Jackson:—

"Mr. Jackson was a clergyman of the Established Church; he was a native of Ireland, but he had for several years resided out of that country. He spent a part of his life in the family of the noted Duchess of Kingston, and is said to have been the person who conducted that lady's controversy with the celebrated Foote. At the period of the French Revolution he passed over to Paris, where he formed political connexions with the constituted authorities. From France he returned to London, in 1794, for the purpose of procuring information as to the practicability of an invasion of England, and was thence to proceed to Ireland on a similar mission. Upon his arrival in London, he renewed an intimacy with a person named Cockayne, who had formerly been his friend and confidential attorney. The extent of his communications, in the first instance, to Cockayne, did not exactly appear. The latter, however, was prevailed upon to write the directions of several of Jackson's letters, containing treasonable matters, to his correspondents abroad; but in a little time, either suspecting or repenting that he had been furnishing evidence of treason against himself, he revealed to the British minister, Mr. Pitt, all that he knew or conjectured relative to Jackson's objects. By the desire of Mr. Pitt, Cockayne accompanied Jackson to Ireland, to watch and defeat his designs; and as soon as the evidence of his treason was mature, announced himself as a witness for the crown. Mr. Jackson was accordingly arrested, and committed to stand his trial for high treason.

"Mr. Jackson was committed to prison in April, 1794, but his trial was delayed, by successive adjournments, till the same month in the following year. In the interval, he wrote and published a refutation of Paine's Age of Reason, probably in the hope that it might be accepted as an atonement. He was convicted, and brought up for judgment on the 30th of April, 1795."

He was indicted for treason in the Summer of 1794; but, sometimes for the crown, and at others for the prisoner, the trial was postponed till the 23rd of April, 1795.

Court—Right Hon. the Earl of Clonmel, Chief Justice; *Hon. Mr. Justice Downes, Hon. Mr. Justice Chamberlaine.

Counsel for the Crown—Mr. Attorney General, Mr. Prime-Sergeant, Mr. Solicitor General, Mr. Frankland, and Mr. Trench. Agent—Thomas Kemmis, Esq. Crown Solicitor.

Counsel assigned to the prisoner—Mr. Curran and Mr. Ponsonby.

Assistant-Counsel—Mr. R. Guinness, Mr. M'Nally, Mr Emmett, Mr. Burton, and Mr. Sampson. Agent—Edward Crookshank Keane, Esq.

The Attorney-General led the prosecution. His chief witness was Cockayne, an English attorney. Among the papers proved was this remarkable VIEW OF IRELAND, by Tone:—

"The situation of Ireland and England is fundamentally different in this: the government of England is national—that of Ireland, provincial. The interest of the first is the same with that of the people; of the last, directly opposite. The people of Ireland are divided into three sects—the Established Church, the Dissenters, and the Catholics. The first—infinitely the smallest portion—have engrossed, besides the whole church patronage, all the profits and honours of the country exclusively, and a very great share of the landed property. They are, of course, aristocrats, adverse to any change, and decided enemies of the French Revolution. The Dissenters—who are much more numerous—are the most enlightened body of the nation; they are steady Republicans, devoted to liberty, and, through all the stages of the French Revolution, have been enthusiastically attached to it. The Catholics—the great body of the people—are in the lowest degree of ignorance, and are ready for any change, because no change can make them worse. The whole peasantry of Ireland, the most oppressed and wretched in Europe, may be said to be Catholic. They have within these two years received a certain degree of information, and manifested a proportionate degree of discontent, by various insurrections, &c. They are a bold, hardy race, and make excellent soldiers. There is nowhere a higher spirit of aristocracy than in all the privileged orders, the clergy and gentry of Ireland, down to the very lowest; to countervail which, there appears now a spirit rising in the people which never existed before, but which is spreading most rapidly, as appears by the Defenders, as they are called, and other insurgents. If the people of Ireland be 4,500,000, as it seems probable they are, the Established Church may be reckoned at 450,000; the Dissenters at 900,000; the Catholics at 3,150,000. The prejudices in England are adverse to the French nation under whatever form of government. It seems idle to suppose the present rancour against the French

---

* Hon. Mr. Justice Boyd was prevented from attending by indisposition.

is owing merely to their being Republicans; it has been cherished by the manners of four centuries, and aggravated by continual wars. It is morally certain that any invasion of England would unite all ranks in opposition to the invaders. In Ireland—a conquered, oppressed, and insulted country—the name of England and her power is universally odious, save with those who have an interest in maintaining it; a body, however, only formidable from situation and property, but which the first convulsion would level in the dust. On the contrary, the great bulk of the people of Ireland would be ready to throw off the yoke in this country, if they saw any force sufficiently strong to resort to for defence until arrangements could be made: the Dissenters are enemies to the English power, from reason and from reflection; the Catholics, from a hatred of the English name. In a word, the prejudices of one country are directly adverse to the other—directly favourable to an invasion. The government of Ireland is only to be looked upon as a government of force: the moment a superior force appears, it would tumble at once, as being founded neither in the interests nor in the affections of the people. It may be said, the people of Ireland show no political exertion. In the first place, public spirit is completely depressed by the recent persecutions of several. The convention act, the gunpowder, &c., &c., declarations of government, parliamentary unanimity, or declarations of grand juries—all proceeding from aristocrats, whose interest is adverse to that of the people, and who think such conduct necessary for their security—are no obstacles; the weight of such men falls in the general welfare, and their own tenantry and dependants would desert and turn against them. The people have no way of expressing their discontent *civiliter*, which is, at the same time, greatly aggravated by those measures; and they are, on the other hand, in that semi-barbarous state, which is, of all others, the best adapted for making war. The spirit of Ireland cannot, therefore, be calculated from newspaper publications, county meetings, &c., at which the gentry only meet and speak for themselves. They are so situated that they have but one way left to make their sentiments known, and that is by war. The church establishment and tithes are very severe grievances, and have been the cause of numberless local insurrections. In a word, from reason, reflection, interest, prejudice, the spirit of change, the misery of the great bulk of the nation, and, above all, the hatred of the English name, resulting from the tyranny of near seven centuries, there seems little doubt but an invasion and sufficient force would be supported by the people. There is scarce any army in the country, and the militia, the bulk of whom are Catholics, would, to a moral certainty, refuse to act, if they saw such a force as they could look to for support."

Curran said:—

My Lords, and Gentlemen of the Jury! I am sure the attention of the court must be a good deal fatigued. I am sure, gentlemen of the jury, that your minds must of necessity be fatigued also. Whether counsel be fatigued or not, is matter very little worth the observation that may be made upon it. I am glad that it is not necessary for me to add a great deal to the labour, either of the court, or the jury. Of the court I must have some knowledge—of the jury, I certainly am not ignorant. I know it is as unnecessary for me to say much, or, perhaps, anything, to inform the court, as it would be ridiculous to affect to lecture a jury of the description I have the honour to address. I know I address a court, anxious to expound fairly and impartially the law of the country, without any apprehension of the consequences and effect of any prosecution. In the jury I am looking to now, I know I address twelve sensible and respectable men of my country, who are as conscious as I am of the great obligation to which they have pledged themselves by their oath, to decide upon the question fairly, without listening to passion, or being swayed by prejudice—without thinking of anything except the charge which has been made, and the evidence which has been brought in support of that charge. They know, as well as I do, that the great object of a jury is to protect the country against crimes, and to protect individuals against all accusation that is not founded in truth. They will remember—I know they will remember, that the great object of their duty is, according to the expression of a late venerated judge, in another country, that they are to come into the box with their minds like white paper, upon which prejudice, or passion, or bias, or talk, or hope, or fear, has not been able to scrawl any thing; that you, gentlemen I come into the box, standing indifferent as you stand unsworn.

In the little, gentlemen, that I shall take the liberty of addressing to you, I shall rest the fate of it upon its intrinsic weight. I shall not leave the case in concealment. If there be no ground on which the evidence can be impeached, I will venture to say I will neither bark at it, nor scold it, in lieu of giving it an answer. Whatever objection I have to make, shall be addressed to your reason. I will not say they are great, or conclusive, or unanswerable objections. I shall submit them to you nakedly as they appear to me. If they have weight, you will give it to them. If they have not, a great promise, on my part, will not give anticipated weight to that whose debility will appear when it comes to be examined.

Gentlemen, you are empannelled to try a charge. It consists of two offences, particularly described in the indictment. The first question is, what is the allegation? In the first branch, the prisoner is indicted upon a statute, which inflicts the pains and penalties of high treason upon any man who shall compass or imagine the King's death. The nature of the offence, if you required any comment on it, has been learnedly, and, I must add, candidly commented upon by Mr. Attorney-General in stating the case. The second part is, that the prisoner did adhere to the King's enemies. By the law of this country, there are particular rules, applicable to cases of prosecutions for high treason, contra-distinguished from all the other branches of the criminal law. The nature of the offence called for this peculiarity of regulation. There is no species of charge to which innocent men may more easily be made victims, than that of offences against the state, and therefore it was necessary to give an additional protection to the subject. There is an honest impulse in the natural and laudable loyalty of every man, that warms his passions strongly against the person who endeavours to disturb the public quiet and security; it was necessary, therefore, to guard the subject against the most dangerous of all abuses—the abuse of a virtue, by extraordinary vigilance. There was another reason:— There is no charge which is so vague and indefinite, and yet would be more likely to succeed, than charging a man as an enemy to the state. There is no case in which the venality of a base informer could have greater expectation of a base reward. Therefore, gentlemen, it was necessary to guard persons accused from the over hasty virtue of a jury on the one hand, and on the other from being made the sacrifice of the base and rank prostitution of a depraved informer. How has the law done this? By pointing out in terms, these rules and orders that shall guide the court, and bind the jury in the verdict they shall give. The man shall be a traitor, if he commits the crime, but it must be a crime of which he should be proveably attaint, by overt acts. And in order that there be an opportunity of investigation and defence, the features of the overt acts should be stated of public record in the very body of the indictment. Justly do I hear it observed, that there cannot be

o

devised a fairer mode of accusation and trial than this is. Gentlemen, I have stated to you how the foundation of it stands in both countries, touching the mode of accusation and trial. I have to add to you, that in Great Britain it has been found necessary still further to increase the sanction of the jury, and the safety of the prisoner, by an express statute in King William's time. By that law it is now settled in that great country, that no man shall be indicted or convicted, except upon the evidence of two witnesses, and it describes what sort of evidence that shall be; either two witnesses swearing directly to the same overt act laid in the indictment, or two witnesses, one swearing to one overt act, and the other to another overt act of the same species of treason So that, in that country, no man can be found guilty, except upon the evidence of two distinct credible witnesses—credible in their testimony, distinct in their persons, and concurring in the evidence of acts of one and the same class of treason; for it must be to the same identical treason, sworn to by both witnesses; or one witness deposing to one act of treason, and the other to another act of the same class of treason. That is the settled law of the neighbouring kingdom, and I state it emphatically to you to be the settled law; because far am I from thinking, that we have not the blessing of living under the same sanction of law—far am I from imagining that the breath which cannot even taint the character of a man in England, shall here blow him from the earth—that the proof, which in England would not wound the man, shall here deprive him of his life—that though the people in England would laugh at the accusation, yet here it shall cause the accused to perish under it. Sure I am that in a country where so few instances of a foul accusation of this sort have occurred, the judges of the court will need little argument to give effect to every thing urged to show that the law is the same in Ireland as in England.

Lord Clonmel—Do you mean to argue that the statute of William is in force in Ireland?

Mr. Curran.—No, my lord; not that the statute of William is in force—but I mean to argue, that the necessity of two witnesses in the case of treason is as strong here as in England. It is the opinion of Lord Coke, founded upon a number of authorities; the opinion of Lord Coke, referring to a judicial confirmation of what he says; the opinion of Lord Coke controverted, if it can be said to be controverted, by the modest and diffident dissent of Sir Michael Foster. It is laid down by Lord Coke, that he conceives it to be the established law, that two witnesses are necessary to convict: 3 Inst. 26. "It seemeth that by the ancient common law, one accuser or witness was not sufficient to convict any person of high treason—and that two witnesses be required, appeareth by our books, and I remember no authority in our books to the contrary." I know of no judicial determination in our books to the contrary of what Lord Coke here states: the common law is grounded upon the principles of reason. I consider the statutes of Edward VI., and William III., as statutes which had become necessary from the abuses occasioned by a departure from the common law. After the statute of Edward VI., expressly declaring the necessity of two witnesses, the courts had fallen into perhaps a well-intentioned departure from the meaning of the statute of Edward VI., so far that the place of two witnesses was supplied in evidence by any thing that the court thought a material additional circumstance in the case; and to the time of William III., such a departure had prevailed, and this was thought sufficient to discharge every thing respecting the obligations of the statute. It became necessary, therefore, to enact and by that enactment to do away the abuse of the principle of the common law, by expressly declaring that no man should be indicted or convicted except by two witnesses to one overt act, or one witness to one act, and a second to another act of high treason of the same species. And there seems to me to be a sound distinction between the case of high treason, and of any other crime. It is the only crime which every subject is sworn against committing: it is the only crime which any subject is sworn to abstain from. In every other case the subject is left to the fear of punishment which he may feel, or to the dictates of his conscience to guard himself against transgressing the law; but treason is a breach of his oath of allegiance, and is so far like the case of perjury: and therefore in the case of treason, no man should be convicted by the testimony of a single witness, because it amounts to no more than oath against oath: so that it is only reasonable there should be another to turn the scale; and therefore it is that I conceive Lord Coke well warranted in laying down this rule, a rule deduced from general justice, and even from the law of God himself. Gentlemen, what I am now stating, I offer to the court as matter of law.

But what were these witnesses? Witnesses in all cases beyond exception in their personal circumstances, and in their personal credit. Therefore it is the law, that no man shall be found guilty of any offence that is not legally proved upon him by the sworn testimony of credible witnesses. Gentlemen, I have submitted my humble ideas of the law— I have stated the charge which the prisoner is called upon to answer. let me now state the overt acts, which in this particular case are necessary to be proved. The first is, that the prisoner did traitorously come to, and land in, Ireland, to procure information concerning the subjects of Ireland, and to send that information to the persons exercising the government in France, to aid them in carrying on the war against the King. I do not recollect that Cockayne said one single word of the prisoner's coming here for such a purpose. The second overt act is, that the prisoner did traitorously intend to raise and levy war, and incite persons to invade Ireland with arms and men; that he did incite Theobald Wolfe Tone to go beyond seas to incite France to invade this kingdom; that he did endeavour to procure persons to go to France and that he agreed with other persons, that they should be sent to France for the same purpose. Having stated these overt acts which are laid in the indictment, you will be pleased to recollect the evidence given by Cockayne. Cockayne did not say that the prisoner came over here for any such purpose as the overt act attributes to him. Then, as to the overt act, of endeavouring to procure persons to go to France for the purpose of giving information to the enemy; the witness said he met Mr. M'Nally; he had known him in England; Jackson was a clergyman; he had known him also. Cockayne had professional business with Mr. M'Nally. Mr. M'Nally paid them a courtesy which any decent person would have been entitled to. They dined at his house, and met three or four persons there; they talked of the politics of Ireland; of the dissatisfaction of the people; but not a syllable of what is stated in the indictment; not one word of any conspiracy; Cockayne did not pretend to be able to give any account of any specific conversation. He went to Newgate; Rowan was then in confinement; he sometimes went by himself: sometimes met Tone, sometimes Jackson; he gave you an account of encouragement; what was it? Was there any thing to support this indictment? Let me remind you that you are to found your verdict on what the witness says and you believe, and not on what learned counsel may be instructed to state. Then what does the witness say? He admits that he did not hear all the conversation. The crying injustice must strike you, of making a man answerable for a part of a conversation, where the witness did not hear it all; but take it as he has stated it, unqualified and unconstrued: how high was he wrought up by it? He heard talk of somebody to go to France; he was to carry papers; he heard an expression of instructions to the French. What French—what instructions? It might be to French manufacturers; it might be to French traitors; it might be to the French King; it might be to the French convention. Do I mean to say that there was nothing by which a credulous or reasonable man might not have his suspicion raised, or that there was nothing in three or four men huddling themselves together in Newgate, and talking of an invasion? No; but my reasoning is this—that your verdict is to be founded on evidence of positive guilt established at the hazard of the personal punishment of the witness; you are not to pick up the conjectures either of his malignity or credulity. I say that this man stands in defiance of your verdict, because it will be affected by nothing but that irresistible evidence on which alone it ought to be founded. But what was the fact which Tone was to do, or any other person? It was an illegal one. By a late act, an English subject going to France is liable to six months' imprisonment. By a clause in the same statute the crime of soliciting a person to go is also punishable. The encouraging any person to go to that country was, therefore, exposing him to danger, but whether it was a motive of trade, or smuggling, or idle adventure, is not the question for you. It is whether the intention was to convey an incitement to the French to make a descent on this kingdom, and endeavour to subvert the constitution of it. You have a simple question before you—has even the prosecutor sworn that he endeavoured to do so? I think not. The next overt act charged is, that he did compose and write a letter in order to be sent to William Stone, in which he traitorously desired Stone to disclose to certain persons in France the scheme and intention of Jackson, to send a person to inform them of the state of Ireland, for the purpose of giving support and effect to a hostile invasion of this country. You have heard these letters read. You must of necessity look on them in one or two important and distinct points of view.

The first, perhaps, that will naturally strike you is, what are these letters? Do they sustain the allegations of the overt act? Are they letters requiring Stone to inform the Convention of this country being in such a state as to encourage an invasion? Does that paper support this allegation? God help us! gentlemen of the jury. I know not in what state the property or life of any man will be if they are always to be at the mercy, and to depend on the possibility of his explaining either the real or pretended circumstances on which he corresponds with persons abroad. The letters are written apparently upon mercantile subjects— he talks of manufactures, of a firm, of prices changed, of different families, of differences among them, of overtures to be accepted of, of disputes likely to be settled by means of common mediation; what is the evidence on which you can be supported in saying that manufactures mean treason—that Nicholas means the war minister of France—the sister-in-law Ireland—that "the firm has been changed," means Danton has been guillotined, but that makes no alteration in the state of the house, meaning the circumstances of the revolution—that the change of prices and manufactures means any thing else necessary to give consistency to the charge of treason. Give me leave to say that this ludicrous and barbarous consequence would follow from a rule of this sort, the idlest letter might be strained to any purpose. The simplicity of our law is, that a man's guilt should be proved by the evidence of witnesses on their oaths, which shall not be supplied by fancy, nor elicited by the ingenuity of any person making suggestions to the wretched credulity of a jury that should be weak enough to adopt them. I come now to this. A letter produced imports on the face of it to be a letter of business, concerning manufactures—another concerning family differences. In which way are they to be understood? I say with confidence, better it should be to let twenty men, that might have a criminal purpose in writing letters of this kind, escape, than fall into the dreadful alternative of making one man a victim to a charge of this kind not supported by such proof as could bring conviction on the mind of a rational jury.

I do not think it necessary to state to you minutely the rest of these allegations of the overt acts. The charge against the prisoner is supported, and this is perhaps the clearest way of calling your attention to the evidence, either by the positive evidence of Cockayne as to these facts, or by the written evidence which stands also on his testimony alone. Touching actual conspiracy he said nothing: somebody was to go to France—he knew not for what—he had an idea on his mind for what it was—but never from any communication with Jackson. There have been other letters read in evidence. Two of them contained duplicates of a sort of representation of the supposed state of Ireland. Cockayne says that he got the packet from Jackson, that he himself wrote the directions; one addressed to Amsterdam, the other to Hamburgh. They were read, and they contain assertions, whether true or false I do not think material, of the state of this country:—if material at all, material only in their falsehood. The public are satisfied that these allegations are false. It is known to every man in this country and must be known with great satisfaction by every honest man, that it is not in that state that could induce any but the most adventurous and wicked folly to try an experiment upon it. It is unnecessary for me to comment on the opinions contained in that paper; there is a matter more material, and calling more loudly for your attention. It is stated to be written for the purpose of inviting the persons governing in France to try a descent upon Ireland. This paper is evidence to support that charge; you have heard it read. On what public subject have you ever heard six men speak, and all to agree? Might not a stranger in a fit of despondency, imagine that an invasion might have a fatal effect on this country. It is not impossible but if ten men were to make a landing, some mischief might happen. Then, again, what do I mean to argue? Is it that this letter bears no marks of the design imputed to it? No such thing. It is a letter that the most innocent man might write, but it is also such a one as a guilty man might write, but unless there was clear evidence of his guilt, he would be entitled to your verdict of acquittal. Though it was not expressly avowed, yet I cannot help thinking that it was meant to lay some little emphasis on certain names which I have met with in the newspapers—I am sure I have met the name of Laignelot in the debates of the convention—I have met the names of Horne Tooke and Stone in the English papers. I have read that Horne Tooke was tried for high treason and acquitted—that Stone made his escape into Switzerland. I believe it is said that there is a person of that name in confinement in England at present. But let me tell you, you are not to draw any inferences from circumstances of this kind against the prisoner: let me tell you, it is the guilt of the man, and not the sound of names, by which his fate is to be decided.

Other papers have been read. One seems to contain some forms of addresses. A letter said to come from Stone has been read to you. The letter to Beresford, said to be written by Jackson, has also been read to you. I have stated the material parts of the evidence. I have endeavoured to submit my poor idea of the rule by which you ought to be guided. I see only one remaining topic to trouble you upon; it appears to me to be a topic of the utmost importance. And, gentlemen, it is this. Who is the man that has been examined to support this charge? One witness! I beseech you to have that engraven on your minds. The charge, in all its parts, stands only on the evidence of Cockayne; there is no other evidence of any conversation, there is not a material letter read in this case that does not rest upon Cockayne's evidence, and that I am warranted in this assertion you will see to a demonstration when I remind the court that he was the only witness, as I recollect, called to prove the handwriting of Jackson. On his testimony alone must depend the fact of their being his hand-writing, of the innuendoes imputed to them, or the purpose with which they were sent.

Gentlemen, I am scarcely justified in having trespassed so long on your patience. It is a narrow case. It is a case of a man charged with the highest and most penal offence known by our law, and charged by one witness only. And let me ask who that witness is. A man, stating that he comes from another country, armed with a pardon for treasons, committed in Ireland, but not in England whence he comes. What! were you never on a jury before? Did you ever hear of a man forfeiting his life on the unsupported evidence of a single witness, and he an accomplice by his own confession? What! his character made the subject of testimony and support!—take his own vile evidence for his character. He was the foul traitor of his own client. What do you think now of his character? He was a spy upon his friend. He was the man that yielded to the tie of three oaths of allegiance, to watch the steps of his client for the bribe of government, with a pardon for the treasons he might commit; and he had impressed on his mind the conviction that he was liable to be executed as a traitor. Was he aware of his crime?—his pardon speaks it. Was he aware of the turpitude of his character?—he came with the cure; he brought his witness in his pocket. To what? To do away an offence which he did not venture to deny, that he had incautiously sworn that which was false in fact, though the jury did not choose to give it the name of wilful and corrupt perjury. Gracious God! Is it, then, on the evidence of a man of this kind, with his pardon in his pocket, and his bribe—not yet in his pocket—that you can venture to convict the prisoner. He was to be taken care of. How so? Jackson owed him a debt—" I was to do the honourable business of a spy and informer, and to be paid for it in the common way; it was common *acreable* work—treason and conspiracy I was to be paid for it by the sheet." Do you find men doing these things in common life? I have now stated the circumstances by which, in my opinion, the credit of Cockayne ought to be reduced to nothing in your eyes. But I do not rest here. Papers were found in the chamber of Mr. Jackson; the door was open—and, by the bye, that carelessness was not evidence of any conscious guilt; the papers were seized. That there were some belonging to Jackson is clear, because he expressed an anxiety about some that are confessed not to have any relation to the subject of this day's trial. I asked Cockayne, if he had any papers in Jackson's room the night before he was arrested? He said not. I asked him, if he had told any person that he had? He said not. Gentlemen, the only witness I shall call, will be one to show you that he na- in that sworn falsely. And let me here make one observation to you, the strength and good sense of which has been repeated an hundred times, and, therefore, rests on better authority than mine. Where a witness swears glibly to a number of circumstances, where it is impossible to produce contradictory proof, and is found to fail in one, it shall overthrow all the others. And see how strongly the observation applies here: he swore to a conversation with Jackson as to what he said and did, well knowing that Jackson could not be a witness to disprove that unless the good sense of the jury should save his life, and enable him to become, in his turn, a prosecutor for the perjury. If on a point of this kind this man should be found to have forsworn himself, it cannot occasion any other sentiment but this, that if you have felt yourselves disposed to give anything like credit to his evidence where he has sworn to facts which he must have known, it is the key-stone of the arch in his testimony, and if you can pluck it from its place, the remainder of the pile will fall in ruins about his head.

I will produce that witness—but, before I sit down, permit me, gentlemen of the jury, to remind you, that if every word which Cockayne has here sworn were sworn in Westminster-Hall, the judges would immediately have said—There is not anything for the jury to decide upon; the evidence of the indictment rests on him alone; there is no second witness. So does the transaction of the letters, for De Joncourt's testimony could not have satisfied the statute; it was not evidence to the same overt act as affecting Jackson personally, nor was it evidence of any distinct overt act; it was merely that species of evidence, the abuse of which had been the cause of introducing the statute of William; a mere collateral concomitant evidence. The overt act was writing and putting into the post-office; that was sworn to by Cockayne, and if he deserved credit, would go so far as to prove the fact by one witness. See what the idea of the statute is; it is that it must be an overt act brought home to the prisoner by each of the two witnesses swearing to it. If De Joncourt's evidence stood single, it could not have brought anything home to Jackson. Cockayne swore the superscription was his writing; he put the letters into the office. De Joncourt said nothing but that he found in the office a letter which he produced, and which Cockayne said was the one he had put into it. This observation appears to collect additional strength from this circumstance. Why did they not produce Tone? It is said they could not. I say they could. It was as easy to pardon him as to pardon Cockayne. But whether he was guilty or not, is no objection. Shall it be said that the argument turns about and affects Jackson as much as it does the prosecutor? I think certainly not. Jackson, I believe it has appeared in the course of the evidence, and is matter of judicial knowledge to the court, has lain in prison for twelve months past, from the moment of his arrest to the moment of his trial. If he is conscious that the charge is false, it is impossible for him to prove that falsehood; he was so circumstanced as that he could not procure the attendance of witnesses; a stranger in the country, he could not tell whether some of the persons named were in existence or not.

I have before apologised to you for trespassing upon your patience, and I have again trespassed—let me not repeat it. I shall only take the liberty of reminding you, that if you have any doubt, in a criminal case doubt should be acquittal; that you are trying a case which if tried in England would preclude the jury from the possibility of finding a verdict of condemnation. It is for you to put it into the power of mankind to say, that that which should pass harmlessly over the head of a man in Great Britain shall blast him here;—whether life is more valuable in that country than in this, or whether a verdict may more easily be obtained here in a case tending to establish pains and penalties of this severe nature.

The trial lasted till four o'clock in the morning, when Jackson was found Guilty. He was brought up for judgment on the 30th of April, but he died in the dock, of arsnic which he had taken. It is noticeable that the rule of allowing one witness to convict for treason in Ireland, as established by this case, enabled the Government to obtain their convictions in '98.

DUBLIN DEFENDERS.

December 22nd, 1795.

TRIAL OF JAMES WELDON, FOR HIGH TREASON

Before the Court holden under a Commission of Oyer and Terminer, and general Gaol delivery, in and for the County of the City of Dublin, in Ireland, on Monday, December 21st, and Tuesday, December 22nd. 36 Geo. III., A.D. *1795.*

COMMISSION.—MONDAY, DECEMBER 14TH, 1795.

Mr. Baron George sat as the Judge of the Commission, and was assisted by Mr. Justice Chamberlaine and Mr. Justice Finucane.

In the latter end of the month of August, 1795, several persons were taken into custody in the city of Dublin, upon charges of High Treason, and in the ensuing commission of Oyer and Terminer held in October, bills of indictment were preferred against them, and others not then in custody which were returned by the grand jury to be true bills.

The prisoners in custody were then brought to the bar of the court, for the purpose of having counsel and agents assigned. They were severally called upon to name their own counsel and agents, and such as they named were assigned by the court, as follows:—

For Thomas Kennedy, George Lewis, Patrick Hart, Edward Hanlon, Thomas Cooke, and John Lowry; Counsel—Messrs. Curran and M'Nally. Agent—Mr. A. Fitzgerald.

For Thomas Murphy and Michael Maguire; Counsel—Messrs. M'Nally and Lysaght. Agent—Mr. M. Kearney.

For Henry Flood; Counsel—Messrs. Fletcher and Ridgeway. Agent—Mr. F. Flood.

In the interval between the October commission and the December, a person of the name of James Weldon was apprehended on a charge of High Treason, and he, together with such as had been previously in custody, were served with copies of the indictments and the captions thereof, five days before the first day of this commission.

This day the prisoners who had been in custody at the last commission were severally arraigned, and pleaded Not Guilty.

On the 21st of December several arguments took place as to the jury, and on the 22nd the trial came on. The Attorney-General stated the case, and examined many witnesses, but especially one William Lawler, a gilder. The crown examination was leading and unfair throughout. Curran said:—

My lords, and gentlemen of the jury, I am of counsel in one of those cases in which the humanity of our law is, very fortunately, joined with the authority and wisdom of the court in alliance with me for the purposes of legal protection. Gentlemen, I cannot, however, but regret that that sort of laudable and amiable anxiety for the public tranquillity, which glows warmest in the breasts of the best men, has, perhaps, induced Mr. Attorney-General to state some facts to the court and the jury, of which no evidence was attempted to be given. And I make the observation only for this purpose, to remind you, gentlemen, that the statement of counsel is not evidence—to remind you, that you are to give a verdict upon this solemn and momentous occasion, founded simply upon the evidence which has been given to you; for such is the oath you have taken. Gentlemen, I make the observation, not only in order to call upon you to discharge any impressions not supported by testimony, but to remind you also of another incontrovertible maxim, not only of the humane law of England, but of eternal justice upon which that is founded—that the more horrid and atrocious the nature of any crime charged upon any man is, the more clear and invincible should be the evidence upon which he is convicted. The charge here is a charge of the most enormous criminality that the law of any country can know—no less than the atrocious and diabolical purpose of offering mortal and fatal violence to the person of the Sovereign, who ought to be sacred. The prisoner is charged with entertaining the guilty purpose of destroying all order, and all society, for the well-being of which the person of the King is held sacred. Therefore, gentlemen, I presume to tell you, that in proportion as the crime is atrocious and horrible, in the same proportion ought the evidence to convict be clear and irresistible. Let me, therefore, endeavour to discharge the duty I owe to the unfortunate man at the bar (for unfortunate I consider him, whether he be convicted or acquitted), by drawing your attention to a consideration of the facts charged, and comparing it with the evidence adduced to support it.

The charge, gentlemen, is of two kinds—two species of treason founded upon the statute 25 Edward III. One is, compassing the King's death; the other is a distinct treason—that of adhering to the King's enemies. In both cases the criminality must be clearly established, under the words of the statute, by having the guilty man convicted of the offence by provable evidence of overt acts. Even in the case, and it is the only one, where by law the imagination shall complete the crime, there that guilt must be proved, and can be provable only by outward acts, made use of by the criminal, for the effectuation of his guilty purpose. The overt acts stated here are, that he associated with traitors unknown, with the design of assisting the French, at war with our government, and therefore a public enemy. 2ndly, consulting with others for the purpose of assisting the French. 3rdly, consulting with other traitors to subvert the government. 4thly, associating with Defenders to subvert the Protestant religion. 5thly, enlisting a person stated in the indictment to assist the French, and administering an oath to him for that purpose. 6thly, enlisting him to adhere to the French. 7thly, corrupting Lawler to become a Defender. 8thly, enlisting him by administering an oath, for similar purposes. In order to warrant a verdict convicting the prisoner, there must be clear and convincing evidence of some one of these overt acts, as they are laid. The law requires that there should be stated upon record such an act as in point of law will amount to an overt act of the treason charged, as matter of evidence, and the evidence adduced must correspond with the fact charged. The uniform rule which extends to every case applies to this, that whether the fact charged be sustained by evidence is for the conscience and the oath of the jury, according to the degree of credit they give to the testimony of it. In treason, the overt act must sustain the crime, and the evidence must go to support the overt act so stated. If this case were tried at the other side of the water, it does not strike me that the very irrelevant evidence given by Mr. Carleton could have supplied what the law requires—the concurring testimony of two witnesses. I cannot be considered, indeed I should be sorry, to put any sort of comparison between the person of Mr. Carleton and the first witness who was called upon the table. Gentlemen of the jury, you have an important province indeed—the life or death of a man—to decide upon. But previous to that, you must consider what degree of credit ought to be given to a man under the circumstances of that witness produced against the prisoner. It does appear to me, that his evidence merits small consideration in point of credibility. But even if he were as deserving of belief as the witness that followed, and that his evidence were as credible as the other's was immaterial, I shall yet rely confidently, that every word, if believed, does leave the accusation unsupported. Gentlemen, I will not affront the idea which ought to be entertained of you, by warning you not be led away by those phantoms which have been created by prejudice, and applied to adorn the idle tales drunk down by folly, and belched up by malignity. You are sensible that you are discharging the greatest duty that law and religion can repose in you, and I am satisfied you will discard your passions, and that your verdict will be founded, not upon passion or prejudice, but upon your oaths and upon justice. Consider what the evidence in point of fact is— Lawler was brought by Brady and Kennedy to Weldon, the prisoner, in Barrack-street; what Brady said to him before, if it had been of moment in itself, I do not conceive can possibly be extended to him, who did not assent to the words, and was not present when they were uttered.— Lawler was carried to the prisoner at the bar to be sworn; and here give me leave to remind you, what was the evidence—to remind you that the expressions proved do not bear that illegal import which real or affected loyalty would attach to them, and therefore you will discharge all that cant of enthusiasm from your minds. I wish that I were so circumstanced as to be entitled to an answer, when I ask Mr. Attorney-General what is the meaning of the word Defender? I wish I were at liberty to appeal to the sober understanding of any man, for the meaning of that tremendous word. I am not entitled to put the question to the counsel or the court—but I am entitled to call upon the wise and grave consideration of the court to say whether the zeal of public accusation has affixed any definite meaning to the word? I would be glad to know, whether that expression, which is annexed to the title of the highest magistrate, marking his highest obligation, and styling him the DEFENDER of the religion of the country, in common parlance acquired any new combination, carrying with it a crime, when applied to any other man in the community? Let me warn you, therefore, against that sort of fallacious lexicography which forms new words, that undergoing the examination of political slander or intemperate zeal, are considered as having a known acceptation. What is the word? A word that should be discarded, when it is sought to affix to it another meaning than that which it bears in the cases where it is used. Let me remind you that a Defender, or any other term used to denote any confraternity, club, or society, like any other word, is arbitrary, but the meaning should be explicit. And therefore with regard to this trial, you are to reject the word, as having no meaning, unless, from the evidence, you find it has in the mind of the party a definite explication; for observe that the witness, such as he is—such as he was, with all his zeal for the furtherance of justice, which he was once ready to violate by the massacre of his fellow-subjects—with all his anxiety for his sovereign's safety, whom he was once ready to assassinate, he, I say, has not told you, that either Brady or Kennedy, or any other person, said what the principles were that denoted a Defender. But I will not rest the case of my client upon that ground. No; it would be a foolish kind of defence, because words might be used as a cloak, and therefore might be colourably introduced. You, gentlemen, are then to consider what this oath, this nonsensical oath, which so far as it is intelligible is innocent, and so far as it is nonsense can prove nothing; you are to consider, whether innocent and nonsensical as it may appear, it was yet a cover and a bond for treasonable association. It is not in my recollection, that any evidence was given, that the oath was conceived in artfully equivocal expressions, for forming, under the sanction of loyal language, a treasonable association. Is one of the parties laughing, evidence that it was treasonable, or the bond of a criminal confederation? It is not. Is it treasonable to say, "that were the King's head off to-morrow, the allegiance to him would be at an end?" It is not The expressions may bring a man into disrepute—to lead the mind of a jury into a suspicion of the morality of the man who used them—but nothing more. It may be asked, why should there be anything insidious? Why but to cover a treasonable purpose, are all these suspicious circumstances? It is not for me, nor is it the prisoner's duty, to account for them in defending himself against this charge, because circumstances are not to render innocence doubtful; but it is full proof establishing the guilt and the treason indubitably which the law requires. Therefore I submit that even if the evidence could be believed, it does not support the overt acts. Was there a word of violating the person of the King? Any affected misrepresentation or any abuse of government? Have you heard a word stated of the King not being an amiable King? Any words contumeliously uttered respecting his person—disrespectful of his government—expressive of any public grievance to be removed, or good to be attained? Not a word of such a subject—nothing of the kind is proved by this solitary witness, in all his accuracy of detail.

Was there any proposition of assisting the French, in case they invaded this kingdom? To support that charge a nonsensical catechism is produced. There it is asked, "Where did the cock crow when all the world heard him?" What kind of old women's stories are these to make an impression upon your minds? Well, but what does that mean? Why, can you be at a loss? It means to—kill the King! Look at the record—it charges the persons with compassing the King's death, and the question about the crowing of a cock is the evidence against them.

Gentlemen, you all know, for you are not of ordinary description, that the statute of Edward III. was made to reduce vague and wandering treasons—to abolish the doctrine of constructive treason, and to mark out some limited boundaries, clear to a court and jury. If a man has been guilty of disrespect in point of expression to the government or the crown, the law has ascertained his guilt and announced the punishment. But all the dreadful uncertainty intended to be guarded against by the statute, and which before the passing of the statute had prevailed in case of treason, and which had shed upon the scaffold some of the best blood in England, would again run in upon us, if a man were to suffer an ignominious death under such circumstances as the present,—if equivocal expressions should be taken as decisive proof, or if dubious words were to receive a meaning from the zeal of a witness, or the heat, passion, or prejudice of a jury. The true rule by which to ascertain what evidence should be deemed sufficient against a prisoner is, that no man should be convicted of any crime except upon the evidence of a man subject to an indictment for perjury, where the evidence is such as if false, the falsehood of it may be so proved as to convict the witness of perjury. But what indictment could be supported for a laugh a shrug, or a wink? Was there any conversation about killing the King? No: but there was a laugh—there was an oath to which we were sworn—and then—there was a wink; by which I understood, we were swearing one thing, and meant another. Why, gentlemen, there can be no safety to the honour, the property, or the life of a man, in a country where such evidence as this shall be deemed sufficient to convict a prisoner. There is nothing necessary to sweep a man from society, but to find a miscreant of sufficient enormity, and the unfortunate accused is drifted down the torrent of the credulity of a well-intending jury. See how material this is; Weldon was present at only one conversation with the witness. It is not pretended by the counsel for the crown, that the guilt as to any personal evidence against Weldon does not stand upon the first conversation. Was there a word upon that conversation of adhering to the King's enemies? It was stated in the case, and certainly made a strong impression, that Lawler was enlisted, in order to assist the French. I heard no such evidence given. The signs of what he called Defenders were communicated to him; the oath which he took was read, and he was told there would be a subsequent meeting, of which the witness should receive notice from Brady.

Gentlemen, before I quit that meeting at Barrack-street, let me put this soberly to you. What is the evidence upon which the court can leave it to you to determine that there is equivocation in the oath? It must be in this way: you are to consider words in the sense in which they are spoken, and in writings words are to be taken in their common meaning. Words have sometimes a technical sense for the purposes of certainty: they may also be made the signs of arbitrary ideas, and therefore I admit a treasonable meaning may be attached to words which, in their ordinary signification, are innocent. But where is the evidence, or what has the witness said to make you believe, that these words in the oath were used in any other than in the common, ordinary acceptation? Not a word, as I have heard. Weldon can be affected only personally, either, first, upon acts by himself, or by other acts brought home to him from the general circumstances of the case. I am considering it in that two-fold way, and I submit, that if it stood upon the evidence respecting the conduct of the prisoner at Barrack-street alone, there could not be a doubt as to his acquittal. It is necessary, therefore, that I should take some further notice of the subsequent part of the evidence. The witness stated, that Weldon informed him that there would be another meeting, of which he, the witness, should have notice. He met Brady and Kennedy; they told him there was a meeting at Plunket-street; and here give me leave to remind the court, that there is no evidence that there was any guilty purpose in agitation to be matured at any future meeting—no proposal of any criminal design. There ought to be evidence to show a connexion between the prisoner and the subsequent meeting, as held under his authority. It is of great moment to recollect, that before any meeting Weldon had left town, and, in the mention of any meeting to be held, let it be remembered he did not state any particular subject, as comprehending the object of the meeting. What happened? There certainly was a meeting in Plunket-street; but there was not a word of assisting the French—of subverting the religion—of massacreing the Protestants—of any criminal design whatever. There was not any consultation upon any such design. I make this distinction, and rely upon it, that where consultations are overt acts of this or that species of treason, it must be a consultation by the members composing that meeting; because it would be the most ridiculous nonsense, that a conversation addressed from one individual to another, not applied to the meeting, should be called a consultation: but, in truth, there is no evidence of anything respecting the French, except in Stoney-batter. There, for the first time, the witness says he heard any mention of the French. Here, gentlemen of the jury, let me beseech you to consider what the force of the evidence is. Supposing that what one man said there to another about assisting the French, to have been criminal, shall Weldon, who was then for a week a hundred miles from the scene, be criminally affected by what was criminally done at Stoney-batter? It is not only that he shall be criminally affected by what was criminally done, but even to the shedding of his blood, shall he be affected by what any individual said, who casually attended that meeting! Have you any feeling of the precipice to which you are hurried, when called upon to extend this evidence in such a manner?—without any one person being present with whom the prisoner had any previous confederation! You will be very cautious, indeed, how you establish such a precedent. How did Weldon connect himself with any other meeting? Why, he said, there will be another meeting, you shall have notice—it would be going a great way to affect him in consequence of that. I lay down the law with confidence, and I say there is no doctrine in it so well ascertained and established, as that a man is to be criminally affected only by his own acts—the man to be charged must be charged with overt acts of his own. There is no law—no security—no reason in that country where a man can be mowed down by foolishly crediting the evidence, not of acts of his own, but of the acts of others, constructively applied to him, who did not attend the meeting, nor was even aware of it. If a man was to be exposed to the penalties of treason hatched and perpetrated in his absence, every member of society becomes liable to be cut off by mere suspicion. I say, no man could go to his bed with an expectation of sleeping in it again, if he were liable to be called upon to answer a charge of suspicious words, spoken when he was a hundred miles off, by miscreants with whom he had no connexion. Good God! gentlemen, only take asunder the evidence upon which you are called upon to take away the life of this man :—" You, Weldon, are chargeable, and shall answer with your blood, for what was done at Stoney-batter." " Why, that is very hard, gentlemen, for I was not there—I was an hundred miles off." " Yes, but you were there in contemplation of law, consulting about the abominable crimes of compassing the King's death, and adhering to his enemies." " How, gentlemen, could I be there?— I knew not that there was any such meeting—I was not present at it." " Aye, but you were there in contemplation of law, because you told Lawler, that Brady would inform him when there would be a meeting in Thomas-street; and because you told him so, you shall be answerable with your life for what is done at any meeting, at any distance of time, at any place, by strangers whom you have never seen or heard of. You have written your name, you have indorsed the treasonable purpose, and through whatever number of persons it may pass, the growing interest of your crime is accumulating against you, and you must pay it with your blood, when it is demanded of you.".

Gentlemen, before we shall have learned to shed blood in sport— while death and slaughter are yet not matter of pastime among us, let us consider maturely, before we establish a rule of justice of this kind. Terrible rules, as we have seen them to be, when weighed upon the day of retribution. I confess it is new to me. Whatever doctrines I have learned, I have endeavoured to learn them from the good sense and humanity of the English law; I have been taught that no man's life shall be sacrificed to the ingenuity of a scholium, and that even he who has heedlessly dropped the seed of guilt, should not answer for it with his blood, when it has grown, under the culture of other hands, from folly to crime, and from crime to treason; he shall not be called upon to answer for the wicked faults of casual and accidental folly. No, gentlemen; I say it with confidence, the act which makes a man guilty must be his own; or if it be by participation it must be by actual participation, not by construction; a construction which leads to an endless confounding of persons and things. If I do not act myself, I am answerable for it: if I do it by another, I am answerable also. If I strike the blow, I am answerable: if I send an assassin, and he strikes the blow, it is still my act, and I ought to be charged with the criminality of it. But if I go into a society of men, into a club, or playhouse, and a crime be there committed, there is no principle of law which shall bring home to me the guilty conduct of these men which they may pursue at any distance of time. What protection can a miserable man have from my discharging perhaps the ineffectual office of my duty to him, if the rule laid down, that every word he said, or was said by a man with whom he ever had a conversation, shall affect him at any distance of time? Consider what will be the consequence of establishing the precedent, that a man shall always be responsible for the act of the society to which he has once belonged. Suppose a man heedlessly brought into an association where criminal purposes are going forward—suppose there was, what has been stated, a society of men calling themselves Defenders, and answering in fact to the very singular picture drawn of them. Will you give it abroad, that if a man once belongs to a criminal confederacy, his case is desperate—his retreat is cut off—that every man once present at a meeting to subvert the government, shall be answerable for every thing done at any distance of time by this flagitious association? What is the law in this respect? As in the association there is peril, so in the moment of retreat there is safety. What could this man have done? He quitted the city—he went to another part of the kingdom, when the treasonable acts were committed; yes, but he was virtually among them! What constitutes a man virtually present, when he is physically absent? What is the principle of law by which he shall be tried? It can alone be tried by that, by which the mandate or authority of any man is brought home to him. By previously suggesting the crime, by which he becomes an accessary before the fact, and therefore a principal in treason; for by suggesting the crime he proves the concurrence of his will with that of the party committing the crime. This is a maxim of law: that which in ordinary felonies makes a man an accessary, in treason will constitute him a principal, because in treason there are no accessaries. Suppose a meeting held for one purpose, and a totally distinct crime is committed, are those who were at the first meeting accessaries? Certainly not; because they must be procurers of the fact done. To make a man a principal, he must be *quodammodo* aiding and assisting—that is not proved. What, then, is the accessorial guilt? Did the prisoner write to the others? Does he appear to be the leader of any fraternity—the conductor of any treasonable meeting? No such thing. I say when he quitted Dublin he had no intention of giving aid or countenance to any meeting; the connexion between him and the society ceased, and there is no evidence that he had any knowledge of any of their subsequent acts. Unless there be positive evidence against him, you ought to consider him out of the sphere of any association. But still you make him answerable for what was done. If you do that, you establish a rule unknown to the sense or humanity of the law; making him answerable for what was done, not by himself but by other persons.

Gentlemen, I feel that counsel, anxious as they ought to be, may be led further than they intend; in point of time I have pressed further than I foresaw upon the patience of the jury and the court. I say the object of this part of the trial is whether the guilt of any thing which happened in that society be in point of law brought home to the prisoner? I have endeavoured to submit that the charge ought to be clear, and the evidence explicit, and that though the meetings at which Lawler attended were guilty, yet the prisoner, being absent, was not affected by their criminality. Give me leave now, with deference, to consider the case in another point of view. I say then, from what has appeared in evidence, the meetings themselves cannot in the estimation of the law be guilty. If these meetings are not provably guilty of treason, there can be no retroactive guilt upon the prisoner, even if the communication between them and him were proved. If there be no direct and original guilt—if they do not that, which, if done by him, would amount to an overt act of treason, *a fortiori*, it cannot extend to him. Therefore, let me suppose, that the prisoner was at the time present at these meetings. Be pleased to examine this, whether if he were, the evidence given would amount to the proof required. I conceive that nothing can be more clear than the distinction between mere casual, indiscreet language, and language conveying a deliberated and debated purpose. To give evidence of overt acts, the evidence must be clear and direct. How is Hensey's case?* A species of evidence was adduced, which it was impossible for any man to deny—actual proof of correspondence found in his own writing and possession. How was it in Lord Preston's case?† Evidence equally clear of a purpose acted upon—going to another country for that treasonable purpose.— In every case of which we read memorials in the law, the act is such, that no man could say it is not an overt act of the means used by the party in effectuation of his guilty intent. But I said, that a deliberate purpose, expressed and acted upon, is different from a casual, indiscreet expression. Suppose now, that the meeting were all indicted for compassing the King's death, and that the overt act charged is, that they consulted about giving aid to the King's enemies, actually at war; the guilt of all is the guilt of each—there is no distinction between them. If that meeting held that consultation, they are all guilty of that species of high treason. But if the evidence were, that at that meeting which consisted of as many as are now here, one individual turned about to another, and said, " we must get arms to assist the French, when they come here." Would any reasonable man say, that was a consultation to adhere to the King's enemies?—a mere casual expression, not answered by any one—not addressed to the body. Can it be sustained for a moment in a court of justice, that it was a consultation to effect the death of the King, or adhere to his enemies? No, gentlemen, this is not matter of any deep or profound learning—it is familiar to the plainest understanding. The foolish language of one servant in your hall is not evidence to affect all the other servants in your house—it is not the guilt of the rest. I am aware it may be the guilt of the rest; it may become such. But I rely upon this; I address it to you with the confidence that my own conviction inspires, that your lordships will state to the jury, that a consultation upon a subject is a reciprocation of sentiment upon the same subject. Every man understands the meaning of a consultation; there is no servant that cannot understand it. If a man said to another, " we will conspire to kill the King," no lacquey could mistake it. But what is a consultation? Why such as a child could not mistake if it passed before him. One saying to ano-

---

* 19 Howell's State Trials, 1341.   † 12 Howell's State Trials, 646.

ther, "We are here together, private friends—we are at war—the
French may land, and if they do, we will assist them." To make that
a consultation there must be an assent to the same thought; upon that
assent, the guilt of the consultation is founded. Is that proved by
a casual expression of one man, without the man to whom it was
directed making any answer, and when, in fact, every other man but
the person using the expression was attending for another purpose?—
But if there be any force in what I have said, as applied to any man
attending there, how much more forcible will it appear, when applied
to a man who was an hundred miles distant from the place of meeting.
If the law be clear, there is no treason in hearing treasonable designs
and not consenting thereto (though it be another offence), unless he
goes there, knowing beforehand what the meeting was to be. Here,
gentlemen, see how careful the law is, and how far it is from being
unprovided as to different cases of this kind. If a man go to a meeting, knowing that the object is to hatch a crime, he shall be joined in
the guilt. If he go there and takes a part, without knowing previously, he is involved; though that has been doubted. Foster says,
"this is proper to be left to the jury, though a party do or say nothing
as to the consultation." If, for instance, a man, knowing of a design
to imprison the King, go to a meeting to consult for that purpose, his
going there is an obvious proof of his assent and encouragement. This
is the law, as laid down by one of the most enlightened writers in any
science. Compare that doctrine with what Mr. Attorney-General
wishes to inculcate, when he seeks to convict the prisoner. There was
a meeting in Barrack-street, and it was treason, because they laughed.
As Sancho said, they all talked of me, because they laughed. But,
then, there is a catechism. Aye, what say you to that? The cock
crew in France;—what say you to that? Why, I say, it might be
foolish, it might be indecent to talk in this manner. But what is the
charge?—that he consulted to kill the King. Where was it he did
that?—at Cork! But did he not assist? No; he was not there.—
But he did assist, because he communicated signs, and thus you collect
the guilt of the party, as the coroner upon an inquest of murder, who
thought a man standing by was guilty. Why?—because three drops
of blood fell from his nose. This was thought to be invincible proof of
his guilt. It reminds me also of an old woman who undertook to
prove that a ghost had appeared. "How do you know there was a
ghost in the room?" "Oh! I'll prove to you there must have been
a ghost—for the very moment I went in, I fainted flat on the floor!"
So, says Mr. Attorney-General, "Oh, I'll convince you, gentlemen, he
designed to kill the King, *for he laughed.*" Weldon was chargeable
with all the guilt of the meeting—he laughed when the paper was read,
and said, "When the King's head was off, there was an end of the
allegiance." In answer to that, I state the humane good sense of the
law, that, in the case of the life of a traitor, it is tender in proportion
to the abomination of the crime; for the law of England, while it suspended the sword of justice over the head of the guilty man, threw its
protection around the innocent, to save his loyalty from the danger of

such evidence. It did more—it threw its protection around him whose innocence might be doubted, but who was not proved to be guilty. The mild and lenient policy of the law discharges a man from the necessity of proving his innocence, because otherwise it would look as if the jury were empannelled to condemn upon accusation, without evidence in support of it, but merely because he did not prove himself innocent. Therefore, gentlemen, I come round again to state what the law is. In order to make a general assembling and consultation evidence of overt acts, there must be that assembling; and the guilt must be marked by that consultation, in order to charge any man, who was present and did not say anything concurring, with the guilt of that consultation. It is necessary that he should have notice that the guilty purpose was to be debated upon—that the meeting was convened for that purpose. But let me recal your attention to this, and you will feel it bearing strongly upon that case. The silence of a man at such a meeting is not criminal to the degree here charged. Then suppose his disclaimer necessary—suppose the law considered every man as abetting what he did not disavow—remember that the wretch now sought to be affected by his silence at a meeting, was one hundred miles distant from it. There might have been a purpose from which his soul had recoiled. Is this then evidence upon which to convict the prisoner? There is no statement of any particular purpose—no summons to confer upon any particular purpose—no authority given to any meeting by a deputy named; and let me remind you, that at the last meeting, if there were the gossipings and communications you have heard, there was not any one man present who attended the first meeting, nor is there any evidence to show that the prisoner had ever spoken to any one man who attended the last meeting, upon any occasion; and yet the monstrous absurdity contended for is, that although Weldon proposed no subject for discussion—although he proposed no meeting—although he did not know that any purpose was to be carried into effect, because he was then one hundred miles off, he is still to suffer for the foolish babble of one individual to another. You are to put all proceedings together, and out of the tissue of this talk, hearsay, and conjecture, you are to collect the materials of a verdict, by which you directly swear that the man is guilty of compassing the King's death. But suppose a man were to suggest a treasonable meeting—that the meeting takes place, and he does not go—the first proposal may amount to an evidence of treason, if it went far enough, and amounted to an incitement. But suppose the meeting held be a distinct one from that which was suggested, and the party does not attend, it appears to me, that the act of that meeting cannot be considered as his overt act. The previous incitement must be clearly established by evidence, and I rely upon it, that the subsequent acts of that meeting, to which I am supposing he did not go—particularly if it be a meeting at which many others were present who were not at the first—I rely upon it, I say, that no declaration of any man (and more decidedly, if it be by a man not privy to the original declaration), can be evidence upon which a jury can attach guilt to the party. It is nothing more than misfeasance, which is cer tainly criminal, but not to the extent of this charge. To affect any man by subsequent debate, it must be with notice of the purpose, and if the meeting be dictated by himself it is only in that point he can be guilty; because if you propose a meeting for one purpose, you shall not be affected by any other—no matter what the meeting is—however treasonable or bad. Unless you knew before for what purpose they assembled, you cannot be guilty virtually by what they have done.

Gentlemen, I do not see that anything further occurs to me upon the law of the case, that I have not endeavoured in some way to submit to you. Perhaps I have been going back somewhat irregularly. Gentlemen, there remains only one, and that a very narrow subject of observation. I said that the evidence upon which the life, and the fame, and the property of a man should be decided and extinguished, ought to be of itself evidence of a most cogent and impressive nature. Gentlemen, does it appear to you that the witness whom you saw upon the table comes under that description? Has he sworn truly? If he has, what has he told you? As soon as he discovered the extent of the guilt he quitted the fraternity. Do you believe that? Hart told him that ALL the Protestants were to be massacred. "I did not like," said he, "the notion of massacreing ALL." Here is the picture he draws of himself— he an accomplice in the guilt. I did not ask him—"Have you been promised a pardon?" I did not ask him—"Are you coming to swear by the acre?"—but I appeal to the picture he drew of himself upon the table. What worked his contrition? Is it the massacre of one wretch? He was unappalled at the idea of dipping his hands, and lapping the blood of *part* of the Protestant body—it was only heaps of festering dead that nauseated his appetite, and worked his repentance and conversion. Is your verdict to be founded upon the unsupported evidence of a wretch of that kind? His stomach stood a partial massacre—it was only an universal deluge of blood that made him a convert to humanity! And he is now the honest, disinterested, and *loyal* witness in a court of justice! What said he further? "As soon as I found from Hart, their schemes, I went to Mr. Cowan." You saw, gentlemen, that he felt my motive in asking the question. "You abandoned them as soon as you found their criminality?" Because, had he answered otherwise, he would have destroyed his credit; but as it is, he has thrown his credit, and the foundation of it, overboard. If Lawler be innocent, Weldon must be so. He saw that, and, therefore, he said he thought it no crime to kill the King. Therefore, gentlemen, my conscience told me, that if he felt no remorse at plunging a dagger into the heart of his King, he would feel no trembling hesitation at plunging a dagger into the breast of an individual subject, by perjured testimony. Those workings of the heart which agitate the feelings at the untimely fate of a fellow-creature touch not him, and he could behold with delight the perishing of that man who had a knowledge of *his* guilt. He has no compunction, and he betrays no reluctance at drinking deep in the torrent of human blood, provided it leaves a remnant of the class. What stipulation can you make between a wretch of that kind and the sacred obligation of an oath? You are to swear upon his oath; a verdict is not to be founded upon your own loyalty—not upon what you have seen or heard spoken disrespectfully of the government or the King. Your honest, pure, and constitutional verdict can be founded only upon that sympathy that you feel between your own hearts and the credibility of the witness. It is a question for you. Will you hazard that oath upon the conscience of such a man? A man influenced by hope and agitated with fear—anxious for life and afraid to die, that you may safely say, "We have heard a witness, he stated facts which we could not believe; he is a wretch, for he thought it no crime to murder his King: and a partial massacre appeared to him to be meritorious!" Is it upon the testimony of that nefarious miscreant —the ready traitor—the prompt murderer—I retract not the expression, if I did, it would be to put in its place a word of more emphatic and combined reprobation; is it upon that evidence, I say, you will pronounce a verdict, establishing the most aggravated degree of criminality known to our law, upon the person of that man, supposed by the law to be innocent, until his guilt be proved? I know not whether the man be a good subject or a bad one: it is not necessary for me to know nor for you to inquire; but I exhort you finally to remember, that in Great Britain, so anxious has the law been to guard against the perfidiousness of such men, that no less than two concurrent witnesses are necessary there in cases of treason. I call not upon you to adopt that law; but to show you the principle, that there should be strong evidence satisfying the mind of a jury. I commit the decision of this case to your consciences, not to your humanity—I commit it to your determination upon the sound principles of justice and law.

After Mr. Curran had sat down, he rose again, and said he had closed without stating any evidence, from a conviction that it would be unnecessary; and added—"It is desired to produce some evidence which I will not oppose in a case of life. There is evidence to show that Lawler is not credible."

Curran examined witnesses to this effect, but Weldon was found GUILTY, and though Leary, another prisoner, was acquitted, under precisely similar facts, Weldon was hanged.

CATHOLIC EMANCIPATION.

May 4th, 1795.

ON the 4th of January, 1795, Lord Fitzwilliam was sent to Ireland, charged with the carrying of Catholic Emancipation and the pacification of Ireland. The causes of this proposed concession were the rapid progress of the United Irishmen, and the still more rapid progress of the French armies, who had driven the Spaniards behind the Pyrenees, the Austrians behind the Rhine, destroyed the Duke of York's army, and prepared the occupation of Holland, in the winter of 1794—5.

On the 22nd of January, Parliament met, and heard a most plausible speech. It imposed on Grattan; he outdid ministers in loyalty to the stupid and barbarous King, and illiberal and insolent government of England. An Emancipation Bill was read a first time, but ample supplies were voted, and anti-Gallican frenzy got up among certain classes, before it was found that Beresford and the King were too strong for Fitzwilliam and Pitt. The Viceroy was recalled, the Emancipation Bill defeated, but the supplies and the frenzy were appropriated by the ministers. On the second reading of the bill a debate of great length and ability took place. I regret the inferiority of the report of Curran's speech.—

I mean not, at this late hour, to trouble the house at large on the question. I have from the first been a friend to the deliverance of the Catholics. I think their claims irresistible on every principle of policy and justice. I have more than once given my reasons for that opinion. It is not necessary now to repeat them. Never did a cause stand less in need of additional defence. Very little therefore will I now add; particularly as the speech of a right honourable gentleman has made it manifest that gentlemen have come with their minds prepared upon the subject, and that it is a question of division and not of debate. I feel myself forced to rise to set right some things that have been asserted in the debate. An honourable and learned gentleman has been pleased to mix the names of the Catholics with that of Mr. Jackson, who was lately tried for treason. It is only justice to that body of our fellow-subjects to say, in the presence of the Attorney-General, who conducted that prosecution, that not one syllable was said upon the trial, nor did any circumstance whatsoever appear, that could warrant even a suspicion of the most distant intercourse between any one Catholic and that unfortunate man; and I am glad of being able to make this assertion in this public place, in order that if any calumny of that sort should be ever uttered against them, it might be known to be most malicious and unfounded. I must animadvert on the impropriety of talking so familiarly of the names of individuals in parliament. It is abusing the absent, who ought to have at least opportunity of answering—or of saying, what they probably would say—that they thought such aspersions unworthy of reply. It is also asserted, that the bill was penned in a particular quarter, on which the learned gentleman has been very liberal of contemptuous language—I beg to assure him he is mistaken; the bill was not penned by those persons.

If it be blameable, it is only just to say where the guilt is chargeable. Part of the guilt is with myself—I have assisted in framing this bill. The right honourable mover has the greater part of the guilt to answer for; I am at a loss, however, to find out in what this guilt consists. I have thought of it much, but I cannot find out the criminality. The nation is of my opinion—every persuasion is of my opinion; I am convinced, therefore, not of its guilt, but of its justice. I am satisfied that if Ireland is to be saved, it can be done only by the emancipation of the Catholics, and the union of the people. It is no longer a question between the Protestants and the Catholics, but between the minister and the country; the mode of the debate has shown this. Gentlemen have not even touched upon the first arguments upon which they had formerly supported their opposition—namely, the danger to property. They have this night confined themselves to idle aspersions on the persons of the Catholics, or to idle boasting of their own loyalty and orthodoxy. For my own part, I think there is no great merit in having the one, nor any great certainty of having the other, to boast of. If I were not convinced the present bill is perfectly reconcileable with both, I should not think of giving it the warm support which I have given, and will, while I live, continue to give it.

I feel myself falling into the merits of the debate, contrary to my resolution when I rose. I have heard a learned gentleman use a very celebrated and respected name in a most extraordinary manner. I had heard something like it before, and suffered it to pass unnoticed. I am unwilling to rise as the advocate of that gentleman's person or character; they are too high above such censure to require defence. There might seem as much egotism as zeal or respect in taking the province of his defender; but I cannot, for the honour of the house, suffer an idea to go abroad, that the name of Mr. Edmund Burke has been treated with disrespect, without expressing the strongest indignation at such a breach of decorum. I should lament that this house could be thought so dead to all sense of such exalted merit, as tamely to endure a language, the disgrace of which could fall only on themselves. But it seems to be a night of unmerited imputation. A young member (Mr. Stuart) has been pleased to say, he hoped the present administration would relieve this country from the bad conduct of the last. It is a subject on which I will enter the lists with the honourable member. I am sorry so young a man could entertain so mean an opinion of the house, as to use such language.

I am surprised that the young member should, at so early an age, give the house credit for so much levity and inconsistency as they must possess, if they should listen quietly to such an aspersion on the character of a viceroy whom they have declared unanimously to deserve the thanks of this house and the confidence of the people. As for my part, I should think it time very much mispent to go into any detail of that noble lord's merits with this country; I regret the consequences of their being so universally felt as they are.

The same honourable member has noticed the existence of office without responsibility or place; it was a circumstance, I confess, which marked the government of Lord Fitzwilliam. I see not much likelihood of its being repeated. It would, I fear, be as difficult to find the talents, as the disinterestedness of the right honourable member to whom the gentleman has alluded; he has lent his great powers to his country, without the emolument of office. I am sorry to find the honourable young member not more sensible of that merit. As he advances in years, I trust that he will think more justly, and perhaps improve so much as to make a splendid model the object of more respect—perhaps of imitation. I shall take the liberty of saying to him—

> Disce, Puer, virtutem ex illo,
> Verumque laborem;
> Fortunam ex aliis.

The second reading was rejected by 155 to 84.—*Debates*, vol. xv., pp. 367—368.

STATE OF THE NATION.

15th May, 1795.

On this day Curran spoke and proposed as follows :—

The present is the most awful and important crisis that Ireland ever saw, considering the actual state of the nation, of the empire, and of the war in which we are engaged. As to the original motives of the war, this is not the time to inquire into them; they are lost in the events; if they were as pure as they have been represented, how much is it to be regretted that the issue has proved only that it is not in mortals to command success. The armies of Europe have poured into the field, and surrounded the devoted region of France on every side; but far from achieving their purpose, they have only formed an iron hoop about her, which instead of quelling the fury of her dissensions, has compressed their spring into an irresistible energy, and forced them into co-action. During its progress we saw the miserable objects for whom it was undertaken consumed in nameless thousands in the different quarters of Europe, by want, and misery, and despair; or expiring on the scaffold, or perishing in the field. We have seen the honest body of the British manufacturer tumbled into the common grave with the venal carcass of the Prussian hireling; we have seen the generous Briton submit to the alliance and servitude of venality, and submit to it in vain. The sad vicissitudes of each successive campaign have been marked by the defeat of our armies, the triumph of our enemies, and the perfidy of our allies. What was the situation of the contending parties at the beginning of the contest?—England, with Spain, with Austria, with Prussia, with Holland, with Ireland on her side; while France had to count the revolt of Toulon, the insurrection of La Vandee, the rebellion of Lyons, and her whole eastern territory in the hands of her enemies; how direful the present reverse! England exhausted, Holland surrendered, Austria wavering, Prussia fled, and Spain fainting in the contest; while France, triumphant and successful, waves a military and triumphant sceptre over an extent of territory that stretches from the ocean and the Rhine to the Pyrennees and the ocean. I shall not dwell upon this miserable picture; I will only observe, that during this long succession of disaster and defeat, Ireland alone, of all the allies Great Britain had, neither trafficked, nor deceived, nor deserted. The present distresses of her people attest her liberality of her treasure, while the bones of her enemies, and of her children, bleaching upon all the plains of Europe, attest the brilliancy of her courage, and the steadfastness of her faith. In this state was the war at the commencement of this session. Shortly before that period it was thought prudent by his majesty's ministers in Great Britain to remove the chief governor of this kingdom, and to appoint a successor; of that successor it would be presumptuous in me to be the panegyrist; of his predecessor it would be neither consistent with the decorum of this house, nor with my own feelings, to speak with any personal reproach; to the acts of both it is impossible not to advert. That the commencement of this session was a most awful period, has been stated from the throne, and admitted by the addresses of both houses of parliament; the causes that made it awful were clearly understood by the new viceroy—the disasters of the war, and the discontents of the Irish nation. Of these discontents this house cannot possibly be ignorant, because you cannot be ignorant of the cause, namely, the abuses in our government. Upon this subject you must see that you have much to redress, and you feel that you have not little to atone; your situation is most critical. Your conduct then, if it could be looked at distinctly from your conduct afterwards, I would have considered as highly dignified. Lord Fitzwilliam found it necessary to demand a supply to an unexampled amount; this house felt the necessity, and complied with the demand; but you are the trustees of the nation, and must feel that so extraordinary an exertion of supply ought to be accompanied by a most extensive measure of redress. You cannot, as honest men, give the money of the people, and give a sanction to the continuance of their grievances; you may bestow your own money, if you will, without equivalent; but to act so with the money and the blood of the nation, would not be generosity, but the most abominable dishonesty and fraud;—you can give it only upon the terms of redress, and upon these terms only was it demanded by Lord Fitzwilliam, or given by this house. It is inconsistent with the purity of his mind; it is inconsistent with the character which you ought to preserve in the nation, to put this compact into express terms. He could not have said to you expressly, I will cure those corruptions, which have depressed and impoverished your people, which have enriched the most unworthy, and have been connived at by a majority of yourselves. He could not thus hold you out as criminals and penitents to the nation; it was a compact, therefore, expressed rather by acts than by words. The viceroy set actually about the reform, and the house attested their most zealous gratitude and concurrence. Thus did I consider this house as warranted to say to their constituents:—We have sent the flower of your population to the standard of the empire; we have sent the protector from his habitation, the mechanic from his trade, and the labourer from his field; we have found you weak, and we have made you weaker; we have found you poor, and we have made you poorer; we have laid a load of taxes upon you, of which for years you must feel the depression; we have laid these taxes so as almost to preclude the attainment of those comforts and decencies of life without which you can scarcely exist; but we have not sold you, we have not betrayed you; what we have given has been the pledge of your loyalty, and the price of your redemption; by this pledge you have united yourselves to your king, and your posterity with his for ever; for this price the grievances and the abuses that depressed you shall be corrected and redressed. This I considered to be the meaning of that transaction as fully as if it had been expressed in the strongest terms of contract or stipulation.

It remains for me to state what these abuses and grievances are.— They began with the sale of the honour of the peerage; the open and avowed sale, for money, of the peerage, to any man rich and shameless enough to be a purchaser. Such a course depraves the commons; it profanes the sanctity of the lords; it poisons the sources of legislation, and the fountains of justice; it annihilates the very idea of public honour and public integrity; yet all this was done by the government of Lord Westmoreland. I myself in this house stated the charge; I offered to bring evidence to the bar to prove it; I offered to prosecute the crime at the risk of that punishment which the law denounces against the false accuser; but that government shrunk from the inquiry; the charge was suffocated in the previous question; the truth of the charge was, however, confessed by that very flight from trial; it was like the flight of any ordinary.felon,— an admission of guilt; but it differed from it in this, it was followed by no forfeiture. I shall next refer to the sending of the troops from the country, contrary to law and to compact. That compact and the provision in the money bill, declare that twelve thousand effective men shall be at all times kept up in Ireland for the defence thereof, except in case of actual rebellion in, or invasion of, Great Britain; yet this law was broken by Lord Westmoreland's administration; it was broken in the moment of war, with the enemy at the gate, when the breach of this law might have been the loss of the island. If such a charge of assuming a dispensing power were to be mentioned in the British parliament, that assembly would turn pale at the bare statement of an assumption of power by which the last of the Stuarts had lost, and meritedly lost, his throne; but I have lived to hear the charge made upon an Irish viceroy, either not attempted to be denied by his adherents, or admitted by their justification of the fact, yet eluded by the subterfuge of a motion for adjournment. Of such subterfuges I cannot sufficiently express my abhorrence. It is a desertion of the duty which, as the grand inquest of the nation, this house owes to the public, thus to smother accusation and collude with the accused; it cannot save the viceroy's character. and can only produce a shameful impunity, with the loss of all estimation with the members of this house and with their constituents; it invites offence by discouraging accusation: this effect, however, it shall never have with me; I have often before been baffled by this dexterity of evasion, and I cannot be without apprehension that even this night the most disinterested effort of public duty may be hag-ridden under the weight of a previous question; but I shall persevere, for I know it is to efforts of this sort, made no doubt with very superior talent, but attended with no better success, that Ireland is indebted for the little progress she has made against the torrent of her oppressions. An hundred and fifty thousand pounds of the public money has been expended without any sanction whatsoever of law, but advanced to the colonels of new-raised levies, without security or account. I appeal to your own accounts for the truth of the fact. The law touching the issuing of the public money, proves its criminality. Again; Lord Westmoreland, previous to his departure, granted almost every office at the disposal of government to his own friends and adherents. I and my friends have, session after session, complained of the pernicious excess of influence, and we were opposed as the invaders of a just and necessary patronage. If Lord Westmoreland thought this patronage necessary, upon what ground can

he justify the shameless plunder of it, to the injury of his sovereign and
to the prejudice of his successor? Upon what preteuce shall he be considered in his own country as the friend of the necessary power of his
sovereign, when he must be conscious that he has laboured to reduce
the influence of that sovereign to a state of the most contemptible
imbecility. It is a notorious fact, that he has not left a single office of
value in Ireland, of which a reversion could be granted, that he has not
put out of the power of the crown for a number of years to come. And
now, I call upon this house, I call upon his friends within it, (if any
friends he have within it,)—vindicate him if you can; deny the fact if
you can; justify it if you can; and relieve him from the distressing situation in which he must feel himself, if a fact of this kind shall be admitted,
and confirmed, while it is screened by the interposition of a previous
question. Let me warn you how you will exhibit this anxiety for the
prorogation, like the zeal of honest servants who stand at the windows
with their muskets, to oppose the executions of creditors, that when
they have beaten off the sheriff, they may steal the furniture themselves.
I now pass to the subject of the Roman Catholics. I have been the
apologist of this house for the great concessions made in 1793, and for
the perfect emancipation to which, in the beginning of the session, the
house assented, with an unanimity uninterrupted only by the dissent by
two honourable members, whose diversity of opinion I cannot but respect
and regret, but which I cannot adopt. [He enforced very strongly, and
at large, the injustice, the absurdity, and the danger of denying that
emancipation.] But the question, such as it is, has not been left for
discussion in the present session; it was decided in 1793. By giving
the elective franchise, the principle of their full claim was admitted;
the man who is constitutionally fit to be a constituent must be equally
so to be a representative. The concessions of 1793 authorised their
pretensions, and put their claims into a progress which it will be just as
easy to stop as it would be the revolution of the heavens or the earth;
that measure for which the great mass of the people felt themselves ripe,
and demanded as the great bond of their union and anchor of their
safety, (however it may, by sinister interference, be impeded or delayed),
cannot be finally withheld or refused; you were pledged to it before by
your duty to the public, you are now doubly pledged for the vindication
of your character. The defeat of your laudable intentions upon this
subject is stated as the reason of the recal of Lord Fitzwilliam. In
plain English, Mr. Pitt might as well have said, " The lords of Ireland
have no will of their own; the commons of Ireland have no will of their
own; they are the representatives only of their own wants and of their
own venality. If Lord Fitzwilliam remain in Ireland the Catholics will
be emancipated; if we send another in his place, that tame and sequa-
cious parliament will move like puppets by his wires, and the nation
will still continue divided and depressed, to the great advantage of English patronage—to the great credit of English justice." This house, in
emancipating the Catholics, would have only ratified the engagement
of its previous concessions; Lord Fitzwilliam had acted wisely by concurring in the performance of that engagement, and it only now remained

with the house to vindicate its honour and its character by expressing a becoming resentment at the interference which had frustrated that performance; for where, if such interference is endured, where shall the legislature of Ireland be found? Not in the Commons, not in the Lords, not the King, but it will be found one and indivisible in the sacred person of an Irish Minister! There remains to be mentioned one grievance more, of which we expected the redress, and which redress might have justified our extraordinary grants; the unjust and impolitic restraints upon our commerce. Without our own concurrence, those restraints could not exist an hour—and how at this moment shall we justify such a concurrence to the people? We are the trustees of the people; we are the trustees of their properties and their rights; we have only the power of trustees; we have the power to manage, the duty to defend, but we have neither the power to abuse, to bestow, or to surrender. Every wise man in this country is now convinced, that with respect to commerce, the old adage of "*honesty is the best policy*" is peculiarly true; and that the wealth of one country can never be effectually secured by the poverty of another. The first inventions of commerce, like those of all other arts, are cunning and shortsighted, and the perfection of the machine is too generally supposed to consist in the complexity of its wheels; it is only in the course of progressive improvement that they are unfolded with simplicity and comprehension. The abolition, therefore, of these restraints, is what we owe to policy; but we owe it, also, in common honesty, to our constituents. We have loaded their poverty with taxes; we have sent away from them those whose labour might produce for them the necessaries of life, of which we have thereby doubly diminished the production, and increased the price. With what face shall we approach them, if we say that we have done all this without attaining the redress of a single grievance? With what face, if we abandon them in parliament, shall we turn them over to the tax-gatherer for consolation? I know this is no time, when the passions of the public ought to be inflamed—nor do I mean to inflame them—[Here a murmur was heard from the opposite side of the house.] Yes, I speak not to inflame; but I address you, in order to allay the fever of the public mind. If I had power to warn you, I would exert that power, in order to diminish the public ferment—in order to show the people that they have more security in your warmth than they can have in their own heat—that the ardour of your honest zeal may be a salutary ventilator to the ferment of your country—in order that you may take the people out of their own hands, and bring them within your guidance. Trust me, at this momentous crisis, a firm and tempered sensibility of injury would be equally honourable to yourselves, and beneficial to the nation. Trust me, if, at a time when every little stream is swoln into a torrent, we alone should be found to exhibit a smooth, and listless and frozen surface, the folly of the people may be tempted to walk across us; and whether they should suppose that they were only walking upon ice, or treading upon corruption, the rashness of the experiment might be fatal to us all. I do, therefore, think it is time for you to speak out. You granted the property of our constituents; you granted their persons to Great Britain; you did so in a war most unpopular in Ireland—in the disaster of which she might lose everything—in the best event of which she could gain nothing; you embarked yourselves and your country in her cause, and your loyalty and attachment grew with her distresses, and seemed to rise upon her defeats. You did so, upon the faith that the grievances under which she laboured, and the abuses of which she complained, would, under the administration of a viceroy, in whose virtues and character you could not but confide, have been redressed. Your honest confidence has been defrauded, and your honest zeal insulted with a blow, while your grants have been accepted—I think dishonestly accepted.

The viceroy, in whom your addresses attested your so just and unlimited a confidence, while he was employed in the correction of those abuses, was recalled in a manner the most ignominious; not to him—for the bold, and simple, and manly integrity of a conduct, directed by a mixed regard to prudence, to loyalty, and to justice, placed him far above the aspersion of low intrigue or interested cabal—but in a manner most ignominious to you. It is a reproach which he may repel by silent and contemptuous disdain; but it is an ignominy which you would adopt by silence, and which you can only repel by speaking out. The measures for which your constituents paid the most invaluable purchase have been most impudently intercepted in their progress; you owe it, therefore, to Lord Fitzwilliam—you owe it to yourselves—you owe it to your country—you owe it to the British nation, to speak out. Already has too much been sacrificed to your submission to ministers. Let me advise you now to make some atonement, by consulting the interests of your king and your country. Do not meanly flatter those ministers with an idea that their insolence does not, and must not, damp the zeal and alienate the affections of a loyal, a proud, a brave, and an injured people; do not dishonestly lead that beloved, and justly beloved sovereign into the fatal delusion of supposing that Ireland either does or can glow with the same affection, or beat with the same ardour, if these indignities shall continue to be wantonly inflicted upon her; do not be guilty of keeping Great Britain in ignorance of the exact disposition of the last ally whose fidelity has survived this eventful war. State to her honestly the sentiment of your country—a sentiment which you can attest, but which you cannot control—that Ireland, even in the hour of British adversity, remembers and plights anew her solemn covenant of "standing and falling with the British nation," but that she remembers too that it is a covenant of "equal fate," upon the terms of "equal liberty"—that it is a covenant which Ireland is to cement with her blood but which Great Britain must ratify with her justice. I conclude with moving the following address:—

"That an humble address be presented to his Majesty, to assure his Majesty of our attachment to his person and family—of our inviolable regard for the monarchical form of government—and of our determination to support the connexion with Great Britain for ever.

"That we humbly presume to hope we have, on all occasions, manifested those sentiments abundantly.

"That we are the more inclined to do so, from a conscious sense of the value of Ireland in the present critical situation of the empire.

"That, in consequence of the part taken by Great Britain, under the advice of his Majesty's ministers, Ireland was involved in the present most eventful war.

"That, in consequence of this war, we have greatly added to our annual taxes, and increased, near three-fold, the debt of the nation.

"That we have also assisted the army and navy of the empire with vast numbers of our people, who have, in the different quarters of the globe, asserted, what his Majesty must ever command, the courage and loyalty of their country.

"That, in this year, we continued to increase the annual taxes; voted a loan of nearly two millions; granted a greater force than ever was paid by Ireland; and made these unexampled exertions with the unanimity of the parliament and the approbation of the people.

"That we were the more induced to this, from a zeal for his Majesty's service, and an attachment to Great Britain, but accompanied with an expectation that our extraordinary grants would be justified to our constituents by a reform, under a patriot viceroy, of the various and manifold abuses that had taken place in the administration of the Irish government—a reformation which we conceived, in the present times, and under such an increase of debt and taxes, indispensable, and which we do, therefore, most humbly persist to implore and expect.

"That after the supply was granted, and the force voted, and whilst the Chief Governor, possessing the entire confidence of both houses of parliament and the approbation of all the people, was reforming abuses, and putting the country in a state of defence, he was suddenly and prematurely recalled, and our unparalleled efforts for the support of his Majesty, answered by the strongest marks of the resentment of his ministers.

"That, in consequence of such a proceeding, the business of government was interrupted—the defence of the country suspended—the unanimity which had, under the then Lord Lieutenant, existed, converted into just complaint and remonstrance—and the energy, confidence, and zeal of the nation, so loudly called for by his Majesty's ministers, were, by the conduct of those very ministers themselves, materially affected.

"That this their late proceedings aggravated their past system; in complaining of which we particularly refer to the notorious traffic of honours—to the removal of the troops, contrary to law, and in total disregard of the solemn compact with the nation, and safety of the realm—to the criminal conduct of government respecting the Irish army —to the disbursement of sums of money without account or authority —to the improvident grant of reversions at the expense of his Majesty's interest, sacrificed for the emoluments of his servants—to the conduct of his Majesty's ministers in both countries, toward his Catholic and Protestant subjects of Ireland, alternately practising on their passions, exciting their hope, and procuring their disappointment.

"That, convinced by the benefits which we have received under his Majesty's reign, that the grievances of which we complain are as

unknown to his Majesty as abhorrent from his paternal and loyal disposition—
" We, his Commons of Ireland, beg leave to lay ourselves at his feet, and, with all humility to his Majesty, to prefer, on our part, and on the part of our constituents, this our just and necessary remonstrance against the conduct of his ministers ; and to implore his Majesty, that he may be graciously pleased to lay his commands upon his minister to second the zeal of his Irish parliament in his Majesty's services, by manifesting, in future, to the people of Ireland, due regard and attention."—*Debates*, vol. xv., pp. 389—398

Grattan seconded, and Ponsonby supported, the motion; but the adjournment of the house, moved by the Chancellor of the Exchequer, was carried without a division.

INDEMNITY BILL.

February 3rd, 1796.

On the Indemnity Bill, Grattan moved that Justice Chamberlain and Baron Smith, the judges who had gone circuit in the disturbed districts, should be first examined. Curran supported him :—

Some excesses, I believe, have taken place, which no friend to his country can see without the deepest concern. But it is not from hearsay that the belief of a general confederacy against the state should be adopted—it should not be a belief founded on a mere hatred of the lower orders. Of Bills of Indemnity I admit the principle ; that is, the breach of the law for the safety of the state. Was it so in the last year that is the purpose of the inquiry. It is to see if such necessity existed whether such breach and to such a degree has been necessary. I know from public evidence, on oath, that most flagrant oppression has been practised upon some poor people by magistrates ; taken from their beds at midnight, and transported no man knew whither, without the colour of accusation, or form of trial. No such acts were done in England at any of the times alluded to, nor does any Act of Indemnity there extend to any arbitrary sentence or execution of any man, or anything not inevitable at times of convulsion. Nothing has been done to separate the rich from the poor, and to make wealth a proof of innocence, and poverty itself a crime. I wish to have the report of the Judges on the state of the country, and the general conduct of the magistrates. They must have observed coolly ; they had the best means of observing ; they could not be misled by malignity or panic. I appeal to the candour of gentlemen themselves, whether they do not feel some warmth on this subject ? and whether men who have the power of judging in their own cars, ought also to pronounce on their own evidence, against those who could not speak for themselves. As to myself I abhor outrages as much as any man ; I wish for no delay, but I wish for information, for temper, and therefore for inquiry.—*Debates*, vol. xvi., p. 51.

The amendment was lost, without a division

CHANNEL TRADE

February 15th, 1796.

GRATTAN moved a resolution for the Equalization of Trade Duties between England and Ireland. Mr. Vandeleur seconded the motion; and Sir L. Parsons, Mr. Fletcher, Mr. W. Smith, and Mr. O'Hara supported it. The Chancellor of the Exchequer moved the order of the day, and was sustained by Sir H. Langrishe, who nevertheless defended the principle of Grattan's motion. Curran said:—

I will not trouble the house long; it is, indeed, to no purpose to trouble the house long. I see that the only object of the other side of the house is a division, and that an early division; and I doubt not there are at this moment forty cooks in Dublin who are apprised that it is not necessary to keep dinner back. I lament, however, that a gentleman of character should be thrust forward to move so ungraciously the order of the day upon such a question. This method of treating a matter of so much moment to the interest of the country, excites my warmest indignation. It is peculiarly unwise and improper under the critical circumstances of the present times, which call at least, as much for the probity as for the authority of parliament. Disturbances exist in different parts of the kingdom, but the conduct of an honest and prudent government would be to inquire seriously into the causes of the people's discontent, and at one and the same time to redress their grievances, if they should appear to have any, and to repress with vigour, and, if necessary, to punish with rigour, their excesses; whereas the system of the present administration is to exasperate, if not provoke the latter, by obstinately and contumeliously refusing to remove or to investigate the former; and representing government to the people as nothing but an object of terror and dislike. Gentlemen, in the confidence of administration to-night, instead of conciliating the affections of the people, by a temperate assertion of their rights, and by showing a disposition to advance gradually to the attainment of them, contemptuously turn even from the discussion of them, and refuse to enter into the consideration of a measure, of all others perhaps most calculated to allay popular discontent, at the very moment they are forced to confess the justice of its principle; thus at once acknowledging, or shamefully betraying, or as shamefully deserting the interests and the rights of their country. It has been argued (if an argument it can be called, instead of an insult), that it is presumption in an inexperienced and uncapitaled country like this, immediately to attempt coping with, and rivalling the commerce that is sustained by the skill, and the enterprise, and the experience, and the opulence of the traders of Great Britain. Our rights must be made equal, but our advantages must continue to be inferior to those of that country; and this, I insist is an incontrovertible answer to that narrow, illiberal, and dishonest policy, which we ought rather to disdain to answer, and which was said (and I hope and believe untruly said), to be the actuating principle of the trading interest of England. I am too much a friend to that country to believe that such is its principle; but if it is, however mistaken and unjust I may think it, I cannot but feel some respect for the minister (and I recommend that sentiment to the consideration of those who are called the ministry here), who feels in the disposition and the wishes of a great body of the people, a powerful and a formidable restraint upon his conduct. But if that really were the case,—if the Lancashire and Warwickshire manufacturers are such potentates, as that their prejudices cannot be resisted, nor even reasoned with by the English minister instead of an expostulation with him, I would propose one with them I would recommend that a bare-legged deputation from this country should be sent to their high mightinesses, the lords of the buckle and button manufactory, humbly to represent to them, that the welfare of the two kingdoms is not absolutely incompatible, that we are only seeking to benefit ourselves in a small and a gradual increase, without injuring them in the smallest degree, and to entreat that they will be graciously pleased to permit their minister to permit our parliament to act with some regard for the interests of its constituents, and with some respect for its own independence.

I repeat, that I am aware by what has fallen from the other side of the house, and the manner in which these gentlemen have treated the subject, that I am trespassing upon their time in vain, and wasting my own, by which I argue the question with them; the truth is, the question must be decided by votes, and there are two modes of influencing votes, in neither of which, perhaps, could I venture to hope for much success. One method is by argument, and another by motive. Argument certainly does influence the votes of a great number of gentlemen in this house; and if an argument is opposed to me, I may answer it well or ill as I can; and, if truth, and justice, and reason are with me, I may entertain some hopes of succeeding; but if argument be altogether abandoned, and a motive opposed to me, I must examine the nature of it, because it might happen to be of such a nature as that it must be impossible for me to reply to it with any effect. For example, if a gentleman's motive should turn out to be a pension of five hundred pounds a year, it would be impossible to be answered by any logic but that of the treasury bench; but there is a motive of another, and of a very different nature—the sense of general and collective, instead of private and individual, interest; and never was there a time when such a motive ought to operate so powerfully upon the house as the present, when its own honour and the prosperity and the peace of the country alike depend upon the respect of the people for parliament. [He again pressed, with great energy, the gross and shameful inconsistency of at once admitting the justice of the principle of the resolution, and shrinking from an honest declaration of that principle; and concluded a short, but forcible and very animated speech, by giving his cordial assent to the motion.]—*Debates,* vol. xvi., pp. 85—88.

The order of the day was carried by 82 to 16.

INSURRECTION BILL.

February 25th, 1796.

On the second reading of this bill Sir Laurence Parsons said he would vote for the second reading, but objected to much of the bill, especially to the right of arbitrary transportation which it gave magistrates, and contrasted the misery of the peasantry with the luxury of the aristocracy. For this he was angrily attacked by Mr. Cuffe, Col. Stewart, Col. Hutchinson, and Mr. Archdall. The bill was also generally supported by Mr. Ogle, Mr. Ruxton, and Mr. Ormsby. Mr. Jephson concurred with Sir L. Parsons. Arthur Browne, of College, denounced the bill as tyrannical, and Sir L. Parsons' description of the peasantry as untrue. Curran followed him:—

Notwithstanding the liberality, and even zeal, with which gentlemen have yielded to every measure that administration has thought necessary for the defence of the country, and the support of the war, it is yet evident that they made it part of their system to throw out, on almost every occasion, language the most abusive, and charges the most false, on the motives of those who dared to dissent from them, even on questions the most indifferent. With respect to myself, it is a work of no great difficulty to show, that the motion, which I had the honour of proposing at the commencement of the session, could not have been suggested by any wish to inflame or to embarrass. It is plain to every reasonable man, that when the poor of Ireland were in a state of extreme discontent, whether with or without just cause, the most obvious and natural remedy for legislature to apply would be, in the first instance, to inquire into their situation, in order that, if they were under the pressure of no extraordinary evils, the inquiry might at once evince the watchful solicitude of Parliament over their interest, and show them that they were discontented without reason. And if, on the other hand, the result of the inquiry should turn out to be, that the poor were suffering under grievances which admitted of redress, what could be more effectual to prevent the spreading of disaffection, or to restore tranquillity to the public mind, than to grant that redress? Such were my motives; and I appeal to the recollection of every gentleman who assisted at that debate, whether I did not touch on the subject of it, with a degree of coolness and temperance, which, indeed, ill befitted such a topic; but which, at least, showed how studious I was to avoid meriting the imputation of a design to inflame the minds of the poor—already discontented. Indeed, so very careful have I been, lest the touch of even a feeble finger might irritate, that when I perceived the sense of the house to be against the inquiry, I did not attempt to say another word on the subject, and from the first introduction of the question, till the present hour. it has been (with respect to me) at rest.

But why do gentlemen charge opposition with a design to irritate the public mind, when even administration themselves cannot deny that it is to the persevering efforts of opposition that THEY owe whatever popularity they possess? Little as that popularity is, they should be grateful to the opposition for that little; for opposition it was which forced them to adopt, one after another, every beneficial measure they can boast of. If it was praiseworthy in his Majesty's ministers to give those measures to the country, it could not have been inflammatory in gentlemen to propose them; but if the measures were such as ought to have been given, then the administration, who for a series of years opposed, abused, and rejected these measures, were guilty; and on them must be charged the disaffection of the country they injured, and to them must be attributed the design of inflaming discontent.

The honourable gentleman has alluded to Lord Fitzwilliam—has talked of his having embodied himself with the mob—of the Catholics, too, and their want of zeal in repressing the disturbances. It is my opinion, that had not Lord Fitzwilliam been removed, the kingdom, at this day, would be in a state of perfect tranquillity. To the folly of removing that nobleman, on whom the hearts and wishes of the nation, particularly of the poor, were fixed, every wise man attributes, at least in a very great degree, the present state of the country; and with respect to the Catholics, had they not been wounded by the aggravated insult which, on that occasion, had been given to their most tender feelings, they would have continued still active and zealous in preserving the peace of the kingdom. It is to be regretted, as the honourable gentleman observed, that they did not continue their exertions; but it would have been somewhat unreasonable to expect that men who have been publicly insulted by the administration of the country, should not retire in disgust. Even the honourable gentleman himself would not serve government with the same zeal, did he meet no reward but disgrace and reprehension, as he would for the honours and emoluments of a good place—it is not in human nature.

The imputations, then, which have been openly charged on me by one gentleman, and insinuated by another, were founded only in that perversion of understanding which sees every object inverted, and that habit of mind, which, from frequently contemplating the obliquity of its own workings, cannot believe that any thing is straight. With regard to other honourable gentlemen, with whom I generally agree, the charges were equally false, and particularly with respect to a right honourable gentleman (Mr. Grattan), who is not now present, and who, indeed, I cannot help congratulating on his absence, as it saves him the pain of hearing the torrent of irritating folly which has been so copiously poured forth by the honourable member who has thought proper, again, to allude to his celebrated address. It would become that honourable gentleman (Mr. Archdall) to remember that on that subject he has already been *answered;* and though the right honourable gentleman to whom he alluded was not present—*stat nominis umbra!*

That honourable gentleman deals as well in panegyric as invective. He has declared love to the secretary, and seems displeased that other gentlemen have not blazoned the perfections of his charmer with the same zeal as himself. The praises he has lavished on the right honourable gentleman, in this instance, brings to my mind the marriage ceremony which is performed among some savages I have read of, where the priest pours on the bride a hornful of strong smelling mixtures; it strikes me very forcibly that this ceremony is performed at the Cape of Good Hope.

As to the bill, I contend that however a young and honourable member's blood may run cold at the idea, it is a bill *for* the *rich*, and *against* the *poor*. What is a bill which puts the liberty of the poor man, who has no visible means of living but labour, in the discretion of the magistrates? In England, where no man need be poor, but because he is idle, such a law may be useful and necessary, and certainly is not oppressive; but in Ireland, where he who is willing to labour, cannot always find employ, such a bill lays the poor prostrate at the rich man's feet—it does what in Ireland, of all countries on the face of the earth, government should be most careful to avoid—it constitutes *poverty* a *crime*, and leaves it in the discretion of wealth to apportion the punishment. Such a law in any country is dangerous; in the present circumstances of Ireland, it threatens dreadful mischief. That there must be poor in every country, no man will doubt; but it is a principle which I imbibed in early youth, and in which I have the authority of Helvetius to support me, that there may be too great a disproportion between the property of the poor and rich. Who will deny that this is the case of Ireland? and who that acknowledges it will say, that in such a state of things, it would not be hazardous to the last degree to exasperate the feelings of excessive poverty, by laws that lie heavy, most heavy, on the poor alone? Such a law may, perhaps, for a time, produce a momentary suppression of disturbance; but like pressure on an elastic body, it will only prepare it for expanding itself with still greater force. Let the rich men of Ireland, therefore, fear when they enact a law against poverty, lest poverty should enact a counter-law against wealth. It is an age of wonders, and strange mischiefs have been produced by intemperate laws. Gentlemen have reasoned very ingeniously to prove that he who should be transported by this law would only be sent into an honourable retirement, where he might gain glory by fighting for the country from which his poverty had expelled him; but I believe there would be but few men found who would be reconciled, by these arguments, to transportation; and I again conjure the house to weigh well the danger of abrogating the constitution, by a law so little likely to attain the end it aims at.—*Debates*, vol. xvi., pp. 143—46.

Mr. Maxwell, the Attorney-General, &c., supported the bill, Mr. Hoare and Lord Edward Fitzgerald earnestly resisting it; but the second reading was carried, and the bill committed, without a division.

FRENCH WAR.

13th October, 1796.

PARLIAMENT was opened this day, by a speech from the Lord Lieutenant (Earl Camden), holding out a hope of successful negociation with France, but bidding them prepare to resist invasion.* It also referred to the Orange wreckings in Armagh as "outrages."

* Hoche's force was just assembling at Brest; and the reader will remember that Wolfe Tone, Grouchy, and a part of that expedition, reached Bantry Bay on the 22nd December, and did not leave it till the 28th.

Grattan moved, as an amendment to the address—" To represent to his Majesty, that the most effectual method for strengthen'ng the country, and promoting unanimity, was to take such measures and to enact such laws, as to ensure to all his Majesty's subjects the blessings and privileges of the constitution, without any distinction of religion." The Right Hon. W. B. Ponsonby, seconded the amendment, which was resisted by George Knox, Dominick Browne, Sir H. Langrishe, Egan, and others, as untimely. Curran supported it:—

I am surprised at the apathy of government, which can leave a question of such importance to the idle skirmishing of their dependants. I might attribute their dumbness to their discretion, if I did not remark the mischievous and foolish approbation which, in the disconcertion of their surprise, they have given to the most foolish and mischievous assertions. I would give them credit for their silence and their contrition, had they been struck mute by a consciousness that the present disastrous crisis had found its maturity in their folly, and could hope for no cure from their capacity; but I own I am shocked to find that exposed and detected perverseness should reserve their dumb show for the expression of a speechless and incorrigible impenitence. It is, indeed, an awful subject; it is the call of the minister of the sister country in the hour of her distress—a distress brought upon her by his incapacity and ambition—upon a nation uniformly insulted and abused, but which still feels the warm sentiment of interest for her difficulties, and for her safety. When the speech has informed us of the alarming symptoms of disaffection in this country, not only in the lower orders who may act from the mere feeling of suffering—when it tells us that within we have to dread the union of popular passion and popular opinion—that the empire is obliged to sue for peace, and that the enemy is actually at our gates —I do not wonder that the house is solemnly called upon for advice at such a crisis. It is its duty to give it; and I cannot but regret that the speech has furnished so little to direct your judgments, and whether you are to advise upon the idea of continuing war, or of a probable peace. I did, indeed, expect that the sad succession of disaster and defeat, which have extinguished all hopes of success against the enemy, would have tempted the minister to try again the only talents to which he could aspire, the talents of peace; the first of which is, an undisguised sincerity with the country; but he has been equally insincere in the motives which he avowed in this statement of its events, and his hopes of its termination. It was first a war of our allies, the Dutch, for the opening of the Scheldt; it was next, together with our faithful ally, the plunderer of Poland, a war to support the rights of property; with our ally the emperor, it was a war for the true principles of liberty; with his Holiness the Pope, it was a war for orthodoxy and the Protestant religion; in Corsica it was a war in support of elective monarchy and arbitrary despotism; it was next a war against certain principles and opinions, in which the polemics of the minister had been rather unfortunate; it was next a war of indemnity for the past, and security for the future. At length the object of the war has become sole and unequivocal, it is now a war for peace—no doubt a better peace than he had before; the former peace was encumbered by alliances, by commerce, by access to every port in Europe, and, no doubt, plethoric, by the sur plus of blood and population. We are now likely to have a peace without any of these disadvantages, and additionally secured by the fortunate increase of one hundred millions of debt! I do not wish to raise a lauph at such a time, and upon such a subject; on the contrary, I regret the perplexity which this silly train of juggling has cast upon the subject of debate. No man can judge from the speech, whether the minister has any reasonable prospect either of war or peace: the enemy is beaten and are suing for peace: the enemy is beaten, and the enemy is at our gate. We must consult, therefore, and advise with a view to either event; that advice is contained in the amendment proposed; it consists of two parts; it recommends the union of the country in its defence, and, next, it recommends a cure of that disunion which the speech has stated, by giving the people equal rights, and thereby irresistible union in the common cause; put into plain words it is this: The enemy is at the gate, what do you advise? We advise to arm the nation against them. But, says the minister, the nation is divided. Then, adds the advice, reconcile them to yourself by common justice, and unite them in the cause, by giving them liberty to defend. The question now is, is this advice honest and wise, or is it, as has been charged, seditious and impolitic? The first part of the charge is supported by weak and silly imputations upon the character of the mover; but I will not condescend to notice them. With the present age the accusers will be a sufficient answer to the accusation, and with the time to come, the character of the right honourable mover is not likely to meet either the accusation or the accusers. One allegation only in point of fact I must contradict. It has been stated that the right honourable member, when in power, moved the supply, unaccompanied by the emancipation of the Catholics. The fact was directly otherwise. The supply was presented with one hand, and, with the other, the just and fair compensation of unqualified franchise to our Catholic brethren; and the former would never have been presented if he had not supposed that no shameless perfidy could have deprived the latter of effect. But is the advice contained in the amendment impolitic? Can those who say so find any way by which an invader can be resisted, except by the force and courage of the country invaded? Believe me, Sir, an invader can look to nothing but certain destruction where he is opposed by the wishes and passions of the people. It is not garrisons, it is not generals, nor armies, upon which we can repose in safety. It is on the union and zeal of the general inhabitants, removing provisions, discovering the designs, marring the projects, and hanging upon the retreats of an enemy, that baffles and defeats him more than any regular force can do. The speech insinuates, and gentlemen have asserted, that of this powerful alliance we should not have the aid. Wisely it is ordained that there shall be only one way of possessing it; that government shall be just in order that subjects shall be loyal; and that statesmen learn, if they would be safe they must be honest. That honesty is recommended by the amendment; but gentlemen have insinuated, though they cannot be hardy enough to assert, that the Irish nation has been honestly dealt with. What has been the system pursued with respect to the Catholics during the administration of the present minister? Their petitions to parliament were contumeliously rejected. I arraign that rejection upon the authority of parliament, which is ashamed of what it has done, and received that very petition the subsequent session, and so far abolished the brutal code of proscription and of blood. To your own wisdom and justice I fondly attribute your repentance of your mistake, and it is seriously for you now to consider whether you will suffer the perverseness of a giddy and incapable government to lead you into the degradation of repenting of that repentance. To parliament I wish to ascribe the merit of the justice that was done to the Catholics; to the government only could be ascribed the vengeance that has been excited against them by that justice. Government have resorted to the mean artifice of excluding them from all offices and franchises, of encouraging every attack upon their reputation, and encouraging the most wicked and groundless prosecutions against their lives. Of the trials of Mr. Fay, and of the principal Catholic merchants of Drogheda, I can speak as an eye-witness; and I declare them to be scenes of more atrocity and horror than I have ever seen exhibited in a court of justice. It was what the Catholics might have expected when they found their avowed enemies continued in authority, and the malice of an implacable government left to indemnify itself by vengeance for what it had lost by law. But why do I state those sufferings of my countrymen? Is it to inflame their passions? Far from it; if I wished them inflamed, it is expressly stated that they are so already. I am therefore stating those errors which have led to that inflammation, as an argument for supporting the amendment, which proposes a correction of them. As to the disease, I cannot but admit that gentlemen are right in saying that it exists, and I warn the administration against placing themselves in so ridiculous a light as a government must appear in, by refusing the remedy proposed, and that without having any plausible objection or any rational substitute. The disease and the remedy are found in the nature of man: by injuries he is alienated, and by kindnesses conciliated. You have tried the former part of this maxim at the hazard of every thing that is dear to a nation, the amendment advises you to give the latter part of it a fair trial in mercy to the nation and to yourselves. But if you are not reconciled to this advice by any intrinsic mark of its wisdom, try it by your own objections. One gentleman says that the government has been just, and that the people are united. If that be so, to refuse the amendment is to libel your own justice, and to deny the consequences of your own wisdom.

Another gentleman says they are disaffected, but thinks our own swords an unfailing protection. I cannot but regret that such an idea should have fallen from him. The idea of an enemy, and of a country, combined against those swords, would be too terrible in its consequence —surely, surely it cannot be seriously even insinuated to be true. Gentlemen say the Catholics have got every thing but seats in parliament. Are we really afraid of giving them that privilege? Are we seriously afraid that Catholic venality might pollute the immaculate integrity of the House of Commons?—that a Catholic member would be more accessible to a promise, or a pension, or a bribe, than a Protestant? Lay your hands upon your hearts, look in one another's faces and say, Yes, and I will vote against this amendment. But is it the fact that they have every thing? Is it the fact that they have the common benefit of the constitution, or the common protection of the law? Look at the scene that has been exhibited for two years in one of your counties, of robbery, and rape, and murder, and extermination; and why has that disgraceful practice existed? Because the law can give them no protection under a hostile and implacable government; because they have not struck those natural roots into their own soil, that can secure them against the storm that has mercilessly raged against them. But a right honourable gentleman has said, it is not yet the time. Low indeed must the topics of objection have been drained, when even talents like this descend to such an objection. One merit it certainly has; it is an argument for ever equally true, with only one unlucky circumstance,— that it is for ever equally false—an argument in support of which the whole force of prospective eternity may be put into requisition, and made to sustain the onset with such obstinate courage, that no single moment will be found to consult its safety in retreat, or decline the alternative of victory or death.

Another gentleman has said, the Catholics have got much, and ought to be content. Why have they got that much? is it from the minister? is it from the parliament, which threw their petition over its bar? No, they got it by the great revolution of human affairs, by the astonishing march of the human mind; a march that has collected too much moment in its advance, to be now stopped in its progress. The bark is still afloat, it is freighted with the hopes and liberties of millions of men; she is already under weigh—the rower may faint, or the wind may sleep, but rely upon it, she has already acquired an energy of advancement that will support her course, and bring her to her destination; rely upon it, whether much or little remains, it is now vain to withhold it; rely upon it, you may as well stamp your foot upon the earth, in order to prevent its revolution. You cannot stop it! you will only remain a silly gnomon upon its surface to measure the rapidity of rotation, until you are forced round and buried in the shade of that body, whose irresistible course you would endeavour to oppose.

One honourable gentleman has put the question upon its true grounds —namely, the effect which the adoption or rejection of the amendment must have upon England, upon Ireland, upon France; it must be so considered. I ask what have ministers to say to England at the hour of her danger—can they tell her that Ireland is unnecessary to her defence? No; separate Ireland from her, and she sinks to the bottom, and only finds a grave in the ocean that was before the theatre of her triumphs and her pride. Will they assure England of a zealous assistance in this hour of her calamity? If their own assertions here be true, they dare not make her such a promise. Will they dare to tell her that the disaffection of which they complain has been occasioned by their own malignity and folly? Will they dare to avow that they have goaded the great body of this nation into such an extreme of detestation and contempt, that they prefer the last and worst of evils, the ravages and horrors of a hostile invader, to the hope of safety, by arming under so odious and despised a banner? Will they dare to aggravate the avowal with a confession that their implacable malice had rejected the only resource that remained to her—namely, justice and conciliation?

The honourable gentleman has asked, what effect it would have on France? What effect must it have upon enemies, to be told upon the authority of our governors, that our people are not to be trusted—that they are hostile to our cause—that they are favourable to them, and that they are ready to receive from them, as rebels, those arms which we are afraid to trust them with, as subjects? Such is the encouragement which you trumpet to them by the rejection of this amendment; the contrary is the terror with which you would inspire them by its adoption. But what must be the effect upon this unhappy country? Have ministers seriously considered the consequences of that unfeeling and incorrigible oppression, which turns even the wisdom of the wisest into madness? Are they willing to say to them, We hate your persons, we abominate your rights, we detest your claims, we abhor your religion, and we are determined rather to spurn you to the enemy, to expose your country to a bondage more fierce than we have practised upon it, to expose the glory and pride of Britain to utter extinction, rather than condescend to treat you as fellow-subjects, or arm you in the defence of anything but the continuance of your own subjection and degradation? But I will not nominate so fatal an idea, as I cannot refuse to profit by the interval, before a decision takes place, and still hope that wiser counsels will be adopted, and that more auspicious projects will arise; that we may still cling to the hope of national prosperity and imperial stability; that we may be yet permitted to show to England that we feel the endearing ties of common language, common constitution, common interest, and common fate; that in her distress we are willing to forget any injury of the past; that our last shilling and the last drop of our blood are ready to be expended in her cause; and that, in that prompt and cordial tender, we do not stop to parley for contract or stipulation; that we look only to the means by which that tender could be carried into effect, by bringing to the aid of the common cause that irresistible support which must be ever found in a concentrated and united people.—*Debates*, vol. xvii., pp. 28—34.

George Ponsonby most skilfully defended Grattan's amendment, but it was defeated by 149 to 12! and then the Attorney-General moved for leave to bring in a bill, similar to such as have been enacted on like occasions when invasion threatened the coasts in England, to empower the Lord Lieutenant, or other Chief Governor or Governors of this kingdom, to take up and detain all such persons as were suspected of treasonable practices; and leave being given, the bill was forthwith presented, read a first and second time, and committed for the morrow.

SUSPENSION OF THE HABEAS CORPUS.

October 14th, 1796.

In Committee Ponsonby opposed the bill; so did Curran:—

I conjure the house to reflect seriously upon the moment that has been chosen by administration for the bringing in of this bill; I think it a melancholy proof of their want of temper, and their want of judgment. My right honourable friend moved an amendment to the address in favour of the Roman Catholics; it was a motion of the very utmost importance; in the debates upon that motion the rights of the Roman Catholics were strongly urged, and as strongly opposed; the disposition of the administration towards them was fully manifested, and the motion was rejected. Of the propriety of that rejection I will not speak—I cannot but lament it; I lament still more the effect that I am sure the making of the present bill the immediate sequel to that rejection, will have on the public mind. [He dwelt strongly upon the indiscretion of ministers, in thus appearing to make the bill be an attack and an insult upon the Catholics; and then replied to the arguments that had been used in support of the measure; he adverted to the bills of the last session.] The Habeas Corpus act is almost the only remaining guardian of our liberties; and the ministry have stabbed the guardian upon its post and in the dark. The house was exhausted by a long debate upon a subject of the last importance to the union and to the peace of the country; those members of parliament who were likely to defend this last privilege of the people were withdrawn, and it was not till the next morning that they were told in their beds, that the Habeas Corpus act was repealed. That sacred palladium of our liberties which was never suffered to sleep, ought not to have been stolen from us while we slumbered. I ask why the wisdom of our ancestors has opposed so many checks to the progress of a bill through parliament? I ask whether those checks are intended only to prevent the precipitation of measures of no moment, and that the dearest interests, and most sacred privileges of the subject, are to be left exposed to all the fatal consequences of rashness and intemperance? Before a bill can be laid before the house, its leave must be asked, and obtained, for bringing it in—here it may be debated and opposed in its very first onset. It is then, by the leave of the house, to be read a first time, and upon this reading its principle is to be discussed; a day is then appointed for the further discussion of its principle upon a second reading; it is then, if so far approved of, to be considered, and, if possible, to be amended by a committee of the whole house. Has the constitution no object in all these provisions for deliberation, or is such deliberation intended to be only upon trifles?

At two o'clock in the morning the house was moved for leave to bring in a bill to repeal the Habeas Corpus act; at five minutes past two in the morning the bill was read a first time; and, after *grave* and *mature* deliberation, the bill was ordered to be read, and was accordingly read, a second time at ten minutes after two in the morning. Its principle was then *fully considered* and approved of; and at fifteen minutes after two in the morning, it was laid before a committee of the whole house! I ask, what peculiar and extraordinary urgency has been stated for refusing to such a bill the deliberation of eight-and-forty hours ? and I insist, that whatever arguments have been offered for the necessity of passing such a bill at all, not one has been even insinuated for forcing it into a law, without examination and without reflection. I believe there was but one motive for it, and that was to create an unfounded alarm in the country, and, if possible, to silence the murmurs of the people. If ministers wish to excite alarm, they may succeed—they have already succeeded. Their industrious reports of an invasion, of which I am convinced they have no apprehension, have nearly destroyed public credit in the South. I have it from what I believe the best authority, and upon such matters I can only speak from information, that in Cork and Waterford discount is wholly stopped. If ministers hope to dismay the people into silence, I tell them they cannot terrify them into apathy, and that they may exasperate their abhorrence into violence.

It remains now to consider the nature of what has been adduced as evidence of a treasonable confederation at present existing in the country, and which has been urged as the justification of the measure before the house. It cannot be denied that there has been treason in the country, because several men have been long since tried and convicted and executed as traitors: but I do deny that there is any evidence whatever before the house of a treasonable confederation now subsisting. I cannot too strongly reprobate the idea of considering a passage in the speech from the throne as evidence upon which to pass a bill or attainder against the constitution; if such a doctrine were to be endured, it would be at any time in the power of a corrupt minister to lay the people at his feet. I insist that the assertions of the Attorney-General, even if they could be admitted as evidence, amount to no more than that informations have been sworn against certain individuals for crimes, the nature of which has not been disclosed, and that they have been apprehended. As to the late imprisonment of persons in the North, I will not say it was a mere pretext for the introduction of this bill ; I disclaim the idea of making so horrid a charge, but I cannot but say it is no foundation whatever for such a bill : to say that it is, would be to say, these persons are guilty—to pronounce them guilty without the forms of trial. Whatever facts have been stated to the house have only tended to show that the bill is unnecessary ; men suspected of treason against the government may be apprehended and detained without the bill ; but confederation for the mere purpose of obtaining, by constitutional means, a reform in the representation, is not a circumstance that can justify the house in abandoning the people, and laying their liberty at the mercy of the executive power. I shall vote for Mr Mason's leaving the chair.—*Debates*, vol. xvii., pp. 56—9.

The division was 137 to 7.

CATHOLIC EMANCIPATION.

October 17*th,* 1796.

THE opposition (consisting of Grattan, Curran, the two Ponsonbys, Duquery, Fle' her &c.,) placed between a government bent on despotism, and The United Irishmen preparing for revolution, made incessant efforts at accommodation—restraining the people, and endeavouring to check the government; but the attempts were almost useless. The opposition was too small and punctilious to impede the cabinet seriously.

On the 17th of October, Grattan moved "that the admissibility of persons professing the Roman Catholic religion to seats in parliament is consistent with the safety of the crown and the connexion of Ireland with Great Britain." George Ponsonby seconded it, and it was opposed with fury by the government. The speaker immediately preceding Curran was Dr. Duigenan, who attacked the Catholics collectively and individually, past, present, and future, in most insolent language, and supported the amendment for the order of the day. Curran said:—

I declare, sir, that I have no words to express the indignation I feel at the despicable attempt to skulk from the discussion of so important and so necessary a question, by the affectation of an appeal to our secrecy and our discretion; the ludicrous, the ridiculous secrecy of a public assembly; the nonsense of pretending to conceal from the world what they know as well, or better, than ourselves; the rare discretion of an Irish parliament hiding from the Executive Directory of the French Republic the operations of their own armies; concealing from them their victories in Italy, or their humiliation of Great Britain; concealing from them the various coquetry of her negotiations, and her now avowed solicitations for a peace. As ridiculous and as empty is the senseless parade of affecting to keep our own deliberations a secret. Rely upon it, sir, if our enemies condescend to feel any curiosity as to our discussion, you might as well propose to conceal from them the course of the Danube, or the course of the Rhine, as the course of a debate in this assembly, as winding, perhaps, and perhaps as muddy as either. But the folly of the present advocates for silence and for secrecy go still farther,—it proposes to keep all these matters a profound secret from ourselves; it goes to the extravagant length of saying, that if we be beaten, we are not to deliberate upon the means of repairing our disasters, because that would be to own that we were beaten; that if the enemy were at our gates it would not be prudent to acknowledge so terrifying a fact, even in considering the means of repelling him; that if our people are disaffected, we ought to be peculiarly cautious of any measures that can possibly tend to conciliation and union, because the adoption, or even the discussion, of such measures, would be in effect to tell ourselves, and to tell all the world, that the people are disaffected. The infatuation or the presumption of ministers goes even further than this—it insists upon the denial and the avowal of the very same facts; that we are to be alarmed with an invasion, for the purpose of making us obsequious to all the plans of ministers for intrenching themselves in their places; that we are to be panicstruck for them, but disdainful for ourselves; that our people are to be disaffected, and the consequences of that disaffection to be the most dangerous and the most imminent, for the purpose of despoiling ourselves of our best and most sacred privileges. So imminent is this danger, that it is declared by ministers and by their adherents, that in order to preserve our liberties for ever, it is absolutely necessary to surrender them for a time ; the surrender has been actually made. So frightfully disunited and divided are we, that we cannot venture to trust ourselves with the possession of our freedom, but we are all united as one man against redressing the grievances of the great majority of ourselves; we are all united as one man against the conciliation of our animosities, and the consolidation of our strength. I, for one, will never submit to be made the credulous dupe of an imposture so gross and so impudent. I know that the times are critical indeed ; I know that it is necessary to open our eyes to our danger, and to meet it in the front ; to consider what that danger is, and to consider of the best, and, perhaps, the only, possible means of averting it. For these reasons I consider the resolution not only a measure of justice and of honesty, but of the most pressing necessity.

[Mr. Curran entered largely into the state of the empire, and of its allies—of the disposition of our enemies towards Great Britain—of the nature of their political principles, and of the rapid dissemination of those principles.] It is difficult to tell whether the dissemination of these principles is likely to be more encouraged by the continuance of the war or by the establishment of a peace ; and if the war be, as has been repeatedly insisted on, a war on our part for the preservation of social order and of limited monarchy, an immediate necessity exists of making those objects the common interest and the common cause of every man in the nation. I spurn the idea of any disloyalty in the Catholics,—an idea which is sometimes more than intimated, and sometimes as vehemently disclaimed, by the enemies of Catholic emancipation. But the Catholics are men, and are, of course, sensible to the impression of kindness and injury, and of insult ; they know their rights, and feel their wrongs, and nothing but the grossest ignorance, or the meanest hypocrisy, can represent them as cringing with a slavish fondness to those who oppress and insult them. I sought to remove their oppressions, in order to make the interests of the whole nation one and the same; to this great object the resolution moved by my right honourable friend, manifestly tends; and I lament exceedingly that so indecent and so disingenuous a way of evading that motion has been resorted to, as passing to the order of the day—a conduct that however speciously the gentlemen who have adopted it may endeavour to excuse, can be regarded by the Catholics, and by the public, no otherwise than as an expression of direct hostility to the Catholic claims. It has been asserted that the Catholics are already in possession of civil liberty, and are only seeking for political power. What is it, then, that we are so anxiously withholding, and so greedily monopolising ? The answer which has been given to that assertion, by a learned and honourable friend near me (Mr. W. Smith) is that of a true patriot, and of a sound constitutional lawyer ; namely,—that civil liberty was a shadow, without a sufficient portion of political power to protect it.

[Having replied to the arguments of several members who had pre-

ceded him in the debate, Mr. Curran came to the speech that had been
delivered by Mr. Duigenan, and entertained the house, for about half
an hour, with one of the most lively sallies of wit and humour that we
remember to have heard.*] The learned doctor has made himself a
very prominent figure in this debate. Furious, indeed, has been his
anger, and manifold his attack ; what argument, or what man, or what
thing has he not abused ? Half choked by his rage in refuting those
who have spoken, he has relieved himself by attacking those who have
not spoken. He has abused the Catholics, he has abused their ancestors, he has abused the merchants of Ireland, he has abused Mr. Burke,
ne has abused those who voted for the order of the day. I do not know
but I ought to be obliged to the learned doctor, for honouring me with
a place in the invective ; he has called me the bottle-holder of my right
honourable friend. Sure I am, that if I had been the bottle-holder of
both, the learned doctor would have less reason to complain of me
than my right honourable friend ; for him I should have left perfectly
sober, whilst it would very clearly appear, that, with respect to the
learned doctor, the bottle had not only been managed fairly, but generously ; and if, in furnishing im with liquor, I had not furnished him
with argument, I had, at least, furnished him with a good excuse for
wanting it ; with the best excuse for that confusion of history and divinity, and civil law and canon law—that rollicking mixture of politics
and theology, and antiquity, with which he has overwhelmed the debate;
for the havoc and carnage he has made of the population of the last
age, and the fury with which he seemed determined to exterminate,
and even to devour the population of this ; and which urged him, after
tearing and gnawing the characters of the Catholics, to spend the last
efforts of his rage with the most unrelenting ferocity, in actually gnawing their names—[Alluding to Dr. Duigenan's pronunciation of the
name of Mr. Keogh, and which, Mr. Curran said, was a kind of pro-
nunciatory defamation.] In truth, Sir, I felt some surprise, and some
regret, when I heard him describe the sceptre of lath, and the tiara of
straw, and mimic his bedlamite Emperor and Pope with such refined
and happy gesticulation, that he could be prevailed on to quit so congenial a company. I should not, however, be disposed to hasten his
return to them, or to precipitate the access of his fit, if, by a most
unlucky felicity of indiscretion, he had not dropped some doctrines
which the silent approbation of the minister seemed to have adopted.
I do not mean, amongst these doctrines, to place the learned doctor's
opinions touching the revolution, nor his wise and valorous plan, in
case of an invasion, of arming the beadles and the sextons, and putting
himself in wind for an attack upon the French, by a massacre of the
Papists ; the doctrine I mean is, that Catholic franchise is inconsistent
with British connexion. Strong, indeed, must the minister be in so
wild and desperate a prejudice, if he can venture, in the fallen state of
the empire, under the disasters of the war, and with an enemy at the
gate- -if he can dare to state to the great body of the Irish nation, that

So in the Report.

their slavery is the condition of their connexion with England; that she is more afraid of yielding to Irish liberty than of losing Irish connexion The denunciation is not yet upon record; it might yet be left with the learned doctor, who, I hope, has embraced it only to make it odious—has hugged it in his arms with the generous purpose of plunging with it into the deep, and exposing it to merited derision, even at the hazard of the character of his own sanity. It is yet in the power of the minister to decide whether a blasphemy of this kind shall pass for the mere ravings of frenzy, or for the solemn and mischievous lunacy of a minister. I call, therefore, again to rouse that minister from his trance, and in the hearing of the two countries, to put this question to him, which must be heard by a third—Whether at no period, upon no event at no extremity, we are to hope for any connexion with Britain, except that of the master and the slave, and this, even without the assertion of any fact that could support such a proscription? It is necessary, I find, to state the terms and the nature of the connexion; it has been grossly misrepresented; it is a great federal contract between perfectly equal nations, pledging themselves to equal fate, upon the terms of equal liberty—upon perfectly equal liberty. The motive to that contract is the mutual benefit to each—the object of it their mutual and common benefit; the condition of the compact is, the honest and fair performance of it, and from that honest and fair performance, and from that only, arises the obligation of it. If England show a decided purpose of invading our liberty, the compact, by such an act of foulness and perfidy is broken, and the connexion utterly at an end; but I say, the resolution moved for by my right honourable friend, to the test of this connexion, to invade our liberty, is a dissolution of it. But what is liberty, as known to our constitution? It is a portion of political power necessary to its conservation; as, for instance, the liberty of the Commons of those kingdoms is that right, accompanied with a portion of political power to preserve it against the crown and against the aristocracy. It is by invading the power that the right is attacked in any of its constituent parts; hence it is, that if the crown show a deliberate design of so destroying it, it is an abdication; and let it be remembered that by our compact we have given up no constitutional right. Therefore I am warranted, as a constitutional lawyer, in stating, that if the crown or its ministers, by force or by fraud, destroy that fair representation of the people, by which alone they can be protected in their liberty, it is a direct breach of the contract of connexion; and I do not scruple to say, that if a House of Commons could be so debased as to deny the right stated in the resolution, it is out of their own mouths conclusive evidence of the fact. I insist that the claim of the Catholics to that right is directly within the spirit of the compact. And what are the arguments advanced against the claim? One is an argument which, if founded on fact, would have some weight; it is, that the Catholics did not make the claim at all. Another argument is used, which, I think, has as little foundation in fact, and is not very easily to be reconciled to the other—it is, that the Catholics make their claim with insolence, and attempt to carry their object by intimidation. Let gentlemen take this fact, if they please, in opposition to their own denial of it. The Catholics then do make the demand. Is their demand just?—is it just that they should be free?—is it just that they should have franchise? The justice is expressly admitted. Why not give it, then? The answer is, they demand it with insolence. Suppose that assertion, false as it is in fact, to be true, is it any argument with a public assembly, that any incivility of demand can cover the injustice of refusal? How low must that assembly be fallen which can suggest as an apology for the refusal of an incontestible right, the answer which a bankrupt buck might give to the demand of his tailor—he will not pay the bill, because "the rascal had dared to threaten his honour."

As another argument against their claims, their principles have been maligned; the experience of a century is the refutation of the aspersion. The articles of their faith have been opposed, by the learned doctor, to the validity of their claims. Can their religion be an objection, where a total absence of all religion, where atheism itself, is none? The learned doctor, no doubt, thought he was praising the mercy with which they have been governed, when he dilated upon their poverty; but can poverty be an objection in an assembly whose humble and Christian condescension shut not its doors even against the common beggar? He has traduced some of them by name: "Mr. Byrne, Mr. Keogh, and four or five ruffians from the Liberty;" but this is something better than frenzy; this is something better than the want of mere feeling and decorum; there cannot, perhaps, be a better way of evincing a further and more important want of the Irish nation, the want of a reformed representation of the people in Parliament. For what can impress the necessity of it more strongly upon the justice, upon the humanity, the indignation, and the shame of an assembly of Irish gentlemen, than to find the people so stripped of all share in the representation, as that the most respectable class of our fellow-citizens, men who have acquired wealth upon the noblest principle, the practice of commercial industry and integrity, could be made the butts of such idle and unavailing, such unworthy, such shameful abuse, without the possibility of having an opportunity to vindicate themselves—when men of that class can be exposed to the degradation of unanswered calumny, or the more bitter degradation of eleemosynary defence? [Mr. Curran touched upon a variety of other topics, and concluded with the most forcible appeal to the Minister, to the house, and to the country, upon the state of public affairs at home and abroad.] I insist that the measure is not, as it has been stated to be, a measure of mere internal policy; it is a measure that involves the question of right and wrong, of just and unjust; but it is more; it is a measure of the most absolute necessity, which cannot be denied, and which cannot safely be delayed. I cannot foresee future events; I cannot be appalled by the future, for I cannot see it; but the present I can see, and I cannot but see that it is big with danger: it may be the crisis of political life, or political extinction; it is a time fairly to state to the country whether they have anything, and what, to fight for; whether they are to struggle for a connexion of tyranny or of privilege; whether the administration of England will let us condescend to forgive the insolence of her happier days; or whether, as the beams of her prosperity have wasted and consumed us, so even the frost of her adversity shall perform the deleterious effects of fire, and burn upon our privileges and our hopes for ever.—*Debates*, vol. xvii., pp. 104—10.

Duquery's speech on the same side was most noble, but the motion was lost by 143 to 19.

HOCHE'S EXPEDITION.

January 6th, 1797.

SECRETARY PELHAM having brought down a message from the Lord Lieutenant full of English palaver, in reference to France and especially to the Expedition of Hoche. Grattan moved an amendment, censuring the inactivity of the British navy during the recent danger. Ponsonby supported, and Pelham and others resisted the amendment. There is a short speech of Sir Jonah Barrington's, then Mr. Barrington, and a *hopeful* lawyer, which I give as I find it:—

"Mr. Barrington (in full uniform) was also against the amendment literally, *vi et armis*. He repeated those arguments which he generally uses, drawn from the tendency of opposition speeches to inflame the public mind, and encourage the *disciplined banditti* of France again to attack us. He informed the house that on the present occasion he talked to them only as an *Irish soldier*; when he should have taken off his uniform he would talk to them in *his other capacity*. He confessed his surprise that the right honourable gentleman who moved the amendment did not at this time of danger become an *Irish soldier*—he was astonished that at such a crisis the right honourable gentleman's *hand hid its head*."—*Debates*, vol. xvii., pp. 171, 2.

Duquery replied to his impertinence with over much apology, saying that Grattan was an enrolled Volunteer. After some further debate Curran said:—

I strongly reprobate the mode used to hurry the house into a decision on subjects which require to be very maturely considered. The address may be considered, as it relates to the defence of the country by the British fleet; the negotiation with France; and as pledging the country to continue the war. With respect to the first, nothing is more clear than that it is a subject which deserves inquiry, and which the house cannot as yet have examined. All that is yet known on the subject is, that it has been understood for three months past that a design was entertained to invade Ireland. The British minister affected, indeed, not to believe this, and went so far as to say, on the very day when the French fleet were in Bantry Bay, that the report was but the frenetic rumour of the day. The armament, however, arrived, and on the whole coast of the kingdom of Ireland, a British line-of-battle ship was not to be seen. Why was this? I do not mean to criminate the admirals who commanded, nor the British cabinet; but I contend for it, the affair at first view appears such as deserves to be inquired into; and I will say more, that if parliament do not inquire, they will abandon their duty to their country and to themselves. Ireland has a right to protection from Great Britain, and if it is not given, it becomes her parliament to inquire. I know, indeed, that the contributions of Ireland in a pecuniary way are laughed at by the great monied interest of Great

R

Britain; but if the proportion of our wealth to hers were considered, it would be found we contribute a full share. But, besides our wealth, we contribute what to Britain is more essential than wealth—we contribute that, without which wealth would be useless to her—we give one hundred thousand men to her navy and to her armies. Ireland is entitled then to protection, but she receives it not. If parliament neglect, or refuse to inquire why she did not receive it, let them answer it to their country.

The house is also called on to decide on the negotiation—to say that it was broken off by the arrogance of France. What proofs are there of that? The house must be omniscient, if they can determine, without having read any one paper in support of or against that proposition. To me it seems that the case is far from being a clear one, that the fault was in the French. Lord Malmesbury goes to Paris, and tells the Directory that he is come to negotiate for peace. They ask him, has he a power to treat for the allies? Oh, no—he has no power to treat for the allies. Has he any powers to treat for a separate peace? No, he has no power to treat for separate peace; but he comes to treat for *peace*—but whether a *general* or a *separate* peace he cannot say. It is exactly such a case, to use a professional illustration, as if a man came to compromise a suit between two parties without having powers from either. So bungling a contrivance was never before made use of to attempt deceit, and gain a colourable pretext for continuing a quarrel! The French are charged in the address with terminating the negotiation arrogantly. I do not exactly know in what that arrogance appears. If it was arrogant in France to insist on, as a *sine qua non*, the retaining of Holland, it was surely equally arrogant in England to insist on the cession of Holland, as a *sine qua non*. I cannot, therefore, unprepared as I am, determine at the moment, that the negotiation was broken off by the fault of France; so far as I am yet informed, I think the contrary.

On the subject of the war, I feel most deeply the danger and the mischief of pledging the country to support it until the Netherlands are restored. I confess I am of the number of those who originally agreed to support the war. I never approved of its principle; but when once Great Britain had embarked in it, I feared it might damp her ardour and give vigour to her enemies if it were opposed in Ireland. Of the merits of the war, my opinion has never changed—I have always thought it, and will always think it, a war begun in interested ambition, and carried on against the liberty of mankind; but had a powerful opposition risen against it in the Irish parliament, it might have rather been taken by the enemies as a signal for turning the tide of war upon our island, than been looked on by the minister of Great Britain as a salutary admonition to his folly. Now the circumstances are changed— the minister has been taught wisdom, if he be capable of instruction, by four years' calamities—and France is now too well acquainted with our situation for me to fear that any new information may be conveyed to her by what passes in this house. How France came to know our supposed weakness and distraction, let *them* answer who passed a gunpowder bill and a convention act, as if the people of Ireland were too ill affected to be trusted with arms or suffered to speak their sentiments. Let them answer who at midnight came to this house, and, as if in the tumult of a rebellion, passed an Habeas Corpus Act, making the crown the arbiter of the subject's liberty, and suspending, as if treason stalked through the land, every privilege of the laws and the constitution. What are the feelings of those gentlemen at this hour, when, after thus treating the people of Ireland as traitors and rebels, by acts which reduced them, as to suffering and disqualification, to a level with the rebel,—what are now, I ask, the feelings of those men when they are now forced to come forward and declare, that to the loyalty, the zeal and affection of those very men they owe the safety and the existence of the country which the neglect of his Majesty's ministers left exposed to the enemy during a space of twenty days? The people have saved the country—the administration have destroyed the constitution. What is there left of Irish freedom?—what is there left in Ireland of the British constitution? Have not the people been deprived of every valuable privilege of speaking and acting in a public way?—have they not been subjected to prison and massacre? If any gentleman thinks I am declaiming, let him set down and tell me in written characters what remains to Ireland of her constitution. He will find on that examination that I am speaking truth without exaggeration. Ireland has lost her freedom—England has partly lost it; she has mistaken wealth for power, and power for liberty. She is now beginning to learn the lesson of adversity. Her blood is flowing, and when the wound stiffens she will feel it; she will then learn that there are physical bounds to the wealth of a nation as well as that of individuals— she will find that with her burden of £400,000,000 of debt, her small remains of liberty will be unable to support her. What is the force of Britain? France has natural strength—she has extensive territory— she reckons climates under her dominion—and exults in her thirty millions of population. The force of Britain is her spirit of liberty, her commercial enterprise, and her commercial connexion. Her liberty is gone—her commerce is bending under an accumulated load of debt. Strip her of her commercial territory, and compress her within her natural dimensions, and where is she? The calamities of Great Britain are the calamities of Ireland, though unhappily her benefits and her advantages she has not shared with us. But as Ireland is at least to suffer with Great Britain, it is wise to stop her in her race towards ruin; therefore it is, that I would rather repress than encourage her rage for a war which evidently tends to involve her still more deeply in destruction. Gentlemen are encouraged to be liberal in support of the war. Why? Because the martial spirit of the people is up. We have so many thousands brave loyal subjects in arms. I will ask gentlemen, do they think that the compliments of a Lord Lieutenant's secretary, or of a House of Commons, can continue to support these men in neglecting their ordinary and indispensable avocations? Can those men live in idleness, or feed their families by the produce of their military exhibitions? Gentlemen are too wise to think so; they must know that a country in arms will soon be a ruined country." Industry alone can produce wealth, or the necessaries of life, and a military life is incompatible with industry. But the resources of the country flourish. Where are they? You have already laid a shilling on the brogues of your beggar peasants; will you impose another shilling on them, or, if you do, who will be able to purchase? Those peasants, already so rich in loyalty, and zeal for the constitution, what other wealth have they? Seven pence per day! Can they, with all their loyalty—and loyal they are—bear any diminution of this scarcity? This has been a war for religion; has the church contributed, or will it contribute? If not, it behoves you to look out for your resources, before you pledge yourselves still farther to support the war.—*Debates*, vol. xvii., pp. 276-80.

Grattan replied to the ministers, and he and Ponsonby told seven members against ninety.

INTERNAL DEFENCE

24th February, 1797.

SIR LAURENCE PARSONS moved an address for an increase of the domestic army, especially the Yeoman infantry, grounding his motion on the power of France, the ' eglect and weakness of England, and the danger and loyalty (!) of Ireland. Grattan supported, and the Ministers opposed, the address. Neither party foresaw how the patriots of the Clubs would turn into the scourges of the people—traitors to their country and their oath, when under the bribe of payment, the compulsion of discipline, and the spirit of array. Curran said :—

I confess I never was more surprised than at the incredible fatuity of a House of Commons, who, when they are deliberating on a question, which determines whether we are to be Irish emigrants or Irish legislators, seems ready to pay obeisance to the silly nonsense which has been uttered by a man in office.

The right honourable gentleman has asked, why has not the house confidence in his exertion for the defence of the country? I answer, because the right honourable gentleman had advice of an intended invasion for three months before it took place; and in that time took no steps to repel the enemy, but left the defence of the country to the winds. I expect—there is every reason to expect—another attack from the enemy, and with much greater force than before. I expect this, from the known conduct of the French, who have not, except in one instance, been known to desist from an undertaking. What, then, must we look to? Not to England certainly. We have had a trial— we were in danger, and received no assistance. Besides, the west wind, which lets out the fleet of France, wi keep that of England locked up. As a proof of the culpable negligence of administration. which shou'd teach the house to think of protecti g themselves, I will mention a fact, of which I have been informed by authority I cannot doubt: it is, that when the French fleet arrived in Bantry, there were not, in that quarter of the country, including Cork, one thousand men fit to meet the enemy; hence the consternation which prevailed in that city, wher they received intelligence of their arrival. Another instance of the contemptible unsteadiness of the administration ; a gentleman of most respectable family, of hereditary loyalty, and great wealth, in the neighbourhood of Cork, had solicited leave to form a corps. For several weeks his request remained unanswered ; at length, on Christmas eve, he received his commission, but without either sword, gun, or bayonet for his men ; the very next day he received a letter from the minister, desiring to know how many of his corps were ready to march against the enemy.

What are the preparations which should be made against the enemy? It is not on this or on that army we should depend, but on the energy of the whole people. Would gentlemen wish to risk the fate of the country on a battle, with whatever prospect of a victory? Would they not rather wish to deter the enemy, if possible, by previous arrangements? But how deter them? By no mode but that to the use of which they owe their conquests—not by discipline, or by skill, but by rousing that enthusiastic zeal in your people, for the cause in which they engage. That enthusiasm it was, which taught Austria the lesson, that when it urges forward a furious crowd they will overcome the most matured efforts of discipline and regulated valour. Unless Ireland, in embodying her people, excites something of this spirit, she can find no safety against her invading enemy.

In order to evince how little is to be expected from the fleet of Britain, just consider the present situation of the minister, after four campaigns, in which he has gained nothing but debt and defeat, has lost all his allies, and forfeited the confidence of the people, if not in his integrity, at least in his ability and success. Is it possible that a minister, so circumstanced, floating in the torrent which is just ready to swallow him up, would venture to send to the assistance of Ireland the fleet of Britain, if Britain herself were in danger of being attacked? Is it not natural to suppose that he would make this country the theatre of war, rather than incur the danger of instant destruction, from the resentment of his countrymen, should he risk their safety to save Ireland? On these grounds it is clear that this country should think of providing a force within its own shores, to repel the enemy. I am of opinion that the force proposed by the motion is the most eligible that can be had— it is a speedy, a numerous, and a constitutional force. I could have wished that the augmentation, which has been made to the regulars, had rather been made to the militia: for that, too, is a constitutional force ; not that I fear a standing army—the soldier has of late wonderfully changed his character—he seems to have now learned that his duty is to meet death without delay, and to inflict it without remorse— but only for the purpose of protecting others from that danger which he encounters. Such has been found the soldier's character in France, and in various instances which have occurred in the present war. Such has been found to be the character of a standing army, even in the northern parts of our own kingdom, where they have been struck with reverence at the industry of its inhabitants, softened by their hospitality, and moved to pity at the sufferings they have witnessed.

In order to oppose France, it is necessary we should have an armed people; it is still more necessary we should have a people united and content. What, then, must have been the exultation of France, when she read in the official accounts by administration, of the late invasion; when they state so many corps as accepted and so many as rejected?— What notion must not the French have of the discordant state in which we are, when they find that a man offering his breast against the bayonet of an enemy, is not thought fit to be trusted? The best means for restoring union and confidence to the people, is to reform their representation, and to emancipate the Catholics. I caution administration against the fatal error, in times like these, of identifying the abuses of the constitution with the constitution itself. Such a conduct only tends to make treason, in their sense of it, the glory of every honest man.— At this moment the gaols are crowded. Gentlemen should take care, that in their zeal to punish crimes, they do not make a demand of redress an act of treason. Before those unfortunate men—unfortunate, if guilty, but fortunate and honourable men, if innocent, inasmuch as suffering for resistance to public abuse is in the highest degree gratifying to the feeling of an independent mind—before they are tried, care should be taken not to give such a description of their crime as may excite not hatred but sympathy in the minds of the people, and turn what was considered guilt into glory.—*Debates*, vol. xv., pp. 530—4.

23 persons voted for the address; 125 against it.

DISARMING OF ULSTER.

March 20th, 1797.

CURRAN spoke on the 27th of February for Ponsonby's motion of Censure on Ministers, and on the 28th for Vandeleur's motion for an Absentee Tax, but I could not get reports of these speeches. His speech on the Disarming of Ulster is very ill reported, but the subject is most important, and the peroration seems preserved. In order to make this speech intelligible, I prefix the following proceedings in the house, on Saturday, the 18th of March, 1797:—

MESSAGE FROM THE LORD LIEUTENANT.

Mr. Secretary Pelham delivered to the house a message from his Excellency, stating that the insurrectionary spirit which had manifested itself in certain districts in the province of Ulster, had rendered it necessary to the Lord Lieutenant and Council to issue a proclamation, declaring those districts in a state of disturbance; and his Excellency had in consequence conveyed instructions to General Lake, to assist the magistrates in disarming the inhabitants of those districts in which the General had already succeeded in a considerable extent.

Mr. Pelham moved that the house do on Monday resolve itself into a committee, in order to take his Excellency's message into consideration Ordered accordingly.

The following is a copy of General Luke's proclamation, in consequence of the instructions above alluded to, addressed to the people of the province of Ulster.

"Belfast, March 13th, 1797.

"Whereas, the daring and horrid outrages in many parts of this province, evidently perpetrated with a view to supersede the laws and the administration of justice, by an organised system of murder and robbery, have increased to such an alarming degree, as from their atrocity and extent to bid defiance to the civil power, and to endanger the lives and properties of his Majesty's faithful subjects. And whereas, the better to effect their traitorous purposes, several persons who have been enrolled under the authority of his Majesty's commissions, and others, have been forcibly and traitorously deprived of their arms; it is therefore become indispensably necessary for the safety and protection of the well-disposed, to interpose the King's troops under my command: and I do hereby give notice that I have received authority and directions to act in such a manner as the public safety may require.

"I do therefore hereby enjoin and require all persons in this district (peace officers and those serving in a military capacity excepted) forthwith to bring in and surrender up all arms and ammunition which they may have in their possession, to the officer commanding the king's troops in their neighbourhood.

"I trust that an immediate compliance with this order may render any act of mine to enforce it unnecessary.

"Let the people seriously reflect, before it is too late, on the ruin into which they are rushing; let them reflect on their present prosperity, and the miseries into which they will inevitably be involved by persisting in acts of positive rebellion; let them instantly, by surrendering up their arms, and by restoring those traitorously taken from the King's forces, rescue themselves from the severity of military authority. Let all the loyal and well-intentioned act together with energy and spirit, in enforcing subordination to the laws and restoring tranquillity in their respective neighbourhoods, and they may be assured of protection and support from me.

"And I do hereby invite all persons who are enabled to give information touching arms and ammunition which may be concealed, immediately to communicate the same to the several officers commanding his Majesty's forces in their respective districts; and for their encouragement and reward, I do hereby promise and engage that strict and inviolate secrecy shall be observed, with respect to all persons who shall make such communication; and that every person who shall make it, shall receive as a reward the full value of all such arms and ammunition as shall be seized in consequence thereof.

"G. LAKE, Lieut-Gen.
"Commanding the Northern District."

On Monday, accordingly, Mr. Annesley being Chairman of a Committee of the whole house, Mr. Ogle moved an address approving the preceding message, and Grattan moved an amendment. I give his noble opening, and the words of his amendment:—

"The worst news I have heard of late, and I have heard much bad news of late, is the message from the Lord Lieutenant, attainting one entire province of Ireland of high treason. This parliament is desired to assent to that attainder forthwith, and to put the province of Ulster under military execution. We are called to do this without inquiry of any sort; and without the delay of a moment, we are called upon to do that with respect to the most flourishing part of our country which could not be done in the case of an individual: we are called upon to attaint a *people*—to attaint a *people* for high treason, on the charge preferred by a *minister*: we are called upon to do this without evidence, inquiry, trial, or the delay of a moment, to proceed against our own country with less justice or ceremony than were observed by the revolutionary tribunals of France. An Irish parliament is called upon to take the word of a minister, and on that word to attaint their country of treason. Who are the people whom they attaint of treason, and consign to military execution? They are the men who placed William III. on the throne of this kingdom; they are the men who, when the English parliament had trampled on your rights, enabled you to claim those rights, and armed as Volunteers to defend their country against foreign enemies and domestic tyrants, and carried you on their back while you preferred your claim of right. Yes, you were carried on the back of an armed people, to the sounding of martial music—better harmony than such addresses as these; you were carried on the back of an armed people, and forced or indeed ravished into the temple of freedom. And now you are to 'sell your redeemer, and deliver him up to bondage!' You are now to deprive of their arms, those very men, at the desire of some of those who would have hanged you for disputing the usurpations of the British parliament, but for those arms.'—*Debates*, vol. xvii. pp. 131, 32.

AMENDMENT.

"That we cannot avoid expressing our profound, heartfelt concern, that his Excellency should have been advised to issue an order contrary to the law of the land and the principles of the constitution, which cannot be enforced without violating every thing which is dear to a free people, and without the introduction of military government, and military execution. We do, therefore, most humbly entreat his Excellency to recall the same. We shall, on our parts, inquire into the present state of the country, to enable us to take such measures as her interest may require."

After a very long debate, in which Col. Blacquiere, Mr. Alexander, Mr. Sergeant Stanley, Mr. Archdall, Mr. John Claudius Beresford, the Attorney-General, the Prime-Sergeant, Mr. Egan, Mr. Maxwell, Mr. Pelham, supported the government address, and Sir Thomas Osborne, Mr. W. Smith, Mr. Jephson, Mr. Fletcher, Mr. Hoare, Mr. Ponsonby, sustained Grattan's amendment, Curran said:—

The weakness of my health has kept me silent in the early stage of the debate. As it advanced I felt less inclination to rise, because I saw clearly, whatever a majority might think, how it was resolved to vote. The speech, however, of the last speaker made it impossible for me to sit silent, or to withhold my reprobation of the doctrines which the right honourable gentleman (Mr. Pelham) has advanced. That gentleman has stated, that the prerogative was wisely left undefined and unlimited, and warranted the disarming the North, if such an act was expedient Before the honourable member becomes a teacher in constitution, he would do well to begin by becoming a learner, and he will easily learn that his idea is an utter mistake. A prerogative without limit is a dispensing power; he will learn that for having assumed such a power James II. lost his crown. It is the great merit of the British constitution that no such power exists. It is, on the contrary, the limitation of the prerogative by law that distinguishes a lawful magistrate from a tyrant, and a subject from a slave. Every prerogative is defined in its nature and extent, though the exercise of it, so defined and limited, is very properly left to the discretion of the crown. The King, for example, has the prerogative of making peace or war—or calling or dissolving a parliament. This prerogative rests merely on the authority of law, but the time or manner of doing any of these things is wisely left to the discretion of the crown; nor is that discretion wild and arbitrary, for the minister is responsible with his head. The honourable gentleman has made two assertions: first, that the crown has the power of disarming the people by its prerogative; and, next, that in the present instance the act was just and necessary. In fact, the second position of the honourable member is a complete abandonment of his first; for if the people are disarmed by virtue of the prerogative, why come to this house? The truth is, the gentleman's conduct shows he does not know the constitution on this subject. The Right Hon. Attorney-General has done right in declaring that the Viceroy has broken the law in the order to disarm the people. The order, as to any man acting under it, was a perfect nullity, and any man was answerable for what he might commit under such an order, as a mere common offender. But examine the second position itself, that at this time it is just and necessary. Why? Because the North is in a state of rebellion, and rebellion may be resisted by an armed force. Are they in open arrayed rebellion? Not so; but they are in secret and organized rebellion, and the prevention is necessary. See the horrors that result when government are suffered to desert the known laws, and to wander into their own stupid and fantastic analogies. We find the same exactness of knowledge which the minister has shown in the doctrine of prerogative displayed in his curious distinction in the law of treason; he thinks a secret system of treason, unattended by any act, the same with treason arrayed in arms. Having assumed so monstrous a position in defiance of the known law, that calls nothing treason that is not proveable by overt act, see whither his own reasoning must lead him. If open rebellion, and this mere treason in intention be the same, then the same remedies must be lawful in both cases You may assist and resist open rebellion by armed force; you may mow it down in the field—you may burn it in its camp. By the gentleman's own doctrine—having first assumed this intentional treason—he would be justified in covering the North with massacre and conflagration. [On this part of the subject, Mr. Curran went into a variety of observations. He next examined the evidence on which we were to publish to the world, to the enemy, that the most valuable and enlightened part of the nation was in rebellion, without inquiry, without even the assertion of any specific fact!] How can we look the public in the face, if we surrender ourselves so meanly to a British agent, or surrender our country to military law, without evidence or inquiry? I will put a serious question:—if the government think fit to supersede all law, and to substitute the bayonet, what must be the consequence? It freezes my blood to think of it; I cannot bring myself to state it in a public assembly. But the government are loud in their invectives on the North. Is it possible that the detection of their folly can drive ministers, not into self-conviction or amendment, but into fury? The North, I am sure, is deeply discontented; but owing to what cause? To your own laws; to your convention act, to your gunpowder act, to your insurrection act. The first denies the natural right of sufferers—the right of petition or complaint; the second, the power of self-defence by arms against brutal force; and the third, the defence of a jury against the attempts of power. What else could you expect? You were in vain warned that you would at last bring the nation to the state in which it is said to be. Such laws can only deprave and infect the people. Put a spaniel in the chain, and you corrupt the gentleness of his nature, and make him fierce and ferocious; put a people in the chain, and you do the same. And what is the remedy? Only one. Set them both at large, and liberty will infallibly effect a cure. Repeal your cruel and foolish laws—restore the constitution to its natural mildness, and you will soon find the natural effects. Gentlemen have condemned the idea of an appeal to the sister nation for assistance, and condemned the interference of Lord Moira and Mr. Fox, as trenching on our independence. I commend their conduct as that of the most generous sympathy to our sinking situation, and the most patriotic to their own country. It was not an interference with the freedom of our legislation, but with the ruinous corruption of our own government, in which, as subjects of the empire, they have an interest, and therefore a right of saying to their sovereign—" Sir, your ministers are degrading the common constitution of Ireland—they are enslaving the people, debauching its parliament, and driving the country to madness." To censure such a conduct strikes my mind as the last and lowest extreme of degeneracy and shame. To bark at those who had virtue to make a struggle for our safety, which we had not virtue to make for ourselves.— Rare pride! Oh, rare and proud spirit of independence! Oh, pure and jealous representatives of your country! Oh, dignified assertion of a right of suicide! Oh, glorious assertion of your sacred right of abandoning your country, and selling its representation! Oh, high-souled declaration, worthy to be recorded, and worthy of those that make it ; We *will* be drowned, and nobody *shall* save us. A gentleman said, sneeringly, he was pleased we were reduced to seven ; I now thank him for his taunt—I am grateful for the reproach. Never did I feel it as a charge; I now feel it as an acquittal from all participation of such perverseness and degradation. My sentiments are decidedly in favour of the amendment.—*Debates*, vol. xvii., pp. 160—163.

Grattan followed, and, after a violent altercation between him and Egan, the motion was rejected by 127 to 16.

LAST SPEECH IN THE IRISH COMMONS.

May 15th, 1797.

The reader has seen the decreasing minorities of the party who gallantly struggled to maintain the parliamentary constitution of Ireland. But they grew daily more powerless. The people looked to the United Irish Executive, to France, to arms, to revolution. The government persisted in refusing Reform and Emancipation, continued the suspension of the constitution, and incessantly augmented the despotism of their laws, the profligacy of their administration, and the violence of their soldiery—they trusted to intimidation. Under these circumstances, the opposition determined to abandon the contest. They did unwisely. They might have embarrassed ministers seriously in the following year, and they did not so, nor did they join the military organization of the patriots.

The pre-determined secession took place on the 15th May, 1797. As the proceedings are of peculiar interest, I copy them from the *Debates* :—

The expectation of the very important business which was announced for this evening, the Reform in the Representation, had filled the galleries at three o'clock. The speaker took the chair at four, and proceeded to business. Two debates followed—the one on the Lords' address, the other on the Reform. The house continued to sit until past five next morning.

Lord Castlereagh pre-occupied the attention of the house by moving, that the address of the Lords on the subject of the treasonable papers, be now taken into consideration. The address contained strong expressions of the loyalty and affection of the house—alluded in very strong terms to the enormity and extent of this traitorous conspiracy—thanked his Majesty for the measures which had been already taken for restoring the due observation of the laws, and recommended to his adoption the most severe measures for the complete suppression of these dangerous disorders. His lordship animadverted on the danger of the conspiracy which had given occasion to this address—stated its object to be the overthrow of our most excellent constitution, and the separation of this country from Great Britain—that the evidence in proof of these assertions had been so full that even the most sceptic could not doubt, and so plain that no man could question the inferences which had been made by their lordships. His lordship then entered into a long and minute history of the society of United Irishmen, repeating nearly what had been said on that subject in the report of the Secret Committee. He deprecated, in any debate which might arise on this question, the admixture of any foreign matter with this particular subject, which was simply an inquiry into the most extraordinary mass of treason which had ever appeared in the country; to introduce any other matter into the debate would be construed by the ignorance of the country as a proof that treason and traitors had abettors even within those walls. A speech of much vehemence against the United Irishmen, &c., was concluded by a motion—" that the Commons should agree with their Lordships in this address."

Mr. Grattan declared that he did not on this subject wish to bring on a debate, as he would reserve the opinion which he meant to give at large on the state of the country, for the debate on the question of Reform. He could not help, however, declaring, that to that part of the address which expressed approbation of the measures of government, he was bound in consistency not to give any approbation, neither could he do so of that part which prayed for a continuance of coercion, because he believed in his conscience that such measures could be productive of no good.

Mr. Smith, after a short preface, moved an amendment, which alone could reconcile him to the address. His amendment was in substance a request that his Majesty would use conciliatory measures to remove every pretext of discontent from the well-disposed, as well as measures of coercion for the prevention and punishment of conspiracy and treason— urging the necessity of correcting abuses, as well as adopting strong laws to repress disaffection, &c.

This amendment introduced much very animated conversation from Mr George Ponsonby, Mr. Fletcher, Mr. Jephson, Mr Grattan, and Mr. Hoare, who supported the amendment, which was opposed by the Attorney-General, Denis Browne, Mr. Egan, Sir B. Roche, Mr. Alexander, Messrs. J. and M. Beresford, Mr. Ogle, Mr. Toler, and Mr. Annesley.

The most contentious topic in the debate was an expression which fell from Mr. Fletcher in the course of his speech, in which he said, that if coercive measures were to be pursued, the whole country must be coerced, for the *spirit of insurrection had pervaded every part of it.*

Mr. M. Beresford ordered the clerk to take down these words, and the gallery was instantly cleared. When strangers were again admitted, the debate on the address still continued, and in the course of it Mr. J. C. Beresford thought himself called on to defend the Secret Committee against an assertion which had fallen from Mr. Fletcher in the course of his speech. The assertion was in substance that he feared the people would be led to look on the report of the committee as fabricated rather to justify the past measures of Government, than to state facts!

Mr. Fletcher contended that he had a right to animadvert on the report, but disclaimed any design of imputing anything unfair to the members of that committee individually.

In the course of the altercation which followed on this subject, Mr. Toler threatened, and actually did move an abstract resolution, declaring that the imputation conveyed in these words (of Mr. Fletcher) was an unfounded calumny on the report. He was at length, however, persuaded to withdraw his motion. The house then divided on Mr. Smith's amendment which was ost without a division.

PARLIAMENTARY REFORM.

Mr W. Ponsonby in a short prefatory speech, proposed his Resolutions on Parliamentary Reform. Before he moved any of them specifically, he read them all to the house. They are in substance as follow:—

" Resolved, that it is indispensably necessary to a fundamental reform of the representation, that all disabilities on account of religion be for ever abolished, and that Catholics shall be admitted into the legislature, and all the great offices of state in the same extent, &c., as Protestants now are.

" That it is the indispensable right of the people of Ireland to be fully and fairly represented in Parliament.

" That in order that the people may be fully enabled to exercise that right, the privilege of returning members for cities, boroughs, &c., in the present form shall cease; that each county be divided into districts, consisting of 6000 houses each, each district to return two members to parliament.

" That all persons possessing freehold property to the amount of 40s. per annum; all possessed of household interests, of the value of   ; all possessed of a house of the value of   ; all who have resided for a certain number of years in any great city or town, following a trade; and all who shall be free of any city, &c., by birth, marriage, or servitude, shall vote for members of parliament.

" That seats in parliament shall endure for   number of years. (The blanks were left to be filled up by the discretion of the house.)"—*Debates,* vol. xvii., pp. 527-30.

Mr. Pelham moved and spoke for an adjournment, and was supported by Mr. D. Browne, Mr. M. Beresford, Sir H. Langrishe, Sir Frederick Flood, Mr. M. Mason, Mr C. Osborne, Mr. William Smyth (afterwards judge, whom Curran followed): some opposing emancipation, some reform, some resisting the proposal of Ponsonby as ill-timed, or as Browne said " thatching a house in a hurricane." The original motion was sustained by Mr. Stewart (of Killymoon), Sir J. Freake, George Ponsonby, Mr. Jephson, the Knight of Kerry (Mr. Fitzgerald), Mr. Fletcher (afterwards judge), and Counsellor Hoare (of whom Curran used to say, his smile was like the shining of the brass plate on a coffin).

I consider this as a measure of justice, with respect to the Catholics, and the people at large. The Catholics in former times groaned under the malignant folly of penal laws—wandered like herds upon the earth —or gathered under some thread-bare grandee, who came to Dublin, danced attendance at the Castle, was smiled on by the secretary, and carried back to his miserable countrymen the gracious promise of favour and protection. They are no longer mean dependants, but owners of their country, and claiming simply and boldly, as Irishmen, the national privileges of men, and natives of their country. [Upon this part of the question, he went into a variety of very interesting topics, descriptive of their importance and their oppressions, which he attributed wholly to the wicked propagation of religious antipathies, and concluded that their claim to perfect freedom in their own land could be denied only by the grossest malignity and tyranny.]

I now proceed to answer the objections to the measure. I was extremely shocked to see the agent of a foreign cabinet rise up in the assembly that ought to represent the Irish nation, and oppose a motion that was made on the acknowledged and deplored corruption which has been imported from his country. Such an opposition is a proof of the charge, which I am astonished he could venture upon at so awful a crisis. I doubt whether the charge, or this proof of it, would appear most odious. However, I will examine the objections. It is said—It is not the time. This argument has become a jest in Ireland, for it has been used in all times; in war, in peace, in quiet, and in disturbance. It is the miserable, dilatory plea of persevering and stupid corruption, that wishes to postpone its fate by a promise of amendment, which it is resolved never to perform. Reform has become an exception to the proverb that says, there is a time for all things; but for Reform there is no time, because at all times corruption is more profitable to its authors that public virtue and propriety, which they know must be fatal to their views. As to the present time, the objections to it are a compound of the most unblushing impudence and folly. Forsooth it would seem as if the house had yielded through fear. Personal bravery or fear are inapplicable to a public assembly. I know no cowardice so despicable as the fear of seeming to be afraid. To be afraid of danger is not an unnatural sensation; but to be brave in absurdity and injustice, merely from fear of having your sense or honesty imputed to your own apprehension, is a stretch of folly which I have never heard of before. But the time is pregnant with arguments very different, indeed, from those I have heard; I mean the report of the Secret Committee, and the dreadful state of the country. The allegation is, that the people are not to have justice, because a rebellion exists within, and because we have an enemy at our gates—because, forsooth, reform is only a pretext, and separation is the object of the leaders. If a rebellion exist, every good subject ought to be detached from it. But if an enemy threaten to invade us, it is only common sense to detach every subject from the hostile standard, and bring him back to his duty and his country.

The present miserable state of Ireland—its distractions, its distresses, its bankruptcy, are the effects of the war, and it is the duty of the authors of that war to reconcile the people by the most timely and liberal justice; the utmost physical strength should be called forth, and that can be done only by union. This is a subject so tremendous, I do not wish to dwell on it, I will therefore leave it; I will support a Reform on its own merits, and as a measure of internal peace at this most momentous juncture. Its merits are admitted by the objection to the time, because the objection admits that at any other time it would be proper. For twenty years past there was no man of any note in England or Ireland who did not consider the necessity of it as a maxim; they all saw and confessed that the people are not represented, and that they have not the benefit of a mixed monarchy. They have a monarchy which absorbs the two other estates, and, therefore, they have the insupportable expense of a monarchy, an aristocracy, and a democracy, without the simplicity or energy of any one of those forms of government. In Ireland this is peculiarly fatal, because the honest representation of the people is swallowed in the corruption and intrigue of a cabinet of another country. From this may be deduced the low estate of the Irish people; their honest labour is wasted in pampering their betrayers, instead of being employed, as it ought to be, in accommodating themselves and their children. On these miserable consequences of corruption, and which are all the fatal effects of inadequate representation, I do not wish to dwell. To expatiate too much on them might be unfair, but to suppress them would be treason to the public. It is said, that reform is only a pretence, and that separation is the real object of leaders; if this be so, confound the leaders by destroying the pretext, and take the followers to yourselves. You say there are one hundred thousand; I firmly believe there is three times the number. So much the better for you: if these seducers can attach so many followers to rebellion, by the hope of reform, through blood, how much more readily will you engage them, not by the promise, but the possession, and without blood? You allude to the British fleet; learn from it to avoid the fatal consequence that may follow even a few days' delay of justice. It is said to be only a pretext; I am convinced of the contrary—I am convinced the people are sincere, and would be satisfied by it. I think so from the perseverance in petitioning for it for a number of years; I think so, because I think a monarchy, properly balanced by a fair representation of the people, gives as perfect liberty as the most celebrated republics of old. But, of the real attraction of this object of reform, you have a proof almost miraculous: the desire of reform has annihilated religious antipathy, and united the country. In the history of mankind it is the only instance of so fatal a religious fanaticism being discarded by the good sense of mankind, instead of dying slowly by the development of its folly. And I am persuaded the hints thrown out this night, to make the different sects jealous of each other, will be a detected trick, and will only unite them still more closely. The Catholics have given a pledge to their countrymen of their sincerity and their zeal, which cannot fail of producing the most firm reliance; they have solemnly disclaimed all idea of what is called emancipation, except as a part of that reform without which their Presbyterian brethren could not be free. Reform is a necessary change of mildness for coercion. The latter has been tried; what is its success? The convention bill was passed to punish the meetings at Dungannon, and those of the Catholics: the government considered the Catholic concessions as defeats that called for vengeance, and cruelly have they avenged them. But did that act, or those which followed it, put down those meetings? The contrary was the fact. It concealed them most foolishly. When popular discontents are abroad, a wise government should put them into a hive of glass. You hid them. The association, at first, was small; the earth seemed to drink it as a rivulet, but it only disappeared for a season. A thousand streams, through the secret windings of the earth, found their way to one course, and swelled its waters, until at last, too mighty to be contained, it burst out a great river, fertilizing by its exudations, or terrifying by its cataracts. This is the effect of our penal code: it swelled sedition into rebellion. What else could be hoped from a system of terrorism? Fear is the most transient of all the passions—it is the warning that nature gives for self-preservation. But when safety is unattainable, the warning must be useless, and nature does not, therefore, give it. Administration, therefore, mistook the quality of penal laws; they were sent out to abolish conventions, but they did not pass the threshold—they stood sentinels at the gates. You think that penal laws, like great dogs, will wag their tails to their masters, and bark only at their enemies. You are mistaken—they turn and devour those they are meant to protect, and are harmless where they are intended to destroy. I see gentlemen laugh; I see they are still very ignorant of the nature of fear; it cannot last; neither while it does can it be concealed. The feeble glimmering of a forced smile is a light that makes the cheek look paler. Trust me, the times are too humanised for such systems of government. Humanity will not execute them, but humanity will abhor them, and those who wish to rule by such means. This is not theory; the experiment has been tried, and proved. You hoped much, and, I doubt not, meant well by those laws; but they have miserably failed you—it is time to try milder methods. You have tried to force the people: the rage of your penal laws was a storm that only drove them in groups to shelter. Your convention law gave them that organization which is justly an object of such alarm; and the very proclamation seems to have given them arms. Before it is too late, therefore, try the better force of reason, and conciliate them by justice and humanity. The period of coercion in Ireland is gone, nor can it ever return until the people shall return to the folly and to the natural weakness of disunion. Neither let us talk of innovation; the progress of nature is no innovation. The increase of people, with the growth of the mind, is no innovation; it is no way alarming, unless the growth of our minds lag behind. If we think otherwise, and think it an innovation to depart from the folly of our infancy, we should come here in our swaddling-clothes, we should not innovate upon the dress, more than the understanding of the cradle. As to the system of peace now proposed, you must take it on principles—they are simply two, the abolition of religious disabilities, and the representation of the people. I am confident the effects would be everything to be wished. The present alarming discontent will vanish, the good will be separated from the evil-intentioned; the friends of mixed government in Ireland are many; every sensible man must see that it gives all the enjoyment of rational liberty if the people have their due piace in the state. This system would make us invincible against a foreign or domestic enemy; it would make the empire strong at this important crisis; it would restore to us liberty, industry, and peace, which I am satisfied can never by any other means be restored. Instead, therefore, of abusing the people, let us remember that there is no physical strength but theirs, and conciliate them by justice and reason. I am censured heavily for having acted for them in the late prosecutions. I feel no shame at such a charge, except that, at such a time as this, to defend the people should be held out as an imputation upon a king's counsel, when the people are prosecuted by the state. I think every counsel is the property of his fellow-subjects. If, indeed, because I wore his Majesty's gown, I had declined my duty, or done it weakly or treacherously—if I had made that gown a mantle of hypocrisy, and betrayed my client, or sacrificed him to any personal view, I might, perhaps, have been thought wiser by those who have blamed me, but I should have thought myself the basest villain upon earth. The plan of peace, proposed by a Reform, is the only means that I and my friends can see left to save us. It is certainly a time for decision, and not for half measures. I agree that unanimity is indispensable. The house seems pretty nearly unanimous for force; I am sorry for it, for I bode the worst from it. I will retire from a scene where I can do no good—where I certainly would interrupt that unanimity. I cannot, however, go, without a parting entreaty, that gentlemen will reflect on the awful responsibility in which they stand to their country and to their conscience, before they set the example to the people of abandoning the constitution and the law, and resorting to the terrible expedient of force.—*Debates*, vol. xvii., pp. 553—8.

Grattan followed him, closing the debate, his speech, and the attendance of the opposition, in these words:-

Before they are to be reformed, rebellion, you tell us, must be subdued. You tried that experiment in America. America required self-legislation; you attempted to subdue America by force of angry laws, and by force of arms—you exacted of America unconditional submission—the stamp act and the tea tax were only pretexts. So you said. The object, you said, was separation. So here the Reform of Parliament, you say, and Catholic Emancipation are only pretexts: the object you say is separation. And here you exact unconditional submission: "YOU MUST SUBDUE BEFORE YOU REFORM"—indeed! Alas, you think so: but you forget you subdue by reforming. It is the best conquest you can obtain over your own people. But let me suppose you succeed; what is your success? A military government, a perfect despotism, a hapless victory over the principles of a mild government and a mild constitution. But what may be the ultimate consequence of such a victory?—a separation. Let us suppose that the war continues, and that your conquest over your own people is interrupted by a French invasion. What would be your situation then? I do not wish to think of it; but I wish you to think of it, and to make a better preparation against such an event than such conquests and such victories. When you consider the state of your arms abroad, and the ill-assured state of your government at home, precipitating on such a system, surely you should pause a little. Even on the event of a peace you are ill-secured against a future war, which the state of Ireland, under such a system, would be too apt to invite; but in the event of the continuation of the war, your system is perilous, indeed. I speak without asperity—I speak without resentment; I speak, perhaps, my delusion, but it is my heart-felt conviction—I speak my apprehension for the immediate state of our liberty, and for the ultimate state of the empire. I see, or I imagine I see, in this system, everything which is dangerous to both. I hope I am mistaken—at least, I hope I exaggerate; possibly I may. If so, I shall acknowledge my error with more satisfaction than is usual in the acknowledgment of error. I cannot, however, banish from my memory the lesson of the American war: and yet at that time the English government was at the head of Europe, and was possessed of resources comparatively unbroken. If that lesson has no effect on ministers, surely I can suggest nothing that will. We have offered you our measure—you will reject it; we deprecate yours—you will persevere. Having no hopes left to persuade or dissuade, and having discharged our duty, we shall trouble you no more, and, AFTER THIS DAY, SHALL NOT ATTEND THE HOUSE OF COMMONS!—*Debates*, vol. xvii., pp. 569—70.

The question being put on the adjournment it was carried:—for it, 170; against it, 30.

The opposition ceased to attend, and the parliament, after a few sittings, was adjourned in a speech from the Lord Lieutenant, of unusual length, on the 3rd of July, 1797. Thus, in the twilight of his country, ended Curran's parliamentary career; but in the awful night which followed, he was a beacon.

FOR PETER FINNERTY,
PUBLISHER OF "THE PRESS."
[LIBEL.]
December 22nd, 1797.

THE Government and the United Irishmen were now face to face, the former armed with a full code of coercion and a large army and unscrupulous agents to support it—the latter with a good cause, the organization given by Tone, and the prospect of French aid. Each party tried to strengthen itself by conciliation and intimidation. Among the government instruments were spies (such as Magnane and others, chronicled in Dr. Madden's work), "the battalion of testimony" (Bird, Newell, O'Brien, &c.), free quarters, prosecutions, bribery, patronage, and calumny.

One of the best auxiliaries summoned by the United Irishmen was "*The Press*" newspaper.

The first number of it was published in Dublin, on Thursday, the 28th of September, 1797, and was thence continued on Tuesdays, Thursdays, and Saturdays, until Tuesday the 13th of March, 1798, when the 69th and last number was seized by the government. It was not, like the *Northern Star*, a chronicle of French politics. It was a true propagandist organ of Liberal and National opinions, filled with essays, letters, and addresses of great ability. Arthur O'Connor mainly originated it, and he, Thomas Emmet, Drennan, Sampson, &c., wrote it.

Government naturally longed to crush such a paper, as it had done the *Northern Star*, but raw force was premature for Dublin, so they waited for a libel, and, as they gave plenty of provocation, they waited not long. They found one, which irritated them deeply, while it gave them a good opening, in a letter published on Thursday, the 26th of October, 1797, addressed to the Lord Lieutenant, signed "Marcus." Most of the letter is set out in the indictment; so are the legal facts which were the text of it, but it is right to say something more of them.

William Orr was a Presbyterian farmer, resident at Farranshane, in the County of Antrim—a man of pious, gentle, and gallant character; a tall, athletic, and hearty fellow, too, and popular exceedingly. He was arrested in 1796, under the Insurrection Act (passed in the February of that year), for having, in April, 1796, administered the United Irish oath to Hugh Wheatly, a private in the Fifeshire Fencibles. He was indicted at Carrickfergus, on the 17th April, 1797, and tried on Saturday, 16th of September, 1797, before Chief Baron Lord Yelverton. The chief witness was Wheatly, who deposed that Orr acted as chairman or Secretary of a Baronial Committee in Antrim, where Wheatly was induced to go, and was there forced to take the oath. Lindsay, a private in the same corps, swore that he *saw* the oath administered, but did not hear it. Curran and Sampson, Orr's counsel, contended that this was a case for a prosecution for high treason, but Yelverton decided otherwise, and charged for a conviction. The jury retired at seven at night, and came into court at six o'clock on Sunday morning, and after much confusion (from conscience or intoxication) gave in a verdict of Guilty, with a recommendation to mercy, which Yelverton sent by express to the Castle. On Monday, the 18th, Curran moved for a new trial, on the affidavit of two of the jurors, stating the drunkenness of some of the jurors, and the intimidation used to one of the deponents. He had an affidavit from a third juror, swearing that he was deceived into the verdict, but Orr was sentenced to be hanged on the 7th of October. Orr declared at the close of the trial that he was innocent. Various attempts were made to save him. His brother James signed a declaration of his guilt and a prayer for mercy, in William's name, and got it backed by the gentry; but William disclaimed it. It was also sworn by a Presbyterian clergyman that Wheatly had confessed himself guilty of murder, perjury, and other crimes. In consequence of all this, Orr was thrice respited, and judging from the conciliatory and beseeching tone of *The Press* (No. 5), Government seems to have had an opportunity of making themselves popular, and weakening the United Irishmen by a just lenience. They preferred the harsh course, and on Saturday, the 14th of October, Orr was hanged, outside Carrickfergus, amid a mass of troops. He distributed a written paper, declaring his innocence, and died calmly and nobly. He left five children, and a wife, about again to be a mother.

Indignation was nigh universal. Medals with "Remember Orr!" were circulated; his name became a watchword (and continued so, as Sheares' proclamation proves); "The Ministers in Orr's place" was a toast even in England, and Fox spoke of him as a martyr. That he was a United Irishman is clear; but that he gave Wheatly the oath, or was therefore guilty in law is not probable. Guilty or not, his execution for such a crime, on such evidence, and after such a verdict, was a murder! So it was treated in the letter of "Marcus." The author was a Mr Deane Swift, a frequent contributor to "*The Press.*"

On Tuesday, the 31st of October, Major Sirr arrested Peter Finnerty, at 62, Abbey-street, (The *Press* office), for this publication, under a Judge's warrant, and put him into Newgate, and on Thursday he was brought, handcuffed, before Mr. Jameson, K.C., acting Judge at the Commission Court; true bills were found; he was indicted in the dock, being refused liberty to bail. He was thence sent back to Newgate, where he was exposed to threats to force a confession, but he was steady, and on Friday, the 22nd of December, was tried before Justice Downes at the Commission Court. The indictment stated,

"That at a general assizes and general gaol delivery, holden at Carrickfergus, in and for the County of Antrim, on the 17th day of April, in the thirty-seventh year of the King, before the Honourable Mathias Finucane, one of the Judges of his Majesty's Court of Common Pleas in Ireland, and the Honourable Denis George, one of the Barons of his Majesty's Court of Exchequer in Ireland, Justices and Commissioners assigned to deliver the gao. of our said Lord the King, in and for the County of Antrim, of the several prisoners and malefactors therein, one William Orr, late of Farranshane, in said county of Antrim, yeoman, was in lawful manner indicted for feloniously administering a certain oath and engagement, upon a book, to one Hugh Wheatly; which oath and engagement imported to bind the said Hugh Wheatly, who then and there took the same, to be of an association, brotherhood, and Society, formed for seditious purposes; and also for feloniously causing, procuring, and inducing said Hugh Wheatly, to take an oath of said import last mentioned; and also for feloniously administering to said Hugh Wheatly another oath, importing to bind said Hugh Wheatly not to inform or give evidence against any brother, associate, or confederate, of a certain society then and there formed; and also for feloniously causing, procuring, and seducing said Hugh Wheatly to take an oath of said import last mentioned. And afterwards at Carrickfergus aforesaid, before the Right Honourable Barry Lord Yelverton, Lord Chief Baron of his Majesty's Court of Exchequer in Ireland, and the Honourable Tankerville Chamberlain, one of his Majesty's Justices of his Court of Chief Pleas in Ireland, at a general assizes, &c., on the 16th day of September, in the 37th year of the King, said William Orr, by the verdict of a certain jury of said county of Antrim, between our said Lord the King and said William Orr, taken of and for the felony aforesaid in due manner, was tried, convicted, and attainted, and for the same was duly executed: and that he, the said Peter Finnerty, well knowing the premises, but being a wicked and ill-disposed person, and of unquiet conversation and disposition, and devising and intending to molest and disturb the peace and public tranquillity of this kingdom of Ireland; and to bring and draw the trial aforesaid, and the verdict thereon, for our said Lord the King against this William Orr given, and the due course of law in that behalf had, as aforesaid, into hatred, contempt, and scandal, with all the liege subjects of our said Lord the King; and to persuade, and cause the subjects of our said Lord the King to believe that the trial aforesaid was unduly had, and that the said William Orr did undeservedly die in manner aforesaid and that his Excellency John Jefferys, Earl Camden, the Lord Lieutenant of this kingdom, after the conviction aforesaid, ought to have extended to the said William Orr, his Majesty's gracious pardon of the felonies aforesaid; and that in not so extending such pardon, he, the said Lord Lieutenant, had acted inhumanly, wickedly, and unjustly, and in a manner unworthy of the trust which had been committed to him by our said Lord the King in that behalf; and that the said Lord Lieutenant in his government of this kingdom, had acted unjustly, cruelly, and oppressively, to his Majesty's subjects therein: And the said Peter Finnerty, to fulfil and bring to effect his most wicked and detestable devices and intentions aforesaid, on the 26th of October, in the 37th year of the King, at Mountrath-street aforesaid, city of Dublin aforesaid, falsely, wickedly, maliciously, and seditiously did print and publish, and cause and procure to be printed and published, in a certain newspaper entitled '*The Press*,' a certain false, wicked, malicious and seditious libel, of and concerning the said trial, conviction, attainder, and execution of the said William Orr, as aforesaid, and of and concerning the said Lord Lieutenant and his government of this kingdom, and his Majesty's Ministers employed by him in his government of this kingdom, according to the tenor and effect following, to wit:—

"'The death of Mr. Orr, (meaning the execution of the said William Orr) the nation has pronounced one of the most sanguinary and savage acts that had disgraced the laws. In perjury, did you not hear, my Lord (meaning the said Lord Lieutenant,) the verdict (meaning the verdict aforesaid) was given? Perjury accompanied with terror, as terror has marked every step of your government (meaning the government of this kingdom aforesaid, by the said Lord Lieutenant). Vengeance and desolation were to fall on those who would not plunge themselves in blood. These were not strong enough: against the express law of the land, not only was drink introduced to the jury (meaning the jury aforesaid), but drunkenness itself, beastly and criminal drunkenness, was employed to procure the murder of a better man (meaning the said execution of the said William Orr) than any that now surrounds you (meaning the said Lord Lieutenant).'

"'And in another part thereof, according to the tenor and effect following, to wit:—
"'Repentance, which is a slow virtue, hastened, however, to declare the innocence of the victim (meaning the said William Orr); the mischief (meaning the said conviction of the said William Orr) which perjury had done, truth now stepped forward to repair. Neither

S

was she too late, had humanity formed any part of your counsels (meaning the counsels of the said Lord Lieutenant). Stung with remorse, on the return of reason, part of his jury (meaning the jury aforesaid) solemnly and soberly made oath that their verdict (meaning the verdict aforesaid) had been given under the unhappy influence of intimidation and drink; and in the most serious affidavit that ever was made, by acknowledging their crime, endeavoured to atone to God and to their country, for the sin into which they had been seduced."

" And in another part thereof, according to the tenor and effect following, to wit :—

"'And though the innocence of the accused (meaning the said William Orr) had even remained doubtful, it was your duty (meaning the duty of the said Lord Lieutenant), my Lord, and you, (meaning the said Lord Lieutenant) had no exemption from that duty, to have interposed your arm, and saved him (meaning the said William Orr) from the death (meaning the execution aforesaid) that perjury, drunkenness, and reward had prepared for him (meaning the said William Orr.) Let not the nation be told that you (meaning the Lord Lieutenant) are a passive instrument in the hands of others ; if passive you be, then is your office a shadow indeed. If an active instrument, as you ought to be, you (meaning the said Lord Lieutenant) did not perform the duty which the laws required of you; you (meaning the said Lord Lieutenant) did not exercise the prerogative of mercy ; that mercy which the constitution had entrusted to you (meaning the said Lord Lieutenant) for the safety of the subject, by guarding him from the oppression of wicked men. Innocent it appears he (meaning the said William Orr) was; his blood (meaning the blood of the said William Orr) has been shed, and the precedent indeed is awful.

" And in another part thereof, according to the tenor and effect following, to wit :—

"' But suppose the evidence of Wheatly had been true, what was the offence of Mr. Orr (meaning the said William Orr) ? Not that he had taken an oath of blood and extermination, for then he had not suffered ; but that he (meaning the said William Orr) had taken an oath of charity and of union, of humanity and of peace, he meaning the said William Orr) has suffered. Shall we then be told that your government (meaning the government of this kingdom aforesaid, by the said Lord Lieutenant) will conciliate public opinion, or that the people will not continue to look for a better ?'

" And in another part thereof, according to the tenor and effect following, that is to say :—

"' Is it to be wondered that a successor of Lord Fitzwilliam should sign the death-warrant of Mr. Orr (meaning the said William Orr) ? Mr. Pitt had learned that a merciful Lord Lieutenant was unsuited to a government of violence. It was no compliment to the native clemency of a Camden, that he sent you (meaning the said Lord Lieutenant) into Ireland, and what has been our portion under the change, but massacre and rape, military murders, desolation and terror.'

" And in another part thereof, according to the tenor and effect here following, that is to say :—

"' Feasting in your castle, in the midst of your myrmidons and bishops, you (meaning the said Lord Lieutenant) have little concerned yourself about the expelled and miserable cottager whose dwelling, at the moment of your mirth, was in flames, his wife and his daughter then under the violation of some commissioned ravager, his son agonising on the bayonet, and his helpless infants crying in vain for mercy. These are lamentations which stain not the house of carousal. Under intoxicated counsels (meaning the counsels of the said Lord Lieutenant), the constitution has reeled to its centre, justice is not only blind drunk, but deaf, like Festus, to the words of soberness and truth.'

" And in another part thereof, according to the tenor and effect here following, to wit :—

"' Let, however, the awful execution of Mr. Orr (meaning the execution aforesaid of the said William Orr) be a lesson to all unthinking juries, and let them cease to flatter themselves that the soberest recommendation of theirs, and of the presiding judge, can stop the course of carnage, which sanguinary, and I do not fear to say, unconstitutional laws have ordered to be loosed. Let them remember, that, like Macbeth, the servants of the crown have waded so far in blood, that they find it easier to go on than to go back.'

' In contempt, &c., and against the peace, &c."

The Counsel for the prosecution were the Attorney-General (Arthur Wolfe), Prime Serjeant, Solicitor-General (Toler), Messrs. Ridgeway, Townshend, and Worthington ; for the defence, Curran, Fletcher, M'Nally, Sampson, Sheares and Orr. The Attorney General stated the case, and produced witnesses, who proved printing and publication. Mr. Fletcher opened the defence, and called Lord Yelverton and Mr. E. Cooke (Chief Clerk in the Secretary's office) to prove the truth of the libel ; but the evidence was soon stopped, as illegal, and then Curran spoke as follows :—

Never did I feel myself so sunk under the importance of any cause. To speak to a question of this kind, at any time, would require the greatest talent and the most mature deliberation ; but to be obliged, without either of those advantages, to speak to a subject that has so deeply shaken the feelings of this already irritated and agitated nation is a task that fills me with embarrassment and dismay.

Neither my learned colleague nor myself received any instruction or licence until after the jury were actually sworn, and we both of us came here under an idea that we should not take any part in the trial. This circumstance I mention, not as an idle apology for an effort that cannot be the subject of either praise or censure, but as a call upon you, gentlemen of the jury, to supply the defects of my efforts, by a double exertion of your attention.

Perhaps I ought to regret that I cannot begin with any compliment that may recommend me or my client personally to your favour. A more artful advocate would probably begin his address to you by compliments on your patriotism, and by felicitating his client upon the happy selection of his jury, and upon that unsuspected impartiality in which, if he was innocent, he must be safe. You must be conscious, gentlemen, that such idle verbiage as that, could not convey either my sentiments, or my client's upon that subject. You know, and we know, upon what occasion you are come, and by whom you have been chosen; you are come to try an accusation professedly brought forward by the state, chosen by a sheriff who is appointed by our accuser.

The Attorney-General, interrupting Mr. Curran, said the sheriff was elected by the city and that the observation was therefore unfounded.

Be it so [continued Mr. Curran]: I will not now stop to inquire whose property the city may be considered to be; but the learned gentleman seems to forget, that the election by that city, to whomsoever it may belong, is absolutely void without the approbation of that very Lord Lieutenant, who is the prosecutor in this case. I do therefore repeat, gentlemen, that not a man of you has been called to that box by the voice of my client; that he has had no power to object to a single man among you, though the crown has; and that you yourselves must feel under what influence you are chosen, or for what qualifications you are particularly selected. At a moment when this wretched land is shaken to its centre by the dreadful conflicts of the different branches of the community; between those who call themselves the partisans of liberty, and those that call themselves the partisans of power; between the advocates of infliction and the advocates of suffering; upon such a question as the present, and at such a season, can any man be at a loss to guess to what class of character and opinion, a friend to either party would resort for that jury, which was to decide between both? I trust gentlemen, you know me too well to suppose that I could be capable of treating you with any personal disrespect: I am speaking to you in the honest confidence of your fellow-citizen. When I allude to those unworthy imputations of supposed bias, or passion, or partiality, that may have marked you out for your present situation, I do so, in order to warn you of the ground on which you stand, of the point of awful responsibility in which you are placed, to your conscience, and to your country; and to remind you, that if you have been put into that box from any unworthy reliance on your complaisance or your servility, you have it in your power, before you leave it, to refute and to punish so vile an expectation, by the integrity of your verdict; to remind you, too, that you have it in your power to show to as many Irishmen as yet linger in this country, that all law and justice have not taken their flight with our prosperity and peace; that the sanctity of an oath, and the honesty of a juror are not yet dead amongst us; and that if our courts of justice are superseded by so many strange and terrible tribunals, it is not because they are deficient either in wisdom or virtue.

Gentlemen, it is necessary that you should have a clear idea, first, of the law by which this question is to be decided; secondly, of the nature and object of the prosecution. As to the first, it is my duty to inform you, that the law respecting libels has been much changed of late. Heretofore, in consequence of some decisions of the judges in Westminster-hall, the jury was conceived to have no province but that of finding the truth of the inuendos, and the fact of publication; but the libellous nature of that publication, as well as the guilt or innocence of the publication, were considered as exclusively belonging to the court.

In a system like that of law, which reasons logically, no one erroneous principle can be introduced, without producing every other that can be deducible from it. If in the premises of any argument you admit one erroneous proposition, nothing but bad reasoning can save the conclusions from falsehood. So it has been with this encroachment of the court upon the province of the jury with respect to libels. The moment the court assumed as a principle that they, the court, were to decide upon every thing but the publication; that is, that they were to decide upon the question of libel or no libel, and upon the guilt or innocence of the intention, which must form the essence of every crime, the guilt or innocence must of necessity have ceased to be material.

You see, gentlemen, clearly, that the question of intention is a mere question of fact.

Now the moment the court determined that the jury was not to try that question, it followed of necessity that it was not to be tried at all; for the court cannot try a question of fact. When the court said that it was not triable, there was no way of fortifying that extraordinary proposition, except by asserting that it was not material. The same erroneous reasoning carried them another step, still more mischievous and unjust; if the intention had been material, it must have been decided upon as a mere fact, under all its circumstances. Of these circumstances, the meanest understanding can see that the leading one must be the truth or the falsehood of the publication; but having decided the intention to be immaterial, it followed that the truth must be equally immaterial, and under the law so distorted, any man in England who published the most undeniable truth and with the purest intention, might be punished for a crime in the most ignominious manner without imposing on the prosecutor the necessity of proving his guilt, or his getting any opportunity of showing his innocence.

I am not in the habit of speaking of legal institutions with disrespect; but I am warranted in condemning that usurpation upon the right of juries, by the authority of that statute by which your jurisdiction is restored. For that restitution of justice, the British subject is indebted to the splendid exertions of Mr. Fox and Mr. Erskine, those distinguished supporters of the constitution and of the law; and I am happy to say to you, that though we can claim no share in the glory they have so justly acquired, we have the full benefit of their success; for you are now sitting under a similar act passed in this country, which makes it your duty and right to decide on the entire question upon the broadest grounds, and under all its circumstances, and of course, to determine by your verdict, whether this publication be a false and scandalous libel; false in fact, and published with the seditious purpose alleged, of bringing the government into scandal, and instigating the people to insurrection.

Having stated to you, gentlemen, the great and exclusive extent of your jurisdiction, I shall beg leave to suggest to you a distinction that will strike you at first sight; and that is, the distinction between public animadversions upon the character of private individuals, and those which are written upon measures of government, and the persons who conduct them.

The former may be called personal, and the latter political publications. No two things can be more different in their nature, nor in the point of view in which they are to be looked on by a jury. The criminality of a mere personal libel consists in this, that it tends to a breach of the peace; it tends to all the vindictive paroxysms of exasperated vanity, or to the deeper or more deadly vengeance of irritated pride. The truth is, few men see at once that they cannot be hurt so much as they think by the mere battery of a newspaper. They do not reflect that every character has a natural station, from which it cannot be effectually degraded, and beyond which it cannot be raised by the bawling of a news-hawker. If it is wantonly aspersed, it is but for a season, and that a short one, when it emerges, like the moon from a passing cloud, to its original brightness. It is right, however, that the law, and that you, should hold the strictest hand over this kind of public animadversion, that forces humility and innocence from their retreat into the glare of public view; that wounds and terrifies, that destroys the cordiality and the peace of domestic life, and that, without eradicating a single vice, or single folly, plants a thousand thorns in the human heart.

In cases of that kind, I perfectly agree with the law as stated from the bench; in such cases, I hesitate not to think, that the truth of a charge ought not to justify its publication. If a private man is charged with a crime, he ought to be prosecuted in a court of justice, where he may be punished, if it is true, and the accuser, if it is false. But far differently do I deem of the freedom of political publication. The salutary restraint of the former species, which I talked of, is found in the general law of all societies whatever; but the more enlarged freedom of the press, for which I contend, in political publication, I conceive to be founded in the peculiar nature of the British constitution, and to follow directly from the contract on which the British government hath bee placed by the Revolution. By the British constitution, the power of the state is a trust, committed by the people, upon certain conditions; by the violation of which, it may be abdicated by those who hold, and resumed by those who conferred it. The real security, therefore, of the British sceptre, is, the sentiment and opinion of the people, and it is, consequently, their duty to observe the conduct of the government; and it is the privilege of every man to give them full and just information upon that important subject. Hence the liberty of the press is inseparably twined with the liberty of the people.

The press is the great public monitor: its duty is that of the historian and the witness, that "*nil falsi audeat, nil veri non audeat dicere;*" that its horizon shall extend to the farthest verge and limit of truth; that it shall speak truth to the king in the hearing of the people, and to the people in the hearing of the king; that it shall not perplex either the one or the other with false alarm, lest it lose its characteristic veracity, and become an unheeded warner of real danger; lest it should vainly warn them of that sin, of which the inevitable consequence is death. This, gentlemen, is the great privilege upon which you are to decide; and I have detained you the longer, because of the late change of the law, and because of some observations that have been made, which I shall find it necessary to compare with the principles I have now laid down

And now, gentlemen, let us come to the immediate subject of the trial, as it is brought before you, by the charge in the indictment, to which it ought to have been confined; and also, as it is presented to you by the statement of the learned counsel who has taken a much wider range than the mere limits of the accusation, and has endeavoured to force upon your consideration extraneous and irrelevant facts, for reasons which it is not my duty to explain.

The indictment states simply that Mr. Finnerty has published a false and scandalous libel upon the Lord Lieutenant of Ireland, tending to bring his government into disrepute, and to alienate the affections of the people; and one would have expected, that, without stating any other matter, the counsel for the crown would have gone directly to the proof of this allegation; but he has not done so; he has gone to a most extraordinary length, indeed, of preliminary observation, and an allusion to facts, and sometimes an assertion of facts, at which, I own, I was astonished, until I saw the drift of these allusions and assertions. Whether you have been fairly dealt with by him, or are now honestly dealt with by me, you must be judges.

He has been pleased to say, that this prosecution is brought against this letter signed "Marcus," merely as a part of what he calls a system of attack upon the government, by the paper called "*The Press.*" As to this, I will only ask you whether you are fairly dealt with? whether it is fair treatment to men upon their oaths, to insinuate to them, that the general character of a newspaper (and that general character founded merely upon the assertion of the prosecutor), is to have any influence upon their minds, when they are to judge of a particular publication? I will only ask you, what men you must be supposed to be, when it is thought, that even in a court of justice, and with the eyes of the nation upon you, you can be the dupes of that trite and exploded expedient, so scandalous of late in this country, of raising a vulgar and mercenary cry against whatever man, or whatever principle, it is thought necessary to put down ; and I shall, therefore, merely leave it to your own pride to suggest upon what foundation it could be hoped, that a senseless clamour of that kind could be echoed back by the yell of a jury upon their oaths. I trust you see that this has nothing to do with the question.

Gentlemen of the jury, other matters have been mentioned, which I must repeat for the same purpose ; that of showing you that they have nothing to do with the question. The learned counsel has been pleased to say, that he comes forward in this prosecution as the real advocate for the liberty of the press, and to protect a mild and a merciful government from its licentiousness ; and he has been pleased to add, that the constitution can never be lost while its freedom remains, and that its licentiousness alone can destroy that freedom. As to that, gentlemen, he might as well have said, that there is only one mortal disease of which a man can die: I can die the death inflicted by tyranny ; and when he comes forward to extinguish this paper, in the ruin of the printer, by a state prosecution, in order to prevent its dying of licentiousness, you must judge how candidly he is treating you, both in the fact and in the reasoning. Is it in Ireland, gentlemen, that we are told licentiousness is the only disease that can be mortal to the press ? Has he heard of nothing else that has been fatal to the freeom of publication ? I know not whether the printer of the *Northern Star* may have heard of such things in his captivity ; but I know that his wife and children are well apprised that a press may be destroyed in the open day, not by its own licentiousness, but by the licentiousness of a military force.

As to the sincerity of the declaration, that the state has prosecuted, in order to assert the freedom of the press, it starts a train of thought— of melancholy retrospect and direful prospect—to which I did not think the learned counsel would have wished you to commit your minds. It leads you naturally to reflect at what times, from what motives, and with what consequences, the government has displayed its patriotism, by prosecutions of this sort. As to the motives, does history give you a single instance in which the state has been provoked to these conflicts, except by the fear of truth and by the love of vengeance ? Have you ever seen the rulers of any country bring forward a prosecution from motives of filial piety, for libels upon their departed ancestors ? Do you read that Elizabeth directed any of those state prosecutions against the libels which the divines of her times had written against her Catholic sister, or against the other libels which the same gentlemen had written against her Protestant father ? No, gentlemen, we read of no such thing ; but we know she did bring forward a prosecution from motives of personal resentment ; and we know that a jury was found time-serving and mean enough to give a verdict which she was ashamed to carry into effect.

I said the learned counsel drew you back to the times that have been marked by these miserable conflicts. I see you turn your thoughts to the reign of the second James. I see you turn your eyes to those pages of governmental abandonment, of popular degradation, of expiring liberty, of merciless and sanguinary persecution; to that miserable period, in which the fallen and abject state of man might have been almost an argument in the mouth of the atheist and the blasphemer, against the existence of an all-just and an all-wise First Cause; if the glorious era of the Revolution that followed it had not refuted the impious inference, by showing that if a man descends, it is not in his own proper motion; that it is with labour and with pain; that he can continue to sink only until, by the force and pressure of the descent, the spring of his immortal faculties acquires that recuperative energy and effort that hurries him as many miles aloft; that he sinks but to rise again. It is at that period that the state seeks for shelter in the destruction of the press; it is in a period like that, that the tyrant prepares for an attack upon the people, by destroying the liberty of the press; by taking away that shield of wisdom and of virtue, behind which the people are invulnerable; in whose pure and polished convex, ere the lifted blow has fallen, he beholds his own image, and is turned into stone. It is at those periods that the honest man dares not speak, because truth is too dreadful to be told; it is then humanity has no ears, because humanity has no tongue. It is then the proud man scorns to speak, but, like a physician baffled by the wayward excesses of a dying patient, retires indignantly from the bed of an unhappy wretch, whose ear is too fastidious to bear the sound of wholesome advice, whose palate is too debauched to bear the salutary bitter of the medicine that might redeem him; and therefore leaves him to the felonious piety of the slaves that talk to him of life, and strip him before he is cold.

I do not care, gentlemen, to exhaust too much of your attention, by following this subject through the last century with much minuteness; but the facts are too recent in your mind not to show you, that the liberty of the press and the liberty of the people sink and rise together; that the liberty of speaking and the liberty of acting have shared exactly the same fate. You must have observed in England, that their fate has been the same in the successive vicissitudes of their late depression; and sorry I am to add, that this country has exhibited a melancholy proof of their inseparable destiny, through the various and fitful stages of deterioration, down to the period of their final extinction, when the constitution has given place to the sword, and the only printer in Ireland who dares to speak for the people is now in the dock.

Gentlemen, the learned counsel has made the real subject of this prosecution so small a part of his statement, and has led you into so wide a range—certainly as necessary to the object, as inapplicable to the subject of this prosecution—that I trust you will think me excusable in having somewhat followed his example. Glad am I to find that I have the authority of the same example for coming at last to the subject of this trial. I agree with the learned counsel that the charge made against the Lord Lieutenant of Ireland is that of having grossly and inhumanly abused the royal prerogative of mercy, of which the King is only the trustee for the benefit of the people. The facts are not controverted. It has been asserted that their truth or falsehood is indifferent, and they are shortly these, as they appear in this publication.

William Orr was indicted for having administered the oath of a United Irishman. Every man now knows what the oath is: that it is simply an engagement, first, to promote a brotherhood of affection among men of all religious distinctions; secondly, to labour for the attainment of a parliamentary reform; and thirdly, an obligation of secrecy, which was added to it when the convention law made it criminal and punishable to meet by any public delegation for that purpose.

After remaining upwards of a year in gaol, Mr. Orr was brought to his trial; was prosecuted by the state; was sworn against by a common informer of the name of Wheatly, who himself had taken the obligation; and was convicted under the Insurrection Act, which makes the administering such an obligation felony of death. The jury recommended Mr. Orr to mercy, and the judge, with a humanity becoming his character, transmitted the recommendation to the noble prosecutor in this case. Three of the jurors made solemn affidavit in court, that liquor had been conveyed into their box; that they were brutally threatened by some of their fellow-jurors with criminal prosecution if they did not find the prisoner guilty; and that under the impression of those threats, and worn down by watching and intoxication, they had given a verdict of guilty against him, though they believed him in their consciences to be innocent. That further inquiries were made, which ended in a discovery of the infamous life and character of the informer; that a respite was therefore sent once, and twice, and thrice, to give time, as Mr. Attorney-General has stated, for his Excellency to consider whether mercy *could* be extended to him or not; and that with a knowledge of all these circumstances, his Excellency did finally determine that mercy should not be extended to him; and that he was accordingly executed upon that verdict.

Of this publication, which the indictment charges to be false and seditious, Mr. Attorney-General is pleased to say, that the design of it is to bring the courts of justice into contempt. As to this point of fact, gentlemen, I beg to set you right.

To the administration of justice, so far as it relates to the judges, this publication has not even an allusion in any part mentioned in this indictment; it relates to a department of justice, that cannot begin until the duty of the judge closes. Sorry should I be, that, with respect to this unfortunate man, any censure should be flung on those judges who presided at his trial, with the mildness and temper that became them upon so awful an occasion as the trial of life and death. Sure am I, that if they had been charged with inhumanity or injustice, and if they had condescended at all to prosecute the reviler, they would not have come forward in the face of the public to say, as has been said this day, that it was immaterial whether the charge was true or not. Sure I am, their first object would have been to show that it was false, and readily should I have been an eye-witness of the fact, to have discharged the debt of ancient friendship, of private respect, and of public duty, and upon my oath to have repelled the falsehood of such an imputation.

Upon this subject, gentlemen, the presence of those venerable judges restrains what I might otherwise have said, nor should I have named them at all, if I had not been forced to do so, and merely to undeceive you, if you have been made to believe their characters to have any community of cause whatever with the Lord Lieutenant of Ireland. To him alone it is confined, and against him the charge is made, as strongly, I suppose, as the writer could find words to express it, that the Viceroy of Ireland has cruelly abused the prerogative of royal mercy, in suffering a man under such circumstances to perish like a common malefactor. For this Mr. Attorney-General calls for your conviction as a false and scandalous libel; and after stating himself every fact that I have repeated to you, either from his statement, or from the evidence, he tells you, that you ought to find it false and scandalous, though he almost in words admits that it is not false, and has resisted the admission of the evidence by which we offered to prove every word of it to be true.

And here, gentlemen, give me leave to remind you of the parties before you.

The traverser is a printer, who follows that profession for bread, and who at a time of great public misery and terror. when the people are restrained by law from debating under any delegated form; when the few constituents that we have are prevented by force from meeting in their own persons, to deliberate or to petition: when every other newspaper in Ireland is put down by force, or purchased by the administration (though here, gentlemen, perhaps I ought to beg your pardon for stating without authority; I recollect when we attempted to examine as to the number of newspapers in the pay of the castle, that the evidence was objected to); at a season like this, Mr. Finnerty has had the courage, perhaps the folly, to print the publication in question, for no motive under heaven of malice or vengeance, but in the mere duty which he owes to his family, and to the public.

His prosecutor is the King's minister in Ireland; in that character does the learned gentleman mean to say, that his conduct is not a fair subject of public observation? Where does he find his authority for that in the law or practice of the sister country? Have the virtues, or the exalted station, or the general love of his people preserved the sacred person even of the royal master of the prosecutor, from the asperity and intemperance of public censure, unfounded as it ever must be, with any personal respect to his Majesty, in justice or truth? Have the gigantic abilities of Mr. Pitt, have the more gigantic talents of his great antagonist, Mr. Fox, protected either of them from the insolent familiarity, and for aught we know, the injustice with which writers have treated them? What latitude of invective has the King's minister escaped upon the subject of the present war? Is there an epithet of contumely, or of reproach, that hatred or that fancy could suggest, that is not publicly lavished upon them? Do you not find the words, advocate of despotism, robber of the public treasure, murderer of the King's subjects, debaucher of the public morality, degrader of the constitution, tarnisher of the British empire, by frequency of use lose all meaning whatsoever, and dwindle into terms, not of any peculiar reproach, but of ordinary appellation?

And why, gentlemen, is this permitted in that country? I'll tell you why; because in that country they are yet wise enough to see that the measures of the state are the proper subject for the freedom of the press; that the principles relating to personal slander do not apply to rulers or to ministers; that to publish an attack upon a public minister, without any regard to truth, but merely because of its tendency to a breach of the peace, would be ridiculous in the extreme. What breach of the peace, gentlemen, I pray you, in such a case? Is it the tendency of such publications to provoke Mr. Pitt or Mr. Dundas to break the head of the writer, if they should happen to meet him? No, gentlemen; in that country this freedom is exercised, because the people feel it to be their right; and it is wisely suffered to pass by the state, from a consciousness that it would be vain to oppose it; a consciousness confirmed by the event of every incautious experiment. It is suffered to pass from a conviction that, in a court of justice at least, the bulwarks of the constitution will not be surrendered to the state; and that the intended victim, whether clothed in the humble guise of honest industry, or decked in the honours of genius, and virtue, and philosophy, whether a Hardy or a Tooke, will find certain protection in the honesty and spirit of an English jury.

But, gentlemen, I suppose Mr. Attorney-General will scarcely wish to carry his doctrine altogether so far. Indeed, I remember, he declared himself a most zealous advocate for the liberty of the press. I may, therefore, even according to him, presume to make some observations on the conduct of the existing government. I should wish to know how far he supposes it to extend; is it to the composition of lampoons and madrigals, to be sung down the grates by ragged balladmongers to kitchen-maids and footmen? I will not suppose that he means to confine it to the ebullitions of Billingsgate, to those cataracts of ribaldry and scurrility, that are daily spouting upon the miseries of our wretched fellow-sufferers, and the unavailing efforts of those who have vainly laboured in their cause. I will not suppose that he confines it to the poetic licence of a birth-day ode; the *Laureat* would not use such language! In which case I do not entirely agree with him, that the truth or the falsehood is as perfectly immaterial to the law, as it is to the *Laureat*; as perfectly unrestrained by the law of the land, as it is by any law of decency or shame, of modesty or decorum.

But as to the privilege of censure or blame, I am sorry that the learned gentleman has not favoured you with his notion of the liberty of the press.

Suppose an Irish Viceroy acts a very little absurdly, may the press venture to be respectfully comical upon that absurdity? The learned counsel does not, at least in terms, give a negative to that. But let me treat you honestly, and go further, to a more material point; suppose an Irish Viceroy does an act that brings scandal upon his master, that fills the mind of a reasonable man with the fear of approaching despotism; that leaves no hope to the people of preserving themselves and their children from chains, but in common confederacy for common safety. What is that honest man in that case to do?

I am sorry *the right honourable advocate for the liberty of the press* has not told you his opinion, at least in any express words. I will therefore venture to give you my far humbler thoughts upon the subject.

I think an honest man ought to tell the people frankly and boldly of their peril; and I must say I can imagine no villany greater than that of his holding a traitorous silence at such a crisis, except the villany and baseness of prosecuting him, or of finding him guilty for such an honest discharge of his public duty. And I found myself on the known principle of the revolution of England, namely, that the crown tself may be abdicated by certain abuses of the trust reposed; and that there are possible excesses of arbitrary power, which it is not only the right, but the bounden duty, of every honest man to resist, at the risk of his fortune and his life.

Now, gentlemen, if this reasoning be admitted, and it cannot be denied; if there be any possible event in which the people are obliged to look only to themselves, and are justified in doing so; can you be so absurd as to say, that it is lawful for the people to act upon it when it unfortunately does arrive, but that it is criminal in any man to tell them that the miserable event has actually arrived, or is imminently approaching? Far am I, gentlemen, from insinuating that (extreme as it is) our misery has been matured into any deplorable crisis of thi; kind, from which I pray that the Almighty God may for ever preserve us! But I am putting my principles upon the strongest ground, and most favourable to my opponents, namely, that it never can be criminal to say any thing of government but what is false; and I put this in the extreme, in order to demonstrate to you, *a fortiori*, that the privilege of speaking truth to the people, which holds in the last extremity, must also obtain in every stage of inferior importance; and that, however a court may have decided, before the late act, that the truth was immaterial in case of libel, since that act, no honest jury can be governed by such principle.

Be pleased now, gentlemen, to consider the grounds upon which this publication is called a libel, and criminal.

Mr. Attorney-General tells you it tends to excite sedition and insurrection. Let me again remind you, that the truth of this charge is not denied by the noble prosecutor. What is it then that tends to excite sedition and insurrection? "The act that is charged upon the prosecutor, and is not attempted to be denied?" And, gracious God! gentlemen of the jury, is the public statement of the King's representative this, "I have done a deed that must fill the mind of every feeling or thinking man with horror and indignation; that must alienate every man that knows it from the King's government, and endanger the separation of this distracted empire: the traverser has had the guilt of publishing this fact, which I myself acknowledge, and I pray you to find him guilty?" Is this the case which the Lord Lieutenant of Ireland brings forward? Is this the principle for which he ventures, at a dreadful crisis like the present, to contend in a court of justice? Is this the picture which he wishes to hold out of himself to the justice and humanity of his own countrymen? Is this the history which he wishes to be read by the poor Irishmen of the South and of the North, by the sister nation, and the common enemy?

With the profoundest respect, permit me humbly to defend his Excellency, even against his own opinion. The guilt of this publication he is pleased to think consists in this, that it tends to insurrection. Upon what can such a fear be supported? After the multitudes that have perished in this unhappy nation within the last three years, unhappiness which has been borne with a patience not paralleled in the history of nations, can any man suppose that the fate of a single individual could lead to resistance or insurrection?

But suppose that it might, what then ought to be the conduct of an honest man? Should it not be to apprise the government of the country and the Viceroy—you will drive the people to madness, if you persevere in such bloody councils; you will alienate the Irish nation; you will distract the common force; and you will invite the common enemy? Should not an honest man say to the people—the measure of your affliction is great, but you need not resort for remedy to any desperate expedients. If the King's minister is defective in humanity or wisdom, his royal master, your beloved sovereign, is abounding in both. At such a moment, can you be so senseless as not to feel, that any one of you ought to hold such language; or is it possible you could be so infatuated, as to punish the man who was honest enough to hold it?—or is it possible that you could bring yourselves to say to your country, that at such a season the press ought to sleep upon its post, or to act like the perfidious watchman on his round, that sees the villain wrenching the door, or the flames bursting from the windows, while the inhabitant is wrapt in sleep, and cries out that "'tis past five o'clock, the morning is fair, and all well?"

On this part of the case I shall only put one question to you. I do not affect to say it is similar in all its points; I do not affect to compare the humble fortunes of Mr. Orr with the sainted names of Russell or Sidney; still less am I willing to find any likeness between the present period and the year 1688. But I will put a question to you, completely parallel in principle: When that unhappy and misguided monarch had shed the sacred blood, which their noble hearts had matured into a fit cement of revolution, if any honest Englishman had been brought to trial for daring to proclaim to the world his abhorrence of such a deed, what would you have thought of the English jury that could have said —we know in our hearts what he said was true and honest, but we will say, upon our oaths, that it was false and criminal; and we will, by that base subserviency, add another item to the catalogue of public wrongs, and another argument for the necessity of an appeal to heaven for redress?

Gentlemen, I am perfectly aware that what I say may be easily misconstrued; but if you listen to me, with the same fairness that I address you, I cannot be misunderstood. When I show you the full extent of your political rights and remedies ; when I answer those slanderers of British liberty, who degrade the monarch into a despot, who pervert the steadfastness of law into the waywardness of will ; when I show you the inestimable stores of political wealth, so dearly acquired by our ancestors, and so solemnly bequeathed ; and when I show you how much of that precious inheritance has yet survived all the prodigality of their posterity, I am far from saying that I stand in need of it all upon the present occasion. No, gentlemen, far am I indeed from such a sentiment. No man more deeply than myself deplores the present melancholy state of our unhappy country. Neither does any man more fervently wish for the return of peace and tranquillity, through the natural channels of mercy and of justice. I have seen too much of force and of violence to hope much good from the continuance of them on the one side or the retaliation of them on another. I have of late een too much of political rebuilding, not to have observed, that to demolish is not the shortest way to repair. It is with pain and anguish that I should search for the miserable right of breaking ancient ties, or going in quest of new relations, or untried adventures. No, gentlemen the case of my client rests not upon these sad privileges of despair. I trust, that as to the fact, namely, the intention of exciting insurrection, you must see it cannot be found in this publication ; that it is the mere idle, unsupported imputation of malice, or panic, or falsehood. And that as to the law, so far has he been from transgressing the limits of the constitution, that whole regions lie between him and those limits, which he has not trod, and which I pray to heaven it may never be necessary for any of us to tread.

Gentlemen, Mr. Attorney-General has been pleased to open another battery upon this publication, which I do trust I shall silence, unless I flatter myself too much in supposing that hitherto my resistance has not been utterly unsuccessful.

He abuses it for the foul and insolent familiarity of its address. I do clearly understand his idea ; he considers the freedom of the press to be the licence of offering that paltry adulation which no man ought to stoop to utter or to hear ; he supposes the freedom of the press ought to be like the freedom of a king's jester, who, instead of reproving the faults of which majesty ought to be ashamed, is base and cunning enough, under the mask of servile and adulatory censure, to stroke down and pamper those vices of which it is foolish enough to be vain. He would not have the press presume to tell the Viceroy, that the prerogative of mercy is a trust for the benefit of the subject, and not a gaudy feather stuck into the diadem to shake in the wind, and by the waving of the gorgeous plumage to amuse the vanity of the wearer. He would not have it to say to him, that the discretion of the crown as to mercy, is like the discretion of a court of justice as to law ; and that in the one case, as well as the other, wherever the propriety of the exercise of it appears, it is equally a matter of right He would have the press all fierceness to the people, and all sycophancy to power ; he would consider the mad and frenetic outrages of authority, like the awful and inscrutable dispensations of Providence, and say to the unfeeling and despotic spoiler, in the blasphemed and insulted language of religious resignation, " the Lord hath given, and the Lord hath taken away, blessed be the name of the Lord."

But let me condense the generality of the learned gentleman's invective into questions that you can conceive. Does he mean that the air of this publication is rustic and uncourtly? Does he mean, that when " Marcus" presumed to ascend the steps of the castle, and to address the Viceroy, he did not turn out his toes as he ought to have done? But, gentlemen, you are not a jury of dancing-masters: or does the learned gentleman mean that the language is coarse and vulgar? If this be his complaint, my client has but a poor advocate.

I do not pretend to be a mighty grammarian, or a formidable critic; but I would beg leave to suggest to you, in serious humility, that a free press can be supported only by the ardour of men who feel the prompting sting of real or supposed capacity; who write from the enthusiasm of virtue, or the ambition of praise, and over whom, if you exercise the rigour of a grammatical censorship, you will inspire them with as mean an opinion of your integrity as of your wisdom, and inevitably drive them from their post; and if you do, rely upon it, you will reduce the spirit of publication, and with it the press of this country, to what it for a long interval has been—the register of births, and fairs, and funerals, and the general abuse of the people and their friends.

Gentlemen, in order to bring this charge of insolence and vulgarity to the test, let me ask you, whether you know of any language which could have adequately described the idea of mercy denied, where it ought to have been granted; or of any phrase vigorous enough to convey the indignation which an honest man would have felt upon such a subject?

Let me beg of you for a moment to suppose that any one of you had been the writer of this very severe expostulation with the Viceroy, and that you had been the witness of the whole progress of this never-to-be-forgotten catastrophe.

Let me suppose that you had known the charge upon which Mr. Orr was apprehended—the charge of abjuring that bigotry which had torn and disgraced his country—of pledging himself to restore the people of his country to their place in the constitution—and of binding himself never to be the betrayer of his fellow-labourers in that enterprise: that you had seen him upon that charge removed from his industry, and confined in a gaol; that through the slow and lingering progress of twelve tedious months you had seen him confined in a dungeon, shut out from the common use of air and of his own limbs; that day after day you had marked the unhappy captive cheered by no sound but the cries of his family, or the clinking of chains; that you had seen him at last brought to his trial; that you had seen the vile and perjured informer deposing against his life; that you had seen the drunken, and worn-out, and terrified jury give in a verdict of death; that you had seen the same jury when their returning sobriety had brought back their conscience, prostrate themselves before the humanity of the bench, and pray that the mercy of the crown might save their characters from the reproach of an involuntary crime, their consciences from the torture of eternal self-condemnation, and their souls from the indelible stain of innocent blood.

Let me suppose that you had seen the respite given, and that contrite and honest recommendation transmitted to that seat where mercy was presumed to dwell—that new and before unheard-of crimes are discovered against the informer—that the royal mercy seems to relent, and that a new respite is sent to the prisoner—that time is taken, as the learned counsel for the crown has expressed it, to see whether mercy could be extended or not!—that after that period of lingering deliberation passed, a third respite is transmitted—that the unhappy captive himself feels the cheering hope of being restored to a family that he had adored, to a character that he had never stained, and to a country that he had ever loved—that you had seen his wife and children upon their knees, giving those tears to gratitude, which their locked and frozen hearts could not give to anguish and despair, and imploring the blessings of Eternal Providence upon his head, who had graciously spared the father, and restored him to his children—that you had seen the olive branch sent into his little ark, but no sign that the waters had subsided.

"Alas!
Nor wife, nor children more shall he behold—
Nor friends, nor sacred home!"

No seraph mercy unbars his dungeon, and leads him forth to light and life; but the minister of death hurries him to the scene of suffering and of shame, where, unmoved by the hostile array of artillery and armed men collected together, to secure, or to insult, or to disturb him, he dies with a solemn declaration of his innocence, and utters his last breath, in a prayer for the liberty of his country.

Let me now ask you, if any of you had addressed the public ear upon so foul and monstrous a subject, in what language would you have conveyed the feelings of horror and indignation? Would you have stooped to the meanness of qualified complaint?—would you have checked your feelings to search for courtly and gaudy language?—would you have been mean enough—but I entreat your forgiveness—I do not think meanly of you. Had I thought so meanly of you, I could not suffer my mind to commune with you as it has done; had I thought you that base and vile instrument, attuned by hope and by fear into discord and falsehood, from whose vulgar string no groan of suffering could vibrate, no voice of integrity or honour could speak, let me honestly tell you, I should have scorned to fling my hand across it—I should have left it to a fitter minstrel. If I do not, therefore, grossly err in my opinion of you, I could use no language upon such a subject as this, that must not lag behind the rapidity of your feelings, and that would not disgrace those feelings, if it attempted to describe them.

Gentlemen, I am not unconscious that the learned counsel for the crown seemed to address you with a confidence of a very different kind·

he seemed to expect from you a kind and respectful sympathy with the feelings of the Castle, and with the griefs of chided authority. Perhaps gentlemen, he may know you better than I do. If he does, he has spoken to you as he ought ; he has been right in telling you, that if the reprobation of this writer is weak, it is because his genius could not make it stronger ; he has been right in telling you, that his language has not been braided and festooned as elegantly as it might—that he has not pinched the miserable plaits of his phraseology, nor placed his patches and feathers with that correctness of millinery which became so exalted a person.

If you agree with him, gentlemen of the jury—if you think that the man who ventures, at the hazard of his own life, to rescue from the deep the drowning honour of his country, you must not presume upon the guilty familiarity of plucking it up by the locks. I have no more to say ; do a courteous thing. Upright and honest jurors, find a civil and obliging verdict against the printer ! And when you have done so, march through the ranks of your fellow-citizens to your own homes, and bear their looks as you pass along. Retire to the bosom of your families and your children, and when you are presiding over the morality of the parental board, tell those infants, who are to be the future men of Ireland, the history of this day. Form their young minds by your precepts, and confirm those precepts by your own example—teach them how discreetly allegiance may be perjured on the table, or loyalty be forsworn in the jury-box ; and when you have done so, tell them the story of Orr—tell them of his captivity, of his children, of his crime, of his hopes, of his disappointments, of his courage, and of his death; and when you find your little hearers hanging from your lips—when you see their eyes overflow with sympathy and sorrow—and their young hearts bursting with the pangs of anticipated orphanage—tell them that you had the boldness and the justice to stigmatize the monster who had dared to publish the transaction !

Gentlemen, I believe I told you before, that the conduct of the Viceroy was a small part, indeed, of the subject of this trial. If the vindication of his mere personal character had been, as it ought to have been, the sole object of this prosecution, I should have felt the most respectful regret at seeing a person of his high consideration come forward in a court of public justice in one and the same breath to admit the truth, and to demand the punishment of a publication like the present, to prevent the chance he might have had of such an accusation being disbelieved, and, by a prosecution like this, to give to the passing stricture of a newspaper that life and body, and action and reality, to prove it to all mankind, and make the record of it indelible. Even as it is, I do own I feel the utmost concern that his name should have been soiled by being mixed in a question of which it is the mere pretext and scape goat.

Mr. Attorney-General was too wise to state to you the real question, or the object which he wished to be answered by your verdict. Do you remember that he was pleased to say that this publication was a base and foul misrepresentation of the virtue and wisdom of the government, and a false and audacious statement to the world, that the King's government in Ireland was base enough to pay informers for taking away the lives of the people? When I heard this statement to-day, I doubted whether you were aware of its tendency or not. It is now necessary that I should explain it to you more at large.

You cannot be ignorant of the great conflict between prerogative and privilege which hath convulsed the country for the last fifteen years: when I say privilege, you cannot suppose that I mean the privilege of the House of Commons,—I mean the privileges of the people.

You are no strangers to the various modes by which the people laboured to approach their object. Delegations, conventions, remonstrances, resolutions, petitions to the parliament, petitions to the throne.

It might not be decorous in this place to state to you, with any sharpness, the various modes of resistance that were employed on the other side; but you, all of you, seem old enough to remember the variety of acts of parliament that have been made, by which the people were deprived, session after session, of what they had supposed to be the known and established fundamentals of the constitution, the right of public debate, the right of public petition, the right of bail, the right of trial, the right of arms for self-defence; until the last, even the relics of popular privilege became superseded by a military force; the press extinguished; and the state found its last entrenchment in the grave of the constitution. As little can you be strangers to the tremendous confederations of hundreds of thousands of your countrymen, of the nature and objects of which such a variety of opinions have been propagated and entertained.

The writer of this letter presumed to censure the recal of Lord Fitzwilliam, as well as the measures of the present Viceroy. Into this subject I do not enter; but you cannot yourselves forget that the conciliatory measures of the former noble lord had produced an almost miraculous unanimity in this country; and much do I regret, and sure I am that it is not without pain you can reflect, how unfortunately the conduct of his successor has terminated. His intentions might have been the best; I neither know them nor condemn them, but their terrible effects you cannot be blind to. Every new act of coercion has been followed by some new symptom of discontent, and every new attack provoked some new paroxysm of resentment, or some new combination of resistance.

In this deplorable state of affairs—convulsed and distracted within, and menaced by a most formidable enemy from without—it was thought that public safety might be found in union and conciliation; and repeated applications were made to the parliament of this kingdom, for a calm inquiry into the complaints of the people. These applications were made in vain.

Impressed by the same motives, Mr. Fox brought the same subject before the Commons of England, and ventured to ascribe the perilous state of Ireland to the severity of its government. Even his stupendous abilities, excited by the liveliest sympathy with our sufferings, and animated by the most ardent zeal to restore the strength with the union of the empire, were repeatedly exerted without success. The fact of discontent was denied—the fact of coercion was denied—and the consequence was, the coercion became more implacable, and the discontent more threatening and irreconcilable.

A similar application was made in the beginning of this session in the Lords of Great Britain, by our illustrious countryman,* of whom I do not wonder that my learned friend should have observed, how much virtue can fling pedigree into the shade; or how much the transient honour of a body inherited from man, is obscured by the lustre of an intellect derived from God. He, after being an eye-witness of this country, presented the miserable picture of what he had seen; and, to the astonishment of every man in Ireland, the existence of those facts was ventured to be denied; the conduct of the Viceroy was justified and applauded; and the necessity of continuing that conduct was insisted upon, as the only means of preserving the constitution, the peace, and the prosperity of Ireland. The moment the learned counsel had talked of this publication as a false statement of the conduct of the government, and the condition of the people, no man could be at a loss to see that the awful question, which had been dismissed from the Commons of Ireland, and from the Lords and Commons of Great Britain, is now brought forward to be tried by a side wind, and, in a collateral way, by a criminal prosecution.

The learned counsel has asserted that the paper which he prosecutes is only part of a system formed to misrepresent the state of Ireland and the conduct of its government. Do you not, therefore, discover that his object is to procure a verdict to sanction the parliaments of both countries in refusing an inquiry into your grievances? Let me ask you, then, are you prepared to say, upon your oath, that those measures of coercion, which are daily practised, are absolutely necessary and ought to be continued? It is not upon Finnerty you are sitting in judgment; but you are sitting in judgment upon the lives and liberties of the inhabitants of more than half of Ireland. You are to say that it is a foul proceeding to condemn the government of Ireland; that it is a foul act, founded in foul motives, and originating in falsehood and sedition; that it is an attack upon a government, under which the people are prosperous and happy; that justice is administered with mercy; that the statements made in Great Britain are false—are the effusions of party or of discontent; that all is mildness and tranquillity; that there are no burnings—no transportations; that you never travel by the light of conflagrations; that the gaols are not crowded month after month, from which prisoners are taken out, not for trial, but for embarkation! These are the questions upon which, I say, you must virtually decide. It is in vain that the counsel for the crown may tell you that I am misrepresenting the case—that I am endeavouring to raise false fears, and to take advantage of your passions—that the question is, whether this paper be a libel or not—and that the circumstances of the country have nothing to do with it. Such assertions

* Lord Moira.

must be vain. The statement of the counsel for the crown has forced the introduction of those important topics; and I appeal to your own hearts whether the country is misrepresented, and whether the government is misrepresented.

I tell you, therefore, gentlemen of the jury, it is not with respect to Mr. Orr, or Mr. Finnerty, that your verdict is now sought. You are called upon, on your oaths, to say, that the government is wise and merciful—the people prosperous and happy; that military law ought to be continued; that the constitution could not with safety be restored to Ireland; and that the statements of a contrary import by your advocates, in either country, are libellous and false.

I tell you these are the questions; and I ask you, if you can have the front to give the expected answer in the face of a community who know the country as well as you do? Let me ask you, how you could reconcile with such a verdict, the gaols, the tenders, the gibbets, the conflagrations, the murders, the proclamations that we hear of every day in the streets, and see every day in the country? What are the prosecutions of the learned counsel himself, circuit after circuit? Merciful God! what is the state of Ireland, and where shall you find the wretched inhabitant of this land! You may find him, perhaps, in a gaol, the only place of security—I had almost said of ordinary habitation! If you do not find him there, you may see him flying with his family from the flames of his own dwelling—lighted to his dungeon by the conflagration of his hovel; or you may find his bones bleaching on the green fields of his country; or you may find him tossing on the surface of the ocean, and mingling his groans with those tempests, less savage than his persecutors, that drift him to a returnless distance from his family and his home, without charge, or trial, or sentence. Is this a foul misrepresentation? Or can you, with these facts ringing in your ears, and staring in your face, say, upon your oaths, they do not exist? You are called upon, in defiance of shame, of truth, of honour, to deny the sufferings under which you groan, and to flatter the persecution that tramples you under foot.

Gentlemen, I am not accustomed to speak of circumstances of this kind; and though familiarized as I have been to them, when I come to speak of them, my power fails me—my voice dies within me. I am not able to call upon you. It is now I ought to have strength—it is now I ought to have energy and voice. But I have none; I am like the unfortunate state of the country—perhaps, like you. This is the time in which I ought to speak, if I can, or be dumb for ever; in which, if you do not speak as *you* ought, *you* ought to be dumb for ever.

But the learned gentleman is further pleased to say, that the traverser has charged the government with the encouragement of informers. This, gentlemen, is another small fact that you are to deny at the hazard of your souls, and upon the solemnity of your oaths. You are upon your oaths to say to the sister country, that the government of Ireland uses no such abominable instruments of destruction as informers. Let me ask you honestly, what do you feel, when in my hearing, when in the face of this audience, you are called upon to give a verdict that every man of us, and every man of you know, by the testimony of your own eyes, to be utterly and absolutely false? I speak not now of the public proclamation for informers, with a promise of secrecy, and of extravagant reward; I speak not of the fate of those horrid wretches who have been so often transferred from the table to the dock, and from the dock to the pillory; I speak of what your own eyes have seen, day after day, during the course of this commission, from the box where you are now sitting; the number of horrid miscreants, who acknowledged, upon their oaths, that they had come from the seat of government—from the very chambers of the Castle—where they had been worked upon, by the fear of death and the hope of compensation, to give evidence against their fellows; that the mild, the wholesome, and merciful councils of this government are holden over these catacombs of living death, where the wretch that is buried a man, lies till his heart has time to fester and dissolve, and is then dug up a witness!

Is this a picture created by a hag-ridden fancy, or is it fact? Have you not seen him, after his resurrection from that region of death and corruption, make his appearance upon the table, the living image of life and of death, and the supreme arbiter of both; Have you not marked when he entered, how the stormy wave of the multitude retired at his approach? Have you not seen how the human heart bowed to the supremacy of his power, in the undissembled homage of deferential horror? how his glance, like the lightning of heaven, seemed to rive the body of the accused, and mark it for the grave, while his voice warned the devoted wretch of woe and death—a death which no innocence can escape, no art elude, no force resist, no antidote prevent. There was an antidote—a juror's oath!—but even that adamantine chain, that bound the integrity of man to the throne of eternal justice, is solved and molten in the breath that issues from the informer's mouth; conscience swings from her moorings, and the appalled and affrighted juror consults his own safety in the surrender of the victim:—

"Et quæ sibi quisque timebat,
Unius in miseri exitium conversa tulere."

Informers are worshipped in the temple of justice, even as the devil has been worshipped by Pagans and savages—even so in this wicked country, is the informer an object of judicial idolatry—even so is he soothed by the music of human groans—even so is he placated and incensed by the fumes and by the blood of human sacrifices.

Gentlemen, I feel I must have tired your patience; but I have been forced into this length by the prosecutor, who has thought fit to introduce those extraordinary topics, and to bring a question of mere politics to trial, under the form of a criminal prosecution. I cannot say I am surprised that this has been done, or that you should be solicited by the same inducements, and from the same motives, as if your verdict was a vote of approbation. I do not wonder that the government of Ireland should stand appalled at the state to which we are reduced I wonder not that they should start at the public voice, and labour to stifle or contradict it. I wonder not that at this arduous crisis, when the very existence of the empire is at stake, and when its strongest and most precious limb is not girt with the sword for battle, but pressed by the tourniquet for amputation; when they find the coldness of death already begun in those extremities where it never ends; that they are terrified at what they have done, and wish to say to the surviving parties of that empire, "they cannot say that we did it." I wonder not that they should consider their conduct as no immaterial question for a court of criminal jurisdiction, and wish anxiously, as on an inquest of blood, for the kind acquittal of a friendly jury.

I wonder not that they should wish to close the chasm they have opened, by flinging you into the abyss. But trust me, my countrymen, you might perish in it, but you could not close it; trust me, if it is yet possible to close it, it can be done only by truth and honour; trust me, that such an effect could no more be wrought by the sacrifice of a jury, than by the sacrifice of Orr.

As a state measure, the one would be as unwise and unavailing as the other; but while you are yet upon the brink, while you are yet visible, let me, before we part, remind you once more of your awful situation.

You are upon a great forward ground, with the people at your back, and the government in your front. You have neither the disadvantages nor the excuses of jurors a century ago. No, thank God! never was there a stronger characteristic distinction between those times, upon which no man can reflect without horror, and the present. You have seen this trial conducted with mildness and patience by the court. We have now no Jefferies, with scurvy and vulgar conceits, to browbeat the prisoner and perplex his counsel. Such has been the improvement of manners, and so calm the confidence of integrity, that during the defence of accused persons, the judges sit quietly, and show themselves worthy of their situation, by bearing, with a mild and merciful patience, the little extravagancies of the bar, as you should bear with the little extravagancies of the press. Let me then turn your eyes to that pattern of mildness in the bench. The press is your advocate; bear with its excess—bear with every thing but its bad intention. If it come as a villanous slanderer, treat it as such; but if it endeavour to raise the honour and glory of your country, remember that you reduce its power to a nonentity, if you stop its animadversions upon public measures. You should not check the efforts of genius, nor damp the ardour of patriotism. In vain will you desire the bird to soar, if you meanly or madly steal from it its plumage. Beware lest, under the pretence of bearing down the licentiousness of the press, you extinguish it altogether. Beware how you rival the venal ferocity of those miscreants, who rob a printer of the means of bread, and claim from deluded royalty the reward of integrity and allegiance. Let me, therefore, remind you, that though the day may soon come when our ashes shall be scattered before the winds of heaven, the memory of what you do cannot die; it will carry down to your posterity your honour or your shame.— In the presence and in the name of that ever living God, I do therefore conjure you to reflect, that you have your characters, your consciences, that you have also the character, perhaps the ultimate destiny of your country, in your hands. In that awful name, I do conjure you to have mercy upon your country and yourselves, and so judge now, as you will hereafter be judged; and I do now submit the fate of my client, and of that country which we have yet in common, to your disposal.

The Prime Sergeant (Hon. James Fitzgerald) shortly replied; Judge Downes charged weakly, but not rudely; and, after a short absence, the jury returned "Guilty" on the issue paper.

On the following day, the 23rd of December, Mr. Finnerty was brought up for judgment. Mr. Finnerty stated that he had been taken out of prison to Alderman Alexander's office, and there threatened with public whipping, if he did not give up the author of the libel. He boldly defended the letter, but was most respectful to the Bench. Judge Downes sentenced him to two years' imprisonment from the day of his arrest, to stand in the pillory for an hour, pay a fine of £20, and at the expiration of his imprisonment to give security, himself in £500, and two bailsmen in £250 each for his good behaviour. On the 30th of December, Mr. Finnerty did actually stand in the pillory, and the rest of this miscellaneous and iniquitous sentence was also carried out.

FOR MR. PATRICK FINNEY.

[HIGH TREASON.]

January 16th, 1798.

On the 31st of May, 1797, Patrick Finney was arrested at Tuite's public house, in Thomas-street. He was indicted for High Treason, at the Commission held in Dublin, in July, 1797, and on Tuesday, the 16th of January, 1798, was brought to trial. Mr. Ridgeway opened the indictment, which was in substance as follows:—

The first count of the indictment charged—"That Patrick Finney, yeoman, on the 30th day of April, in the 37th year of the King, and divers other days, at the city of Dublin, being a false traitor, did compass and imagine the death of our said Lord the King, and did traitorously and feloniously intend our said Lord the King to kill, murder, and put to death."

The overt acts laid were as follows:—"1. Adhering to the persons exercising the powers of government in France, in case they should invade, or cause to be invaded this kingdom of Ireland, they being enemies to the King, and at war. 2. That the conspirators afore said did meet, &c., confer, consult, and deliberate, about adhering to the persons exercising the powers of government in France. 3. Adhering to the persons exercising the powers of government in France. 4. Conspiring that one or more persons should be sent into France, to excite an invasion of Ireland. 5. Conspiring that one or more persons should be sent into France, to excite an invasion of this kingdom, and to make war therein; and for that purpose did ask, levy, and receive, &c., from other traitors, money, to wit, from each £20, to defray the expenses of the persons to be sent. 6. That conspiring, &c., they did send into France four persons unknown, to excite the persons exercising the powers of government in France to invade this kingdom, and make war therein. 7. Conspiring to send, and sending, four persons into France, to persuade invasion, and to aid them in invading, and raising, and making war; and Finney, then and there, demanding and receiving money, viz. £20 t defray the charges of said persons. 8. That said Patrick Finney became a United Irishman for the purpose of assisting the persons exercising the powers of government in France, and being met to the number of forty-eight other traitors, did divide into four splits, each of which contained twelve traitors, and each split did then choose one to be secretary, to consult on behalf thereof with other splits, under the denomination of baronial meetings, for the purpose of adhering and making war, in case of an invasion of Ireland from France, and then and there conspiring an attack upon the Castle of Dublin, &c., and to deprive his Majesty of the stores and ammunition therein; and said Finney, to facilitate such attack did advise and commend other traitors to view White's Court, &c., and give their opinion to their several splits, so that their secretaries might report the same to their baronial meetings. 9. Adhering to the persons exercising the powers of government in France, &c., and with forty-eight other conspirators, divided into four splits, each containing twelve, each split choosing a secretary to confer for the purpose of adhering to the enemy in case of invasion, and confederating and agreeing that a violent attack should be made on the ordnance stores, &c. 10. Consulting, &c., to procure an invasion. 11. Consulting to raise insurrection, rebellion, and war, in case of invasion of Ireland or Great Britain, from France. 12. Conspiring to assist the persons exercising the powers of government in France, in case of their invading this realm with ships and arms."

There was a second count, for "adhering to the King's enemies within the realm;" and in support of this count, the overt acts laid were exactly the same as those above recited.

The Attorney-General (Wolfe) stated the case, describing the United Irish organization, and alleging their communication with France. He introduced the charge against the prisoner and the chief witness—the eminent informer, Jemmy O'Brien, in these words:—

"A man of the name of James O'Brien, upon the 25th of April, 1797, was passing through Thomas-street, in this city; he met a man who was his acquaintance, named Hyland standing at the door of one Blake, who kept a public-house. The prisoner at the bar, then, as I believe, a stranger to O'Brien, was standing at the door; Hyland asked O'Brien was he *up?*—which is, I presume, a technical expression to signify that a man is a member of the society. They tried O'Brien by the signs, whether he was or not. They told him that no man's life was safe if he was not *up*; and, particularly the prisoner at the bar, told O'Brien his life would not be safe, if he were not *up*: they desired O'Brien to go into the house, in a room of which eight people were sitting. There, after some discourse, O'Brien was sworn to secrecy, and afterwards he was sworn to that oath which is called the oath of the United Irishmen. They talked much of their strength—of the number of men and arms provided in various parts of the kingdom, so great as to render the attainment of their object certain; and after much other discourse, which it is unnecessary to state, they adjourned their meeting to the house of one Coghran, in Newmarket on the Coombe, to be held the next Sunday, the 30th of April; they agreed that the password to gain admittance at Coghran's should be "Mr. Green." And it appears (for the trade is attended with some profit) that O'Brien was called upon to pay, and did pay the prisoner one shilling for swearing him.

"As soon as O'Brien left the house, and escaped the danger he imagined he was in, he went to Mr. Higgins, a magistrate of the Queen's county, to whom he was known, then in Dublin, and disclosed to him what had passed. Mr. Higgins told O'Brien he was right to reveal the matter, and brought him to Lord Portarlington, who brought him to one of the committee-rooms of the House of Lords, where he was examined by one of the Lord Lieutenant's secretaries. It was then thought expedient, that attention should be paid to this society, seeing its dangerous tendency, in order to counteract the designs entertained. O'Brien, conceiving that he might be in some danger from a society formed upon such principles, was advised to enlist in one of the regiments of dragoons then quartered in Dublin, and to attend the society, to learn their designs. With this view, O'Brien attended at Coghran's house, in Newmarket, and was admitted on giving the password "Mr. Green."

He there found the prisoner at the bar, with forty others assembled; he was desired to pay sixpence to the funds of the Society; he said he had not then sixpence; they told him he was to return in the evening, and that it made no difference, whether he then paid, or brought it in the evening. Finney informed him and the society that the money collected was to constitute a fund for the purpose of the society; that upon that day there was to be a collection from the United societies in Dublin, sixpence from each man, and that there was to be collected that evening from the various societies, 10,000 sixpences; and he further informed them (for he was an active man at that meeting) that there was to be a great funeral, that of one Ryan, a millwright, whose corpse lay at Plinlico, which was to be attended by all the societies in Dublin; that after the funeral, that particular society was again to assemble at the same place, Coghran's."

Various other meetings were stated in a very moderate speech, and O'Brien swore firmly to the facts. Curran cross-examined the man calmly, and tempted him into confidential insolence. The ruffian described his career as the hanger-on of an excise officer, drinking and extorting in public houses; he candidly avowed not only that he had practised coining, but he identified a receipt for coining, which he had, in a missionary spirit, given to another person; he admitted that, when told that Mr. Roberts of Stradbally would give evidence against his character, he (having a sword and pistol in his hands,) had said he "would settle him." For this he made a trivial explanation. Peter Clarke swore that on the 31st of May, Finney gave him a copy of the United Irish test, and Lord Portarlington swore that O'Brien told him of one or two of the early meetings. Curran was to have opened the defence; but a principal witness being absent, a chaise was despatched for him, and Mr. M'Nally set to speak against time.* The court had then to adjourn for twenty minutes' rest. Then Curran, after examining some persons of the middle class to prove O'Brien's infamy of character, and one to Finney's general loyalty, spoke as follows:—

My Lords, and Gentlemen of the Jury. In the early part of this trial, I thought I should have had to address you on the most important

---

* Mr. M'Nally has marked, on his copy of the speech, that he spoke for an hour and three quarters, and that the speech was reported by "Leonard M'Nally, jun."

occasion possible, on this side of the grave, a man labouring for life, on the casual strength of an exhausted, and, at best, a feeble advocate. But, gentlemen, do not imagine that I rise under any such impressions; do not imagine that I approach you sinking under the hopeless difficulties of my cause. I am not now soliciting your indulgence to the inadequacy of my powers, or artfully enlisting your passions at the side of my client. No, gentlemen; but I rise with what of law, of conscience, of justice, and of constitution, there exists within this realm, at my back, and, standing in front of that great and powerful alliance, I *demand* a verdict of acquittal for my client! What is the opposition of evidence? It is a tissue which requires no strength to break through; it vanishes at the touch, and is sundered into tatters.

The right honourable gentleman who stated the case in the first stage of this trial, has been so kind as to express a reliance, that the counsel for the prisoner would address the jury with the same candour which he exemplified on the part of the crown; readily and confidently do I accept the compliment, the more particularly, as in my cause I feel no temptation to reject it. Life can present no situation wherein the humble powers of man are so awfully and so divinely excited, as in defence of a fellow-creature placed in the circumstances of my client; and if any labours can peculiarly attract the gracious and approving eye of heaven, it is when God looks down on a human being assailed by human turpitude, and struggling with practices against which the Deity has placed his special canon, when he said "Thou shalt not bear false witness against thy neighbour; thou shalt do no murder."

Gentlemen, let me desire you again and again to consider all the circumstances of this man's case, abstracted from the influence of prejudice and habit; and if aught of passion assumes dominion over you, let it be of that honest, generous nature that good men must feel when they see an innocent man depending on their verdict for his life; to this passion I feel myself insensibly yielding; but unclouded, though not unwarmed, I shall, I trust, proceed in my great duty.

Wishing to state my client's case with all possible succinctness which the nature of the charge admits, I am glad my learned colleague has acquitted himself on this head already to such an extent, and with such ability, that anything I can say will chance to be superfluous; in truth, that honesty of heart, and integrity of principle, for which all must give him credit, uniting with a sound judgment and sympathetic heart, have given to his statement all the advantages it could have derived from these qualities.

He has truly said that "the declaratory act, the 25th of Edward III., is that on which all charges of high treason are founded;" and I trust the observation will be deeply engraven on your hearts. It is an act made to save the subject from the vague and wandering uncertainty of the law. It is an act which leaves it no longer doubtful whether a man shall incur conviction by his own conduct, or the sagacity of crown construction: whether he shall sink beneath his own guilt, or the cruel and barbarous refinement of crown prosecution. It has been most aptly called the blessed act: and oh! may the great God of justice and of mercy give repose and eternal blessing to the souls of those honest men by whom it was enacted! By this law, no man shall be convicted of high treason, but on proveable evidence; the overt acts of treason, as explained in this law, shall be stated clearly and distinctly in the charge; and the proof of these acts shall be equally clear and distinct, in order that no man's life may depend on a partial or wicked allegation. It does every thing for the prisoner which he could do himself, it does every thing but utter the verdict, which alone remains with you, and which, I trust, you will give in the same pure, honest, saving spirit, in which that act was formed. Gentlemen, I would call it an omnipotent act, if it could possibly appal the informer from our courts of justice; but law cannot do it, religion cannot do it, the feelings of human nature frozen in the depraved heart of the wretched informer, cannot be thawed!

Law cannot prevent the envenomed arrow from being pointed at the intended victim; but it has given him a shield in the integrity of a jury! Every thing is so clear in this act, that all must understand: the several acts of treason must be recited, and proveable conviction must follow. What is proveable conviction? Are you at a loss to know? Do you think if a man comes on the table, and says, "By virtue of my oath, I know of a conspiracy against the state, and such and such persons are engaged in it," do you think that his mere allegation shall justify you in a verdict of conviction? A witness coming on this table, of whatsoever description, whether the noble lord who has been examined, or the honourable judges on the bench, or Mr. James O'Brien, who shall declare upon oath that a man bought powder, ball, and arms, intending to kill another, this is not proveable conviction; the unlawful intention must be shown by cogency of evidence, and the credit of the witness must stand strong and unimpeached. The law means not that infamous assertion or dirty ribaldry is to overthrow the character of a man; even in these imputations, flung against the victim, there is fortunately something detergent, that cleanses the character it was destined to befoul.

In stating the law, gentlemen, I have told you that the overt act must be laid and proved by positive testimony of untainted witnesses; and in so saying, I have only spoken the language of the most illustrious writers on the law of England.

I should, perhaps, apologize to you for detaining your attention so long on these particular points, but that in the present disturbed state of the public mind, and in the abandonment of principle, which it but too frequently produces, I think I cannot too strongly impress you with the purity of legal distinction, so that your souls shall not be harrowed with those torturing regrets, which the return of reason would bring along with it, were you, on the present occasion, for a moment to resign it to the subjection of your passions; for these, though sometimes amiable in their impetuosity, can never be dignified and just, but under the control of reason.

The charge against the prisoner is two-fold: compassing and imagining the King's death, and adhering to the King's enemies. To be accurate on this head is not less my intention than it is my interest; for if I fall into errors, they will not escape the learned counsel who is to come after me, and whose detections will not fail to be made in the correct spirit of crown prosecution

Gentlemen, there are no fewer than thirteen overt acts, as described, necessary to support the indictment; these, however, it is not necessary to recapitulate. The learned counsel for the crown has been perfectly candid and correct in saying, that if any of them support either species of treason charged in the indictment, it will be sufficient to attach the guilt. I do not complain that on the part of the crown it was not found expedient to point out which act or acts went to support the indictment: neither will I complain, gentlemen, if you fix your attention particularly on the circumstances.

Mr. Attorney-General has been pleased to make an observation which drew a remark from my colleague, with which I fully agree, that the atrocity of a charge should make no impression on you. It was the judgment of candour and liberality, and should be yours; nor though you should more than answer the high opinion I entertain of you, and though your hearts betray not the consoling confidence which your looks inspire, yet do not disdain to increase your stock stock of candour and liberality, from whatsoever source it flows; though the abundance of my client's innocence may render him independent of its exertions, your country wants it all. You are not to suffer impressions of loyalty, or an enthusiastic love for the sacred person of the King, to give your judgments the smallest bias. You are to decide from the evidence which you have heard; and if the atrocity of the charge were to have any influence with you, it should be that of rendering you more incredulous to the possibility of its truth.

I confess I cannot conceive a greater crime against civilized society, be the form of government what it may, whether monarchial, republican, or, I had almost said, despotic, than attempting to destroy the life of the person holding the executive authority; the counsel for the crown cannot feel a greater abhorrence against it than I do; and happy am I, at this moment, that I can do justice to my principles, and the feelings of my heart, without endangering the defence of my client, and that defence is, that your hearts would not feel more reluctant to the perpetration of the crimes with which he is charged, than the man who there stands at the bar of his country, waiting until you shall clear him from the foul and unmerited imputation, until your verdict, sounding life and honour to his senses, shall rescue him from the dreadful fascination of the informer's eye.

The overt acts in the charge against the prisoner are many, and all apparently of the same nature, but they, notwithstanding, admit of a very material distinction. This want of candour I attribute to the base imposition of the prosecutor on those who brought him forward.

You find at the bottom of the charge a foundation-stone attempted to be laid by O'Brien,—the deliberations of a society of United Irishmen, and on this are laid all the overt acts. I said the distinction was of moment, because it is endeavoured to be held forth to the public, to all Europe, that, at a time like this, of peril and of danger, there are, in one province alone, one hundred and eleven thousand of your countrymen combined for the purpose of destroying the King, and the tranquillity of the country, which so much depends on him, an assertion which you should consider of again and again, before you give it any other existence than it derives from the attainting breath of the informer. If nothing should induce that consideration but the name of *Irishman*, the honours of which you share, a name so foully, and, as I shall demonstrate, so falsely aspersed, if you can say that one fact of O'Brien's testimony deserves belief, all that can from thence be inferred is, that a great combination of mind and will exists on some public subject.

What says the written evidence on that subject?

What are the obligations imposed by the test-oath of the society of United Irishmen? Is it unjust to get rid of religious differences and distinctions? Would to God it were possible. Is it an offence against the state, to promote a full, free, and adequate representation of all the people of Ireland in parliament? If it be, the text is full of its own comment, it needs no comment of mine. As to the last clause, obliging to secrecy: Now, gentlemen of the jury, in the hearing of the court, I submit to the opposite counsel this question. I will make my adversary my arbiter. Taking the test-oath, as thus written, is there any thing of treason in it? However objectionable it may be, it certainly is not treasonable.

I admit there may be a colourable combination of words to conceal a really bad design; but to what evils would it not expose society, if, in this case, to *suppose* were to *decide*. A high legal authority thus speaks on this subject: "Strong, indeed, must the evidence be which goes to prove that any man can mean, by words, any thing more than what is conveyed in their ordinary acceptation." If the test of any particular community were an open one—if, like the London Corresponding Society, it was to be openly published, then, indeed, there might be a reason for not using words in their common application; but, subject to no public discussion, at least not intended to be so, why should the proceedings of those men, or the obligation by which they are connected, be expressed in the phraseology of studied concealment? If men meet in secret, to talk over how best the French can invade this country, to what purpose is it that they take an engagement different in meaning? Common sense rejects the idea!

Gentlemen, having stated these distinctions, I am led to the remaining divisions of the subject you are to consider. I admit, that because a man merely takes this obligation of union, it cannot prevent his becoming a traitor if he pleases; but the question for you to decide on would then be, whether every man who takes it must necessarily be a traitor?

Independent of that engagement, have any superadded facts been proved against the prisoner? What is the evidence of O'Brien? What has he stated? Here, gentlemen, let me claim the benefits of that great privilege, which distinguishes trial by jury in th' —untry from all the world. Twelve men, not emerging from the must and cobwebs of a study, abstracted from human nature, or only acquainted with its extravagancies; but twelve men, conversant with life, and practised in those feelings which mark the common and necessary intercourse between man and man, such are you, gentlemen.

How, then, does Mr. O'Brien's tale hang together? Look to its commencement. He walks along Thomas-street, in the open day (a street not the least populous in this city), and is accosted by a man, who, without any preface, tells him he'll be murdered before he goes *half* the street, unless he becomes a United Irishman! Do you think this is a probable story? Suppose any of you, gentlemen, be a United Irishman, or a Freemason, or a Friendly Brother, and that you meet me walking *innocently* along, just like Mr. O'Brien, and meaning *no harm*, would you say, " Stop, Mr. Curran, don't go further, you'll be murdered before you go half the street, if you do not become a United Irishman, a Freemason, or a Friendly Brother." Did you ever hear so *coaxing* an invitation to *felony* as this? " Sweet Mr. James O'Brien' come in and save your precious life—come in and take an oath, or you'll be murdered before you go half the street! Do, sweetest, dearest Mr. James O'Brien, come in, and do not risk your valuable existence." What a loss had he been to his King, whom he loves so marvellously! Well, what does poor Mr. O'Brien do? Poor, dear man, he stands petrified with the magnitude of his danger,—all his members refuse their office,—he can neither run from the danger, nor call out for assistance; his tongue cleaves to his mouth, and his feet incorporate with the paving-stones; it is in vain that his expressive eye silently implores protection of the passenger; he yields at length, as men have done, and resignedly submits to his fate. He then enters the house, and being led into a room, a parcel of men *make faces* at him; but mark the metamorphosis: well may it be said, that " miracles will never cease;" he who feared to resist in open air, and in the face of the public, becomes a *bravo* when pent up in a room, and environed by *sixteen* men, and one is obliged to bar the door, while another swears him, which after some resistance, is accordingly done, and poor Mr. O'Brien becomes a United Irishman, for no earthly purpose whatever, but merely to save his sweet life.

But this is not all,—the pill so bitter to the percipiency of his loyal palate, must be washed down; and, lest he should throw it off his stomach, he is filled up to the neck with beef and whiskey. What further did they do?

Mr. O'Brien, thus persecuted, abused, and terrified, would have gone and lodged his sorrows in the sympathetic bosom of the Major; but to prevent him even this little solace, they made him drunk. The *next* evening they used him in the like barbarous manner; so that he was not only sworn against his will, but,—poor man,—he was made drunk against his inclination. Thus was he besieged with *united* beefsteaks and whiskey; and against such potent assailants not even Mr. O'Brien could prevail.

Whether all this whiskey that he has been *forced* to drink has produced the effect or not, Mr. O'Brien's loyalty is better than his memory. In the spirit of loyalty he became prophetic, and told Lord Portarlington the circumstances relative to the intended attack on the ordnance stores full three weeks before he had obtained the information through moral agency. Oh! honest James O'Brien, honest James O'Brien! Let others vainly argue on logical truth and ethical falsehood; but if I can once fasten him to the ring of perjury, I will bait him at it, until his testimony shall fail of producing a verdict, although human nature were as vile and monstrous in you as she is in him! He has made a *mistake!* but surely no man's life is safe if such evidence were admissible: what argument can be founded on his testimony, when he swears he has perjured himself, and that any thing he says must be false? I must not believe him at all, and by a paradoxical conclusion, suppose, against "the damnation" of his own testimony, that he is an *honest man!*

Strongly as I feel my interest keep pace with that of my client, I would not defend him at the expense of truth; I seek not to make the witness worse than he is: whatever he may be, God Almighty convert his mind! May his reprobation,—but I beg his pardon,—let your verdict stamp that currency on his credit; it will have more force than any casual remarks of mine. How this contradiction in Mr. O'Brien's evidence occurred, I am at no loss to understand. He started from the beginning with an intention of informing against some person, no matter against whom; and whether he ever saw the prisoner at the time he gave the information to Lord Portarlington, is a question; but none, that he fabricated the story for the purpose of imposing on the honest zeal of the law officers of the crown.

Having now glanced at a part of this man's evidence, I do not mean to part with him entirely; I shall have occasion to visit him again; but before I do, let me, gentlemen, once more impress upon your minds the observation which my colleague applied to the laws of high treason, that if they are not explained on the statute-book, they are explained on the hearts of all honest men; and, as St. Paul says, "though they know not the law, they obey the statutes thereof." The essence of the charge submitted to your consideration tends to the dissolution of the connexion between Ireland and Great Britain.

I own it is with much warmth and self-gratulation that I feel this calumny answered by the attachment of every good man to the British constitution. I feel,—I embrace its principles; and when I look on you, the proudest benefit of that constitution, I am relieved from the fears of advocacy, since I place my client under the influence of its sacred shade. This is not the idle sycophancy of words. It is not crying "Lord! Lord!" but doing "the will of my Father who is in heaven." If my client were to be tried by a jury of Ludgate-hill shopkeepers, he would, ere now, be in his lodging. The law of England would not suffer a man to be cruelly butchered in a court of justice. The law of England recognises the possibility of villains thirsting for the blood of their fellow-creatures; and the people of Ireland have no cause to be incredulous of the fact.

In that country, St. Paul's is not more public than the charge made against the poorest creature that crawls upon the soil of England. There must be two witnesses to convict the prisoner of high treason. The prisoner must have a copy of the jurors' names, by whom he may eventually be tried; he must have a list of the witnesses that are to be produced against him, that they may not, vampire-like, come crawling out of the grave to drink his blood; but that, by having a list of their names and places of abode, he may inquire into their characters and modes of life, that, if they are infamous, he may be enabled to defend himself against the attacks of their perjury, and their subornation. There must, I say, be two witnesses, that the jury may be satisfied, if they believe the evidence, that the prisoner is guilty; and if there be but one witness, the jury shall not be troubled with the idle folly of listening to the prisoner's defence. If there be but one witness, there is the less possibility of contradicting him; he the less fears any detection of his murderous tale, having only infernal communication between him and the author of all evil; and when on the table, which he makes the altar of his sacrifice, however common men may be affected at sight of the innocent victim, it cannot be supposed that the prompter of his perjury will instigate him to retribution: this is the law in England, and God forbid that Irishmen should so differ, in the estimation of the law, from Englishmen, that their blood is not equally worth preserving. I do not, gentlemen, apply any part of this observation to you; you are Irishmen yourselves, and I know you will act proudly and honestly. The law of *England* renders two witnesses necessary, and one witness insufficient, to take away the life of a man on a charge of high treason. This is founded on the principle of common sense, and common justice; for, unless the subject were guarded by this wise prevention, every wretch who could so pervert the powers of invention, as to trump up a tale of treason and conspiracy, would have it in his power to defraud the crown into the most abominable and afflicting acts of cruelty and oppression.

Gentlemen of the jury, though from the evidence which has been adduced against the prisoner, they have lost their value, yet had they been necessary, I must tell you, that my client came forward under disadvantage of great magnitude, the absence of two witnesses very material to his defence; I am not now at liberty to say, what I an instructed would have been proved by May, and Mr. Roberts.

But, you will ask, why is not Mr. Roberts here? Recollect the admission of O'Brien, that he threatened to *settle* him, and you cease to wonder at his absence, when, if he came, the dagger was preparation to be plunged into his heart I said Mr. Roberts absent, I correct myself; no! in effect he is here: I appeal to the heart of that obdurate man (O'Brien), what would have been his (Roberts's) testimony, if he had dared to venture a personal evidence on this trial? Gracious God! is a tyranny of this kind to be borne with, where law is said to exist? Shall the horrors which surround the informer, the ferocity of his countenance, and the terrors of his voice, cast such a wide and appalling influence, that none dare approach and save the victim, which he marks for ignominy and death!

Now, gentlemen, be pleased to look to the rest of O'Brien's testimony: he tells you there are one hundred and eleven thousand men in one province, added to ten thousand of the inhabitants of the metropolis, ready to assist the object of an invasion! Gentlemen, are you prepared to say that the kingdom of Ireland has been so forsaken by all principles of humanity and of loyalty, that there are now no less than 111,000 men sworn by the most solemn of all engagements, and connected in a deadly combination to destroy the constitution of the country, and to invite the common enemy, the French, to invade it—are you prepared to say this by your verdict? When you know not the intentions or the means of that watchful and insatiable enemy, do you think it would be wise by your verdict of guilty, to say, on the single testimony of a common informer, that you do believe upon your oaths that there is a body consisting of no less a number than 111,000 men ready to assist the French, if they should make an attempt upon this country, and ready to fly to their standard whenever they think proper to invade it? This is another point of view in which to examine this case. You know the distress and convulsion of the public mind for a considerable length of time; cautiously will I abstain from making observations that could refresh the public memory, situated as I am, in a court of justice. But, gentlemen, this is the first, the only trial for high treason, in which an informer gives his notions of the propriety or impropriety of public measures; I remember none—except the trial of that unfortunate wanderer, that unhappy fugitive, for so I may call him, Jackson, a native of this country—guilty he was, but neither his guilt nor innocence had any affinity with any other system. But this is the first trial that has been brought forward for high treason, except that, where such matters have been disclosed; and, gentlemen, are you prepared to think well of the burden of embarking your character, high and respectable, on the evidence of an abandoned, and I will show you, a perjured and common informer, in declaring you are ready to offer up to death 111,000 men, one by one, by the sentence of a court of justice? Are you ready to meet it? Do not suppose I am base or mean enough to say anything to intimidate you, when I talk to you of such an event; but if you were prepared for such a scene, what would be your private reflections were you to do any such thing? Therefore I put the question fairly to you—have you made up your minds to tell the public, that as soon as James O'Brien shall choose to come forward again, to make the same charge against 111,000 other men, you are ready to see so many men, so many of your fellow-subjects and fellow-citizens, drop one by one into the grave, dug for them by his testimony?

Do not think I am speaking disrespectfully of you when I say, that while an O'Brien may be found, it may be the lot of the proudest among you to be in the dock instead of the jury-box. If you were standing there, how would you feel if you found that the evidence of such a wretch would be admitted as sufficient to attaint your life, and send you to an ignominious death? Remember I do beseech you, that great mandate of your religion—" Do thou unto all men as you would they should do unto you."

Give me leave to put another point to you—what is the reason that you deliberate—that you condescend to listen to me with such attention? Why are you so anxious, if, even from me, any thing should fall tending to enlighten you on the present awful occcasion? it is, because, bound by the sacred obligations of an oath, your heart will not allow you to forfeit it. Have you any doubt that it is the object of O'Brien to take down the prisoner for the reward that follows? Have you not seen with what more than instinctive keenness this blood-hound has pursued his victim? how he has kept him in view from place to place, until he hunts him through the avenues of the court to where the unhappy man stands now, hopeless of all succour but that which your verdict shall afford. I have heard of assassination by sword, by pistol, and by dagger; but here is a wretch who would dip the Evangelists in blood; if he thinks he has not sworn his victim to death, he is ready to swear, without mercy and without end: but oh! do not, I conjure you, suffer him to take an oath ; the hand of the murderer should not pollute the purity of the gospel: if he will swear, let it be on the *knife*, the proper symbol of his profession

Gentlemen, I am again reminded of that tissue of abominable slander and calumny with which O'Brien has endeavoured to load so great a portion of the adult part of your country. Is it possible you can believe the report of that wretch, that no less than 111,000 men are ready to destroy and overturn the government? I do not believe the abominable slander. I may have been too quick in condemning this man ; and I know the argument which will be used, and to a certain degree, it is not without sense—that you cannot always expect witnesses of the most unblemished character, and such things would never be brought to light if witnesses like O'Brien were rejected altogether. The argument is of some force ; but does it hold here? or are you to believe it as a truth, because the fact is sworn to by an abominable and perjured witness? No ; the law of England, the so-often-mentioned principle upon which that important statute is framed, denies the admission. An English judge would be bound to tell you, and the learned judges present will tell you, that a single accomplice is not to be believed without strong corroborative confirmation—I do not know where a contrary principle was entertained : if such has been the case, I never heard of it. O'Brien stated himself to have been involved in the guilt of the prisoner, in taking the obligation which was forced on him, and which he was afterwards obliged to wash down ; but may not the whole description given by him be false? May he not have fabricated that story, and come forward as an informer in a transaction that never happened, from the expectation of pay and profit? How does he stand? He stands divested of a single witness to support his character or the truth of his assertions, when numbers were necessary for each. You would be most helpless and unfortunate men, if everything said by the witness laid you under a necessity of believing it. Therefore he must be supported either by collateral or confirmatory evidence. Has he been supported by any collatera.

evidence, confirming what was sworn this day? No. Two witnesses have been examined, they are not additional witnesses to the overt acts; but if either of them should carry any conviction to your minds, you must be satisfied that the evidence given by O'Brien is false. I will not pollute the respectable and honourable character of Lord Portarlington, by mentioning it with the false and perjured O'Brien. Does his lordship tell you a single word but what O'Brien said to him? Because, if his lordship told all here that O'Brien told to him, O'Brien has done the same too; and though he has told Lord Portarlington every word which he has sworn on the table, yet still the evidence given by his lordship cannot be corroborative, because the probability is that he told a falsehood; you must take that evidence by comparison. And what did he tell Lord Portarlington? or, rather, what has Lord Portarlington told you? That O'Brien did state to him the project of robbing the ordnance some time before he could possibly have known it himself. And it is material that he swore on the table that he did not know of the plot till his third meeting with the societies; and Lord Portarlington swears that he told it to him on the first interview with him; there the contradiction of O'Brien by Lord Portarlington is material; and the testimony of Lord Portarlington may be put out of the case, except so far as it contradicts that of O'Brien.

Mr. Justice Chamberlain—It is material, Mr. Curran, that Lord Portarlington did not swear positively it was at the first interview, but that he was inclined to believe it was so.

Mr. Curran—Your lordship will recollect that he said O'Brien did not say anything of consequence at any of the other interviews; but I put his lordship out of the question, so far as he does not contradict O'Brien, and he does so. If I am stating anything through mistake, I would wish to be set right; but Lord Portarlington said he did not recollect anything of importance at any subsequent meeting; and as far as he goes, he does beyond contradiction, establish the false swearing of O'Brien. I am strictly right in stating the contradiction; so far as it can be compared with the testimony of O'Brien, it does weaken it; and, therefore, I will leave it there, and put Lord Portarlington out of the question—that is, as if he had not been examined at all, but where he differs from the evidence given by O'Brien.

As to the witness Clarke, after all he has sworn, you cannot but be satisfied he has not said a single word materially against the prisoner; he has not given any confirmatory evidence in support of any one overt act laid in the indictment. You have them upon your minds—he has not said one word as to the various meetings—levying money, or sending persons to France; and, therefore, I do warn you against giving it that attention for which it has been introduced. He does not make a second witness. Gentlemen, in alluding to the evidence of Lord Portarlington, which I have already mentioned, I was bound to make some observations. On the evidence of Clarke I am also obliged to do the same, because he has endeavoured to prejudice your minds by an endeavour to give a sliding evidence of what does not by any means come within this case; that is, a malignant endeavour to impute a horrid transaction—the murder of a man of the name of Thompson—

to the prisoner at the bar; but I do conjure you to consider what motives there can be for insinuations of this sort, and why such a transaction, so remote from the case before you, should be endeavoured to be impressed on your minds. Gentlemen, I am not blinking the question; I come boldly up to it; and I ask you, in the presence of the court and of your God, is there one word of evidence that bears the shadow of such a charge, as the murder of that unfortunate man, to the prisoner at the bar? Is there one word to show how he died—whether by force, or by any other means? Is there a word how he came to his end? Is there a word to bring a shadow of suspicion that can be attached to the prisoner? Gentlemen, my client has been deprived of the benefit of a witness, May, (you have heard of it,) who, had the trial been postponed, might have been able to attend; we have not been able to examine him, but you may guess what he would have said—he would have discredited the informer O'Brien. The evidence of O'Brien ought to be supported by collateral circumstances. It is not; and though Roberts is not here, yet you may conjecture what he would have said. But, gentlemen, I have examined five witnesses, and it does seem as if there had been some providential interference carried on in bringing five witnesses to contradict O'Brien in his testimony, as to direct matters of fact, if his testimony could be put in competition with direct positive evidence. O'Brien said, he knew nothing of ordering back any money to Margaret Moore; he denied that fact. The woman was examined—what did she say on the table in the presence of O'Brien. That "an order was made, and the money refunded, after the magistrate had abused him for his conduct." What would you think of your servant, if you found him committing such perjury—would you believe him? What do you think of this fact? O'Brien denies he knew anything of the money being refunded! What does Mrs. Moore say? That after the magistrate had abused him for his conduct, the money was refunded, and that "she and O'Brien walked down stairs together!" Is this an accidental trip, a little stumble of conscience, or, is it not downright, wilful perjury? What said Mr. Clarke? I laid the foundation of the evidence by asking O'Brien, did you ever pass for a revenue officer? I call, gentlemen, on your knowledge of the human character, and of human life, what was the conduct of the man? Was it what you would have acted, if you had been called on in a court of justice? Did he answer me candidly? Do you remember his manner? "Not, sir, that I remember; it could not be when I was sober." "Did you do it at all?" What was the answer—"I might, sir, have done it; but I must have been drunk. I never did anything dishonest." Why did he answer thus? Because he did imagine he would have been opposed in his testimony, he not only added perjury to his prevarication, but he added robbery to both. There are thousands of your fellow-subjects waiting to know, if the fact charged upon the imtion of 111,000 men ready to assist the common enemy be true; if upon the evidence of an abandoned wretch, a common cheat, a robber, and a perjurer, you will convict the prisoner at the bar. As to his being a coiner, I will not pass that felony in payment among his other crimes, but I will offer it by itself: I will offer it as an emblem of his conscience, copper-washed—I will offer it by itself.

What has O'Brien said? "I never remember that I did pretend to be a revenue officer; but I remember there was a man said something about whiskey; and I remember I threatened to complain, and he was a little frightened—and he gave me three and three pence!" I asked him, "Did his wife give you anything?" "There was three and three pence between them." "Who gave you the money?" "It was all I got from both of them!" Gentlemen, would you let him into your house as a servant? Suppose one of you wanted a servant, and went to the other to get one; and suppose that you heard that he personated a revenue officer; that he had threatened to become an informer against persons not having licences, in order to extort money to compromise the actions, would you take him as a servant? If you would not take him as a servant in exchange for his wages, would you take his perjuries in exchange for the life of a fellow-subject? Let me ask you, how would you show your faces to the public, and justify a barter of that kind, if you were to establish and send abroad his assignats of perjury to pass current as the price of human blood? How could you bear the tyranny your consciences would exercise over you; the dagger that would turn upon your heart's blood, if in the moment of madness you could suffer by your verdict the sword of justice to fall on the head of a victim committed to your sworn humanity, to be massacred in your presence by the perjured and abominable evidence that has been offered! But does it stop there? Has perjury rested there?—No. What said the honest-looking, unlettered mind of the poor farmer? What said Cavanagh? "I keep a public-house,—O'Brien came to me, and pretended he was a revenue officer;—I knew not but it might be so;—he told me he was so—he examined the little beer I had, and my cask of porter." And, gentlemen, what did the villain do? While he was dipping his abandoned tongue in perjury and in blood, he robbed the wretched man of two guineas. Where is he now? Do you wonder he is afraid of my eye? that he has buried himself in the crowd? that he has shrunk into the whole of the multitude, when the witness endeavoured to disentangle him and his evidence? Do you not feel that he was appalled with horror by that more piercing and penetrating eye that looks upon him, and upon me, and upon us all? The chords of his heart bore testimony by its flight, and proved that he fled for the same. But does it rest there? No. Witness upon witness appeared for the prisoner, to whom, I dare say, you will give that credit you must deny to O'Brien. In the presence of God they swore, that they "would not believe him upon his oath, in the smallest matter." Do you know him, gentlemen of the jury? Are you acquainted with James O'Brien? If you do, let him come forward from that crowd where he has hid himself, and claim you by a look. Have you been fellow companions? If you have, I dare say you will recognize him. Have I done with him yet? No; while there is a thread of his villany together, I will tatter it, lest you should be caught with it. Did he dare to say to the solicitor for the crown, to the counsel that are prosecuting the prisoner, that "there is some one witness on the surface of the globe that will say, he believes I am not a villain; but I am a man that deserves some credit on my oath in a court of justice?" Did he venture to call one human being to that fact? But why did they not venture to examine the prisoner's witnesses, as to the reasons of their disbelief? What, if I was bold enough to say to any of you, gentlemen, that I did not think you deserved credit on your oath, would not the first question you would ask be the reason for that opinion? Did he venture to ask that question? No. I think the trial has been fairly and humanely carried on. Mrs. Moore was examined; she underwent cross-examination—the object was to impeach her credit. I offered to examine to her character; no—I would not be suffered to do it; they were right in the point of law. Gentlemen, let me ask you another question:—Is the character of O'Brien such, that you think he did not know that any human creature was to attack it? Did you not see him coiling himself in the scaly circles of his perjury, making anticipated battle against the attack, that he knew would be made, and spitting his venom against the man that might have given such evidence of his infamous character, if he had dared to appear.

Gentlemen, do you feel now that I was maliciously aspersing the character of O'Brien? What language is strong enough to describe the mixture of swindling and imposition which, in the face of justice, this wretch has been guilty of? Taking on himself the situation of one of the King's officers, to rob the King's subjects of the King's money; but that is not enough for him—in the vileness and turpitude of his character he afterwards wants to rob them of their lives by perjury. Do I speak truly to you, gentlemen, when I have shown you the witness in his real colours—when I have shown you his habitual fellowship with baseness and fraud? He gave a recipe for forging money. "Why did you give it to him?" "He was an inquisitive man, and I gave it as a matter of course." "But why did you do it?" "It was a light, easy way of getting money—I gave it as a humbug." He gave a recipe for forging the coin of the country, because it was a light, easy way of getting money! Has it, gentlemen, ever happened to you in the ordinary passages of life, to have met with such a constellation of atrocities and horrors, and that in a single man? What do you say to Clarke? Except his perjury, he has scarcely ground to turn on. What was his cross-examination? "Pray, sir, were you in court yesterday?" "No, sir, I was not." "Why?" "Mr. Kemmis sent me word not to come." There happened to be several persons who saw him in court—one of them swore it—the rest were ready. Call up "little Skirmish" again.* "Pray, Skirmish, why did you say you were not in court yesterday, when you were?" "Why, it was a little bit of a mistake, not being a lawyer. It being a matter of law, I was mistaken." "How did it happen you were mistaken?" "I was puzzled by the hard questions that Mr. M'Nally asked me." What was the hard question he was asked? "Were you in court yesterday?" "No; Mr. Kemmis

---

* "Little Skirmish," a character in *The Deserter*.

sent me word I need not come?" Can you, gentlemen of the jury, suppose that any simple, well-meaning man would commit such a gross and abominable perjury? I do not think he is a credible man; that is, that he swore truer than Lord Portarlington did, because his lordship stands on a single testimony; he may be true, because he has sworn on both sides: he has sworn positively that he was not in the court yesterday; and he has sworn positively he was! so that, wherever the truth is, he is found in it; let the ground be clean or dirty, he is in the midst of it. There is no person but deserves some little degree of credit; if the soul was as black as night, it would burn to something in hell. But let me not appear to avoid the question by any seeming levity upon it. O'Brien stands blackened by the unimpeached proofs of five positive perjuries. If he was indicted on any one of them, he could not appear to give evidence in a court of justice; and I do call upon you, gentlemen of the jury, to refuse him on his oath that credit which never ought to be squandered on the evidence of an abandoned and self-convicted perjurer.

The charge is not merely against the prisoner at the bar; it takes in the entire character of your country. It is the first question of the kind for ages brought forward in this nation to public view, after an expiration of years. It is the great experiment of the informers of Ireland, to see with what success they may make this traffic of human blood. Fifteen men are now in gaol, depending on the fate of the unfortunate prisoner, and on the same blasted and perjured evidence of O'Brien. I have stated at large the case, and the situation of my client; I make no apology for wasting your time; I regret I have not been more able to do my duty; it would insult you if I were to express any such feeling to you. I have only to apologize to my client for delaying his acquittal. I have blackened the character of O'Brien in every point of view; and, though he anticipated the attack that would be made on it, yet he could not procure one human being even base enough to depose that he was to be believed on his oath.

The character of the prisoner has been given. Am I warranted in saying, that I am now defending an innocent and unfortunate fellow-subject, on the grounds of eternal justice and immutable law? and on that eternal law I do call upon you to acquit my client. I call upon you for your justice! Great is the reward, and sweet is the recollection in the hour of trial, and in the day of dissolution, when the casualties of life are pressing close upon your heart, and when in the agonies of death, you look back to the justifiable and honourable transactions of your life. At the awful foot of eternal justice I do, therefore, invite you to acquit my client; and may God, of his infinite mercy, grant you that great compensation which is a reward more lasting than that perishable crown we read of, which the ancients gave to him who saved the life of a fellow citizen in battle. In the name of public justice! I do implore you to interpose between the perjurer and his intended victim; and, if ever you are assailed by the villany of an informer, may you find refuge in the recollection of that example, which, when jurors, you set to those that might be called to pass judgment upon your lives; to repel at the human tribunal the intended effects of hireling perjury, and premeditated murder! If it should be the fate of any of you to count the tedious moments of captivity, in sorrow and in pain, pining in the damps and gloom of a dungeon, recollect there is another more awful tribunal than any on earth, which we must all approach, and before which the best of us will have occasion to look back to what little good he has done on this side the grave; I do pray, that Eternal Justice may record the deed you have done, and give to you the full benefit of your claims to an eternal reward, a requital in mercy upon your souls!

After a reply from the Solicitor-General (Toler), Justice Chamberlain and Baron Smith charged, inclining to the prisoner, and in a quarter of an hour the jury returned a verdict of *Not Guilty*. On the 19th, fifteen other persons, who had been indicted on the same charge were formally tried and acquitted, and, on taking the oath of allegiance, and filing recognizances for good behaviour, were discharged. So ended the first of the '98 trials.

HENRY SHEARES.

[HIGH TREASON.]

SPECIAL COMMISSION, DUBLIN.

4th and 12th July, 1798.

I NOTICED the formation of the United Irish Society, in 1791, for the achievement of Catholic Emancipation and Parliamentary Reform, and its increase, in 1792–3, retaining its original objects. In 1794, the views of Tone and Neilson, who both desired an independent republic, spread; but the formal objects were unchanged, when, on the 10th of May, 1795,* the organization of Ulster was completed. The recal of Lord Fitzwilliam, and the consequent disappointment of the Roman Catholics—the accumulation of coercive laws—the prospect of French alliance, and the natural progress of a quarrel, rapidly spread the influence, and altered the whole character of the Society. The Test of the Society was made more decisive, and less constitutional. In the Autumn of 1796 the organization was made military in Ulster. Twelve neighbours formed a society, whose secretary was called "a petty officer;" the petty officers of five societies elected one of themselves into the lower baronial, as representative and captain of sixty; the members of ten lower baronials sent a delegate to the upper baronial. This last delegate was, therefore, colonel of a battalion of six hundred men. Towards the middle of 1797, this system spread to Leinster. Each baronial sent a delegate to a county committee, and the provincial committee consisted of two or three delegates from each of the counties. The provincial committee ballotted for five members of an executive; the secretary alone examined the ballot, and reported it to the persons elected, but not to the electors.

Though so far back as May, 1796, the then Executive had *formally* communicated with France, through Lord Edward Fitzgerald, it was not till 19th February, 1798, that it was resolved—"That they would not be diverted from their purpose by anything which could be done in parliament."

The Executive consisted then of Dr. MacNevin, Arthur O'Connor, Thomas Addis Emmet, Richard M'Cormack, Oliver Bond, and Lord Edward.

In the Winter of 1796-7, the coming of the French was urged as a reason for immediate insurrection; but it did not prevail. In May, 1797, the order for the execution of the four soldiers of the Monaghan Militia, at Blaris Mór, was regarded by the Militias as a sufficient motive for action; but not so thought the Executive.

In the Summer of 1797, the Militia regiments sent a deputation, offering to seize the Castle. The Northern leaders were for an outbreak; so was Lord Edward. Still nothing was done. And again, in the beginning of '98, the people, subjected to free quarters, whipping, burnings, and transportation, pressed for insurrection; and Lord Edward was disposed

---

* Neilson's Evidence—Report of Secret Committee. Appendix, No. 3L.

to it. Emmet wanted to wait for French aid (though no man was more adverse to, or took more precautions against. French authority in Ireland); and thus they were, when the sleek traitor, Reynolds of Kilkee, glided into their councils (through Lord Edward's weak kindness), and betrayed them to the Castle for money.

Arthur O'Connor was arrested at Maidstone, in the act of embarking for France; and, on the 12th of March, a meeting of Leinster delegates, including Oliver Bond, M'Cann, &c., &c. were arrested at Oliver Bond's woollen warehouse, in Bridge-street. MacNevin, Thomas Emmet, and Sampson, were in the warrant with Bond; but not being punctual at the meeting, were not taken for some days.

A warrant had, at the same time, been issued against Lord Edward; but he escaped, and lay concealed. The places of MacNevin, Emmet, and O'Connor were filled. John Sheares was one of the New Directory. But Reynolds, though suspected, retained his intimacy On the 19th of May, just four days before the rising was to take place. Lord Edward was pounced on, and, on the 21st, the two Sheares were arrested. Thus the insurrection began, without its designers to lead it, and without time to replace them.

On the night of the 23rd May, the stopping of the mail coaches was the signal for insurrection. Next day the peasantry of Kildare, Wicklow, and parts of Meath arose. They were generally met and defeated; but they succeeded at Prosperous, and partially in other places. On the 26th, the Meath people were defeated at Tara. On the 27th, the Wexford men won the battle of Oulard—the next day, stormed Enniscorthy—on the 30th, got Wexford town by capitulation, and immediately swept the county. On the 5th June, the insurgents stormed Ross, got drunk in the town, and were driven out with much execution and, on the 9th, another of their masses failed in an attack on Arklow. The Wexford insurrection began thenceforth to decline. On the 21st of June, the battle of Vinegar Hill was gained by General Lake. Meantime, the Antrim rising had been stopped by a battle in that town, on the 7th of June; and the success of that of Down, at Saintfield, on the 10th June, was over-balanced by the total defeat of Munroe and his Presbyterians, at Ballinahinch, on the 12th. Kildare and Wicklow continued a partizan war; and a column of Wexford fugitives forced their way to the Boyne, and there, utterly worn out, were cut to pieces. This was on the 13th of July, the morning when the Sheares were convicted. On the 17th July, Lord Castlereagh announced the final defeat of the rebellion.*

Perhaps the reader will forgive these dates, as he may better appreciate, by means of them, the moral atmosphere wherein these next speeches of Curran were spoken.

Henry and John Sheares were the sons of a Cork banker. The elder was a man of fine person—vain and weak face, and vainer and weaker mind—some eloquence and warmth, and showy manners. In '98, he was forty-five years old, and was married to a second wife, by whom he had a large family. John was thirty-two—a man of firmness, feeling, and ready intellect. He was, at the time of his death, engaged to a Miss Steele.

Henry's property was £1,200 a-year, which he encumbered; John's £3,000, on which he lived, after lending his brother money. Miss Steele says he bought "nothing but books." They resided in Baggot-street (now No. 130), and there Henry was arrested. John was arrested at Surgeon Lawless's, in French-street. They had been United Irishmen from 1793, and John was a frequent chairman, and apparently a man of weight in "The Union." He contributed to "*The Press*"—was peculiarly active with his brother in pushing the organization in Cork—and became, as we have seen, one of the Executive, after the arrests at Bond's, in March, '98.

Strange to say, it was not till the 10th of May that they first met their betrayer; but he was a skilful and zealous artist, and in eleven days he contrived to win their intimacy, share their hospitality, gain their secrets, and hand them to the executioner! Unrivalled Armstrong!

This John Warneford Armstrong was a man of good family, and a Captain in the King's County Militia, then stationed at Loughlinstown Camp, between Dublin and Bray. On the 10th May, he went to the shop of Byrne, a bookseller, in Grafton-street, and a notorious member of the United Irish Society. He was in the habit of buying there the books current among the Republicans, and Byrne (a feeble, but not treacherous, man) was absurd enough to introduce him to Henry Sheares.† Henry declined communication, and went away; but John (who had before noticed Armstrong in the shop) soon came in, was introduced, and plunged headlong into communication with Armstrong. Frequent interviews followed. The means of taking the Castle, Island-bridge Barracks, and Lehaunstown

---

* If I add, that the French, under Humbert, entered Killala Bay on the 22nd of August—carried Castlebar on the 27th of August—and surrendered, at Ballinamuck, on the 8th September; and that Hardy's flotilla was taken on the 11th October, with Tone, who died on the 19th of November, the reader will have a short chronology of the "Rebellion of '98."

† At Armstrong's request, says the brief; at Byrne's own desire, said Captain Armstrong, in a conversation with Dr. Madden, which will appear in the Third, and most interesting Series of "The United Irishmen."

(Loughlinstown) Camp, were constant topics. On the 20th (Sunday) he dined at Baggot-street, on John's invitation, and with the earnest approval of Lord Castlereagh; was informed by John, on the part of the Executive, that he was to command the King's County force, and discussed many raw, but important, projects. Armstrong had formed the acquaintance to get them in his clutches; they were so, and on the 21st of May they were taken.

On the 26th of June, Chief Justice Lord Carleton, Baron George, and Justices Crookshank, Chamberlain, and Daly, opened the Special Commission. After the Grand Juries for Dublin City and County were sworn, they were addressed by Lord Carleton; and then numerous prisoners were arraigned. True bills were found against Samuel Neilson, Michael Byrne, Henry and John Sheares, John M'Cann, and Oliver Bond. The Court assigned* Mr Curran and Mr. M'Nally to John Sheares; Mr. Plunket, for Henry Sheares; and Mr. Armstrong Fitzgerald, as agent for both; and then adjourned to the 4th July.

On the 4th July, Lord Carleton, Barons Smith and George, and Justices Crookshank and Daly, sat; and Henry and John Sheares being put to the bar, their indictment for High Treason was read by the Clerk of the Crown. The first count stated sixteen overt acts The second count was for associating as United Irishmen, &c.

Mr. M'Nally objected, after some delay, that John Decluzeau, one of the grand jurors who found the bills, was an alien, not naturalized, and filed a plea in court. The Crown replied and Curran supported the plea as follows:—

My lords, we have looked over this replication, and we find that the gentlemen concerned for the crown have thought proper to plead in three ways. The subject matter of our plea in abatement came very recently to our knowledge. To suppose that an alien had been upon the grand jury finding a bill of indictment involving the duty of allegiance was a rare thing; the suspicion of it came late to our knowledge. It would have been our duty to be prepared, had we known it in time; but as we did not, and as it is a plea of great novelty, we hope the court will not think it unreasonable to give us time till to-morrow to answer this pleading.

The Court over-ruled the application.

Mr. Curran—My lords, before we rejoin, it may be prudent to consider, whether this replication should not be *quashed*. There are three distinct matters in the replication, and they are repugnant to one another One is, that the juror is *not an alien;* the second and third contain averments that he *is an alien.* Clearly, in civil cases, a party cannot plead double matter, without the leave of the court; even the statute which gives that benefit, does not admit it without a special motion, in order that the court may see whether the pleas can stand together. But even that holds only in civil cases, and by the authority of an act of parliament. Therefore, your lordships will consider, whether a replication of this kind, consisting of three parts, contradictory and repugnant, ought to be answered.

Lord Carleton—In civil cases, certainly, the right of pleading double arises from the act of parliament. As to the objection you now make, you must avail yourself of it in some other way. We will not quash the replication upon motion.

A rejoinder and demurrer of insufficiency were then filed on the part of the prisoners.

Mr. Curran—My lords, it is my duty to suggest such reasons as occur to me in support of the demurrer filed here on the part of the prisoners My lords, the law of this country has declared that in order to the conviction of any man, not only of any charge of the higher species of criminal offences, but of any criminal charge whatsoever, he must be con-

---

* The right to have counsel assigned, and to get a copy of the indictment, was conceded to prisoners by the 5th George III., an act introduced by the father of the Sheares, when a member of the Irish parliament.

victed upon the finding of two juries; first, of the grand jury, who determine upon the guilt in one point of view; and, secondly, by the corroborative finding of the petty jury, who establish that guilt in a more direct manner; and it is the law of this country, that the jurors who shall so find, whether upon the grand, or whether upon the petty inquest, shall be *probi et legales homines omni exceptione majores*. They must be open to no legal objection of personal incompetence. They must be capable of having freehold property; and, in order to have freehold property, they must not be open to the objection of being born under the jurisdiction of a foreign prince, or owing allegiance to any foreign power. Because the law of this country, and, indeed, the law of every country in Europe, has thought it an indispensable precaution, to trust no man with the weight or influence which territorial possession may give him, contrary to that allegiance which ought to flow from every man having property in the country.

This observation is emphatically forcible in every branch of the criminal law; but in the law of treason, it has a degree of force and cogency that fails in every inferior class of offence, because the verpoint to be inquired into in treason, is the nature of allegiance.

The general nature of allegiance may be pretty clear to every man. Every man, however unlearned he may be, can easily acquire such a notion of allegiance, whether natural and born with him, or whether it be temporary, and contracted by emigration into another country, he may acquire a vague, untechnical idea of allegiance, for his immediate personal conduct.

But I am warranted in saying, that the constitution does not suppose, that any foreigner has any direct idea of allegiance, but what he owes to his original prince. The constitution supposes, and takes for granted, that no foreigner has such an idea of our peculiar and precise allegiance, as qualifies him to act as a juror, where that is the question to be inquired into; and I found myself upon this known principle, that though the benignity of the English law has in many cases, where strangers are tried, given a jury half composed of foreigners and half natives, that benefit is denied to any man accused of treason, for the reason I have stated; because, says Sir W. Blackstone, " aliens are very improper judges of the breach of allegiance." A foreigner is a most improper judge of what the allegiance is which binds an English subject to his constitution. And, therefore, upon that idea of utter incompetency in a stranger, is every foreigner directly removed and repelled from the possibility of exercising a function that he is supposed utterly unable to discharge.

If one Frenchman shall be suffered to find a bill of indictment between our Lord the King and his subjects, by a parity of reasoning, may twenty-three men of the same descent be put into the box, with authority to find a bill of indictment. By the same reason that the court may communicate with one man, whose language they do not know, may they communicate with twenty-three natives of twenty-three different countries and languages.

How far do I mean to carry this? Thus far: that every statute, or means by which allegiance may be shaken off, and any kind of benefit or privilege conferred upon an emigrating foreigner, is for ever to be considered by a court of justice with relation to that natural incompetency to perform certain trusts, which is taken for granted, and established by the law of England. I urge it with this idea, that whether the privilege is conferred by letters patent, making the foreigner a denizen, or whether by act of parliament, making him as a native subject, the letters patent, or act of parliament, should be construed *secundum subjectam materiam*; and a court of justice will take care, that no privilege be supposed to be granted, incompatible with the original situation of the party to whom, or the constitution of the country in which, it is conferred.

Therefore, my lords, my clients have pleaded, that the bill of indictment to which they have been called upon to answer, has been found, among others, by a foreigner, born under a foreign allegiance, and incapable of exercising the right of a juror, upon the grand, or the petty inquest. That is the substance of the plea in abatement. The counsel for the crown have replied, and we have demurred to the second and third parts of the replication.

My lords, I take it to be a rule of law, not now to be questioned, that there is a distinction in our statute laws; some are of a public, some of a private nature.

That part of the legislative edict which is considered as of a public nature, is supposed to be recorded in the breasts of the King's judges. As the King's judges, you are the depositories and the records of the public law of the country.

But wherever a private indulgence is granted, or a mere personal privilege conferred, the King's judges are not the depositories of such laws, though enacted with the same publicity; you are not the repositories of deeds or titles which give men franchises or estates, nor of those statutes which ease a man of a disability, or grant him a privilege. With regard to the individual to whom they relate, they are mere private acts, muniments, or deeds, call them by what name you please; they are to be shown as private deeds, to such courts as it may be thought necessary to bring them forward. Therefore, if there be any act of parliament, by which a man is enabled to say he has shaken off the disability which prevented him from intermeddling in the political or judicial arrangement of the country; if he says he is no longer to be considered as an alien, he must show that act specially to the court in his pleading. The particular authority, whether by letters of denization, or act of parliament, must be set forth, that the court may judge of them, that if it be by act of parliament, the court may see whether he comes within the provisions of the act. This replication does no such thing.

The second and the third parts were intended to be founded upon the statute of Charles II., and also, I suppose, upon the subsequent statute, made to give it perpetuity, with certain additional requisites. The statute of Charles recites, that the kingdom was wasted by the unfortunate troubles of that time; and that trade had decreased, for want of merchants. After thus stating generally the grievances which had afflicted the trade and population of the country, and the necessity of encouraging emigration from abroad, it goes on and says, that strangers may be induced to transport themselves and families, to replenish the country, if they may be made partakers of the advantages and free exercise of their trades, without interruption and disturbance

The grievance was the scarcity of men; the remedy was tne encouragement of foreigners to transport themselves: and the encouragement given was such a degree of protection, as was necessary to the full exercise of their trades, in dealing, buying, and selling, and enjoying the fullest extent of personal security. Therefore, it enacts, that all foreigners, of the Protestant religion, and all merchants, &c., who shall, within the *term of seven years*, transport themselves to this country, shall be deemed and reputed natural-born subjects, and *may implead and be impleaded, and prosecute and defend suits*.

The intention was, to give them protection for the purposes for which they were encouraged to come here; and therefore the statute, instead of saying generally they shall be subjects *to all intents and purposes*, specifically enumerates the privileges they shall enjoy. If the legislature intended to make them subjects *to all intents and purposes*, it had nothing more to do than say so. But not having meant any such thing, the statute is confined to the enumeration of the mere hospitable rights and privileges to be granted to such foreigners as come here for special purposes. It states, that he may implead, and shall be answered unto, that he may prosecute and defend suits. Why go on and tell a man, who is *to all intents and purposes* a natural-born subject, that he may implead and bring actions? I say, it is to all intents and purposes absurd and preposterous. If *all* privileges be granted in the first instance, why mention *particular* parts afterwards? A man would be esteemed absurd, who by his grant gave a thing under a general description, and afterwards granted the particular parts. What would be thought of a man who gave another his horse, and then said to the grantee, "I also give you liberty to ride him when and where you please?"

What was the case here? The government of Ireland said, we want men of skill and industry, we invite you to come over, our intention is, that if you be Protestants, you shall be protected: but you are not to be judges, or legislators, or kings. We make an act of parliament giving you protection and encouragement to follow the trades for your knowledge in which we invite you; you are to exercise your trade as a natural-born subject. How? With full power to make a bargain and enforce it: we invest you with the same power, and you shall have the same benefit, as if you were appealing to your own natural form of public justice; you shall be here as a Frenchman in Paris, buying and selling the commodities appertaining to your trade.

Look at another clause in the act of parliament, which is said to make a legislator of this man, or a juror, to pass upon the life and death of a fellow-subject, no, not a fellow-subject, but a stranger. It says, "you may purchase an estate and you may enjoy it, without being

a trustee for the crown." Why was that necessary, if he were a subject *to all intents and purposes?*
This statute had continuance for the period of seven years only: that is, it limited the time in which a foreigner might avail himself of its benefits to seven years. The statute 4 George I. revives it, and makes it perpetual. I trust I may say, that whenever an act of parliament is made, giving perpetuity to a former act, no greater force or operation can be given to the latter, than would have been given to the former, had it been declared perpetual at the time of its enactment. An act of that kind is merely to cure the defect of continuance; therefore, it does no more than is necessary to that end. Then how will it stand? Thus: that any man, who, within seven years after the passing of the act of Charles II. performing the requisites there mentioned, shall have the privileges thereby granted for ever thereafter. The court would assume the office of legislation, not of construction, if they inferred or supplied by intendment, a longer period than seven years; there is nothing in the subsequent act, changing the term of seven years limited in the former; it is not competent to a court of justice to alter or extend the operation of a statute by the introduction of clauses not to be found in it. It is the business of the legislature to enact laws, of the court to expound them.

It is worthy of observation, my lords, that this subsequent statute has annexed certain explicit conditions to be performed by the person who is to take the benefit of the preceding act; for it is provided, that no person shall have the benefit of the former act, unless he take the several oaths appointed to be taken by the latter; among which, is the oath against the Pretender, which is not stated in the replication.

There is a circumstance in the latter act, which, with regard to the argument, is extremely strong, to show, that the legislature did not intend to grant the universal franchise and privilege to all intents and purposes. It revives every part of the former, save that part exempting aliens from the payment of excise. Will it be contended, that an alien should be considered as a natural-born subject *to all intents and purposes,* and yet be exempt from the payment of excise? It is absurd, and impossible.

Put it in another point of view. What is an act of naturalization? It is an encroachment upon the common law rights, which every man born in this country has in it; those rights are encroached upon and taken away by a stranger. The statute therefore should be construed with the rigour of a penal law. The court, to be sure, will see, that the stranger has the full benefit intended for him by the statute; but they will not give him any privilege inconsistent with the rights of the natural-born subjects, or incompatible with the fundamental principles of the constitution into which he is admitted; and I found myself upon this, that after declaring that he shall be considered as a natural-born subject, the act states such privileges only as are necessary to the exercise of trade and the enjoyment of property.

Therefore, it comes back to the observation just now made. Is not any man pleading a statute of naturalization, by which he claims to be considered as a natural-born subject, bound to set forth a compliance with all the requisites pointed out by that statute? He is made a native to a certain extent, upon complying with certain conditions; is he not bound to state that compliance? Here he has not stated them. But I go farther; I say, that every condition mentioned in the statute of Charles, should be set forth in the second part of the replication; that he came with an intent of settling; that he brought his family and his stock; that he took the oaths before the proper magistrates; and after a minute statement of every fact, he should state the additional oath required by the statute George I.

But, my lords, a great question remains behind to be decided upon. I know of no case upon it. I do not pretend to say, that the industry of other men may not have discovered a case. But I would not be surprised, if no such case could be found; if since the history of the administration of justice in all its forms in England, a stranger had not been found intruding himself into its concerns; if through the entire history of our courts of justice, an instance was not to be found, of the folly of a stranger interfering upon so awful a subject, as the breach of allegiance between a subject and his king.

My lords, I beg leave upon this part to say, that it would be a most formidable thing, if a court of justice would pronounce a determination big with danger, if they said that an alien may find a bill of indictment involving the doctrine of allegiance. It is permitting him to intermeddle in a business of which he cannot be supposed to have any knowledge. Shall a subject of the Irish crown be charged with a breach of his allegiance upon the saying of a German, an Italian, a Frenchman, or a Spaniard? Can any man suppose any thing more monstrous or absurd, than that of a stranger being competent to form an opinion upon the subject? I would not form a supposition upon it. At a time when the generals, the admirals, and the captains of France are endeavouring to pour their armies upon us, shall we permit their petty detachments to attack us in judicial hostility? Shall we sit inactive, and see their skirmishers take off our fellow-subjects by explosions in a jury room?

When did this man come into the country? Is the raft upon which he floated now in court? What has he said upon the back of the bill? What understanding had he of it? If he can write more than his own name, and had wrote *ignoramus* upon the back of the indictment, he might have written truly; he might say, he knew nothing of the matter.

He says he is naturalized; I am glad of it; you are welcome to Ireland, Sir; you shall have all the privileges of a stranger, independent of the invitation by which you came; if you sell, you shall recover the price of your wares, you shall enforce the contract; if you purchase an estate, you shall transmit it to your children, if you have any—if not, your devisee shall have it. But you must know, that in this constitution, there are laws binding upon the court as strongly as upon you; the statute itself which confers the privileges you enjoy, makes you incapable of discharging offices. Why? Because they go to the fun¡

damentals of the constitution, and belong only to those men who have an interest in that constitution transmitted to them from their ancestors.

Therefore, my lords, the foreigner must be content; he shall be kept apart from the judicial functions; in the extensive words of the act of parliament, he shall be kept from "all places of trust whatsoever." If the act had been silent in that part, the court would notwithstanding be bound to say, that, it did not confer the power of filling the high departments of the state. The alien would still be incapable of sitting in either house of parliament, he would be incapable of advising with the king, or holding any place of constitutional trust whatever. What! shall it be said, there is no trust in the office of a grand juror? I do not speak or think lightly of the sacred office confided to your lordships, of administering justice between the crown and the subject, or between subject and subject : I do not compare the office of a grand juror to that. But, in the name of God, with regard to the issues of life and death, with regard to the consequences of imputed or established criminality, what difference is there, in the importance of the constitution, between the juror who brings in a verdict, and the judge who pronounces upon that verdict the sentence of the law? Shall it be said, that the former is no place of trust? What is the place of trust meant by the statute ? It is not merely giving a thing to another, or depositing for safe custody, it means *constitutional trust*, the trust of executing given departments, in which the highest confidence must be reposed in the man appointed to perform them. It means not the trust of keeping a paltry chattel, it means the awful trust of keeping the secrets of the state, and of the king.

Look at the weight of the obligation imposed upon the juror ; look at the enormous extent of the danger, if he violate or disregard it. At a time like the present, a time of war, what! is the trust to be confided to the conscience of a Frenchman? But I am speaking for the lives of my clients, and I do not choose, even here, to state the terms of the trust, lest I might furnish as many hints of mischief, as I am anxious to furnish arguments of defence. But shall a Frenchman, at this moment, be entrusted with those secrets upon which your sitting upon that bench may eventually depend. What is the inquiry to be made? Having been a pedlar in the country, is he to have the selling of the country, if he be inclined to do so? Is he to have confided to him the secrets of the state ? He *may* remember to have had a *first* allegiance, that he has sworn to it: he might find civilians to aid his perfidious logic, and to tell him, that a secret communicated to him by the humanity of the country which received him, might be disclosed to the older and better matured allegiance sworn to a former power! He might give up the perfidious use of his conscience to the integrity of the older title. Shall the power of calling upon an Irishman to take his trial before an Irish judge, before "the country," be left to the broken speech, the *lingua franca*, of a stranger coming among you and saying, " I was naturalized by act of parliament, and I cannot carry on my trade, without dealing in the blood of your citizens ?"

He holds up your statute as his protection, and flings it against you.

liberty, claiming the right of exercising a judicial function, feeling at the same time the honest love for an older title to allegiance. It is a love which every man ought to feel, and which every subject of this country would feel if he left this country to-morrow, and were to spend his last hour among the Hottentots of Africa. I do trust in God there is not a man who hears me, who does not feel, that he would carry with him to the remotest part of the globe, the old ties which bound him to his original friends, his country, and his king : I do, as the advocate of my clients, of my country—as the advocate for you, my lords, whose elevation prevents you from the possibility of being advocates for yourselves,—for your children, stand up and rely upon it, that this act of parliament has been confined to a limited operation; it was enacted for a limited purpose, and will not allow this meddling stranger to pass upon the life, fame, or fortune of the gentlemen at the bar,—of me, their advocate,—of you, their judges,—or of any man in the nation. It is an intrusion not to be borne.

My lords, you deny him no advantage that strangers ought to have. By extending the statute, you take away a right from a native of the country, and you transfer one to an intermeddling stranger. I do not mean to use him with disrespect; he may be a respectable and worthy man; but whatever he may be, I do, with humble reliance upon the justice of the court, deprecate the idea of communicating to him that high, awful, and tremendous privilege, of passing upon life, of expounding the law in case of treason; it being a fundamental maxim that strangers will, most improperly, be called upon to judge of breaches of allegiance between a subject and his sovereign.

The objection being over-ruled, the Court adjourned.

On Thursday, the 12th July, at nine o'clock, the trial came on. Mr. Webber opened, and the Attorney-General (Toler) stated, the case. Alderman Alexander proved that he found in John's open desk, in Baggot-street, the following paper. (The words in *italics* were interlined; those between crotchets were struck across with a pen):—

"IRISHMEN,

[" Your country is free; all those monsters who usurped its government to oppress its people are in our hands, except such as have]

" Your country is free and you are about to be avenged [already] that vile government which has so long and so cruelly oppressed you is no more; some of its most atrocious monsters have already paid the forfeit of their lives, and the rest are in our hands [waiting their fate.] The national flag, *the sacred green*, is at this moment flying over the ruins of despotism, and that capital which a few hours past [was the scene] witnessed the debauchery, [the machinations] plots and crimes of your tyrants, is now the citadel of triumphant patriotism *and virtue* Arise, then, united sons of Ireland; arise like a great and powerful people, determined to [live] be free or die; arm yourselves by every means in your power, and rush like lions on your foes; consider, that [in disarming your enemy] for every enemy you disarm, you arm a friend, and thus become doubly powerful; in the cause of liberty, inaction is cowardice, and the coward shall forfeit the property he has not the courage to protect. Let his arms be seized and transferred to those gallant [patriots] *spirits* who want, and will use them; yes, Irishmen, we swear by that eternal justice, in whose cause you fight, that the brave patriot, who survives the present glorious struggle, and the family of him who has fallen, or shall fall hereafter in it, shall receive from the hands of a grateful nation, an ample recompense out of [those funds] that property which the crimes of our enemies [shall] have forfeited into its hands, and his name [too] shall be inscribed on the national record of Irish revolution, as a glorious example to all posterity ; *but we likewise swear to punish robbery with death and infamy.*

" We also swear that we will never sheath the sword until every [person] being in the country is restored to those equal rights, which the God of nature has given to all men until an order of things shall be established, in which no superiority shall be acknowledged among the citizens of Erin, but that [which] of virtue and talent [shall entitle to].

"[As for those degenerate wretches who turn their swords against their native country the national vengeance awaits them. "Let them find no quarter unless they shall prove their repentance by speedily deserting, exchanging from the standard of slavery, for that of freedom, under which their former errors may be buried, and they may share the glory and advantages that are due to the patriot bands of Ireland.]

"Many of the military feel the love of liberty glow within their breasts, and have [already to] joined the national standard: receive [those] with open arms, such as shall follow so glorious an example, they can render signal service to the cause of freedom, and shall be rewarded according to their deserts: but for the wretch who turns his sword against his native country, let the national vengeance be visited on him, let him find no quarter, two other crimes demand——

"Rouse all the energies of your souls; call forth all the merits and abilities which a vicious government consigned to obscurity, and under the conduct of your chosen leaders march with a steady step to victory; heed not the glare of [a mercenary] hired soldiery, of *aristocratic yeomanry*, they cannot stand the vigorous shock of freemen, [close with them man to man, and let them see what vigour the cause of freedom can.] Their trappings and their arms will soon be yours, and the detested government of England to which we vow eternal hatred, shall learn, that the treasures [she, it] *they* exhaust on [their mercenary] its accoutered slaves for the purpose of butchering Irishmen, shall but further enable us to turn their swords on its devoted head.

"Attack them in every direction by day and by night; avail yourselves of the natural advantages of your country, which are innumerable, *and with which you are better acquainted than they*; where you cannot oppose them in full force, constantly harass their rear and their flanks; cut off their provisions and magazines, and prevent them as much as possible from uniting their forces; let whatever moments you cannot [pass in] devote to fighting for your country, be [devoted to] passed in learning how to fight for it, or preparing the means of war; for war, war alone must occupy every mind, and every hand in Ireland, until its long oppressed soil be purged of all its enemies.

"Vengeance, Irishmen, vengeance on your oppressors. Remember what thousands of our dearest friends have perished by their [murders, cruel plots] *merciless orders*; remember their burnings, their rackings, their torturings, their military massacres, and their legal murders. Remember ORR."

The kindness of a Conservative:friend has put me in possession of the briefs in this case. The present owner of them was, in '98, an apprentice to Mr. A. Fitzgerald, agent for the defence, and was employed to write down the defence, from *John Sheares'* dictation. These briefs (for the 4th and, 12th July) possess, therefore, unusual interest. They are clear masculine, and sagacious. In them John Sheares plainly enough tells his counsel to save his brother at his expense.

The back is torn off the brief for the 4th, which contains the main case for the defence; but the "additional brief, on behalf of the Prisoners," is directed to "George Ponsonby Esq.," and "with you, J. P. Curran, Wm. C. Plunket, Leonard M'Nally;" yet formally Curran only spoke for Henry Sheares.

The brief must have struck dismay into the counsel's heart. Covered in the usual language of advocacy, it disclosed that, on the 10th of May, John had undertaken to find out what United Men were in Armstrong's regiment; that Armstrong entreated secrecy; that the two brothers were called on in Baggot-street, at four o'clock, on same day, by Armstrong, and there discussed with him the taking of Lehaunstown. On the evening of the 11th, and twice on the 12th, they met. On Sunday, Armstrong dined with them, and John wrote down many names of officers and men, including Captain Crofton. Lieutenant Wilkinson, &c., who could be relied on. A return of the number of organised men of armed men in the different counties was also on the same paper. This paper was found on John's person when he was arrested. It seems to have greatly alarmed him and his agent. It was not only proved, but A. Kearney swore that he and John Sheares were at a meeting in Werburgh-street, where the calculations were made.

Armstrong *may* for a moment have doubted which to sell himself to—the United Irish, or the Castle; for he expressed great anxiety about his commission in case of a revolution, and "to which the prisoner John replied, that it was more than probable they would make him Colonel, as Colonel Lestrange was a violent man against them." So it ran first in the brief, but was altered to, "that they ought rather make him Colonel, as Sir Laurence Parsons had resigned."

He had a bargainer's eye on every one—even on Parsons, his patron and benefactor: so he asked John Sheares, if Sir Laurence was "united," and that he'd like to talk to him on the subject.

Here is Armstrong at home with the family on Sunday night, whom he crunched like a shark next day:—

"During dinner, and until the females withdrew, the most perfect picture of domestic happiness, that could soften the most obdurate heart, was presented in the family then collected together. It consisted of the prisoners' mother and sister, and the wife and three young children of the prisoner Henry, on all of whom he doats with the tenderest affection. Yet could not this scene move the prosecutor from his purposed treachery! On the

X

trary, he was very lively, and seemed to enjoy the ruin he meditated. When the wine had circulated pretty freely, the prosecutor again renewed the political theme—spoke in the harshest terms of the government, and particularly of the Chancellor, Speaker, and some others, whom he termed the prime movers of all the cruelties, military and civil, that were inflicted on the people. Among many other instances which he cited to inflame the passions of the prisoners, he mentioned one that deserves notice. He said he was on guard one night at the Castle, when a guard was demanded of him to quell some tumult in the Liberties; that the orders expressly given by Major Sirr to him were, to desire the officer who was to command the party going on that service, *to be sure to shed blood enough—to spare neither man, woman, nor child—and, at his peril, to take no prisoners*; that he did, accordingly, give those orders, and that the officer entirely disobeyed them, and brought back some prisoners, for which he was violently abused by Major Sirr."

In nothing does John's superiority appear more than in his self-sacrificing care for his brother. Surely this is a clear direction to his counsel to save Henry at *any* rate

"It is suggested to counsel, that as the only means by which any of the overt acts, committed *exclusively* by the said John, can attach upon the said Henry, arise from the alleged conversation, &c., of both the prisoners, in presence of the prosecutor, for the purpose of overturning the government, &c., the entire force of the prisoners' defence should be directed to show, in the first instance, that at those interviews nothing occurred but conversations started by the prosecutor himself, and afterwards distorted by him into criminal consultations; and, secondly, that whatever consultations can be expected to have passed between the prosecutor and John, Henry had no concern in—none of the overt acts laid in the indictment having been committed in his presence, nor with his concurrence or knowledge. Possessed of complete domestic happiness, he felt it a duty he owed his family and self, to avoid engaging in any political controversy, by which he had already so severely injured them. The same motives actuated the said John to preserve to the said Henry the full advantage of this prudent resolution, though more addicted, from nature and situation, to indulge his own political propensities; he endeavoured to avert from the said Henry any inconvenience or injury that might result from his (the said John's) conduct. But the artifice of the prosecutor baffled him, and apparently connected both in this transaction. Yet when it is considered, that at the first introduction between the prosecutor and the prisoner Henry, which certainly was entirely unsought for by the latter, no political conversation whatsoever took place; that he, Henry, was never present when any of the names of officers or sergeants were written or produced; that at two of the meetings between the prosecutor and John, Henry was absent; that in no instance did Henry take upon him any part, *or promise to do any act*, nor to procure any of the information sought for; that no writing, or other document whatsoever, was found in *his possession*; that though John, his brother, lived in his house, their papers were wholly distinct, and those of each secret and unknown to the other; that it can in no instance be shown that Henry associated with any individual suspected of being concerned in this rebellion."

In reference to the proclamation, after many palliations, and speaking of it as a rude and hypothetical "scroll," as it surely was, the brief (or rather John Sheares) says:—

"But what the real object of it was cannot appear, but by explanation and evidence of the writer's opinions, relative to points mentioned therein. (The justification of his opinions on some of these points is considered by the prisoner, in whose desk these papers were found, of more importance than his personal safety.)"

Poor fellow! every one's testimony, man's and woman's, goes to show that he was the more humane, as he was the braver and the more earnest, of the brothers.

There is one other fact about Armstrong, better told in the brief than in any narrative:—

"When taken to the guard-room at the Castle, another instance occurred of the prisoner John's total unconsciousness that any intercourse he had had with the prosecutor was of a criminal nature. While there in custody, the prosecutor entered—expressed his surprise and concern at seeing the prisoner there—inquired if there was any danger of prisoner, or if the government had any charge against him—offered his services in the most friendly manner. Prisoner, instead of suspecting or fearing him, as he naturally would have done, if conscious he could injure him, felt and expressed himself as highly grateful for such friendly attention. Said all he feared was that a certain paper had been found in his desk; that if it was, he would certainly be committed; recommended to the prosecutor to withdraw immediately from the room, lest any injurious suspicion might attach upon him, if seen in conversation with the prisoner; (prisoner thought that prosecutor's anxiety for him made him forget his former caution relative to their acquaintance;) prisoner requested prosecutor that he would call upon his family and pacify their fears, which he promised to do, and departed."*

* Captain Armstrong was accused in Dr. Madden's "United Irishmen," and in Mr. William Curran's noble Memoir of his Father, of having played with Henry Sheares' children. He considered this error so important as to seek two interviews for the correction of it. The minutes of one of these meetings will appear in Dr. Madden's Third Series, and will amuse or amaze the reader of it.

Tyler's* speech was as sanguinary and confused as possible.
Armstrong was examined by Saurin, and swore to the facts we have stated (he had no occasion for perjury); and his cross-examination only proved him blood-thirsty, an Atheist and a traitor. He was good enough for crown and jury.
Application was made for adjournment, but in vain. Mr. G. Ponsonby opened for Henry and Mr. Plunket for John Sheares. Mr. M'Nally pressed some law points with little effect. Three witnesses were examined to prove Captain Armstrong an Atheist; two that he was an avowed Republican and rebel. Several witnesses were examined to the character of the Sheares.
It was then twelve at night—the trial had began at nine; and worn with fifteen hours of anxiety, in a crowded court, in the midst of a red hot summer, Curran rose and said:—

My Lord, before I address you or the Jury, I would wish to make one preliminary observation; it may be an observation only, it may be a request; for myself, I am indifferent, but I feel I am now unequal to the duty—I am sinking under the weight of it. We all know the character of the jury; the interval of their separation must be short, if it should be deemed necessary to separate them. I protest I have sunk under this trial. If I must go on, the court must bear with me, the jury may also bear with me: I will go on, until I sink. But after a sitting of sixteen hours, with only twenty minutes' interval, in these times, I should hope it would not be thought an obtrusive request, to hope for a few hours' interval for repose, or rather for recollection

Lord Carleton—What say you, Mr. Attorney General?
Mr. Attorney-General—My lords, I feel such public inconvenience from adjourning cases of this kind, that I cannot consent. The counsel for the prisoners cannot be more exhausted than those for the prosecution. If they do not choose to speak to the evidence, we shall give up our right to speak, and leave the matter to the court altogether. They have had two speeches already [Mr. Ponsonby had spoken], and leaving them unreplied to is a great concession.
Lord Carleton—We would be glad to accommodate as much as possible. I am as much exhausted as any other; but we think it better to go on.

Mr. Curran—Gentlemen of the jury, it seems that much has been conceded to us. God help us! I do not know what has been conceded to me, if so insignificant a person may have extorted the remark. Perhaps it is a concession, that I rise in such a state of mind and body, of collapse and deprivation, as to feel but a little spark of indignation raised by the remark, that much has been conceded to the counsel for the prisoner; much has been conceded to the prisoners! Almighty and merciful God who lookest down upon us, what are the times to which we are reserved, when we are told, that much has been conceded to prisoners who are put upon their trial at a moment like this, of more darkness and night of the human intellect, than a darkness of the natural period of twenty-four hours; that public convenience cannot spare a respite of a few hours to those who are accused for their lives, and that much has been conceded to the advocate, almost exhausted in the poor remark which he has endeavoured to make upon it.

My countrymen, I do pray you, by the awful duty which you owe your country, by that sacred duty which you owe your character (and I know how you feel it), I do obtest you, by the Almighty God, to have mercy upon my client, to save him, not from guilt, but from the baseness of his accuser, and the pressure of the treatment under which I am sinking.

* He had been made Attorney, and Stewart Solicitor-General on the 10th of July.

With what spirit did you leave your habitations this day? with what state of mind and heart did you come here from your families? with what sentiments did you leave your children, to do an act of great public importance, to pledge yourselves at the shrine of eternal justice, by the awful and solemn obligation of an oath, to do perfect, equal, impartial and steady justice, between the accuser and the accused? Have you come abroad under the idea, that public fury is clamorous for blood, that you are put there under the mere formality or memorial of death, and ought to gratify that fury, with the blood for which it seems to thirst? If you are, I have known some of you, more than one, or two, or three, in some of those situations, where the human heart speaks in honest sentiments. I think I ought to know you well, you ought to know me, and there are some of you, who ought to listen to what so obscure an individual may say, not altogether without some degree of personal confidence and respect. I will not solicit your attention by paying the greatest compliment which man can pay to man; but I say I hold you in regard as being worthy of it; I will speak such language as I would not stoop to hold, if I did not think you worthy of it.

Gentlemen, I will not be afraid of beginning with what some may think I should avoid, the disastrous picture which you must have met previous or way to this court. A more artful advocate might endeavour to play with you, in supposing you to possess a degree of pity and of feeling beyond that of any other human being. But I, gentlemen, am not afraid of beginning by warning you against those prejudices which I must possess; by speaking strongly against them; by striking upon the string, if not strong enough to snap it, will wake it into vibration. Unless you make an exertion beyond the power almost of men to make, you are not fit to try this cause. You may preside at such an execution as the witness would erect himself for—at the sentence flowing from a very short inquiry into reason; but you are not fit to discharge the solid trust of honest men, coming into the box, indifferent as they stand unsworn, to pronounce a verdict of death and infamy, or of existence and of honour. You have only the interval between this and pronouncing your verdict to reflect, and the other interval when you are resigning up your last breath, between your verdict and your grave, when you may lament that you did not act as you ought.

Do you think I want to flatter your passions? I would scorn myself for it. I want to address your reason, to call upon your consciences, to remind you of your oaths, and the consequence of that verdict, which, upon the law and the fact, you must give between the accuser and the accused. Part of what I shall say must of necessity be addressed to the court, for it is matter of law; but upon this subject, every observation in point of law is so inseparably blended with the fact, that I cannot pretend to say, that I can discharge your attention, gentlemen, even when I address the court. On the contrary, I shall the more desire your attention, not so much that you may understand what I shall say, as what the court shall say.

Gentlemen, this indictment is founded upon the statute 25th Edward III.

The statute itself begins with a melancholy observation on the proneness to deterioration which has been found in all countries unfortunately to take place in their criminal law, particularly in the law respecting high treason. The statute begins with reciting, that in the uncertainty of adjudications, it became difficult to know what was treason, and what was not; and to remove further difficulty, it professes to declare all species of treason, that should thereafter be so considered; and by thus regulating the law, to secure the state and the constitution, and the persons of those interested in the executive departments of the government, from the common acts of violence that might be used to their destruction.

The three first clauses of the statute seem to have gone a great way indeed upon the subject; because the object of the provisions was to protect the person, and I beg of you to understand what I mean by person, I mean the *natural person*; I mean no figure of speech, not the monarch in the abstract, but the natural man. The first clause was made without the smallest relation to the executive power, but solely to the natural body and person. The words are "when a man doth compass or imagine the death of the King, or of our lady his Queen, or their eldest son and heir, and thereof be, upon sufficient proof, attainted of open deed by men of his condition, he shall be a traitor." This I say relates only to the natural person of the King. The son and heir of the King is mentioned in the same manner, but he has no power and therefore a compassing his death, must mean the death of his natural person, and so must it be in the case of the King. To conceive the purpose of destroying a common subject, was once a felony of death and that was expressed in the same language, compassing and imagining the death of the subject. It was thought right to dismiss that severe rigour of the law in the case of the subject, but it was thought right to continue it in the case of the King, in contradistinction to all the subjects within the realm.

The statute, after describing the persons, describes what shall be evidence of that high and abominable guilt: it must appear by open deed; the intention of the guilty heart must be proved by evidence of the open deed committed towards the accomplishment of the design. Perhaps in the hurry of speaking, perhaps from the mistakes of reporters, sometimes from one, and sometimes from the other, judges are too often made to say, that such or such an overt act is, if proved to have been committed, ground upon which the jury must find the party guilty of the accusation. I must deny the position, not only in the reason of the thing, but I am fortified by the ablest writers upon the law of treason. In the reason of the thing, because the design entertained, and act done, are matters for the jury. Whether a party compassed the King's death or not, is matter for the jury: and therefore if a certain fact be proved, it is nonsense to say, that such a conclusion *must* follow; because a conclusion of law would then be pronounced by the jury, not by the court. I am warranted in this by the writers cited by Mr. Justice Foster; and therefore, gentlemen, upon the first count in the indictment you are to decide a plain matter of fact, 1st, whether the prisoner did compass and imagine the death of the King? and whether there be any act proved, or apparent means taken, which he resorted to for the perpetration of the crime?

Upon this subject, many observations have already been made before me. I will take the liberty of making one, I do not know whether it has been made before. Even in a case where the overt act stated has of its own nature gone to the person of the King, still it is left to the jury to decide, whether it was done with the criminal purpose alleged, or not. In Russell's case, there was an overt act of a conspiracy to seize the guards; the natural consequence threatened from an act of gross violence so immediately approaching the King's person, might fairly be said to affect his life; but still it was left to the jury to decide, whether that was done for the purpose of compassing the King's death.

I mention this, because I think it a strong answer to those kind of expressions, which in bad times fall from the mouths of prosecutors, neither law nor poetry, but sometimes half metaphysical. Laws may be enacted in the spirit of sound policy, and supported by superior reason; but when only half considered, and their provisions half enumerated, they become the plague of the government, and the grave of principle. It is that kind of refinement and cant which overwhelmed the law of treason, and brought it to a metaphysical death; the laws are made to pass through a contorted understanding, vibratory and confused, and, therefore, after a small interval from the first enactment of any law in Great Britain, the dreams of fancy get around, and the law is lost in the mass of absurd comment. Hence it was that the statute gave its awful declarations to those glossaries; so that if any case arise, apparently within the statute, they were not to indulge themselves in conjecture, but refer to the standard, and abide by the law as marked out for them. Therefore, I say, that the issue for the jury here is to decide in the words of the statute, whether the prisoners did compass the death of the King; and whether they can say, upon their oaths, that there is any overt act proved in evidence, manifesting an intention of injury to the natural person of the King?

I know that the semblance of authority may be used to contradict me: if any man can reconcile himself to the miserable toil of poring over the records of guilt, he will find them marked, not in black, but in red, the blood of the unfortunate, leaving the marks of folly, barbarity, and tyranny. But I am glad that men, who in some situations appear not to have had the pulse of honest compassion, have made sober reflections in the hour of political disgrace. Such has been the fate of Lord Coke, who, in the triumph of insolence and power, pursued a conduct which, in the hour of calm retreat, he regretted in the language of sorrow and disappointment. He then held a language which I willingly repeat, "that a conspiracy to levy war, was no act of compassing the murder of the King." There he spoke the language of law and of good sense; for a man shall not be charged with one crime, and convicted of another. It is a narrow and a cruel policy, to make a conspiracy to levy war an act of compassing the King's death; because it is a separate and distinct offence; because it is calling upon the bones!

affections of the heart, and creating those pathetical effusions, which confound all distinct principles of law, a grievance not to be borne in a state where the laws ought to be certain.

This reasoning is founded upon the momentary supposition that the evidence is true; for you are to recollect the quarter from whence it comes; there has been an attempt by precipitate confession, to transfer guilt to innocence, in order to escape the punishment of the law.— Here, gentlemen, there is evidence of levying war, which act, it is said, tends to the death of the King: that is a constructive treason, calculated as a trap for the loyalty of a jury; therefore you should set bounds to proceedings of that kind; for it is an abuse of the law, to make one class of offence, sufficiently punished already, evidence of another. Every court, and every jury, should set themselves against crimes, when they come to determine upon distinct and specified guilt: they are not to encourage a confusion of crimes, by disregarding the distinction of punishments; nor show the effusion of their loyalty, by an effusion of blood.

I cannot but say, that when cases of this kind have been under judgment in Westminster-hall, there was some kind of natural reason to excuse this confusion in the reports—the propriety of making the person of the King secure. A war immediately adjoining the precincts of the palace, a riot in London, might endanger the life of the King; but can the same law prevail in every part of the British empire? It may be an overt act of compassing the King's death to levy war in Great Britain; but can it be so in Jamaica, in the Bahama isles, or in Corsica, when it was annexed to the British empire? Suppose at that time a man had been indicted there for compassing the King's death, and the evidence was, that he intended to transfer the dominion of that island to the Genoese, or the French; what would you say, if you were told, that was an act by which he intended to murder the King? By seizing Corsica, he was to murder the King? How can there be any immediate attempt upon the King's life, by such a proceeding? It is not possible, and therefore no such consequence can be probably inferred; and therefore I call upon you to listen to the court with respect, but I also call upon you to listen to common sense, and consider, whether the conspiring to raise war can in this country be an overt act of compassing the King's death in this country? I will go further: if the statute of Edward III. had been conceived to make a conspiracy to levy war an overt act of compassing the King's death, it would be unnecessary to make it penal by any subsequent statute; and yet subsequent statutes were enacted for that purpose; which I consider an unanswerable argument, that it was not considered as coming within the purview of the clause against compassing the King's death.

Now, gentlemen, you will be pleased to consider what was the evidence brought forward to support this indictment. I do not think it necessary to exhaust your attention, by stating at large the evidence given by Captain Armstrong. He gives an account which we shall have occasion to examine, with regard to its credibility. He stated his introduction, first to Mr. Henry Sheares, afterwards to his brother; and he stated a conversation which you do not forget, so strange has it been! But in the whole course of his evidence, so far from making any observation, or saying a word in connexion with the power at war with the King, he expressly said, that the insurrection, by whomsoever prepared, or by what infatuation encouraged, was to be a home exertion, independent of any foreign interference whatever. And therefore I am warranted in saying, that such an insurrection does not come within the first clause of the statute. It cannot come within the second, of adhering to the King's enemies; because that means his foreign enemies; and here, so far from any intercourse with them, they were totally disregarded.

Adhering to the King's enemies means co-operating with them, sending them provisions, or intelligence, or supplying them with arms. But I venture to say, that there has not been any one case deciding that any act can be an adherence to a foreign enemy, which was not calculated for the advantage of that enemy. In the case of Jackson, Hensey, and Lord Preston, the parties had gone as far as they could in giving assistance. So it was in Quigley's. But in addition to this, I must repeat, that it is utterly unnecessary the law should be otherwise; for levying war is, of itself, a crime; therefore it is unnecessary, by a strained construction, to say, that levying war, or conspiring to levy war, should come within any other clause equally penal, but not so descriptive.

But, gentlemen, suppose I am mistaken in both points of my argument; suppose the prisoners (if the evidence were true) did compass the King's death, and adhere to the King's enemies; what are you to found your verdict upon? Upon your oaths: what are they to be founded upon? Upon the oath of the witness: and what is that founded upon? Upon this, and this only, that he does believe that there is an eternal God, an intelligent supreme existence, capable of inflicting eternal punishment for offences, or conferring eternal compensation, upon man, after he has passed the boundary of the grave! But where the witness believes he is possessed of a perishing soul, and that there is nothing upon which punishment or reward can be exerted, he proceeds regardless of the number of his offences, and undisturbed by the terrors of exhausted fancy, which might save you from the fear, that your verdict is founded upon perjury. I suppose he imagines that the body is actuated by some kind of animal machinery. I know not in what language to describe his notions. Suppose his opinion of the beautiful system framed by the Almighty hand to be, that it is all folly and blindness, compared to the manner in which he considers himself to have been created; or his abominable heart conceives its ideas; or his tongue communicates his notions. Suppose him, I say, to think so; what is perjury to him? He needs no creed, if he thinks his miserable body can take eternal refuge in the grave, and the last puff of his nostrils can send his soul into annihilation! He laughs at the idea of eternal justice, and tells you that the grave, into which he sinks as a log, forms an entrenchment against the throne of God, and the vengeance of exasperated justice!

Do you not feel, my fellow-countrymen, a sort of anticipated consolation, in reflecting, that Religion—which gave us comfort in our early days, enabled us to sustain the stroke of affliction, and endeared us to one another,—when we see our friends sinking into the earth, fills us with the expectation that we rise again; that we but sleep for a while, to wake for ever? But what kind of communion can you hold, what interchange expect, what confidence place, in that abject slave, that condemned, despaired of wretch, who acts under the idea that he is only the folly of a moment, that he cannot step beyond the threshold of the grave, that that which is an object of terror to the best, and of hope to the confiding, is to him contempt or despair?

Bear with me, my countrymen; I feel my heart run away with me— the worst men only can be cool. What is the law of this country?— If the witness does not believe in God, or a future state, you cannot swear him. What swear him upon? Is it upon the book, or the leaf? You might as well swear him by a bramble, or a coin. The ceremony of kissing is only the external symbol, by which man seals himself to the precept, and says, "May God so help me, as I swear the truth." He is then attached to the divinity, upon the condition of telling truth; and he expects mercy from heaven, as he performs his undertaking. But the infidel!—By what can you catch his soul, or by what can you hold it? You repulse him from giving evidence; for he has no conscience, no hope to cheer him, no punishment to dread!

What is the evidence touching that unfortunate young man? What said his own relation, Mr. Shervington? He had talked to him freely, had known him long. What kind of character did he give of him? Paine was his creed and his philosophy. He had drawn his maxims of politics from the vulgar and furious anarchy broached by Mr. Paine. His ideas of religion were adopted from the vulgar maxims of the same man, the scandal of inquiry, the blasphemer of his God as of his King. He bears testimony against himself, that he submitted to the undertaking of reading both his abominable tracts, that abominable abomination of all abominations, Paine's "Age of Reason," professing to teach mankind, by acknowledging that he did not learn himself! working upon debauched and narrow understandings. Why not swear the witness upon the vulgar maxims of that base fellow, that wretched outlaw and fugitive from his country and his God? Is it not lamentable to see a man labouring under an incurable disease, and fond of his own blotches?

"Do you wish," says he, "to know my sentiments with regard to politics? I have learned them from Paine! I do not love a King, and if no other executioner could be found, I would myself plunge a dagger into the heart of George III., because he is a King, and because he is my King. I swear by the sacred missal of Paine, I would think it a meritorious thing to plunge a dagger into his heart, to whom I had devoted a soul, which Mr. Paine says I have not to lend." Is this the casual effusion of a giddy young man, not considering the meaning of what he said? If it were said among a parcel of boarding-school misses, where he might think he was giving specimens of his courage by nobly denying religion, there might be some excuse. There is a latitude assumed upon some such occasions. A little blasphemy and a little obscenity passes for wit in some companies. But recollect it was not to a little miss, whom he wished to astonish, that he mentioned these sentiments; but a kinsman, a man of boiling loyalty. I confess I did not approve of his conduct in the abstract, talking of running a man through the body; but I admired the honest boldness of the soldier who expressed his indignation in such warm language. If Mr. Shervington swore true, Captain Armstrong must be a forsworn witness; it comes to that simple point. You cannot put it upon other ground. I put it to your good sense, I am not playing with your understandings, I am putting foot to foot, and credit to credit. One or other of the two must be perjured: which of them is it? If you disbelieve Captain Armstrong, can you find a verdict of blood upon his evidence?

Gentlemen, I go further: I know your horror of crime—your warmth of loyalty. They are among the reasons why I respect and regard you. I ask you, then, will you reject such a witness? or would you dismiss the friend you regarded, or the child you loved, upon the evidence of such a witness? Suppose him to tell his own story :—" I went to your friend, or your child—I addressed myself in the garb of friendship—in the smile of confidence, I courted confidence, in order to betray it—I traduced you, spoke all the evil I could against you, to inflame him—I told him, your father does not love you." If he went to you, and told you all this—that he inflamed your child, and abused you to your friend, and said, " I come now to increase it, by the horror of superadded cruelty," would you dismiss from your love and affection the child or the friend you had loved for years? You would not prejudge them. You would examine the consistency of the man's story—you would listen to it with doubt, and receive it with hesitation.

Says Captain Armstrong—" Byrne was my bookseller; from him I bought my little study of blasphemy and obscenity, with which I amused myself." " Shall I introduce Mr. Sheares to you ?"—not saying which What is done then ? He thought it was not right till he saw Captain Clibborn. Has he stated any reason why he supposed Mr. Sheares had any wish at all to be introduced to him?—any reason for supposing that Byrne's principles were of that kind ?—or any reason, why he imagined the intercourse was to lead to anything improper? It is most material that, he says, he never spoke to Byrne upon political subjects; therefore, he knew nothing of Byrne's principles, nor Byrne of his. But the proposal was made, and he was so alarmed, that he would not give an answer till he saw his Captain. Is not this incredible.

There is one circumstance which made an impression upon my mind: that he assumed the part of a public informer, and, in the first instance, came to the field with pledgets and bandages; he was scarcely off the table, when a witness came to his credit. It is the first time that I saw a witness taking fright at his own credit, and sending up a person to justify his character.

Consider how he has fortified it: he told it all to Captain Clibborn He saw him every evening when he returned, like a bee, with his thighs loaded with evidence. What is the defence? That the witness is unworthy of belief. My clients say, their lives are not to be touched by such a man; he is found to be an informer—he marks the victim! You know the world too well, not to know that every falsehood is reduced to a certain degree of malleability by an alloy of truth. Such stories as these are not pure and simple falsehoods: look at your Oateses, your Bedloes, and Dugdales!

I am disposed to believe, shocking as it is, that this witness had the heart, when he was surrounded by the little progeny of my client—when he was sitting in the mansion in which he was hospitably entertained— when he saw the old mother supported by the piety of her son, and the children basking in the parental fondness of the father—that he saw the scene, and smiled at it; contemplated the havoc he was to make, consigning them to the storms of a miserable world, without having an anchorage in the kindness of a father! Can such horror exist, and not waken the rooted vengeance of an eternal God? But it cannot reach this man beyond the grave. Therefore, I uphold him here. I can imagine it, gentlemen, because, when the mind becomes destitute of the principles of morality and religion, all within the miserable being is left a black and desolate waste, never cheered by the rays of tenderness and humanity. When the belief of eternal justice is gone from the soul of man, horror and execution may set up their abode. I can believe that the witness—with what view, I cannot say—with what hope, I cannot conjecture—you may—did meditate the consigning of these two men to death, their children to beggary and reproach, abusing the hospitality with which he was received, that he might afterwards come here and crown his work, having obtained the little spark of truth by which his mass of falsehood was to be animated.

I talked of the inconsistency of the story. Do you believe it, gentlemen? The case of my client is, that the witness is perjured; and you are appealed to, in the name of that ever-living God, whom you revere, but whom he despiseth, to consider, that there is something to save him from the baseness of such an accuser.

But I go back to the testimony; I may wander from it, but it is my duty to stay with it. Says he: "Byrne makes an important application —I was not accustomed to it; I never spoke to him, and yet he, with whom I had no connexion, introduces me to Sheares—this is a *true brother.*" You see, gentlemen, I state this truly—he never talked to Byrne about politics. How could Byrne know his principles? By inspiration? He was to know the edition of the man, as he knew the edition of books. "You may repose all confidence." I ask not is this true; but I say it can be nothing else than false. I do not ask you to say it is doubtful; it is a case of blood, of life or death; and you are to add to the terrors of a painful death, the desolation of a family—overwhelming the aged with sorrow, and the young with infamy. Gentlemen, I should disdain to reason with you; I am pinning your minds down to one point, to show you to demonstration, that nothing can save your minds from the evidence of such perjury; not because you may think it may be false, but because it is impossible it can be true. I put into one of the scales of justice that execrable perjury, and I put into the other, the life, the fame, the fortune, the children of my client. Let not the balance tremble as you hold it; and, as you hold it now, so may the balance of eternal justice be held for you.

But is it upon his inconsistency only I call upon you to reject him? I call in aid the evidence of his own kinsman, Mr. Shervington, and Mr. Drought; the evidence of Mr. Bride and Mr. Graydon. Before you can believe Armstrong, you must believe that all those are perjured. What are his temptations to perjury? The hope of bribery and reward. And he did go up with his sheets of paper in his hand : here is one, it speaks treason—here is another, the accused grows paler—here is a third, it opens another vein. Had Shervington any temptation of that kind? No; let not the honest and genuine soldier lose the credit of it. He has paid a great compliment to the proud integrity of the King, his master, when he did venture, at a time like this, to give evidence, " I would not have come for one hundred guineas." I could not refuse the effusion of my heart, and exclaiming, may the blessings of God pour upon you, and may you never want a hundred guineas!

There is another circumstance. I think I saw it strike your attention, my lords; it was the horrid tale of the three servants whom he met upon the road. They had no connexion with the rebels; if they had, they were open to a summary proceeding. He hangs up one, shoots a second, and administers torture to the body of the third, in order to make him give evidence. Why, my lords, did you feel nothing stir within you? Our adjudications had condemned the application of torture for the extraction of evidence. When a wild and furious assassin had made a deadly attempt upon a life of much public consequence, it was proposed to put him to the torture, in order to discover his accomplices. I scarcely know whether to admire most the awful and impressive lesson given by Felton, or the doctrine stated by the judges of the 'and. "No," said he, " put me not to the torture; for in the extravagance of my pain, I may be brought to accuse yourselves." What say the judges? " It is not allowable by the law and constitution of England, to inflict torture upon any man, or to extract evidence under the coercion of personal sufferings." Apply that to this case: if the unfortunate man did himself dread the application of such an engine for the extraction of evidence, let it be an excuse for his degradation, that he sought to avoid the pain of body by public infamy. But there is another observation more applicable :—Says Mr. Drought, " Had you no feeling, or do you think you will escape future vengeance?" "Oh, Sir, I thought you knew my ideas too well, to talk in that way." Merciful God! Do you think it is upon the evidence of such a man that you ought to consign a fellow-subject to death? He who would hang up a miserable peasant, to gratify caprice, could laugh at remonstrance, and say, " You know my ideas of futurity."

If he thought so little of murdering a fellow-creature, without trial and without ceremony, what kind of compunction can he feel within himself, when you are made the instruments of his savage barbarity? He kills a miserable wretch, looking, perhaps, for bread for his children, and who falls, unaccused, uncondemned. What compunction can he feel at sacrificing other victims, when he considers death as eternal sleep, and the darkness of annihilation. These victims are at this moment led out to public execution; he has marked them for the grave —he will not bewail the object of his own work: they are passing through the vale of death, while he is dozing over the expectancy of annihilation.

Gentlemen, I am too weak to follow the line of observation I had marked out; but I trust I am warranted in saying, that if you weigh the evidence, the balance will be in favour of the prisoners.

But there is another topic, or two, to which I must solicit your attention. If I had been stronger, in a common case, I would not have said so much; weak as I am here, I must say more.

It may be said that the parole evidence may be put out of the case; attribute the conduct of Armstrong to folly, or passion, or whatever else you please, you may safely repose upon the written evidence. This calls for an observation or two. As to Mr. Henry Sheares, that written evidence, even if the hand-writing were fully proved, does not apply to him. I do not say it was not admissible. The writings of Sydney found in his closet were read, justly, according to some; but I do not wish to consider that now. But I say, the evidence of Mr. Dwyer has not satisfactorily established the hand-writing of John. I do not say it is not proved to a certain extent; but it is proved in the very slightest manner that you ever saw paper proved: it is barely evidence to go to you; and the witness might be mistaken.

An unpublished writing cannot be an overt act of treason; so it is laid down expressly by Hale and Foster. A number of cases have occurred, and decisions have been pronounced, asserting that writings are not overt acts, for want of publication; but if they plainly relate to an overt act proved, they may be left to the jury for their consideration. But here it has no reference to the overt act laid; it could not be intended for publication until after the unfortunate event of revolution had taken place; and therefore, it could not be designed to create insurrection. Gentlemen, I am not counsel for Mr. John Sheares, but I would be guilty of cruelty, if I did not make another observation. This might be an idle composition, or the translation of idle absurdity from the papers of another country. The manner in which it was found leads me to think that the more probable. A writing designed for such an event as charged, would hardly be left in a writing-box, unlocked, in a room near the hall-door. The manner of its finding also shows two things: that Henry Sheares knew nothing of it, for he had an opportunity of destroying it, as Alderman Alexander said he had; and further that he could not have imagined his brother had such a design; and it is impossible, if the paper had been designed for such purposes, that it would not be communicated to him.

There is a point to which I will beseech the attention of your lordships. I know your humanity, and it will not be applied merely because I am exhausted or fatigued. You have only one witness to an overt act of treason. There is no decision upon the point in this country. Jackson's case was the first; Lord Clonmel made allusion to the point; but a jury ought not to find guilty upon the testimony of a single witness. It is the opinion of Foster, that by the common law one witness, if believed, was sufficient. Lord Coke's opinion is, that two were necessary: they are great names; no man looks upon the works of Foster with more veneration than myself, and I would not compare him with the deprociated credit of Coke; I would rather leave Lord Coke to the character which Foster gives him; that he was one of the ablest lawyers, independent of some particulars, that ever existed in England. In the wild extravagance, heat, and cruel reign of the Tudors, such doctrines of treason had gone abroad, as drenched the kingdom with blood. By the construction of crown lawyers, and the shameful complaisance of juries, many sacrifices had been made, and therefore, it was necessary to prune away these excesses, by the statute of Edward VI., and, therefore, there is every reason to imagine, from the history of the times, that Lord Coke was right in saying, not by new statute, but by the common law, confirmed and redeemed by declaratory acts, the trials were regulated.

A law of Philip and Mary was afterwards enacted: some think it was a repeal of the statute of Edward VI., some think not. I mention this diversity of opinions, with this view, that in this country, upon a new point of that kind, the weight of criminal prosecution will turn the scale in favour of the prisoner, and that the court will be of opinion, that the statute 7th Wm. III. did not enact any new thing, unknown to the common law, but redeemed it from abuse. What was the state of England? The King had been declared to have abdicated the throne; prosecutions, temporizing juries, and the arbitrary construction of judges, condemned to the scaffold those who were to protect the crown, men who knew, that after the destruction of the cottage, the palace was endangered. It was not, then, the enactment of anything new; it was founded on the caution of the times, and derived from the maxims of the constitution. I know the peevishness with which Burnet observed upon that statute; he is reprehended in a modest manner by Foster; but what says Blackstone, of great authority, of the clearest head and the profoundest reading? He agrees with Montesquieu the French philosopher:—

"In cases of treason, there is the accused's oath of allegiance to counterpoise the information of a single witness; and that may perhaps be one reason, why the law requires a *double* testimony to convict him: though the principal reason undoubtedly is, to secure the subject from being sacrificed to fictitious conspiracies, which have been the engines of profligate and crafty politicians in all ages."*

Gentlemen, I do not pretend to say, that you are bound by an English act of parliament. You may condemn upon the testimony of a single witness. You, to be sure, are too proud to listen to the wisdom of an English law! Illustrious independents! You may murder under the semblance of judicial forms, because you are proud of your blessed indo-

*, Blackstone's Commentaries, 358.

pendence! You pronounce that to be legally done which would be murder in England, because you are proud! You may imbrue your hands in blood, because you are too proud to be bound by a foreign act of parliament; and when you are to look for what is to save you from the abuse of arbitrary power, you will not avail yourselves of it, because it is a foreign act of parliament! Is that the independence of an Irish jury? Do I see the heart of any Englishman move, when I say to him, "Thou servile Briton, you cannot condemn upon the perjury of a single witness, because you are held in by the cogency of an act of parliament."

If power seeks to make victims by judicial means, an act of parliament would save you from the perjury of abominable malice. Talk not of proud slavery to law, but lament that you are bound by the integrity and irresistible strength of right reason; and at the next step bewail, that the all-powerful Author of nature has bound himself in the illustrious servitude of his attributes, which prevent him from thinking what is not true, or doing what is not just. Go, then, and enjoy your independence. At the other side of the water, your verdict upon the testimony of a single witness would be murder. But here you can murder without reproach, because there is no act of parliament to bind you to the ties of social life, and save the accused from the breath of a perjured informer. In England, a jury could not pronounce conviction upon the testimony of the purest man, if he stood alone; and yet, what comparison can that case bear with a blighted and marred informer, where every word is proved to be perjury, and every word turns back upon his soul?

I am reasoning for your country and your children. Let me not reason in vain. I am not playing the advocate; you know I am not— your conscience tells you I am not. I put this case to the Bench: The statute 7 Henry III. does not bind this country by its legislative cogency; and will you declare positively, and without doubt, that it is not common law, the enactment of a new one? Will you say it has no weight to influence the conduct of a jury, from the authority of a great and exalted nation—the only nation in Europe where liberty has seated herself? Do not imagine, that the man who praises liberty is singing an idle song; for a moment, it may be the song of a bird in his cage— I know it may. But you are now standing upon an awful isthmus, a little neck of land, where liberty has found a seat. Look about you— look at the state of the country—the tribunals that dire necessity has introduced. Look at this dawn of law, admitting the functions of a jury; I feel a comfort—methinks I see the venerable forms of Holt and Hale looking down upon us, attesting its continuance. Is it your opinion that bloody verdicts are necessary—that blood enough has not been shed—that the bonds of society are not to be drawn close again, nor the scattered fragments of our strength bound together, to make them of force, but they are to be left in that scattered state, in which every little child may break them to pieces? You will do more towards tranquillizing the country, by a verdict of mercy. Guard yourselves against the sanguinary excesses of prejudice or revenge; and though you think there is a great call of public justice, let no unmerited victim fall.

Gentlemen, I have tired you—I durst not relax. The danger of my client is from the hectic of the moment, which you have fortitude, I trust, to withstand. In that belief, I leave him to you; and as you deal justice and mercy, so may you find it; and I hope that the happy compensation of an honest discharge of your duty may not be deferred til' a future existence, which this witness* does not expect, but that you may speedily enjoy the benefits you will have conferred upon your country

Mr. Prime-Sergeant replied in a long and not candid speech.

Mr. Henry Sheares—My lord. I wish to say a word.

Lord Carleton—It is not regular, after the counsel for the crown have closed. I aske) you at the proper time, you then declined. However, go on.

Mr. Henry Sheares—My lord, after the able and eloquent defence which has been made for me by my counsel, it would ill become me to add anything to it. But there is one part of it which appears to me not to have been sufficiently dwelt upon. It is respecting that paper. I protest most solemnly, my lords, I knew nothing of it; to know of it, and leave it where it was when the magistrate came, were a folly so glaring, that I cannot be supposed to have been guilty of it. When the Alderman rapped at the door, I asked, what was the matter? After he was admitted, he said he wanted my papers; I told him they were there. My lords, is it possible, I could commit myself and all I hold dear, by so egregious an act of folly? Having the dearest sources of happiness around me, should I sacrifice them and myself, by leaving such a document in an open writing box?

My lords, I beg your lordships' pardon. I thank you for this indulgence; it would be irregular for me to expatiate further. The evidence of Captain Armstrong is one of the most ingenious and maliciously fabricated stories, with respect to me, I ever heard of. My lords, I should think, I could not be legally implicated by any paper found in that way.

Lord Carleton charged elaborately, reading the evidence thoroughly, and Justice Crookshank and Baron Smith concurred.

The jury asked for the papers, which, with the prisoner's consent, were taken to the jury room. They then retired for seventeen minutes, and brought in a verdict, finding both the prisoners GUILTY.

As soon as the verdict was pronounced, the prisoners clasped each other in their arms.

It being now near eight o'clock on Friday morning, the Court adjourned to three o'clock.

When the Court met in the afternoon, the Attorney-General moved that the prisoners be brought up for judgment. Mr. M'Nally tried to make a point, on the want of venue for the "war" alleged in the indictment. The point was at once set aside, as at best only affecting one count, and then the prisoners were brought up

The Clerk of the Crown read the indictment, and asked them what they had to say, why judgment of death and execution should not be awarded against them, according to law.

Mr. Henry Sheares—My lord, as I had no notion of dying such a death as I am about to meet, I have only to ask your lordship for sufficient time to prepare myself and family for it. I have a wife and six children, and hope your humanity will allow me some reasonable time to settle my affairs. and make a provision for them. *(Here he was so overwhelmed with tears that he could not proceed.)*

Mr. John Sheares—My lord, I wish to say a few words before the sentence is pronounced, because there is a weight pressing upon my heart, much greater than that of the sentence which is to come from the Court. There has been, my lord, a weight pressing upon my mind from the first moment I heard the indictment read upon which I was tried; but that weight has been more peculiarly and heavily pressing upon my heart, when I found the accusation in the indictment enforced and supported upon the trial; and that weight would be left insupportable, if it were not for this opportunity of discharging it. It should be insupportable, since a verdict of my country has stamped that evidence as well founded.

Do not think, my lords, that I am about to make a declaration against the verdict of the jury, or the persons concerned in the trial; I am only about to call to your recollection a part of the charge, which my soul shudders at; and if I had not this opportunity of renouncing it before your lordships and this auditory, no courage would be sufficient to support me. The accusation, my lords, to which I allude, is one of the blackest kind, and peculiarly painful, because it appears to have been founded upon my own act and deed, and to be given under my own hand. The accusation of which I speak. while I linger here yet a minute, is, "that of holding out to the people of Ireland a direction to give no quarter to the troops

---

* Armstrong.

fighting for its defence." My lords, let me say this and if there be any acquaintances !˙ this crowded court, I will not say my intimate frie..,s, but acquaintances, who do not know that what I say is truth, I should be rep:ited the wretch which I am not, I say: If any acquaintance of mine can believe, that I could utter a recommendation of giving no quarter to a yielding and unoffending foe, it is not the death that I am about to suffer which I deserve—no punishment could be adequate to such a crime. My lords, I can not only acquit my soul of such an intention, but I declare in the presence of that God, before whom I must shortly appear, that the favourite doctrine of my heart was, *that no human being should suffer death, but where absolute necessity required it.*

My lords, I feel a consolation in making this declaration, which nothing else could afford me; because it is not only a justification of myself, but where I am sealing my life with that breath, which cannot be suspected of falsehood, what I say may make some impression on the minds of men not holding the same doctrine. I declare to God, I know no crime but assassination, which can eclipse or equal that of which I am accused. I discern no shade of guilt between that, and taking away the life of a foe, by putting a bayonet to his breast, when he is yielding and surrendering. I do request the bench to believe that of me, I do request my country to believe that of me, I am sure God will think that of me.

Now, my lords, I have no favour to ask of the Court: my country has decided that I am guilty, and the law says that I shall suffer: it sees that I am ready to suffer.

But, my lords, I have a favour to request of the Court, that does not relate to myself My lords, I have a brother whom I have ever loved dearer than myself; but it is not from any affection for him alone that I am induced to make the request. He is a man, and therefore I hope, prepared to die, if he stood as I do, though I do not stand unconnected, but he stands more dearly connected. In short, my lords, to spare your feelings and my own, I do not pray that I should not die; but, that the husband, the father, the brother, and the son, all comprised in one person, holding these relations, dearer in life to him, than to any other man I know, for such a man I do not pray a pardon, for that is not in t! power of the Court, but I pray a respite for such time as the Court in its humanity and discretion shall think proper. You have heard, my lords, that his private affairs require arrangement. I have yet a farther room for asking; if immediately both of us be taken off, an aged and revered mother, a dear sister, and the most affectionate wife that ever lived, and six children, will be left without protection, or provision of any kind. When I address myself to your lordships, it is with the knowledge you will have of all the sons of our aged mother being gone. Two have perished in the service of the King; one very recently. I only request, that, disposing of me with what swiftness either the public mind or justice requires, a respite may be given to my brother, and that the family may acquire strength to bear it all. That is all I wish, I shall remember it to my last breath, and I will offer up my prayers for you to that Being, who has endued us all with sensibility to feel. This is all I have to ask. I have nothing more to say.

Lord Carleton passed sentence of death in a feeling and considerate manner.

Mr. Attorney-General—My lord, I could, with great sincerity, allow any indulgence c? time, if the circumstances of the case could by possibility admit of it. But, my lords, I have a great public duty to discharge, and must pray that execution may be done upon the prisoners to-morrow.

Court—Be it so.

Henry Sheares wrote a letter full of supplication and promise to Barrington, to carry to the Chancellor. Barrington says, that through a set of trivial accidents, a delay occurred in acting on this, but that he finally reached Green-street, *with a respite*, in time to see the hangman holding his old friend's dripping head, and crying, "behold the head of a traitor."

John wrote a letter of deep love and comfort to his sister Julia, and he died (as did Henry, too, when he rea..., came to his doom), placidly and well.

FOR OLIVER BOND.

[HIGH TREASON.]

SPECIAL COMMISSION, GREEN-STREET.

24th July, 1798.

THREE days after the Sheares died, John M'Cann was tried, defended by Curran, convicted and hanged. On the 20th, Byrne was tried, and similarly defended, with a like fate. Curran's speeches are not reported.

On the 23rd of July, Oliver Bond, an eminent woollen draper, of Bridge-street, and a shrewd, kind man, was put to the bar.

The officer of the court charged the prisoner as follows:—

"Mr. Oliver Bond, you stand indicted, for, that not having the fear of God before your eyes, nor the duty of your allegiance considering, but being moved and seduced by the instigation of the devil, you did, with other false traitors, conspire and meet together, and contriving and imagining with all your strength this kingdom to disturb, and to overturn by force of arms, &c., the government of this kingdom, on the 20th day of May, in the thirty-eighth year of the reign of the present King, in the parish of St. Michael the Archangel, did conspire and meet together about the means of overturning the government; and his Majesty of and from his royal state, power, and government of this country to deprive and put; and that you, Oliver Bond, with other false traitors, did meet together, and make resolutions to procure arms and ammunition, for the purpose of arming men to wage war against our Sovereign Lord the King; and did conspire to overturn by force the lawful government of this kingdom, and to change by force the government thereof; and did assemble and meet together to raise a rebellion in this kingdom; to procure arms to aid and assist in said rebellion; and that you, Oliver Bond, did aid and cause Thomas Reynolds to be a colonel in the county of Kildare, to aid and assist in the said rebellion: and did administer unlawful oaths to said Thomas Reynolds, and to certain other persons, to be United Irishmen, for the purpose of overturning by force the government of this kingdom; and that you, the said Oliver Bond, did collect sums of money to furnish arms and ammunition to the persons in said rebellion, against the duty of your allegiance, contrary to his Majesty's peace, his crown, and dignity, and contrary to the form of the statute in that case made and provided. And whereas a public war, both by land and sea, is and hath been carried on by persons exercising the powers of government in France, that you, the said Oliver Bond, not having the fear of God before your eyes, did aid and assist the French and men of France to invade this kingdom, to overturn by force the government of this kingdom, and to compass and imagine the death of the King, and so forth. On this indictment, you, Oliver Bond, have been this day arraigned, and have pleaded not guilty, and for trial have put yourself on God and your country."

The principal witness was Thomas Reynolds, of Kilkea Castle, in the County Kildare. He had been a silk-mercer in Dublin, and was "united" at an early period. In 1797, he was Treasurer, and a Colonel, of Kildare. Soon after he became one of the Leinster Delegates.

His son was ill-advised enough to write the monster's memoirs, which has provoked Dr. Madden to a review of his career. A few specimens of him will suffice. He stole jewels and silks belonging to his mother, swindled a servant out of a bond for £175, and was accused by his brother-in-law, under circumstances of the strongest suspicion, of having poisoned his wife's mother for the sake of robbing her of £300. A number of persons of good position in Dublin swore he was not credible on his oath. He had been benefitted by Lord Edward, and betrayed him. He had not only taken all the United Irish oaths, but being suspected after the arrests at Bond's, swore his innocence, and tried to get Felix Rourke put to death for his own treason. For his treachery he was honoured with two consular commissions, and got in all £45,000. One of his family still *enjoys* the reversion of his pension. *Nearly* all his infamy came out on the trial.

There is nothing peculiar in the indictment, nor did any facts additional to what have been stated in Sheares' case appear.

The court was crowded with armed military and yeomen, licentious with power. They frequently interrupted and threatened Curran.

Curran spoke as follows:—

My lords, and gentlemen of the jury, I am counsel for the prisoner at the bar, and it is my duty to lay his case before you. It is a duty that at any time would be a painful one to me, but at present peculiarly so; having in the course of this long trial, experienced great fatigue both of mind and of body—a fatigue I have felt in common with the learned judges who preside on the bench, and with my brethren of the bar; I feel, as an advocate, for my client, the duty of the awful obligation that has devolved on me. I do not mean, gentlemen of the jury, to dilate on my own personal fatigues; for I am not in the habit of considering my personal ill state of health, or the anxiety of my mind, in discharging my duty to clients in such awful situations as in the present momentous crisis; I have not been in the habit, gentlemen of the jury, to expatiate to you on personal ill health. In addressing myself to jurors on any common subject, I have been in the habit of addressing myself to the interposition of the Court, or to the good-natured consideration of the jury, on behalf of my client. I have mentioned, indeed, my own enfeebled worn-out body, and my worn-out state of mind, not out of any paltry respect to myself, nor to draw your attention to myself, but to induce you to reflect upon this, that in the weakness of the advocate, the case of my client, the prisoner at the bar, is not implicated; for his case is so strong in support of his innocence, that it is not to be weakened by the imbecility or the fatigue of the advocate.

Gentlemen of the jury, I lament that this case has not been brought forward in a simple, and in the usual way, without any extraneous matter being introduced into it, as I think in justice, and as I think in humanity, it ought to have been. I lament that any little artifices should be employed upon so great and solemn a case as this, more especially in desperate times, and upon a more than ordinary occasion; and that some allegations of criminality have been introduced, as to persons and things, that ought not, in my opinion, to have been adverted to in a case like this.

What, for instance, has this case to do with the motion made by Lord Moira, in the House of Lords in Ireland, in February last, or the accidental conversations with Lord Edward Fitzgerald? If you have a feeling for virtue, I trust that Lord Moira will be revered as a character that adds a dignity to the peerage. What made that noble character forego his great fortune, quit his extensive demesnes, and the tranquillity of the philosophic mind, but the great and glorious endeavour to do service to his country? I must repeat, he is an honour to the Irish peerage. Let me ask, why was the name of Lord Moira or Lord Wycombe (who happened to dine at Duke Giffard's), introduced into this trial? what has that motion which Lord Moira introduced into the House of Lords to do with the trial of Mr. Oliver Bond on a charge of high treason?

Gentlemen, much pains have been taken to warn you, and then you are entreated to be cool; when the fire has been kindled, it has been spoken to, and prayed to be extinguished. What is that?

This question was occasioned by a clash of arms among the military that thronged the court. Some of those who were nearest to the advocate, appeared, from their looks and gestures, about to offer him personal violence, upon which, fixing his eye sternly upon them, he exclaimed—

You may assassinate, but you shall not intimidate me.

Here Mr. Curran was again interrupted by the tumult of the auditors; it was the third time that he had been obliged to sit down. On rising, he continued:—

I have very little, scarcely any, hope of being able to discharge my duty to my unfortunate client—perhaps most unfortunate in having me for his advocate. I know not whether to impute these inhuman interruptions to mere accident; but I greatly fear they have been excited by prejudice.

The Court said they would punish any person who dared to interrupt the counsel for the prisoner:—"Pray, Mr. Curran, proceed in stating your case; we will take care, with the blessing of God, that you shall not be interrupted."

You have been cautioned, gentlemen, against prejudice. I also urge the caution, and not with less sincerity. But what is the prejudice against which I would have you armed? I will tell you: it is that pre-occupation of mind that tries the accused before he is judicially heard—that draws those conclusions from passion which should be founded on proof—and that suffers the temper of the mind to be dissolved and debased in the heat of the season. It is not against the senseless clamour of the crowd, feeling impatient that the idle discussion of fact delays the execution, that I warn you. No; you are too proud, too humane, to hasten the holiday of blood. It is not against any such disgraceful feelings that I warn you. I wish to recall your recollections to your own minds, to guard you against the prejudice of elevated and honest understandings—against the prejudice of your virtues. I shall lay before you the case of my client, to controvert the evidence given on the part of the prosecution, and shall offer to your consideration some observations in point of law, under the judicial control of the Court. I will strip my client's case from the extraneous matter that has been attempted to be fastened on it. I feel myself, gentlemen, warmed, when I speak to you in favour of my client's innocency, and to bring his innocency home to your judgments. I know the honesty and rectitude of your characters, and I know my client has nothing to fear from your understandings.

It is my duty to state to you, we have evidence to prove that the witness on the part of the prosecution is undeserving of credit; and it is my duty to examine into the moral character of the witness that has been produced. It is of the utmost concern you should do this, as your verdict is to decide on the life or death, the fame or dishonour of the prisoner at the bar. With respect to prosecutions brought forward by the state, I have ever been of opinion that the decision is to be by the jury; and that as to any matter of law, the jury do derive information from the court: for jurors have by the constitution, a fixed and permanent power to decide on matter of fact; while the letter of the law the Sovereign leaves to be expounded by the mouth of the King's judges. Some censure upon past occasions has fallen on former judges, for a breach of this doctrine.

Upon a former occasion I differed in opinion from the learned judge who then presided, as to what I construed to be the law of high treason, touching the compassing or imagining the death of the King. I am not ashamed of the opinion I entertained. As a point of law, I never shall be ashamed of it. I am extremely sorry I should differ from the bench on a point of law; but judges have had different opinions upon the same subject.

Where an overt act is laid, of compassing and imagining the death of the King, it does not mean, in construction of law, the natural dissolution of the King; but where there was not the fact acted upon, but confined merely to the intention a man had, such intention must, according to Lord Coke and Sir M. Foster, be proved by two witnesses. In England, the statute of Edward III. provides against the event of the death of the King by any person levying war, whereby his life might become endangered; and the proof of such overt act must be substantiated by two witnesses; how it comes not to be settled and required in Ireland, is not accounted for.

Before the statute of Edward III. the law relative to high treason was undefined, which tended to oppress and harass the people; for, by the common law of England, it was formerly a matter of doubt whether it was necessary to have two witnesses to prove an overt act of high treason. Lord Coke says, that in England there must be two witnesses to prove an overt act; it seems he was afterwards of a contrary opinion. In the reign of William III. a statute passed, and by that statute in England there must be two witnesses. When that statute came to be enacted here, the clause relative to there being two witnesses to an overt act of high treason was not made the law in Ireland; but why it was not required in Ireland is not explained. By the English act of William III., the overt act must be proved by two witnesses in England, but it does not say in Ireland.

Surely, as the common law of England and the common law of Ireland are the same, the consciences of an Irish jury ought to be fully satisfied by the testimony of two witnesses to an overt act. On this point, however, some of the Irish judges are of opinion, that two witnesses are not, in Ireland, required to substantiate an overt act, therefore their opinion must be acquiesced in.

It has been insinuated, and with artful applications to your feelings of national independence, that I have advanced, on a former occasion the doctrine that you should be bound in your decisions by an English act of parliament, the statute of William III. Reject the unfounded accusation; nor believe that I assail your independence, because I instruct your judgment and excite your justice. No; the statute of William III. does not bind you, but it instructs you upon a point which before was enveloped in doubt. The morality and wisdom of Confucius, of Plato, of Socrates, or of Tully, do not bind you, but they may elevate and illumine you; and in the same way have British acts of parliament reclaimed you from barbarism. By the statute of Wm. III., two witnesses are necessary, in cases of high treason, to a just and equal trial between the Sovereign and the subject; and Sir Wm. Blackstone, one of the wisest and best authorities on the laws of England, states two witnesses to be but a necessary defence of the subject against the profligacy of ministers. In this opinion he fortifies himself with that of Baron Montesquieu, who says, that where one witness is sufficient to decide between the subject and the state, the consequences are fatal to liberty; and a people so circumstanced cannot long maintain their independence. The oath of allegiance, which every subject is supposed to have taken, stands upon the part of the accused against the oath of his accuser; and no principle can be more wise or just than that a third oath is necessary to turn the balance. Neither does this principle merely apply to the evidence of a common and impeached informer such as you have heard this day, but to that of any one witness, however high and respectable his character.

And now, gentlemen of the jury, let me state to you, in the clearest point of view, the defence of the prisoner at the bar, and see what has been the nature of the evidence adduced. The prisoner at the bar is accused of compassing or imagining the death of the King, and of adhering to the King's enemies; the evidence against him is parole and written evidence.

Gentlemen of the jury, I will venture to observe to you, that as to the written evidence, if suffered to go before you by the court, it is only as evidence at large; but as to the credibility of it, that is for you to decide upon.

Mr. Reynolds, in his parole testimony, has sworn that he was made a United Irishman by the prisoner at the bar. Mr. Reynolds says, he was sworn to what he considered to be the objects of that society; he stated them to you; but whether true or false, is for you to determine, by the credit you may give to his testimony. This is the third time Mr. Reynolds has appeared in a court of justice, to prosecute prisoners. He says, the objects of the United Irishmen are to overturn the present government, and to establish a republican form of government in its stead, and to comfort and abet the French, on their invading this kingdom, should such an event take place. You have heard his testimony; let me ask, do you think him incapable of being a villain? do you think him to be a villain? You observed with what kind of pride he gave his testimony? Do you believe his evidence, by the solemn oath that you have taken? or do you believe it was a blasted perjury? Can you give credit to any man of a blasted character?

It has been the misfortune of many former jurors to have given their verdict founded upon the evidence of a perjured witness, and on their death-bed they repented of their credulity, in convicting a man upon false testimony. The history of former ages is replete with such conduct, as may be seen in the state trials. In the case of Lord Kimbolton and Titus Oates, the then jurors convicted that nobleman; but some time after his death, the jurors discovered they had given implicit credit to a person unworthy of it; and the lawyers of those times might have said, "I thank God, they have done the deed." Does not the history of human infirmity give many instances of this kind?

Gentlemen, let me bring you more immediately to the case before you.

Had we no evidence against Reynolds, but his own solitary evidence, then, I say, from the whole of his evidence, you cannot establish the guilt of the prisoner at the bar; take the whole of his evidence into your consideration, and it will appear he is unworthy of credit. He told you he got information from M'Cann on the Sunday morning, that the meeting was to be on Monday morning, at ten o'clock. Reynolds goes immediately to Mr. Cope, and gives him that information. On Sunday afternoon, he goes to Lord Edward Fitzgerald, and shows him the orders issued by Captain Saurin to the lawyers' corps: then, said Lord Edward, I fear government intend to arrest me; I will go to France, and hasten them to invade this country; government has no information of the meeting of the provincial delegates at Bond's. No, no, says Reynolds, that is impossible. Reynolds wrote to Bond, that he could not attend the meeting, as his wife was ill; Reynolds did not go to the meeting. Bond was arrested on the Monday morning: on Monday evening, at eight at night, Reynolds goes to Lord Edward, in Aungier-street, meets him, and goes again to him the next night; and Lord Edward conversed with Reynolds about his (Lord Edward's) going to France. Reynolds then went to Kildare; he gave the most solemn assurances to the delegates at a meeting there, that he never gave information of the meeting at Bond's.

Now see how many oaths Reynolds has taken. He admits he took two of the oaths of the obligations to the society of United Irishmen. He told you Lord Edward advised him to accept the appointment of colonel in the Kildare United Irishmen's army; and yet he says he afterwards went to Bond's, and Bond advised him to be a colonel. It appears in evidence, that Reynolds' was treasurer; he took two more oaths, one as colonel, and one as treasurer, and he took the oath of allegiance also, and he took oath to the truth of his testimony, at the two former trials, and at this. On which do you give him credit? Gentlemen, in order to narrow the question under your consideration, I may observe that what Reynolds said, relative to Lord Edward's conversation, is totally out of this case: it can have no weight at all on the trial of Mr. Bond for high treason, in the finding of your verdict. How or in what manner, is the prisoner at the bar to be affected by it? I submit to your lordship, that the declaration of Lord Edward to Reynolds, when Bond was not present, is not attachable to the prisoner.

Mr. Reynolds has given you a long account of a conversation he had with Mr. Cope, relative to the proceedings of the society of United Irishmen; and Mr. Cope said, if such a man could be found, as described by Mr. Reynolds, who would come forward and give information, he would deserve the epithet of saviour of his country. Thus, by Reynolds' evidence, it would seem that Mr. Cope was the little pony of repentance to bear away the gigantic crimes of the colossus Reynolds. But remember, said Mr. Reynolds, though I give information I won't sacrifice my morality; I won't come forward to prosecute any United Irishman. No, no; like a bashful girl, higgling about the price of her virginity, I am determined, says Reynolds, to preserve my character; I will give the communications, but do not think I will descend to be an informer, I will acquaint you of every thing against the United Irishmen, but I must preserve my credit; I tell you the design of the United Irishmen is to overturn the constitution, I will lead you to the threshold of discovery, but I won't name any price for reward. "Pray don't mention it at all," says Mr. Cope, "a man would deserve a thousand or fifteen hundred a year, and a seat in parliament, or any thing, if he could give the information you mention." No such thing is required, no such thing, says Reynolds, you mistake me; I will have nothing in the world, but merely a compensation for losses, do you think I would take a bribe? I ask only of you to give me leave to draw a little bit of a note on you for five hundred guineas, only by way of indemnity; that is all: merely for indemnity of losses I have sustained, or am liable to sustain.

Gentlemen of the jury, don't you see the vast distinction between bribe and gratification? What says Foigard?* Consider my con-

* *.* Foigard in one of the vile comedies of that time.

science; do you think I would take a bribe? it would grieve my conscience, if I was to take a bribe. To be a member of parliament, and declare for the ayes or the noes, I will accept of no bribe. I will once take a little indemnity for claret that may be spilt; for a little furniture that may be destroyed; for a little wear and tear; for boots and for shoes, for plate destroyed, for defraying the expenses of some pleasurable jaunts, when out of this country: for if I become a public informer against the United Irishmen, and should continue here for some time, I may chance at some time to be killed by some of them, for I have sworn to be true to them, although I also took the oath of allegiance to be true to my Sovereign. I have taken all sorts of oaths; if I frequent the company of those who are loyal to the King, they will despise the man who broke his oath of allegiance; and between the loyalist and the United Irishman I may chance to be killed.

As I am in the habit of living in the world, says Mr. Reynolds to Mr. Cope, you will give me leave to draw a bit of paper on you, only for three hundred guineas at present. It will operate like a bandage to a sore leg; though it won't cure the sore, or the rottenness of the bone, it may hide it from the public view. I will, says Mr. Reynolds, be newly baptised for a draught of three hundred guineas; and become a public informer for a further bit of paper, only for another two hundred guineas; yet I trust you will excuse me, I will not positively take any more.

He might, I imagine, be compared to a bashful girl, and say, "What! shall the brutal arms of man attack a country maid?" and when her gown shortens, and her apron bursts asunder, and she shrinks at the view of public prostitution, shall she not stipulate for full wages? Perhaps he practised upon her virtue, when the innocent dupe thought she was gaining his affections. Do you think that Reynolds would touch a bribe, and become an informer? No, no; he said he would be no informer. But did he not consent to do a little business in private, and did he not get money for it? Perhaps he said, I thought to be no villain.—I would not have the world to think me a villain. I can confide in myself; why should I mind what the world says of me, though it should call me villain? Even though I should become the talk of all the porter-houses—though I should become the talk of all the tea-tables—yet perjury is not brought home to me; no—no human being has knowledge of what is rankling within. Has it not been said I was an honest man, to come upon the public board as a public informer? They called me an honest man, and a worthy, a respectable informer; and thus my character is at bay,

Mr. Reynolds was, unfortunately a United Irishman. He told you there was a provincial meeting of delegates; but he has not ventured to tell you where the provincial committee met—he has simply said, there was a provincial committee. The meeting, he says, was on a question of great concern. I have doubts upon it; it is not stated to me what these important consultations were about. From M'Cann he heard that a baronial meeting was to be at Bond's, on the 12th of March, and that there was material business to transact. He desired Reynolds to attend. That is all Reynolds heard from M'Cann. M'Cann is now no more and this part of the case is in doubt and obscurity. For my part, I am not satisfied that any thing criminal passed at the meeting at Bond's, on the 12th of March. No man can say so on the evidence produced: they do not say it—they only suppose there was. If the jury were to judge by their own present view, I do not think they would, or could, come justly to a verdict of condemnation.

The question is not, whether there was any meeting at Bond's, but what was the object of that meeting? Bond was in the warehouse, in the custody of the guard; afterwards he came up to the room with Mr. Swan. At Bond's there was a meeting of the United Irishmen; and though Bond was not taken in that room, yet Bond's charge is mixed with the guilt of that meeting.

The overt act in the indictment is, of conspiring to levy war, &c. It is material to observe, in this part of the case, it is a bare conspiracy to levy war. That is not, as I conceive, high treason. The bare intention does not amount to compassing or imagining the death of the King; it is not adhering to the King's enemies. Under certain circumstances, compassing the death of the King is not high treason. This is the great hinge, as I apprehend, in this case.

Gentlemen, what was the evidence given? That there was a meeting, for a dangerous purpose. M'Cann said, there was to be a meeting of the delegates at Bond's, on the 12th of March; he did not tell Reynolds the purport of that meeting. Therefore, gentlemen, my objection is, was that a provincial meeting? It rests on the hearsay of other witnesses. It was M'Cann told Reynolds, "You must be at the convention, on the 12th of March, to compass the death of the King, and overturn the government." But Bond did not tell him any such thing. Bond only said, M'Cann was able to give information of what was going forward at that meeting. But Bond knew nothing about it.

Admitting a meeting was held in Bond's house for a guilty purpose, yet Bond might be perfectly innocent; he was not in the room till Mr. Swan came. There was to be a watch-word—"Is M'Cann here?"— From thence, it would seem, it was a meeting at M'Cann's suggestion. Mr. Bond probably did not know the motive why he gave the use of the room, for there was not one word of conversation between Bond and Reynolds. Reynolds says M'Cann told him the watch-word, M'Cann did not get the watch-word from Bond, the prisoner at the bar. The watch-word was, "Is M'Cann here?" It was for the admission of no person that M'Cann did not know; it had no relation to Mr. Bond.

Has this no weight with you, gentlemen of the jury? Do you feel anxious to investigate the truth? If you believe Reynolds, the meeting was for the worst purpose. But was it with the knowledge of Bond? —for Bond said to Reynolds, "I can give you no information; go to M'Cann, he can inform you." Upon the evidence, therefore, of Reynolds rests this man's life; for the written evidence found in the room cannot, in my apprehension, affect Bond, if you be, as no doubt you will be, of opinion, Bond was not in the room where the papers were found. There is not any evidence of the conversation before Mr. Swan came: and he found on the table a paper written on, and the ink not dry, "I,

A. B., was duly elected." It was not found upon the prisoner at the bar: the papers found might affect the persons in the room; but, at the time of the seizure of the papers Bond was in the warehouse, in custody of Sergeant Dugan, and was not brought up stairs until after the arrest. The papers found upon Bond might be read in evidence against him, but I conceive not those found in the room. What was the intention of mentioning the letter from Reynolds, found on the prisoner at the bar? It was stated, but not read in evidence, merely to apologize for Reynolds' not attending the meeting on the 12th of March. Reynolds says he got it again, and burnt it. Reynolds did not pretend to state to you, that he knew from Bond what the object of the meeting was; and it is material to observe, that Bond's name was not found entered in the list of the persons who made returns, and attended the meeting.

I know that Reynolds has laboured to establish a connexion between the prisoner and the meeting held at his house. But how does he manage it? He brings forward asserted conversations with persons who cannot confront him—with M'Cann, whom he has sent to the grave —and with Lord Edward Fitzgerald, whose premature death leaves his guilt a matter upon which justice dares not to pronounce. He has never told you that he has spoken to any of these in the presence of the prisoner. Are you then prepared, in a case of life and death—of honour and of infamy—to credit a vile informer, the perjurer of a hundred oaths—a wretch whom pride, honour, or religion could not bind? The forsaken prostitute of every vice calls upon you, with one breath, to blast the memory of the dead, and to blight the character of the living. Do you think Reynolds to be a villain? It is true he dresses like a gentleman; and the confident expression of his countenance, and the tones of his voice, savour strong of growing authority. He measures his value by the coffins of his victims; and, in the field of evidence, appreciates his fame as the Indian warrior does in fight—by the number of scalps with which he can swell his triumphs. He calls upon you, by the solemn league of eternal justice, to accredit the purity of a conscience washed in his own atrocities. He has promised and betrayed— he has sworn and forsworn; and, whether his soul shall go to heaven or to hell, he seems altogether indifferent, for he tells you that he has established an interest in both. He has told you that he has pledged himself to treason and to allegiance, and that both oaths has he contemned and broken.* At this time, when reason is affrighted from her

* The following is the list of Reynolds' oaths.—
Q. (By Mr. Curran)—Can you just tott up the different oaths that you took upon either side. A. I will give the particulars.
Q. No: you may mention the gross? A. No; I will mention the particulars. I took an oath of secrecy in the county meeting—an oath to my captains, as colonel. After this I took an oath, it has been said—I do not deny it, nor do I say I took it, I was so alarmed, but I would have taken one if required—when the United Irishmen were designing to kill me, I took an oath before a county member, that I had not betrayed the meeting at Bond's. After this I took an oath of allegiance.
Q. Had you ever taken an oath of allegiance before? A. After this, I took an oath before the Privy Council. I took two, at different times, upon giving informations respecting these trials. I have taken three since—one upon each of the trials; and, before, I took any of them, I had taken the oath of allegiance.
If to these we add his oaths on the trials, we may get a glimpse of the conscience whose strength slew so many.

heat, and giddy prejudice takes the reins—when the wheels of society are set in conflagration by the rapidity of their own motion—at such a time does he call upon a jury to credit a testimony blasted by his own accusation. Vile, however, as this execrable informer must feel himself, history, alas! holds out too much encouragement to his hopes; for, however base, and however perjured, I recollect few instances, in cases between the subject and the crown, where informers have not cut keen, and rode awhile triumphant on public prejudice. I know of few instances wherein the edge of his testimony has not been fatal, or only blunted by the extent of its execution, and retiring from the public view beneath a heap of its own carnage.

Bond has been resident in this city twenty years; in your walks of life, gentlemen of the jury, you never heard anything to his prejudice before this charge. I know my duty to my client, and must tell you, if you have had prejudices, I know you will discard them. I am not paying you any compliment —I have spoken under the feelings of an Irishman.

During the course of these trials, I have endeavoured to speak to your understandings. I have not ventured to entreat you on behalf of my client, because I am sure you will give your justice and your merits free operation in your minds and consciences at this trial. I am sure you will try the cause fairly, and admit every circumstance into your reflections. In a case between the crown and the prisoner, I have not ventured to address you on the public feelings. At this important crisis, you will preserve the subject for the sake of the law, and preserve the law for the sake of the crown. You are to decide by your sober and deliberate understandings, and hold the balance equal between the crown and the subject.

You have been emphatically called upon to secure the state by a condemnation of the prisoner. I am less interested in the condition and political happiness of this country than you are, for probably I shall be a shorter while in it. I have, then, the greater claim on your attention and your confidence, when I caution you against the greatest and most fatal revolution—that of putting the sceptre in the hands of the informer. These are probably, the last words I shall ever speak to you; but these last are directed to your salvation, and that of your posterity. I tell you that the reign of the informer is the suppression of the law. My old friends, I tell you, that, if you surrender yourselves to the mean and disgraceful instrumentality of your own condemnation, you will mark yourselves fit objects of martial law—you will give an attestation to the British minister that you are fit for, and have no expectation of any other than, martial law—and your liberties will be flown, never, never to return! Your country will be desolated, or only become the gaol of the living; until the informer, fatigued with slaughter and gorged with blood, shall slumber over the sceptre of perjury. No pen shall be found to undertake the disgusting office of your historian; and some future age shall ask —What became of Ireland? Do you not see that the legal carnage which takes place day after day has already depraved the feelings of your wretched population, which seems impatient and clamorous for the amusement of an execution. It remains with you—in your determination it lies—whether that population shall be alone composed of four species of men: the informer, to accuse—the jury, to find guilty—the judge, to condemn—and the prisoner, to suffer. It regardeth not me what impressions your verdict shall make on the fate of this country but you it much regardeth. The observations I have offered—the warning I have held forth—I bequeath you with all the solemnity of a dying bequest; and, oh! may the acquittal of your accused fellow-citizen, who takes refuge in your verdict from the vampire who seeks to suck his blood, be a blessed and happy promise of speedy peace, confidence, and security, to this wretched, distracted, and self-devouring country!

By the common law, no subject can be deprived of life, but by a trial of his fellow-subjects; but in times when rebellion prevails in any country, men may suffer without the semblance of a trial by their equals. From the earliest period of history down to the present, there have been seen in some parts of the earth, instances where jurors have done little more than record the opinions given to them by the then judges; out that is the last scene of departing liberty.

I have read that, in the period of the rebellion, in the last century, in England, jurors on trials, by the common law of the land, have been swayed in their determination by the unsupported evidence of an informer; and after-times have proved their verdict was ill-founded, the innocency of the convicted persons afterwards appearing.

Trials on charges of high treason are of the utmost moment to the country, not merely in respect of any individual, but of the necessity there is that the public should know the blessings of trial by jury, and that the jurors should solely determine on their verdict by the evidence, and maturely weigh the *credit of the witnesses* against any prisoner.— At several of these trials of late date some of you have been present, and you know that the object of the court and the jurors is to investigate the truth from the evidence produced. The jurors are sworn to try, and to bring in a true verdict according to the evidence.

One witness has been examined on this trial, who, I think, does not deserve credit; but it is you who are the sole judges whom you will give credit to. Though you know this witness has given evidence on two former trials, and though the then jury did give credit to his testimony; yet you are not to determine on your verdict, on the faith or precedent of any former jurors, but you are to be solely guided by your own consciences. You will observe we have had here two witnesses to impeach the character of Mr. Reynolds, that were not produced on the former trials, and you will no doubt throw out of your minds whatever did not come this day before you in evidence, on the part of the prosecution, and recollect that which will come before you on the part of the prisoner's defence. You will find your verdict flowing from conscious integrity, and from the feelings of honourable minds, notwithstanding the evidence of the witness Reynolds, who has been examined upon the table, and whose testimony I need not repeat to you. Perhaps you may be inclined to think he is a perjured witness; perhaps you will not believe the story he has told against the prisoner at the bar, and of his own turpitude. You will do well to consider it was through a perjured witness that a Russell and a Sydney were convicted in the reign of James II. If juries are not circumspect to determine *only* by the evidence adduced before them, and not from any extraneous matter, nor from the slightest breath of prejudice, then what will become of our boasted trial by jury; then what will become of our boasted constitution of Ireland? In former times, when jurors decided contrary to evidence, it created great effusion of blood. Let me ask, will you, gentlemen, give a verdict through infirmity of body, or through misrepresentation, or through ignorance? You, by your verdict, will give an answer to this.

Gentlemen of the jury, you will weigh in your minds, that many inhuman executions did take place in former times, though the then accused underwent the solemnity of a trial. The verdicts of those jurors are not in a state of annihilation, for they remain on the page of history, as a beacon to future jurors. The judges before whom the then accused were tried, have long since paid the debt of nature; they cannot now be called to account, why they shrunk from their duty.

I call upon you, gentlemen of the jury, to be firm in the exercise of the solemn duty you are now engaged in. Should you be of opinion to bring in a verdict of condemnation against my unfortunate client, for myself I ought to care nothing, what impressions may actuate your minds to find such verdict; it is not for me, it is for you, to consider what kind of men you condemn to die, and before you write his bloody sentence to weigh maturely, whether the charge against the prisoner is fully proved. If you should, on the evidence you have heard, condemn the prisoner to death, and afterwards repent it, I shall not live among you to trace any proof of your future repentance.

I said I rose to tell you what evidence we had to produce on behalf of my client, the prisoner at the bar. We shall lay evidence before you, from which you can infer, that the witness produced this day was a perjured man. We have only to show to you, as honest men, that the witness is not deserving of credit on his oath, we have nothing more to offer on behalf of my client, the prisoner at the bar. It is your province to deliberate in your consciences on the evidence you will hear, whether you will believe the witness you have heard, on his oath, or not. And now I ask you, will you, upon the evidence you have heard, take away the life of the prisoner at the bar, separate him from his wife and from his little children for ever?

I told you I was to state to you the evidence which we had to bring forward on behalf of my unfortunate client. I tell you it is to discredit the testimony of Mr. Reynolds. When you have heard our evidence to this point, I cannot suppose you will give your verdict to doom to death the unhappy and unfortunate prisoner at the bar, and entail infamy upon his posterity. We will also produce respectable witnesses to the hitherto unimpeached character of the prisoner at the bar, and prove that he was a man of fair honest character. You, gentlemen of the jury, have yourselves known him a number of years in this city; let me ask you, do you not know that the prisoner at the bar has always borne the character of a man of integrity, and of honest fame? and, gentlemen of the jury, I call upon you to answer my question by your verdict.

I feel myself impressed with the idea in my bosom, that you will give your verdict of acquittal of the prisoner at the bar; and that by your verdict you will declare on your oaths, that you do not believe one syllable that Mr. Reynolds has told you. Let me entreat you to put .n one scale, the base, the attainted, the unfounded, the perjured witness; and in the opposite scale, let me advise you to put the testimony of the respectable witnesses produced against Mr. Reynolds, and the witnesses to the prisoner's hitherto unimpeached character; and you will hold the balance with justice, tempered with mercy, so as your consciences in future will approve.

Let me depart from the scene of beholding human misery, should the life of my client by your verdict be forfeited!

Should he live, by your verdict of acquittal, he would rank as the kindest father, and protector of his little children; as the best of husbands and of friends; and ever maintain that irreproachable character he has hitherto sustained in private life. Should our witnesses exculpate the prisoner from the crimes charged on him, to the extent charged in the indictment, I pray to God to give you the judgment and understanding to acquit him. Do not imagine I have made use of any arguments to mislead your consciences, or to distress your feelings: no, but if you conceive a doubt on your minds, that the prisoner is innocent of the crime of high treason, I pray to God to give you firmness of mind to acquit him. I now leave you, gentlemen of the jury, to the free exercise of your own judgments in the verdict you may give. I have not by way of supplication addressed you in argument; I do not wish to distress your feelings by supplications; it would be most unbefitting to your candour and understanding; you are bound by your oaths to find a true verdict according to the evidence; and you do not deserve the station of jurors, in which the constitution has placed you, if you do not discharge the trust the constitution has vested in you, to give your verdict freely and indifferently, according to your consciences.

Mr. Bond was found GUILTY.

It was said at the time that Bond died of apoplexy in prison, during the negociation which followed his conviction; but there is much evidence to show he was murdered.*

On the following morning (the insurrection being hopelessly suppressed), the state prisoners opened a negociation with government, and a compact made by Lord Clare, Lord Castlereagh, and Mr. Cooke, on behalf of ministers, securing the lives of all the leaders who wished to agree to the treaty. On the other hand, these leaders were to describe the state of the United Irish affairs, so far as they could, without implicating individuals. Byrne, however, was hanged; but the compact was finally settled on the 29th, at the Castle, by "deputies from the gaols." The government broke the compact. They, not only in their press, but by their indemnity act, described the United Leaders, as confessing guilt, and craving pardon, neither of which they did. Instead of being allowed to go abroad, they were kept in gaol here for a year, and then thrust into Fort George, from whence they were not released, till the Treaty of Amiens, in 1802.

* See Madden's "United Irishmen," 2nd series, vol. 1., p. 214.

FOR LADY PAMELA FITZGERALD AND HER CHILDREN.
[AGAINST ATTAINDER BILL.]
BAR OF THE IRISH COMMONS.—IN COMMITTEE.
August 20th, 1798.

In the very agony caused by Lord Edward's death, his dear noble brother Henry wrote to Lord Lieutenant Camden a letter ending thus:—"One word more, and I have done, as I alone am answerable for this letter. Perhaps you will still take compassion on his wife and three babes, the eldest not four years old. The opportunity that I offer is to protect their estate for them from violence and plunder. You can do it if you please."

The appeal was vain, and on the 27th of July, Toler introduced a bill into the Commons, to attaint Lord Edward Fitzgerald, Cornelius Grogan, and Bagenal Harvey. It was read a second time on the 9th of August, and on the same day Lord Caulfield presented Lady Pamela Fitzgerald's petition against it. On the 13th Arthur Moore, in a sound and feeling speech, moved a clause to exempt the heirs from attaint. Barrington and Plunket supported him, but the motion was lost. On the 14th the case was gone into against Harvey, and, on the 18th, witnesses were heard at the bar for the bill, the principal one being Reynolds of Kilkea. He proved the same facts as on Bond's trial, with some special ones as to Lord Edward. There was no doubt of the facts or the evidence, for Fitzgerald had frankly madly trusted the villain.

On the 20th Curran was heard against the bill, and spoke as follows:—

I appear in support of a petition presented on behalf of Lord Henry Fitzgerald, brother of the deceased Lord Edward Fitzgerald: of Pamela, his widow; Edward, his only son and heir, an infant of the age of four years; Pamela, his eldest daughter, of the age of two years; and Lucy, his youngest child, of the age of three months, against the bill of attainder now before the committee.

The bill of attainder has formed the division of the subject into two parts. It asserts the fact of the late Lord Edward's treason, and, secondly, it purports to attaint him, and to vest his property in the crown. I shall follow the same order.

As to the first part of the bill, I must remark upon the strange looseness of its allegation. The bill states that he had, during his life, and since the 1st of November last, committed several acts of high treason, without stating what, or when, or where, or with whom: it then affects to state the different species of treason of which he had been guilty; namely, conspiring to levy war, and endeavouring to persuade the enemies of the King to invade the country. The latter allegation they did not attempt to prove. The conspiring, without actually levying war, is clearly no high treason, and has been repeatedly so determined.

Upon this previous and important question, namely, the guilt of Lord Edward (without the full proof of which no punishment can be just), I was asked by the committee, if I had any defence to go into?

I was confounded by a question which I could not answer; but upon a very little reflection, I saw in that very confusion the most conclusive proof of the injustice of the bill. For what can be more flagrantly unjust, than to inquire into a fact, of the truth or falsehood of which no human being can have knowledge, save the informer who comes forward to assert it.

Sir, I now answer the question.

I have no defensive evidence! I have no case! it is impossible I should: I have often of late gone to the dungeon of the captive, but never have I gone to the grave of the dead, to receive instructions for his defence, nor in truth have I ever before been at the trial ot a dead man! I offer, therefore, no evidence upon this inquiry: against the perilous example of which I do protest on behalf of the public, and against the cruelty and injustice of which I do protest in the name o the dead father, whose memory is sought to be dishonoured; and of his infant orphans, whose bread is sought to be taken away.

Some observations, and but a few, upon the assertions of Reynolds, I will make. I do verily believe him in this instance, even though I have heard him assert it upon his oath. By his own confession he is an informer—a bribed informer: a man whom seven respectable witnesses have sworn in a court of justice, upon their oaths, not to be credible on his oath; a man upon whose single testimony no jury ever did, nor ever ought, to pronounce a verdict of guilty; a kind of man to whom the law resorts with abhorrence, and from necessity, in order to set the criminal against the crime; but who is made use of by the law for the same reason that the most noxious poisons are restored to in medicine.

If such be the man, look for a moment at his story; he confines himself to mere conversation only, with a dead man! He ventures not to introduce any third person, living or even dead! he ventures to state no act whatever done. He wishes, indeed, to asperse the conduct of Lady Edward Fitzgerald; but he well knew that, even were she in the country, she could not be adduced as a witness to disprove him. See, therefore, if there be any one assertion to which credit can be given, except this, that he has sworn and forsworn, that he is a traitor; that he has received five hundred guineas to be an informer; and that his general reputation is, to be utterly unworthy of credit.

As to the papers, it is sufficient to say, that no one of them, nor even all of them, were even asserted to contain any positive proof against Lord Edward; that the utmost that could be deduced from them is nothing more than doubt or conjecture, which, had Lord Edward been living, might have been easily explained, to explain which is now impossible, and upon which to found a sentence of guilt would be contrary to every rule of justice or humanity?

Is this bill of attainder warranted by the principles of reason, the principles of forfeiture in the law of treason, or the usage of parliament in bills of attainder? The subject is, of necessity, very long; it has nothing to attract attention, but much to repel it. But I trust that the anxiety of the committee for justice, notwithstanding any dulness either in the subject or in the speaker, will secure to me their attention.

Mr. Curran then went into a minute detail of the principles of the law of forfeiture for high treason, of which no report appears to exist.

The laws of the Persians and Macedonians extended the punishment of a traitor to the extinction of all his kindred. The law subjected the property and life of every man to the most complicated despotism, because the loyalty of every individual of his kindred was as much a matter of wild caprice, as the will of the most arbitrary despot could be.

This principle was never adopted in any period of our law. At the earliest times of the Saxons, the law of treason acted directly only on the person of the criminal: it took away from him what he actually had to forfeit, his life and property. But as to his children, the law disclaimed to affect them directly; they suffered, but they suffered by a necessary consequence of their father's punishment, which the law could not prevent, and never directly intended. It took away the inheritance, because the criminal, at the time of taking it away, had absolute dominion over it, and might himself have conveyed it away from his family. This is proved by the instances of conditional fees at the common law, and estates tail since the statute *de Donis*. In the former case the tenant did not forfeit until he had acquired an absolute dominion over the estate by the performance of the condition. Neither in the latter case is the estate tail made forfeitable, until the tenant in tail has become enabled in two ways to obtain the absolute dominion, by a common recovery, or by a fine. Until then the issue in tail, though not only the children of the tenant, but taking from him his estate by descent, could not be disinherited by his crime. Here is a decisive proof, that even the early law of treason never intended to extend the punishment of the traitor to his children as such; but even this direct punishment upon the traitor himself, is to take effect only upon a condition suggested by the unalterable rules of natural justice, namely, a judgment founded upon conviction, against which he might have made his defence or upon an outlawry, where he refused to abide his trial. In that case he is punished, because during his life the punishment could act directly upon his person; because during his life the estate was his to convey and therefore his to forfeit.

But if he died without attainder, a fair trial was impossible, because a fair defence was impossible; a direct punishment upon his person was impossible, because he could not feel it; and a confiscation of his estate was equally impossible, because it was then no longer his, but was vested in his heir, to whom it belonged by a title as good as that by which it had ever belonged to him in his lifetime, namely, the known law of the country.

As to a posthumous forfeiture of lands, that appears to have been attempted by inquest after death. But so early as the 8th of Edward III., the legality of such presentments was disallowed by the judges. And there is no lawyer at this day who can venture to deny, that since the 25th and 34th of Edward III. no estate of inheritance can regularly be forfeited, save by attainder in the life of the party; therefore, the law of the country being, that unless the descent is interrupted by an actual attainder in the lifetime of the criminal, it becomes vested in the heir, the moment it did descend, the heir became seized by a title the most favoured in law. He might, perhaps, have been considered as a purchaser for the most valuable consideration, his mother's marriage, of which he was the issue. Why, then, was posthumous attainder excluded from the protective law of treason? why has it never since been enacted by a prospective law? clearly for this reason, that in its own nature it is inhuman, impolitic, and unjust.

But it is said, this may be done by a bill of attainder; that the parliament is omnipotent, and therefore may do it; and that it is a perceeding familiar to our constitution. As to the first, it cannot be denied that the parliament is the highest power of the country, but an argument from the existence of a power to the exercise of it in any particular instance, is ridiculous and absurd. From such an argument it would follow, that it must do whatever it is able to do; and that it must be stripped of the best of all power—the power of abstaining from what is wrong.

Such a bill ought not to pass. First, because every argument against the justice or the policy of a prospective, is tenfold strong against a retrospective law; because every *ex post facto* law is in itself an exercise of despotic power. When it alters the law of property, it is peculiarly dangerous; when it punishes the innocent for the guilty, it is peculiarly unjust; when it affects to do that which the criminal law, as it now stands, could not do, it acts peculiarly against the spirit of the constitution; which is to contract and restrain penal law by the strictest construction, and not to add to it by vindictive innovation. But, I am warranted to go much further, upon the authority of the British legislature itself, and to say, that the principle of forfeiture, even in the prospective law, is altogether repugnant to the spirit of the British constitution.

The statutes of Anne and of George the Second have declared, that after the death of the Pretender and of his sons, no such forfeiture should or ought to exist. In favour of that high authority, every philosophical and theoretic writer, Baron Montesquieu, the Marquis Beccaria, and many others, might be cited; against it, no one writer of credit or character, that has come to my hands. Of the late Mr. Yorke, I do not mean to speak with disrespect; he was certainly a man of learning and genius; but it must be observed, he wrote for a party and for a purpose; he wrote against the repeal of the law of forfeiture, more than for its principle; of that principle he expressly declines entering into a direct defence. But for the extending of that principle farther than it is already law, the slightest insinuation cannot be found in his treatise.

But it is asserted to be the usage of the constitution in both countries. Of bills of attainder, the instances are certainly many, and most numerous in the worst times, and rising above each other in violence and injustice. The most tolerable of them was that which attainted the man who fled from justice, which gave him a day to appear, had he chosen to do so, and operated as a legislative outlawry. That kind of act has been passed, though but rarely, within the present century. There have been many acts of attainder when the party was willing but not permitted to appear and take his trial. In these two kinds of bills of attainder, however, it is to be observed, that they do not any violence to the common law, by the declaring of a new crime or a new punishment, but only by creating a new jurisdiction, and a new order of proceedings.

Of the second kind that has been mentioned, many instances are to be found in the violent reigns of the Plantagenets and Tudors, and many of them revised by the wisdom of cooler and juster times. Of such unhappy monuments of human frailty, Lord Coke said, " *auferat oblivio, si non silentium tegat.*" I beg leave to differ in that from the learned judge: I say, let the record upon which they are written be indelible and immortal: I say, let the memory that preserves them have a thousand tongues to tell them; and when justice, even late and slow, shall have robbed their fellow principle of life, let them be interred in a monument of negative instruction to posterity for ever.

A third kind of bill of attainder might be found, which for the first time declared the law, and attainted the criminal upon it: such was the attainder of Strafford. A fourth, which did not change the law as to the crime, but as to the evidence upon which it was to be proved; such was the attainder of Sir John Fenwick.

Of these two last species of attainder, no lawyer has ever spoken with respect; they were the cruel effect of the rancour and injustice of party spirit; nor could anything be said in their excuse, except that they were made for the direct punishment of the actual criminals, and whilst they were yet living.

The only other attainder that remains possible to be added to this catalogue is that of a bill like the present, which affects to try after a party's death, when trial is impossible; to punish guilt, when punishment is impossible; to inflict punishment where crime is not even pretended; change the settled law of property; to confiscate the widow's pittance! to plunder the orphan's cradle! and to violate the religion of the dead man's grave!

For this, too, there was a precedent: but for the honour of humanity let it be remembered, that an hundred and forty years have elapsed in which that precedent has not been thought worthy of imitation in Great Britain. I mean the attainder of the regicides. Upon the Restoration, four of them were included in that bill of attainder, which was passed after their death.

But, what were the circumstances of that period?

A king restored, and by his nature disposed to mercy, a ministry of uncommon wisdom, feeling that the salvation of the state could be secured only by mildness and conciliation; a bigoted, irritated, and interested faction in parliament: the public mind in the highest state of division and agitation. For what, then, is that act of attainder resorted to as a precedent? Surely it cannot be as a precedent of that servile paroxysm of simulated loyalty, with which the same men, who a few days before had shouted after the wheels of the good Protector, now raked out the grave of the traitorous usurper, and dragged his wretched carcass through the streets; that servile and simulated loyalty, which affected to bow in obsequious admiration of the salutary lenity which their vindictive folly was labouring to frustrate; that servile and interested hypocrisy, which gave a hollow and faithless support to the power of the monarch, utterly regardless alike of his character or his safety.

That the example, which this act of attainder held forth, was never respected, appears from this, that it never has been followed in Great Britain, although that country has since that time been agitated by one revolution, and vexed by two rebellions. So far from extending forfeiture or attainder beyond the existing law, the opinion of that wise and reflecting country was gradually maturing into a dislike of the principle altogether; until at last, by the statutes of Anne and George II., she declared, that no forfeiture or attainder for treason should prejudice any other than the actual offender, nor work any injury to the heir or other person, after the death of the pretenders to the throne. Why has Great Britain thus condemned the principle of forfeiture? Because she felt it to be unjust, and because she found it to be ineffectual

Need I prove the impolicy of severe penal laws? They have ever been found more to exasperate than to restrain. When the infliction is beyond the crime, the horror of the guilt is lost in the horror of the punishment; the sufferer becomes an object of commiseration; and the injustice of the state, of public odium. It was well observed, that in England the highwayman never murdered, because there the offender was not condemned to torture! but in France, where the offender was broken on the wheel, the traveller seldom or never escaped!* What then, is it in England that sends the traveller home with life, but the comparative mildness of English law? What, but the merciless cruelty of the French law, that gives the atrocious aggravation of murder to robbery? The multiplication of penal laws lessens the value of life, and when you lessen the value of life, you lessen the fear of death.

Look to the history of England upon this subject with respect to treason. Notwithstanding all its formidable array of death, of Saxon forfeiture, and of feudal corruption of blood; in what country do you read of more treasons or of more rebellions? And why? Because these terrors do not restrain the traitor. . Beyond all other delinquents he is likely to be a person of that ardent, enthusiastic and intrepid spirit, that is roused into more decisive and desperate daring by the prospect of peril.

Mr. Yorke thinks the child of the traitor may be reclaimed to his loyalty by the restitution of his estate. Mr. Yorke perhaps might have reasoned better if he had looked to the still greater likelihood of making him a deadly enemy to the state by the ignominy inflicted on his father, and by the loss of his own inheritance. How keenly did Hannibal pursue his vengeance which he had sworn against Rome? How much more enthusiastically would he have pursued his purpose, had that oath been taken upon a father's grave, for the avenging of a father's sufferings, for the avenging of a father's wrongs!

If I am called upon to give more reasons why this precedent has not been for more than a century and a half repeated, I will say, that a bill of attainder is the result of an unnatural union of the legislative and judicial functions; in which the judicial has no law to restrain it; in which the legislative has no rule to guide it, unless passion and prejudice, which reject all rule and law, be called rule and law. It puts the lives and properties of men completely at the mercy of an arbitrary and despotic power.

* Beccaria on Crimes and Punishments.

Such were the acts of posthumous attainder in Ireland, in the reign of the arbitrary Elizabeth, who used these acts as a mere moue of robbing an Irish subject, for the benefit of an English minion. Such was the act of 9th William III., not passed for the same odious and despicable purpose, but for a purpose equally arbitrary and unjust—the purpose of transferring the property of the country from persons professing one religion into the hands of those professing another—a purpose manifested and avowed by the remarkable clause in that act, which saves the inheritance to the heir of the traitor, provided that heir be a Protestant! Nor was it so brutally tyrannical in its operation, inasmuch as it gave a right to traverse and a trial by jury to every person claiming a right; and protected the rights of infants, until they should be of age, and capable to assert those rights.

There are yet other reasons why that precedent of the regicides was not followed in Great Britain. A government that means honestly will appeal to the affections, not to the fears of the people. A state must be at the last gasp, when it is driven to seek protection in the abandonment of the law—that melancholy avowal of its weakness and its fear. Therefore it was not done in the rebellion of 1715, nor in that of 1745.

I have hitherto abstained from adverting to the late transactions o. Ireland: but I could not defraud my clients, or their cause, of so pregnant an example.

In this country, penal laws have been tried beyond any example of any former times. What was the event? the race between penalty and crime was continued, each growing fiercer in the conflict, until the penalty could go no further, and the fugitive turned upon the breathless pursuer.

From what a scene of wretchedness and horror have we escaped!

But I do not wish to annoy you by the stench of those unburied and unrotted examples of the havoc and the impotence of penal law pushed to its extravagance. I am more pleased to turn your attention to the happy consequences of temperate, conciliatory government—of equal law Compare the latter with the former, and let your wisdom decide between the tempest and the calm. I know it is a delicate subject, but let me presume to suggest what must be the impression upon this grieved and anxious country, if the rigour of the parliament shall seem at war with the mildness of the government, if the people shall have refuge in the mercy of the crown from the rigour of their own representatives. But if, at the same moment, they shall see the convicted and attainted secured in their lives and in their property by the wise lenity of the crown, while the parliament is visiting shame, and misery, and want, upon the cradle of the unprotected infant, who could not have offended—but I will not follow the idea, I will not see the inauspicious omen: I pray that heaven may avert it.

One topic more you will permit me to add. Every act of the sort ought to have a practical morality flowing from its principle. If loyalty and justice require that these infants should be deprived of bread, must it not be a violation of that principle, to give them food or shelter

Must not every loyal and just man wish to see them, in the words of the famous Golden Bull, "always poor and necessitous, and for eve. accompanied by the infamy of their father, languishing in continued indigence, and finding their punishment in living, and their relief in dying?" If the widowed mother should carry the orphan heir of her unfortunate husband to the gate of any man who might feel himself touched with the sad vicissitudes of human affairs, who might feel a compassionate reverence for the noble blood that flowed in his veins, nobler than the royalty that first ennobled it, that like a rich stream rose till it ran and hid its fountain;—if, remembering the many noble qualities of his unfortunate father, his heart melted over the calamities of the child; if his heart swelled, if his eyes overflowed, if his too precipitate hand were stretched out by his pity or his gratitude to the poor excommunicated sufferers, how could he justify the rebel tear, or the traitorous humanity?

I shall trespass no longer upon the patience for which I am grateful one word only, and I have done; and that is, once more earnestly and solemnly to conjure you to reflect, that the fact, I mean the fact of guilt or innocence, which must be the foundation of this bill, is not now, after the death of the party, capable of being tried, consistently with the liberty of a free people, or the unalterable rules of eternal justice; and that as to the forfeiture and the ignominy which it enacts, that only can be punishment which lights upon guilt, and that can be only vengeance which breaks upon innocence!

Though great exertions were made to stop the bill, it reached the Lords, and passed in September.

A final effort was now made by Lady Edward's friends. A memorial was presented to the King, setting out with the tenderest and most eloquent wisdom the reasons, from the constitution, from justice, and from clemency, for stopping this bill. The names to the Memorial are "Richmond" (the Duke), "W. Ogilvie" (Lord Edward's step-father), "Henry Fitzgerald." "Charles James Fox," "Henry Edward Fox," "Holland." This document, and many letters written by the Duchess of Leinster to the Royal Family, will be found in the appendix to Moore's touching and simple narrative of "The Life and Death of Lord Edward Fitzgerald." This too was for the time unsuccessful, and the bill received the Royal assent in October; but the execution of the attainder was delayed, and the estate was sold in Chancery for a mortgage, and bought for £10,500, by Mr. Ogilvie, who cleared the property, and restored it to Lady Edward. She, a sensitive, vehement creature, went to France, and married there imprudently. She separated from her second husband, and after living long in retirement at Toulouse, died in poor lodgings in the Rue Richepanse, Paris, in November, 1831. An application for the reversal of the attainder was made in 1799; Government agreed to bring it forward in the United Parliament; but it did not pass till 1819.

NAPPER TANDY

[FOR NOT SURRENDERING ON A CHARGE OF HIGH TREASON, UNDER AN ATTAINDER ACT.]

COURT OF KING'S BENCH.

May 19th, 1800.

In the case of the Dublin Mayoralty, we have already noticed James Napper Tandy. He now presents himself again—no longer the fierce Tribune of the Common Council, but a chained prisoner, under a double accusation of treason. He was declared a traitor by act of parliament—it was easy to prove him so in fact; he was dragged to Ireland as a man already condemned.

He was a Dublin merchant, of respectable family, and obtained much civic influence by his bustling and patriotic conduct. In 1773-4 he became a Common Councilman, and a member of the Trinity Guild.* He commanded the Volunteer Artillery, and had his guns cast with "Free Trade or else——" on them. He became the head of the Radical party in the Common Council, and, as we have seen, materially aided their triumph in the Lord Mayor's case. In 1790. He was secretary to the first Dublin meeting of the United Irish Society, held on November 9th, 1791, at "The Eagle," in Eustace Street, and there Tone's Declaration and Test (which had been first agreed to in Belfast, on October 14th, 1791) were adopted.† His signature is to two other documents of theirs.

At the meeting of the Dublin Volunteers, at Pardons. In Cope-street, and or which so much appears in Rowan's case, Tandy was busy distributing Drennan's "Citizen Soldiers" proclamation; and during the discussions which followed on it in Parliament, Toler spoke insolently of Tandy. For this Tandy challenged him ;‡ but Toler took it into his head not to fight, and complained to the House of Commons. The speaker issued his warrant against Tandy, who was arrested at his house in Chancery lane ; but he went into a back-room, shut the door on the Commons' officer, and escaped through a window. The Privy Council issued a proclamation, offering £50 reward for Tandy's arrest, and Tandy brought action against the Lord Lieutenant (Westmorland) and the Privy Councillors who signed the proclamation ; but after long discussions, in which Simon Butler and Thomas Addis Emmet most ably supported Tandy's case, the subpœnas were quashed.§ In February, 1793, Tandy and Rowan were prosecuted as Defenders. Tandy fled to America Francis Graham, a magistrate, was prosecuted for having suborned Corbally, a tailor, to swear this charge against them ; but Graham was acquitted, and on his acquittal prosecuted and convicted Corbally for perjury.‖

Thus he lived in perpetual turmoil, and enjoyed it. He was employed by the United Irish in the French negociation. and for this left America in '98, and having been marked out by the Secret Committee, he was the first of fifty-one persons¶ included in an attainder act (38th George III., c 80), by which it was declared that unless the persons named in it surrendered on or before the 1st December, 1798. they would be held convict traitors, and suffer death, confiscation of goods, and corruption of blood accordingly. He tried to join Humbert's Expedition in the Autumn of that year, but, fortunately for himself, missed doing so, and after being part of a day on the Donegal coast, sailed safely to Norway. On the 24th of November he and Harvey Morris** (Montmorenci), Corbet, and Blackwall, were arrested by English agents in Hamburgh, put in prison, and finally brought to Ireland. A habeas corpus was issued ; but it was not until the 10th of February that the parties were brought from Kilmainham to the King's Bench. On that day they were arraigned, and on the 12th pleaded specially that they had been arrested within the time allowed by the act of parliament. Issue was joined on the facts, and after delays, allowed to the prisoners to procure the attendance of Sir James Crawford (British envoy at Hamburgh at the time of the arrest) the trial of both Tandy and Morris took place on the 19th of May, 1800, before Lord Kilwarden. Mr Ridgeway opened the prisoner's plea, and Curran supported it as follows :—

My Lords, and you, Gentlemen of the Jury, I am in this case of counsel for Mr. Tandy, the prisoner at the bar. I could have wished it had been the pleasure of the gentlemen who conduct this business on the part of the crown, to have gone on first. The subject itself is of a very novel nature in this country ; but certainly it is the right of the crown, and which the gentlemen have thought proper to follow, to call on the counsel for the prisoner to begin ; and, therefore, it is my duty, my lords, to submit to you, and to explain, under the direction of the court, to you, gentlemen of the jury, what the nature of the question is that you are sworn to try.

An act of parliament was passed in this country, which began to be

* He then resided in Dorset-street.
† See the proceedings of the "Society of United Irishmen of Dublin," published in Dublin, by the Society, in 1794, with this motto, "Let the Nation stand."
‡ See his letter to Rowan on the subject in Drummond's Life of Rowan, page 164.
§ The proceedings are in the "United Irish" volume, referred to in the last note but one. These cases exist in pamphlet reports, and are highly interesting.
¶ Among the 51, were Wolfe Tone, Lewins, Surgeon Lawless, M'Cormick, Michael Reynolds, and several Presbyterian clergymen.
** Of Knockalton, in the county Tipperary. He became a General Officer in the French Service.—See O'Connor's "Military Memoirs of the Irish Nation."

a law on the 6th of October, 1798. On that day it received the royal assent. By that law it is stated, that the prisoner at the bar had been guilty of acts of treason of many different kinds ; and it is enacted, that he shall stand attainted of high treason, except he should, on or before the 1st day of December following, surrender himself to one of the judges of this court, or to one of his Majesty's justices of the peace, for the purpose of becoming amenable to that law, from which he was supposed to have fled, in order to abide his trial for any crime that might be alleged against him.

It was a law not passed for the purpose of absolutely pronouncing any judgment whatsoever against him, but for the purpose of compelling him to come in and take his trial ; and nothing can show more strongly, that that act of parliament has not established anything touching the fact of the prisoner's guilt ; because it would be absurd, in one and the same breath, to pronounce that he was guilty of high treason, and then call upon him to come in and abide his trial ; and the title of the act speaks that it is an act not pronouncing sentence against the prisoner, but that it is an act in order to compel him to come forward.

This act creates a parliamentary attainder, not founded on the establishment of the prisoner's guilt of treason, but on his contumacious avoidance of trial, by standing out against a trial by law. I make this observation to you, gentlemen of the jury, in order that you may, in the first instance, discharge from your minds any actual belief of any criminality in the prisoner at the bar ; and that for two reasons: first, because a well-founded conviction of his guilt, on the authority of this statute, might have some impression on the minds of men sitting in judgment on the prisoner ; but for a more material reason, I wish to put it from your minds, because his guilt or innocence has nothing to do with the issue you are sworn to try.

Gentlemen, the issue you are called to try is not the guilt or the innocence of the prisoner : it is therefore necessary you should understand exactly what it is

The prisoner was ca led on to show cause why he should not suffer death pursuant to the enacting clause of the statute, and he has put in a plea, in which he states, that before the time for surrender had expired, namely, on the 24th of November, 1798, seven days before the day he had for surrendering had expired, he was, by order of his Majesty, arrested, and made a prisoner, in the town of Hamburgh ; and, in consequence of such arrest, it became impossible for him to surrender himself, and become amenable to justice within the time prescribed ; and the counsel for the crown have rested the case on the denial, in point of fact, of this allegation ; and, therefore, the question that you are to try is simplified to this—" I was arrested," says the prisoner, " whereby it became impossible for me to surrender"—to which the counsel for the crown reply—" You were not arrested at the time alleged by you, whereby it would have become impossible for you to surrender." This I conceive to be the issue, in point of fact, joined between the parties, and on which it is my duty to explain the evidence that will be offered.

Mr. Tandy is a subject of this country, ar l has never been in it from the time this act of parliament passed until he was brought into it after his arrest, on the 24th of November, 1798. On that day he was in the town of Hamburgh. He had seven days, in which time it was practicable for him to arrive in this country, and surrender himself, according to the requisitions of the act of attainder. Every thing that could be of value to man was at stake, and called on him to make that surrender. If he did not surrender, his life was forfeited—if he did not surrender, his fortune was confiscated—if he did not surrender, the blood of his family was corrupted; and he could leave them no inheritance, but the disgrace of having suffered as a traitor.

Your common sense, gentlemen, will show you, that where a man is to forfeit his life unless he complies with the conditions of an Act of Parliament—your common sense, your common humanity must show you, that a man ought to be suffered to perform the conditions on which his life depends. It can require no argument to impress upon your minds, that to call on a man to surrender himself on pain of death, and by force to prevent him from surrendering, goes to an atrocity of oppression that no human mind can contemplate without horror.

But it seems that the prisoner at the bar was a man of too much consequence to the repose of all civilized nations, to the great moral system—I might almost say, to the great physical system of the universe, to be permitted to act in compliance with the statute that called upon him to surrender himself upon pain of death. The wisdom of the entire Continent was called upon to exercise its mediation on this most momentous circumstance. The diplomatic wisdom of Germany was all put into action on the subject. The enlightened humanity of the North was called on to lend its aid. Gentlemen, you know as well as I the princely virtues and imperial qualifications, the consummate wisdom and sagacity of our steadfast friend and ally, the Emperor of all the Russias; you must feel the awe with which he ought to be mentioned; his sacred person has become embodied in the criminal law of England, and it has become almost a misprision to deem of him or speak of him but with reverence. I feel that reverence for him; and I deem of him and conceive him to be a constellation of all virtue, compared with whose radiance the Ursa-major twinkles only as the glow-worm.

And, gentlemen, what was the result of the exercise of this combination of wisdom? That James Napper Tandy ought to be got rid of in the ordinary way. They felt an honest and a proper indignation, that a little community like Hamburgh should embezzle that carcase which was the property of a mild and merciful government; they felt a proper indignation, that the senate of Hamburgh, under the present sublime system, should defraud the mercy of the government of the blood of the prisoner, or cheat the gibbet of his bones, or deprive the good and loyal ravens of this country of his flesh: and accordingly, by an order issued to these miserable inhabitants of the town of Hamburgh, who were made to feel that common honesty and common humanity can only be sustained by a strength not to be resisted, they were obliged to break the ties of justice and hospitality—to trample on the privileges that every stranger claims; they were obliged to suffer the prisoner to be trampled on, and meanly and cruelly, and pitiably to give up this unfortunate man to the disposal of those who could demand him at such a price.

If a surrender, in fact, had been necessary on the part of the prisoner, certainly a very material object was achieved by arresting him; because they thereby made it impossible for him to avail himself of the opportunity. They made it impossible for him to avail himself of the surrender, if the reflection of his mind led him to it. If a sense of the duty he owed his family led him to a wish, or to an intention, of availing himself of the remaining time he had to surrender, they determined he should not take advantage of it. He had been guilty of what the law deems a crime, that is, of flying from justice, though it does not go to the extent of working a corruption of blood; but by this act of power, by this act of tyrannic force, he was prevented from doing that which every court of justice must intend he was willing do—which the law intends he would have done—which the law gave him time to do—which the law supposes he might have done the last hour, as well as the first. He was on his passage to this country: that would not have taken up a third part of the time that was yet to elapse; but by seizing on him in the manner that he was arrested, it became impossible for him to surrender himself, or become amenable to justice.

The prisoner, when he was arrested, was treated in a manner that made it impossible for him to do any act that might have been considered as tantamount to a surrender. He was confined in a dungeon, little larger than a grave; he was loaded with irons; he was chained by an iron that communicated from his arm to his leg; and that so short as to grind into his flesh. In such a state of restriction did he remain for fifteen days; in such a situation did he lie in a common vault; food was cut into shapeless lumps, and flung to him by his filthy attendants as he lay on the ground, as if he had been a beast; he had no bed to lie on, not even straw to coil himself up in, if he could have slept. In that situation he remained in a foreign country for fifteen days of his long imprisonment; and he is now called to show good cause why he should not suffer death, because he did not surrender himself and become amenable to the law. He was debarred all communication whatsoever: if he attempted to speak to the sentinels that guarded him, they could not understand him; he did make such kind of indications of his misery and his sufferings as could be conveyed by signs, but he made them in vain; and he is now called on to show good cause, wherefore he did contumaciously and traitorously refuse to surrender himself, and become amenable to the law.

Gentlemen of the jury, I am stating facts that happened in a foreign country; will you expect that I should produce witnesses to lay those abominable offences before you in evidence? It was not in the power of the prisoner at the bar to procure witnesses; he was not of importance enough to call on the armed civilization of Europe, or on the armed barbarity of Europe, to compel the inhabitants of the town where he was imprisoned, to attend at the bar of this court to give evidence for the preservation of his life; but though such interposition could not be obtained to preserve his life, it could be procured for the purposes of blood.

And this is an additional reason why the rights of neutral states should be respected; because, if an individual, claiming those privileges, be torn from that sanctuary, he comes without the benefit of the testimony of those that could save his life. It is a maxim of law that no man shall lose any thing, much less his life, by the non-performance of a condition, if that non-performance have arisen by the act of God or of the party who is to avail himself of the condition, that the impossibility so imposed shall be an excuse for the non-performance of the condition; that is the defence the prisoner relies upon here. "Why did you not surrender, and become amenable to justice? Because I was in chains." "Why did you not come over to Ireland? Because I was in prison, in a grave in the town of Hamburgh." "Why did you not do something tantamount to a surrender? Because I was unpractised in the language of the strangers, who could not be my protectors, because they were also my fellow-sufferers."

But he may push this reasoning much further; the statute was made for the express purpose of making him amenable. When the crown seized him at Hamburgh, it thereby made him amenable, and so satisfied the law. It could not seize him for execution as an attainted person, for the time had not arrived at which the attainder could attach. The King, therefore, seized him as a man liable to be tried, and yet he calls upon him to suffer death, because he did not make himself amenable by voluntary surrender; that is, because he did not do that which the King was pleased to do for him, by a seizure, which made it at once unnecessary and impossible for him to do so by any voluntary act.

Such is the barbarity and folly that must ever arise, when force and power assume the functions of reason and justice.

As to his intention after the arrest it is clearly out of the question. The idea of intention is not applicable to an impossible act. To give existence to intention, the act must be possible, and the agent must be free. Gentlemen, this, and this only, is the subject on which you are to give a verdict. I do think it is highly honourable to the gentleman who has come over to this country, to give the prisoner at the bar the benefit of his evidence; no process could have compelled him; the inhabitants of foreign countries are beyond the reach of process to bring witnesses to give evidence. But we have a witness, and that of the highest respectability, who was himself at Hamburgh at the time Mr. Tandy was arrested, in an official situation. We will call Sir J. Crawford, who was then the King's representative in the town of Hamburgh. We will show you by his evidence the facts that I have stated; that before the time allowed to the prisoner to surrender had elapsed, Sir J. Crawford did, in his official situation, and by orders from his own government, cause the person of Mr. Tandy to be arrested in Hamburgh. Far am I from suspecting, or insinuating against Sir James Crawford, that any of the cruelties that were practised on that abused and helpless community, or on my abused client, were committed at his instance or personal sanction; certain am I that no such fact could be possible.

I told you before, gentlemen, that the principal question you had to try was, the fact on which the parties had joined issue: the force and arrest alleged by the prisoner; and the denial of that force by the counsel for the crown. There is one consideration that I think necessary to give some attention to. What you may think of the probable guilt or innocence of the prisoner, is not within the question that you are to decide; but if you should have any opinion of that sort, the verdict given in favour of the prisoner can be no preclusion to public justice, if after your verdict they still call for his life; the utmost that can follow from a verdict in his favour would be, that he will be considered as a person who has surrendered to justice, and must abide his trial for any crime that may be charged against him. There are various ways of getting rid of him, if it be necessary to the repose of the world that he should die.

I have said, if he has committed any crime he is amenable to justice, and in the hands of the law; he may be proceeded against before a jury, or he may be proceeded against in another and more summary manner; it may so happen that you may not be called upon to dispose finally of his life or of his character.

Whatever verdict a jury can pronounce upon him can be of no final avail. There was, indeed, a time when a jury was the shield of liberty and life: there was a time when I never rose to address it without a certain sentiment of confidence and pride; but that time is past. I have now no heart to make any appeal to your indignation, your justice, or your humanity. I sink under the consciousness that you are nothing. With us the trial by jury has given place to shorter, and no doubt better modes of disposing of life. Even in the sister nation, a verdict can merely prevent the duty of the hangman; but it never can purge the stain which the first malignity of accusation, however falsified by proof, stamps indelibly on the character of an " acquitted felon." To speak proudly of it to you would be a cruel mockery of your condition; but let me be at least a supplicant with you for its memory. Do not, I beseech you, by a vile instrumentality, cast any disgrace upon its memory.

I know you are called out to-day to fill up the ceremonial of a gaudy pageant, and that to-morrow you will be flung back again among the unused and useless lumber of the constitution: but trust me, the good old trial by jury will come round again; trust me, gentlemen, in the revolution of the great wheel of human affairs, though it is now at the bottom, it will re-ascend to the station it has lost, and once more assume its former dignity and respect; trust me, that mankind will become tired of resisting the spirit of innovation, by subverting every ancient and established principle, and by trampling upon every right of individuals and of nations. Man, destined to the grave, nothing that appertains to him is exempt from the stroke of death—his life fleeth as a dream, his liberty passeth as a shadow. So, too, of his slavery; it is not immortal; the chain that grinds him is gnawed by rust, or it is rent by fury, or by accident, and the wretch is astonished at the intrusions of freedom, unannounced even by the harbinger of hope. Let me, therefore, conjure you, by the memory of the past, and the hope o' the future, to respect the fallen condition of the good old trial by jury, and cast no infamy upon it. If it be necessary to the repose of the world that the prisoner should die, there are many ways of killing him —we know there are; it is not necessary that you should be stained with his blood. The strange and still more unheard-of proceedings against the prisoner at the bar, have made the business of this day a subject of more attention to all Europe, than is generally excited by the fate or the suffering of any individual. Let me, therefore, advise you seriously to reflect upon your situation, before you give a verdict of meanness and of blood, that must stamp the character of folly and barbarity upon this already disgraced and degraded country.

Sir James Crawford (examined by Mr. Ponsonby) proved the facts of the arrest, and that the prisoner might have come from Hamburgh to Dublin in thirty-seven hours, with fair winds. The Attorney-General (Toler) attempted a most unfair and illegal cross-examination, to prove that Tandy was in the act of treason when arrested. Toler and the Prime-Sergeant then spoke for the crown; Ponsonby and M'Nally replied for Tandy. Lord Kilwarden charged decidedly for acquittal, and so the jury found. Morris's case was then abandoned.

Tandy was afterwards sent to Lifford, tried* for his hostile landing on the Donegal coast, convicted, and sentenced to be hanged. This sentence the Government had no intention of executing; they dared not do so. General Don, whom the Duke of York had employed as a spy during the Helder expedition, had been taken prisoner, and though liable to death, had been released by General Brune (the French Commander), expressly in exchange for Tandy. Napoleon, too, had shown the greatest indignation at the arrest of Tandy in a neutral state; and when the Senate of Hamburgh tried to propitiate him by a long memorial, he amerced the city four millions of marks, and wrote this letter:—

" *Bonaparte, First Consul of the Republic, to the Burgomaster and Senate of the Free and Imperial City of Hamburgh.*
"Paris. Ninth Nivose (eighth year),
30th December, 1799.
"SIRS,—We have received your letter. It does not justify your conduct. Courage and virtue preserve states; cowardice and vice destroy them. You have violated the laws of hospitality. Such an event could not have happened among the most barbarous hordes of the desert. Your fellow-citizens must for ever reproach you. The two unfortunate men whom you have delivered up will die illustrious; but their blood shall work more evil on the heads of their persecutors than a whole army would have done.
" Signed, " BONAPARTE.
" HUGUES B. MARET, Secretary of State."

Napoleon said he would hang two field-officers for Tandy; but Government concealed the negotiation, and attempted by threats, first of execution, then of transportation, to make Tandy inform or succumb. They failed, and he was at last allowed to sail to France. Tandy was attacked by Lord Pelham, Lord Limerick, and Mr. Elliot in the British Parliament, and described as an informer, and in Mr. Elliot's words as "an ignorant man, o' an advanced age, and insignificant rank in life." Tandy was sixty-two years old, and thc made one part of the description true. Tandy was enraged, and in printed letters bearing various dates (the last being Bourdeaux, 5th of February, 1803), disproved the charges, and after useless challenges, branded Elliot as " a calumniator! a liar! a poltroon and a scoundrel!"

He died soon after. His son James, a man of opposite politics, behaved admirably during his father's peril, and amid apparently conflicting duties, observed all. He was persecuted for this, calumniated, and thrown into prison. Against one of his defamers, a Mr. Brabazon Morris, he brought an action, which was tried on the 30th of June, 1806; Curran replied for him, but the report of the speech is inferior, and full of errors, nor did it gain a verdict.†

---

* On Tuesday, the 7th April, 1801.
† James Tandy published an "Appeal to the Public," dated "Dublin, 20th October, 1807,' detailing these facts. It is a valuable pamphlet, and is drily but largely analysed in Plowden's "Ireland from its Union," vol. I.

AGAINST SIR HENRY HAYES.

[ABDUCTION OF MISS PIKE.]

CORK SPRING ASSIZES.

April 13th, 1801.

SIR HENRY BROWN HAYES, Knight, was the son of Mr. Attwell Hayes, a wealthy citizen of Cork. At the time of the occurrence for which Curran prosecuted him, Sir Henry was a widower, with several children, and being a man of address and fortune, and "cutting a great dash," was popular in Cork. It is said that his expenses had exceeded his means, and that he was induced to the abduction of Miss Pike, to retrieve his affairs. The attempt at such an offence was then a capital felony under the statute law.

Mary Pike was the only child of Mr. Samuel Pike, a Cork banker, of a respectable Quaker family, who had died some time before, leaving her a fortune of over £20,000. Her mother was in weak health, resident in the city of Cork, and maintaining her connection with the Society of Friends, which Miss Pike and many of her relatives had abandoned.

In 1797, Miss Pike, then twenty-one years old, resided with a relation, Mr. Cooper Penrose, at a beautiful demesne, called Wood-hill, near Cork. Sir Henry Hayes rode there on Sunday, the 2nd July, 1797, and professing a desire to see the place, it was shown to him by Mr. Penrose, and he was finally (though previously unknown) asked to dinner by Mr. Penrose, and then met Miss Pike for the first time. Mr. Penrose proved on the trial that Miss Pike sat at a side-table, with one of his daughters.

Sir Henry was captivated or content with this acquaintance. He wrote to Dr. Gibbings, Mrs. Pike's physician: and having learned Dr. Gibbings' handwriting from the reply, this letter, in close imitation of that writing, was sent to Wood-hill:—

"TO COOPER PENROSE, ESQ.

"DEAR SIR,—Our friend, Mrs. Pike, is taken suddenly ill; she wishes to see Miss Pike. We would recommend dispatch, as we think she has not many hours to live.

" Yours, &c., 'ROBERT GIBBINGS."

This precious document reached Mr. Penrose after midnight of July the 22nd, and as soon as possible, Miss Pike, accompanied by Miss Penrose, and a Mrs. Richard Pike, set off in Mr. Penrose's carriage. The night was wet and stormy. They had not gone far when their carriage was stopped by armed men, Miss Pike's name ascertained, and her person identified by a muffled man. The traces of their carriage were then cut; and Miss Pike, placed in a chaise with a lady, who seems to have been a sister of Sir Henry's, was driven off under a mounted escort, to Mount-Vernon. She was carried from the gate up the steep avenue by the muffled man. Her treatment then, Miss Pike thus describes in her evidence:—

Q. How did you get into the house? A. He took me in his arms into the parlour.
What happened after you got into the house; were there lights in the parlour? There was a snuff of a candle just going out.
Miss Pike, be so good as to tell what happened after you got into the parlour; did any other persons make their appearance? Yes, two women.
Did you see any body else in the house that night, but Sir Henry and the two women? I did not until the next morning.
Did you see any other persons in that house at any time after? Yes, a man in priest's habits.
Was it that night or next morning? It was next morning.
At break of day, was it? Yes.
Did anything particular happen then? Before that, I was forced up stairs.
By whom? By Sir Henry Hayes and his sister.
After you were forced up stairs, did anything particular happen? Before that, there was a kind of ceremony read, and they forced a ring on my finger ; before I was taken up stairs, there was a kind of ceremony of marriage, and a man appeared dressed in the habit of a clergyman.
Court—You said something about a ring? A ring was attempted to be forced on my finger, which I threw away.
After you were forced up stairs, and after this kind of a ceremony of marriage was performed, did anything particular happen above stairs? I was locked into a room.
What sort of a room? A small room with two windows.
What happened after that; do you recollect anything more? There was tea brought up, and after that Sir Henry Hayes came up.

SIR HENRY HAYES.

After tea was brought up, and after Sir Henry came up stairs, did anything happen? Court—It is now about four years ago; and, therefore, mention only what you remember. I remember his father coming up.
It was after that? Before my uncle came to take me home.
Court -Was the room furnished or unfurnished? There was a bed and a table in it.
Do you recollect anything that passed after Sir Henry's coming up: and if you do, state it to the Court? I recollect perfectly his coming in and out, and behaving in the rudest manner, and saying I was his wife.
Were you restored shortly after? About eight o'clock next morning.
Was or was not any part of that transaction between you and Sir Henry Hayes with your consent or against it? Against it entirely.
Did you write anything while at Vernon-Mount? Yes; I wrote a note directed to my uncle.
How did you come to write that letter? I was anxious to get to my friends, and repeatedly asked for pen and ink.
It was at length brought to you? Yes; and as well as I can recollect, I wrote to my uncle, to let him know where I was.

Sir Henry Hayes absconded. Government offered £1000 for his apprehension, and Miss Pike's relatives offered another reward—both in vain. He was outlawed, but returned to Cork, and lived there without concealment, and Miss Pike went to reside in Bath. About two years after, Hayes wrote to her a polite letter, offering to stand his trial at the next assizes. Upon this the outlawry was reversed by consent, and an application to remove the venue to Dublin city having failed, the case came on at the Spring assizes of Cork, on the 13th day of April, 1801, before Mr. Justice Day.
There were two indictments, one for the abduction, another for procuring it, but on coming into court the Crown quashed the second indictment. The sustained indictment had two counts, one for abduction with intent to marry, the other charging a still baser purpose.
The Counsel for the prosecution were—Messrs. Curran, Hoare, Townsend, Goold, Burton, Waggett, and Wilmott: the agent, Mr. Richard Martin. The prisoner's Counsel were Messrs. Quin, Keller White, Grady, Fitzgerald, Hitchcock, Franks, and Dobbin: the agent was Mr. Fleming.
The trial excited great interest, and Sir Henry came into court attended by numerous nd influential friends.
Witnesses having been ordered out of court, Curran spoke as follows :—

My Lord and Gentlemen of the Jury—It is my duty, as one of the counsel in this prosecution, to state to your lordship, and to you, gentlemen of the jury, such facts as I am instructed will be established by evidence, in order that you may be informed of the nature of the offence charged by the indictment, and be rendered capable of understanding that evidence, which, without some previous statement, might appear irrelevant or obscure. And I shall make a few such observations, in point of law, on the evidence we propose to adduce, with respect to the manner in which it will support the charge, if you shall believe it to be true, as may assist you in performing that awful duty which you are now called upon to discharge. In doing so, I cannot forget upon what very different ground from that of the learned counsel for the prisoner, I find myself placed. It is the privilege, it is the obligation, of those who have to defend a client on a trial for his life, to exert every force, and to call forth every resource, that zeal, and genius, and sagacity can suggest. It is an indulgence in favour of life—it has the sanction of usage—it has the permission of humanity; and the man who should linger one single step behind the most advanced limit of that privilege, and should fail to exercise every talent that heaven had given him, in that defence, would be guilty of a mean desertion of his duty, and an abandonment of his client.

Far different is the situation of him who is concerned for the crown. Cautiously should he use his privileges—scrupulously should he keep within the duties of accusation. His task is to lay fairly the nature of the case before the court and the jury. Should he endeavour to gain a verdict otherwise than by evidence, he were unworthy of speaking in a court of justice. If I heard a counsel for the crown state anything that I did not think founded in law, I should say to myself, "God grant that the man who has stated this may be an ignorant man, because his ignorance can be his only justification." It shall, therefore, be my endeavour, so to lay the matters of fact and of law before you, as shall enable you clearly to comprehend them, and finally, by your verdict, to do complete justice between the prisoner and the public.

My Lord, and Gentlemen of the Jury, this is an indictment, found by the grand jury against the prisoner at the bar, for having feloniously carried away Mary Pike, with intent against her will to marry her; there is another charge also, that he did feloniously carry her away with intent to defile her.

There was a former statute made on this subject, enacting the punishment of death against any man that should, by violence, carry away a female, and actually marry or defile her. But it was found that young creatures, the victims of this sort of crime, from their natural timidity, and the awful impression made upon them in an assembly like the present, were often unequal to the task of prosecution, and that offences against that statute often passed unpunished, because the natural delicacy and modesty of the sex shrunk from the revolting details that were unavoidable on such trials. It, therefore, became necessary to enact a new law upon the subject, making the taking away with intent to marry or defile, although, in fact, no such marriage or defilement had taken place, felony of death. Thus was suppressed the necessity of a those shocking, but necessary, details, that were otherwise required.

Of the enormity of the crime, I trust I need say but little. I trust in God there could not be found in this great city twelve men, to whom it could be necessary to expatiate on the hideous enormity of such an offence. It goes to sap the foundation of all civil society; it goes to check the working of that natural affection, which heaven has planted in the breast of the parent for the child. In fact, gentlemen of the jury, if crimes like this shall be encouraged and multiplied by impunity, why should you defraud your own gratifications of the fruits of your industry?—why lay up the acquisitions of self-denying toil, as an advancement for your child?—why check your own appetites to give her all?—why labour to adorn her person or her mind with useless, with fatal accomplishments? You are only decking her with temptations for lust and rapine; you are refining her heart, only to make her feel more profoundly the agony of violation and of dishonour. Why, then, labour to multiply the inducements of the ravisher?—why labour to augment and to perpetuate the sufferings of the victim? Instead of telling you my opinion of the enormity of this crime, I will tell you that of the legislature upon it:—the legislature has deemed it a crime deserving the punishment of death.

I will now state to you the facts as I am instructed they will appear to you in evidence.

The prisoner at the bar, and considering his education, his age, his rank, and situation in society, I do regret, from my soul, that he is there), married many years ago ; his wife died, leaving him the surviving parent of, I believe, many children. Miss Mary Pike is the only child of a person, whom, I suppose, you all knew—Mr. Samuel Pike, of this city. He had devoted a long life to a very persevering and successful industry, and died advanced in years, leaving this his only child, entitled to all the fruits of his laborious and persevering application. The property she is entitled to, I understand, is very great, indeed.— At the time of the transaction, to which your attention must be called, she was living in the house, and under the protection, of an universally respected member of society, Mr. Cooper Penrose. From the moment her mind was susceptible of it, no expense was spared to give her every accomplishment that she was capable of receiving; and in the house of her own father, while he lived, and in the house of Mr. Penrose, when she came under his protection, her mind was formed to the most correct principles of modesty, and delicacy, and decorum, with those additional characteristics, humility and reserve, that belong to that most respectable sect of which her father was a member. The prisoner at the bar, it seems, had heard of her, and had heard of her property ; for it is a material circumstance in this case, that he never by any accident had seen her, even for a moment, until he went to see and identify her person, and mark her out the victim of his projected crime.

He was not induced by the common motives that influence young men—by any individual attachment to the mind or the person of the lady. It will appear, that his first approach to her was meanly and perfidiously contrived, with the single purpose of identifying her person, in order that he might feloniously steal it, as the title-deed of her estate.

Some time before the 22nd of July, in the year 1797, he rode down to the residence of Mr. Penrose. Mr. Penrose has a country-house, built in a very beautiful situation, and which attracts the curiosity of strangers, who frequently go to see it.

The prisoner at the bar went into the grounds as one of these, and seemed to observe every thing with great attention. Mr. Penrose immediately came out to him, and conducted him to whatever objects he supposed might gratify his curiosity. He affected to be much entertained ; he lingered about the grounds until the hour of Mr. Penrose's dinner approached. Mr. Penrose, quite a stranger to the prisoner at the bar, was not, I suppose, very anxious to invite a perfect stranger in among his family, more desirous, probably, of enjoying the little exclusive confidential intercourse of that family. However with that good nature, which any man of his cordial and honest turn of mind will feel it his duty to exercise, he did invite Sir Henry Hayes to dinner. The invitation was accepted of ; and thus the first step towards the crime he meditated, was an abuse of the sacred duty which the hospitality of his host imposed upon him, as a man, and as a gentleman. He placed himself at the friendly and unsuspecting board, in order to the accomplishment of his design, by the most unfeeling and unextenuated violation of the rights of the host, whom he made his dupe—of the lady, whom he marked as

2 A

his victim—and of the law, which he determined to trample upon, and disgrace by the commission of a felony of death. There, when the eye of the prisoner could escape from the smiles that were lavished upon him —those honest smiles of respect and cordiality, that come only from the heart— it was to search the room, to find out who probably was the person that he had come to identify. He made his observation, and took his departure; but it was not a departure for the last time.

Mrs. Pike, the widow, mother of the prosecutrix, was then in Cork, in a dangerous state of health. In order to get Miss Pike out of the hands of her protector, a stratagem was adopted. Dr. Gibbings was the attending physician upon her mother; it does not appear that the prisoner knew Dr. Gibbings' hand-writing: it was necessary that a letter should be sent, as if from Dr. Gibbings; but to do so with effect, it was necessary that a letter should be written to Mr. Penrose in a hand-writing, bearing such such a similitude to the doctor's, as might pass for genuine. To qualify himself for this, the prisoner at the bar made some pretext for sending a written message to Dr. Gibbings, which procured in return, a written answer from the doctor. Thus was he furnished with the form of the hand-writing of Dr. Gibbings, which he intended to counterfeit; and accordingly there was written, on the 22nd day of July, 1797, a letter, so like the character of Dr. Gibbings' that he himself on a slight glance would be apt to take it for his own. It was in these words:—"Dear Sir,—Our friend, Mrs. Pike, is taken suddenly ill; she wishes to see Miss Pike; we would recommend despatch, as we think she has not many hours to live. Yours Robert Gibbings." Addressed "to Mr. Cooper Penrose." The first step to the crime was a flagrant breach of hospitality, and the second, towards the completion, was the inhuman fraud of practising upon the piety of the child, to decoy her into the trap of the ravisher, to seduce her to destruction by the angelic impulses of that feeling that attaches her to the parent—that sends her after the hour of midnight, from the house of her protector, to pay the last duty, and to receive the parting benediction. Such was the intention with which the prosecutrix, of a rainy night, between one and two o'clock in the morning, rose from her bed; such was her intention; it was not her destination; it was not to visit the sick bed of a parent; it was not to carry a daughter's duty of consolation to her dying mother; it was not for that she came abroad; it was that she might fall into the hands of preconcerted villany; that she should fall into that trap, which was laid for her, with the intention to despoil her of every thing that makes human existence worth the having, by any female who has any feeling of delicacy or honour.

I should state to you, that she left the house of Mr. Penrose, in his carriage, attended by two female relations, one of them his daughter and when they had advanced about half way to Cork, the carriage was suddenly met by four or five men. They ordered the coachman to stop. One of them was dressed in a great coat, and armed with pistols, and had the lower part of his face concealed, by tying a handkerchief round it.

The ladies, as you may suppose, were exceedingly terrified at such a circumstance as this. They asked, as well as extreme terror would permit, what they sought for; they were answered, "they must be searched." On looking about, they observed another chaise, stationed near the place where they were detained. It will appear to you, that Miss Pike was taken forcibly out of the carriage from her friends; that she was placed in the other chaise which I have mentioned; in which she found, shame to tell it—she found a woman. The traces of Mr. Penrose's chaise were then cut; and the ladies that came in it, left of course to find their way, as well as they could, and return in the dark.

The carriage, into which the prosecutrix was put, drove off towards Cork; the female that was with her will appear to you to have been the sister of the prisoner. Happy! happy for her! that death has taken her away from being the companion of his trial, and of his punishment, as she was the accomplice of his guilt: but she is dead. The carriage drove on to the seat belonging to the prisoner at the bar, called Mount-Vernon, in the liberties of the city; at the bottom of his avenue, which it seems is a steep ascent, and of considerable length, the horses refused to go on; upon which the prisoner rode up to the chaise, dismounted from his horse, which he gave to one of his attendants, opened the door, took the prosecutrix out, and carried her, struggling in his arms, the whole length of the avenue, to his house. When he arrived there, he carried her up stairs, where she saw a man, attired in somewhat like the dress of a priest; and she was then told that she was brought there to marry the prisoner at the bar. In what frame of mind the miserable wretch must have been, any man, that has feelings, must picture to himself. She had quitted the innocent and respectable protection of her friends, and family, and found herself—good God! where?—in the power of an inexorable ravisher, and surrounded by his accomplices: she looked in every mean and guilty countenance; she saw the base unfeeling accomplices induced by bribe, and armed for present force, bound and pledged by the community of guilt and danger, by the felon's necessity, to the future perjury of self-defence.

Thus situated, what was she to look to for assistance? What was she to do? Was she to implore the unfeeling heart of the prisoner? As well might she have invoked her buried father, to burst the cerements of the grave, and rise to the protection of his forlorn and miserable child. There, whatever sort of ceremony they thought right to perform, took place, something was muttered in a language which she partly did not hear, and partly could not understand; she was then his wife—she was then Lady Hayes.

A letter was then to be written to apprise her miserable relations of their new affinity. A pen was put into her hand, and she consented to write, in hopes that it might lead to her deliverance; but when the sad scroll was finished and the subscription only remained, neither entreaties nor menaces could prevail upon her, desolate and forlorn as she was, to write the odious name of the ravisher. She subscribed herself by the surname of her departed father; as if she thought there was some mysterious virtue in the name of her family, to which she could cling in that hour of terror, as a refuge from lawless force and unmerited suffering.

A ceremony of marriage had taken place: a ring was forced upon her anger; she tore it off, and indignantly dashed it from her; she was then forced into an adjoining chamber, and the prisoner brutally endeavoured to push her towards the bed.

My lord, and gentlemen of the jury, you will soon see this young lady. You will see that whatever grace or proportion her person possesses, it does not seem formed for much power of resistance, or self-defence. But there is a last effort of sinking modesty, that can rally more than the powers of nature to the heart, and send them to every fibre of the frame, where they can achieve more than mere vulgar strength can do upon any ordinary occasion: that effort she did make, and made it with effect; and in that instance, innocence was crowned with success.

Baffled and frustrated in his purposes of force, he sought to soften, to conciliate. "And do you not know me?" said he. "Don't you know who I am?" "Yes," answered she, "I do know you; I do now remember you did go to my cousin's, as you say you did. I remember your mean intrusion, you are Sir Henry Hayes." How natually do the parties support their characters! The criminal puts his questions under the consciousness of guilt, as if under the forecast of his present situation. The innocent victim of that guilt regards him already as his prosecutrix; she recognizes him, but it is only to identify him as a malefactor, and to disclaim him as a husband.

Gentlemen, she remained in this captivity, until her friends got intelligence of her situation. Justice was applied to. A party went to the house of the prisoner, for the purpose of enlarging her. The prisoner at the bar had fled. His sister, his accomplice, had fled. They left behind them Miss Pike, who was taken back by her relations. Informations were lodged immediately. The prisoner absconded. It would be base and scandalous to suffer a crime of that kind to pass with impunity, without doing every thing that could be done to bring the offender to justice. Government was apprised of it. Government felt as it ought. There was offered by proclamation, a reward to a considerable amount for taking the prisoner. The family of Miss Pike did as they ought. They offered a considerable additional sum, as the reward for his apprehension. For some time he kept in concealment; the rewards were offered in vain; the process of the law went on; an indictment, to the honour of this city, to the honour of the national character, was found; they proceeded to the outlawry of the prisoner.

What I have stated hitherto reflects honour upon all persons concerned, except the unhappy man at the bar, and his accomplices; but what I am about to relate, is a circumstance that no man of feeling or humanity can listen to without indignation. Notwithstanding that outlawry; notwithstanding the publicly-offered rewards, to the amount of near one thousand pounds, for the apprehension of the prisoner at the bar, (would to God the story could not be told in a foreign country! would to God it were not in the power of those so ready to defame us, to adduce such a circumstance in corroboration of their charge!) for near two years did the prisoner live in public, almost in the heart of your city; reading in every newspaper, over his tea, the miserable proclamation of impotent public justice, of the laws defied and trampled upon. The second city in the nation was made the hiding-place—no! no! not the hiding-place, where guilt hid its head—but the receptacle where it walked abroad, unappalled, and threw your degraded city into the odious predicament of being a sort of public accessory and accomplice in his crime, by giving it that hideous appearance of protection and impunity. Here he stayed, basking in the favour of a numerous kindred and acquaintance, in a widely-extended city.

Sad reverse! It was not for guilt to fly! It was for guilt to stand, and bay at public justice! It was only for innocence to betake itself to flight! It was not the ravisher that fled. It was the helpless female, the object of his crime, the victim of his felony! It was hers to feel that she could despair of even personal protection in that country which harboured and cherished the delinquent! It was she who was hunted, a poor fugitive from her family and her home; and was forced to fling herself at the feet of a foreign nation, a suppliant for personal protection. She fled to England, where she remained for two years.

A few months ago, previous to the last term, a letter was written and sent to Miss Pike, the prosecutrix, by the prisoner. The purport of it was, to state to her, that his conduct to her had been honourable and delicate, and asserting, that any lady, possessed of the smallest particle of humanity, could not be so sanguinary as to wish for the blood of an individual, however guilty; intimating a threat, that her conduct upon this occasion would mark her fate through life; desiring her to withdraw her advertisements, saying, he would abide his trial at the assizes of Cork; boasting his influence in the city in which he lived, thanking God he stands as high as any man in the regards of rich and poor, of which the inefficacy of her present and former rewards must convince her.

He thought, I suppose, that an interval of two years, during which he had been an outlaw, and had resided among his friends, had brought the public mind to such a state of honourable sympathy in his favour as would leave any form of trial perfectly safe. After this he thought proper to appear, and the outlawry was reversed without opposition by counsel for the prosecution; because their object was not to take advantage of any judgment of outlawry, upon which he might be executed; but to admit him to plead to the charge, and take his trial by a jury of his country. He pleaded to that indictment in the court above, and accordingly he now stands at the bar of this court for the purpose of trial.

The publicity of his living in this city, of his going to festivals and entertainments, during the course of two years, did impress the minds of the friends of this unhappy lady, with such a despair of obtaining public justice, that they did struggle hard, not, as it is said, to try the offence by a foreign jury; but, to try the offence at a distant place, in the capital where the authority of the court might keep public justice in some sort of countenance. That application was refused: and justly did you, my lord, and the learned judges, your brethren, ground yourselves upon the reason which you gave. "We will not," said you, "give " judicial sanction to a reproach of such a scandalous atrocity upon any county in the land, much less upon the second city in it." "I do remember," said one of you, "a case, which happened not twenty years since. A similar crime was committed on two young women of the name of Kennedy; it was actually necessary to guard them through two counties with a military force as they went to prosecute; that mean and odious bias, that the dregs of every community will feel by natural sympathy with every thing base, was in favour of the prisoners. Every means were used to try and baffle justice, by practising upon the modesty and constancy of the prosecutrixes, and their friends: but the infatuated populace, that had assembled together to celebrate the triumph of an acquittal, were the unwilling spectators of the vindication of the law. The court recollected, that particular respect is due to the female, who nobly comes forward to vindicate the law, and give protection to her sex. The jury remembered what they owed to their oaths, to their families, to their country. They felt as became the fathers of families, and foresaw what the hideous consequence would be of impunity, in a case of manifest guilt. They pronounced that verdict which saved their characters; and the offenders were executed."

I am glad that the Court of King's Bench did not yield to the despair which had taken place in the minds of those who were anxious to bring the prosecution forward. I am glad the prisoner was sent to this bar, in order that you may decide upon it.

I have stated to you, gentlemen of the jury, the facts that I conceive material; I have stated that it was necessary, and my duty, as counsel for the crown, to give you an exact idea of the nature of the offence, of the evidence, and of the law; that you may be enabled to combine the whole case together, and to pronounce such a verdict as shall fairly decide the question, which you are sworn to try, between the public and the prisoner. Any thing I say, either as to the fact, or as to the law, ought not to attract any thing more than bare attention for a single moment; it should make no impression upon your belief, unless confirmed by credible evidence. I am merely stating facts from instruction; but I am not a witness.

I am also obliged, as I told you, to make observations as to the law, but that is wholly submitted to the court; to which it is your duty, as well as mine, to bow with all becoming deference and respect.

My lord, the prisoner is indicted as a principal offender, upon the statute; and therefore, it is necessary that the jury shall understand what kind of evidence is necessary to sustain that charge. Formerly there was a distinction taken by courts of justice between two species of principals; the one, a principal at the doing of the very act; the other, a principal in the second degree, who was then considered as an accessory at the fact: a distinction in point of law, which, as Mr. Justice Forster observes, was a great inconvenience in the course and order of proceeding against accomplices in felony; tending, as it plainly did, to the total obstruction of justice in many cases, and to great delay in others; and which induced the judges, from a principle of true political justice, to come into the rule now established: "That all persons present, aiding and abetting, are principals"

I now proceed to show what kind of presence it is that will make a man concurring in the crime, in judgment of the law, "present, aiding and assisting:" which to explain, I shall read the words of the last-mentioned writer, as follows: "When the law requireth the presence of the accomplice at the perpetration of the fact, in order to render him a principal, it doth not require a strict, actual, immediate presence such a presence as would make him an eye or ear witness of what passeth." And I may thus exemplify this case: "Several persons set out together, or in small parties, upon one common design, be it murder, or other felony; or for any other purpose, unlawful in itself; and each taketh the part assigned him: one to commit the fact, others to watch at proper stations, to prevent a surprise, or favour, if need be, the escape of those who are more immediately engaged; they are all (provided the fact be committed,) in the eye of the law, present at it. For it was made a common cause with them; each man operated in his station, at one and the same instant, towards the same common end: and the part each man took, tended to give countenance, encouragement, and protection, to the whole gang, and to ensure the success of their common enterprise."

If the prisoner at the bar formed a design of doing the illegal act with which he is charged, namely, running away with Miss Pike, in order to marry or defile her; if he projected the perpetration of it by dividing his accomplices in such manner, as that each might contribute his part to its success; that it was made a common cause; that what each man did, tended to secure the success of the common enterprise; then every person so acting, although not an eye or ear witness of what was done, yet in the eye of the law is guilty. He is a principal, and punishable as such.

Suppose, that some should guard at Mr. Penrose's bounds; others guard at different stations on the road; others guard at the bridge; others remain at the house at Mount-Vernon. In that case, I should not hesitate to say, in point of law, that the man stationed at the back door of Mr. Penrose's house (supposing her to be taken out by violence,) the men guarding on the road and at the bridge; nay, the priest that waited at Mount-Vernon to celebrate the marriage, were all a combination of one common power; acting each man in his station, to produce the intended effect; and, as such, were all equally principals in the offence.

But in the present case it is not necessary to argue upon a constructive presence; for here is an actual presence. If what I have stated should be supported by the witnesses, there is full ground to convince the jury, that Sir Henry Hayes was the person in disguise, who put her into his carriage, when taken out of Mr. Penrose's; particularly when the circumstance is considered, that he went to the house in order to identify her person, for that knowledge of her person would have been useless, unless he had been present at the first taking of her.

If the jury believe he was there at such first taking, he was actually present and guilty. But, supposing the jury to doubt, strange as the doubt must be, yet if there shall be evidence to satisfy them, that the prisoner, at the bottom of the hill leading to his house, took her out of his carriage, and led her to the house, that is, as to him, a taking and carrying away, clearly within the statute. There cannot be the least doubt, that every step the chaise proceeded from Mr. Penrose's to Mount-Vernon, that every man who joined the cavalcade, and became an assistant in the project, became a principal in the entire transaction, and guilty of carrying her away, contrary to the statute.

In further illustration, suppose this case. A highwayman stops a traveller, and proceeds to rob him; and another comes up to the assistance of that robber; there is not the least doubt, that the man who joins in the robbery a little later, is equally guilty with the former in the eye of the law. This is applicable to the present case.

Thus I have stated the nature of the case, and what I conceive to be the law touching that case. I know not what kind of defence may be set up. There are some defences which, if they can be established clearly, must acquit the prisoner. If he did not do this, if she was not taken away, or if Sir Henry took no share in the transaction, there can be no doubt in the case. It will be for your consciences to say, whether this be a mere tale of the imagination, unsupported by truth, and uncorroborated by evidence. It is material, however, to state to you, that, as soon as guilt is once established in the eye of the law, nothing that the party can do can have any sort of retrospect, so as to purge that criminality, if once completed. It is out of the power of the expiring victim of a death-blow, to give any release or acquittal to his murderer; it is out of the power of any human creature, upon whom an illegal offence has been committed, by any act of forgiveness to purge that original guilt; and, therefore, the semblance of a marriage is entirely out of the case.

In the case of the Misses Kennedy, the young ladies had been obliged to submit to a marriage, and cohabitation for a length of time, yet the offenders were most justly convicted, and suffered death.

It is, therefore, necessary for you to keep your minds and understandings so fixed upon the material points of the charge, as that, in the course of the examination, no sidelong view of the subject may mislead or divert your attention.

The point before you is, whether the crime was once committed; and if so, nothing happening after can make any sort of difference upon the subject. It has been my most anxious wish to abstain, as far as was consistent with my duty, from every the remotest expression of contumely or disrespect to the unhappy prisoner at the bar; or to say or to do anything that might unhinge his mind or distract his recollection, so as to disable him from giving his whole undisturbed reflection to the consideration of his defence; but it is also a sacred duty, which every man placed in my situation owes to public justice, to take care, under the affectation of false humanity, not to suffocate that charge which it is his duty to unfold, nor to frustrate the force of that evidence which it is his duty to develop. Painful must it be to the counsel, to the jury, and the court, who are bound by their respective duties to prosecute, to convict, and to pronounce and to draw down the stroke of public justice, even upon the guilty head; but despicable would they all be, if, instead of surrendering the criminal to the law, they could abandon the law to the criminal; if, instead of having mercy upon outraged justice and injured innocence, they should squander their disgraceful sympathy upon guilt alone. Justice may weep; but she must strike where she ought not to spare. We, too, may lament; but, when we mourn over crimes, let us take care that there be no crimes of our own, upon which our tears should be shed.

Gentlemen, you cannot be surprised that I hold this language to you. Had this case no reference to any country but our own, the extraordinary circumstances attending it, which are known to the whole nation, would well warrant much more than I have said. But you cannot forget that the eyes of another country also are upon you: another country, which is now the source of your legislation. You are not ignorant what sort of character is given of us there; by what sort of men, and from what kind of motive. Alas! we have no power of contradicting the cruel calumnies that are there heaped upon us, in defiance of notorious truth, and of common mercy and humanity; but, when we are there charged with being a barbarous race of savages, with whom no measures can be held, upon whose devoted heads legislation can only pour down laws of fire, we can easily, by our own misconduct, furnish proof that to a much less willing belief may corroborate their base evidence, and turn their falsehood into truth.

Once more, and for the last time, let me say to you, you have heard the charge. Believe nothing upon my statement. Hear and weigh the evidence. If you doubt its truth, acquit without hesitation. By the laws of every country, because by those of eternal justice, doubt and acquittal are synonymous terms. If, on the other hand, the guilt of the prisoner shall unhappily be clearly proved, remember what you owe to your fame, your conscience, and your country. I shall trouble you no further, but shall call evidence in support of the indictment; and I have not a doubt, that there will be such a verdict given, whether of conviction or acquittal, as may hereafter be spoken of, without kindling any shame in yourselves, or your country.

Before the witnesses were called Mr. Curran objected to any person but the prisoner being suffered to stand at the bar. Prisoner's counsel declared they were not anxious about it, but mentioned the case of Mr. Horne Tooke, where the Court allowed him to be attended by his counsel. The Court said, the prisoner here should have that indulgence, when he came to his defence: but, for the present, all other persons, save his attorney, and one of his counsel, were ordered to withdraw from the bar.

Miss Pike proved the facts stated before, but her cross-examination by Mr. Quin contained some inconsistencies:—

Q. Can you swear that, at that time, you knew any one of the persons who took and carried you away from that part of the Glanmire Road, where you were stopped? *A.* No, I cannot.

Your uncle mentioned something as you went along of the necessity of giving immediate informations—did he not? I said before he did.

When did you give the informations? The Monday morning following.

Do you recollect what day of the week it happened? I believe Saturday.

And you gave informations on Monday? I did.

Where did you swear them? At my aunt's.

Who drew them out? Indeed I do not know who wrote them.

Do you recollect whether you swore in the informations, that Sir Henry took, and carried you away on the Glanmire Road? I believe I did not.

Was there any interposition used with you to induce you to come into court this morning? No, there was not.
Did any person describe the dress or person of Sir Henry to you before you came into court? No, sir.
Will you now say upon your oath, that if, at the time you came into court and sat upon the table, you were asked the question, that you could have said positively you knew Sir Henry Hayes? No. I could not, because he might have been very much disguised.
Mr. and Miss Penrose, Dr. Gibbings, and Mr. Richard Pike proved the other facts. Mr. Quin spoke for the prisoner, but declined to call witnesses, and pressed for an acquittal in law, from the insufficiency of the evidence under the statute of abduction. Curran shortly replied, as follows:—

It is the undoubted privilege of the crown to reply in all criminal cases, not only to a point of law, but if the prisoner's counsel speak to evidence, the crown is warranted to reply. I might by law have prevented such speaking altogether; but I will never oppose such indulgence to a prisoner. The evidence adduced upon the part of the crown has not been attempted to be denied by a single witness, and therefore I think it would be absurd to go about to establish the credibility of testimony uncontroverted, even by the prisoner. I feel myself, therefore, only called upon to answer the objections in point of law. Much has been said about that indictment which was quashed; the observations on that, as far as they go, are a complete answer to themselves. It is undoubted law, that if a man be indicted as a principal, and acquitted, and afterwards indicted as an accessory before the fact, that the former acquittal is a conclusive plea in bar. The law is clearly settled in that case, and an acquittal upon the present indictment would be a complete bar to any prosecution upon the second; therefore it was, that the second indictment was quashed. We sent up that indictment in fact, because we did not, with precise exactness, know how the evidence would turn out upon the trial. The second indictment was a mere charge of an accessorial offence; but feeling, that to bring forward the real merits of the case, we should go upon the first indictment, we thought it would be an act of unwarrantable vexation not to apprise the prisoner, the court, and the jury, that that was the only charge against him. And therefore, it is, that that indictment should be dismissed entirely from the subject. The argument contended for is, that the evidence adduced does not support the indictment; to that, and that alone, it is necessary for me to reply: the only question is, whether there is sufficient evidence to maintain the indictment. [Reads the indictment.] On this a question of law occurs. What is a taking and carrying away? I see no possibility that the jury can disbelieve that the man who took her out of Mr. Penrose's carriage was the prisoner at the bar, who went before to identify her. He could not make use of that knowledge of her person on that occasion, if he was not there; he should have shown that he was then in some other place, but to do so was not attempted. Observe upon the latter part of the transaction, on the carriage proceeding with her in it to the passage leading to Mount-Vernon, that there a man dressed as the lady describes, alit from his horse; but there has been strong evidence that he did not come from the house; took the handkerchief from his face, took her in his arms, and carried her in his arms from the foot of the hill to Mount-Vernon house, and where that marriage was absolutely solemnized. Upon this part of the question there does, to be sure, arise a question—Was that a taking and carrying away within the statute? I do admit that the taking and carrying away are essential; but it is not being the first taker that is necessary within the act of parliament: for if ten different persons had rescued her from one another, and another had taken her into the place, where, &c., he would be guilty, because he had taken her, and carried her away. The question, therefore, is, Was there a taking within the act or not? Mr. Quin has argued from two cases, that he supposes similar to the present; the one was burglary, the other was murder. They differ materially in this from the present, that they are things done at one moment of time, and in the present case, a continuance of the force is a continuance of the taking, upon the statute of Henry VII.; there must be an actual marriage in order to constitute the offence; but in England, as well as here, there must be a previous taking and carrying away; therefore, what is there considered as such, must be in this country, a taking and carrying away. 2 Hawkins, 315. Also, if a woman be taken away by force in one county, and carried into another, and there married, the offender may be indicted, and tried in the second county upon the statute of Henry VII., because it is a continuation of force, and of such kind as amounts to forcibly taking within the statute; and so it is, if the prisoner at the bar had taken her by force in an adjoining county, and brought her into this.

You have an unquestionable authority, and a most respectable one, stating that a continuance of force in the county where the indictment is laid, is a sufficient taking and carrying away within the statute.

Suppose a man hires a gang of people to seize a woman in Dublin, and bring her down by force; in the last stage, he goes and takes her in his arms, and carries her into his house; will any one say that because he had not seized her in the first instance himself, that his seizing her by force, in the last stage, is not a taking within the statute?

The simple question to be decided upon is this, in point of law, whether the taking her out of that chaise, in which she was brought to the avenue of the prisoner, was a sufficient taking, and whether the carrying her up to his house, was such a carrying away, as, added to the taking, brought the present case within the statute.

To support this, I shall cite the case of the King and Lapyard, an indictment on which the facts were,—" That Mrs. Hobart, coming out of the play-house, had an attempt made by the prisoner to snatch her ear-ring from her ear; it appeared that the snatch at it was so violent, that it tore through her ear. When she went home, she found not only that the ear-ring had not been taken away by the prisoner, but actually found it sticking in the curls of her hair." It was necessary, then, that there should be a taking, and also a carrying away; and the question was, whether the facts did amount to that carrying and taking away. The judge gave into the doubts proposed by the prisoner's counsel. I shall mention two cases, one where a man turned a cart from a horizontal to a perpendicular position to get at the goods; the other case was, where a person removed a parcel into the head of a wagon, in order to steal it, which had been before in the tail of it, and in each case there was judged a sufficient taking and carrying away. A man lodged at an inn, and in the morning took the sheets out of his bed, and carried them into the stable and another stole them. The jury found the prisoner guilty; but judgment was respited, and the case submitted to the consideration of the twelve judges, who were of opinion that he was guilty of the charge of felony laid in the indictment. Compare these to the present case. Miss Pike was taken by force out of the chaise; she was carried by force up the avenue; she was taken by force into a room. What would become of the law, if miserable subterfuges of this kind could have any effect? The circumstances of this case make it ridiculous to suppose that the conduct of the prisoner was from any motive of hospitality, as has been insinuated, for she stated other facts inconsistent with such a defence. Every fact, if the jury believed the prosecution, was by force, and against her consent. Let me remind the jury that such an idea as this ought not to go abroad, that a gang may be hired by a man, to force away a woman, and that that man, meeting her in the last stage of the transaction, shall completely commit a felony against the statute, with impunity.

The judge charged fairly, and after an hour's deliberation the jury found the prisoner Guilty, but recommended him to mercy. The law point on the insufficiency of the evidence was referred to the twelve judges, and decided against Sir Henry, but the recommendation to mercy was acceded to, and he was transported.

HEVEY v. MAJOR SIRR.

KING'S BENCH.

May 17th, 1802.

As an illustration of the abominable government of Ireland at the time of the trial, and for some years before, this case is most interesting, and Curran's speech equal to the occasion.

Hevey was a brewer in Dublin, and in '98 acted as a yeoman in the Roebuck cavalry, Happening to be in court during a trial, and seeing a rascal whom he had once employed, on the table, he said what he thought of him, and was then obliged to give evidence against the witness's character, and the prisoner was acquitted. For this he was seized on by Major Sirr and his gang, forced into prison, obliged to give up a valuable mare to Sandys, a comrade of Sirr's, was then hurried to Kilkenny, tried by Court-martial, and sentenced to be hanged. Lord Cornwallis saw the report of the trial, and released Hevey. In September, 1801, Major Sirr met Hevey in the Commercial Buildings, threatened him, and when Hevey defied him, Sirr thrust the unfortunate man into the provost prison in the Castle, till he signed a submission. For this the action was brought.

Lord Kilwarden (Arthur Wolfe) and a special jury tried the case. Curran opened for the plaintiff:—

This is the most extraordinary action I have ever met with. It must proceed from the most unexampled impudence in the plaintiff, if he has brought it wantonly, or the most unparalleled miscreancy in the defendant, if it shall appear supported by proof. The event must stamp the most condign and indelible disgrace on the guilty defendant, unless an unworthy verdict should shift the scandal upon another quarter.

On the record the action appears short and simple. It is an action of trespass, *vi et armis* for an assault, battery, and false imprisonment.

But the facts that led to it, that explain its nature, and its enormity, and, of course, that should measure the damages, are neither short nor simple. The novelty of them may surprise, the atrocity must shock your feelings, if you have feelings to be shocked. But I do not mean to address myself to any of your proud feelings of liberty—the season for that is past. There was, indeed, a time, when, in addressing a jury upon very inferior violations of human rights, I have felt my bosom glow and swell with the noble and elevating consciousness of being a freeman, speaking to free-men, and in a free-country; where, if I was not able to communicate the generous flame to their bosoms, I was not at least so cold as not to catch it from them. But that is a sympathy which I am not now so foolish as to affect either to inspire, or to participate. I shall not insult you by the bitter mockery of such an affectation; buried as they are, I do not wish to conjure up the shades of departed freedom to flutter round their tomb, to taunt or to reproach them. Where freedom is no more, it is a mischievous profanation to use her language; because it tends to deceive the man who is no longer free, upon the most important of all points—that is, the nature of the situation to which he is reduced; and to make him confound the licentiousness of words with the real possession of freedom. I mean not, therefore, to call for a haughty verdict, that might humble the insolence of oppression, or assert the fancied rights of independence. Far from it; I only ask for such a verdict as may make some reparation for the most extreme and unmerited suffering, and may also tend to some probable mitigation of the public and general destiny. For this purpose I must carry back your attention to the melancholy period of 1798. It was at that sad crisis that the defendant, from an obscure individual, started into notice and consequence. It is in the hot-bed of public calamity that such portentous and inauspicious products are accelerated without being matured. From being a town-major, a name scarcely legible in the list of public incumbrances, he became at once invested with all the real powers of the most absolute authority. The life and the liberty of every man seemed to be given up to his disposal. With this gentleman's extraordinary elevation begins the story of the sufferings and ruin of the plaintiff.

It seems, a man of the name of M'Guire was prosecuted for some offence against the state. Mr. Hevey, the plaintiff, by accident was in court; he was then a citizen of wealth and credit, a brewer, in the first line of that business. Unfortunately for him, he had heretofore employed the witness for the prosecution, and found him a man of infamous character. Unfortunately for himself, he mentioned this circumstance in court. The counsel for the prisoner insisted on his being sworn; he was so   The jury were convinced that no credit was due to the witness for the crown, and the prisoner was accordingly acquitted. In a day or two after, Major Sirr met the plaintiff in the street, asked how he dared to interfere in his business, and swore, "By God, he would teach him now to meddle with his people."

Gentlemen, there are two classes of prophets, one that derive their predictions from real or fancied inspiration, and are sometimes mistaken;

and another who prophecy what they are determined to bring about themselves. Of this second, and by far the most authentic class, was the Major; for heaven, you see, has no monopoly of prediction.

On the following evening, poor Hevey was dogged in the dark into some lonely alley; there he was seized, he knew not by whom, nor by what authority—and became in a moment to his family and his friends, as if he had never been. He was carried away in equal ignorance of his crime and of his destiny, whether to be tortured, or hanged, or transported. His crime he soon learned; it was the treason which he had committed against the majesty of Major Sirr. He was immediately conducted to a new place of imprisonment in the Castle-yard, called the Provost. Of this mansion of misery, of which you have since heard so much, Major Sandy was, and I believe yet is, the keeper—a gentleman of whom I know how dangerous it is to speak, and of whom every prudent man will think and talk with all due reverence. He seemed a twin star of the defendant,—equal in honour, in confidence;—equal also (for who could be superior?) in probity and humanity. To this gentleman was my client consigned, and in his custody he remained about seven weeks, unthought of by the world as if he had never existed. The oblivion of the buried is as profound as the oblivion of the dead; his family may have mourned his absence or his probable death; but why should I mention so paltry a circumstance? The fears or the sorrows of the wretched give no interruption to the general progress of things. The sun rose and the sun set, just as it did before—the business of the government, the business of the castle, of the feast, or the torture went on with their usual exactness and tranquillity.

At last Mr. Hevey was discovered among the sweepings of the prison, and was to be disposed of. He was at last honoured with the personal notice of Major Sandys. "Hevey (says the Major), I have seen you ride, I think, a smart sort of a mare; you can't use her here; you had better give me an order for her." The plaintiff, you may well suppose, by this time had a tolerable idea of his situation; he thought he might have much to fear from a refusal, and something to hope from compliance; at all events, he saw it would be a means of apprising his family that he was not dead;—he instantly gave the order required. The Major graciously accepted it, saying, "Your courtesy will not cost you much: you are to be sent down to-morrow to Kilkenny, to be tried for your life; you will most certainly be hanged; and you can scarcely think that your journey to the other world will be performed on horseback." The humane and honourable Major was equally a prophet with his compeer. The plaintiff on the next day took leave of his prison, as he supposed for the last time, and was sent under a guard to Kilkenny then the head-quarters of Sir Charles Asgil, there to be tried by a court-martial for such crime as might chance to be alleged against him.

In any other country the scene that took place on that occasion might excite no little horror and astonishment; but with us, these sensations have become extinguished by frequency of repetition. I am instructed that a proclamation was sent forth, offering a reward to any man who would come forward and give any evidence against the traitor Hevey.

An unhappy wretch who had been shortly before condemned to die, and was then lying ready for execution, was allured by the proposal. His integrity was not firm enough to hesitate long between the alternative proposed; pardon, favour, and reward, with perjury on one side—the rope and the gibbet on the other. His loyalty decided the question against his soul. He was examined, and Hevey was appointed by the sentence of a mild, and no doubt enlightened court-martial, to take the place of the witness, and succeed to the vacant halter.

Hevey, you may suppose, now thought his labours at an end; but he was mistaken; his hour was not yet come. You, probably, gentlemen, or you, my lords, are accounting for his escape, by the fortunate recollection of some early circumstances that might have smote upon the sensibility of Sir Charles Asgil, and made him believe that he was in debt to Providence for the life of one innocent, though convicted victim. But it was not so; his escape was purely accidental.

The proceedings upon this trial happened to meet the eye of Lord Cornwallis. The freaks of fortune are not always cruel; in the bitterness of her jocularity, you see she can adorn the miscreancy of the slave in the trappings of power, and rank, and wealth. But her playfulness is not always inhuman; she will sometimes in her gambols, fling oil upon the wounds of the sufferer; she will sometimes save the captive from the dungeon and the grave, were it only that she might afterwards re-consign him to his destiny, by the reprisal of capricious cruelty upon fantastic commiseration. Lord Cornwallis read the transmiss of Hevey's condemnation; his heart recoiled from the detail of stupidity and barbarity; he dashed his pen across the odious record, and ordered that Hevey should be forthwith liberated. I cannot but highly honour him for his conduct in this instance; nor, when I recollect his peculiar situation at that disastrous period, can I much blame him for not having acted towards that court with the same vigour and indignation which he hath since shown with respect to those abominable jurisdictions.

Hevey was now a man again—he shook the dust off his feet against his prison gate; his heart beat the response to the anticipated embrace of his family and his friends, and he returned to Dublin. On his arrival here, one of the first persons he met with, was his old friend Major Sandys. In the eye of poor Hevey, justice and humanity had shorn the Major of his beams—he no longer regarded him with respect or terror. He demanded his mare; observing, that though he might have travelled to heaven on foot, he thought it more comfortable to perform his earthly journeys on horseback. "Ungrateful villain," says the Major; "is this the gratitude you show to his Majesty and to me, for our clemency to you? You shan't get possession of the beast, which you have forfeited by your treason; nor can I suppose, that a noble animal that had been honoured with conveying the weight of duty and allegiance, could condescend to load her loyal loins with the vile burden of a convicted traitor." As to the Major, I am not surprised that he spoke and acted as he did. He was no doubt astonished at the impudence and novelty of one calling the privileges of official plunder into question. Hardened by numberless instances of that mode of unpunished acquisition, he had erected the frequency of impunity into a sort of warrant of spoil and rapine.

One of these instances I feel I am now bringing to the memory of your lordship. A learned and respected brother barrister* had a silver cup; the Major heard that for many years it had borne an inscription of "*Erin go Bragh,*" which meant "*Ireland for ever.*" The Major considered this perseverance in guilt for such a length of years, as a forfeiture of the delinquent vessel. My poor friend was accordingly robbed of his cup. But upon writing to the then Attorney-General, that excellent officer felt the outrage, as it was his nature to feel everything that was barbarous or base; and the Major's sideboard was condemned to the grief of restitution.

And here, let me say, in my own defence, that this is the only occasion upon which I have ever mentioned this circumstance with the least appearance of lightness. I have often told the story in a way that it would not become me to tell it here. I have told it in the spirit of those feelings which were excited at seeing that one man could be sober and humane at a crisis when so many thousands were drunk and barbarous. And probably my statement was not stinted by the recollection that I held that person in peculiar respect and regard. But little does it signify, whether acts of moderation and humanity are blazoned by gratitude, by flattery, or by friendship; they are recorded in the heart from which they sprung; and in the hour of adverse vicissitude, if it should ever come, sweet is the odour of their memory, and precious is the balm of their consolation.

But to return: Hevey brought an action for his mare. The Major, not choosing to come into court, and thereby suggest the probable success of a thousand actions, restored the property, and paid the costs of the suit to the attorney of Mr. Hevey.

It may perhaps strike you, my lord, as if I were stating what was not relevant to the action. It is materially pertinent; I am stating a system of concerted vengeance and oppression. These two men acted in concert; they were Archer and Aimwell.† You master at Lichfield and I at Coventry. You are plunderer in the gaol, and I tyrant in the street. And in our respective situations we will co-operate in the common cause of robbery and vengeance. And I state this, because I see Major Sandys in court: and because I feel I can prove the fact beyond the possibility of denial. If he does not dare to appear, so called upon, as I have called upon him, I prove it by his not daring to appear. If he does venture to come forward, I will prove it by his own oath, or if he ventures to deny a syllable that I have stated, I will prove it by irrefragable evidence that his denial was false and perjured. Thus far, gentlemen, we have traced the plaintiff through the strange vicissitudes of barbarous imprisonment, of atrocious condemnation, and of accidental deliverance.

Here Mr. Curran described the feelings of the plaintiff and of his family upon his restoration: his difficulties on his return, his struggle against the aspersions on his character, his renewed industry, his gradual success, the implacable malignity of Sirr and of Sandys, and the immediate cause of the present action.‡

---

* Mr M'Nally   † Two characters in the "Beaux Stratagem."   ‡ So in the Report.

Three years had elapsed since the deliverance of my client; the public atmosphere had cleared—the private destiny of Hevey seemed to have brightened—but the malice of his enemies had not been appeased. On the 8th of September last, Mr. Hevey was sitting in a public coffee-house; Major Sirr was there. Mr. Hevey was informed that the Major had at that moment said, that he (Hevey) ought to have been hanged. The plaintiff was fired at the charge, he fixed his eye on Sirr, and asked, if he had dared to say so? Sirr declared that he had, and had said it truly Hevey answered that he was a slanderous scoundrel. At the instant, Sirr rushed upon him, and, assisted by three or four of his satellites, who had attended him in disguise, secured him, and sent him to the castle guard, desiring that a receipt might be given for the villain. He was sent thither. The officer of the guard chanced to be an Englishman, but lately arrived in Ireland; he said to the bailiffs,—If this were in England, I should think this gentleman entitled to bail, but I don't know the laws of this country: however, you had better loosen those irons on his wrists, or I think they may kill him.

Major Sirr, the defendant, soon arrived, went into his office, and returned with an order which he had written, and by virtue of which Mr. Hevey was conveyed to the custody of his old friend and gaoler, Major Sandys. Here he was flung into a room of about thirteen feet by twelve—it was called the hospital of the provost. It was occupied by six beds, in which were to lie fourteen or fifteen miserable wretches, some of them sinking under contagious diseases. On his first entrance, the light that was admitted by the opening of the door, disclosed to him a view of the sad fellow-sufferers, for whose loathsome society he was once more to exchange the cheerful haunts of men, the use of open air and of his own limbs; and where he was condemned to expiate the disloyal hatred and contempt which he had dared to show to the overweening and felonious arrogance of slaves in office, and minions in authority here he passed the first night, without bed or food.

The next morning his humane keeper, the Major, appeared. The plaintiff demanded "why he was so imprisoned;" complained of hunger, and asked for the gaol allowance. Major Sandy's replied with a torrent of abuse, which he concluded by saying—"Your crime is your insolence to Major Sirr; however, he disdains to trample upon you—you may appease him by proper and contrite submission : but unless you do so, you shall rot where you are. I tell you this, that if government will not protect us, by God we will not protect them. You will probably (for I know your insolent and ungrateful hardiness,) attempt to get out by a Habeas Corpus; but in that you will find yourself mistaken, as such a rascal deserves."

Hevey was insolent enough to issue a Habeas Corpus, and a return was made upon it—"that Hevey was in custody under warrant from General Craig, on a charge of treason." That this return was a gross falsehood, fabricated by Sirr, I am instructed to assert. Let him prove the truth of it if he can. The Judge before whom this return was brought, felt that he had no authority to liberate the unhappy prisoner and thus, by a most inhuman and malicious lie, my client was again remanded to the horrid mansion of pestilence and famine.

Mr. Curran proceeded to describe the feelings of Mr. Hevey—the despair of his friends—the ruin of his affairs—the insolence of Sandys—his offer to set him at large, on condition of making an abject submission to Sirr—the indignant rejection of Hevey—the supplication of his father and sister, rather to submit to an enemy, however base and odious, than perish in such a situation; the repugnance of Hevey—the repetition of kind remonstrances; and the final submission of Hevey to their entreaties—his signing a submission dictated by Sandys, and his enlargement from confinement.

Thus was he kicked from his gaol into the common mass of his fellow-slaves, by yielding to the tender entreaties of the kindred that loved him, to sign, what was in fact, a release of his claim to the common rights of a human creature, by humbling himself to the brutal arrogance of a pampered slave. But he did suffer the dignity of his nature to be subdued by its kindness: he has been enlarged, and he has brought the present action.

As to the facts I have stated, I shall make a few observations. It might be said for the defendant, that much of what was stated may not appear in proof. To that I answer, that I would not have so stated, if I had not seen Major Sandys in court. I therefore put the facts against him in a way which I thought, the most likely to rouse him to a defence of his own character, if he dared to be examined as a witness. I have, I trust, made him feel that he has no way of escaping universal detestation, but by denying those charges, if false. And if they are not denied, being thus publicly asserted, my entire case is admitted—his original oppression in the provost is admitted—his robbery of the cup is admitted—his robbery of the mare is admitted—the lie so audaciously forged on the Habeas Corpus is admitted—the extortion of the infamous apology is admitted. Again, I challenge this worthy compeer of the worthy Major to make his election between proving his guilt by his own corporal oath, or by the more credible modesty of his silence.

I have now given you a mere sketch of this extraordinary history. No country, governed by any settled laws, or treated with common humanity, could furnish any occurrences of such unparalleled atrocity; and if the author of Caleb Williams,* or of the Simple Story,† were to read the tale of this man's sufferings, it might, I think, humble the vanity of their talents (if they are not too proud to be vain), when they saw how a much more fruitful source of incident could be found in the infernal workings of the heart of a malignant slave, than in the richest copiousness of the most fertile and creative imagination. But it is the destiny of Ireland to be the scene of such horrors, and to be stung by such reptiles to madness and to death.

And now I feel a sort of melancholy pleasure, in getting nearly rid of this odious and nauseous subject. It remains for me only to make a few observations as to the damages you ought to give, if you believe the case of the plaintiff to be as I have stated. I told you before, that neither pride nor spirit belong to our situation; I should be sorry to influence you into any apish affectation of the port or stature of freedom or independence.

* Godwin.   † Mrs Inchbald

But my advice to you is, to give the full amount of the damages laid in the declaration; and I will tell you why I give you that advice; I think no damages could be excessive, either as a compensation for the injury of the plaintiff, or as a punishment for the savage barbarity of the defendant; but my reasons for giving you this advice lie much deeper than such considerations; they spring from a view of our present most forlorn and disastrous situation. You are now in the hands of another country; that country has no means of knowing your real condition, except by information that she may accidentally derive from transactions of a public nature. No printer would dare to publish the thousand instances of atrocity which we have witnessed, as hideous as the present, nor any one of them, unless he did it in some sort of confidence, that he could scarcely be made a public sacrifice by brutal force, for publishing what was openly proved in a court of justice.

<small>Mr. Curran here made some pointed observations on the state of a country where the freedom of the press is extinguished, and where another nation, by whose indolent mercy, or whose instigated fury, it may be spared or sacrificed, can know nothing of the extent of its sufferings, or its delinquency, but by casual hearsay.</small>

I know that those philosophers have been abused, who think that men are born in a state of war. I confess I go further, and firmly think they cannot be reclaimed to a state of peace. When I see the conduct of man to man I believe it. When I see the list of offences in every criminal code in Europe—when I compare the enormity of their crimes with the still greater enormity of their punishments, I retain no doubt upon the subject.

But if I could hesitate as to men in the same community, I have no doubt of the inextinguishable malignity that will for ever inflame nation against nation. Well was it said, that a "nation has no heart."— Towards each other, nations are uniformly envious, vindictive, oppressive, and unjust. What did Spain feel for the murders or robberies of the West? nothing. And yet, at that time, she prided herself as much as England ever did on the elevation of her sentiment, and the refinement of her morality. Yet what an odious spectacle did she exhibit her bosom burning with all the fury of rapine and tyranny; her mouth full of the pious praises of the living God, and her hands red with the blood of his innocent and devoted creatures. When I advise you, therefore, to mark your feeling of the case before you, do not think I mean that you could make any general impression on the morality or tenderness of the country whose property we are become. I am not so foolish as to hope any such effect; practical justice and humanity are virtues that require laborious acts, and mortifying privations; expect not, therefore, to find them,—appeal not to them.

But there are principles and feelings substituted in their place, a stupid preference and admiration of self, an affectation of humanity, and a fondness for unmerited praise; these you may find, for they cost nothing, and upon them you may produce some effect. When outrages of this kind are held up to the world, as done under the sanction of their authority, they must become odious to mankind, unless they let fall some reprobation on the immediate instruments and abettors of such deeds. An Irish Lord Lieutenant will shrink from the imputation of countenancing them. Great Britain will see that it cannot be her interest to encourage such an infernal spirit of subaltern barbarity, that reduces man to a condition lower than that of the beast of the field. They will be ashamed of employing such instruments as the present defendant. When the government of Ireland lately gave up the celebrated O'Brien* to the hands of the executioner, I have no little reason to believe that they suffered as they deserved on the occasion. I have no doubt but that your verdict this day, if you act as you ought to do, will produce a similar effect. And as to England, I cannot too often inculcate upon you that she knows nothing of our situation.— When torture was the daily and ordinary system of the executive government, it was denied in London, with a profligacy of effrontery equal to the barbarity with which it was exhibited in Dublin; and if the facts that shall appear to-day should be stated on the other side of the water, I make no doubt that very near one hundred worthy persons would be ready to deny their existence upon their honour, or, if necessary, upon their oaths.

I cannot but observe also to you, that the real state of one country is more forcibly impressed on the attention of another by a verdict on such a subject as this, than it could be by any general description.— When you endeavour to convey an idea of a great number of barbarians practising a great variety of cruelties upon an incalculable multitude of sufferers, nothing defined or specific finds its way to the heart; nor is any sentiment excited, save that of a general, erratic, unappropriated commiseration.

If, for instance, you wished to convey to the mind of an English matron the horrors of that direful period, when, in defiance of the remonstrance of the ever-to-be-lamented Abercromby, our poor people were surrendered to the licentious brutality of the soldiery, by the authority of the state, you would vainly endeavour to give her a general picture of lust, and rapine, and murder, and conflagration. By endeavouring to comprehend every thing, you would convey nothing.

When the father of poetry† wishes to pourtray the movements of contending armies, and an embattled field, he exemplifies only, he does not describe; he does not venture to describe the perplexed and promiscuous conflicts of adverse hosts, but by the acts and fates of a few individuals he conveys a notion of the vicissitudes of the fight, and the fortunes of the day.

So should your story to her keep clear of generalities; instead of exhibiting the picture of an entire province, select a single object; and even in that single object do not release the imagination of your hearer from its task, by giving more than an outline. Take a cottage; place the affrighted mother of her orphan daughter at the door, the paleness of death upon her face, and more than its agonies in her heart; her aching eye, her anxious ear struggling through the mist of closing day, to catch the approaches of desolation and dishonour. The ruffian

---

See ante, Curran's defence of Finney   † Homer.

gang arrives; the feast of plunder begins; the cup of madness kindles in its circulation. The wandering glances of the ravisher become concentrated upon the shrinking and devoted victim. You need not dilate, you need not expatiate; the unpolluted mother, to whom you tell the story of horror, beseeches you not to proceed; she presses her child to her heart, she drowns it in her tears; her fancy catches more than an angel's tongue could describe; at a single view she takes in the whole miserable succession of force, of profanation, of despair, of death.

So it is in the question before us. If any man shall hear of this day's transaction, he cannot be so foolish as to suppose that we have been confined to a single character, like those now brought before you. No, gentlemen; far from it; he will have too much common sense not to know that outrages like this are never solitary; that where the public calamity generates imps like these, their number is as the sands of the sea, and their fury as insatiable as its waves.

I am therefore anxious that our *masters* should have one authenticated example of the treatment which our unhappy country suffers under the sanction of their authority; it will put a strong question to their humanity, if they have any—to their prudence, if their pride will let them listen to it; or, at least, to that anxiety for reputation, to that pretension to the imaginary virtues of mildness and mercy, which even countries the most divested of them are so ready to assert their claim to, and so credulously disposed to believe that claim allowed.

There are some considerations respecting yourselves, and the defendant, to which I should wish to say a word. You may, perhaps, think your persons unsafe, if you find a verdict against so considerable a person. I know his power, as well as you do—I know he might send you to the Provost, as he has done the plaintiff, and forge a return on any writ you might issue for your deliverance—I know there is no spot on the devoted nation (except that on which we now are), where the story of oppression can be told or heard; but I think you can have no well-founded apprehensions There is a time when cruelty and oppression become satiated and fatigued; in that satiety at least you will find yourselves secure. But there is still a better security for you—the gratitude of the worthy defendant. If anything could add to his honours and his credit, and his claims, it would be your verdict for the plaintiff; for in what instance have you ever seen any man so effectually accredited and recommended, as by the public execration?—what a man, for instance, might not O'Brien have been, if the envy of the gibbet had not arrested the career of his honours and preferments!

In every point of view, therefore, I recommend to you to find, and to find liberally, for the plaintiff; I have founded my advice upon the real circumstances of your situation; I have not endeavoured to stimulate you into any silly hectic of fancied liberty. I do not call upon you to expose yourselves by the affectation of vindicating the cause of freedom and humanity; much less do I wish to exhibit ourselves to those, whose property we are, as indignant or contumacious under their authority. Far from it: they are unquestionably the proprietors of us; they are entitled of right to drive us, and to work us: but we may be permitted modestly to suggest, that for their own sakes, and for their own interest, a line of moderation may be drawn—that there are excesses of infliction that human nature cannot bear.

With respect to her western negroes, Great Britain has had the wisdom and humanity to feel the justice of this observation, and in some degree to act upon it; and I have too high an opinion of that great and philosophic nation, not to hope that she might think us not undeserving of equal mildness—provided it did not interfere with her just authority over us. It would, I should even think, be for her credit, that having the honour of so illustrious a rider, we should be kept in some sort of condition, somewhat bordering upon spirit, which cannot be maintained, if she suffers us to be utterly broken down by the malicious wantonness of her grooms and jockeys.

This cause is of no inconsiderable expectation; and in whatever light you regard it,—whether with respect to the two countries or to Ireland singly, or to the parties concerned, or to your own sense of character and public duty, or to the natural consequences that must flow from the event, you ought to consider it with the most profound attention before you agree upon your verdict.

James Molloy, Esq., Samuel Rainey, and Patrick Maguire were examined, to prove the occurrences in the Commercial Buildings, and the facts of the imprisonment and release. Mr. William Fletcher opened the defence, and examined Mr. Hall, to show that Hevey was the aggressor, but this he failed to do. Mr. W. C. Plunket replied for the defendant; Mr. Jonah Barrington followed for the plaintiff. After a just charge from Lord Kilwarden the jury retired, and shortly returned with a verdict for the plaintiff, £150 damages, with costs. Counsel for the plaintiff—Messrs. Curran, Barrington, Ball, Orr, M'Nally, and Wallace; agent, Mr. Cooke. Counsel for the defendant—Messrs. Fletcher. Plunket, Jonas Greene, Ridgeway, and Kemmis, agent, Mr. Thomas Kemmis, Crown-Solicitor.

On the publication of the trial, by Stockdale, Major Sandys wrote him a letter, dated "Dublin Barracks, October 13th, 1802," in which he abused Curran and Stockdale, and said he was "subpœnaed" by the plaintiff, and was in court, ready to be examined. Stockdale's reply is very sharp. It affirms the accuracy of the report, and denies his liability for Mr. Curran. Two of the paragraphs are worth preserving:—

"It is certainly very wonderful, and perhaps might appear incredible, if the fact did not stand upon the authority of Major Sandys himself, that considering all the circumstances of the transaction, the part that he took in it, and the light in which he appeared at the trial, he was not examined as a witness on the part of the plaintiff. This must, I am persuaded, have been a great disappointment to him—but I can only feel for his disappointment, I cannot remedy it; nor can I, any more than he can himself, account for it; if I were to presume to offer a conjecture as to the cause of that extraordinary omission, I should, perhaps, ascribe it to the polite indiscretion of the counsel on both sides, each of whom seemed disposed to make a compliment of the Major to the other, and each of whom seemed also obstinately determined not to accept that compliment.

"Major Sandys has very stoutly and manfully declared, that as he utterly denies the charges that have been brought forward against him, so he is ready to meet and refute any further charges that may be brought forward; that is, I presume, by utterly denying them —a mode of refutation that should always have great weight, but which, in the present instance, after unluckily missing the only opportunity that has occurred of putting that denial into the most solemn form, in a court of justice, and after a serious deliberation of several months upon the subject, ought, in the judgment of every rational and candid man, to be absolutely conclusive."

Spite of this success, Hevey was victimized; the long imprisonment made him a bankrupt. Poverty and sorrow broke his mind; he died a pauper lunatic shortly after.

FOR OWEN KIRWAN
[HIGH TREASON.]
SPECIAL COMMISSION GREEN-STREET

Thursday, 1st September, 1803.

THE failure of the risings and invasions of 1798 broke the faith of some, the principles of others, and the hopes of many; but the causes of discontent increased. The horrid revenge which followed the defeat of the rebels—the treachery of Government to the United Irish leaders in 1798, and to the Catholics in 1801—and the extinction of the Constitution of '82, were added to the political slavery of the Catholics, and the desperate poverty of the people. The revival of the war after the short peace of Amiens,, and the alienation from England caused by the first blight of the Union, increased the strength and hopes of revolution.

Robert Emmet's insurrection was, then, not so ill-timed as most writers allege.

His friends were far higher than is commonly supposed; but he did not sufficiently allow for the effects of religious feud in Ulster, or the depression of the people elsewhere. Still his chances were not slight; and the insufficiency of his agents, not of his friends, joined to his own rashness and softness of character. were the main causes of his defeat.

I shall not repeat the common mistakes as to this insurrection, nor attempt to anticipate the full and most strangely true account of it, about to appear in the Third Series of Dr Maddens, "United Irishmen."

Robert Emmet and his associates accumulated pikes, guns, cartridges, materials for street defences, and considerable camp equipage, in different stores in Dublin, the principal of them being in Mass-lane. He had arranged for the arrival in Dublin of bodies of peasantry from the neighbouring counties, and the commencement of the insurrection there on the 23rd July, 1803; while Thomas Russell was to head another movement in the county Down Government were in possession of much vague information; yet so conceited and absolute was Mr. Secretary Marsden (then the real governor of Ireland). that he allowed the Lord Lieutenant to go to the Lodge in the Phœnix Park, late on the 23rd, without an additional guard, and left the public functionaries, military and civil, without distinct instructions. The night was unusually dark for the time of the year, and, favoured by it, a mob assembled about nine o'clock, and at ten (the hour agreed on) a number of them received arms from the depot, in Mass-lane. A signal rocket was then fired—Emmet and some of his friends turned out, and a rush was made towards the Castle. The mob acted like a mob—got confused, violent, and alarmed—paused and wavered—butchered Colonel Brown, Lord Kilwarden, and some others, who could not fight- and ran from the fire of a few small bodies of troops who were first hurried against them. The leaders, in disgust, abandoned them; the insurrection was over long before morning. All that remained was for Government to proclaim, try, hang, and oppress. They did all vigorously.

A Special Commission was issued, and it opened its sittings on the 31st of August, the Judges being Lord Norbury Mr. Justice Finucane, and Barons George and Daly. Nineteen persons were tried before the Commission :—one, Walter Clare, was respited; another, Joseph Doran, was acquitted; the rest, including Robert Emmet, were hanged. Russell shared the same fate in Downpatrick.

Curran, aided by Ponsonby and M'Nally, was counsel for several of the prisoners; but his only speech was for Owen Kirwan.

Kirwan was tried on the 1st day of September. He was a tailor and clothes dealer, resident at 64, Plunket-street, Dublin, and exercised no influence in the insurrection.

The Attorney-General (O'Grady,[*] afterwards Viscount Guillamore), stated the case.

The witnesses called were Edward Wilson and Mr. Douglas, who proved the scene in Thomas-street; Lieutenant Coltman, who proved the taking of arms, stores, and especially rockets, in Mass-lane; Thomas Rice, who proved Emmet's proclamations; Benjamin Adams, who swore that, on the firing of the signal rocket, he saw Kirwan turn out from his shop, with a pike on his shoulder at the head of several men; and Joseph Adams, who confirmed Benjamin's evidence.

Curran then, hopeless it would seem of saving the prisoner, but anxious to serve the country (for which he then hoped, at best, a slavish repose) spoke as follows:—

---

[*] He was appointed Attorney-General June the 7th, 1803. John Stewart, made Attorney-General on the 6th of December, 1800, came between Toler and O'Grady. James M'Clelland was Solicitor-General during these trials, and continued so till November, when Plunket succeeded him.

It has become my duty to state to the court and jury the defence of the prisoner at the bar. I was chosen for that very unpleasant task, without my concurrence or knowledge ; but as soon as I was apprised of it, I accepted it without hesitation. To assist a human being, labouring under the most awful of all situations—trembling in the dreadful alternative of honourable life or ignominious death—is what no man, worthy of the name, could refuse to man ; but it would be peculiarly base in any person who had the honour of wearing the King's gown, to leave the King's subject undefended, until a sentence pronounced upon him had shown, that neither in fact nor in law could any defence avail him.

I cannot, however, but confess, that I feel no small consolation when I compare my present with my former situation upon similar occasions. In those sad times to which I allude, it was frequently my fate to come forward to the spot where I now stand, with a body sinking under infirmity and disease, and a mind broken with the consciousness of public calamity, created and exasperated by public folly. It has pleased heaven that I should live to survive both those afflictions, and I am grateful to its mercy.

I now come here through a composed and quiet city—I read no expression in any face, save such as marks the ordinary feelings of social life, or the various characters of civil occupation—I see no frightful spectacle of infuriated power or suffering humanity—I see no tortures —I hear no shrieks—I no longer see the human heart charred in the flame of its own wild and paltry passions, black and bloodless, capable only of catching and communicating that destructive fire by which it devours, and is itself devoured.

I no longer behold the ravages of that odious bigotry by which we were deformed, and degraded, and disgraced—a bigotry against which no honest man should ever miss an opportunity of putting his countrymen, of all sects and of all descriptions, upon their guard. It is the accursed and promiscuous progeny of servile hypocrisy—of remorseless lust of power—of insatiate thirst of gain, labouring for the destruction of man under the specious pretences of religion. Her banner stolen from the altar of God, and her allies congregated from the abysses of hell, she acts by votaries, to be restrained by no compunctions of humanity, for they are dead to mercy—to be reclaimed by no voice of reason, for refutation is the bread on which their folly feeds : they are outlawed alike from their species and their Creator—the object of their crime is social life, and the wages of their sin is social death.

Though it may happen that a guilty individual should escape from the law that he has broken, it cannot be so with nations—their guilt is too unwieldy for such escape. They may rest assured that Providence has, in the natural connexion between causes and their effects, established a system of retributive justice, by which the crimes of nations are sooner or later avenged by their own inevitable consequences. But hat hateful bigotry, that baneful discord, which fired the heart of man, nd steeled it against his brother, has fled at last, and, I trust, for ever. Even in this melancholy place, I feel myself restored and recreated, by breathing the mild atmosphere of justice, mercy, and humanity—I feel I am addressing the parental authority of the law—I feel I am addressing a jury of my countrymen, my fellow-subjects, and my fellow-Christians, against whom my heart is waging no ill-concealed hostility—from whom my face is disguising no latent sentiment of repugnance or disgust. I have not now to touch the chords of an angry passion in those that hear me, nor have I the terror of thinking, that if those chords cannot be snapt by the stroke, they will be only provoked into a more instigated vibration. Whatever I address to the Court in point of law, or to the jury in point of fact, will be heard not only with patience, but with an anxious desire to supply what may be defective in the defence.

This happy change in the minds and feelings of all men is the natural consequence of that system of mildness and good temper which has been recently adopted, and which I strongly exhort you, gentlemen of the jury, to imitate, and to improve upon, that you may thereby demonstrate to ourselves, to Great Britain, and to the enemy, that we are not that assemblage of fiends which we have been alleged to be, unworthy of the ordinary privilege of regular justice or the lenient treatment of a merciful government.

It is of the utmost importance to be on your guard against the wicked and mischievous representation of the circumstances which call you now together ; you ought not to take from any unauthenticated report those facts which you can have directly from sworn evidence.

I have heard much of the dreadful extent of the conspiracy against this country—of the narrow escape of the government. You now see the fact as it is. By the judicious adoption of a mild and conciliatory system of conduct, what was six years ago a formidable rebellion, has now dwindled down to a drunken riotous insurrection, disgraced, certainly, by some odious atrocities; its objects, whatever they were, were, no doubt, highly criminal, but as an attack upon the state, of the most contemptible insignificance. I do not wonder that the patrons of burning and torture should be vexed that their favourite instruments were not employed in recruiting for the rebellion. I have no doubt that had they been so employed, the effect would have followed ; and that an odious, drunken insurrection would have been easily swelled into a formidable rebellion. Nor is it strange that persons so mortified should vent themselves in wanton, exaggerated misrepresentation, and in unmerited censure—in slandering the nation in the person of the Viceroy, and the Viceroy in the character of the nation—and that they should do so, without considering that they were weakening the common resources against the common danger, by making the different parts of the empire odious to each other, and by holding out to the enemy, and falsely holding out, that we were too much absorbed in civil discord to be capable of effectual resistance.

In making this observation, my wish is merely to refute a slander upon my country   I have no pretensions to be the vindicator of the Lord Lieutenant of Ireland, whose person I do-not know that I have ever seen. At the same time, when I am so necessarily forced upon the subject, I feel no disposition to conceal the respect and satisfaction with which I see the King's representative comport himself as he does, at a crisis of no little anxiety, though of no considerable danger, if we may believe the evidence we have heard. I think it was a proof of his Excellency's firmness and good sense, not to discredit his own opinion of his confidence in the public safety, by an ostentatious display of unnecessary open preparation; and I think he did himself equal honour by preserving his usual temper, and not suffering himself to be exasperated by the event, when it did happen, into the adoption of any violent or precipitate measures

Perhaps, I may even be excused if I confess that I was not wholly free from some professional vanity, when I saw that the descendant of a great lawyer* was capable of remembering, what, without the memory of such an example, he perhaps might not have done, that even in the moment of peril, the law is the best safeguard of the constitution. At all events, I feel, that a man, who at all times has so freely censured the extravagancies of power and force, as I have done, is justified, if not bound, by consistency of character, to give the fair attestation of his opinion to the exercise of wisdom and humanity, wherever he finds them, whether in a friend or in a stranger.

I hope, that these preliminary observations are not wantonly and irrelevantly delaying you from the question which you are to try, and which I am ready to enter into; but there still remains a circumstance to be observed upon for a moment before you proceed to the real subject of your inquiry, the guilt or innocence of the prisoner, the fact that has been so impressively stated—the never to be too much lamented fate of that excellent man, Lord Kilwarden, whose character was as marked by the most scrupulous anxiety for justice as by the mildest and tenderest feelings of humanity.

Let us not wantonly slander the character of the nation, by giving any countenance to the notion, that the horror of such a crime could be extended farther than the actual perpetrators of the deed. The general indignation, the tears that were shed at the sad news of his fate, show that we are not that nest of demons on whom any genera stigma could attach from such an event; the wicked wretch himself, perhaps, has cut off the very man, through whose humanity he might have escaped the consequences of other crimes; and, by a hideous aggravation of his guilt, has given another motive to Providence to trace the murderer's steps, and secure the certainty of his punishment. But on this occasion, the jury should put it out of their minds, and think nothing of that valuable man, save his last advice, "That no person should perish but by the just sentence of the law;" and that advice I hope you will honour, not by idle praise, but by strict observance.

As to the evidence, give me leave to advert to one circumstance which ought to be removed from your minds; it was adverted to before, and I do not believe it was resisted by the officers of the crown: it occurred in the former case. No act of parliament or commission under the great seal can be evidence in such a case as this.

* Lord Hardwicke.

Mr. Attorney-General—My lord, I hope Mr. Curran will excuse me for interrupting him. No allusion was made to the act of parliament, or the commission in this case; and although I did advert to them in the former, no attempt was made to rely upon them as evidence.

Mr. Curran—I mentioned the circumstance in the confidence that it would be given up as not applicable in evidence, and the learned gentleman will please to recollect, that he referred to the first statement made by him, and even to the verdict found yesterday, and therefore it is right upon my part to take notice of that which might make an impression upon the jury.

Lord Norbury—This much we must say, that no notice has been taken by the Bench of any act of parliament or any other document but what has been proved in evidence before us.

Mr. Curran—If I had not been interrupted by the anxiety of the Attorney-General, I should have added, that as the statute, if offered, would not be evidence, much less was the statement evidence. He also suggested that notoriety would be evidence; but however that may be with respect to a grand jury, it can have no influence with a petit jury. It may as well be said, that the notoriety of a man having committed a crime is evidence of his guilt. Notoriety is at best another name for reputation, which cannot even by law be given in evidence in any criminal case, and which, *a fortiori*, could not sustain a verdict of conviction.

Mr. Justice Finucane—Public war is always taken from notoriety.

Mr. Curran—But I do not think, that insurrection can take its character of innocence or guilt from notoriety. And I will add to the jury what I am certain will meet the acquiescence of the Bench, that though the jury should leave their homes without any doubt of the fact, yet it is their duty to forget the notoriety, and, attending to their oaths, to decide according to the evidence, the probability of such a conspiracy at the present time.

It is clear from the evidence that it could not be imputed to any particular sect, or party, or faction; because no sect or faction could fail, had they acted in it, of engaging one hundred times the number of deluded instruments in their design.

We may then fairly ask, is it likely that the country at large, setting even apart all moral tie of duty, or allegiance, or the difficulty, or the danger, could see any motive of interest to recommend to them the measure of separating from England, or fraternizing with France? Is there any description of men in Ireland who could expect any advantage from such a change? And this reasoning is more pertinent to the question, because politics are not now, as heretofore, a dead science, in dead language; they have now become the subject of the day, vernacular and universal: and the repose which the late system of Irish government gave the people for reflection, has enabled them to consider their own condition, and what they, or any other country, could have to hope from France, or rather from its present master. I scorn to allude to that personage, merely to scold or to revile him: unbecoming obloquy may show that we do not love the object, but certainly not that we do not fear him. Buonaparte, a stranger, an usurper, getting possession of a numerous, proud, volatile, and capricious people; getting that possession by military force, able to hold it only by force, to secure his power, found, or thought he found, it necessary to abolish all religious establishments, as well as all shadow of freedom. He has completely subjugated all the adjoining nations. Now, it is clear that there are but two modes of holding states, or the members of the same state, together; namely, community of interest, or predominance of force. The former is the natural bond of the British empire; their interest, their hopes, their dangers, can be no other than one and the same, if they are not stupidly blind to their own situation; and stupidly blind indeed must they be, and justly must they incur the inevitable consequences of that blindness and stupidity, if they have not fortitude and magnanimity enough to lay aside those mean and narrow jealousies which have hitherto prevented that community of interest and unity of effort, by which alone we can stand, and without which we must fall together.

But force only can hold the acquisitions of the French Consul. What community of interest can he have with the different nations that he has subdued and plundered? Clearly none. Can he venture to establish any regular and protected system of religion among them? Wherever he erected an altar, he would set up a monument of condemnation and reproach upon those wild and fantastic speculations which he is pleased to dignify with the name of philosophy, but which other men, perhaps, because they are endowed with a less aspiring intellect, conceive to be a desperate anarchical atheism, giving to every man a dispensing power for the gratification of his passions, teaching him that he may be a rebel to his conscience with advantage, and to his God with impunity.

Just as soon would the government of Britain venture to display the crescent in its churches, as an honorary member of all faiths show any reverence to the cross in his dominions.

Apply the same reasoning to liberty: can he venture to give any reasonable portion of it to his subjects at home, or his vassals abroad? The answer is obvious: sustained merely by military force, his unavoidable policy is to make the army every thing, and the people nothing. If he ventured to elevate his soldiers into citizens, and his wretched subjects into freemen, he would form a confederacy of mutual interest between both, against which he could not exist a moment.

If he relaxed in like manner with Holland, or Belgium, or Switzerland, or Italy, and withdrew his armies from them, he would excite and make them capable of instant revolt. There is one circumstance which just leaves it possible for him not to chain them down still more rigorously than he has done, and that is, the facility with which he can pour military reinforcements upon them, in case of necessity. But destitute as he is of a marine, he could look to no such resource with respect to any insular acquisition; and of course he should guard against the possibility of danger, by so complete and merciless a thraldom as would make an effort of resistance physically impossible.

Perhaps, my lords, and gentlemen, I may be thought the apologist, instead of the reviler of the ruler of France. I affect not either character—I am searching for the motives of his conduct, and not for the topics of his justification. I do not affect to trace those motives to any depravity of heart or of mind, which accident may have occasioned for a season, and which reflection or compunction may extinguish or allay, and thereby make him a completely different man, with respect to France and to the world; I am acting more fairly and more usefully by my country, when I show, that his conduct must be so swayed by the permanent pressure of his situation, by the control of an unchangeable and inexorable necessity, that he cannot dare to relax or relent, without becoming the certain victim of his own humanity or contrition.

I may be asked, are these merely my own speculations, or have others in Ireland adopted them? I answer freely, *non meus hic sermo est.* It is, to my own knowledge, the result of serious reflection in numbers of our countrymen. In the storm of arbitrary sway, in the distraction of torture and suffering, the human mind had lost its poise and its tone, and was incapable of sober reflection; but, by removing those terrors from it, by holding an even hand between all parties, by disdaining the patronage of any sect or faction, the people of Ireland were left at liberty to consider her real situation and interest; and happily for herself, I trust in God, she has availed herself of the opportunity.

With respect to the higher orders, even of those who thought they had some cause to complain, I know this to be the fact, they are not so blind as not to see the difference between being proud, and jealous, and punctilious in any claim of privilege or right between themselves and their fellow-subjects, and the mad and desperate depravity of seeking the redress of any dissatisfaction that they might feel, by an appeal to force, or by the dreadful recourse to treason and to blood.

As to the humbler orders of our people, for whom I confess I feel the greatest sympathy, because there are more of them to be undone, and because, from want of education, they must be more liable to delusion; I am satisfied the topics to which I have adverted, apply with still greater force to them, than to those who are raised above them.

I have not the same opportunity of knowing their actual opinions; but if their opinions be other than I think they ought to be, would to God they were present in this place, or that I had the opportunity of going into their cottages—and they well know I should not disdain to visit them—and to speak to them the language of affection and candour on the subject; I should have little difficulty in showing to their quick and apprehensive minds, how easy it is, when the heart is incensed, to confound the evils which are inseparable from the destiny of imperfect man, with those which arise from the faults or errors of his political situation. I would put a few questions to their candid and unadulterated sense. I would ask them,—Do you think that you have made no advance to civil prosperity within the last twenty years? Are your opinions of modern and subjugated France the same that you entertained of popular and revolutionary France fourteen years ago? Have you any hope, that if the First Consul got possession of your island, he would treat you half so well as he does those countries at his door, whom he must respect more than he can respect or regard you?

And do you know how he treats those unhappy nations? You know hat in Ireland there is l'tt'e personal wealth t) plunder, that there are few churches to rob Can you then doubt that he would reward his rapacious gener; ls and soldiers by parcelling out the soil of the island among them, d by dividing you into lots of serfs, to till the respective lands to which you belong, or sending you as graziers to enjoy the rocks of Malta and Gibral r? Can you suppose that the perfidy and treason of surrendering your country to an invader, would, to your new master, be any pledge of your new alliegance? Can you suppose that while a single French soldier was willing to accept an acre of Irish ground, that he would leave that acre in the possession of a man, who had shown himself so wickedly and so stupidly dead to the suggestions of the most obvious interest, and to the ties of the most imperious moral obligations?

To what do you look forward with respect to the aggrandizement of your sect? Are you Protestants? he has abolished Protestantism with Christianity. Are you Catholics? do you think he will raise you to the level of the Pope? Perhaps, and I think, he would not; but, if he did, could you hope more privilege than he has left his Holiness? And what privilege has he left him? he has reduced his religion to be a mendicant for contemptuous toleration, and he has reduced his person to beggary and to rags.

Let me ask you a further question. Do you think he would feel any kind-hearted sympathy for you? Answer yourselves by asking, what sympathy does he feel for Frenchmen, whom he is ready by thousands to bury in the ocean, in the barbarous gambling of his wild ambition? What sympathy, then, could bind him to you? He is not your countryman. The scene of your birth and your childhood is not endeared to his heart, by the reflection, that it was also the scene of his: he is not your fellow-Christian; he is not, therefore, bound to you by any similarity of duty in the world, or by any union of hope beyond the grave. What, then, could you suppose the object of his visit, or the consequence of his success? Can you be so foolish as not to see, that he would use you as slaves, while he held you; and that when he grew weary, which he soon would become, of such a worthless and precarious possession, he would carry you to market in some treaty of peace, barter you for some more valuable concession, and surrender you to expiate, by your punishment and degradation, the advantage you had given him by your follies and your crimes.

There is another topic on which a few words might be addressed to the deluded peasant of this country: he might be asked,—What could you hope from the momentary success of any effort to subvert the government by mere intestine convulsion? Could you look forward to the hope of liberty or property? Where are the characters, the capacities, and the motives of those that have embarked in those chimerical projects? you see them a despicable gang of needy adventurers; desperate from guilt and poverty; uncountenanced by a single individual of probity or name; ready to use you as the instruments, and equally ready to abandon you by treachery or flight, as the victims of their crimes. For a short interval, murder and rapine might have their sway; but do not be such fools as to think, that though robbing might make a few persons poor, it could make many rich.

Do not be so silly as to confound the destruction of property with the partition of wealth. Small must be your share of the spoil, and short your enjoyment of it. Soon, trust me, very soon, would such a state of things be terminated by the very atrocities of its authors. Soon would you find yourselves subdued, ruined, and degraded. If you looked back, it would be to character destroyed, to hope extinguished. If you looked forward, you could see only the dire necessity you had imposed upon your governors, of acting towards you with no feelings but those of abhorrence and self-preservation, of ruling you by a system of coercion, of which alone you would be worthy, and of loading you with taxes (that is, selling the food and raiment which your honest labour might earn for your family,) to defray the expense of that force, by which only you could be restrained.

Say not, gentlemen, that I am inexcusably vain when I say, would to God that I had an opportunity of speaking this plain, and, I trust, not absurd, language to the humblest orders of my countrymen. When I see what sort of missionaries can preach the doctrines of villany and folly with success, I cannot think it very vain to suppose, that they would listen with some attention and some respect to a man who was addressing plain sense to their minds, whose whole life ought to be a pledge for his sincerity and affection, who had never in a single instance deceived, or deserted, or betrayed them, who had never been seduced to an abandonment of their just rights, or a connivance at any of their excesses, that could threaten an injury to their character or their condition.

But perhaps I have trespassed too much upon your patience, by what may appear a digression from the question. The motive of my doing so, I perceive by your indulgent hearing, you perfectly comprehend. But I do not consider what I have said as a mere irrelevant digression, with respect to the immediate cause before you. The reasoning comes to this: the present state of this country shows, that nothing could be so stupidly and perversely wicked as a project of separation, or of French connexion; and, of course, nothing more improbable than the adoption of such a senseless project. If it be then so senseless, and therefore so improbable, how strong ought the evidence to be on which you should be warranted in attesting on your oaths, to England and France, so odious an imputation on the good sense and loyalty of your country. Let me revert again to the evidence which you have heard to support so incredible a charge. I have already observed on the contemptible smallness of the number, a few drunken peasants, assembled in the outlets; there, in the fury of intoxication, they committed such atrocities as no man can be disposed to defend or extenuate; and having done so, they flee before a few peace-officers, aided by the gallantry of Mr. Justice Drury, who, even if he did retreat, as has been insinuated, has at least the merit of having no wish to shed the blood of his fellow-Christians, and is certainly entitled to the praise of preserving the life of a most valuable citizen and loyal subject.

In this whole transaction, no attempt, however feeble or ill directed, is made on any place belonging to or connected with the government. They never even approach the barrack, the castle, the magazines. No leader whatsoever appears; nothing that I can see to call for your verdict, except the finding the bill, and the uncorroborated statement of the Attorney-General. In that statement, too, I must beg leave to guard you against mistake in one or two particulars. As to what he said of my Lord Kilwarden, it was not unnatural to feel as he seemed to do at the recollection, or to have stated that sad event as a fact that took place on that occasion, but I am satisfied he did not state it with the least intention of agitating your passions, or of letting it have the smallest influence on your judgment.]

In your inquiry into a charge of treason, you are to determine upon evidence; and what is there in this case to connect the prisoner with the general plan or the depôt which was found? I do not say that the account of these matters was not admissible evidence; but I say, that the existence of these things without a design, or proof of a design, without connexion with the prisoner, cannot affect his life; for you cannot found a verdict upon construction or suspicion.

The testimony of Adams seemed to have been brought forward as evidence of greater cogency. He saw the prisoner go out with a bag half full, and return with it empty. I am at a loss to conjecture what they would wish you to suppose was contained in it:—but men are seen at his house; does it follow that he was connected with the transactions in Thomas-street? The elder Adams does not appear to have stated any thing material but his own fears. The proclamation may be evidence of a treasonable conspiracy existing; but it is no evidence against the prisoner, unless he be clearly connected with it; and in truth when I see the evidence on which you are to decide, reduced to what is legal or admissible, I do not wonder that Mr. Attorney-General himself should, upon the first trial, have treated this doughty rebellion with the laughter and contempt it deserved.

Where now is this providential escape of the government and the castle? why, simply in this, that nobody attacked either the one or the other; and that there were no persons that could have attacked either. It seems not unlike the escape which a young man had of being shot through the head at the battle of Detongen, by the providential interference by which he was sent twenty miles off on a foraging party, only ten days before the battle.

I wish from my heart that there may be now present some worthy gentleman, who may transmit to Paris a faithful account of what has this day passed.

If so, I think some loyal absentee may possibly find an account of it in the *Publiciste* or the *Moniteur*, and perhaps somewhat in this way: "On the 23rd of July last, a most splendid rebellion displayed her standard in the metropolis of Ireland, in a part of the city, which, in their language, is called the *Poddle*. The band of heroes that came forth at the call of patriotism, capable of bearing arms, at the lowest calculation must have amounted to little less than two hundred persons. . The rebellion advanced with a most intrepid step, till she came to the site of the old Four Courts and Tholsel. There she espied a decayed pillory, on which she mounted, in order to reconnoitre, but she found to her great mortification, that the rebels had staid behind. She therefore judged it right to make her escape, which she effected in a masterly manner down *Dirty Lane;* the rebels at the same time retiring in some disorder from the *Poddle,* being hard pressed by the poles and lanterns of the watchmen, and being additionally galled by Mr. Justice Drury, who came to a most unerring aim on their rear, on which he played without any intermission, with a spy-glass from his dining-room window *Raro antecedentem scelestum deseruit pœna pede claudo.*

"It is clearly ascertained that she did not appear in her own clothes, for she threw away her regimental jacket before she fled, which has been picked up, and is now to be seen at Mr. Carleton's, at sixpence a head for grown persons, and threepence for a nurse and child. It was thought at first to be the work of an Irish artist, who might have taken measure in the absence of the wearer; but by a bill and receipt found in one of the pockets, it appears to have been made by the actual body-tailor of her August Highness the Consort of the First Consul. At present it is but poorly ornamented, but it is said that the Irish Volunteers have entered into a subscription to *trim* it, if it shall be ever worn again."

Happy, most happy, it is for those islands, that those rumours which are so maliciously invented and circulated, to destroy our confidence in each other, to invite attack, and dispirit resistance, turn out, upon inquiry, to be so ludicrous and contemptible, that we cannot speak of them without laughter, or without wonder that they did not rather form the materials of a farce in a puppet-show, than of a grave prosecution in a court of justice.

There is still, gentlemen, another topic material to remind you of; this is the first trial for treason that has occurred since the union of these islands. No effectual union can be achieved by the mere letter of a statute. Do not imagine that bigotry can blend with liberality, or barbarism with civilization. If you wish to be really united with Great Britain, teach her to respect you, and do so by showing her that you are fit objects of wholesome laws—by showing that you are as capable of rising to a proud equality with her in the exercise of social duties and civil virtues, as every part of the globe has proved you to be in her fleets and her armies; show her that you can try this cause as she would try it; that you have too much sense and humanity to be borne away in your verdict by despicable panic, or brutal fury; show her, that in prosecutions by the state, you can even go a step beyond her, and that you can discover and act upon those eternal principles of justice, which it has been found necessary in that country to enforce by the coercion of law: you cannot but feel that I allude to their statute which requires two witnesses in treason.

Our statute does not contain that provision; but if it were wise to enact it there as a law, it cannot be other than wise to adopt it here as a principle; unless you think it discreet to hold it out as your opinion, that the life of man is not so valuable here, and ought not to be as secure as in the other part of the empire; unless you wish to prove your capability of equal rights and equal liberty with Britain, by consigning to the scaffold your miserable fellow-subject, who if tried in England on the same charge and the same evidence, would by law be entitled to a verdict of acquittal.

I trust you will not so blemish yourselves—I trust you will not be satisfied even with a cold imitation of her justice, but on this occasion you will give her an example of magnanimity, by rising superior to the passion or the panic of the moment.

If in any ordinary case, in any ordinary time, you have any reasonable doubt of guilt, you are bound by every principle of law and justice to acquit. But I would advise you, at a time like this, rather to be lavish than parsimonious in the application of that principle; even though you had the strongest suspicion of his culpability, I would advise you to acquit; you would show your confidence in your own strength, that you felt your situation too high to be affected in the smallest degree by the fate of so insignificant an individual. Turn to the miserable prisoner himself—tainted and blemished as he possibly may be, even him you may retrieve to his country and his duty, by a salutary effort of seasonable magnanimity. You will inspire him with reverence for that institution which knows when to spare, as well as when to inflict; and which, instead of sacrificing him to a strong suspicion of his criminality, is determined, not by the belief, but by the possibility of his innocence, and dismisses him with indignation and contemptuous mercy.

A feeble attempt was made to prove that Kirwan slept at home on the 23rd; and witnesses were also examined to prove his general loyalty. Baron George then charged, and in five minutes after, the jury found a verdict of GUILTY. He was sentenced on the 2nd of September, and hanged in Thomas-street, on the 3rd.

AGAINST ENSIGN JOHN COSTLEY.

[CONSPIRACY TO MURDER.]

ESSIONS-HOUSE, GREEN-STREET.

February 23rd, 1804.

THE following speech is chiefly valuable, as illustrating the placid and just manner in which so vehement an advocate as Curran could discharge his duty as prosecutor.

Costley was an ensign in the Roscommon Militia.

He was arraigned before Baron George and Mr. Justice Day at Green-street, Dublin, on the 21st of February, 1804, on an indictment, charging him and Charles Frazer Frizell with having conspired to murder the Rev. William Ledwich, parish priest of Rathfarnham, in the county Dublin. Other indictments charged burglary in the house of Catherine Byrne, with intent to murder. There was one count for a common assault.

On Thursday, the 23rd, the trial came on, and after Mr. O'Grady, jun., had opened the pleadings, Curran stated the case for the crown as follows:—

My lords, and gentlemen of the jury, I am concerned in this cause as counsel for the crown—that is, as counsel for the law and for the public peace. by putting the charge, that has been found by the indictment into a course of sober, humane, firm, and dispassionate inquiry, before you, Gentlemen of the Jury, to enable you to fulfil to the public the awful, heavy, and severe duty of finding the prisoner at the bar guilty, if he be guilty, and that awful, solemn, and equally bounden duty you owe to the prisoner himself, to acquit him, if he shall appear to be innocent of the charges brought against him.

It becomes my duty at present, and painful is that duty, and painful must it be to every man who acts as counsel for the crown against the life of a fellow-subject, painful must it be in proportion to the sad conviction that he feels in his mind that the prosecution must be successful.

It is my duty, gentlemen of the jury, to apprise you of the nature of the charge, as well as to apprise you of the circumstances that will be given in evidence to support that charge, that you may understand, in some previous degree, the law by which you are to be directed, and that you should have some previous knowledge of the nature of the evidence that shall be adduced for the purpose of substantiating that charge.

The prisoner has been given in charge to the jury on an indictment stating, that he, with others, did conspire to kill and murder William Ledwich, who is prosecutor in this cause. That offence is made capital by the statute laws of the country; and, gentlemen, I would be glad to guard you against a mistake, that in common parlance arises on this subject. A conspiracy to kill and murder does not owe its criminality to the length of time it may occupy in its progress, from its first conception to its ultimate adoption—a conspiracy may be formed the very instant before the step is taken to put it into effect. If a number of people meet accidentally in the street, and conspire together to kill and murder at the moment, it is as essentially the crime of conspiracy as if it had been intended for a year before, and hatched for that year to the moment of its accomplishment.

On the charge of burglary alleged against the prisoner at the bar, it becomes requisite to be equally clear and explicit, that you may comprehend how essential it is, that two circumstances shall go to compose this species of crime, which is also made capital, and consequently liable to the punishment of death. It becomes necessary before you can decide on a verdict of guilt on this indictment, that two circumstances shall be proved to your satisfaction. The first of these is, the breaking open of the dwelling or habitation of any of his Majesty's subjects any time after night-fall; and the next essential ingredient is, that such breaking must have been effected with design or intent to commit a felony. These distinct and separate facts you must combine in proof before the charge of burglary can be sustained; so far, that should you be satisfied that a breaking into a dwelling or habitation at a late hour of the night was accomplished, it becomes necessary, in addition, that you should have as strong and forcible a conviction on your minds, that such breaking into the house or dwelling was designed and perpetrated with the intent to commit a felony, before you can venture to bring in a verdict of guilty. As to the burglary charged against the prisoner at the bar, you will perceive that the indictment lays the breaking into the habitation of the prosecutor, with intent to kill and murder him; an act, which, if perpetrated, would constitute a capital felony in itself, and the intention of which, connected with the fact of breaking into the house, forms an indictment on grounds sufficiently firm to form the capital crime of burglary.

It may be equally necessary to hint to you, gentlemen of the jury, that the statute which makes burglary a capital offence, does not lay down a distinct species of felony, the commission of which must previously occupy the intention—it does not discriminate between the intention of committing a murder and committing a robbery; so that, on this principle, if you shall reconcile it to your minds in the course of the evidence which shall be adduced, that the prisoner at the bar broke into the habitation alluded to, with intent to murder, the crime of burglary is effectually constituted; and you are bound, by the sacred oath you have taken, to bring in a sentence of conviction. But if the evidence shall not appear to you sufficiently strong to reconcile your consciences to the belief, that the prisoner at the bar, let the fact of his breaking open the house be ever so incontrovertible, did form the design or intention to commit the murder alleged, then, gentlemen of the jury, your understandings will suggest to you, that it becomes an imperious duty on you to bring in a verdict of acquittal.

I feel it is my duty to make these preliminary observations by which you might at least be directed to that more minute and precise exposition of the law, which you will have the satisfaction of hearing from the court. I also feel, that the man who stands up in a court of justice, owes to the jury whom he addresses, the duty of elucidating any matter of law suggested by the nature of the case in which he becomes an advocate, and a studied anxiety not to aggravate or strain its circumstances beyond a fair and liberal construction of that law. I repeat, gentlemen, that I feel it becomes a duty equally awful and imperious on his conscience, to view the object of explanation in all its points and bearings, with uniform and impartial investigation. The more momentous and important the object of inquiry becomes, the more ardent must his anxiety be not to mislead; and the delicacy, which that advocate must feel in a predicament of this nature, becomes a principle to govern the consciences and the oaths of persons delegated to expound the law in more exalted situations.

I have hitherto stated two material charges against the prisoner at the bar, in which your judgments will be exercised. Those of a less important or inferior nature, I do not think it equally necessary to dilate upon; and will therefore proceed to state the particular circumstances that attended this extraordinary and unfortunate transaction.

I understand, gentlemen of the jury, it will appear in evidence before you, that on the night of the 3rd of the present month of February, about the hour of ten o'clock, this attempt was made on the Rev. William Ledwich, a Roman Catholic clergyman of the parish of Rathfarnam, where he resided for more than twenty-five years, an edifying and respected pattern of innocence of heart, mildness of manners, of exemplary piety, and conduct the most inoffensive and irreproachable.

As this venerated and innocent man was preparing to seek that undisturbed and calm repose, which he should look for, after a conscientious and precise discharge of the functions and duties of the preceding day, he heard a tumultuous noise under the window of the chamber in which he was about to sleep. He naturally went to the window, which he raised, to see what created the unusual disturbance with which he was annoyed from below, when he recollected a voice, and immediately asked, Is not that Mr. Frizell? He also knew the prisoner by his voice, and asked, " Is not that Ensign Costley?" They answered to their names, and ordered him to come down. Astonished at this kind of proceeding, he asked for what he should come down? The reply was, that he must go to the guard-house. Mr. Ledwich began to expostulate. " You know, Mr. Frizell, that I am an infirm man, and that I am to be at all times found on any occasion for me. I entreat of you not to disturb me this night, and you shall find me punctual in attendance at your guard-house on to-morrow." The party below were still vociferous, urging that he must come to the guard-house. This infirm gentleman then put his head out of the window, to try the effect of further entreaty, on which a stroke of a drawn sword was made at him, which fortunately missed his head, but made a deep cut in the window-frame from which he looked out. On this he retired to his room, unconscious how to act, but at length yielded to the half advice, and half persuasions of a fellow-lodger, who was roused by the tumult in the street, and in suspense what opinion to give, as to the most effectual mode for Mr. Ledwich to adopt, in order to save his life. At length he made his way through a back door, and secured a retreat over Lord Ely's park wall, glassed at the top, the sense of peril giving to his feeble bodily powers that concentrated effort which a hard struggle for life will often produce. Having clambered to the top of this wall, he precipitated himself at the other side to a dangerous and most extraordinary depth. Here, it becomes requisite, gentlemen of the jury, to animadvert, but to do it with candour, and not with a view to stimulate your indignation, on a military officer, wearing his Majesty's garb, entrusted with an armed force, for the important purpose of defending his fellow-subjects, and preserving the public peace, degrading that commission, and disgracing the honour of those forces under his command, by converting the arms given to them for protection into vile instruments of annoyance, seeking by their means to take away a life it was his duty to preserve. Nor is the aggravation of this horrible outrage small, when offered against a man advanced in years, infirm in health, a priest in orders, preaching the same faith with others, upon the same authorised system of social duty on this side of the grave, in order to realize those hopes in the next world, given to Christians to entertain by that wise Redeemer, whose last charge, on leaving this earth, tended most sublimely and emphatically to enforce the obligation of mutual affection between man and man, and whose last awful and divine command was, that we should love one another.

It is not my custom, however, to say anything that might embitter the voice of accusation. I know the unhappy circumstances under which the young man at the bar labours: and I have endeavoured, in the conduct of this prosecution to take off the pressure of that peculiar predicament under which he unfortunately stands. But 1 cannot permit a relaxation of duty so flagrant, from any individual consideration, let the object of that consideration be what it may.

When I perceive those violent struggles to distort and tear asunder all the social ties which bind man to man—not by the wantonness of aggravating description, or offering of cruel taunts at the prisoner's situation—but by some system of conduct operating as a remote but sure cause of so lamentable an effect, I should think myself indeed an unworthy and unfeeling co-operator in the conduct every honest mind must reprobate, and an accessory to the consequences which flow from it, were I, from the affectation of false feelings of humanity, to sink parts of that detail, which it becomes my duty to disclose.

I understood that the conduct attributable, and perhaps justly so, to certain parties labouring under the present accusation, might have indicated something like an excuse under the unhappy pretext of intoxication. If any of you, gentlemen of the jury, have permitted an opinion to get hold of your understanding, that a voluntary privation of reason amounts to an extenuation of a crime committed, permit me to remove so egregious a mistake from your minds. It is the law of this country, touching the subject of intoxication as apology for crimes, that so far from contributing any excuse or apology for the perpetration of crimes, such state of mind is considered as a high aggravation of any offence committed under its influence. This being the law of the land, you are bound most solemnly on your oaths strictly to abide by it—in deciding by the same law, which unequivocally says, that intoxication is no excuse for or palliation of guilt. I am afraid that circumstance will come out in evidence of complicated aggravation in the offence charged against the prisoner at the bar. It will appear that he ordered a party of the military under his command to fire into the windows of the prosecutor's bed-chamber, and that some of the bullets were found lodged in the walls of his apartment, while others passed through the curtains of his bed. It will also appear that other shots took effect in an adjacent apartment, where other lodgers were asleep. If it shall be suggested as a defence of the prisoner's conduct, that he acted, or thought he acted, under the orders of a magistrate, it is a weak pretext and a gross mistake, to suppose that the company even of a real magistrate, which it appears that Mr. Frizell, however qualified, is not, could give a man sanction to break into a habitation, in order to commit a murder. On the contrary it is a most hideous aggravation of such offence. The system of our laws uniting a degree of wisdom and a principle of equity not to be equalled, or perhaps found, in the laws of any other country in the world, divides the criminal code into different branches, and on that principle it is left to the judge to expound the law, while the jury are confined to the investigation of facts, on which alone they must decide. There may be cases where a higher authority interferes,—cases for which a wise provision is also made by appealing to a branch of the judicial authority, invested with a power to turn off from a culprit, the bitter edge of the law. A portion of that power is delegated in the first instance to persons who soften the rigour of the law, by the emotions peculiar to kind and sympathetic hearts liberally imbued with the finer feelings of humanity. The judges of the land are therefore wisely permitted to exercise those principles of social affections and compassion towards proper objects, which will ultimately terminate with a higher power, who is bound to administer justice in mercy.

Gentlemen of the jury, I have endeavoured to state to you those principles and maxims of the criminal laws of your country, by which you cannot fail to perceive the boundaries which the sound policy of our general law has affixed to each department. Finding the facts against the prisoner at the bar, according to the evidence which shall be laid before you, will not preclude him from mercy, should he be conceived a proper subject for it, a consideration which you, as honest and humane men, must feel a superior gratification in contemplating. But, on the other hand, reflect that it is not because you suspect a culprit, that you must find him guilty; for the wise policy of the law itself has it, that the more hideous are the circumstances of the offence, so much the more shall Christian charity induce you to be incredulous as to its perpetration. And, on that principle, the practice of the courts is grounded, which requires that solemn and pathetic appeal to God, from the officer, praying to send the culprit a good deliverance. Therefore, unless a true conviction shall remove all rational doubt from your minds before you take upon you to pass a verdict on the life or liberty of your fellow-creature, it will be, as I before have stated, your bounden duty unreservedly to acquit. But if conviction shall supersede all doubt, and clear up all embarrassment, you are equally bound to consider that pardon and mercy to the culprit are lodged in other breasts than yours. I shall conclude, gentlemen of the jury, with only one observation, that is, in your discussion of the several charges exhibited against the prisoner at the bar, you will not permit anything I have said, or any statement of the evidence I have laid before you to make an exclusive impression on you.

The Rev. William Ledwich proved that on the 3rd of February he was lodging at Catherine Byrne's house at Rathfarnham, that about ten o'clock on that night Frizell and Costley with a party of their yeomen, came to the house, and endeavoured to force him away to the guard-house; that he resisted, was struck at with a sword, and finally escaped over Lord Ely's wall at the back of the house. Other witnesses proved that the prisoner and his party fired into the house, and also broke the doors and windows to force their way in.

Mr. Egan opened the defence, using the cross-examination of the prosecutor's witnesses, to prove that Costley was only drunk and intemperate, and had got into a riot, and called Lord Erris and Colonel Caulfield to testify to his character. After a reply from Mr. M'Nally and a charge from Judge Day, the jury acquitted the prisoner on all the charges except the assault. On that he was found Guilty, and for it he was sentenced to two years' imprisonment, and a trifling fine.

MASSY v. HEADFORT.
[FOR CRIMINAL CONVERSATION.]
ENNIS SUMMER ASSIZES.
July 27th, 1804.

THE Rev. Charles Massy, second son of Sir Hugh Massy, Bart., was a clergyman, deriving a large income from church livings. In March, 1796, he married against his father's wish, a Miss Rosslewin, then eighteen years of age, and of remarkable beauty. By her he had one son. He was residing, in 1803, at Doonas, on the Clare bank of the Shannon, about five miles above Limerick. The Marquis of Headfort, with his regiment of Meath Militia, was then quartered in Limerick, his lordship residing in the Earl of Limerick's house. Mr Massy, when at one time a rector in Meath, had known the dowager Lady Bective and the Headfort family; so, when his wife became acquainted with Lord Headfort in Limerick, he very naturally asked the Marquis to Doonas—his wife was rather fond of society and display, but, then, Lord Headfort was fifty years old.

The result of the visit was, that on a Sunday morning after the Christmas of 1803, while Mr. Massy was performing service in his church, Mrs. Massy eloped with Lord Headfort, and for this the action was brought. Damages were laid at £40,000, and the case was tried at the Clare Summer Assizes before Baron Smith and a special jury.

An immense bar was employed for the plaintiff; they were—John Philpot Curran, Bartholomew Hoare, Henry Deane Grady, Thomas Carey, John Whyte, Amory Hawksworth, William O'Regan, Thomas Lloyd, William M'Mahon, and George Bennet, Esqrs.; agent, Anthony Hogan, Esq. The Counsel for the defence were George Ponsonby, Thomas Quin, Thomas Goold, John Francks, Charles Burton, Richard Pennefather, Esqrs.; agent, James Simms, Esq.

Mr. George Bennet opened the pleadings. Mr. Hoare stated the case, describing Lord Headfort as "this hoary veteran in whom, like Etna, the snow above did not quench the flames below." His speech throughout is masculine, original, and to the point; while his Cornish plunderer has been cited as an instance of the highest eloquence. Here it is:—

"The noble lord proceeded to the completion of his diabolical project, not with the rash precipitancy of youth, but with the most cool and deliberate consideration. The Cornish plunderer, intent on spoil, callous to every touch of humanity, shrouded in darkness, holds out false lights to the tempest-tossed vessel, and lures her and her pilot to that shore upon which she must be lost for ever, the rock unseen, the ruffian invisible, and nothing apparent but the treacherous signal of security and repose; so this prop of the throne, this pillar of the state, this stay of religion, the ornament of the peerage, this common protector of the people's privileges and of the crown's prerogatives, descends from these high grounds of character to muffle himself in the gloom of his own base and dark designs, to play before the eyes of the deluded wife and the deceived husband the falsest lights of love to the one, and of friendly and hospitable regards to the other, until she is at length dashed upon that hard bosom, where her honour and happiness are wrecked and lost ever; the agonised husband beholds the ruin with those sensations of misery and of horror which you can better feel than I describe; she, upon whom he had embarked all his hopes and all his happiness in this life, the treasure of all his earthly felicities, the rich fund of all his hoarded joys, sunk before his eyes into an abyss of infamy, or if any fragment escape, escaping to solace, to gratify, to enrich her vile destroyer."

Five witnesses proved the marriage and elopement, the happiness of Mr. Massy's home, and the fortune of Lord Headfort.

Mr. Quin opened the defence, not denying the fact, but the injury. He alleged that Mrs. Massy's character was so light that it was gross folly or worse of her husband, to have thrown her into Lord Headfort's way. To prove this he examined Colonel Pepper, Captain Charleton, and Mr. George Evans Bruce.* Mr. Ponsonby followed on the same side, with great skill, and then Curran said:—

Never so clearly as in the present instance have I observed that safeguard of justice, which Providence hath placed in the nature of man. Such is the imperious dominion with which truth and reason wave their sceptre over the human intellect, that no solicitations, however artful, no talent, however commanding, can reduce it from its allegiance. In

---

* Struck at for (amongst other things), his evidence in this case, by Harry Deane Grady, in the "Nosegay," a once celebrated, but now happily forgotten satire.

proportion to the humility of our submission to its rule, do we rise into some faint emulation of that ineffable and presiding divinity, whose characteristic attribute it is, to be coerced and bound by the inexorable laws of its own nature, so as to be all-wise and all-just from necessity, rather than election. You have seen it in the learned advocate,* who has preceded me, most peculiarly and strikingly illustrated. You have seen even his great talents, perhaps the first in any country, languishing under a cause too weak to carry him, and too heavy to be carried by him. He was forced to dismiss his natural candour and sincerity, and having no merits in his case, to substitute the dignity of his own manner, the resources of his own ingenuity, against the overwhelming difficulties with which he was surrounded. Wretched client! unhappy advocate! what a combination do you form! But such is the condition of guilt, its commission mean and tremulous, its defence artificial and insincere, its prosecution candid and simple, its condemnation dignified and austere. Such has been the defendant's guilt, such his defence, such shall be my address, and such, I trust, your verdict.

The learned counsel has told you, that this unfortunate woman is not to be estimated at forty thousand pounds. Fatal and unquestionable is the truth of this assertion. Alas! gentlemen, she is no longer worth anything—faded, fallen, degraded, and disgraced, she is worth less than nothing! But it is for the honour, the hope, the expectation, the tenderness, and the comforts that have been blasted by the defendant, and have fled for ever, that you are to remunerate the plaintiff, by the punishment of the defendant. It is not her present value which you are to weigh, but it is her value at that time, when she sat basking in a husband's love, with the blessing of heaven on her head, and its purity in her heart: when she sat amongst her family, and administered the morality of the parental board: estimate that past value, compare it with its present deplorable diminution, and it may lead you to form some judgment of the severity of the injury, and the requisite extent of the compensation.

The learned counsel has told you, you ought to be cautious, because your verdict cannot be set aside for excess. The assertion is just; but has he treated you fairly by its application? His cause would not allow him to be fair—for, why is the rule adopted in this single action? Because this being peculiarly an injury to the most susceptible of all human feelings—it leaves the injury of the husband to be ascertained by the sensibility of the jury, and does not presume to measure the justice of their determination by the cold and chilly exercise of his own discretion.

In any other action it is easy to calculate. If a tradesman's arm is cut off, you can measure the loss which he has sustained; but the wound of feeling, and the agony of the heart cannot be judged by any standard with which I am acquainted. And you are unfairly dealt with, when you are called on to appreciate the present suffering of the husband, by the present guilt, delinquency, and degradation of his wife. As well might you, if called on to give compensation to a man for the murder

* Mr. Ponsonby.

of his dearest friend, find the measure of his injury, by weighing the ashes of the dead. But it is not, gentlemen of the jury, by weighing the ashes of the dead, that you would estimate the loss of the survivor.

The learned counsel has referred you to other cases, and other countries, for instances of moderate verdicts. I can refer you to some authentic instances of just ones. In the next country, £15,000 against a subaltern officer. In Travers and M'Carthy, £5,000 against a servant. In Tighe against Jones, £10,000 against a man not worth a shilling.

What then ought to be the rule, where rank, and power, and wealth, and station, have combined to render the example of his crime more dangerous,—to make his guilt more odious—to make the injury to the plaintiff more grievous, because more conspicuous? I affect no levelling familiarity, when I speak of persons in the higher ranks of society —distinctions of orders are necessary, and I always feel disposed to treat them with respect—but when it is my duty to speak of the crimes by which they are degraded, I am not so fastidious as to shrink from their contact, when to touch them is essential to their dissection. In this action, the condition, the conduct, and the circumstances of the party, are justly and peculiarly the objects of your consideration.

Who are the parties?

The plaintiff, young, amiable, of family, and education. Of the generous disinterestedness of his heart you can form an opinion even from the evidence of the defendant, that he declined an alliance, which would have added to his fortune and consideration, and which he rejected for an unportioned union with his present wife. She, too, at that time, was young, beautiful, and accomplished; and felt her affection for her husband increase, in proportion as she remembered the ardour of his love, and the sincerity of his sacrifice.

Look now to the defendant!—I blush to name him! I blush to name a rank which he has tarnished—and a patent that he has worse than cancelled. High in the army—high in the state—the hereditary councillor of the king—of wealth incalculable :—and to this last I advert with an indignant and contemptuous satisfaction, because, as the only instrument of his guilt and shame, it will be the means of his punishment, and the source of compensation for his guilt.

But let me call your attention, distinctly, to the questions you have to consider. The first is the fact of guilt. Is this noble lord guilty? His counsel knew too well how they would have mortified his vanity, had they given the smallest reason to doubt the splendour of his achievement. Against any such humiliating suspicion he had taken the most studious precaution by the publicity of the exploit. And here, in this court, and before you, and in the face of the country, has he the unparalleled effrontery of disdaining to resort even to a profession of innocence.

His guilt established, your next question is, the damages you should give. You have been told, that the amount of damages should depend on circumstances. You will consider these circumstances, whether of aggravation or mitigation.

His learned counsel contend, that the plaintiff has been the author of his own suffering, and ought to receive no compensation for the ill consequences of his own conduct. In what part of evidence do you find any foundation for that assertion? He indulged her, it seems, in dress —generous and attached, he probably indulged her in that point beyond his means; and the defendant now impudently calls on you to find an excuse for the adulterer in the fondness and liberality of the husband.

But you have been told that the husband connived. Odious and impudent aggravation of injury, to add calumny to insult, and outrage to dishonour. From whom, but a man hackneyed in the paths of shame and vice—from whom, but from a man having no compunctions in his own breast to restrain him, could you expect such brutal disregard for the feelings of others; from whom, but from the cold-blooded veteran seducer—from what, but from the exhausted mind, the habitual community with shame—from what, but the habitual contempt of virtue and of man, could you have expected the arrogance, the barbarity, and folly of so foul, because so false an imputation? He should have reflected, and have blushed, before he suffered so vile a topic of defence to have passed his lips.

But ere you condemn him, let him have the benefit of the excuse, if the excuse be true.

You must have observed how his counsel fluttered and vibrated, between what they call connivance and injudicious confidence; and how in affecting to distinguish, they have confounded them both together.

If the plaintiff has connived, I freely say to you, do not reward the wretch who has prostituted his wife, and surrendered his own honour do not compensate the pander of his own shame, and the willing instrument of his own infamy. But as there is no sum so low to which that defence, if true, ought not to reduce your verdict, so neither is any so high to which such a charge ought not to inflame it, if the charge be false.

Where is the single fact in this case on which the remotest suspicion of connivance can be hung? Odiously has the defendant endeavoured to make the softest and most amiable feelings of the heart the pretext of his slanderous imputations. An ancient and respectable prelate, the husband of his wife's sister, is chained down to the bed of sickness, perhaps to the bed of death; in that distressing situation, my client suffered that wife to be the bearer of consolation to the bosom of her sister: he had not the heart to refuse her, and the softness of his nature is now charged on him as a crime. He is now insolently told, that he connived at his dishonour, and that he ought to have foreseen, that the mansion of sickness and sorrow would have been made the scene of assignation and of guilt. On this charge of connivance I will not further weary you or exhaust myself; I will add nothing more, than that it is as false as it is impudent, that in the evidence it has not a colour of support and that by your verdict you should mark it with reprobation.

The other subject, namely, that he was indiscreet in his confidence, does, I think, call for some discussion, for I trust you see that I affect not any address to your passions, by which you may be led away from the subject—I presume merely to separate the parts of this affecting case, and to lay them item by item before you, with coldness of detail and not with any colouring or display of fiction or of fancy. Honourable to himself was his unsuspecting confidence, but fatal must we admit it to have been, when we look to the abuse committed upon it. But where was the guilt of this indiscretion? He did admit this noble lord to pass his threshold as his guest. Now the charge which this noble lord builds on this indiscretion is, " Thou fool! thou hadst confidence in my honour, and that was a guilty indiscretion: thou simpleton! thou thoughtest that an admitted and cherished guest would have respected the laws of honour and hospitality, and thy indiscretion was guilt; thou thoughtest that he would have shrunk from the meanness and barbarity of requiting kindness with treachery, and thy indiscretion was guilt."

Gentlemen, what horrid alternative in the treatment of wives would such reasoning recommend? Are they to be immured by worse than eastern barbarity? Are their principles to be depraved, their passions sublimated, every finer motive of action extinguished by the inevitable consequences of thus treating them like slaves? Or is a liberal and generous confidence in them to be the passport of the adulterer, and the justification of his crimes?

Honourably, but fatally for his own repose, he was neither jealous, suspicious, nor cruel. He treated the defendant with the confidence of a friend, and his wife with the tenderness of a husband. He did leave to the noble Marquis the physical possibility of committing against him the greatest crime which can be perpetrated against a being of an amiable heart and refined education. In the middle of the day, at the moment of divine worship, when the miserable husband was on his knees, directing the prayers and thanksgiving of his congregation to their God, that moment did the remorseless adulterer choose to carry off the deluded victim from her husband, from her child, from her character, from her happiness, as if not content to leave his crime confined to its miserable aggravations, unless he gave it a cast and colour of factitious sacrilege and impiety.

Oh! how happy had it been when he arrived at the bank of the river with the ill-fated fugitive, ere yet he had committed her to that boat, of which, like the fabled bark of Styx, the exile was eternal—how happy at that moment, so teeming with misery and with shame, if you, my lord, had met him, and could have accosted him in the character of that good genius which had abandoned him. How impressively might you have pleaded the cause of the father, of the child, of the mother, and even of the worthless defendant himself. You would have said: " Is this the requital that you are about to make for respect and kindness, and confidence in your honour? Can you deliberately expose this young man, in the bloom of life, with all his hopes before him—can you expose him, a wretched outcast from society, to the scorn of a merciless world? Can you set him adrift upon the tempestuous ocean of his own passions, at this early season, when they are most headstrong; and can you cut him out from the moorings of those domestic obligations by whose cable he might ride at safety from their turbulence? Think of, if you can conceive it, what a powerful influence arises from the sense of home, from the sacred religion of the heart in quelling the passions, in reclaiming the wanderings, in correcting the discords of the human heart; do not cruelly take from him the protection of these attachments.

"But if you have no pity for the father, have mercy at least upon his innocent and helpless child; do not condemn him to an education scandalous or neglected; do not strike him into that most dreadful of all human conditions, the orphanage that springs not from the grave, that falls not from the hand of Providence, or from the stroke of death, but comes before its time, anticipated and inflicted by the remorseless cruelty of parental guilt."

For the poor victim herself, not yet immolated, while yet balancing upon the pivot of her destiny, your heart could not be cold, nor your tongue be wordless. You would have said to him: "Pause, my lord, while there is yet a moment for reflection. What are your motives, what your views, what your prospects from what you are about to do? You are a married man, the husband of the most amiable and respectable of women; you cannot look to the chance of marrying this wretched fugitive; between you and such an event there are two sepulchres to pass. What are your inducements? Is it love, think you? No, do not give that name to any attraction you can find in the faded refuse of a violated bed. Love is a noble and generous passion; it can be founded only on a pure and ardent friendship, on an exalted respect— on an implicit confidence in its object. Search your heart, examine your judgment, do you find the semblance of any one of these sentiments to bind you to her? What could degrade a mind to which nature or education had given port, or stature, or character, into a friendship for her? Could you repose upon her faith? Look in her face, my lord; she is at this moment giving you the violation of the most sacred of human obligations as the pledge of her fidelity. She is giving you the most irrefragable proof, that as she is deserting her husband for you, so she would without a scruple abandon you for another. Do you anticipate any pleasure you might feel in the possible event of your becoming the parents of a common child? She is at this moment proving to you that she is as dead to the sense of parental as of conjugal obligation and that she would abandon your offspring to-morrow, with the same facility with which she now deserts her own. Look then at her conduct, as it is, as the world must behold it, blackened by every aggravation that can make it either odious or contemptible, and unrelieved by a single circumstance of mitigation, that could palliate its guilt, or retrieve it from abhorrence.

"Mean, however, and degraded as this woman must be, she will still (if you take her with you), have strong and heavy claims upon you. The force of such claims does certainly depend upon circumstances; before, therefore, you expose her fate to the dreadful risk of your caprice or ingratitude, in mercy to her, weigh well the confidence she can place in your future justice and honour: at that future time, much nearer than you think, by what topics can her cause be pleaded to a sated appetite, to a heart that repels her, to a just judgment in which she never could have been valued or respected? Here is not the case of an unmarried woman, with whom a pure and generous friendship may insensibly have ripened into a more serious attachment, until at last her heart became too deeply pledged to be reassumed. If so circumstanced, without any husband to betray, or child to desert, or motive to restrain, except what related solely to herself, her anxiety for your happiness made her overlook every other consideration, and commit her history to your honour; in such a case, the strongest and the highest that man's imagination can suppose, in which you at least could see nothing but the most noble and disinterested sacrifice; in which you could find nothing but what claimed from you the most kind and exalted sentiment of tenderness, and devotion, and respect; and in which the most fastidious rigour would find so much more subject for sympathy than blame; let me ask you, could you even in that case, answer for your own justice and gratitude?

"I do not allude to the long and pitiful catalogue of paltry adventures, in which it seems your time has been employed; the coarse and vulgar succession of casual connexions, joyless, loveless, and unendeared. but do you not find upon your memory some trace of an engagement of the character I have sketched? Has not your sense of what you would owe in such a case, and to such a woman, been at least once put to the test of experiment? Has it not once, at least, happened that such a woman, with all the resolution of strong faith, flung her youth, her hope, her beauty, her talent, upon your bosom, weighed you against the world, which she found but a feather in the scale, and took you as an equivalent? How did you then acquit yourself? Did you prove yourself worthy of the sacred trust reposed in you? Did your spirit so associate with hers, as to leave her no room to regret the splendid and disinterested sacrifice she had made? Did her soul find a pillow in the tenderness of yours, and support in its firmness? Did you preserve her high in her own consciousness, proud in your admiration and friendship, and happy in your affection? You might have so acted; and the man that was worthy of her would have perished rather than not so act, as to make her delighted with having confided so sacred a trust to his honour. Did you so act? Did she feel that, however precious to your heart, she was still more exalted and honoured in your reverence and respect? Or did she find you coarse and paltry, fluttering and unpurposed, unfeeling, and ungrateful? You found her a fair and blushing flower, its beauty and its fragrance bathed in the dew of heaven. Did you so tenderly transplant it, as to preserve that beauty and fragrance unimpaired? Or did you so rudely cut it, as to interrupt its nutriment, to waste its sweetness, to blast its beauty, to bow its faded and sickly head? And did you at last fling it like 'a loathsome weed away?' If then to such a woman, so clothed with every title that could ennoble, and exalt, and endear her to the heart of man, you would be cruelly and capriciously deficient, how can a wretched fugitive like this, in every point her contrast, hope to find you just? Send her then away. Send her back to her home, to her child, to her husband, to herself."

Alas! there was no one to hold such language to this noble defendant; he did not hold it to himself. But he paraded his despicable prize in his own carriage, with his own retinue, his own servants; this veteran Paris hawked his enamoured Helen from this western quarter of the island to a sea-port in the eastern, crowned with the acclamations of a senseless and grinning rabble, glorying and delighted, no doubt, in the leering and scoffing admiration of grooms, and ostlers, and waiters, as he passed.

In this odious contempt of every personal feeling, of public opinion, of common humanity, did he parade this woman to the sea-port, whence he transported his precious cargo to a country, where her example may be less mischievous than in her own; where I agree with my learned colleague in heartily wishing he may remain with her for ever. We are too poor, too simple, too unadvanced a country, for the example of such achievements. When the relaxation of morals is the natural growth and consequence of the great progress of arts and wealth, it is accompanied by a refinement that makes it less gross than shocking; but for such palliations we are at least a century too young. I advise you, therefore, most earnestly to rebuke this budding mischief, by letting the wholesome vigour and chastisement of a liberal verdict speak what you think of its enormity.

In every point of view in which I can look at the subject, I see you are called upon to give a verdict of bold, and just, and indignant, and exemplary compensation. The injury of the plaintiff demands it from your justice; the delinquency of the defendant provokes it by its enormity. The rank on which he has relied for impunity calls upon you to tell him, that crime does not ascend to the rank of the perpetrator, but the perpetrator sinks from his rank, and descends to the level of his delinquency. The style and mode of his defence is a gross aggravation of his conduct, and a gross insult upon you.

Look upon the different subjects of his defence as you ought, and let him profit by them as he deserves. Vainly presumptuous upon his rank, he wishes to overawe you by that despicable consideration. He next resorts to a cruel aspersion upon the character of the unhappy plaintiff, whom he had already wounded beyond the possibility of reparation: he has ventured to charge him with connivance. As to that, I will only say, gentlemen of the jury, do not give this vain boaster a pretext for saying, that if her husband connived in the offence, the jury also connived in the reparation.

But he has pressed another curious topic upon you. After the plaintiff had cause to suspect his designs, and the likelihood of their being fatally successful, he did not then act precisely as he ought. Gracious God! what an argument for him to dare to advance! It is saying this to him:—" I abused your confidence, your hospitality; I laid a base plan for the seduction of the wife of your bosom; I succeeded at last, so as to throw in upon you that most dreadful of all suspicions to a man fondly attached, proud of his wife's honour, and tremblingly alive to his own; that you were possibly a dupe to the confidence in the wife, as much as in the guest. In this so pitiable distress, which I myself had studiously and deliberately contrived for you, between hope and fear, and doubt and love, and jealously and shame; one moment shrinking from the cruelty of your suspicion; the next, fired with indignation at the facility and credulity of your acquittal; in this labyrinth of doubt, in this frenzy of suffering, you were not collected and composed; you did not act as you might have done, if I had not worked you to madness; and upon that very madness which I have inflicted upon you, upon the very completion of my guilt, and of your misery, I will build my defence. You will not act critically right, and therefore are unworthy of compensation."

Gentlemen, can you be dead to the remorseless atrocity of such a defence! And shall not your honest verdict mark it as it deserves.

But let me go a little further; let me ask you, for I confess I have no distinct idea—What should be the conduct of a husband so placed, and who is to act critically right? Shall he lock her up, or turn her out, or enlarge or abridge her liberty of acting as she pleases? Oh, dreadful Areopagus of the tea-table! how formidable thy inquests, how tremendous thy condemnations! In the first case, he is brutal and barbarous; an odious eastern despot. In the next; what! turn an innocent woman out of his house, without evidence or proof, but merely because he is vile and mean enough to suspect the wife of his bosom, and the mother of his child! Between these extremes, what intermediate degree is he to adopt? I put this question to you—Do you at this moment, uninfluenced by any passion as you now are, but cool and collected, and uninterested as you must be, do you see clearly this proper and exact line, which the plaintiff should have pursued? I much question if you do. But if you did or could, must you not say, that he was the last man from whom you should expect the coolness to discover, or the steadiness to pursue it? And yet this is the outrageous and insolent defence that is put forward to you. My miserable client, when his brain was on fire, and every fiend of hell was let loose upon his heart, should then, it seems, have placed himself before his mirror: he should have taught the stream of agony to flow decorously down his forehead: he should have composed his features to harmony; he should have writhed with grace, and groaned in melody.

But look farther to this noble defendant, and his honourable defence. The wretched woman is to be successively the victim of seduction, and of slander. She, it seems, received marked attentions. Here, I confess, I felt myself not a little at a loss. The witnesses could not describe what these marked attentions were, or are. They consisted, not, if you believe the witness that swore to them, in any personal approach, or contact whatsoever, nor in any unwarrantable topics of discourse. Of what materials, then, were they composed? Why, it seems a gentleman had the insolence at table to propose to her a glass of wine; and she, oh, most abandoned lady! instead of flying like an angry parrot at his head, and besmirching and bescratching him for his insolence, tamely and basely replies, "Port, sir, if you please."

But, gentlemen, why do I advert to this folly, this nonsense? Not surely to vindicate from censure the most innocent and the most delightful intercourse of social kindness, or harmless and cheerful courtesy "where virtue is, these are most virtuous." But I am soliciting your attention, and your feeling, to the mean and odious aggravation, to the unblushing and remorseless barbarity, of falsely aspersing the wretched woman he had undone.

One good he has done, he has disclosed to you the point in which he can feel; for how imperious must that avarice be, which could resort to so vile an expedient of frugality? Yes, I will say, that, with the common feelings of a man, he would have rather suffered his thirty thousand a year to go as compensation to the plaintiff, than have saved a shilling of it by so vile an expedient of economy. He would rather have starved with her in a gaol, he would rather have sunk with her into the ocean, than have so vilified her—than have so degraded himself.

But it seems, gentlemen, and indeed you have been told, that long as the course of his gallantries has been, and he has grown gray in the service, it is the first time he has been called upon for damages. To how many might it have been fortunate, if he had not that impunity to boast? Your verdict will, I trust, put an end to that encouragement to guilt, that is built upon impunity.

The devil, it seems, has saved the noble Marquis harmless in the past; but your verdict will tell him the term of that indemnity is expired—that his old friend and banker has no more effects in his hands—and that if he draws any more upon him, he must pay his own bills himself. You will do much good by doing so: you may not enlighten his conscience, nor touch his heart; but his frugality will understand the hint. It will adopt the prudence of age, and deter him from pursuits, in which, though he may be insensible of shame, he will not be regardless of expense. You will do more—you will not only punish him in his tender point, but you will weaken him in his strong one, his money. We have heard much of this noble Lord's wealth, and much of his exploits, but not much of his accomplishments or his wit; I know not that his verses have soared even to the "poet's corner." I have heard it said, that an ass laden with gold could find his way through the gate of the strongest city. But, gentlemen, lighten the load upon his back, and you will completely curtail the mischievous faculty of a grave animal, whose momentum lies, not in his agility, but his weight; not in the quantity of his motion, but the quantity of his matter.

There is another ground on which you are called upon to give most liberal damages, and that has been laid by the unfeeling vanity of the defendant. This business has been marked by the most elaborate publicity. It is very clear that he has been allured by the glory of the chase, and not the value of the game. The poor object of his pursuit could be of no value to him, or he could not have so wantonly, and cruelly, and unnecessarily abused her. He might easily have kept this unhappy intercourse an unsuspected secret. Even if he wished for elopement, he might easily have so contrived it, that the place of her retreat would be profoundly undiscoverable.

Yet, though even the expense, a point so tender to his delicate sensibility, of concealing, could not be one-fortieth of the cost of publishing her, his vanity decided him in favour of glory and publicity. By that election, he has, in fact, put forward the Irish nation, and its character, so often and so variously calumniated, upon its trial before the tribunal of the empire; and your verdict will this day decide whether an Irish jury can feel with justice and spirit upon a subject that involves conjugal affection and comfort, domestic honour and repose, the certainty of issue, the weight of public opinion, the gilded and presumptuous criminality of overweening rank and station.

I doubt not but he is at this moment reclined on a silken sofa, anticipating that submissive and modest verdict, by which you will lean gently on his errors; and expecting from your patriotism, no doubt, that you will think again, and again, before you condemn any great portion of the immense revenue of a great absentee, to be detained in the nation that produced it, instead of being transmitted, as it ought, to be expended in the splendour of another country. He is now probably waiting for the arrival of the report of this day, which I understand a famous notetaker has been sent hither to collect. Let not the gentleman be disturbed.

Gentlemen, let me assure you, it is more, much more, the trial of you, than of the noble Marquis, of which this imported recorder is at this moment collecting materials. His noble employer is now expecting a report to the following effect:—" Such a day came on to be tried at Ennis, by a special jury, the cause of Charles Massy against the most noble the Marquis of Headfort. It appeared that the plaintiff's wife was young, beautiful, and captivating; the plaintiff himself, a person fond of this beautiful creature to distraction, and both doating on their child. But the noble Marquis approached her; the plume of glory nodded on his head. Not the goddess Minerva, but the goddess Venus, had lighted up his casque with 'the fire that never tires, such as many a lady gay had been dazzled with before' At the first advance she trembled; at the second, she struck to the redoubted son of Mars, and pupil of Venus. The jury saw it was not his fault (it was an Irish jury); they felt compassion for the tenderness of the mother's heart, and for the warmth of the lover's passion. The jury saw on one side, a young, entertaining gallant; on the other, a beauteous creature, of charms irresistible. They recollected that Jupiter had been always successful in his amours, although Vulcan had not always escaped some awkward accidents. The jury was composed of fathers, brothers, husbands, but they had not the vulgar jealousy, that views little things of that sort with rigour; and, wishing to assimilate their country in every respect to England, now that they are united to it, they, like English gentlemen, returned to their box, with a verdict of 6d. damages, and 6d. costs."

Let this be sent to England. I promise you, your odious secret will not be kept better than that of the wretched Mrs. Massy. There is not a bawdy chronicle in London, in which the epitaph which you would have written on yourselves will not be published; and our enemies will delight in the spectacle of our precocious depravity, in seeing that we can be rotten before we are ripe. I do not suppose it; I do not, cannot, will not believe it; I will not harrow up myself with the anticipated apprehension.

There is another consideration, gentlemen, which I think most imporiously demands even a vindictive reward of exemplary damages—and that is, the breach of hospitality.

To us peculiarly does it belong to avenge the violation of its altar. The hospitality of other countries is a matter of necessity or convention—in savage nations, of the first; in polished, of the latter but the hospitality of an Irishman is not the running account of posted and legered courtesies, as in other countries; it springs like all his qualities, his faults, his virtues, directly from his heart. The heart of an Irishman is by nature bold, and he confides; it is tender, and he loves; it is generous, and he gives; it is social, and he is hospitable. This sacrilegious intruder has profaned the religion of that sacred altar so elevated in our worship, so precious to our devotion: and it is our privilege to avenge the crime. You must either pull down the altar, and abolish the worship; or you must preserve its sanctity undebased. There is no alternative between the universal exclusion of all mankind from your threshold, and the most rigorous punishment of him who is admitted and betrays. This defendant has been so trusted, has so betrayed, and you ought to make him a most signal example.

Gentlemen, I am the more disposed to feel the strongest indignation and abhorrence at this odious conduct of the defendant, when I consider the deplorable condition to which he has reduced the plaintiff, and perhaps the still more deplorable one that the plaintiff has in prospect before him. What a progress has he to travel through, before he can attain the peace and tranquillity which he has lost? How like the wounds of the body are those of the mind! how burning the fever! how painful the suppuration! how slow, how hesitating, how relapsing the process to convalescence! Through what a variety of suffering, what new scenes and changes must my unhappy client pass, ere he can re-attain, should he ever re-attain, that health of soul of which he has been despoiled by the cold and deliberate machinations of this practised and gilded seducer?

If, instead of drawing upon his incalculable wealth for a scanty retribution, you were to stop the progress of his despicable achievements, by reducing him to actual poverty, you could not even so punish him beyond the scope of his offence, nor reprise the plaintiff beyond the measure of his suffering. Let me remind you, that in this action, the law not only empowers you, but that its policy commands you to consider the public example, as well as the individual injury, when you adjust the amount of your verdict. I confess I am most anxious that you should acquit yourselves worthily upon this important occasion. I am addressing you as fathers, husbands, brothers. I am anxious that a feeling of those high relations should enter into and give dignity to your verdict.

But I confess, I feel a ten-fold solicitude when I remember that I am addressing you as my countrymen, as Irishmen, whose characters as jurors, as gentlemen, must find either honour or degradation in the result of your decision. Small as must be the distributive share of that national estimation, that can belong to so unimportant an individual as myself, yet I do own I am tremblingly solicitous for its fate. Perhaps it appears of more value to me, because it is embarked on the same bottom with yours; perhaps the community of peril, of common safety, or common wreck, gives a consequence to my share of the risk, which I could not be vain enough to give it, if it were not raised to it by that mutuality. But why stoop to think at all of myself, when I know that you, gentlemen of the jury—when I know that our country itself are my clients on this day, and must abide the alternative of honour or of infamy, as you shall decide. But I will not despond, I will not dare to despond. I have every trust, and hope, and confidence in you. And to that hope I will add my most fervent prayer to the God of all truth and justice, so to raise, and enlighten, and fortify your minds, that you may so decide, as to preserve to yourselves while you live, the most delightful of all recollections—that of acting justly; and to transmit to your children the most precious of all inheritances—the memory of your virtue.

Baron Smith charged, and after a trial of twelve hours' duration, the jury at midnight found for the plaintiff, £10,000 damages, with costs.

FOR JUDGE JOHNSON.

[HABEAS CORPUS.]

COURT OF EXCHEQUER.

BEFORE CHIEF BARON LORD AVONMORE AND THE OTHER BARONS.

February 4th, 1805

ROBERT JOHNSON was called to the Irish Bar in Michaelmas Term, 1776, and obtained an early reputation for ability. Notwithstanding the prevalent opinion that Mr. Jebb wrote the letters of "Guatimozin and Considicus"—those admirable arguments for nationality*— there is much evidence in favour of Mr. Johnson's authorship of some of them at least.⁴ In June, 1800, he was made one of the Justices of the Court of Common Pleas in Ireland.

On the 5th of November, 1803, a letter, signed "Juverna," was published in *Cobbett's Political Register*. It was written in a bold and bitter style, and having narrated the story of the Trojan Horse, applied it to Lord Hardwicke's stupid, plausible, and vicious rule in Ireland. In that and subsequent papers Lord Hardwicke was described as "a very eminent breeder of sheep in Cambridgeshire ;" Lord Chancellor Redesdale is called "a very able and strong-built Chancery pleader from Lincoln's Inn ;" Mr. Secretary Marsden appears as "a corrupt, unprincipled, rapacious plunderer, preying upon the property of the state;" and Justice Osborne as "the most corrupt instrument of a debased and degraded government, lending himself as a screen to conceal them from the disgrace their actions would naturally bring upon them."

These are the strongest passages, and what were relied on in the prosecution.

Cobbett was prosecuted for these publications, as libelling Lords Hardwicke and Redesdale, Mr. Marsden, and Judge Osborne; he was tried at Westminster, before Lord Ellenborough, on the 4th of May, 1804. The Attorney-General prosecuted, Mr. Adam defended Cobbett, and called Lord Minto, Charles Yorke, Windham, Lord Henry Stewart, &c., to swear to Cobbett's ultra-loyalty; but in ten minutes the jury found him guilty of the libel.

In one of the "Juverna" articles (that published on the 10th of December), Plunket, then Solicitor-General for Ireland, was attacked on many grounds, but especially for his

---

* They were originally published in the *Freeman's Journal*. The first is dated 16th of April, 1779. They were reprinted in a pamphlet, which ranks with Pollock's "Letters of Owen Roe," and Drennan's "Orellana," at the head of Irish political literature during the Volunteer Revolution. Indeed for the union of strong sense, and clear, impetuous eloquence, they have hardly, if ever, been surpassed.

† See Mr. H. Grattan's Memoirs of Grattan, vol. 5, now at press, for these proofs.

speech in reply on Emmet's trial. "Juverna" represents Emmet as describing Plunket thus: "That viper, whom my father nourished! He it was from whose lips I first imbibed those principles and doctrines which now by their effects drag me to my grave, and he it is who is now brought forward as my prosecutor, and who, by an unheard of exercise of the prerogative, has wantonly lashed with a speech to evidence the dying son of his former friend, when that son had produced no evidence, had made no defence; but, on the contrary, had acknowledged the charge, and submitted to his fate."

For publishing this libel, and it was a false and cruel charge, Plunket brought a civil action against Cobbett; the case was heard by Lord Ellenborough on the 26th of May, 1804. Erskine opened for the plaintiff; Adam defended Cobbett ably, quoting Plunket's words on the nullity of the Union; but the jury, after twenty minutes' deliberation, found a verdict for the plaintiff, and £500 damages.

These verdicts were not enforced. Cobbett gave up the manuscript of the libellous articles, alleging that they were written by Mr. Justice Johnson. The offended parties believed the statement, and it was resolved to ruin Johnson.

For this purpose a vast and abominable machinery was resorted to.

On the 20th of July, 1804, an act was passed, entitled, "an act to render more easy the apprehending and bringing to trial offenders *escaping* from one part of the United Kingdom to the other, and also from one county to another," by which, amongst other things, it was enacted, that a warrant from a court in Great Britain might be transmitted to Ireland, be endorsed and executed there by a Justice of the Peace, and the accused party transferred for trial to the court from which the warrant issued.

That all the persons concerned in pushing this act knew its object, it would be wrong to say; but it was brought in by Perceval, Lord Redesdale's brother-in-law, and by Charles Yorke, the brother of Lord Hardwicke, and was mainly and speedily used against Johnson —a case for strong suspicion, at least, against the Irish government.

The act was soon used. Bills were found against Johnson for Libel by the Middlesex Grand Jury, and on the 24th of November, 1804, a warrant was issued against him from the King's Bench at Westminster, founded on a charge of libel; this warrant was endorsed by Robert Bell, Esq., J.P. for the county Dublin, and under it the Judge was conditionally arrested at his house at Milltown, on the 17th, and absolutely on the 18th of January, 1805 Johnson procured delay,* a Habeas Corpus was at once issued, and on the 19th of January he was brought before the Chief Justice and six other Judges, at the Chief's house, and the case immediately gone into. Johnson was ill and sought delay, but O'Grady (the Attorney-General) refused it, and Johnson read a statement showing that he had sought to go to Bath for his health (then very feeble) and had obtained leave, though warned that he would be held to bail, and that the whole proceeding was a tyrannical and illegal contrivance. Counsel argued the case, the Attorney-General replied on the 22nd, and an eighth judge having come in that day, their lordships divided, three for and three against, allowing the cause shown on the writ of Habeas Corpus, and two were neuter. The question, therefore, went into the King's Bench, and was there argued, on the 26th, 28th, and 29th of January, by Curran, M'Cartney, William Johnson for the judge, and by Arthur Browne (the Prime-Sergeant) and the Attorney-General, O'Grady, for the crown. Justice Day decided for release, Chief Justice Downes and Justice Daly against it.

Curran's speech contains nothing of argument additional to the speech he afterwards made in the Exchequer, on the same subject; nor has it any pretensions to brilliant eloquence, except, perhaps, in the concluding passage, which is as follows:—

But suppose him arrived in London. What defence can he make there? Yes, I think there is one; there is an inborn enthusiasm for liberty—an innate love of freedom—a hatred of oppression and tyranny, that would redeem the victim and secure him from the attack of the oppressor. But give such a power to a prosecutor, as the construction put upon this statute would give, and there is not a man in England, from the Archbishop of Canterbury to the lowest mechanic, who may not be brought here under colour of this statute, and *vice versa*, and tried upon trivial accusations without the possibility of giving bail.— The minister going to the House of Commons may be arrested upon the information of an Irish chairman, and a warrant granted by a

---

* The fact that he was communicated with on the 17th, negatives the charge against government, of having tried to kidnap him—expedition they were bound under the act to use.

trading justice. Mr. Pitt is brought over here *in vinculis*. What to do?—to see whether he should be bailed or not. I remember Mr. Fox was here during the lifetime of this country: in the same way he might be brought over. It may facilitate the intercourse between the islands —any man may travel at the public expense. Suppose I gave an Irishman in London a small assault in trust; when the vacation arrives, he knocks at the door of a trading justice, and tells him he wants a warrant against the counsellor. "What counsellor?" "Oh, sure every body knows the counsellor." "Well, friend, and what is your name?" "Thady O'Flanagan, please your honour." "What countryman are you?" "An Englishman, by construction." "Very well, I'll draw upon my correspondent in Ireland for the body of the counsellor."

What! my lords, is there no apprehension of an outrage of that kind? There is nothing against it but the great expense. The two warrants cannot be obtained for less than five shillings of our money. But the expense of the journey must be defrayed by the public; and can it be supposed that the legislature intended, that the public money should be thus drawn upon at the good will of every petty prosecutor, either to gratify his malice or supply his necessities?

<small>Lord Chief Justice Downes—Give me leave to ask, whether this mischief might not arise in the case of an unfounded charge of felony?</small>

Mr. Curran—No, my lord; accusers are not so easily found in such cases. The atrocity of the charge deters the party from making it. I have witnessed many trials, and I seldom knew a false charge of a capital crime; but there are a thousand instances of false charges of petty misdemeanor.

I shall add to that head of observation, that this is a state prosecution. Yet it must be proceeded upon as every common case between subject and subject. But if anything can impress this particular case more upon the Court than any other, it is the circumstance that it is a prosecution by the state for a libel; see then what a power is put into the hands of a minister, or the rival of a minister. An experiment must first be made in the province, remote from the seat of government, where it may be supposed to pass *sub silentio*. They would not venture to try it in London, to give up an inhabitant of England to an Irish catchpole, and send him upon a voyage to Ireland, to know whether he should be bailed or not. It would appal the English nation to have such an artillery opened upon them; it would be to stand before a loaded cannon, while a child with a lighted torch was sitting at the touch-hole. If my client must undertake this voyage, let the messenger perform the obsequies by night, and take him to the water-edge in the dark, that his countrymen may not see his last look upon his native shore, which he is never to see again. Let not his wife or children witness his departure. He is to be taken to a place, where his innocence cannot appear, for there is no process to produce the witness who can attest it.

My lords, this is an odious experiment. It is of late that this perplexed doctrine of constructions has been revived; it flourished before science had attained its full maturity, and when there was nothing but commentators, and scholiasts, and constructors. Are acknowledged principles to be explained away by some godfather, producing his adopted manuscript—"nullus liber homo capiatur, vel imprisonetur, nisi per legale judicium parium suorum, vel per legem terræ." A manuscript is produced—it came into the hands of a grandfather's executor— by which it appears, that *lex terræ* is for the common people, but *judicium parium* means something more; it means the judgment of the upper house—the judgment of the peers. This exposes the freedom of the subject, and his dearest rights, to the uncertainties of caprice and the vagaries of speculation. It is admitted there are real hardships imposed by this statute; but it is suggested it may be amended Perhaps it may—perhaps it may not. But under the construction contended for by the prosecutor, they are desperate and formidable. If you see one construction which is destructive of former rights, and another which is sanative of those rights, I hope you will adopt the latter. I hope that you will not think this a doubtful case—that it will be understood abroad that it is not—that the prosecutor will be pleased with his failure—that he will feel a gratifying consciousness at going out of court mercifully triumphant. If there be any latent motive against the accused, it will be defeated by persisting in the present measure; they will exhibit him as a persecuted man, rousing and arming every principle of the human heart to pity and protect him. If they have any object, they will lose it by an odious and abominable prosecution. But grieved should I be to look to the compunction of humanity, or await the satiated vengeance of the prosecutor, instead of the honourable and upright justice of the Court, which is to pass sentence one way or the other.

Therefore, I leave my client with you. He has fled to the temple of justice—he has fallen upon its steps. I trust in Divine Providence, that he will find there a sanctuary, and that your lordships will order him to be discharged from the custody in which he is now detained.

Pending this, another writ had been issued from the Exchequer. Under it Johnson was brought up on the 4th of February, before Barry Viscount Yelverton, Barons George (William) Smith, and M'Clelland. Mr. Peter Burrowes shortly and argumentatively moved the release of Judge Johnson, and then Curran rose and said :—

My Lords, it has fallen to my lot, either fortunately or unfortunately, as the event may be, to rise as counsel for my client, on this most important and momentous occasion. I appear before you, my lords, in consequence of a writ issued by his Majesty, commanding that cause be shown to this his court, why his subject has been deprived of his liberty; and upon the cause shown in obedience to this writ, it is my duty to address you on the most awful question—if awfulness is to be judged by consequences and events—on which you have ever been called upon to decide. Sorry am I that the task has not been confided to more adequate powers; but, feeble as mine are, they will, at least, not shrink from it. I move you, therefore, that Mr. Justice Johnson be released from illegal imprisonment.

I cannot but observe the sort of scenic preparation with which this sad drama is sought to be brought forward. In part, I approve it; in part, it excites my disgust and indignation. I am glad to find that the Attorney-General and the Solicitor-General, the natural and official prosecutors for the state, do not appear; and I infer from their absence, that his Excellency the Lord Lieutenant disclaims any personal concern in this execrable transaction. I think it does him much honour; it is a conduct that equally accords with the dignity of his character and the feelings of his heart. To his private virtues, whenever he is left to their influence, I willingly concur in giving the most unqualified tribute of respect. And I do firmly believe, it is with no small regret that he suffers his name to be even formally made use of, in avowing for a return of one of the judges of the land, with as much indifference and *nonchalance*, as if he were a beast of the plough.

I observe, too, the dead silence into which the public is frowned by authority for the sad occasion. No man dares to mutter, no newspaper dares to whisper, that such a question is afloat. It seems an inquiry among the tombs, or rather in the shades beyond them.

Ibant sola sub nocte **per** um

I am glad it is so—I am glad of this factitious dumbness: for if murmurs dared to become audible, my voice would be too feeble to drown them. But when all is hushed, when nature sleeps—

"Cum quies mortalibus ægris"—

the weakest voice is heard—the shepherd's whistle shoots across the listening darkness of the interminable heath, and gives notice that the wolf is upon his walk; and the same gloom and stillness that tempt the monster to come abroad, facilitate the communication of the warning to beware. Yes, through that silence the voice shall be heard; yes, through that silence the shepherd shall be put upon his guard; yes, through that silence shall the felon savage be chased into the toil. Yes, my lords, I feel myself impressed and cheered by the composed and dignified attention with which I see you are disposed to hear me on the most important question that has ever been subjected to your consideration—the most important to the dearest rights of the human being—the most deeply interesting and animating that can beat in his heart, or burn upon his tongue.

Oh! how recreating is it to feel that occasions may arise, in which the soul of man may resume her pretensions—in which she hears the voice of nature whisper to her, "*os homini sublime dedi cœlumque tueri*"—in which even I can look up with calm security to the court, and down with the most profound contempt upon the reptile I mean to tread upon! I say, reptile; because, when the proudest man in society becomes so much the dupe of his childish malice, as to wish to inflict on the object of his vengeance the poison of his sting, to do a reptile's work, he must shrink into a reptile's dimension; and, so shrunk, the only way to assail him is to tread upon him.

But to the subject. This writ of habeas corpus has had a return. That return states, that Lord Ellenborough, Chief Justice of England, issued a warrant, reciting the foundation of this dismal transaction, that one of the clerks of the crown office had certified to him, that an indictment had been found at Westminster, charging the Honourable Robert

Johnson, late of Westminster, one of the Justices of his Majesty's Court of Common Pleas in Ireland, with the publication of certain slanderous libels against the government of that country; against the person of his Excellency Lord Hardwicke, Lord Lieutenant of that country; against the person of Lord Redesdale, the Chancellor of Ireland; and against the person of Mr. Justice Osborne, one of the Justices of the Court of King's Bench in Ireland. One of the clerks of the crown office, it seems, certified all this to his lordship. How many of those there are, or who they are, or which of them so certified, we cannot presume to guess, because the learned and noble lord is silent as to those circumstances. We are only informed that one of them made that important communication to his lordship.

It puts me in mind of the information given to one of Fielding's justices: "Did not," says his worship's wife, "the man with the valet make his *fidavy* that you was *a vagram*?" I suppose it was some such petty-bag officer who gave Lord Ellenborough to understand that Mr. Justice Johnson was indicted.

And being thus given to understand and be informed, he issued his warrant to a gentleman, no doubt of great respectability, a Mr. Williams, his tipstaff, to take the body of Mr. Justice Johnson, and bring him before a magistrate, for the purpose of giving bail to appear within the first eight days of this term, so that there might be a trial within the sittings after; and if, by the blessing of God, he should be convicted then to appear on the return of the *postea*, to be dealt with according to law.

Perhaps it may be a question for you to decide, whether that warrant such as it may be, is not now absolutely spent; and if not, how a man can contrive to be hereafter in England on a day that is past? And high as the opinion may be in England of Irish understanding, it will be something beyond even Irish exactness, to bind him to appear in England, not a fortnight hence, but a fortnight ago. I wish, my lords, we had the art of giving time this retrograde motion. If possessed of the secret we might possibly be disposed to improve it from fortnights into years

There is something not incurious in the juxta-position of signatures The warrant is signed by the Chief Justice of all England. In music, the ear is reconciled to strong transitions of key, by a preparatory resolution of the intervening discords; but here, alas! there is nothing to break the fall: the august title of Ellenborough is followed by the unadorned name of brother Bell, the sponsor of his Lordship's warrant Let me not, however, be suffered to deem lightly of the compeer of the noble and learned lord. Mr. Justice Bell ought to be a lawyer; ' remember him myself long a crier,* and I know his credit with the state he has had a *noli prosequi*. I see not, therefore, why it may not be fairly said, "*fortunati ambo!*" It appears by this return, that Mr. Justice Bell endorses this bill of lading to another consignee. Mr. Medlicot, a most respectable gentleman; he describes himself upon the warrant, and he gives a delightful specimen of the administration of justice.

* This gentleman was formerly crier to the late Baron Hamilton, when the Baron went circuit as a Judge

and the calendar of saints in office; he describes himself a justice and a peace-officer, that is, a magistrate and a catchpole. So he may receive informations as a justice; if he can write, he may draw them as a clerk; 'f not, he can execute the warrant as a bailiff; and, if it be a capital offence, you may see the culprit, the justice, the clerk, the bailiff, and the hangman, together in the same cart; and, though he may not write, he may " ride and tie." What a pity that their journey should not be further continued together! That, as they had been " lovely in their lives, so in their deaths they might not be divided!" I find, my lords I have undesignedly raised a laugh: never did I less feel merriment Let not me be condemned—let not the laugh be mistaken. Never was Mr. Hume more just than when he says, that "in many things the extremes are nearer to one another than the means." Few are those events that are produced by vice and folly, that fire the heart with indignation, that do not also shake the sides with laughter. So when the two famous moralists of old beheld the sad spectacle of life, the one burst into laughter, the other melted into tears; they were each of them right, and equally right.

"Si credas utrique
" Res sunt humanæ debile ludibrium."

But these are the bitter ireful laughs of honest indignation—or they are laughs of hectic melancholy despair.

It is stated to you, my lords, that these two justices, if justices they are to be called, went to the house of the defendant. I am speaking to judges, but I disdain the paltry insult it would be to them were I to appeal to any wretched sympathy of situation. I feel I am above it. I know the bench is above it. But I know, too, that there are ranks, and degrees, and decorums to be observed, and, if I had a harsh communication to make to a venerable judge, and a similar one to his crier, I should certainly address them in very different language indeed. A judge of the land, a man not young, of infirm health, has the sanctuary of his habitation broken open by these two persons, who set out with him for the coast, to drag him from his country, to hurry him to a strange land by the " most direct way," till the King's writ stopped the malefactors, and left the subject of the King a waif dropped in the pursuit.

Is it for nothing, my lords, I say this? Is it without intention, I state the facts in this way? It is with every intention. It is the duty of the public advocate not so to put forward the object of public attention, as that the skeleton only shall appear, without flesh, or feature, or complexion. I mean everything that ought to be meant in a court of justice. I mean not only that this execrable attempt shall be intelligible to the court as a matter of law, but shall be understood by the world as an act of state. If advocates had always the honesty and the courage, upon occasions like this, to despise all personal considerations, and to think of no consequence but what may result to the public from the faithful discharge of their sacred trust, these frenetic projects of power, these atrocious aggressions on the liberty and happiness of men, would not be so often attempted; for, though a certain class of delinquents may be screened from punishment, they cannot be protected from hatred and derision.

The great tribunal of reputation will pass its inexorable sentence upon their crimes, their follies, or their incompetency; they will sink themselves under the consciousness of their situation; they will feel the operation of an acid so neutralizing the malignity of their natures, as to make them at least harmless, if it cannot make them honest. Nor is there anything of risk in the conduct I recommend. If the fire be hot, or the window cold, turn not your back to either; turn your face. So, if you are obliged to arraign the acts of those in high stations, approach them not in malice, nor favour, nor fear. Remember, that it is the condition of guilt to tremble, and of honesty to be bold; remember, that your false fear can only give them false courage; that while you nobly avow the cause of truth, you will find her shield an impenetrable protection; and that no attack can be either hazardous or inefficient, if it be just and resolute. If Nathan had not fortified himself in the boldness and directness of his charge, he might have been hanged for the malice of his parable.

It is, my lords, in this temper of mind-- befitting every advocate who is worthy of the name, deeply and modestly sensible of his duty, and proud of his privilege, equally exalted above the meanness of temporizing or of offending, most averse from the unnecessary infliction of pain upon any man or men whatsoever—that I now address you on a question, the most vitally connected with the liberty and well-being of every man within the limits of the British empire; which being decided one way, he may be a freeman; which being decided the other, he must be a slave.

It is not the Irish nation only that is involved in this question; every member of the three realms is equally embarked: and would to God all England could listen to what passes here day! They would regard us with more sympathy and respect, when the proudest Briton saw that his liberty was defended in what he would call a provincial court, and by a provincial advocate.

The abstract and general question for your consideration is this. My Lord Ellenborough has signed with his own hand a warrant, which has been endorsed by Mr. Bell, an Irish Justice, for seizing the person of Mr. Justice Johnson, in Ireland, for conveying his person by the most direct way, in such manner as these bailiffs may choose, across the sea, and afterwards to the city of Westminster, to take his trial for an alleged libel against the persons entrusted with the government of Ireland, and to take that trial in a country where the supposed offender did not live at the time of the supposed offence, nor, since a period of at least eighteen months previous thereto, has ever resided; where the subject of his accusation is perfectly unknown; where the conduct of his prosecutors, which has been the subject of the supposed libel, is equally unknown; where he has not the power of compelling the attendance of a single witness for his defence.

Under that warrant, he has been dragged from his family; under that warrant, he was on his way to the water's edge; his transportation has been interrupted by the writ before you, and upon the return of that writ arises the question upon which you are to decide the legality or illegality of so transporting him for the purpose of trial. I am well aware, my lords, of the limits of the present discussion; if the law were clear in favour of the prosecutors, a most momentous question might arise—how far they may be delinquents, in daring to avail themselves of such a law for such a purpose? But I am aware that such is not the present question; I am aware that this is no court of impeachment; and, therefore, that your inquiry is, not whether such a power hath been criminally used, but whether it doth in fact exist?

The arrest of the defendant has been justified by the advocates of the crown, under the forty-fourth of his present Majesty. I have had the curiosity to inquire into the history of that act, and I find that in the month of May, 1804, the brother-in-law of one of the present prosecutors obtained leave to bring in a bill, to " render more easy the apprehending and bringing to trial offenders escaping from one part of the United Kingdom to another, and also from one county to another:" that bill was brought in; it travelled in the caravan of legislation unheeded and unnoticed, retarded by no difficulties of discussion or debate, and in due fulness of season it passed into a law, which was to commence from and after the 1st of August, 1804.

This act, like a young Hercules, began its exploits in the cradle. In the November following, the present warrant was issued, under its supposed authority. Let me not be understood to say that the act has been slided through an unsuspecting legislature, under any particular influence, or for any particular purpose: that any such man could be found, or any such influence exist, or any such lethargy prevail, would not, perhaps, be decent to suppose. Still less do I question the legislative authority of parliament. We all know that a parliament may attaint itself; and that its omnipotence may equally extend in the same way to the whole body of the people. We know also that most unjust and cruel acts of attainder have been obtained by corrupt men in bad times; and if I could bring myself to say, which I do not, that this act was contrived for the mere purpose of destroying an obnoxious individual, I should not hesitate to call it the most odious species of attainder that could be found upon the records of legislative degradation; because, for the simple purpose of extinguishing an individual, it would sweep the liberty of every being in the state into the vortex of general and undistinguished destruction.

But these are points of view upon which the minds of the people of Ireland and England may dwell with terror, or indignation, or apathy, according as they may be fitted for liberty or for chains: but they are not points for the court; and so I pass them by. The present arrest and detention are defended under the forty-fourth of the King: are they warranted by that act? That is the only question for you to decide; and you will arrive at that decision in the usual course, by inquiring, first, how the law stood before upon the subject; next, what the imperfection or grievance of that law was; and, thirdly, what is the remedy intended to be applied by the act in question?

First, then, how stood the law before? Upon this part, it would be a parade of useless learning to go farther back than the statute of Charles, the Habeas Corpus Act, which is so justly called the second Magna Charta of British liberty: what was the occasion of the law? the arbitrary transportation of the subject beyond the realm; that base and malignant war, which the odious and despicable minions of power are for ever ready to wage against all those who are honest and bold enough to despise, to expose, and to resist them.

Such is the oscitancy of man, that he lies torpid for ages under these aggressions, until at last some signal abuse—the violation of Lucrece, the death of Virginia, the oppression of William Tell—shakes him from his slumber. For years had those drunken gambols of power been played in England; for years had the waters of bitterness been rising to the brim; at last, a single drop caused them to overflow,—the oppression of a single individual raised the people of England from their sleep. And what does that great statute do? It defines and asserts the right, it points out the abuse, and it endeavours to secure the right, and to guard against the abuse, by giving redress to the sufferer, and by punishing the offender.

For years had it been the practice to transport obnoxious persons out of the realm into distant parts, under the pretext of punishment, or of safe custody. Well might they have been said, to be sent "to that undiscovered country, from whose bourne no traveller returns;" for of these wretched travellers, how few ever did return?

But of that flagrant abuse, this statute has laid the axe to the root It prohibits the abuse; it declares such detention or removal illegal; it gives an action against all persons concerned in the offence, by contriving, writing, signing, countersigning, such warrant, or advising or assisting therein.

That you may form a just estimate of the rights which were to be secured, examine the means by which the infringement was in future to be prevented and punished. The injured party has a civil action against the offenders; but the legislature recollected, that the sneaking unprincipled humility of a servile packed jury might do homage to ministerial power, by compensating the individual with nominal damages. The statute does that, of which I remember no other instance—it leaves the jury at liberty to give damages to any extent, above five hundred pounds; but expressly forbids them to find a verdict of damages below it. Was this sufficient? No. The offenders incur a *præmunire*.— They are put out of the King's protection; they forfeit their lands and goods; they are disabled from bearing any office of trust or profit. Did the statute stop there? The legislature saw, in their prospective wisdom, that the profligate favourite, who had committed treason against the King by the oppression of his subjects, might acquire such a dominion over the mind of his master, as by the exertion of prerogative to interrupt the course of justice, and prevent the punishment of his crime; if, therefore, the guilty minister of such abuse should attempt to pour poison into the sovereign's ear, and talk to him of mercy, this statute dashes the phial from his hand—it takes away the prerogative of pardon. Are bulwarks like these ever constructed to repel the incursions of a contemptible enemy? Was it a trivial and ordinary occasion which raised this storm of indignation in the parliament of that day? Is the ocean ever lashed by the tempest, to waft a feather, or to drown a fly?

Thus haughtily and jealously does the statute restrain the abuses that may be committed against the liberty of the subject by the judge, the jury, or the minister.

One exception, and one exception only, does it contain: it excepts from its protection, by the sixteenth section, persons who may have committed any capital offence in Scotland or Ireland. If the principle of that exception were now open to discussion, sure I am, that much might be said against its policy. On the one side, you would have to consider the mischief of letting this statute protect a capital offender from punishment, by prohibiting his transmission to that jurisdiction where his crime was committed, and where alone he could be tried. On the other, you would have to weigh the danger to be feared from the abuse of such a power, which, as the Habeas Corpus A stood, could not be resorted to in any ordinary way, but was confined to the sole and exclusive exercises of the advisers of the prerogative. You would have to consider whether it was more likely that it would be used against the guilty or the obnoxious; whether it was more likely to be used as an instrument of justice against the bad, or a pretext of oppression against the good; and, finally, whether you might not apply to the subject the humane maxim of our law, that better it is that one hundred guilty men should escape, than that one innocent, and, let me add, meritorious man, should suffer. But our ancestors have considered the question; they have decided; and, until we are better satisfied than I fear we can be, that we have not degenerated from their virtue, it can scarcely become us to pass any light or hasty condemnation upon their wisdom.

In this great statute, then, my lords, you have the line of demarcation between the prerogative and the people, as well as between the criminal law and the subject, defined with all the exactness, and guarded by every precaution, that human prudence could devise. Wretched must that legislature be, whose acts you cannot trace to the first unchangeable principles of rational prerogative, of civil liberty, of equal justice! In this act you trace them all distinctly.

By this act you have a solemn legislative declaration, "that it is incompatible with liberty to send any subject out of the realm, under pretence of any crime supposed or alleged to be committed in a foreign jurisdiction, except that crime be capital." Such were the bulwarks which our ancestors placed about the sacred temple of liberty, such the ramparts by which they sought to bar out the ever-toiling ocean of arbitrary power; and thought (generous credulity!) that they had barred it out from their posterity for ever. Little did they foresee the future race of vermin that would work their way through those mounds, and let back the inundation; little did they foresee that their labours were so like those frail and transient works that threatened for a while the haughty crimes and battlements of Troy, but so soon vanished before the force of the trident and the impulse of the waters; or that they were still more like the forms which the infant's finger traces upon the beach, the next breeze, the next tide, erases them, and confounds them with the barren undistinguished strand. The ill-omened bird that lights upon it, sees nothing to mark, to allure, or to deter, but finds all one obliterated unvaried waste:—

"Et sola secum sicca spatiatur arena."

Still do I hope that this sacred bequest of our ancestors will have a more prosperous fortune, and be preserved by a more religious and successful care, a polar star to the wisdom of the legislator, and the integrity of the judge.

As such will I suppose its principle not yet brought into disgrace ; and as such, with your permission, will I still presume to argue upon that principle.

So stood the law, till the two acts of the twenty-third and twenty-fourth of George II. which relates wholly to cases between county and county in England. Next followed the act of the thirteenth of his present Majesty, which was merely a regulation between England and Scotland. And next came the act of the forty-fourth of the present reign, upon which you are now called on to decide, which, as between county and county, is an incorporation of the two acts of George II. and as between England, Scotland, and Ireland, is nearly a transcript of the thirteenth of the King.

Under the third and fourth section of this last act, the learned counsel for the learned prosecutors (for really I think it candid to acquit the Lord Lieutenant of the folly or the shame of this business, and to suppose that he is as innocent of the project, from his temper, as he must, from his education, be ignorant of the subject) endeavour to justify this proceeding.

The construction of this act they broadly and expressly contend to be this :—First, they assert that it extends not only to the higher crimes. but to all offences whatsoever. Secondly, that it extends not only to persons who may have committed offences within any given jurisdictions, and afterwards escaped or gone out of such jurisdictions, but to all persons, whether so escaping or going out, or not. Thirdly, that it extends to constructive offences, that is, to offences committed against the laws of certain jurisdictions, committed in places not within them, by persons that never put their feet within them, but, by construction of law, committing them within such jurisdiction, and of course triable therein. Fourthly, that it extends peculiarly to the case of libels against the persons entrusted with the powers of government, or with offices in the state. And, fifthly, that it extends not only to offences committed after the commencement of the act, but also to offences at any period, however remotely, previous to the existence of the statute; that is, that it is to have an *ex post facto* operation.

The learned prosecutors have been forced into the necessity of supporting these last monstrous positions, because, upon the return of the writ, and upon the affidavits, it appears, and has been expressly admitted in the argument: First, that the supposed libel upon these noble and learned prosecutors relates to the unhappy circumstances that took place in Ireland, on the twenty-third of July, 1803, and of course must have been published subsequent thereto. And, secondly, that Mr. Justice Johnson, from the beginning of 1802 to the present hour, was never for a moment in England, but was constantly a resident in Ireland; so that his guilt, whatever it be, must arise from some act, of necessity committed in Ireland, and by no physical possibility committed, or capable of being committed, in England.

These are the positions upon which a learned chancellor and a learned judge come forward to support their cause, and to stake their character, each in the face of his country, and both in the face of the British empire; these are the positions, which, thank God, it belongs to my nature to abhor, and to my education to despise, and which it is this day my most prompt and melancholy duty to refute and to resist—most prompt in obeying, most grieved at the occasion that calls for such obedience.

We must now examine this act of the forty-fourth of the King, and in doing so, I trust you will seek some nobler assistance than can be found in the principles or the practice of day-rules or side-bar motions; something more worthy a liberal and learned court, acting under a religious sense of their duty to their King, their country, and their God, than the feeble and pedantic aid of a stunted verbal interpretation, straining upon its tip-toe to peep over the syllable that stands between it and meaning. If your object was merely to see if its words could be tortured into a submission to a vindictive interpretation, you would have only to endorse the construction that these learned prosecutors have put upon it, and that with as much grave deliberation as Mr. Justice Bell has vouchsafed to endorse the warrant, which my Lord Ellenborough has thought fit to issue under its authority. You would then have only to look at it, "*ut leguleius quidam cautus atque acutus, præcentor.*"

Lord Avonmore—No, Mr. Curran, you forget; it is not *præcentor;* it is "*leguleius quidam cautus atque acutus, præco actionum cantor formarum, auceps syllabarum.*"

Mr. Curran—I thank you, my lord, for the assistance; and I am the more grateful, because, when I consider the laudable and successful efforts that have been made of late to make science domestic and familiar, and to emancipate her from the trammels of scholarship, as well as the just suspicion under which the harbourers and abettors of those outlawed classics have fallen; I see at what a risk you have ventured to help me out. And yet see, my lord, if you are prudent in trusting yourself to the honour of an accomplice. Think, should I be prosecuted for this misprision of learning, if I could resist the temptation of escaping, by turning evidence against so notorious a delinquent as you, my good lord, and so confessedly more criminal than myself, or perhaps than any other man in the empire.

To examine this act, then, my lords, we must revert to the three English statutes, of which it is a transcript. The first of these is the 23rd of Geo. II., cap. 26, sec. 11.

So much of the title as relates to our prese_ inquiry is, "for the appreben, ing of persons in any county or place upon warrants granted by justices of the peace in any county or place."

See now sect. 11, that contains the preamble and enactment as to this subject:—

"And, whereas, it frequently happens that persons, against whom warrants are granted by justices of the peace, for the several counties within this kingdom, escape into other counties or places out of the jurisdiction of the justices of the peace, granting such warrants, and thereby avoid being punished for the offences wherewith they are charged: for remedy whereof be it enacted by the authority aforesaid, that from and after the 24th day of June, 1750, in case any person against whom legal warrant shall be issued by any justice or justices of the peace for any county, riding, division, city, liberty, town or place, within this kingdom, shall escape or go into any other county, riding, division, city, liberty, town or place out of the jurisdiction of the justice or justices granting such warrant, as afor said, it shall and may be lawful for any justice of the peace of the county, riding, division, city, liberty, town or place, to which such person shall have gone or escaped, to endorse such warrant, upon application made to him for that purpose, and to cause the person against whom the same shall have been issued to be apprehended and sent to the justice or justices who granted such warrant, or some other justice or justices of the county, riding, division, city, liberty, town or place, from whence such person shall have gone or escaped, to the end that he or she may be dealt with according to law, any law or usage to the contrary notwithstanding."

This act was amended by the 24th of the same reign, the title of which was, "An act for amending and making more effectual a clause in an act passed in the last session of parliament, for the apprehending of person in any county or place, upon warrants granted by justices of the peace of any county or place."

It then recites the 11th section of the 23d of George II., and proceeds, "And whereas such offender or offenders may reside or be in some other county, riding, division, city, liberty, town, or place, out of the jurisdictions of the justice or justices granting such warrant as aforesaid, before the granting such warrant, and without escaping or going out of the county, riding, division, city, liberty, town, or place, after such warrant granted."

I shall reserve a more particular examination of these two acts, for that head of my argument which will necessarily require it. At present I shall only observe—First, that they are manifestly prospective; Secondly, that they operate only as between county and county in England; Thirdly, that they clearly and distinctly go to all offenders whatsoever, who may avoid trial and punishment of their offences by escaping from the jurisdiction in which they were committed, and were of course triable and punishable; and, Fourthly, that provision is made for bailing the persons so arrested in the place where taken, if the offences charged upon them were bailable by law.

In the 13th of his present Majesty, it was thought fit to make a law with respect to criminals escaping from England to Scotland, and vice versâ; of that act, the present statute of the 44th is a transcript. And upon this statute arises the first question made by the prosecutors; namely, whether, like the acts of the 23d and 24th of George II. which were merely between county and county, it extended indiscriminately to the lowest as well as the highest offences? or whether the 13th and 44th, which go to kingdom and kingdom, are not confined to some and to what particular species of offences? The preamble to these two statutes, so far as they bear upon our present question, is contained in the third section of the 44th, the act now under consideration; and there is not a word in it that is not most material.

It says, " Whereas, it may frequently happen that felons and other malefactors in Ireland, may make their escape into Great Britain, and also that felons and other malefactors in Great Britain may make their escape into Ireland, whereby their crimes remain unpunished." There being no sufficient provision by the laws now in force in Great Britain and Ireland respectively, for apprehending such offenders, and transmitting them into that part of the United Kingdom in which their offences were committed. " For remedy whereof, &c., and if any person against whom a warrant shall be issued by any justice of the peace in Ireland for any crime or offence against the laws of Ireland, shall escape, go into, reside, or be in any place in England or Scotland, it shall be lawful for any justice of the peace for the place whither or where such persons shall escape, &c., to endorse his name on such warrant; which warrant so endorsed shall be a sufficient authority to the person bringing it to execute the same, by apprehending the person against whom it is granted, and to convey him by the most direct way into Ireland, and before a justice living near the place where he shall land, which justice shall proceed with regard to him as if he had been legally apprehended in such county of Ireland."

The fourth section makes the same provision for escapes from England or Scotland into Ireland. The statute goes on and directs that the expenses of such removal shall be repaid to the person defraying the same, by the treasurer of the county in which the crime was committed, and the treasurer is to be allowed for it in his accounts.

To support the construction that takes place in all possible offences of all possible degrees, you have been told, and upon the grave authority of notable cases, that the enacting part of a statute may go beyond its preamble; that it cannot be restrained by the preamble, and still less by the title: that here the enacting clause has the words " any offence," and that " any offence" must extend to every offence, and of course to the offence in question. If the question had been of the lighter kind, you might perhaps have smiled at the parade of authorities produced to establish what no lawyer ever thinks of denying. The learned gentlemen would have acted with more advantage to the justice of the country, though perhaps not to the wishes of their clients, if they had reminded your lordships, that in the construction of a statute, the preamble and even the title itself may give some assistance to the judge in developing its meaning and its extent; if they had reminded you, that remedial laws are to be construed liberally, and penal laws with the utmost strictness and caution.

And when they contended that a supposed libel is within the letter of this law, they would have done well to have added, that it is a maxim that there may be cases within the letter of a statute, which, notwithstanding the judge is bound to reject from its operation, as being incompatible with its spirit.

They would have done well in adding, that the judge is bound so to construe all laws, as not to infringe upon any of the known rules of religion or morality, any of the known rules of distributive justice, any of the established principles of the liberties and rights of the subject ; and that it is no more than a decent and becoming deference to the legislator, to assume as certain, that whatever words he may have used, he could not possibly have meant anything that upon the face of it was palpably absurd, immoral, or unjust.

These are the principles on which I am persuaded this court will always act, because I know them to be the principles on which every court of justice ought to act. And I abstain studiously from appealing to any judicial decisions in support of them; because to fortify them by precedent or authority would be to suppose them liable to be called in question. There is another rule which I can easily excuse the learned gentlemen from adverting to, and that is, that when many statutes are made in *pari materia*, any one of them is to be construed, not independently of the others, but with a reference to the entire code, of which it is only a component part.

On these grounds, then, I say the 44th was not, and could not be intended to go to all offences whatsoever.

First, because the acts of 23rd and 24th George II. had already described "all persons" by words of the most general and comprehensive kind. If the framers of the 13th and 44th meant to carry these acts to the same length, they had the words of the former acts before their eyes, and yet they have used very different words : a clear proof, in my mind, that they meant to convey a very different meaning.

In these latter acts they use very singular words, " felons and other malefactors ;" that these words are somewhat loose and indefinite, I make no difficulty of admitting; but will any man who understands English deny that they describe offences of a higher and most enormous degree? You are told, that felon does not necessarily mean a capital offender, because there are felonies not capital, the name being derived from the forfeiture, not of life, but of property. You are also told that malefactor means generally an ill-doer, and in that sense, that every offender is a malefactor : but the 13th and 44th state this class to be felons and malefactors, for whose transmission from kingdom to kingdom " no sufficient provision was made by the laws now in force."

Now I think it is not unfair reasoning to say, that this act extends to a class of offenders whose transmission was admitted to be not incompatible with the just liberty of the subject of England ; but for whose transmission the legislature could not say there was no provision ; but for whose transmission it was clear that there was not a sufficient provision, though there was some provision. If you can find any class so circumstanced, that is exclusively liable by law to be so transmitted, the meaning of the words "felons and other malefactors" becomes fixed and must necessarily refer to such class..

Now that class is expressly described in the Habeas Corpus Act, because it declares the transmission of all persons to be illegal, except only persons charged with capital crimes; for their apprehension and transmission there was a provision, the *mandatum regis;* that is, the discretionary exercise of the prerogative. That power had, therefore, been used in cases of treason, as in Lundy's case. So in the case of Lord Sanquhar; Carliel, the principal in the murder of Turner, committed in London by the procurement of Lord Sanquhar, was arrested in Scotland, whither he had fled, by the order of King James I., and brought back to England, where he was executed for the crime, as was Lord Sanquhar, the accessory before the fact. But such interference of the prerogative might be granted or withheld at pleasure, could be applied for only with great difficulty and expense, and therefore might well be called an insufficient provision. No provision for such a purpose can be sufficient, unless, instead of depending on the caprice of men in power, it can be resorted to in the ordinary course of law.

You have, therefore, my lords, to elect between two constructions, one, which makes an adequate provision for carrying the exception in the 16th section of the Habeas Corpus Act into effect; and the other, a complete and radical repeal of that sacred security for the freedom of Englishmen.

But further, the spirit and the letter of the Habeas Corpus law is, that the party arrested shall, without a moment's delay, be bailed, if the offence be bailable; but if misdemeanors are within this act, then an English subject arrested under an Irish warrant, cannot be bailed within any part of the realm of England, but must be carried forward in the custody of Irish bailiffs, to the sea-shore of his country, where he is to be embarked in such vessel as they think proper; and, if it should be the good pleasure of his guardians to let him land alive in any part of Ireland, then, and not till then, may he apply to an Irish justice to admit him to bail in a foreign country, where he is a perfect stranger, and where none but an idiot could expect to find any man disposed to make himself responsible for his appearance.

Can you, my lords, bring your minds easily to believe that such a tissue of despotism and folly could have been the sober and deliberate intention of the legislature? but further, under the acts of George II., even from one county to the next, the warrant by the first justice must be authenticated upon oath, before it can be endorsed by the second: but in this act, between, perhaps, the remotest regions of different kingdoms, no authentication is required; and upon the endorsement of, perhaps, a forged warrant, which the English justice has no means of inquiring into, a British subject is to be marched through England, and carried over sea to Ireland, there to learn in the county of Kerry, or Galway, or Derry, that he has been torn from his family, his friends, his business, to the annihilation of his credit, the ruin of his affairs, the destruction of his health, in consequence of a mistake, or a practical joke, or an inhuman or remorseless project of vindictive malice; and that he is then at liberty to return, if he be able; that he may have a good action at law against the worthy and responsible bailiff that abused him, if he is foolish enough to look for him, or unfortunate enough to find him. Can you, my lords, be brought seriously to believe, that such a construction would not be the foulest aspersion upon the wisdom and justice of the legislature?

I said, my lords, that an Englishman may be taken upon the endorsement of a forged warrant. Let me not be supposed to be such a simpleton as to think that the danger of forgery makes a shade of difference in the subject. I know too well that calendar of saints, the Irish justices; I am too much in the habit of prosecuting and defending them every term and every commission, not to be able to guess at what price a customer might have real warrants by the dozen; and, without much sagacity, we might calculate the average expense of their endorsement at the other side of the water. But further yet, the act provides that the expense of such transmission shall be paid at the end of the journey, by the place where the crime has been committed, but, who is to supply the expenses by the way? what sort of prosecutors do you think the more likely to advance those expenses—an angry minister or a vindictive individual?

I can easily see that such a construction would furnish a most effectual method of getting rid of a troublesome political opponent; or a rival in trade; or a rival in love; or of quickening the undutiful lingering of an ancestor that felt not the maturity of his heir; but I cannot bring myself to believe, that a sober legislature, when the common rights of humanity seem to be beaten into their last entrenchment, and to make their last stand,—I trust in God, a successful one,—in the British empire, would choose exactly that awful crisis for destroying the most vital principles of common justice and liberty, or of showing to these nations, that their treasure and their blood were to be wasted in struggling for the noble privilege of holding the right of freedom, of habitation, and of country, at the courtesy of every little irritable officer of state, or of our worshipful Rivets, and Bells, and Medlicots, and their trusty and well-beloved cousins and catchpoles.

But, my lords, even if the prosecutor should succeed, which for the honour and character of Ireland I trust he cannot, in wringing from the bench an admission that all offences whatsoever are within this act, he will have only commenced his honourable cause—he will only have arrived at the vestibule of atrocity. He has now to show that Mr. Johnson is within the description of a malefactor, making his escape into Ireland, whereby his offence may remain unpunished, and liable to be arrested under a warrant endorsed in that place whither or where such person escape, go into, reside, or be. For this inquiry you must refer to the 23rd and 24th of George II. The first of these, 23rd, cap. 11, recites the mischief, "that persons against whom warrants are granted, escape into other countries, and thereby avoid being punished." The enacting part then gives the remedy: "the justice for the place into which such person shall have gone or escaped. shall endorse the original warrant, and the person accused shall thereunder be sent to the justice who granted it, to be by him dealt with," &c.

If words can be plain, these words are so, they extend to persons actually committing crimes within a jurisdiction, and actually escaping into some other, after warrant granted, and thereby avoiding trial. In this act there were found two defects: first, it did not comprehend persons changing there abode before warrant issued, and whose removing as not being a direct flight from pursuit, could scarcely be called a escape; secondly, it did not give the second justice a power to bail. And here you see how essential to justice it was deemed, that the person arrested should be bailed on the spot and at the moment of arrest, if the charge was bailable.

Accordingly, the 24th of George II., cap., 55, was made: after reciting the former act, and the class of offenders thereby described, namely, actual offenders actually escaping, it recites, that "whereas, such offenders may reside, or be in some other county before the warrant granted, and without escaping or going out of the county after such a warrant granted;" it then enacts, "that the justice for such place where such person shall escape, go into, reside, or be, shall endorse, &c. and may bail, if bailable, or transmit," &c.

Now the construction of these two acts taken together is manifestly this: it takes in every person, who being in any jurisdiction, and committing an offence therein, escaping after warrant, or without escaping after warrant, going into some other jurisdiction, and who shall there reside, that is permanently abide, or shall be, that is permanently, so as to be called a resident.

Now here it is admitted, that Mr. Johnson was not within the realm of England since the beginning of 1802, more than a year before the offence existed; and therefore you are gravely called upon to say that he is the person who made his escape from a place where he never was and into a place which he had never left. To let in this wise and humane construction, see what you are called upon to do; the statute makes such persons liable to arrest if they shall have done certain things; to wit, "if they shall escape, go into, reside, or be;" but if the fact of simply being, *i. e.*, existing in another jurisdiction, is sufficient to make them so liable, it follows of course, that the only two verbs that imply doing any thing, that is *escape or go into*, must be regarded as superfluous; that is, that the legislature had no idea whatsoever to be conveyed by them when they used them, and, therefore, are to be altogether expunged and rejected.

Such, my lords, are the strange and unnatural monsters that may be produced by the union of malignity and folly. I cannot but own, that I feel an indignant, and perhaps ill-natured satisfaction, in reflecting that my own country cannot monopolize the derision and detestation that such a production must attract. It was originally conceived by the wisdom of the east; it has made its escape, and come into Ireland, under the sanction of the first criminal judge of the empire; here, I trust in God, we shall have only to feel shame or anger at the insolence of the visit, without the melancholy aggravation of such an execrable guest continuing to reside or to be among us. On the contrary, I will not dismiss the cheering expectation from my heart, that your decision, my lords, will show the British nation, that a country, having as just and as proud an idea of liberty as herself, is not an unworthy ally in the great contest for the rights of humanity; is no unworthy associate in resisting the progress of barbarity and military despotism, and in defending against its enemies that great system of British freedom, in which we have now a common interest, and under the ruins of which, if it should be overthrown, we must be buried in a common destruction.

I am not ignorant, my lords, that this extraordinary construction has received the sanction of another court, nor of the surprise and dismay with which it smote upon the general heart of the bar. I am aware that I may have the mortification of being told in another country of that unhappy decision, and I foresee in what confusion I shall hang down my head when I am told it.

But I cherish, too, the consolatory hope, that I shall be able to tell them that I had old and learned friend, whom I would put above all the sweepings of their hall, who was of a different opinion; who had derived his ideas of civil liberty from the purest fountains of Athens and of Rome; who had fed the youthful vigour of his studious mind with the theoretic knowledge of their wisest philosophers and statesmen; and who had refined that theory into the quick and exquisite sensibility of moral instinct, by contemplating the practice of their most illustrious examples;—by dwelling on the sweet-souled piety of Cimon—on the anticipated Christianity of Socrates;—on the gallant and pathetic patriotism of Epaminondas;—on that pure austerity of Fabricius, whom to move from his integrity would have been more difficult than to have pushed the sun from his course.

I would add, that if he had seemed to hesitate, it was but for a moment; that his hesitation was like the passing cloud that floats across the morning sun, and hides it from the view, and does so for a moment hide it, by involving the spectator, without even approaching the face of the luminary. And this soothing hope I draw from the dearest and tenderest recollections of my life; from the remembrance of those attic nights and those refections of the gods which we have partaken with those admired, and respected, and beloved companions who have gone before us; over whose ashes the most precious tears of Ireland have been shed.

Here Lord Avonmore could not refrain from bursting into tears.

Yes, my good lord, I see you do not forget them; I see their sacred forms passing in sad review before your memory; I see your pained and softened fancy recalling those happy meetings, where the innocent enjoyment of social mirth became expanded into the nobler warmth of social virtue, and the horizon of the board became enlarged into the horizon of man; where the swelling heart conceived and communicated the pure and generous purpose, where my slenderer and younger taper imbibed its borrowed light from the more matured and redundant fountain of yours. Yes, my lord, we can remember those nights, without any other regret than that they can never more return; for—

> "We spent them not in toys, or lust, or wine
> But search of deep philosophy,
> Wit, eloquence, and poesy;
> Arts which I loved, for they, my friend, were thine"*

But, my lords, to return to a subject from which to have thus far departed, I think may not be wholly without excuse. The express object of the 44th was to send persons from places where they were not triable by law, back to the places that had jurisdiction to try them. And in those very words does Mr. Justice Blackstone observe on the 13th of the King, that it was made to prevent impunity by escape, by giving a power of "sending back" such offenders as had so escaped.

This topic of argument would now naturally claim its place in the present discussion. I mention it now, that it might not be supposed that I meant to pretermit so important a consideration. And I only mention it, because it will connect itself with a subsequent head of this inquiry in a manner more forcibly applicable to the object; when I think I may venture to say it will appear to demonstration, that if the offence charged upon the defendant be triable at all, it is triable in Ireland, and no where else; and, of course, that the prosecutors are acting in direct violation of the statute, when they seek to transport him from a place where he can be tried, into another country which can have no possible jurisdiction over him.

Let us now, my lords, examine the next position contended for by these learned prosecutors. Having laboured to prove that the act applies not merely to capital crimes, but to all offences whatsoever; having laboured to show that an act for preventing impunity by escape extends to cases not only where there was no escape, but where escape in fact was physically impossible, they proceeded to put forward boldly a doctrine which no lawyer, I do not hesitate to say it, in Westminster-hall would have the folly or the temerity to advance: that is, that the defendant may, by construction of law, be guilty of the offence in Westminster, though he should never have passed within its limits, till he was sent thither to be tried.

With what a fatal and inexorable uniformity do the tempers and characters of men domineer over their actions and conduct! How clearly must an Englishman, if by chance there be any now listening to us, discern the motives and principles that dictated the odious persecutions of 1794 re-asuming their operations; forgetting that public spirit by which they were frustrated; unappalled by fear, undeterred by shame, and returning again to the charge; the same wild and impious nonsense of constructive criminality—the same execrable application of the ill-understood rules of a vulgar, clerk-like, and illiterate equity, to the sound, and plain, and guarded maxims of the criminal law of England!—the purest, the noblest, the chastest system of distributive justice that was

---

* Lord Avonmore, in whose breast political resentment was easily subdued, by the same noble tenderness of feeling which distinguished the late Mr. Fox, upon a more celebrated occasion, could not withstand this appeal to his heart. At this period there was a suspension of intercourse between him and Mr. Curran; but the moment the court rose, his lordship sent for his friend, and threw himself into his arms, declaring that unworthy artifices had been used to separate them, and that they should never succeed in future.--*Life of Curran by his son*, vol. L, p. 148, *nota*.

ever venerated by the wise, or perverted by the foolish, or that the children of men in any age or climate of the world have ever yet beheld—the same instruments, the same movements, the same artists, the same doctrines, the same doctors, the same servile and infuriated contempt of humanity, and persecution of freedom!—the same shadows of the varying hour that extend or contract their length, as the beam of a rising or sinking sun plays upon the gnomon of self-interest! How demonstratively does the same appetite for mice authenticate the identity of the transformed princess that had been once a cat.

But it seems as if the whole order and arrangement of the moral and the physical world had been contrived for the instruction of man, and to warn him that he is not immortal. In every age, in every country, do we see the natural rise, advancement, and decline of virtue and of science So it has been in Greece, in Rome; so it must be, I fear, the fate of England. In science, the point of its maturity and manhood is the commencement of its old age; the race of writers, and thinkers, and reasoners, passes away, and gives place to a succession of men who can neither write, nor think, nor reason. The Hales, the Holts, and the Somerses, shed a transient light upon mankind, but are soon extinct and disappear, and give place to a superficial and overweening generation of laborious and strenuous idlers, of silly scholiasts, of wrangling mooters, of prosing garrulists, who explore their darkling ascent upon the steps of science, by the balustrade of cases and manuscripts—who calculate their depth by their darkness, and fancy they are profound, because they feel they are perplexed. When the race of the Palladios is extinct, you may expect to see a clumsy hod-man collected beneath the shade of his shoulders—

"ανηρ νευττι μιγαττ
Εξοχος ανεςωπων κιφαλην και ευριας αρ:νς"—

affecting to fling a builder's glance upon the temple, on the proportion of its pillars; and to pass a critic's judgment on the doctrine that should be preached within them.

Let it not, my lords, be considered amiss, that I take this up as an English rather than an Irish question. It is not merely because we have habeas corpus law in existence (the antiquarian may read of it, though we do not enjoy it); it is not merely because my mind refuses itself to the delusion of imaginary freedom, and shrinks from the meanness of affecting an indignant haughtiness of spirit that belongs not to our condition, that I am disposed to argue it as an English question; but it is because I am aware that we have now a community of interest and of destiny that we never had before—because I am aware, that, blended as we now are, the liberty of man must fall where it is highest, or rise where it is lowest, till it finds its common level in the common empire—and because, also, I wish that Englishmen may see, that we are conscious that nothing but mutual benevolence and sympathy can support the common interest that should bind us against the external or the intestine foe—and that we are willing, whenever that common interest is attacked, to make an honest and animated resistance, as in a common cause, and with as cordial and tender anxiety for their safety as for our own.

Let me now briefly, because no subject can be shorter or plainer, consider the principle of local jurisdictions, and constructive crimes.

A man is bound to obedience, and punishable for disobedience of laws:--first, because by living within their jurisdiction, he avails himself of their protection—and this is no more than the reciprocity of protection, and allegiance on a narrower scale; and, secondly, because, by so living within their jurisdiction, he has the means of knowing them, and cannot be excused because of his ignorance of them.

I should be glad to know upon the authority of what manuscript, of what pocket-case, the soundness of these principles can be disputed? I should be glad to know upon what known principle of English law a Chinese, or a Laplander, can be kidnapped into England, and arraigned for a crime which he committed under the pole, to the injury of a country which he had never seen—in violation of a law which he had never known, and to which he could not owe obedience—and perhaps, for an act, the non-performance of which might have forfeited his liberty or his life to the laws of that country which he was bound to know, and was bound to obey?

Very differently did our ancestors think of that subject. They thought it essential to justice, that the jurisdiction of criminal law should be local and defined—that no man should be triable but there, where he was accused of having actually committed the offence; where the character of the prosecutor, where his own character was known, as well as the characters of the witnesses produced against him, and where he had the authority of legal process to enforce the attendance of witnesses for his defence. They were too simple to know anything of the equity of criminal law. Poor Bracton or Fleta would have stared if you had asked them, "What, gentlemen, do you mean to say that such a crime as this shall escape from punishment?" Their answer would have been no doubt, very simple, and very foolish: they would have said, "We know there are many actions that we think bad actions, which yet are not punishable, because not triable by law; and which are not triable, because of the local limits of criminal jurisdictions."

And, my lords, to show with what a religious scrupulosity the locality of jurisdictions was observed, you have an instance in the most odious of all offences, treason only excepted—I mean the crime of wilful murder. By the common law, if a man in one county procured a murder to be committed, which was afterwards actually committed in another, such procuror could not be tried in either jurisdiction, because the crime was not completed in either. This defect was remedied by the act of Edward VI. which made the author of the crime amenable to justice. But in what jurisdiction did it make him amenable? Was it there where the murder was actually perpetrated? By no means; but there only where he had been guilty of the procurement, and where alone his accessorial offence was completed.

And here you have the authority of parliament for this abstract position, that where a man living in one jurisdiction does an act, in consequence of which, a crime is committed within another jurisdiction, he is by law triable only where his own personal act of procurement was committed, and not there where the procured or projected crime actually too : effect. In answer to these known authorities of common law, has any statute, has a single decision, or even dictum of a Court, been adduced ? Or, in an age in which the pastry-cooks and snuff-shops have been defrauded of their natural right to these compositions that may be useful without being read, has even a single manuscript been offered to show the researches of these learned prosecutors, or to support their cause ? No, my lords ; there has not.

I said, my lords, that this was a fruit from the same tree that produced the stupid and wicked prosecutions of 1794 ; let me not be supposed to say it is a mere repetition of that attempt, without any additional aggravation. In 1794, the design—and odious enough it was—was confined to the doctrine of constructive guilt; but it did not venture upon the atrocious outrage of a substituted jurisdiction. The Englishman was tried on English ground where he was known, where he could procure his witnesses, where he had lived, and where he was accused of a crime, whether actual or constructive ; but the locality of the trial defeated the infernal malice of these prosecutions. The speeches of half the natural day, where every juryman had his hour, were the knell of sleep but they were not the knell of death. The project was exposed, and the destined victims were saved. A piece so damned could not safely be produced again on the same stage. It was thought wise, therefore, to let some little time pass, and then to let its author produce it on some other distant, provincial theatre, for his own benefit, and at his own expense and hazard.

To drag an English judge from his bench, or an English Member of Parliament from the senate, and in the open day, in the city of London, to strap him to the roof of a mail-coach, or pack him up in a waggon or hand him over to an Irish bailiff, with a rope tied about his leg, to be goaded forward like an ox, on his way to Ireland, to be there tried for a constructive misdemeanor, would be an experiment, perhaps not very safe to be attempted. These Merlins, therefore, thought it prudent to change the scene of their sorcery :—

"Modo Romæ, modo ponit Athenis!"

The people of England might, perhaps, enter into the feelings of such an exhibition with an officiousness of sympathy not altogether for the benefit of the contrivers :—

"Nec coram populo natos Medea trucidet"—

and it was thought wise to try the second production before spectators whose necks were pliant, and whose hearts were broken : where every man who dared to refuse his worship to the golden calf, would have the furnace before his eyes, and think that it was at once useless and dangerous to speak, and discreet at least, if it was not honest, to be silent. I cannot deny that it was prudent to try an experiment, which if successful, must reduce an Englishman to a state of slavery, more abject and forlorn than that of the helots of Sparta, or the negroes of your plantations.

For see, my lords, the extent of the construction now broadly and directly contended for at your bar :—The King's peace in Ireland, if eems, is distinct from his peace in England, and both are distinct from his peace in Scotland; and, of course, the same act may be a crime against each distinct peace, and severally and successively punishable in each country—so much more inveterate is the criminality of a constructive than of an actual offence.

So that the same man for the same act, against laws that he never heard of, may be punished in Ireland, be then sent to England, by virtue of the warrant of Mr. Justice Bell, endorsed by my Lord Ellenborough; and after having his health, his hopes, and his property destroyed, for his constructive offences against his Majesty's peace in Ireland, and his Majesty's peace in England, he may find, that his Majesty's peace in the Orkneys, has, after all, a vested remainder in his carcass; and, if it be the case of a libel, for the full time and term of fourteen years from the day of his conviction, before the Scottish jurisdiction, to be fully completed and determined.

Is there, my lords, can there be, a man who hears me, that does not feel that such a construction of such a law would put every individual in society under the despotical dominion, would reduce him to be the despicable chattel, of those most likely to abuse their power, the profligate of the higher, and the abandoned of the lower orders; to the remorseless malice of a vindictive minister; to the servile instrumentality of a trading justice? Can any man who hears me, conceive any possible case of abduction, of rape, or of murder, that may not be perpetrated, under the construction now shamelessly put forward.

Let us suppose a case:—By this construction a person in England, by procuring a misdemeanor to be committed in Ireland, is constructively guilty in Ireland, and, of course, triable in Ireland. Let us suppose that Mr. Justice Bell receives, or says he receives, information, that the lady of an English nobleman wrote a letter to an Irish chambermaid, counselling her to steal a row of pins from an Irish pedlar, and that the said row of pins was, in consequence of such advice and counsel, actually stolen, against the Irish peace of our Lord the King suppose my Lord Ellenborough, knowing the signature, and reverencing the virtue of his tried and valued colleague, endorses this warrant; is it not clear as the sun, that this English lady may, in the dead of the night, be taken out of her bed and surrendered to the mercy of two or three Irish bailiffs, if the captain who employed them should happen to be engaged in any contemporary adventure nearer to his heart, without the possibility of any legal authority interposing to save her, to be matronized in a journey by land, and a voyage by sea, by such modest and respectable guardians, to be dealt with during the journey as her companions might think proper, and to be dealt with afterward by the worshipful correspondent of the noble and learned lord, Mr Justice Bell, according to law?

I can without much difficulty, my lords, imagine, that after a year or two had been spent in accounts current, in drawing and re-drawing for human flesh, between our worthy Bells and Medlicots on this side of the water, and their noble or their ignoble correspondents on the other, that they might meet to settle their accounts and adjust their balances. I can conceive that the items might not be wholly destitute of curiosity.—Brother B. I take credit for the body of an English patriot—Brother E. I set off against it that of an Irish judge—Brother B. I charge you in account with three English bishops—Brother L. I set off Mrs. M'Lean and two of her chickens; petticoat against petticoat—Brother B. I have sent you the body of a most intractable disturber, a fellow that has had the impudence to give a threshing to Bonaparte himself: I have sent you Sir Sidney—Dearest Brother E.— But I see my learned opponents smile—I see their meaning. I may be told, that I am putting imaginary and ludicrous, but not probable, and therefore, not supposable cases. But I answer, that that reasoning would be worthy only of a slave, and disgraceful to a freeman. I answer, that the condition and essence of rational freedom is, not that the subject probably will not be abused, but that no man in the state shall be clothed with any discretionary power, under the colour and pretext of which he can dare to abuse him.

As to probability, I answer, that in the mind of man there is no more instigating temptation to the most remorseless oppression, than the rancour and malice of irritated pride and wounded vanity. To the argument of improbability, I adduce in answer, the very fact, the very question in debate; nor to such answer can I see the possibility of any reply, save that the prosecutors are so heartily sick of the point of view into which they have put themselves by their prosecution that they are not likely again to make a similar experiment. But when I see any man fearless of power, because it possibly or probably may not be exercised upon him, I am astonished at his fortitude; I am astonished at the tranquil courage of any man who can quietly see that a loaded cannon is brought to bear on him, and that a fool is sitting at its touch-hole with a lighted match in his hand.

And yet, my lords, upon a little reflection, what is it, after what we have seen, that should surprise us, however it may shock us? What have the last ten years of the world been employed in, but in destroying the land-marks of rights, and duties, and obligations; in substituting sounds in the place of sense; in substituting a vile and canting methodism in the place of social duty and practical honour; in suffering virtue to evaporate into phrase, and morality into hypocrisy and affectation? We talk of the violations of Hamburgh or of Baden; we talk of the despotic and remorseless barbarian, who tramples on the common privileges of the human being; who, in defiance of the most known and sacred rights, issues the brutal mandate of usurped authority; who brings his victim by force within the limits of a jurisdiction to which he never owed obedience, and there butchers him for a constructive offence. Does it not seem as if it were a contest whether we should be more scurrilous in invective, or more atrocious in imitation? Into what a condition must we be sinking, when we have the front to select as the subject of our obloquy, those very crimes which we have flung behind us in the race of profligate rivalry!

My lords, the learned counsel for the prosecutors have asserted that this act of the 44th of the King extends to all offences, no matter how long or previously to it they may have been committed. The words are, "That from and after the 1st day of August, 1804, if any person, &c., shall escape, &c." Now certainly nothing could be more convenient for the purpose of the prosecutors, than to dismiss, as they have done, the words "escape and go into," altogether. If those words could have been saved from the ostracism of the prosecutors, they must have designated some act of the offenders, upon the happening or doing of which the operation of the statute might commence; but the temporary bar of these words they wave by the equity of their own construction, and thereby make it a retrospective law; and having so construed t. a manifestly *ex post facto* law, they tell you it is no such thing, because it creates no new offence, and only makes the offender amenable who was not so before. The law professes to take effect only from and after the 1st of August, 1804; now, for eighteen months before that day, it is clear that Mr. Johnson could not be removed by any power existing from his country and his dwelling; but the moment the act took effect, it is made to operate upon an alleged offence, committed, if at all, confessedly eighteen months before.

But another word as to the assertion, that it is not *ex post facto*, because it creates no new crime, but only makes the party amenable.

The force of that argument is precisely this:—If this act inflicted deportation on the defendant by way of punishment after his guilt had been established by conviction, that would, no doubt, be tyrannical. Law is bound to suppose him perfectly innocent; and that only by way of process to make him amenable, not by way of punishment; and surely he cannot be so unreasonable as not to feel the force of the distinction.

How naturally, too, we find similar outrages resort to similar justifications! Such exactly was the defence of the forcible entry into Baden. Had that been a brutal violence committed in perpetration of the murder of the unfortunate victim, perhaps very scrupulous moralists might find something in it to disapprove of; but his Imperial Majesty was too delicately tender of the rights of individuals and of nations, to do any act so flagrant as that would be if done in that point of view; but his Imperial Majesty only introduced a clause of *ne omittas* into his warrant, whereby the worshipful Bells and Medlicots that executed it were authorized to disregard any supposed fantastical privilege of nations that gave sanctuary to traitors; and he did that from the purest motives, from as disinterested a love of justice as that of the present prosecutors; and not at all in the way of an *ex post facto* law, but merely as process to bring him in, and make him amenable to the competent and unquestionable jurisdiction of the *Bois de Boulogne*.

Such are the wretched sophistries to which men are obliged to have recourse, when their passions have led them to do what no thinking man can regard without horror, what they themselves cannot look at without shame; and for which no legitimate reasoning can suggest either justification or excuse. Such are the principles of criminal justice on which the first experiment is made in Ireland; but I venture to pledge myself to my fellow-subjects of Great Britain, that if the experiment succeeds, they shall soon have the full benefit of that success. I venture to promise them, they shall soon have their full measure of this salutary system for making men "amenable," heaped and running over into their bosoms.

There now remains, my lords, one, and only one topic of this odious subject, to call for observation. The offence here appears by the return and the affidavits, to be a libel upon the Irish government, published by construction in Westminster. Of the constructive commission of a crime in one place by an agent, who, perhaps at the moment of the act, is in another hemisphere, you have already heard enough. Here, therefore, we will consider it simply as an illegal libel upon the Irish government; and whether, as such, it is a charge coming within the meaning of the statute, and for which a common justice of peace in one kingdom, is empowered to grant a warrant for conveying the person accused for trial into the other.

Your lordships will observe, that in the whole catalogue of crimes for which a justice of peace may grant a warrant, there is not one that imposes upon him the necessity of deciding upon any matter of law, involving the smallest doubt or difficulty whatsoever. In treason the overt act; in felony, whether capital or not, the act; in misdemeanors, the simple act. The dullest justice can understand what is a breach of the peace, and can describe it in his warrant. It is no more than the description of a fact, which the informer has seen and sworn to. But no libel comes within such a class; for it is decided over and over, that a libel is no breach of the peace, and upon that ground it was that Mr. Wilkes, in 1763, was allowed the privilege of parliament, which privilege does not extend to any breach of the peace.

See, then, my lords, what a task is imposed upon a justice of the peace, if he is to grant such a warrant upon such a charge: he, no doubt, may easily comprehend the allegation of the informer, as to the fact of writing the supposed libel; in deciding whether the facts sworn amounted to a publication or not, I should have great apprehension of his fallibility; but if he got over those difficulties, I should much fear for his competency to decide what given facts would amount to a constructive publication.

But even if he did solve that question—a point on which, if I were a justice, I should acknowledge myself most profoundly ignorant—he would then have to proceed to a labour, in which I believe no man could expect him to succeed; that is, how far the paper sworn to was in point of legal construction, libellous or not. I trust this court will never be prevailed upon to sanction, by its decision, a construction that would give to such a set of men a power so incompatible with every privilege of liberty or of law. To say it would give an irresistible power of destroying the liberty of the press in Ireland, would, I am well aware, be but a silly argument, where such a thing has long ceased to exist; but I have, for that very reason, a double interest now, as a subject of the empire, in that noble guardian of liberty in the sister nation. When my own lamp is broken, I have a double interest in the preservation of my neighbour's.

But if every man in England who dares to observe, no matter how honestly and justly, upon the conduct of Irish ministers, is liable to be torn from his family, and dragged hither by an Irish bailiff, for a constructive libel against the Irish government and upon the authority of an Irish warrant, no man can be such a fool as not to see the consequence. The inevitable consequence is this, that at this awful crisis, when the weal, not of this empire only, but of the whole civilized world, depends on the steady faith and consolidated efforts of these two countries, when Ireland is become the right arm of England, when every thing that draws the common interest and affection closer gives the hope of life, when every thing that has even a tendency to relax that sentiment is a symptom of death, even at such a crisis may the rashness or folly of those entrusted with its management, so act as to destroy its internal prosperity and repose, and lead it into the two-fold fatal error, of mistaking its natural enemies for its friends, and its natural friends for its natural enemies; without any man being found so romantically daring, as to give notice of the approaching destruction.

My lords, I suppose the learned counsel will do here what they have done in the other court: they will assert that this libel is not triable here; and they will argue that so false and heinous a production surely ought to be triable somewhere.

As to the first position, I say the law is directly against them.

From a very early stage of the discussion, the gentlemen for the prosecution thought it wise for their clients to take a range into the facts much more at large than they appeared on the return to the writ, or even by the affidavits that have been made; and they have done this to take the opportunity of aggravating the guilt of the defendant, and at the same time of panegyrising their clients; they have, therefore, not argued upon the libel generally as a libel, but they have thought it prudent to appear perfectly acquainted with the charges which it contains: they have, therefore, assumed, that it relates to the transactions of the 23rd of July, 1803; and that the guilt of the defendant was, that he wrote that letter in Ireland, which was afterwards published in England, not by himself, but by some other persons.

Now, on these facts, nothing can be clearer than that he is triable here.

If it be a libel, and if he wrote it here, and it was published in England, most manifestly there must have been a precedent publication, not merely by construction of law, in Ireland, but a publication by actual fact. And for this plain reason, if you for a moment suppose the libel in his possession (and if he did in fact write it, I can scarcely conceive that it was not, unless he wrote it perhaps by construction), there were no physical means of transmitting it to England, that would not amount to a publication here. Because, if he put it into the post-office, or gave it to a messenger to carry thither, that would be complete evidence of publication against him.

So would the mere possession of the paper, in the hands of the witness who appeared and produced it, be perfect evidence, if not accounted for, or contradicted, to charge him with the publicat on ; so that really I am surprised how gentlemen could be betrayed into positions so utterly without foundation.

They would have acted just as usefully for their clients, if they had admitted, what every man knows to be the fact, that is, that they durst not bring the charge before an Irish jury. The facts of that period were too well understood. The Irish public might have looked at such a prosecution with the most incredulous detestation ; and if they had been so indiscreet as to run the risk of coming before an Irish jury, instead of refuting the charges against them as a calumny, they would have exposed themselves to the peril of establishing the accusation, and of raising the character of the man whom they had the heart to destroy because he had dared to censure them.

Let not the learned gentlemen, I pray, suppose me so ungracious as to say, that this publication, which has given so much pain to their clients, is actually true; I cannot personally know it to be so, nor do I say so, nor is this the place or the occasion to say that it is so. I mean only to speak positively to the question before you, which is matter of law. But as the gentlemen themselves thought it meet to pronounce an eulogy on their clients, I thought it rather unseemly not to show that I attended to them ; I have most respectfully done so ; I do not contradict any praise of their virtues or their wisdom, and I only wish to add my very humble commendation of their prudence and discretion, in not bringing the trial of the present libel before a jury of this country.

The learned counsel have not been contented with abusing this libel as a production perfectly known to them, but they have wandered into the regions of fancy. No doubt the other judges, to whom those pathetic flights of forensic sensibility were addressed, must have been strongly affected by them. The learned gentlemen have supposed a variety of possible cases. They have supposed cases of the foulest calumniators aspersing the most virtuous ministers. Whether such supposed cases have been suggested by fancy or by fact, is not for me to decide ; but I beg leave to say, that it is as allowable to us as to them to put cases of supposition :—

—" Cur ego si fingere pauca
Possum, invideor ?"

Let me, then, my lords, put an imaginary case of a different kind · let me suppose that a great personage, entrusted with the safety of the citadel (meaning and wishing perhaps well, but misled by those lacquered vermin that swarm in every great hall), leaves it so loosely guarded, that nothing but the gracious interposition of Providence, has saved it from the enemy. Let me suppose another great personage, going out of his natural department, and under the supposed authority of high station, disseminating such doctrines as tend to root up the foundations of society, to destroy all confidence between man and man, and to impress the great body of the people with a delusive and desperate opinion, that their religion could dissolve or condemn the sacred obligations that bind them to their country, that their rulers have no reliance upon their faith, and are resolved to shut the gates of mercy against them.

Suppose a good and virtuous man saw that such doctrines must necessarily torture the nation into such madness and despair, as to render them unfit for any system of mild or moderate government: that if on one side bigotry or folly shall inject their veins with fire, such a fever must be kindled, as can be allayed only by keeping a stream of blood perpetually running from the other; and that the horrors of martial law must become the direful but inevitable consequence. In such a case, let me ask you, what would be his indispensable duty? It would be, to avert such dreadful dangers, by exposing the conduct of such persons, by holding up the folly of such bigoted and blind enthusiasm to condign derision and contempt; and painfully would he feel that on such an occasion he must dismiss all forms and ceremonies; and that to do his duty with effect, he must do it without mercy. He should also foresee, that a person so acting, when he returned to those to whom he was responsible, would endeavour to justify himself by defaming the country which he had abused, for calumny is the natural defence of the oppressor. he should therefore so reduce his personal credit to its just standard, that his assertions might find no more belief than they deserved.

Were such a person to be looked on as a mere private individual, charity and good-nature might suggest not a little in his excuse.

An inexperienced man, new to the world, and in the honeymoon of preferment, would run no small risk of having his head turned in Ireland. The people in our island are by nature penetrating, sagacious, artful, and comic, "*natio comœda est.*" In no country under heaven would an ass be more likely to be hood-winked, by having his ears drawn over his eyes, and acquire that fantastical alacrity that makes dulness disposable to the purposes of humorous malice, or interested imposture.

In Ireland, a new great man could get the freedom of a science as easily as of a corporation, and become a doctor, by construction, of the whole Encyclopædia; and great allowance might be made under such circumstances for indiscretions and mistakes, as long as they related only to himself; but the moment they become public mischiefs, they lose all pretensions to excuse; the very ambition of incapacity is a crime not to be forgiven: and however painful it may be to inflict punishment, it must be remembered, that mercy to the delinquent would be treason to the public.

I can the more easily understand the painfulness of the conflict between charity and duty, because at this moment I am labouring under it myself; and I feel it the more acutely, because I am confident, that the paroxysms of passion that have produced these public discussions have been bitterly repented of. I think, also, that I should not act fairly if I did not acquit my learned opponents of all share whatsoever in this prosecution; they have too much good sense to have advised it; on the contrary, I can easily suppose Mr. Attorney-General sent for to give counsel and comfort to his patient; and after hearing no very concise detail of his griefs, his resentments, and his misgivings, methinks I hear the answer that he gives, after a pause of silence and reflection: "No, sir, do not proceed in such a business; you will only expose yourself to scorn in one country, and to detestation in the other. You know you durst not try him here, where the whole kingdom would be his witness. If you should attempt to try him there, where he can have no witness, you will have both countries upon your back. An English jury would never find him guilty. You will only confirm the charge against yourself, and be the victim of an impotent abortive malice. If you should have any ulterior project against him, you will defeat that also; for they who might otherwise concur in the design, will be shocked and ashamed of the violence and folly of such a tyrannical proceeding, and will make a merit of protecting him, and of leaving you in the lurch. What you say of your own feelings, I can easily conceive. You think you have been much exposed by those letters; but then remember, my dear sir, that a man can claim the privilege of being made ridiculous or hateful by no publication but his own. Vindictive critics have their rights, as well as bad authors. The thing is bad enough at best; but, if you go on, you will make it worse. It will be considered an attempt to degrade the Irish bench and the Irish bar. You are not aware what a nest of hornets you are disturbing. One inevitable consequence you do not foresee: you will certainly create the very thing in Ireland that you are so afraid of—a newspaper. Think of that, and keep yourself quiet. And, in the meantime, console yourself with reflecting, that no man is laughed at for a long time; every day will procure some new ridicule that must supersede him."

Such, I am satisfied, was the counsel given; but I have no apprehension for my client, because it was not taken.

Even if it should be his fate to be surrendered to his keepers—to be torn from his family—to have his obsequies performed by torch-light—to be carried to a foreign land, and to a strange tribunal, where no witness can attest his innocence—where no voice that he ever heard can be raised in his defence—where he must stand mute, not of his own malice, but the malice of his enemies—yes, even so, I see nothing for him to fear. That all-gracious Being that shields the feeble from the oppressor will fill his heart with hope, and confidence, and courage: his sufferings will be his armour, and his weakness will be his strength. He will find himself in the hands of a brave, a just, and a generous nation; he will find that the bright examples of her Russells and her Sydneys have not been lost to her children. They will behold him with sympathy and respect, and his persecutors with shame and abhorrence. They will feel, too, that what is then his situation, may to-morrow be their own; but their first tear will be shed for him, and the second only for themselves—their hearts will melt in his acquittal. They will convey him kindly and fondly to their shore; and he will return in triumph to his country—to the threshold of his sacred home—and to the weeping welcome of his delighted family. He will find that the darkness of a dreary and lingering night hath at length passed away, and that joy cometh in the morning.

No, my lords, I have no fear for the ultimate safety of my client. Even in these very acts of brutal violence that have been committed against him, do I hail the flattering hope of final advantage to him, and not only of final advantage to him, but of better days and more prosperous fortune for this afflicted country—that country of which I have so often abandoned all hope, and which I have been so often determined to quit for ever.

> "Sæpe vale dicto multa sum deinde locutas,
> Et quasi discedens oscula summa dabam,
> Indulgens animo, pes tardus erat."

But I am reclaimed from that infidel despair. I am satisfied that while a man is suffered to live, it is an intimation from Providence that he has some duty to discharge, which it is mean and criminal to decline. Had I been guilty of that ignominious flight, and gone to pine in the obscurity of some distant retreat, even in that grave I should have been haunted by those passions by which my life had been agitated—

> ———"vivis quæ cura
> Eadem sequitur tellure repostos"

And if the transactions of this day had reached me, I feel how my heart would have been agonized by the shame of the desertion : nor would my sufferings have been mitigated by a sense of the feebleness of that aid, or the smallness of that service which I could render or withdraw. They would have been aggravated by the consciousness that, however feeble or worthless they were, I should not have dared to thieve them from my country. I have repented—I have stayed—and I am at once rebuked and rewarded by the happier hopes that I now entertain.

In the anxious sympathy of the public—in the anxious sympathy of my learned brethren—do I catch the happy presage of a brighter fate for Ireland. They see, that within these sacred walls the cause of liberty and of man may be pleaded with boldness and heard with favour. I am satisfied they will never forget the great trust, of which they alone are now the remaining depositories. While they continue to cultivate a sound and literate philosophy—a mild and tolerating Christianity—and to make both the sources of a just, and liberal, and constitutional jurisprudence, I see everything for us to hope. Into their hands, therefore, with the most affectionate confidence in their virtue, do I commit these precious hopes. Even I may live long enough yet to see the approaching completion, if not the perfect accomplishment of them. Pleased shall I then resign the scene to fitter actors ; pleased shall I lay down my wearied head to rest, and say :—" Lord, now lettest thou thy servant depart in peace, according to thy word, for mine eyes have seen thy salvation."

William Johnson then followed on the same side, and Prime-Sergeant Browne on the opposite.

On the 7th of February the judgment of the Court was given against the release, Baron Smith dissenting in a very constitutional and eloquent, but rather showy, speech.

Mr. James Fitzgerald brought the case before the English Commons, on the 8th of February, without effect. On the 27th of May, a bill was brought into the English Commons, to amend the act of the former year, and enabling parties arrested to give bail, and granting subpœnas for witnesses in Ireland. When this bill reached the Lords, Johnson petitioned against it, and was heard by counsel; but it passed.

Pursuant to the decision of the Irish Courts, Judge Johnson was, therefore, removed to England ; and having there pleaded specially to the indictment the non-jurisdiction of the

Court under the act, the Crown demurred, and on the 20th of June, 1805, the plea was argued by Richardson for, and Abbott against, the prisoner, and on the 1st of July his plea was quashed.

On the 23rd of November, 1805, the trial took place before the full Court of King's Bench, in Westminster, and a special jury. Erskine, Garrow, &c., were with the law officers of the Crown. Cobbett swore to the documents, and four Irish officials swore that they were in Johnson's writing. After an argument on non-proof of publication in Middlesex. Mr. Adams spoke for the defence, and called Sir Henry Jebb, Doctor Hodgkinson (S.F.T.C.D.), Mr. Archdall, Mr. John Gifford, and Mr. Cassidy, to prove the handwriting not Judge Johnson's. After a quarter of an hour's deliberation, the jury found a verdict of GUILTY. A *nolle prosequi* was entered on this by the Whig Government in Trinity Term, 1806, and Johnson retired upon his pension.

He then went to live in Paris, and there, in 1828, under the name of "Colonel Philip Roche Fermoy," published his "Commentary on the Memoirs of Wolfe Tone." This pamphlet went much into the military resources of Ireland, and caused some excitement. It is a very fierce, but not a profound military tract. It is said that he printed a second part, which he sent to a relative in Ireland, who burned the whole impression.

DECISION IN MERRY v. POWER.

[CHARITABLE LEGACY.]

ROLLS COURT.

MARY POWER, in 1804, made her will, bequeathing a considerable part of her property to the Rev. John Power, and others, in trust for charitable purposes. Her brother, Joseph Merry, a merchant in Spain, was her next of kin, and residuary legatee; he died intestate, and his son, the now plaintiff, came over and took out administration to his deceased father and brought a suit in the Spiritual Court, to set aside the will, as unduly obtained, and as disposing of a large property to Papists and for superstitious uses.

In that court the plaintiff applied for an administrator, *pendente lite*, and was refused
The present bill, praying that the effects might be brought into court, was filed only a few weeks; and now, before the defendant had answered, a motion was made by Dr. Vavasour, for a receiver, and that Dr. Power, the acting executor, should be ordered forthwith to bring the effects into court; he relied on the affidavit of his client, the plaintiff, charging that the will was obtained by fraud by the defendant, Power, and that at best it could not be sustained, as being a trust altogether for "Popish uses." The motion was opposed by Mr. Prendergast, who strongly argued against the imputations thrown out upon the conduct of Dr. Power, by the name of "one John Power, a Popish Priest." He insisted, that under the whole circumstances, there was no colour for impeaching the transaction; that the bequests were most praiseworthy; that there had already been a decree of this court, obtained by the trustees of charitable donations, affirming the legality of the trusts; and that it would be unprecedented for a court to interfere in this way, before an answer came in, and without delay or resistance on the part of the defendant to put in his answer.

His Honour the Master of the Rolls (Mr. Curran) said:—

If the question had been brought forward upon the mere rule of the court, I should not have thought it necessary to give many reasons for the order I intend to make : but pressed so strongly as it has been, both by the arguments themselves, and perhaps more so by the style and manner of putting them, as well as the supposed policy which has been called in to aid them, I think I ought to state the grounds upon which I mean to act in my decision.

First, then, it is urged, that this is the case of an insolvent and wasting executor having fradulently obtained the will. As to insolvency, to be an executor it is not necessary to be rich; integrity and discretion are the essential qualities of an executor. If the testator thinks he has found these in an executor of humble means, this court has no power to control him. He may bestow his property as a gift to whom he pleases; it would be strange if he could not confide it as a trust to whom he chooses. I know of no necessary connexion between wealth and honesty. I fear that integrity is not always found to be the parent or offspring of riches. To interfere, therefore, as is now sought, with this executor, would be little short of removing the will.

But it is said that this will has been obtained by fraud, practised by this "one John Power." No doubt this court has acted, where strong ground of suspicion of fraud, and danger of the property being made away with, have appeared; but do these grounds now appear to this court?

Here his Honour recapitulated the facts sworn to, and continued:—

I see no semblance of fact to sustain such a charge. Who does this "one John Power, a Popish Priest," turn out to be? I find he is a Catholic clergyman, a doctor in divinity, and the titular bishop in the diocese of Waterford. And yet I am now pressed to believe that this gentleman has obtained this will by fraud.

Every fact now appearing repels the charge; I cannot but say, that the personal character of the person accused repels it still more strongly.

Can I be brought, on grounds like those now before me, to believe that a man, having the education of a scholar, the habits of a religious life, and vested with so a high a character in the ministry of the gospel, could be capable of so detestable a profanation as is flung upon him? Can I forget that he is a Christian bishop, clothed not in the mere authority of a sect, but clothed in the indelible character of the episcopal order, suffering no diminution from his supposed heterodoxy, nor drawing any increase or confirmation from the merits of his conformity, should he think proper to renounce what we call the errors of faith? Can I bring my mind, on slight, or rather on no grounds, to believe, that he could so trample under his feet all the impressions of that education, of those habits, and of that high rank in the sacred ministry of the gospel, which he holds, as to sink to the odious impiety imputed to him? Can I bring myself to believe such a man, at the dying bed of his fellow-creature, would be capable with one hand of presenting the cross before her lifted eye, and with the other, of basely thieving from her those miserable dregs of this world, of which his perfidious tongue was employed in teaching her a Christian's estimate? I do not believe it; on the contrary, I am (as far as it belongs to me, in this interlocutory way, to judge of the fact) as perfectly convinced that the conduct of Dr. Power was what it ought to be, as I am that the testatrix is dead.

But I am called on to interfere, it being a foolish bequest to superstitious and Popish uses! I have looked into those bequests: I find the object of them is to provide shelter and comfortable support for poor helpless females; and clothes, and food, and instruction, for poor orphan children. Would to God I could see more frequent instances of such bequests! Beautiful in the sight of God must it be, beautiful in the right of man ought it be, to see the dying Christian so employed, to see the last moments of human life so spent in acts of gratuitous benevolence, or even of interested expiation. How can we behold such acts, without regarding them as forming a claim to, as springing from a consciousness of, immortality? In all ages the hour of death has been considered as an interval of more than ordinary illumination; as if some rays from the light of the approaching world had found their way to the darkness of the parting spirit, and revealed to it an existence that could not terminate in the grave, but was to commence in death.

But these uses are condemned, as being not only superstitious but Popish uses. As to that, I must say that I feel no disposition to give any assistance even to the orthodox rapine of the living, in defeating even the heterodox charity of the dead. I am aware that this objection means somewhat more than directly meets the ear, if it means any thing. The object of these bequests, it seems, are Catholics, or, as they have been called, Papists: and the insinuation clearly is, that the religion of the objects of this woman's bounty calls upon me to exercise some peculiar rigour of interference to abridge or defeat her intentions.

Upon this point I wish to be distinctly understood: I don't conceive this to be the spirit of our existing law; nor, of course, the duty of this court to act upon that principle in the way contended for. In times, thank God, now past, the laws would have warranted such doctrines: Those laws owed their existence to unfortunate combinations of circumstances that were thought to render them necessary. But if we look back with sorrow to their enactment, let us look forward with kindness and gratitude to their repeal. Produced by national calamity, they were brought by national benevolence, as well as by national contrition, to the altar of public justice and concord, and there offered as a sacrifice to atone, to heal, to conciliate, to restore social confidence, and to give us that hope of prosperity and safety, which no people ever had, or observed, or dared to have, except where it is founded on the community of interests, a perfectly even and equal participation of just rights, and a consequent contribution of all the strength of all the parts so equally interested in the defence of the whole.

I know they have been supposed to originate in religious bigotry, that is, religious zeal carried to excess. I never thought so. The real spirit of our holy religion is too incorruptibly pure and beneficent to be depraved into any such excess. Analyze the bigot's object, and we see he takes nothing from religion but a flimsy pretext in the profanation of its name. He professes the correction of error and the propagation of truth. But when he has gained the victory, what are the terms he makes for himself?—power and profit. What terms does he make for religion?—profession and conformity. What is that profession? The mere utterance of the lips, the utterance of sounds, that after a pulsation or two upon the air, are just as visible and lasting as they are audible. What is the conformity? Is it the practice of any social virtue or Christian duty? Is it the forgiveness of injuries, or the payment of debts, or the practice of charity? No such thing. It is the performance of some bodily gesture or attitude. It is going to come place of worship. It is to stand or to kneel, or to bow to the poor-box. But it is not a conformity that has anything to do with the judgment, or the heart, or the conduct. All these things bigotry meddles not with, but leaves them to religion herself to perform.

Bigotry only adds one more, and that a very odious one, to the number of those human stains which it is the business of true religion not to burn out with the bigot's fire, but to expunge and wash away by the Christian's tears.

Such, invariably, in all countries and ages, have been the motives to the bigot's conflicts, and such the use of his victories; not the propagation of any opinion, but the engrossment of power and plunder, of homage and tribute. Such, I much fear, was the real origin of our Popery laws. But power and privilege must necessarily be confined to very few. In hostile armies you find them pretty equal, the victors and the vanquished, in the numbers of their hospitals and in the numbers of their dead: so it is with nations; the great mass is despoiled and degraded, but the spoil itself is confined to few indeed. The result finally can be nothing but the disease of dropsy and decrepitude.

In Ireland this was peculiarly the case. Religion was dishonoured, man was degraded, and social affection was almost extinguished. A few, a very few still profited by this abasement of humanity.

But let it be remembered, with a just feeling of grateful respect to their patriotic and disinterested virtue, and it is for this purpose that I have alluded as I have done, that that few composed the whole power of the legislature which concurred in the repeal of that system, and left remaining of it, not an edifice to be demolished, but a mere heap of rubbish, unsightly, perhaps pernicious, to be carted away.

If the repeal of those laws had been a mere abjuration of intolerance, I should have given it little credit. The growing knowledge of the world, particularly of the sister nation, had disclosed and unmasked intolerance; had put it to shame, and consequently to flight! But though public opinion may proscribe intolerance, it cannot take away powers or privileges established by law. Those powers of exclusion and monopoly could be given up only by the generous relinquishment of those who possessed them. And nobly were they so relinquished by those repealing statutes. Those lovers of their country saw the public necessity of the sacrifice, and most disinterestedly did they make it. If, too, they have been singular in this virtue, they have been as singularly fortunate in their reward. In general, the legislator, though he sows the seed of public good, is himself numbered with the dead before the harvest can be gathered. With us it has not been so, with us the public benefactors, many of them, at least, have lived to see the blessing of heaven upon their virtue, in an uniformly accelerating progress of industry, and comfort, and liberality, and social affection, and common interest, such as I do not believe that any age or nation has ever witnessed.

Such I do know was the view, and such the hope, with which that legislature, now no more! proceeded so far as they went, in the repeal of those laws so repealed. And well do I know how warmly it is now remembered by every thinking Catholic, that not a single voice for those repeals was or could be given except by a Protestant legislator. With infinite pleasure do I also know and feel, that the same sense of justice and good-will which then produced the repeal of those laws, is continuing to act, and with increasing energy, upon those persons in both countries, whose worth and whose wisdom are likely to explode whoever principle is dictated by bigotry and folly ; and to give currency and action to whatever principle is wise and salutary. Such, also, I know to be the feelings of every court in this hall. It is from this enlarged and humanized spirit of legislation, that courts of justice ought to take their principles of expounding the law.

At another time I should probably have deemed it right to preserve a more respectful distance from some subjects which I have presumed (but certainly with the best intentions, and I hope no unbecoming freedom) to approach ; but I see the interest the question has excited ; and I think it right to let no person carry away with him any mistake, as to the grounds of my decision, or suppose that it is either the duty or the disposition of our courts to make any harsh or jealous distinctions in their judgment, founded on any differences of religious sects or tenets. I think, therefore, the motion ought to be refused ; and I think myself bound to mark still more strongly my sense of its impropriety, by refusing it with full costs.

NEWRY ELECTION.

17th October, 1812.

AT the General Election, in 1812, many of Curran's friends desired to see him enter the English Parliament. His reputation was not firmly established in England ; and a few speeches on great occasions, in the House of Commons, they conceived would win the waverers. Curran himself was anxious to help Grattan in urging the Catholic claims, and he acceded to their wishes. A requisition was addressed to him from Newry, to contest that borough, on the popular interest, against General Needham, the Government candidate.

In the *Dublin Evening Post*, of October 13th, 1812, appears the following address to the Electors from some of Curran's friends : —

" *To the Independent Electors of Newry.*

" CITIZENS OF NEWRY,

" Once more has devolved upon you the exercise of the sole political prerogative vested by the constitution in the people. Your Representatives are no more ; they are melted down in the general mass, and you are now, in your own persons, part of the Commons o: Great Britain, and the third branch of the Legislature. But as you cannot act in your collective capacity, you are again called upon to choose that representative body, to whom you delegate the guardianship of your lives, your liberty, and your property. The constitution has, with parental care, guarded your rights, by restoring to you, at certain intervals, the opportunity of fixing on the most virtuous to represent you : but what its wisdom has conceived, you alone, by your co-operation, can effectuate. 'Tis in vain to cry out against the profligacy and venality of a House of Commons, if we ourselves are not immaculate. 'Tis in vain to talk, when it is too late, of the necessity of Parliamentary Reform, after having, from interested and unworthy motives, betrayed the opportunity which the constitution has afforded us, and, by the authority of our own example, countenanced the corruption we complain against.

" That opportunity has at length arrived—the most glorious that has fallen to the lot o any Electors of the United Kingdom. A large number of your most respectable fellow citizens have sent a requisition to him, on whom, of all other men, the country looks with admiration for his talents, with reverence for his virtues, with gratitude for his past services, and confidence in his future exertions—for his well-known and tried attachment to Ireland. Nor has he refused—he felt that, at this momentous time, when his country calls upon him for his services, he was not permitted to reject her petition. He has offered to exercise in your service his gigantic eloquence, backed by long experience, and supported by invincible honesty, and, with these all-powerful instruments, to work the regeneration of Ireland.

"He has done his part; it only remains for you to perform yours. To the independent and liberal Protestants of Newry is this chiefly addressed. They as they do not suffer the wrongs of their Catholic countrymen, are not so sensible of the degradation of their country. But there cannot surely exist so vile a Catholic, that would, with spaniel crouch, lick the hand that holds the whip of infliction, and kiss the chains that bind themselves and their posterity to endless servitude and disgrace—much less can that Catholic be a man, whose fortune should make him independent, and who can ascribe no motive for his perfidy, but the meanness of his mind, and the debasement of his nature.

"Away! No Irishman could descend so low! but should there be such a wretch, leave him to the torture of self-reproach, the execration of his own party, and the contempt even of that which he debases by his alliance.

"We have already on our side a numerous class of our Protestant fellow-citizens, those who have already came forward, with generous ardour, to support their Catholic brethren in their petition for redress of their grievances. They have thus declared their sentiments—they know full well the chief object of the dissolution of Parliament is to obstruct that cause which they so warmly espoused; and they have not, and, it is hoped will not follow the example of the government candidate, in making professions never to be fulfilled, and with which their conduct in voting for that candidate would be so glaringly inconsistent. It is possible he may again tender such hollow pledges, but we know what value to place upon them; they will not again pass current.

"Citizens of Newry! it is the more particularly necessary for you to be vigilant on the present occasion, when the Government party have resorted to such mean, but fruitless artifices, as to push on this election with unprecedented haste—publishing the notice on the very day the requisition was signed, and before it could be transmitted to the *Man of the People's choice*. But such paltry contrivances will be as ineffectual as they are unworthy—since we behold all that is liberal, all that is independent, all that is noble in the county, coming forward to support the great *advocate* of the people, THE MASTER OF THE ROLLS.

"October 10th, 1812."

A letter from a Correspondent, in the same journal, reports the commencement of the Election:

Extract of a letter from Newry, dated Monday, 12th Oct., 1812.

"The enthusiasm of the people was such as to take the horses from the Master of the Rolls' carriage on Saturday evening, two miles out of town, and about 3000 people drew him in. He made the finest speech I ever heard this day, for an hour and twenty minutes, amid the greatest acclamations; whilst his opponent, who refused the test in favour of the Catholics, was groaned. We only polled twenty this day—we were equal—we will poll fifty each to-morrow, and, on Wednesday or Thursday we will know our chance—his speech has brought us crowds."

But the government influence was too strong, and a few of the Catholic shopkeepers who were creeping into rural importance were cowardly and slavish. They sustained the Government candidate, and turned the scale against Curran. On October 17th, the sixth day of the Election, he saw that the borough was lost, and withdrew from the contest. It was on that occasion, he made the following speech:—

I was induced by some of the most respectable electors of the borough to offer myself a candidate. As to myself, I could have no wish to add to the weight of my public duties; and as to serving the country essentially, I think very moderately indeed of my own powers: and under circumstances like the present, under such rulers, and in such a state of popular representation, or, rather misrepresentation, I am perfectly convinced that no force of any individual, or even of many joined together, could do much to serve us, or to save us.

In addition to personal disinclination, I was ignorant of the exact state of the borough, and, of course, of the likelihood of my success. But yet, though without personal wish or probable hope, I thought myself bound, as a public man, to obey; because, though the victor was doubtful, the value of the contest was incalculable, inasmuch as it must bring before ourselves, and before the rest of Ireland, not only an exact picture of our situation, and of the public malady under which we are sinking, but must also make an infallible experiment. It must lecide, to the commonest observer, the principle of the disease, the weakness and misery of public distraction, the certain success, if the sufferers can be combined by the sense of common danger, in a common effort, to throw off the odious incubus that sits upon the public heart, locking up the wholesome circulation of its blood, and paralysing its action.

The experiment has now been made, and has failed of immediate success; it was an effort nobly supported by every generous and honest man within the limits of the borough; but its triumph has been delayed by the want of union, by the apostacy of the perfidious, by the vile defection of others, whom opulence could not reconcile to duty and independence.

Yet, notwithstanding this sad coalition of miserable men against themselves and their children, I do not hesitate to announce to the generous and honest electors who hear me, that though their triumph is deferred, their borough is from this moment free, and that terror has ceased to reign over it; you have polled a greater number of honest and independent voters than ever appeared heretofore for your most successful candidate.

Look now, for a moment, against what a torrent of adverse circumstances you had to act.

The object of your support, personally a stranger, giving public notice that he would not solicit a single individual; the moment a contest was apprehended, corruption took the alarm; and a public officer, in my opinion most unbecomingly, appointed so early a day for the election as to make all preparation whatsoever on my part impossible. If you remember the indignant laugh that was excited in the course of the poll, when the returning officer demanded of the poll-taker how many had voted for the Master of the Rolls, and how many "for us!" you must, I think, be satisfied that there must be something base in this business. Sad, indeed, is the detail of this odious and ludicrous transaction, but it is too instructive to be passed over in silence.

When the election opened, an old gentleman rose, and proposed my gallant opponent, as being a gentleman of "great influence in the borough," and who had "served it" for three parliaments; that is, in other words, a gentleman who had the dregs of its population under his feet, and who had, for three parliaments, been the faithful adherent of every minister; and upon every vital question, the steady and remorseless enemy, so far as a dumb vote would go, of this devoted island.

And, indeed, what could you expect from a gentleman of another country, who could have neither interest in you, nor sympathy for you, but was perfectly free to sell you, or to bestow you at his pleasure.

This motion was seconded—I blush to think of it, I burn at being obliged to state it—by a merchant of Newry, himself a Catholic, himself the uniform victim, as he, together with his Catholic brethren, had been the uniform victims of the principles of a gentleman whom he thought proper to support.

Never shall I forget the figure which the unhappy man made; hesitating, stammering, making a poor endeavour to look angry, as if anger could cast any veil over conscious guilt, or conscious shame, or conscious fear: and to what extent must he have felt all those sensations, if he looked forward, not merely to the sentiment of indignation and contempt which he was exciting in the minds of those that he betrayed, but the internal horror that he must feel, when thrust forward to the bar of his own conscience, and the dreadful sentence of expiatory torture which that indignant conscience must pronounce upon him? However he was bold enough to second the motion; and I think the General is altogether indebted to the virtue of this independent Catholic, and of two other equally virtuous Catholics of Newry, for his final success, if success it can be called.

The test proposed to my opponent was the most moderate ever witnessed; it was merely that he would not obstinately persevere in betraying the trust reposed in him. What was his answer? Certainly it was fair and candid, and giving you all the fullest notice of what you had to expect: he said, that he was not an orator; that his principles were those of a soldier; and that, whatever question came forward, he would vote as he should think best; that is, in other words, if you returned him, you would send him a mute to parliament, with a parchment in one hand, under the name of a return, containing the terms of your capitulation, and a bow-string in the other; during the debate he would ring the dumb-bell; but, on the division—

"When it became a passing bell,
O! then he'd sing it passing well."

Indeed, to touch but passingly upon the subsequent transactions of the election—they are fresh in your minds.

You saw those who voted for their country; you saw those who voted against their country, and against themselves. Every honourable, every respectable man within your borough, except the unfortunate Mr. Caulfield and his two associates, were in the former class; but why do I except them? They do not belong to that class of public spirit or honour; you saw the class to which these unfortunate men properly belong. You saw a succession of poor creatures, without clothes upon their back, naked, as if they had been stripped for execution, naked, as if they had been landed from their mothers, consigned to the noble General at the moment of their birth—no part of them covered but their chins, as if nature had stuck a beard upon them in derision of their destiny. Such has been the contest—such the adverse forces—such, too, thus far, the result. But I told you that the contest was of more value than the victory; that if it did not give you triumph, it would give you wisdom; and to keep this promise, I must carry back your reflections to times that have passed us; and I must do that to show you that all our miseries and degradation have sprung from a disunion, cruelly and artfully fabricated by a foreign country, for the base purpose of driving us to suicide, and making us the instrument of our own destruction

Let me rapidly sketch the first dawn of dissension in Ireland, and the relations of the conqueror and the conquered. That conquest was obtained, like all the victories over Ireland, by the triumph of guilt over innocence. This dissension was followed up by the natural hatred of the spoiler and the despoiled; followed up further by the absurd antipathies of religious sects; and still further followed by the rivalries of trade, the cruel tyrants of Ireland dreading, that, if Irish industry had not her hands tied behind her back, she might become impatient of servitude, and those hands might work her deliverance.

To this growing accumulation of Irish dissension, the miserable James the Second, his heart rotted by the depravity of that France which had given him an interested shelter from the just indignation of his betrayed subjects, put the last hand; and an additional dissension, calling itself political, as well as religious, was superadded.

Under this sad coalition of confederating dissensions, nursed and fomented by the policy of England, this devoted country has continued to languish with small fluctuations of national destiny, from the invasion of the Second Henry, to the present time.

And here let me be just while I am indignant. Let me candidly own, that to the noble examples of British virtue—to the splendid exertions of British courage—to their splendid sacrifices, am I probably indebted for my feelings as an Irishman, and my devotion to my country. They thought it madness to trust themselves to the influence of any foreign country; they thought the circulation of the political blood could be carried on only by the action of the heart within the body, and could not be maintained from without. Events have shown you that what they thought was just, and that what they did was indispensable. They thought they ought to govern themselves—they thought that at every hazard they ought to make the effort—they thought it more eligible to perish than to fail—and to the God of heaven I pray, that the authority of so splendid an example may not be lost upon Ireland.

Mr. Curran, in adverting to the state of Ireland, from the Revolution to the year 1782, called her a sad continuing spectacle of disgrace, and oppression, and plunder, which she was too enfeebled by dissension to resist; because she was the abject, and, helpless victim of the sordid, insatiable, and implacable tyranny of a foreign country.

At length, in 1782, a noble effort was made—and deathless ought to be the name of him* that made it, and deathless ought to be the gratitude of the country for which it was made—the independence of Ireland was acknowledged.

Under this system of asserted independence, our progress in prosperity was much more rapid than could have been expected, when we remember the conduct of a very leading noble person† upon that occasion. Never was a more generous mind, or a purer heart; but his mind had more purity than strength. He had all that belonged to taste, and courtesy, and refinement; but the grand and the sublime of national reform were composed of colours too strong for his eye, and comprised a horizon too outstretched for his vision. The Catholics of Ireland were, in fact

* Mr. Grattan. † Lord Charlemont.

excluded from the asserted independence of their country. Thus far the result comes to this—that wherever perfect union is not found, complete redress must be sought in vain.

The Union was the last and mortal blow to the existence of Ireland as a nation—a consummation of our destruction, achieved by that perpetual instrument of our ruin, our own dissensions.

The whole history of mankind records no instance of any hostile cabinet, perhaps of any even internal cabinet, destitute of all principles of honour or of shame. The Irish Catholic was taught to believe, that if he surrendered his country, he would cease to be a slave. The Irish Protestant was cajoled into the belief that if he concurred in the surrender, he would be placed upon the neck of a hostile faction. Wretched dupe! You might as well persuade the goaler, that he is less a prisoner than the captives he locks up, merely because he carries the key of the prison in his pocket.

By that reciprocal animosity, however, Ireland was surrendered; the guilt of the surrender was most atrocious—the consequences of the crime most tremendous and exemplary. We put ourselves into a condition of the most unqualified servitude; we sold our country, and we levied upon ourselves the price of the purchase; we gave up the right of disposing of our properties; we yielded to a foreign legislature to decide, whether the funds necessary to their projects or their profligacy should be extracted from us, or be furnished by themselves. The consequence has been, our scanty means have been squandered in her internal corruption, as profusely as our best blood has been wasted in the madness of her aggressions, or the feeble folly of her resistance—our debt has accordingly been increased more than tenfold—the common comforts of life have been vanishing—we are sinking into beggary—our poor people have been worried by cruel and unprincipled prosecutions—and the instruments of our government have been almost simplified into the tax-gatherer and the hangman.

At length, after this long night of suffering, the morning star of our redemption cast its light upon us—the mist was dissolved—and all men perceived that those whom they had been blindly attacking in the dark were, in reality, their fellow-sufferers and their friends. We have made a discovery of the grand principle in politics, that the tyrant is in every instance the creature of the slave—that he is a cowardly and a computing animal—and that, in every instance, he calculates between the expenditure to be made, and the advantage to be acquired.

I, therefore, do not hesitate to say, that if the wretched Island of Man, that *refugium peccatorum*, had sense and spirit to see the force of this truth, she could not be enslaved by the whole power of England. The oppressor would see that the necessary expenditure in whips, and chains, and gibbets, would infinitely countervail the ultimate value of the acquisition; and it is owing to the ignorance of this unquestionable truth, that so much of this agitated globe has, in all ages, been crawled over by a Manx population. This discovery, at last, Ireland has made—the Catholic claimed his rights; the Protestant generously and nobly felt as he ought, and seconded the claim. A silly government was driven to the despicable courage of cowardice, and resorted to the odious artillery of prosecutions; the expedient failed; the question made its way to the discussion of the senate. I will not tire you with a detail. A House of Commons, who, at least, represented themselves—perhaps afraid, perhaps ashamed, of their employers—became unmanageable tools in the hands of such awkward artists, and were dissolved; just as a beaten gamester throws the cards into the fire, in hopes in a new pack to find better fortune.

Gentlemen, I was well aware at my rising, that you expected nothing like amusement from what I had to say; that my duty was to tell you plain and important truths; to lay before you, without exaggeration or reserve, a fair statement of the causes that have acted upon the national fortune—of the causes that have put you down, and that may raise you up; to possess you with a fair idea of your present position—of what you have to fear, of what you have to hope, and how you ought to act. When I speak of your present position, I would not have you suppose that I mean the actual situation of the borough of Newry; or that I think it much worth while to dwell upon the foolish insolence with which a besotted Cabinet has thought fit to insult you, by sending a stranger to your country and your interests, to obtain a momentary victory over your integrity, by means of which none of you are ignorant.

Here Mr. Bell, an agent in opposition to Mr. Curran, stood up, and fixed his eyes upon the Master of the Rolls, with a very peculiar expression of countenance.

Mr. Curran—Mr. Seneschal, I demand of you, as returning-officer, that I, a candidate, shall be protected, as you are in duty bound to do, from being disturbed by the obscene and unnatural grimaces of a baboon.

Mr. Jebb, the counsel for the Seneschal, immediately interposed, and ordered Mr. Bell to sit down.

Mr. Curran resumed—I do not wonder at having provoked interruption, when I spoke of your borough. I told you that from this moment it is free. Never in my life have I so felt the spirit of the people as among you; never have I so felt the throbs of returning life. I almost forgot my own habitual estimate of my own small importance; I almost thought it was owing to some energy within myself, when I was lifted and borne on upon the buoyant surge of popular sympathy and enthusiasm. I, therefore, again repeat it, it is the moment of your new birth unto righteousness. Your proved friends are high among you—your developed enemies are expunged for ever—your liberty has been taken from the grave, and if she is put back into the tomb, it can be only by your own parricide, and she must be buried alive.

I have to add, for your satisfaction, a statement has been laid before me of the grossest bribery, which will be proved, beyond all doubt, and make the return a nullity. I have also received a statement of evidence, to show that more than one-third of those who voted against us had been trained by bribe and terror into perjury, when they swore to the value of their qualifications. Some of those houses had actually no existence whatsoever. They might as well have voted from their pasture to give their suffrage; and Nebuchadnezzar, in the last year of his feeding on grass, would have been as competent as they were to vote in Ireland. But I enlarge not upon this topic. To touch upon it is enough for the present; the detail must be reserved for a future occasion, and another place.

It belongs only to the hopeless to be angry. Do not you, therefore, be angry, where you cannot be surprised. You have been insulted, and oppressed, and betrayed; but what better could you hope from such a ministry as their own nation is cursed withal. They hear the voice of suffering England now thundering in their ears; they feel they cannot retain—they are anxious to destroy—they are acting upon the principle of Russian retreat.

Pressed upon by the people, and beaten back into their fastnesses, they depopulate as they retire. But what better could you have ever hoped from such men: a motley group, without virtue, or character, or talent; the sort of Cabinet that you have laughed at on the stage, where the "potent, grave, and reverend signiors" were composed of scene-shifters, and candle-snuffers, robed in old curtains, and wigged from the stores of the theatre? They affected to profess religious distinctions, but they were too grossly ignorant to conceive any such. There is no science in which a man must not know something to qualify him for misconception. I have myself talked with Englishmen upon this subject. You cannot suppose me to allude to the exalted class of persons in that country, who have done themselves so much honour by their sympathy and liberality. I speak of an inferior order—indeed, of persons like your ministers here; I have asked them, what they could find so formidable in the religious principles of the Irish Catholics? and the answer has uniformly been, "Why, sir, I never know'd nothing at all of the principles of the Hirish Papists, except their lank hair, and long coats, without no arms in the sleeves; and I thinks the most liberal man will allow, that them there are dangerous principles!"

Shall I, my friends, say one serious word to you upon this serious subject? Patriotism is of no one religion; Christianity belongs exclusively to no sect; and moral virtue and social duty are taught with equal exactness by every sect, and practised with equal imperfection by all; and therefore, wherever you find a little interested bustling bigot, do not hate him, do not imitate him, pity him if you can. I scarcely wish you not to laugh when you look at one of these pearl-divers in theology, his head barely under water, his eyes shut, and an index floating behind him, displaying the precise degree of his purity and his depth.

A word or two upon your actual position; and what upon that subject but a word of sadness, the monumental inscription upon the headstone of our grave? all semblance of national independence buried in that grave in which our legislature is interred, our property and our persons are disposed of by laws made in another clime, and made like boots and shoes for exportation, to fit the wearers as they may. If you were now to consult my learned friend here, and ask him how much of your property belongs to yourself, or for what crime you may be whipped, or hanged, or transported, his answer would be, "It is impossible, sir, to tell you now; but I am told that the packet is in the bay." It was, in fact, the real design of a rash, and arbitrary, and shortsighted projector, at once to deprive you of all power, as to your own taxation, and of another power of not very inferior importance, and which, indeed, is inseparably connected with taxation, to rob you of all influence upon the vital question of peace or war; and to bring all within the control of an English minister. This very power, thus acquired by that detested Union, has been a mill-stone about the neck of England. From that hour to this she has been flaring away in her ruinous and wasteful war: her allies no more—her enemies multiplied—her finances reduced to rags—her people depressed and discontented—her artisans reduced to the last ebb, and their discontents methodised into the most terrific combinations; her labourers without employment—her manufactures without a market, the last entrance in the North to which they could have looked, being now shut against them, and fastened by a bar that has been reddened in the flames of Moscow. But this, gentlemen, is a picture too heart-rending to dilate upon; you cannot but know it already; and I no not wish to anticipate the direful consequences by which you are too probably destined to feel it further to the quick. I find it a sort of refuge to pass to the next topic which I mentioned as calling for your attention, namely, what foundation, what ground we had for hope.

Nothing but the noblest and most disinterested patriotism led the Protestants of Ireland to ally themselves, offensively and defensively, with their afflicted, oppressed Catholic countrymen.

Without the aid of its rank, its intellect, and its property, Ireland could do no more for herself now than she has done for centuries heretofore, when she lay a helpless hulk upon the water; but now, for the first time, we are indebted to a Protestant spirit, for the delicious spectacle of seeing her at length equipped with masts, and sails, and compass, and helm—at length she is sea-worthy.

Whether she is to escape the tempest or gain the port, is an event to be disposed of by the Great Ruler of the waters and the winds. If our voyage be prosperous, our success will be doubled by our unanimity; but even if we are doomed to sink, we shall sink with honour. But, am I over sanguine in counting our Protestant allies? Your own country gives you a cheering instance in a noble marquis,* retiring from the dissipation of an English court, making his country his residence, and giving his first entrance into manhood to the cause of Ireland. It is not from any association of place that my mind is turned to the name of Moira; to name him, is to recognise what your idolatry has given to him for so many years.

But a late transaction calls for a word or two. I thought anxiously upon it at the time, and from that time to this, if he required to be raised, he must have been raised in public opinion by the event of that negociation.

* The Marquis of Downshire.

I saw that the public in either country could not have any hope from an arrangement in which the first preliminary was a selfish scramble for patronage, that must have ended in a scramble for power; in which the first efforts of patriotism were for the reformation of water-closets, and the surrender of mopsticks in the palace; to sink the head and to irritate the man that wore the crown; instead of making their first measure a restitution of representation to the people, who, if they were as strong as they ought to be, could have nothing to dread from the tinsel of a robe, or the gilding of a sceptre.

Let me pass to another splendid accession to our force, in the noble conduct of our rising youth in the election of our University. With what tenderness and admiration must the eye dwell upon the exalted band of young men, the rosy blush of opening life glowing upon their cheeks, advancing in patriotic procession, bringing the first fruits of unfolding virtue, a sacred offering on the altar of their country, and conducted by a priest, in every point worthy of the votaries and of the offering. The choice which they have made of a man of such tried public virtue, and such transcendent talents as Mr. Plunket, is a proof of their early proficiency in sense and virtue. If Mr. Plunket had been sent alone, as the representative of his country, and was not accompanied by the illustrious Henry Grattan, I should hesitate to say of him, what the historian said of Gylippus, when he was sent alone as a military reinforcement to a distressed ally, who had applied for aid to Sparta: Gylippus alone (says the writer) was sent, in whom was concentrated all the energies and all the talents of his country. "*Mittitur Gylippus solus in quo omnium instar Lacedaemoniorum erat.*" I have thought it better to quote the words of the writer, as being probably more familiar to the learned supporters of my gallant opponent, than my translation. It is only due to justice, that upon this subject I add, with whatsoever regret, another word; it would not be candid if I left it possibly for you to suspect, that my attestation could have been dictated by mere private attachment, instead of being measured by the most impartial judgment. Little remains for me to add to what I have already said. I said you should consider how you ought to act, I will give you my humble idea upon that point : do not exhaust the resources of your spirit, by idle anger, or idle disgust; forgive those that have voted against you here, they will not forgive themselves. I understand they are to be packed up in tumbrils, with layers of salt between them, and carted to the election for the county, to appear again in patriotic support of the noble projector of the glories of Walchern. Do not envy him the precious cargo of the raw materials of virtuous legislation; be assured all this is of use. Let me remind you, before I go, of that precept, equally profound and beneficent, which the meek and modest author of our blessed religion left to the world: "And one commandent I give you that you love one another." Be assured, that of this love the true spirit can be no other than probity and honour. The great analogies of the moral and the physical world are surprisingly coincident; you cannot glue two pieces of board together, unless the joint be clean—you cannot unite two men together unless the cement be virtue; for vice can give no sanction to compact, she can form no bond of affection.

And now, my friends, I bid you adieu, with a feeling at my heart that can never leave it, and which my tongue cannot attempt the abortive effort of expressing. If my death do not prevent it, we shall meet again in this place. If you feel as kindly to me as I do to you, relinquish the attestations which I know you had reserved for my departure. Our enemy has, I think, received the mortal blow, but, though he reels, he has not fallen; and we have seen too much, on a greater scale, of the wretchedness of anticipated triumph. Let me, therefore, retire from among you, in the way that becomes me, and becomes you, uncheered by a single voice, and unaccompanied by a single man. May the blessing of God preserve you in the affection of one another.

The following were the numbers at the close of the poll:—

General Needham	146
Right Hon. J. P. Curran	144
Majority	—2

THE END.

PATTISON JOLLY, Steam-Press Printer,
22, Essex-st., West, Dublin.

www.ingramcontent.com/pod-product-compliance
Lightning Source LLC
Chambersburg PA
CBHW022112300426
44117CB00007B/686